Beginning Django

Web Application Development and Deployment with Python

Daniel Rubio

Apress®

Beginning Django: Web Application Development and Deployment with Python

Daniel Rubio
F. Bahia, Ensenada, Baja California, Mexico

ISBN-13 (pbk): 978-1-4842-2786-2 ISBN-13 (electronic): 978-1-4842-2787-9
https://doi.org/10.1007/978-1-4842-2787-9

Library of Congress Control Number: 2017958633

Cover image by Freepik (`www.freepik.com`).

Managing Director: Welmoed Spahr
Editorial Director: Todd Green
Acquisitions Editor: Steve Anglin
Development Editor: Matthew Moodie
Technical Reviewer: Tri Phan
Coordinating Editor: Mark Powers
Copy Editor: Karen Jameson

Distributed to the book trade worldwide by Springer Science+Business Media New York, 233 Spring Street, 6th Floor, New York, NY 10013. Phone 1-800-SPRINGER, fax (201) 348-4505, e-mail `orders-ny@springer-sbm.com`, or visit `www.springeronline.com`. Apress Media, LLC is a California LLC and the sole member (owner) is Springer Science + Business Media Finance Inc (SSBM Finance Inc). SSBM Finance Inc is a **Delaware** corporation.

For information on translations, please e-mail `rights@apress.com`, or visit `http://www.apress.com/rights-permissions`.

Apress titles may be purchased in bulk for academic, corporate, or promotional use. eBook versions and licenses are also available for most titles. For more information, reference our Print and eBook Bulk Sales web page at `http://www.apress.com/bulk-sales`.

Any source code or other supplementary material referenced by the author in this book is available to readers on GitHub via the book's product page, located at `www.apress.com/9781484227862`. For more detailed information, please visit `http://www.apress.com/source-code`.

Printed on acid-free paper

To Valentina, Nancy and all my immediate family

To my uncle Alfonso, whose Commodore 64 let me gain an affinity for technology

Contents at a Glance

Contents

About the Author

Daniel Rubio has worked in software development for over 15 years, in roles that include developer, software architect, manager, consultant, and CTO. He has worked with startups, government agencies, as well as corporations in industries that include banking, education, social media, and retail.

He has coauthored the best-selling *Spring Recipes* book and other titles for Apress (2010), in addition to writing for various other online publications. Daniel's expertise in the early part of his career was focused on Java, Linux, and open source technology, whereas more recently he has focused on Python, JavaScript, and Cloud technology.

About the Technical Reviewer

Tri Phan is the founder of Programming Learning Channel on YouTube. He has over 7 years of experience in the software industry. Specifically, he has worked in many outsourcing companies and has written many applications of many fields in different programming languages such as PHP, Java, and C #. In addition, he has over 6 years of experience in teaching at international and technological centers such as Aptech, NIIT, and Kent College.

Acknowledgments

I want to thank the entire team at Apress for making this book a reality. In particular, Steve Anglin to whom I first presented this book as an idea; Mark Powers who was there every step of the way coordinating the work; as well as Matthew Moodie and Tri Phan, both of whom helped me maintain the technical accuracy of the book.

I would also like to thank all the customers and colleagues with whom I've had the pleasure to work with throughout the years. Without all their questions and problems they faced, I would have never discovered many of the solutions and techniques described in this book.

Finally, I would like to thank the entire community behind the Django framework for putting together one the best web application frameworks on the market. Without their endless amount of work, the Django framework and this book would not have come to light.

Introduction

The web framework market is an extremely competitive environment, with many programming languages and framework design philosophies to choose from. But if you need to build web-based software with quick turnaround times and a scripting language, there's a high probability the Django framework - or something built with it - will be your top choice.

Django has competitors, but even its nearest competitor in the Python ecosystem, the Flask framework has about one-fourth the mind share of Django, based on the benchmark of worldwide Google searches made for Django vs. Flask.[1] Outside the Python ecosystem, but still in the scripting language segment, the Ruby on Rails framework - which emerged along the same time as Django and follows a similar design philosophy - has always maintained an almost equal mind share with Django, as it can also be proven by the amount of worldwide Google search activity.

So what makes the Django framework such a strong choice for web development? It provides a rapid development foundation to create complex web applications. A rapidness that is provided by a modular and simple philosophy of not repeating constructs and logic throughout a project's structure (a.k.a. the DRY principle or Don't Repeat Yourself principle).

And it's this DRY principle, which has given way to a thriving community, as well as a multitude of packages and other frameworks based on the Django framework. Over 10 years after its initial release, there's now a full-fledged CMS (Content Management System), a turn-key e-commerce platform and over 3000 packages, all built or designed to work with the Django framework. Not to mention, there are two annual conferences in the United States and Europe to showcase Django innovations.

This book will walk you through the many core concepts associated with the Django framework. It will help you learn standard and best practices that are essential to creating effective Django projects. And if and when you use a Django-based package or framework, these same foundations will help you navigate the more complex concepts and avoid any blind spots that are part of the core Django framework.

[1] `https://g.co/trends/yXpSy`

CHAPTER 1

■ ■ ■

Introduction to the Django Framework

The Django framework started in 2003, as a project done by Adrian Holovaty and Simon Willison at the *Journal-World* newspaper in Lawrence, Kansas, in the United States. In 2005, Holovaty and Willison released the first public version of the framework, naming it after the Belgian-French guitarist Django Reinhardt.

Fast forward to 2017 – the Django framework now operates under the guidance of the Django Software Foundation (DSF), the framework core has over 1000 contributors with more than 15 release versions, and there are over 3000 packages specifically designed to work with the Django framework.[1]

The Django framework has remained true to its origins as a Model-View-Controller (MVC) server-side framework designed to operate with relational databases. Nevertheless, Django has stayed up to date with most web development tendencies – via third-party packages – to operate alongside technologies like non-relational databases (NoSQL), real-time Internet communication, and modern JavaScript practices. All this to the point, the Django framework is now the web development framework of choice for a wide array of organizations, including the photo sharing sites Instagram[2] and Pinterest[3]; the Public Broadcasting System(PBS)[4]; in the United States, National Geographic[5]; and with the help of this book, your organization!

In this chapter you'll learn about the Django framework design principles, which are key to understanding the day-to-day aspects of working with the Django framework. Next, you'll learn how to install Django in various ways: as a tar.gz file, with pip, using git, and with virtualenv.

Once you install the Django framework, you'll learn how to start a Django project and how to set it up with a relational database. Next, you'll learn about the core building blocks in the Django framework – urls, templates, and apps – and how they work with one another to set up content. Finally, you'll learn how to set up the Django admin site, which is a web-based interface designed to access the relational database connected to a Django project.

[1]https://djangopackages.org/
[2]https://engineering.instagram.com/what-powers-instagram-hundreds-of-instances-dozens-of-technologies-adf2e22da2ad#.pui97g5jk
[3]https://www.quora.com/Pinterest/What-is-the-technology-stack-behind-Pinterest-1
[4]http://open.pbs.org/
[5]https://github.com/natgeo

© Daniel Rubio 2017
D. Rubio, *Beginning Django*, https://doi.org/10.1007/978-1-4842-2787-9_1

Django Framework Design Principles

If you work long enough in web development, you'll eventually come to the conclusion that you can produce the same results with just about any web framework and programming language. But while you can, in fact, produce identical results, what will vary drastically is the time you spend creating a solution: the time creating a prototype, the time adding new features, the time doing testing, the time doing debugging, and the time deploying to scale, among other things.

In this sense, the Django framework uses a set of design principles that produces one of the most productive web development processes compared to many other web frameworks. Note, I'm not saying Django is a silver bullet (e.g., the best at prototyping, the most scalable); I'm saying that at the end of the day, the Django framework incorporates a set of design principles and trade-offs that make it one of the most productive frameworks for building the features needed by most medium to large web applications.

Now, while you might think I'm biased - after all I'm writing an entire book about the topic - I'll lay out these design principles first, so you can gain a better understanding of what gives the Django framework this edge.

Don't Repeat Yourself (DRY) Principle

Repetition might be good to emphasize a point, but when it comes to web development, it just leads to additional and time-consuming work. In fact, the very nature of web development, which operates across multiple tiers interacting with one another (e.g., HTML templates, business logic methods, and databases), lends itself to repetition.

The Django framework really tries to force you not to repeat yourself, so let's see how Django enforces not repeating yourself and why this is a good thing.

Let's say you want to build a coffeehouse application to publish information about stores and also have a contact form for customers. The first thing you'll need to do is determine what kind of information is required for stores and the contact form. Figure 1-1 illustrates a mock-up of two Django models for each of these entities.

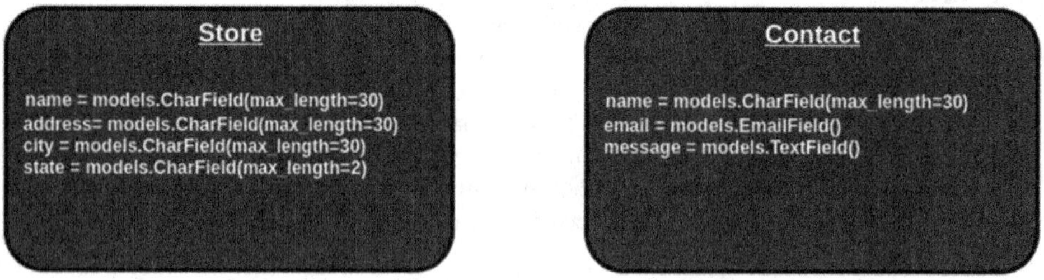

Figure 1-1. *Django models for store and contact entities*

Notice how the Django models in Figure 1-1 each have different field names and a data type to restrict values. For example, the statement `name = models.CharField(max_length=30)` tells Django a store name should have a maximum of 30 characters, while the statement `email = models.EmailField()` tells Django the contact entity should contain a valid email value. If the coffeehouse is like most web applications, you'll generally end up doing the following for the store and contact entities:

- Create relational database tables to save entity information.
- Create business logic to ensure the entities comply with requirements.
- Create HTML forms to allow data to be submitted for the entities.

- Create an interface to allow administrative users to access entities in the database.
- Create REST services to expose entities for a mobile app version.

The crux of doing this last task list is you have the potential of repeating dozens of similar pieces of information (e.g., names, value limits) in database definition language (DDL), HTML forms, business validation logic, and URLs, among other things - process that's not only time consuming, but also error prone.

Wouldn't it be easier that based on a statement like `models.CharField(max_length=30)` you could generate an HTML form input, a DDL statement, and automatically validate information to only contain 30 characters? This is exactly what Django's DRY design principle does.

Figure 1-2 illustrates the same Django models from Figure 1-1 and the various constructs you can generate from the same models without the need to repeat yourself.

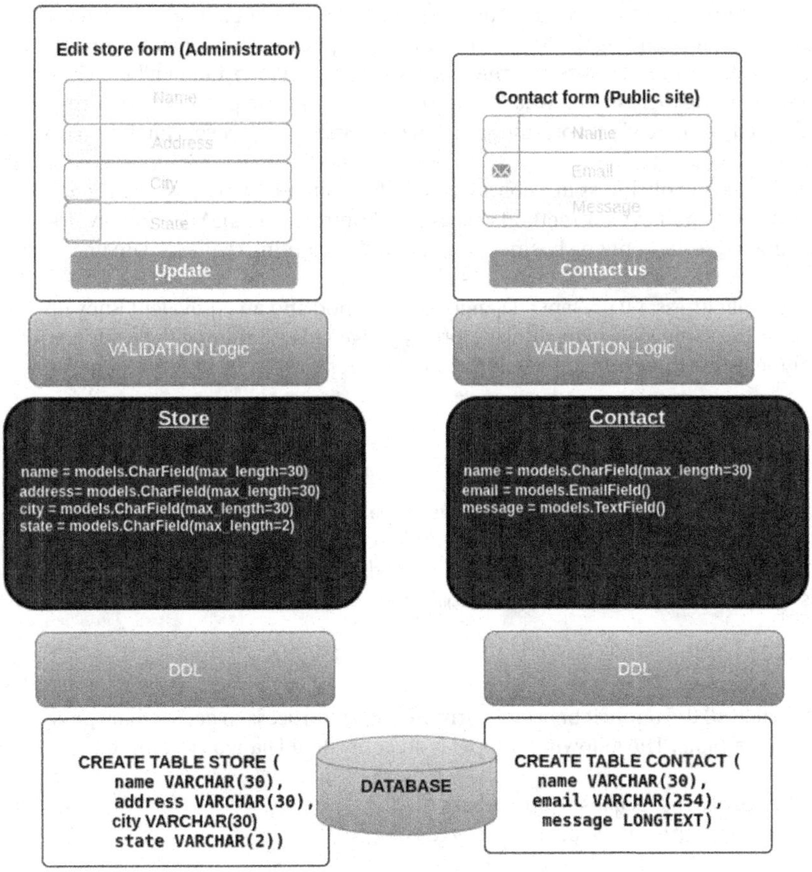

Figure 1-2. *Django models create separate constructs based on DRY principle*

As you can see in Figure 1-2, the entities that represent Django models are capable of generating HTML forms to present to the public, an administrative interface to manage the entities, validation logic to enforce entity values, as well as the DDL to generate database tables representing the entities.

While it's a little premature to discuss the actual techniques to generate such constructs from Django models, needless to say it's much simpler than keeping track of multiple references of the same thing (e.g., name, email) in HTML forms, DDL, validation logic, and other locations.

In this sense, Django really helps you define things in a single place and not have to repeat them elsewhere. Note that it's always possible to repeat yourself to obtain custom behaviors, but by default, Django enforces DRY principles in nearly everything you do with it.

Explicit Is Better Than Implicit

Python, the programming language used by Django, has a mantra-like statement called "The Zen of Python" defined as part of the language's Python Enhancement Proposals (PEP), specifically PEP 20.[6] One of the statements in PEP 20 states "Explicit is better than implicit" and with Django being based on Python, this principle is also taken to heart.

Being explicit leads to web applications that are easily understood and maintained by a greater number of people. Adding new features or understanding the logic behind a web application can be hard enough for someone that didn't write it originally, but if you toss into the mix constructs that have implicit behaviors, users only face greater frustration trying to figure out what's being done implicitly. Explicit does require a little more work typing, but it's well worth it when you compare it to the potential effort you can face trying to debug or solve a problem.

Let's take a quick look at Django's explicitness in a common web development construct used across different MVC frameworks: a view method. A view method acts as the C(ontroller) in an MVC framework, charged with handling incoming requests, applying business logic, and then routing requests with an appropriate response.

To get a better feel for this explicitness, I'll present a Django view method and an equivalent Ruby on Rails view method that performs the same logic of fetching a store by a given id and routing the response to a template. The following snippet is the Ruby on Rails version; note the lines with # that are comments and indicate what's happening.

```
class StoresController < ApplicationController
  def show
    # Automatic access to params, a ruby hash with request parameters and view parameters
    @store = Store.find(params[:id])
    # Instance variables like @store are automatically passed on to view template
    # Automatically uses template views/stores/show.html.erb
  end
end
```

Although very succinct, notice all the implicit behavior surrounding the process to access data, pass data to a template, and assign a template. The following snippet is an equivalent Django view method.

```
# Explicit request variable contains request parameters
# Other view parameters must be explicitly passed to views
def detail(request, store_id):
    store = Store.objects.get(id=store_id)
    # Instance variables must be explicitly passed on to a view template
    # Explicit template must be assigned
    return render(request, 'stores/detail.html', {'store': store})
```

---

[6] https://www.python.org/dev/peps/pep-0020/

Notice in this last snippet there's no guessing where input parameters come from, they're explicitly declared as arguments in the view method. In addition, values are explicitly passed to a template, and the template is also explicitly declared, so the logic is much more amicable to newcomers.

The implicitness of the Ruby on Rails view method is often called 'magic' and is even considered a feature by many. It's called 'magic' because certain behaviors are provided behind the scenes. However, unless you know the framework and application down to a tee, it can be very difficult to pinpoint why certain things are happening, making it more difficult to fix or update things. So even though 'magic' may be able to save you a few minutes or hours in development time at the start, it can end up costing you hours or days in maintenance later.

So just like in Python, the Django framework will always favor an explicit approach over any implicit technique.

It's important to point out explicit doesn't equal verbose or redundant. While you'll certainly end up typing a little more code in Django vs. web frameworks that are implicitly driven (e.g., Rails), as it was described in the prior DRY principle section, the Django framework goes to great lengths to avoid having to introduce more code than necessary in a web application.

Finally, explicit also doesn't mean no defaults. The Django framework does use reasonable defaults where possible, it just doesn't use default values where it isn't obvious they're being used. In essence, the Django framework uses defaults, but avoids using defaults that produce 'magical' outcomes.

Loosely Coupled Architecture

The Django framework being an MVC framework operates across multiple tiers (e.g., HTML templates, business logic methods, and databases). However, Django takes great care of maintaining a loosely couple architecture across all the components that operate across these tiers.

Being loosely coupled means there are no rigid dependencies between the parts that make up a Django application. For example, in Django it's perfectly valid to serve content directly from an HTML template, without the need to use business logic or set up database. Just like in Django it's also perfectly valid to forgo using an HTML template and return raw data directly from a business logic method (e.g., for a REST service).

A later section in this chapter entitled "Set Up Content: Understand URLs, Templates, and Apps" goes into greater detail with examples on how Django's loosely coupled architecture works.

Install Django

There are various ways to install the Django framework. You can download Django from its main site[7] and install it like a regular Python application. You can also download and install Django via an operating system (OS) package administration tool such as `apt-get` - available on Linux distributions.

Yet another option is to install Django is to download it via the Python package manager `pip`. And yet another alternative is to install Django directly from its source on github.[8] The list of Django installation options including their pros and cons is presented in Table 1-1.

[7]`https://www.djangoproject.com/download/`

[8]`https://github.com/django/django/`

Table 1-1. *Django installation options - Pros and Cons*

Approach	Pros	Cons
Download/install with `pip` Python package manager. **(Recommended option)**	Allows install on virtual Python environment. Dependencies are taken care of automatically.	Latest version may not be available.
Download from main site as `tar.gz` file.	Easiest access to latest Django stable release.	Requires manual download and install. Requires additional management of Django dependencies (if not using pip).
Download from Git.	Access to the latest Django features.	Can contain bugs. Requires additional management of Django dependencies (if not using pip).
Download/install from OS package manager (`apt-get`).	Easy to install. Dependencies are taken care of automatically.	Latest version may not be available. Installed on global Python environment.

As emphasized in Table 1-1, the recommended option to install Django is to use the Python `pip` package manager because it provides the most flexibility. Next, I'll describe each of the steps to install Django using this approach and more importantly how to get up and running with `pip`.

Once I finish these steps, I'll also describe the steps to install Django from a `tar.gz` file and from git - using `pip` - which can be helpful if you want to try out the latest Django features.

Install Python (Prerequisite)

Since Django is built on Python, you first need to install Python to run Django. The latest Django long-term release (LTS), which is the focus of this book, is version 1.11. Django 1.11 requires that you either have a Python 2.7.x release or a Python 3.4 or higher release (3.5 or 3.6).

If this is the first time you use Python, it's important to note Python 2 and Python 3 are considerably different. But while it's certainly true Python 3 is the future, be aware the future has been in the making since 2008 - when the first Python 3 release came to light - and Python 2 has remained stubbornly entrenched to the point that Python 2.7.13 came out in December 2016.

So should you use Python 2 or Python 3 with Django? As far as Django's core is concerned, it's compatible with both, so you can easily switch between Python 2 and Python 3. Where it gets a little more tricky is when it comes to third-party Python packages and the Django Python code you plan to write yourself.

While many third-party Python packages have been upgraded to run on Python 3, this process has been sluggish. As I already pointed out, Python 3 has been almost 10 years in the making, so be aware that if you take the Python 3 route, you may encounter third-party Python packages that won't work with Python 3.

When it comes to your own Django application code, the ideal choice is to make your code both Python 2 and Python 3 compatible - just like Django's core - it isn't that hard and I'll use this technique throughout the book. The sidebar contains more details on this topic of writing Python 2 and Python 3 compatible code.

Now, if want to stick to Python 2, just be aware Django 1.11 will be the last Django release to support Python 2 - scheduled to be supported until around April 2020 - so if you eventually upgrade to something higher than Django 1.11, you'll also need to upgrade all your application code to Python 3 - which is why I recommend the dual Python 2 and Python 3 compatibility technique. If you want to stick to Python 3, that's the future, just be aware that as described earlier, some third-party packages might not work with Python 3.

DJANGO COMPATIBILITY WITH PYTHON 2 AND PYTHON 3

Django uses Six[9] to run Python 2 and Python 3 compatible logic. Six is a set of utilities that wraps over the differences between Python 2 and Python 3, allowing that same logic to operate equally in either Python 2 and Python 3. The Django framework's internals – which you'll rarely, if ever, need to inspect or modify – already use this technique.

However, if you plan to write your Django application code to be compatible with both Python 2 and Python 3, then you'll need to be a little more aware of how you write it. Django publishes its own guidelines on the various syntax and techniques you need to follow to make Django application code work with both Python 2 and Python 3,[10] techniques that are also used throughout the book.

If you use a Unix/Linux OS, Python is very likely installed on your system. If you type `which python` on a Unix/Linux terminal and it returns a response (e.g., `/usr/bin/python`), it indicates the location of the Python executable, if there is no response it indicates the Python executable is not available on the system.

If you don't have Python on your system and you're using a Debian or Ubuntu Linux distribution, you can use the OS package manager apt-get to install Python by typing: `apt-get install python`. If you have a Unix/Linux distribution that is not Debian or Ubuntu and you need to install Python, consult your Unix/Linux documentation for available Python packages or download the Python sources from *http://python.org/download/* to do the installation.

If you have a system that runs on a Windows OS or macOS, Python installers are available for download from *http://python.org/download/*.

Irrespective of your system's OS, once you've finished the Python installation, ensure Python is installed correctly and accessible from anywhere on your system. Open a terminal and type `python`, and you should enter a Python interactive session like the one illustrated in Listing 1-1.

Listing 1-1. Python interactive session

```
[user@~]$ python
Python 2.7.12 (default, Nov 19 2016, 06:48:10)
[GCC 5.4.0 20160609] on linux2
Type "help", "copyright", "credits" or "license" for more information.
```

If you aren't able to enter a Python interactive session, review the Python installation process because you will not be able to continue with the following sections.

Update or Install pip Package Manager (Prerequisite)

To make Python package installation and management easier, Python uses a package manager called *pip*. If you're using Python 2.7.9 (or greater 2.x branch) or Python 3.4 (or a greater 3.x branch), pip comes installed by default. Now let's upgrade pip on your system as shown in Listing 1-2, if you don't have pip on your system, I'll provide instructions shortly on how to get it.

[9] https://pythonhosted.org/six/
[10] https://docs.djangoproject.com/en/1.11/topics/python3/

Listing 1-2. Update pip package manager

```
[user@~]$ pip install --upgrade pip
Collecting pip
  Downloading pip-9.0.1-py2.py3-none-any.whl (1.3MB)
Installing collected packages: pip
  Found existing installation: pip 8.1.1
Successfully installed pip-9.0.1
```

As you can see in Listing 1-2, to update pip you invoke the `pip` executable with the arguments `install --upgrade pip`. Upon execution, pip searches for a package by the provided name - in this case pip itself - downloads it and performs an upgrade in case it's already installed. If the installation output on your system is similar to the one in Listing 1-2 - without any errors - you have successfully updated pip.

If you see an error like *The program 'pip' is currently not installed* or *pip not found*, it means your Python installation is not equipped with pip. In this case, you'll need to install the pip executable by downloading *`https://bootstrap.pypa.io/get-pip.py`* and then executing the downloaded file with the command: `python get-pip.py`. Once the `pip` executable is installed, run the pip update procedure from Listing 1-2.

With pip on your system, you're ready to move on to the next step.

Install virtualenv (Optional Prerequisite)

Virtualenv is not essential to develop Django applications, but I highly recommend you use it because it allows you to create virtual Python environments on a single system. By using virtual Python environments, applications can run in their own 'sandbox' in isolation of other Python applications. Initially virtualenv can appear to be of little benefit, but it can be of tremendous help for tasks like replicating a development environment to a production environment and avoiding version conflicts that can arise between different applications.

Without virtualenv you can still proceed to install Django and any other Python package using pip, but the issue is that all packages are installed under the global Python installation. Initially this can seem convenient, because you only need to install packages once in the global Python installation. But it's not that convenient if you think about some of the following questions.

What happens if a new Django version is released after your first project and you want to start a second project? Do you upgrade the first project to run on the new Django version or start the second project as if the new Django version doesn't exist? The first option requires additional work, while the second option requires you to develop on an outdated Django version. By using virtual Python environments you avoid this problem, because each project can run its own Django version in isolation.

If you consider this potential version conflict for any Python package, you'll realize why I recommend you use virtualenv. Many Python packages have specific version dependencies (e.g., package A depends on package B version 2.3 and package C version 1.5). If you update a new package with specific cross-dependency versions, it can be very easy to break a Python installation if you're using a global Python installation. With virtualenv you can have multiple Python installations without them interfering with one another.

Now that I've explained the benefits of virtualenv, let's install the `virtualenv` executable with pip, as show in Listing 1-3.

Listing 1-3. Install virtualenv with pip

```
[user@~]$  pip install virtualenv
Downloading/unpacking virtualenv
  Downloading virtualenv-15.1.0.tar.gz (1.8Mb): 1.8Mb downloaded
  Running setup.py egg_info for package virtualenv
  Installing collected packages: virtualenv
```

```
  Running setup.py install for virtualenv
  Installing virtualenv script to /usr/local/bin
  Installing virtualenv-2.7 script to /usr/local/bin
Successfully installed virtualenv
Cleaning up...
```

As illustrated in Listing 1-3, pip automatically downloads and installs the requested package. Similar to the pip executable, a virtualenv executable is also installed that should be accessible from anywhere on your system. The virtualenv executable allows you to create virtual Python environments. Listing 1-4 illustrates how to create a virtual Python environment with virtualenv.

Listing 1-4. Create virtual Python environment with virtualenv

```
[user@~]$ virtualenv --python=python3 mydjangosandbox
Already using interpreter /usr/bin/python3
Using base prefix '/usr'
New python executable in /mydjangosandbox/bin/python3
Also creating executable in /mydjangosandbox/bin/python
Installing setuptools, pkg_resources, pip, wheel...done.
```

The virtualenv executable accepts several parameters. The task in Listing 1-4 makes use of the --python flag, which tells virtualenv to create a virtual Python based on the python3 executable, creating a Python 3 virtual environment. This is a common option when you have multiple Python versions on an OS (e.g., Python 2 and Python 3) and you need to specify the Python version with which to create the virtualenv. You can omit the --python flag; just be aware that doing so the virtualenv is created with the default OS python executable.

By default, virtualenv creates a pristine virtual Python environment like the one you had when you made the initial Python global installation. Following virtualenv parameters, you only need to specify an argument for the name of the virtual Python environment, which in the case of Listing 1-4 is mydjangosandbox. Upon execution, virtualenv creates a directory with the virtual Python environment whose contents are illustrated in Listing 1-5.

Listing 1-5. Virtual Python environment directory structure

```
+<virtual_environment_name>
|
|
+---+-<bin>
|   |
|   +-activate
|   +-easy_install
|   +-pip
|   +-python
    +-python-config
|   +-wheel
|
+---+-<include>
|
+---+-<lib>
|
+---+-<local>†
|
+---+-<share>
```

■ **Tip** Depending on the Python version used to create the virtualenv, the bin directory can contain multiple aliases or versions of the same command (e.g., In addition to `python`, `python2.7`, and `python3`; in addition to `activate`, `activate.csh`, and `activate_this.py`).

■ **Note†** local folder is only included in a Python 2 virtualenv and links to top-level directories of the virtual directory to simulate a Python installation.

As illustrated in Listing 1-5, a virtual Python environment has a similar directory structure to a global Python installation. The `bin` directory contains executables for the virtual environment, the `include` directory is linked to the global Python installation header files, the `lib` directory is a copy of the global Python installation libraries and where packages for the virtual environment are installed, and the `share` directory is used to place shared Python packages.

The most important part of the virtual environment is the executables under the `bin` directory. If you use any of these executables, such as `pip`, `easy_install`, `python`, or `wheel`, they execute under the context of the virtual Python environment. For example, the `pip` under the `bin` folder installs packages for the virtual environment. Similarly, an application that runs on the `python` executable under the `bin` folder is only able to load packages installed on the virtual Python environment. This is the 'sandbox' behavior I mentioned previously.

Even though access to different virtual Python environments and executables is a powerful feature, having different `pip` and `python` executables for multiple virtual Python environments and the executables of the global Python installation itself, can become confusing due to long access paths and relative paths.

For this reason, virtualenv has a mechanism to load virtual environments so that if you execute `pip`, `python`, or any other executable from anywhere on your system, the executables from a selected virtual environment are used (instead of the default global Python installation executables). This is achieved with the `activate` executable inside the `bin` directory, a process illustrated in Listing 1-6.

Listing 1-6. Activate virtual Python environment

```
[user@~]$ source ./bin/activate
[(mydjangosandbox)user@~] $
# NOTE: source is a Unix/Linux specific command, for other OS just execute activate
```

Notice in Listing 1-6 how after invoking the `activate` executable, the command prompt adds the virtual environment name between parentheses. This means the executables under the `bin` directory of the virtual Python environment `mydjangosandbox` are used over those in the global Python installation. To exit a virtual Python environment just type `deactivate` and you fall back to using the global Python installation executables.

As you've now learned, virtualenv works transparently allowing you to maintain different Python installations each with its own set of executables like the main python interpreter and the pip package manager. You only need to take care of switching between virtual environments so you install and run Python applications in the appropriate virtual environment.

■ **Note** In future sections I won't make any reference to virtualenv (e.g., `mydjangosandbox`) since it isn't directly related to Django. Though I recommend you use virtualenv, I'll leave it up to you if you want to keep using the global Python installation `python` and `pip` executables for everything or if you prefer to keep virtual Python environments with their own executables to make Python application management easier. So when you see Python executables referenced in the book, assume they are global or from a virtualenv, whichever you're using.

Install Django

Once you have all the previous tools working on your system, the actual Django installation is very simple. Listing 1-7 illustrates how to install Django using pip.

Listing 1-7. Install Django with pip

```
[user@~]$ pip install Django==1.11
Downloading/unpacking Django==1.11
Collecting Django==1.11
  Downloading Django-1.11-py2.py3-none-any.whl (6.9MB)
    100% |████████████████████████████████| 6.9MB 95kB/s
Collecting pytz (from Django==1.11)
  Downloading pytz-2017.2-py2.py3-none-any.whl (484kB)
    100% |████████████████████████████████| 491kB 735kB/s
Installing collected packages: pytz, Django
Successfully installed Django-1.11 pytz-2017.2
```

The `pip install` task in Listing 1-7 uses the `Django==1.11` syntax to tell pip to download and install the Django 1.11 version. With this same syntax you can install any specific Django version. If you don't specify a package version, pip downloads and installs the most recent available version for the specified package.

Sometimes a Django release may take a few days to become available through pip, in which case you'll receive an error. In such cases you can download the release directly from the Django main site at *https://www.djangoproject.com/download/*. Once you download the release file in tar.gz format, you can use pip to make the installation as illustrated in Listing 1-8.

Listing 1-8. Install Django from local tar.gz file with pip

```
[user@~]$ pip install /home/Downloads/Django-1.11.tar.gz
Processing /home/Downloads/Django-1.11.tar.gz
Collecting pytz (from Django==1.11)
  Using cached pytz-2017.2-py2.py3-none-any.whl
Building wheels for collected packages: Django
  Running setup.py bdist_wheel for Django ... done
  Stored in directory: /home/ubuntu/.cache/pip/wheels/56/bf/24/
f44162e115f4fe0cfeb4b0ae99b570fb55a741a8d090c9894d
Successfully built Django
Installing collected packages: pytz, Django
Successfully installed Django-1.11 pytz-2017.2
```

Notice in Listing 1-8 how pip is capable of installing Python packages directly from a compressed file on the local file system.

Install Django from Git

If you want to use the most recent functionalities available in Django, then you'll need to install Django from its Git repository. The Git repository contains the latest changes made to Django. Even though the Django Git version can be unstable, it's the only way to develop with the newest Django features or get bug fixes for problems that aren't yet available in public releases.

■ **Note** You need to install Git to execute the following tasks. You can download Git for several OSes at *http://git-scm.com/*

Just like the prior pip installation examples, pip is sufficiently flexible to make a Django installation from Git. There are two alternatives to use pip with Git. You can provide the remote Django Git repository, in which case pip clones the repository locally and discards it after the installation, as illustrated in Listing 1-9. Or you can clone the Django Git repository locally - where you'll be able to make modifications at a later time - and then run pip to do the installation, as illustrated in Listing 1-10.

Listing 1-9. Install Django from remote Git with pip

```
[user@~]$ pip install git+https://github.com/django/django.git
Collecting git+https://github.com/django/django.git
  Cloning https://github.com/django/django.git to ./pip-31j_bcqa-build

Requirement already satisfied: pytz in /python/mydjangosandbox/lib/python3.5/site-packages
(from Django==2.0.dev20170408112615)
Installing collected packages: Django
      Successfully uninstalled Django-1.11
  Running setup.py install for Django ... done
Successfully installed Django-2.0.dev20170408112615
```

Listing 1-10. Download Django from Git and install locally with pip

```
[user@~]$ git clone https://github.com/django/django.git
Cloning into django...
remote: Counting objects: 388550, done.
remote: Compressing objects: 100% (19/19), done.
remote: Total 388550 (delta 5), reused 0 (delta 0), pack-reused 388531
Receiving objects: 100% (388550/388550), 158.63 MiB | 968.00 KiB/s, done.
Resolving deltas: 100% (281856/281856), done.
Checking connectivity... done.

# Assuming Django Git download made to /home/Downloads/django/
[user@~]$ pip install /home/Downloads/django/
Processing /home/Downloads/django
Collecting pytz (from Django==2.0.dev20170408112615)
  Using cached pytz-2017.2-py2.py3-none-any.whl
Installing collected packages: pytz, Django
  Running setup.py install for Django ... done
Successfully installed Django-2.0.dev20170408112615 pytz-2017.2
```

Notice in Listing 1-9 the syntax to download a remote Git repository is `git+` followed by the remote Git location. In this case `https://github.com/django/django.git` represents the Django Git repository. In Listing 1-10 the Django Git repository is cloned locally first, and then `pip` is executed with the argument of the local Git repository directory.

Start a Django Project

To start a Django project you must use the django-admin executable or django-admin.py script that comes with Django. After you install Django, both this executable and script should be accessible from any directory on your system (e.g., installed under /usr/bin/,/usr/local/bin/ or the /bin/ directory of a virtualenv). Note that both the executable and script offer the same functionality; therefore I will use the django-admin term interchangeably going forward.

The django-admin offers various subcommands you'll use extensively for your daily work with Django projects. But it's the startproject subcommand you'll use first, since it creates the initial structure of a Django project. The startproject subcommand receives a single argument to indicate the name of project, as illustrated in the following snippet.

```
#Create a project called coffeehouse
django-admin startproject coffeehouse
#Create a project called sportstats
django-admin startproject sportstats
```

A Django project name can be composed of numbers, letters, or underscores. A project name cannot start with a number, it can only start with a letter or underscore. In addition, special characters, and spaces are not allowed anywhere in a project name, mainly because Django project names serve as a naming convention for directories and Python packages.

Upon executing django-admin startproject <project_name>, a directory called <project_name> is created containing the default Django project structure. The default Django project structure is illustrated in Listing 1-11.

Listing 1-11. Django project structure

```
+<BASE_DIR_project_name>
|
+----manage.py
|
+---+-<PROJECT_DIR_project_name>
    |
    +-__init__.py
    +-settings.py
    +-urls.py
    +-wsgi.py
```

If you inspect the directory layout, you'll notice there are two directories with the <project_name> value. I will refer to the top-level Django project directory as BASE_DIR, which includes the manage.py file and the other subdirectory based on the project name. And I will refer to the second-level subdirectory - which includes the __init__.py, settings.py, urls.py, and wsgi.py files - as PROJECT_DIR. Next, I'll describe the purpose of each file in Listing 1-11.

- manage.py .- Runs project specific tasks. Just as django-admin is used to execute system wide Django tasks, manage.py is used to execute project specific tasks.
- __init__.py .- Python file that allows Python packages to be imported from directories where it's present. Note __init__.py is not Django specific, it's a generic file used in almost all Python applications.

- `settings.py` .- Contains the configuration settings for the Django project.
- `urls.py` .- Contains URL patterns for the Django project.
- `wsgi.py` .- Contains WSGI configuration properties for the Django project. WSGI is the recommended approach to deploy Django applications on production (i.e., to the public). You don't need to set up WSGI to develop Django applications.

■ **Tip** Rename a project's `BASE_DIR`. Having two nested directories with the same name in a Django project can lead to confusion, especially if you deal with Python package import issues. To save yourself trouble, I recommend you rename the `BASE_DIR` to something different than the project name (e.g., rename, capitalize, or shorten the name to make it different than the `PROJECT_DIR`).

■ **Caution** Do not rename the `PROJECT_DIR`. The `PROJECT_DIR` name is hard-coded into some project files (e.g., `settings.py` and `wsgi.py`), so do not change its name. If you need to rename the `PROJECT_DIR` it's simpler to create another project with a new name.

Now that you're familiar with the default Django project structure, let's see the default Django project in a browser. All Django projects have a built-in web server to observe an application in a browser as changes are made to project files. Placed in the `BASE_DIR` of a Django project - where the `manage.py` file is - run the command `python manage.py runserver` as shown in Listing 1-12.

Listing 1-12. Start Django development web server provided by manage.py

```
[user@coffeehouse ~]$ python manage.py runserver
Performing system checks...

System check identified no issues (0 silenced).

You have 13 unapplied migration(s). Your project may not work properly until you apply the
migrations for app(s): admin, auth, contenttypes, sessions.
Run 'python manage.py migrate' to apply them.

May 23, 2017 - 22:41:20
Django version 1.11, using settings 'coffeehouse.settings'
Starting development server at http://127.0.0.1:8000/
Quit the server with CONTROL-C.
```

As illustrated in Listing 1-12, the command `python manage.py runserver` starts a development web server on *`http://127.0.0.1:8000/`* - which is the local address on your system. Don't worry about the `'unapplied migration(s)'` message for the moment, I'll address it in the upcoming section on setting up a database for a Django project. Next, if you open a browser and point it to the address *`http://127.0.0.1:8000/`* you should see the default home page for a Django project illustrated in Figure 1-3.

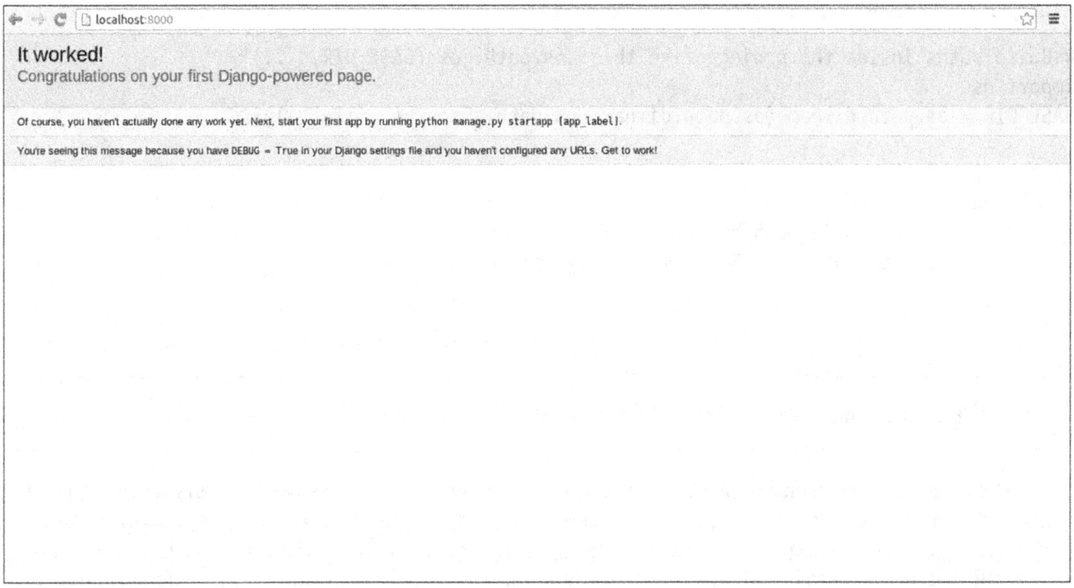

Figure 1-3. *Default home page for a Django project*

Sometimes it's convenient to alter the default address and port for Django's development web server. This can be due to the default port being busy by another service or the need to bind the web server to a non-local address so someone on a remote machine can view the development server. This is easily achieved by appending either the port or full address:port string to the `python manage.py runserver` command, as shown in the various examples in Listing 1-13.

Listing 1-13. Start Django development web server on different address and port

```
# Run the development server on the local address and port 4345 (http://127.0.0.1:4345/)
python manage.py runserver 4345
# Run the dev server on the 96.126.104.88 address and port 80 (http://96.126.104.88/)
python manage.py runserver 96.126.104.88:80
# Run the dev server on the 192.168.0.2 address and port 8888 (http://192.168.0.2:8888/)
python manage.py runserver 192.168.0.2:8888
```

Set Up a Database for a Django Project

Django in its 'out-of-the-box' state is set up to communicate with SQLite - a lightweight relational database included with the Python distribution. So by default, Django automatically creates a SQLite database for your project.

In addition to SQLite, Django also has support for other popular databases that include PostgreSQL, MySQL, and Oracle. The Django configuration to connect to a database is done inside the `setting.py` file of a Django project in the `DATABASES` variable.

If you open the `settings.py` file of a Django project, you'll notice the `DATABASES` variable has a default Python dictionary with the values illustrated in Listing 1-14.

Listing 1-14. Default Django DATABASES dictionary

```
# Build paths inside the project like this: os.path.join(BASE_DIR, ...)
import os
BASE_DIR = os.path.dirname(os.path.dirname(os.path.abspath(__file__)))

DATABASES = {
    'default': {
        'ENGINE': 'django.db.backends.sqlite3',
        'NAME': os.path.join(BASE_DIR, 'db.sqlite3'),
    }
}
```

■ **Tip** Use SQLite if you want the quickest database setup.

A database setup by itself can be time consuming. If you want the quickest setup to enable Django with a database, leave the previous configuration as is. SQLite doesn't require additional credentials or Python packages to establish a Django database connection. Just be aware a SQLite database is a flat file and Django creates the SQLite database based on the `NAME` variable value. In the case of Listing 1-14, under a Django project's `BASE_DIR` and as a flat file named `db.sqlite3`.

■ **Note** If you use SQLite, you can skip to the last step in this section "Test Django database connection and build Django base tables."

The Django `DATABASES` variable defines key-value pairs. Each key represents a database reference name and the value is a Python dictionary with the database connection parameters. In Listing 1-14 you can observe the `default` database reference. The `default` reference name is used to indicate that any database related operation declared in a Django project be executed against this connection. This means that unless otherwise specified, all database CRUD (Create-Read-Update-Delete) operations are done against the database defined with the `default` key.

The database connection parameters for the default database in this case are the keys `ENGINE` and `NAME`, which represent a database engine (i.e., brand) and the name of the database instance, respectively.

The most important parameter of a Django database connection is the `ENGINE` value. The Django application logic associated with a database is platform neutral, which means that you always write database CRUD operations in the same way irrespective of the database selection. Nevertheless, there are minor differences between CRUD operations done against different databases, which need to be taken into account.

Django takes care of this issue by supporting different back ends or engines. Therefore, depending on the database brand you plan to use for a Django application, the `ENGINE` value has to be one of the values illustrated in Table 1-2.

Table 1-2. *Django ENGINE value for different databases*

Database	Django **ENGINE** value
MySQL	`django.db.backends.mysql`
Oracle	`django.db.backends.oracle`
PostgreSQL	`django.db.backends.postgresql_psycopg2`
SQLite	`django.db.backends.sqlite3`

The Django database connection parameter NAME is used to identify a database instance, and its value convention can vary depending on the database brand. For example, for SQLite NAME indicates the location of a flat file, whereas for MySQL it indicates the logical name of an instance.

The full set of Django database connection parameters is described in Table 1-3.

Table 1-3. *Django database connection parameters based on database brand*

Django connection parameter	Default value	Notes
ATOMIC_REQUESTS	False	Enforces (or not) a transaction for each view request. By default set to False, because opening a transaction for every view has additional overhead. The impact on performance depends on the query patterns of an application and on how well a database handles locking.
AUTOCOMMIT	True	By default set to True, because otherwise it would require explicit transactions to perform commits.
CONN_MAX_AGE	0	The lifetime of a database connection in seconds. By default 0 which closes the database connection at the end of each request. Use None for unlimited persistent connections.
ENGINE	''(Empty string)	The database back end to use. See Table 1-2 for value options.
HOST	''(Empty string)	Defines a database host, where an empty string means localhost. For MySQL: If this value starts with a forward slash ('/'), MySQL will connect via a Unix socket to the specified socket (e.g.,"HOST": '/var/run/mysql'). If this value doesn't start with a forward slash, then this value is assumed to be the host. For PostgreSQL: By default("), the connection to the database is done through UNIX domain sockets ('local' lines in pg_hba.conf). If the UNIX domain socket is not in the standard location, use the same value of unix_socket_directory from postgresql.conf. If you want to connect through TCP sockets, set HOST to 'localhost' or '127.0.0.1' ('host' lines in pg_hba.conf). On Windows, you should always define HOST, as UNIX domain sockets are not available.
NAME	''(Empty string)	The name of the database to use. For SQLite, it's the full path to the database file. When specifying the path, always use forward slashes, even on Windows (e.g., C:/www/STORE/db.sqlite3).
OPTIONS	{} (Empty dictionary)	Extra parameters to use when connecting to the database. Available parameters vary depending on database back end, consult the back end module's own documentation. For a list of back-end modules see Table 1-2.
PASSWORD	'' (Empty string)	The password to use when connecting to the database. Not used with SQLite.
PORT	'' (Empty string)	The port to use when connecting to the database. An empty string means the default port. Not used with SQLite.
USER	'' (Empty string)	The username to use when connecting to the database. Not used with SQLite.

Install Python Database Packages

Besides configuring Django to connect to a database, you'll also need to install the necessary Python packages to communicate with your database brand - the only exception to this is SQLite, which is included in the Python distribution.

Each database relies on different packages, but the installation process is straightforward with the pip package manager. If you don't have the pip executable on your system, see the previous section in this chapter "Install Django" in the "Install pip" subsection.

The Python packages for each database supported in Django in its 'out-of-the-box' state are enumerated in Table 1-4. In addition, Table 1-4 also includes the pip command to install each package.

Table 1-4. *Python packages for different databases*

Database	Python package	pip installation syntax
PostgreSQL	`psycopg2`	`pip install psycopg2`
MySQL	`mysql-python`	`pip install mysql-python`
Oracle	`cx_Oracle`	`pip install cx_Oracle`
SQLite	Included with Python 2.5+	N/A

DATABASE DEVELOPMENT LIBRARIES

If you receive an error trying to install one of the Python database packages in Table 1-4, ensure the database development libraries are installed on your system. Database development libraries are necessary to build software that connects to a database.

Database development libraries are not related to Python or Django, so you'll need to consult the database vendor or operating system documentation (e.g., On a Debian Linux or Ubuntu Linux system you can install the MySQL development libraries with the following apt-get task: apt-get install libmysqlclient-dev).

Test Django Database Connection and Build Django Base Tables

Once you update the Django `settings.py` file with database credentials, you can test it to see if the Django application can communicate with the database. There are several tasks you'll do throughout a Django project that will communicate with the database, but one of the most common tasks you can do right now to test a database connection is to migrate the project's data structures to the database.

The Django database migration process ensures all Django project logic associated with a database is reflected in the database itself (e.g., the database has the necessary tables expected by a Django project). When you start a Django project, there are a series of migrations Django requires that create tables to keep track of administrators and sessions. This is always the first migration process a Django project runs against a database. So to test the Django database connection, let's run this first migration on the database to create this set of base tables.

To run a migration on a Django project against a database, use the `manage.py` script in a project's `BASE_DIR` with the `migrate` argument (e.g., `python manage.py migrate`). The first time you execute this command the output should be similar to Listing 1-15.

Listing 1-15. Run first Django migrate operation to create base database tables

```
[user@coffeehouse ~]$ python manage.py migrate
Operations to perform:
  Apply all migrations: admin, auth, contenttypes, sessions
Running migrations:
  Applying contenttypes.0001_initial... OK
  Applying auth.0001_initial... OK
  Applying admin.0001_initial... OK
  Applying admin.0002_logentry_remove_auto_add... OK
  Applying contenttypes.0002_remove_content_type_name... OK
  Applying auth.0002_alter_permission_name_max_length... OK
  Applying auth.0003_alter_user_email_max_length... OK
  Applying auth.0004_alter_user_username_opts... OK
  Applying auth.0005_alter_user_last_login_null... OK
  Applying auth.0006_require_contenttypes_0002... OK
  Applying auth.0007_alter_validators_add_error_messages... OK
  Applying auth.0008_alter_user_username_max_length... OK
  Applying sessions.0001_initial... OK
```

As illustrated in Listing 1-15, if the connection to the database is successful, Django applies a series of migrations that create database tables to manage users, groups, permissions, and sessions for a project. For the moment, don't worry too much about how these Django migrations work or where they are located - I'll provide details later - just be aware these migrations are needed by Django to provide some basic functionality.

■ **Tip** Connect directly to the database. If you receive an error trying to connect to the database or migrating the Django project to create the initial set of database tables, try to connect directly to the database using the same Django parameters.

On many occasions a typo in the Django variables NAME, USER, PASSWORD, HOST, or PORT can cause the process to fail or inclusively the credentials aren't even valid to connect directly to the database.

Set Up Content: Understand Urls, Templates, and Apps

Content in Django projects works with three major building blocks: urls, templates, and apps. You create and configure Django urls, templates, and apps separately, though you connect one to another to fulfill content delivery, which is part of Django's loosely coupled architecture design principles.

Urls define the entry points or where to access content. Templates define the end points that give form to the final content. And apps serve as the middleware between urls and templates, altering or adding content from a database or user interactions. To run static content you only need to create and configure Django urls and templates. To run dynamic content - built from a database or user interactions - you need to create and configure Django apps, in addition to urls and templates.

But before describing how to create and configure urls, templates, and apps, it's very important you understand how each of these parts works with one another. Figure 1-4 shows the Django workflow for user requests and how they work with Django urls, templates, and apps.

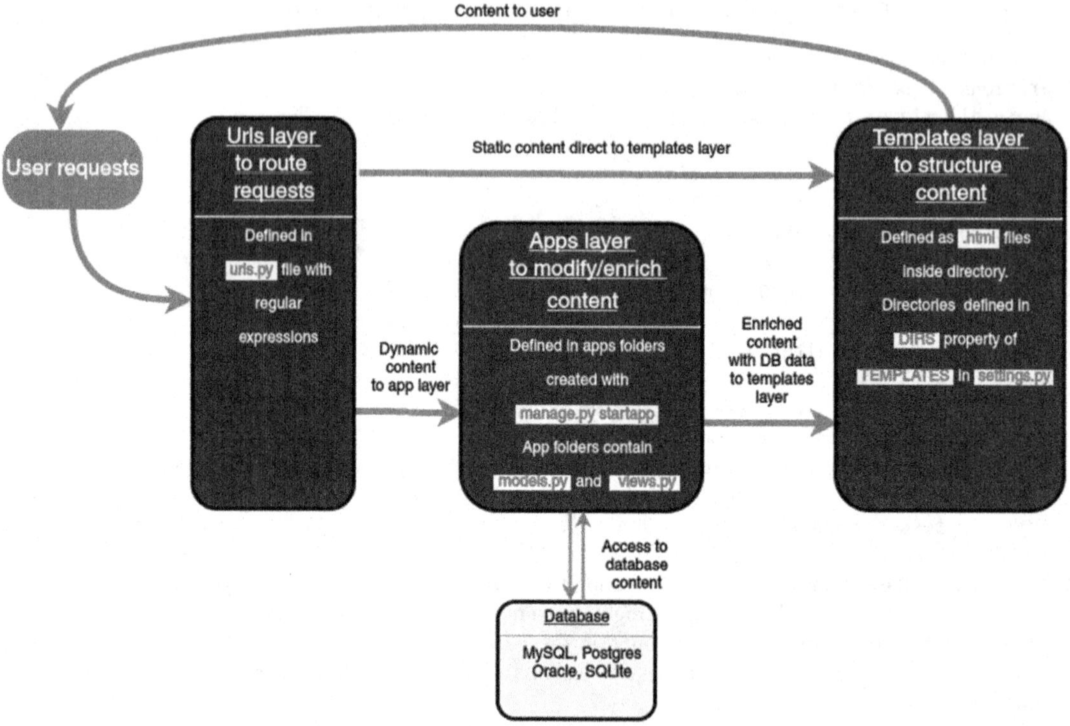

Figure 1-4. *Django workflow for urls, templates, and apps*

As you can see in Figure 1-4, there are two separate pipelines to deliver either static or dynamic content. More importantly, notice how each of the different Django layers is loosely coupled (e.g., you can forgo the apps layer if it isn't required and the urls layer and templates layer are still able to communicate with one another).

Create and Configure Django Urls

The main entry point for Django urls is the `urls.py` file created when you start a project - if you're unfamiliar with a Django project structure, see Listing 1-11 earlier in the chapter. If you open the `urls.py` file, you'll notice it only has one active url to `/admin/` that is the Django admin - I will discuss the Django admin in the next and final section of this chapter.

Now that you're familiar with the `urls.py` file syntax, let's activate a url to view custom content on the home page of a Django project.

Django urls use regular expressions to match incoming requests. The regular expression pattern to match a home page is ^$ - the next chapter includes a dedicated section on the use of regular expression in Django urls. In addition to the regular expression pattern, an action of what to do when a request is intercepted for a matching pattern is also needed (e.g., send the content from a specific template).

Open the `urls.py` file and add line 3 - the one below `django.contrib import admin` - and line 9 - the one below `url(r'^admin/', admin.site.urls),` - as illustrated in Listing 1-16.

Listing 1-16. Django url for home page to template

```
from django.conf.urls import url
from django.contrib import admin
from django.views.generic import TemplateView
...
...

urlpatterns = [
    url(r'^admin/', admin.site.urls),
    url(r'^$',TemplateView.as_view(template_name='homepage.html')),
]
```

As show in Listing 1-16, `urlpatterns` is a Python list of `url()` statements. The `url` method comes from the `django.conf.urls` package. The `url` method you just added defines the pattern for the home page - the regular expression `^$` - followed by the action `TemplateView.as_view(template_name='homepage.html')`. This last action is a helper method to direct the requesting party to a template that takes the argument `template_name='homepage.html'`.

In summary, the `url` method you added in Listing 1-16 tells Django that requests for the home page should return the content in the template `homepage.html`. The `url` method is very versatile and can accept several variations, as I'll describe shortly and extensively in the next chapter.

Now let's test the home page. Start the development web server by executing `python manage.py runserver` on the Django project's `BASE_DIR`. Open a browser on the default address `http://127.0.0.1:8000/`. What do you see? An error page with `Exception Type: TemplateDoesNotExist homepage.html`. This error is caused because Django can't locate the `homepage.html` template defined for the url. In the next section, I'll show you how to configure and create templates.

■ **Caution** If you receive the error `OperationalError - no such table: django_session` instead of the `TemplateDoesNotExist homepage.html` error, this means the database for a Django project is still not set up properly. You'll need to run `python manage.py migrate` in a project's `BASE_DIR` so Django creates the necessary tables to keep track of sessions. See the previous section on setting up a database for more details.

Create and Configure Django Templates

By default, Django templates are interpreted as HTML. This means Django templates are expected to have a standard HTML document structure and HTML tags (e.g., `<html>`, `<body>`). You can use a regular text editor to create Django templates and save the files with an `.html` extension.

Lets create a template for the url in the past section. In a text editor, create a file named `homepage.html` and place the contents of Listing 1-17 into it. Save the file on your system, in a subdirectory called `templates` in your Django project's `PROJECT_DIR`.

Listing 1-17. Template homepage.html

```
<html>
 <body>
  <h4>Home page for Django</h4>
 </body>
</html>
```

Once you have a directory with Django templates, you need to configure a Django project so it can find the templates in this directory. In the settings.py file of the Django project, you need to define the template directory in the DIRS property of the TEMPLATES variable. The DIRS property is a list, so you can define several directories to locate templates, though I recommend you only use a single directory with various subdirectories for classification.

As I recommended previously, you should aim to keep Django templates inside a subdirectory - using an obvious name like templates - in a Django project's PROJECT_DIR. So for example, if the absolute path to a Django project PROJECT_DIR is /www/STORE/coffeehouse/, the recommended location for a DIRS value would be /www/STORE/coffeehouse/templates/. Listing 1-18 illustrates a sample DIRS definition in settings.py using the PROJECT_DIR reference variable set dynamically at the top of settings.py.

Listing 1-18. TEMPLATES and DIRS definition in settings.py

```
BASE_DIR = os.path.dirname(os.path.dirname(os.path.abspath(__file__)))
PROJECT_DIR = os.path.dirname(os.path.abspath(__file__))

TEMPLATES = [
    {
        'BACKEND': 'django.template.backends.django.DjangoTemplates',
        'DIRS': ['%s/templates/' % (PROJECT_DIR),],
        'APP_DIRS': True,
        'OPTIONS': {
            'context_processors': [
                'django.template.context_processors.debug',
                'django.template.context_processors.request',
                'django.contrib.auth.context_processors.auth',
                'django.contrib.messages.context_processors.messages',
            ],
        },
    },
]
```

An important takeaway from Listing 1-18 is that it doesn't use hard-coded directory paths; instead it uses the PROJECT_DIR variable that is determined dynamically. This may seem trivial at the moment, but it's a good practice once the location of a Django project has a tendency to change (e.g., group development, deployment to production).

Finally, start the Django development web server once again and open a browser on the default address http://127.0.0.1:8000/. Instead of the error page you saw in the previous section, you should now see the contents of the template homepage.html on the home page.

Create and Configure Django Apps

Django apps are used to group application functionality. If you want to work with content from a database or user interactions you have to create and configure Django apps. A project can contain as many apps as you need. For example, if you have a project for a coffeehouse, you can create an app for stores, another app for menu items, another app for about information, and create additional apps as they're needed. There's no hard rule to the number of apps in a project. Whether to make code management simpler or delegate app work to a team, the purpose of Django apps is to group application functionality to make work easier.

Django apps are normally contained in subdirectories inside a project. This approach makes it easier to use Python references and naming conventions. If the project name is coffeehouse, the functionality of an app named stores is easily referred through Python packages as coffeehouse.stores.

Because apps provide a modular way to group application functionality, it's common for other people or groups to distribute Django apps with popular functionality. For example, if a Django project requires forum functionality, instead of writing a forum app from scratch, you can leverage one of several Django forum apps. The more general purpose the functionality you're looking for, the more likely you'll be able to find a Django app created by a third party.

YOU ALREADY WORKED WITH DJANGO APPS!

You may not have realized it, but in the previous section when you set up a database for a Django project, you already worked with Django apps when you invoked the migrate operation.

By default, all Django projects are enabled with six apps provided by the framework. These apps are `django.contrib.admin`, `django.contrib.auth`, `django.contrib.contenttypes`, `django.contrib.sessions`, `django.contrib.messages`, and `django.contrib.staticfiles`. When you triggered the migrate operation, Django created the database models for these preinstalled apps.

Next, lets create a small Django app. Go to the `PROJECT_DIR` - where the `urls.py` and `settings.py` files are - and execute the command `django-admin startapp about` to create an app called about. A subdirectory named `about` is created containing the app. By default, upon creating an app its subdirectory includes the following:

- `__init__.py` .- Python file to allow app packages to be imported from other directories. Note `__init__.py` is not a Django specific file, it's a generic file used in almost all Python applications.
- `migrations`.- Directory that contains migrations applied to the app's database definitions (i.e., model classes).
- `admin.py` .- File with admin definitions for the app - such definitions are needed to access model class instances from the Django admin.
- `apps.py` .- File with configuration parameters for the app.
- `models.py` .- File with database definitions (i.e., model classes) for the app.
- `tests.py` .- File with test definitions for the app.
- `views.py` .- File with view definitions (i.e., controller methods) for the app.

Next, open the `views.py` file and add the contents from Listing 1-19.

Listing 1-19. Handler view method in views.py

```
from django.shortcuts import render

def contact(request):
    # Content from request or database extracted here
    # and passed to the template for display
    return render(request,'about/contact.html')
```

The contact method in Listing 1-19 - like all other methods in views.py files - is a controller method with access to a user's web request. Notice the input for the contact method is called request. Inside this type of method you can access content from a web request (e.g., IP address, session) using the request reference or access information from a database, so that toward the end you pass this information to a template. If you look at the last line of the contact method, it finishes with a return statement to the Django helper method render. In this case, the render method returns control to the about/contact.html template.

Because the contact method in Listing 1-19 returns control to the template about/contact.html, you'll also need to create a subdirectory called about with a template called contact.html inside your templates directory (i.e., the one defined in the DIRS property of the TEMPLATES variable).

The contact method by itself does nothing, it needs to be called by a url. Listing 1-20 illustrates how to add a url to the urls.py file linked to the contact method in Listing 1-19.

Listing 1-20. Django url for view method

```
from django.conf.urls import url
from django.contrib import admin
from django.views.generic import TemplateView

from coffeehouse.about import views as about_views

urlpatterns = [
    url(r'^admin/', admin.site.urls),
    url(r'^$',TemplateView.as_view(template_name='homepage.html')),
    url(r'^about/', about_views.contact),
]
```

The first thing that's declared in Listing 1-20 is an import statement to gain access to the contact method in Listing 1-19. In this case, because the app is named about and it's under the coffeehouse project folder, it says from coffeehouse.about, followed by import views which gives us access to the app's views.py file where the contact method is located.

The import statement ends with as about_views to assign a unique qualifier, which is important if you plan to work with multiple apps. For example, import statements without the as keyword, such as from coffeehouse.about import views, from coffeehouse.items import views or from coffeehouse.stores import views can import conflicting view method references (e.g., three methods named index), so the as qualifier is a safeguard to ensure you don't unintentionally use a method with the same name from another app.

The new url definition in Listing 1-20 uses a regular expression to match requests on the about url directory (e.g., *http://127.0.0.1:8000/about/*) and instead of directing the request to a template, control is given to the about_views.contact method - where about_views refers to the imported reference described in the previous paragraph.

Next, start the Django development web server and open a browser on the address *http://127.0.0.1:8000/about/*. Notice how a request on the about url directory displays the underlying about/contact.html template defined in the contact method in views.py.

Finally, although you can now access an app's views.py methods, you also need to configure the app inside a project's settings.py file. This last step is important so Django can find other app constructs you create later (e.g., database model definitions, static resources, custom template tags).

Open the Django project's settings.py file and look for the INSTALLED_APPS variable. You'll see a series of apps already defined on the INSTALLED_APPS. Notice how the installed apps belong to the django.contrib package, this means they're provided by the Django framework itself. Add the coffeehouse.about app to the list as illustrated in line 8 of Listing 1-21.

Listing 1-21. Add app to INSTALLED_APPS in Django settings.py

```
INSTALLED_APPS = [
    'django.contrib.admin',
    'django.contrib.auth',
    'django.contrib.contenttypes',
    'django.contrib.sessions',
    'django.contrib.messages',
    'django.contrib.staticfiles',
    'coffeehouse.about',
]
```

As illustrated in line 8 of Listing 1-21, to add apps to a project you add the app package as a string to the `INSTALLED_APPS` variable. Though the `coffeehouse.about` app is still practically empty, adding the app to the `INSTALLED_APPS` variable is an important configuration step for future actions, such as database operations and static resources associated with the app, among other things.

Set Up the Django admin Site

The Django admin site provides a web-based interface to access the database connected to a Django project. Even for experienced technical administrators, doing database CRUD (Create-Read-Update-Delete) operations directly on a database can be difficult and time consuming, given the need to issue raw SQL commands and navigate database structures. For nontechnical users, doing database CRUD operations directly on a database can be daunting, if not impossible. The Django admin site fixes this problem.

The Django admin site can expose all Django project-related data structures linked to a database, so it's easy for experts and novices alike to perform database CRUD operations. As a Django project grows, the Django admin site can be a vital tool to administer the growing body of information in the database connected to a Django project.

The Django admin site is built as a Django app; this means the only thing you need to do to set up the Django admin site is configure and install the app as any other Django app. If you're unfamiliar with the term Django app, read the previous section "Set Up Content: Understand Urls, Templates, and Apps."

The Django admin site requires that you previously configure a database and also install the Django base tables. So if you still haven't done this, see the prior section "Set Up a Database for a Django Project."

Configure and Install the Django admin site App

By default, the Django admin is enabled on all Django projects. If you open a Django project's `urls.py` file, in the `urlpatterns` variable you'll see the line `url(r'^admin/', admin.site.urls)`. This last regular expression pattern tells Django to enable the admin site app on the `/admin` url directory (e.g., *`http://127.0.0.1:8000/admin/`*).

Next, if you open the project's `settings.py` file and go to the `INSTALLED_APPS` variable, near the top of this variable you'll see the line `django.contrib.admin` that indicates the Django admin site app is enabled.

Start the development web server by executing `python manage.py runserver` on Django's `BASE_DIR`. Open a browser on the Django admin site *`http://127.0.0.1:8000/admin/`*. You'll see a login screen like the one in Figure 1-5.

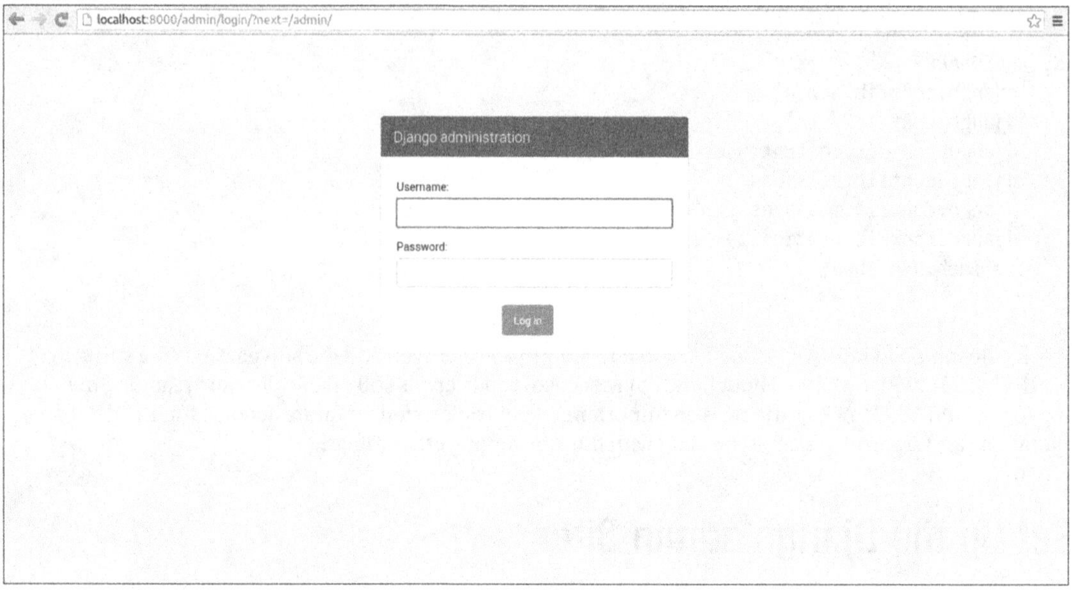

Figure 1-5. *Django admin site login*

Next, let's create a Django superuser or administrator to access the Django admin via the interface in Figure 1-5. To create a Django superuser you can use the `createsuperuser` command from `manage.py` as illustrated in Listing 1-22.

Listing 1-22. Create Django superuser for admin interface

```
[user@coffeehouse ~]$ python manage.py createsuperuser
Username (leave blank to use 'admin'):
Email address: admin@coffeehouse.com
Password:
Password (again):
The password is too similar to the email address.
This password is too short. It must contain at least 8 characters.
This password is too common.
Password:
Password (again):
Superuser created successfully.
```

■ **Caution** If you receive the error `OperationalError - no such table: auth_user`, this means the database for a Django project is still not set up properly. You'll need to run `python manage.py migrate` in a project's BASE_DIR so Django creates the necessary tables to keep track of users. See the previous section "Set Up a Database for a Django Project" for more details.

■ **Tip** By default, Django enforces that user passwords comply with a minimum level of security. For example, in Listing 1-22 you can see that after attempting to use the password coffee, Django rejects the assignment with a series of error messages and forces a new attempt. You can modify these password validation rules in the `AUTH_PASSWORD_VALIDATORS` variable in `setttings.py`.

This last process creates a superuser whose information is stored in the database connected to the Django project, specifically in the `auth_user` table. Now you might be asking yourself, how do you update this user's name, password, or email? While you could go straight to the database table and perform updates, this is a tortuous route; a better approach is to rely on the Django admin, which gives you a very friendly view into the database tables present in your Django project.

Next, introduce the superuser username and password you just created into the interface from Figure 1-5. Once you provide the superuser username and password on the admin site, you'll access the home page for the admin site illustrated in Figure 1-6.

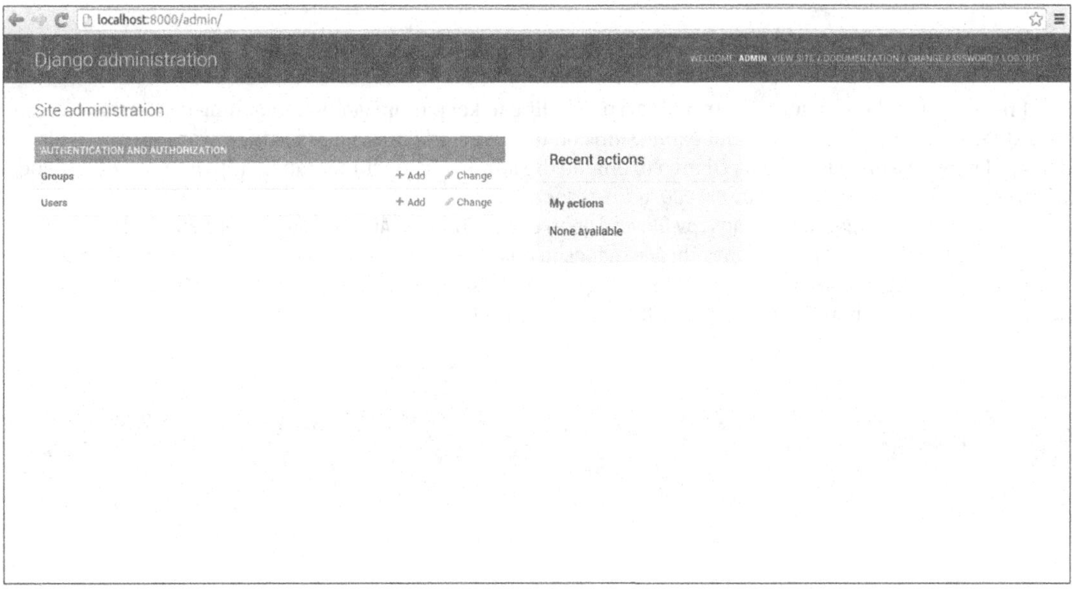

***Figure 1-6.** Django admin site home page*

On the home page of the Django admin site illustrated in Figure 1-6, click on the 'Users' link. You'll see a list of users with access to the Django project. At the moment, you'll only see the superuser you created in the past step. You can change this user's credentials (e.g., password, email, username) or add new users directly from this Django admin site screen.

This flexibility to modify or add records stored in a database that's tied to a Django project is what makes the Django admin site so powerful. For example, if you develop a coffeehouse project and add apps like stores, drinks, or customers, Django admin authorized users can do CRUD operations on these objects (e.g., create stores, update drinks, delete customers). This is tremendously powerful from a content management point of view, particularly for nontechnical users. And most importantly it requires little to no additional development work to enable the Django admin site on a project's apps.

The Django admin site tasks presented here are just the 'tip of the iceberg' in functionality; a future chapter covers the Django admin site functionality in greater detail.

Configure and Install the Django admin site docs App

The Django admin site also has its own documentation app. The Django admin site documentation app not only provides information about the operation of the admin site itself, but also includes other general documentation about Django filters for Django templates. More importantly, the Django admin site documentation app introspects the source code for all installed project apps to present documentation on controller methods and model objects (i.e., documentation embedded in the source code of app `models.py` and `views.py` files).

To install the Django admin site documentation app, you first need to install the docutils Python package with the pip package manager executing the following command: `pip install docutils`. Once you install the docutils package, you can proceed to install the Django admin site documentation app as any other Django app.

Add the url to access the Django admin site documentation app. If you open the project's `urls.py` file, in the `urlpatterns` variable add the following line:

```
url(r'^admin/doc/', include('django.contrib.admindocs.urls'))
```

Ensure you add this before the `url(r'^admin/'`... line to keep more general matching expressions toward the bottom and more granular expressions on the same url path (e.g., `/admin`) toward the top. This last regular expression pattern tells Django to enable the admin site documentation app on the /admin/doc/ url directory (e.g. *`http://127.0.0.1:8000/admin/doc/`*).

Next, open the project's `settings.py` file and go to the `INSTALLED_APPS` variable. Near the final values in this variable add the line `django.contrib.admindocs` to enable the Django admin site documentation app.

With the development web server running, open a browser on the address *`http://127.0.0.1:8000/admin/doc/`* and you should see a page like the one in Figure 1-7.

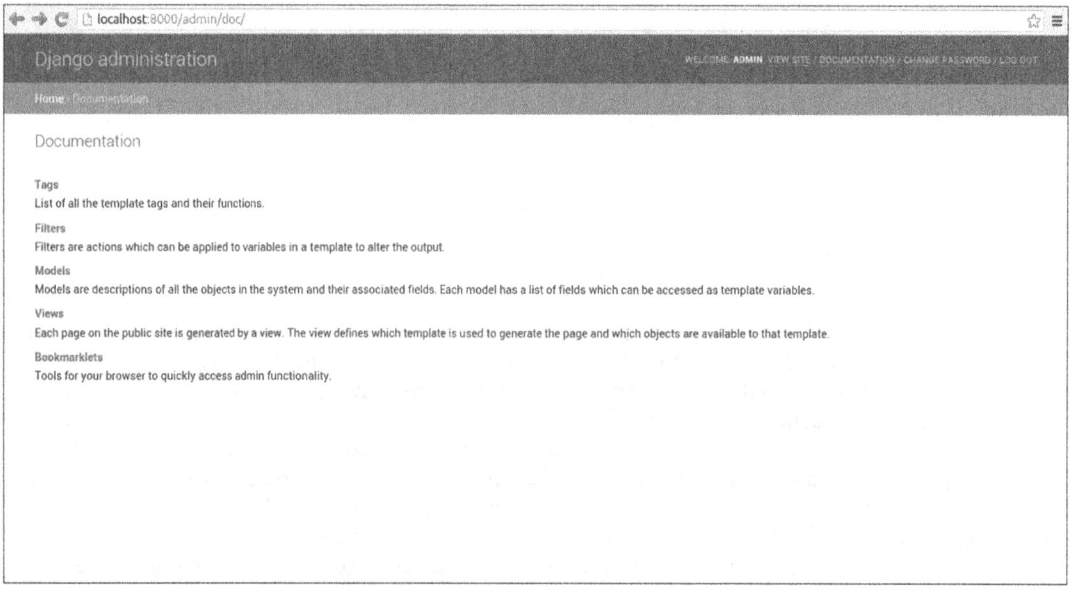

***Figure 1-7.** Django admin site doc home page*

If you logged off the Django admin site, you'll need to log in again to access the documentation since it also requires user authentication. Once you log in, you'll be able to see the documentation home page for the Django admin site - illustrated in Figure 1-7 - as well as the documentation on a project's controller methods and model objects.

CHAPTER 2

■ ■ ■

Django Urls and Views

In Chapter 1 you learned about the core building blocks in Django, inclduing what are views, models, and urls. In this chapter, you'll learn more about Django urls, which are the entry point into a Django application workflow. You'll learn how to create complex url regular expressions, how to use url values in view methods and templates, how to structure and manage urls, and how to name urls.

After urls, Django views represent the next step in almost all Django workflows, where views are charged with inspecting requests, executing business logic, querying a database and validating data, as well as generating responses. In this chapter, you'll learn how to create Django views with optional parameters, the structure of view requests and responses, how to use middleware with views, and how to create class-based views.

Url Regular Expressions

Regular expressions provide a powerful approach in all programming languages to determine patterns. However, with power also comes complexity, to the point that there are entire books written on the topic of regular expressions.[1]

Although most Django urls will never exceed a fraction of the complexity illustrated in many regular expression books, it's important that you understand some of the underlying behaviors and most common patterns of regular expressions in Django urls.

Precedence Rule: Granular Urls First, Broad Urls Last

Django urls need to follow a certain order and syntax to work correctly. Broad url regular expressions should be declared last and only after more granular url regular expressions.

This is because Django url regular expression matching doesn't use short-circuiting behavior, like a nested conditional statement (e.g., if/elif/elif/elif/else) where as soon as one condition is met, the remaining options are ignored. In Django urls if there's more than one matching regular expression for an incoming url request, it will be the top-most one's action that gets triggered. Precedence for matching url regular expressions is given from top (i.e., first declared) to bottom (i.e., last declared).

You shouldn't underestimate how easy it can be to introduce two url regular expressions that match the same pattern, particularly if you've never done regular expressions since the syntax can be cryptic. Listing 2-1 illustrates the right way to declare Django urls, with more granular regular expressions toward the top and broad regular expressions toward the bottom.

[1] http://www.apress.com/la/book/9781590594414

© Daniel Rubio 2017

D. Rubio, *Beginning Django*, https://doi.org/10.1007/978-1-4842-2787-9_2

Listing 2-1. Correct precedence for Django url regular expressions

```
from django.views.generic import TemplateVieww

urlpatterns = [
    url(r'^about/index/',TemplateView.as_view(template_name='index.html')),
    url(r'^about/',TemplateView.as_view(template_name='about.html')),
]
```

Based on Listing 2-1, let's walk through what happens if Django receives a request for the url `/about/index/`. Initially Django matches the last regular expression, which says 'match `^about/`'. Next, Django continues upward inspecting the regular expressions and reaches 'match `^about/index/`' that is an exact match to the request url `/about/index/` and therefore triggers this action to send control to the `index.html` template.

Now let's walk through a request for the url `/about/`. Initially Django matches the last regular expression that says 'match `^about/`'. Next, Django continues upward inspecting the regular expressions for a potential match. Because no match is found - since 'match `^about/index/`' is a more granular regular expression - Django triggers the first action to send control to the `about.html` template, which was the only regular expression match.

As you can see, Listing 2-1 produces what can be said to be expected behavior. But now let's invert the order of the url regular expressions, as shown in Listing 2-2, and break down why declaring more granular regular expressions toward the bottom is the wrong way to declare Django url regular expressions.

Listing 2-2. Wrong precedence for Django url regular expressions

```
from django.views.generic import TemplateVieww

urlpatterns = [
    url(r'^about/',TemplateView.as_view(template_name='about.html')),
    url(r'^about/index/',TemplateView.as_view(template_name='index.html')),
]
```

The issue in Listing 2-2 comes when a request is made for the url `/about/index/`. Initially Django matches the last regular expression, which says 'match `^about/index/`'. However, Django continues inspecting the regular expressions and reaches 'match `^about/`' which is a broader match to the request url `/about/index/`, but nevertheless a match! Therefore Django triggers this action and sends control to the `about.html` template, instead of what was likely expected to be the `index.html` template from the first match.

Exact Url Patterns: Forgoing Broad Matching

In the past section, I intentionally used regular expressions that allowed broad url matching. In my experience, as a Django project grows you'll eventually face the need to use this type of url regular expression - but more on why this is so, shortly.

As it turns out, it's possible to use exact url regular expressions. Exact url regular expressions remove any ambiguity introduced by the order in which Django url regular expression are declared.

Let's rework the url regular expressions from Listing 2-2 and make them exact regular expressions so their order doesn't matter. Listing 2-3 illustrates exact regular expressions on basis of those in Listing 2-2.

Listing 2-3. Exact regular expressions, where url order doesn't matter

```
from django.views.generic import TemplateVieww

urlpatterns = [
    url(r'^about/$',TemplateView.as_view(template_name='about.html')),
    url(r'^about/index/$',TemplateView.as_view(template_name='index.html')),
]
```

Notice the regular expressions in Listing 2-3 end with the $ character. This is the regular expression symbol for end of line, which means the regular expression urls only match an exact pattern.

For example, if Django receives a request for the url `/about/index/` it will only match the last regular expression in Listing 2-3, which says 'match `^about/index/$`'. However, it won't match the higher-up `^/about/$` regular expression because this regular expression says match `about/` *exactly* with nothing else after, since the $ indicates the end of the pattern.

However, as useful as the $ character is to make stricter url regular expressions, it's important you analyze its behavior. If you plan to use url Search Engine Optimization (SEO), A/B testing techniques, or simply want to allow multiple urls to run the same action, stricter regular expressions with $ eventually require more work.

For example, if you start to use urls like `/about/index/`, `/about/email/`,`/about/address/` and they all use the same template or view for processing, exact regular expressions just make the amount of urls you declare larger. Similarly, if you use A/B testing or SEO where lengthier variations of the same url are processed in the same way (e.g., `/about/landing/a/`, `/about/landing/b/`, `/about/the+coffeehouse+in+san+diego/`) broad url matching is much simpler than declaring exact url patterns.

In the end, whether you opt to use exact url regular expression ending in $, I would still recommend you maintain the practice of keeping finer-grained url regulars at the top and broader ones at the bottom, as this avoids the unexpected behaviors described in Listing 2-2 when more than one regular expression matches a url request.

Common Url Patterns

Although url regular expressions can have limitless variations – making it next to impossible to describe each possibility – I'll provide examples on some of the most common url patterns you're more likely to use. Table 2-1 shows individual regular expression characters for Django urls and Table 2-2 shows a series of more concrete examples with url patterns.

Table 2-1. *Regular expression syntax for Django urls: Symbol (Meaning)*

^ (Start of url)	$ (End of url)	\ (Escape for interpreted values)	| (Or)
+ (1 or more occurrences)	? (0 or 1 occurrences)	{n} (n occurrences)	{n,m} (Between n and m occurrences)
[] (Character grouping)	(?P<name>___) (Capture occurrence that matches regexp ___ and assign it to name	. (Any character)	\d+ (One or more digits). Note escape, without escape matches 'd+' literally.
\D+ (One or more non-digits).Note escape, without escape matches 'D+' literally]	[a-zA-Z0-9_]+ (One or more word characters, letter lower or uppercase, number, or underscore)	\w+ (One or more word characters, equivalent to [a-zA-Z0-9_]). Note escape, without escape matches 'w+' literally].	[-@\w]+ (One or more word character, dash. or at sign). Note no escape for \w since it's enclosed in brackets (i.e., a grouping).

Table 2-2. *Common Django url patterns and their regular expressions, with samples*

Url regular expression	Description	Sample urls
url(r'^$',.....)	Empty string (Home page)	Matches: http://127.0.0.1/
url(r'^stores/',.....)	Any trailing characters	Matches: `http://127.0.0.1/stores/` `http://127.0.0.1/stores/long+string+with+anything+12345`
url(r'^about/contact/$',.....)	Exact, no trailing characters	Matches: `http://127.0.0.1/about/contact/` Doesn't match: `http://127.0.0.1/about/`
url(r'^stores/\d+/',.....)	Number	Matches: `http://127.0.0.1/stores/2/` `http://127.0.0.1/stores/34/` Doesn't match: `http://127.0.0.1/stores/downtown/`
url(r'^drinks/\D+/',.....)	Non-digits	Matches: `http://127.0.0.1/drinks/mocha/` Doesn't match: `http://127.0.0.1/drinks/324/`
url(r'^drinks/mocha|espresso/',.....)	Word options, any trailing characters	Matches: `http://127.0.0.1/drinks/mocha/` `http://127.0.0.1/drinks/mochaccino/` `http://127.0.0.1/drinks/espresso/` Doesn't match: `http://127.0.0.1/drinks/soda/`
url(r'^drinks/mocha$\|espresso/$',.....)	Word options exact, no trailing characters	Matches: `http://127.0.0.1/drinks/mocha/` Doesn't match: `http://127.0.0.1/drinks/mochaccino/` Matches: `http://127.0.0.1/drinks/espresso/` Doesn't match: `http://127.0.0.1/drinks/espressomacchiato/`
url(r'^stores/\w+/',.....)	Word characters (Any letter lower or uppercase, number, or underscore)	Matches: `http://127.0.0.1/stores/sandiego/` `http://127.0.0.1/stores/LA/` `http://127.0.0.1/stores/1/` Doesn't match: `http://127.0.0.1/san-diego/`
url(r'^stores/[-\w]+/',.....)	Word characters or dash	Matches: `http://127.0.0.1/san-diego/`
url(r'^state/[A-Z]{2}/',.....)	Two uppercase letters	Matches: `http://127.0.0.1/CA/` Doesn't match: `http://127.0.0.1/Ca/`

DJANGO URLS DON'T INSPECT URL QUERY STRINGS

On certain urls - those made by HTTP GET requests, common in HTML forms or REST services - parameters are added to urls with ? followed by `parameter_name=parameter_value` separated by & (e.g., `/drinks/mocha/?type=cold&size=large`). These set of values are known as query strings and Django ignores them for the purpose of url pattern matching.

If you need to make use of these values as url parameters – a topic explored in the next section – you can access these values in Django view methods through the request reference. Another alternative is to change the url structure to accommodate regular expressions (e.g., `/drinks/mocha/cold/large/` instead of `/drinks/mocha/?type=cold&size=large`).

Url Parameters, Extra Options, and Query Strings

You just learned how to use a wide variety of regular expressions to create urls for your Django applications. However, if you look back at Listings 2-1, 2-2, and 2-3, you'll notice the information provided on the urls is discarded.

Sometimes it's helpful or even necessary to pass url information to the processing construct as a parameter. For example, if you have several urls like `/drinks/mocha/`, `/drinks/espresso/`, and `/drinks/latte/`, the last part of the url represents a drink name. Therefore it can be helpful or necessary to relay this url information to the processing template to display it or use it in some other way in a view (e.g., query a database). To relay this information the url needs to treat this information as a parameter.

To handle url parameters Django uses Python's standard regular expression syntax for named groups.[2] Listing 2-4 shows a url that creates a parameter named `drink_name`.

Listing 2-4. Django url parameter definition for access in templates

```
urlpatterns = [
    url(r'^drinks/(?P<drink_name>\D+)/',TemplateView.as_view(template_name='drinks/index.
    html')),
]
```

Notice the `(?P<drink_name>\D+)` syntax in Listing 2-4. The `?P<>` syntax tells Django to treat this part of the regular expression as a named group and assign the value to a parameter named `drink_name` declared between `<>`. The final piece `\D+` is a regular expression to determine the matching value; in this case the matching value is one or more non-digit characters, as described in Table 2-1.

It's very important you understand a parameter is only captured if the provided value matches the specified regular expression (e.g., `\D+` for non-digits). For example, for the url request `/drinks/mocha/` the value `mocha` is assigned to the `drink_name` parameter, but for a url like `/drinks/123/` the regular expression pattern doesn't match - because `123` are digits - so no action is taken.

If a url match occurs in Listing 2-4, the request is sent directly to the template `drinks/index.html`. Django provides access to all parameters defined in this manner through a Django template context variable with the same name. Therefore to access the parameter you would use the parameter name `drink_type` directly in the template. For example, to output the value of the `drink_name` parameter you would use the standard `{{}}` Django template syntax (e.g., `{{drink_name}}`).

[2]https://docs.python.org/3/howto/regex.html#non-capturing-and-named-groups

In addition to treating parts of a url as parameters, it's also possible to define extra options in the url definition to access them in Django templates as context variables. These extra options are defined inside a dictionary declared as the last part of the url definition.

For example, look at the following modified url Django definition from Listing 2-4:

```
url(r'^drinks/(?P<drink_name>\D+)', TemplateView.as_view(template_name='drinks/index.html'),
{'onsale':True}),
```

Notice how a dictionary with key-values is added at the end of the url definition. In this manner, the onsale key becomes a url extra option, which is passed to the underlying template as a context variable. Url extra options are accessed like url parameters as template context variables. So to output the onsale extra option you would use the {{onsale}} syntax.

Next, let's take a look at another variation of url parameters illustrated in Listing 2-5, which sends control to a Django view method.

Listing 2-5. Django url parameter definition for access in view methods in main urls.py file

```
# Project main urls.py
from coffeehouse.stores import views as stores_views

urlpatterns = patterns[
    url(r'^stores/(?P<store_id>\d+)/',stores_views.detail),
]
```

Notice the (?P<store_id>\d+) syntax in Listing 2-5 is pretty similar to the one in 2-4. The thing that changes is the parameter is now named store_id and the regular expression is \d+ to match digits. So, for example, if a request is made to the url /stores/1/ the value 1 is assigned to the store_id parameter and if a request is made to a url like /stores/downtown/ the regular expression pattern doesn't match - because downtown are letters not digits - so no action is taken.

If a url match occurs for Listing 2-5, the request is sent directly to the Django view method coffeehouse.stores.views.detail. Where coffeehouse.stores is the package name, views.py the file inside the stores app and detail the name of the view method. Listing 2-6 illustrates the detail view method to access the store_id parameter.

Listing 2-6. Django view method in views.py to access url parameter

```
from django.shortcuts import render

def detail(request,store_id):
    # Access store_id with 'store_id' variable
    return render(request,'stores/detail.html')
```

Notice in Listing 2-6 how the detail method has two arguments. The first argument is a request object, which is always the same for all Django view methods. The second argument is the parameter passed by the url. It's important to note the names of url parameters must match the names of the method arguments. In this case, notice in Listing 2-5 the parameter name is store_id and in Listing 2-6 the method argument is also named store_id.

With access to the url parameter via the view method argument, the method can execute logic with the parameter (e.g., query a database) that can then be passed to a Django template for presentation.

Caution Django url parameters are *always* treated as strings, irrespective of the regular expression. For example, \d+ catches digits, but a value of one is treated as '1' (String), not 1 (Integer). This is particularly important if you plan to work with url parameters in view methods and do operations that require something other than strings.

Another option available for url parameters handled by view methods is to make them optional, which in turn allows you to leverage the same view method for multiple urls. Parameters can be made optional by assigning a default value to a view method argument. Listing 2-7 shows a new url that calls the same view method (`coffeehouse.stores.views.detail`) but doesn't define a parameter.

Listing 2-7. Django urls with optional parameters leveraging the same view method

```
from coffeehouse.stores import views as stores_views

urlpatterns = patterns[
    url(r'^stores/',stores_views.detail),
    url(r'^stores/(?P<store_id>\d+)/',stores_views.detail),
]
```

If you called the url `/stores/` without modifying the `detail` method in Listing 2-6, you would get an error. The error occurs because the `detail` view method expects a `store_id` argument, which isn't provided by the first url. To fix this problem, you can define a default value for the `store_id` in the view method, as illustrated in Listing 2-8.

Listing 2-8. Django view method in views.py with default value

```
from django.shortcuts import render

def detail(request,store_id='1'):
    # Access store_id with 'store_id' variable
    return render(request,'stores/detail.html')
```

Notice in Listing 2-8 how the `store_id` argument has the assignment `='1'`. This means the argument will have a default value of `'1'` in case the view method is called without `store_id`. This approach allows you to leverage the same view method to handle multiple urls with optional parameters.

In addition to accessing url parameters inside view methods, it's also possible to access extra options from the url definition. These extra options are defined inside a dictionary declared as the last argument in a url definition. After the view method declaration, you add a dictionary with the key-value pairs you wish to access inside the view method. The following snippet illustrates a modified version of the url statement in Listing 2-7.

```
url(r'^stores/',stores_views.detail,{'location':'headquarters'})
```

In this case, the `location` key becomes a url extra option that's passed as a parameter to the view method. Url extra options are accessed just like url parameters, so to access a url extra option inside a view method you need to modify the method signature to accept an argument with the same name as the url extra option. In this case, the method signature:

```
def detail(request,store_id='1'):
```

needs to change to:

```
def detail(request,store_id='1',location=None):
```

Notice the location argument is made optional by assigning a default value of None.

Finally, it's also possible to access url parameters separated by ? And & - technically known as a query string - inside Django view methods. These type of parameters can be accessed inside a view method using the request object.

Take, for example, the url /stores/1/?hours=sunday&map=flash, Listing 2-9 illustrates how to extract the arguments from this url separated by ? and & using request.GET.

Listing 2-9. Django view method extracting url parameters with request.GET

```
from django.shortcuts import render

def detail(request,store_id='1',location=None):
    # Access store_id param with 'store_id' variable and location param with 'location'
variable
    # Extract 'hours' or 'map' value appended to url as
    # ?hours=sunday&map=flash
    hours = request.GET.get('hours', '')
    map = request.GET.get('map', '')
    # 'hours' has value 'sunday' or '' if hours not in url
    # 'map' has value 'flash' or '' if map not in url
    return render(request,'stores/detail.html')
```

Listing 2-9 uses the syntax request.GET.get(<parameter>, ''). If the parameter is present in request.GET it extracts the value and assigns it to a variable for further usage; if the parameter is not present then the parameter variable is assigned a default empty value of '' - you could equally use None or any other default value - as this is part of Python's standard dictionary get() method syntax to obtain default values.

This last process is designed to extract parameters from an HTTP GET request; however, Django also supports the syntax request.POST.get to extract parameters from an HTTP POST request, which is described in greater detail in the chapter on Django forms and later in this chapter in the section on Django view method requests.

Url Consolidation and Modularization

By default, Django looks up url definitions in the urls.py file inside a project's main directory - it's worth mentioning this is on account of the ROOT_URLCONF variable in settings.py. However, once a project grows beyond a couple of urls, it can become difficult to manage them inside this single file. For example, look at the urls.py file illustrated in Listing 2-10.

Listing 2-10. Django urls.py with no url consolidation

```
from django.conf.urls import url
from django.views.generic import TemplateView
from coffeehouse.about import views as about_views
from coffeehouse.stores import views as stores_views
```

```
urlpatterns = [
    url(r'^$',TemplateView.as_view(template_name='homepage.html')),
    url(r'^about/',about_views.index),
    url(r'^about/contact/',about_views.contact),
    url(r'^stores/',stores_views.index),
    url(r'^stores/(?P<store_id>\d+)/',stores_views.detail,{'location':'headquarters'}),
   ]
```

As you can see in Listing 2-10, there are a couple of urls that have redundant roots - `about/` and `stores/`. Grouping these urls separately can be helpful because it keeps common urls in their own files and avoids the difficulties of making changes to one big `urls.py` file.

Listing 2-11 shows an updated version of the `urls.py` file with the `about/` and `stores/` roots placed in separate files.

Listing 2-11. Django urls.py with include to consolidate urls

```
from django.conf.urls import include, url
from django.views.generic import TemplateView

urlpatterns = [
    url(r'^$',TemplateView.as_view(template_name='homepage.html')),
    url(r'^about/',include('coffeehouse.about.urls')),
    url(r'^stores/',include('coffeehouse.stores.urls'),{'location':'headquarters'}),
   ]
```

Listing 2-11 makes use of the `include` argument to load urls from completely separate files. In this case, `include('coffeehouse.about.urls')` tells Django to load url definitions from the Python module `coffeehouse.about.urls`, which parting from a Django base directory corresponds to the file route / `coffeehouse/about/urls.py`. In this case, I kept using the `urls.py` file name and placed it under the corresponding Django about app directory since it deals with `about/` urls. However, you can use any file name or path you like for url definitions (e.g., `coffeehouse.allmyurl.resturls` to load urls from a file route `/coffeehouse/allmyurls/resturls.py`).

The second include statement in Listing 2-11 works just like the first one, where `include('coffeehouse.stores.urls')` tells Django to load url definitions from the Python module `coffeehouse.stores.urls`. However, notice this second statement appends an additional dictionary as a url extra option, which means all the urls in the include statement will also receive this extra option.

Listing 2-12 illustrates the contents of the file `/coffeehouse/about/urls.py` linked via `include('coffeehouse.about.urls')`.

Listing 2-12. Django /coffeehouse/about/urls.py loaded via include

```
from django.conf.urls import url
from . import views

urlpatterns = [
    url(r'^$',views.index),
    url(r'^contact/$',views.contact),
]
```

A quick look at Listing 2-12 and you can see the structure is pretty similar to the main `urls.py` file; however, there are some minor differences. While the url regular expression `r'^$'` can look like it matches the home page, it isn't. Because the file in Listing 2-12 is linked via `include` in the main `urls.py` file, Django joins the url regular expression with the parent url regular expression. So the first url in Listing 2-12 actually matches `/about/` and the second url in Listing 2-12 actually matches `/about/contact/`. Also because the `urls.py` file in Listing 2-12 is placed alongside the app's `views.py` file, the import statement uses the relative path `from . import views` syntax.

In addition to using the `include` option to reference a separate file with url definitions, the `include` option can also accept url definitions as a Python list. In essence, this allows you to keep all url definitions in the main `urls.py` file, but give it more modularity. This approach is illustrated in Listing 2-13.

Listing 2-13. Django urls.py with inline include statements

```
from django.conf.urls import include, url
from django.views.generic import TemplateView

from coffeehouse.about import views as about_views
from coffeehouse.stores import views as stores_views

store_patterns = [
    url(r'^$',stores_views.index),
    url(r'^(?P<store_id>\d+)/$',stores_views.detail),
]

about_patterns = [
    url(r'^$',about_views.index),
    url(r'^contact/$',about_views.contact),
]

urlpatterns = [
    url(r'^$',TemplateView.as_view(template_name='homepage.html')),
    url(r'^about/',include(about_patterns)),
    url(r'^stores/',include(store_patterns),{'location':'headquarters'}),
   ]
```

The outcome of the url patterns in Listing 2-13 is the same as Listings 2-11 and 2-12. The difference is Listing 2-13 uses the main `urls.py` file to declare multiple url lists, while Listings 2-11 and 2-12 rely on url lists declared in different files.

Url Naming and Namespaces

A project's internal links or url references (e.g., `<a href='/'>Home Page</a>`) tend to be hard-coded, whether it's in view methods to redirect users to certain locations or in templates to provide adequate user navigation. Hard-coding links can present a serious maintenance problem as a project grows, because it leads to links that are difficult to detect and fix. Django offers a way to name urls so it's easy to reference them in view methods and templates.

The most basic technique to name Django urls is to add the `name` attribute to `url` definitions in `urls.py`. Listing 2-14 shows how to name a project's home page, as well as how to reference this url from a view method or template.

Listing 2-14. Django url using name

```
# Definition in urls.py
url(r'^$',TemplateView.as_view(template_name='homepage.html'),name="homepage")

# Definition in view method
from django.http import HttpResponsePermanentRedirect
from django.core.urlresolvers import reverse

def method(request):
    ....
    return HttpResponsePermanentRedirect(reverse('homepage'))

# Definition in template
<a href="{% url 'homepage' %}">Back to home page</a>
```

The url definition in Listing 2-14 uses the regular expression r'^$' that translates into / or the home page, also known as the root directory. Notice the name attribute with the homepage value. By assigning the url a name you can use this value as a reference in view methods and templates, which means any future changes made to the url regular expression, automatically update all url definitions in view methods and templates.

Next in Listing 2-14 you can see a view method example that redirects control to reverse('homepage'). The Django reverse method attempts to look up a url definition by the given name - in this case homepage - and substitutes it accordingly. Similarly, the link sample <a href="{% url 'homepage' %}">Back to home page</a> in Listing 2-14 makes use of the Django {% url %} tag, which attempts to look up a url by its first argument - in this case homepage - and substitute it accordingly.

This same naming and substitution process is available for more complex url definitions, such as those with parameters. Listing 2-15 shows the process for a url with parameters.

Listing 2-15. Django url with arguments using name

```
# Definition in urls.py
url(r'^drinks/(?P<drink_name>\D+)/',TemplateView.as_view(template_name='drinks/index.
html'),name="drink"),

# Definition in view method
from django.http import HttpResponsePermanentRedirect
from django.core.urlresolvers import reverse

def method(request):
    ....
    return HttpResponsePermanentRedirect(reverse('drink', args=(drink.name,)))

# Definition in template
<a href="{% url 'drink' drink.name %}">Drink on sale</a>

<a href="{% url 'drink' 'latte' %}">Drink on sale</a>
```

The url definition in Listing 2-15 uses a more complex regular expression with a parameter that translates into urls in the form /drinks/latte/ or /drinks/espresso/. In this case, the url is given the argument name drink_name.

Because the url uses a parameter, the syntax for the reverse method and {% url %} tag are slightly different. The reverse method requires the url parameters be provided as a tuple to the args variable and the {% url %} tag requires the url arguments be provided as a list of values. Notice in Listing 2-15 the parameters can equally be variables or hard-coded values, so long as it matches the url argument regular expression type - which in this case is non-digits.

For url definitions with more than one argument, the approach to using reverse and {% url %} is identical. For the reverse method you pass it a tuple with all the necessary parameters and for the {% url %} tag you pass it a list of values.

■ **Caution** Beware of invalid url definitions with reverse and {% url %}. Django always checks at startup that all reverse and {% url %} definitions are valid. This means that if you make an error in a reverse method or {% url %} tag definition - like a typo in the url name or the arguments types don't match the regular expression - the application won't start and throw an HTTP 500 internal error.

The error for this kind of situation is `NoReverseMatch at....Reverse for 'urlname' with arguments '()' and keyword arguments '{}' not found. X pattern(s) tried.` If you look at the error stack you'll be able to pinpoint where this is happening and correct it. Just be aware this is a fatal error and if it is not isolated to the view or page where it happens, it will stop the entire application at startup.

Sometimes the use of the name attribute by itself is not sufficient to classify urls. What happens if you have two or three index pages? Or if you have two urls that qualify as details, but one is for stores and the other for drinks?

A crude approach would be to use composite names (e.g., drink_details, store_details). However, the use of composite names in this form can lead to difficult-to-remember naming conventions and sloppy hierarchies. A cleaner approach supported by Django is through the namespace attribute.

The namespace attribute allows a group of urls to be identified with a unique qualifier. Because the namespace attribute is associated with a group of urls, it's used in conjunction with the include method described earlier to consolidate urls.

Listing 2-16 illustrates a series of url definitions that make use of the namespace attribute with include.

Listing 2-16. Django urls.py with namespace attribute

```
# Main urls.py
from django.conf.urls import include, url

urlpatterns = [
    url(r'^$',TemplateView.as_view(template_name='homepage.html'),name="homepage"),
    url(r'^about/',include('coffeehouse.about.urls',namespace="about")),
    url(r'^stores/',include('coffeehouse.stores.urls',namespace="stores")),
]

# About urls.py
from . import views

urlpatterns = [
    url(r'^$',views.index,name="index"),
    url(r'^contact/$',views.contact,name="contact"),
]
```

```
# Stores urls.py
from . import views

urlpatterns = [
    url(r'^$',views.index,name="index"),
    url(r'^(?P<store_id>\d+)/$',views.detail,name="detail"),
)

# Definition in view method
from django.http import HttpResponsePermanentRedirect
from django.core.urlresolvers import reverse

def method(request):
    ....
    return HttpResponsePermanentRedirect(reverse('about:index'))

# Definition in template
<a href="{% url 'stores:index' %}">Back to stores index</a>
```

Listing 2-16 starts with a set of include definitions typical of a main Django urls.py file. Notice both definitions use the namespace attribute. Next, you can see the urls.py files referenced in the main urls.py file that make use of the name attribute described in the past example. Notice both the about and stores urls.py files have a url with name='index'.

To qualify a url name with a namespace you use the syntax <namespace>:<name>. As you can see toward the bottom of Listing 2-16, to reference the index in the about urls.py you use about:index and to reference the index in the stores urls.py file you use stores:index.

The namespace attribute can also be nested to use the syntax <namespace1>:<namespace2>:<namespace3>:<name> to reference urls. Listing 2-17 shows an example of nested namespace attributes.

Listing 2-17. Django urls.py with nested namespace attribute

```
# Main urls.py
from django.conf.urls import include, url
from django.views.generic import TemplateView

urlpatterns = [
    url(r'^$',TemplateView.as_view(template_name='homepage.html'),name="homepage"),
    url(r'^stores/',include('coffeehouse.stores.urls',namespace="stores")),
]

# Stores urls.py
from . import views

urlpatterns = [
    url(r'^$',views.index,name="index"),
    url(r'^(?P<store_id>\d+)/$',views.detail,name="detail"),
    url(r'^(?P<store_id>\d+)/about/',include('coffeehouse.about.urls',namespace="about")),
]

# About urls.py
from . import views
```

```
urlpatterns = [
    url(r'^$',views.index,name="index"),
    url(r'^contact/$',views.contact,name="contact"),
]

# Definition in view method
from django.http import HttpResponsePermanentRedirect
from django.core.urlresolvers import reverse

def method(request):
    ....
    return HttpResponsePermanentRedirect(reverse('stores:about:index', args=(store.id,)))

# Definition in template
<a href="{% url 'stores:about:index' store.id %}">See about for {{store.name}}</a>
```

The url structure in Listing 2-17 differs from Listing 2-16 in that it creates about urls for each store (e.g., `/stores/1/about/`) instead of having a generic about url (e.g., `/about/`). At the top of Listing 2-17 we use `namespace="stores"` to qualify all urls in the stores `urls.py` file.

Next, inside the stores `urls.py` file notice there's another `include` element with `namespace="about"` to qualify all urls in the about `urls.py`. And finally inside the about `urls.py` file, there are urls that just use the `name` attribute. In the last part of Listing 2-17, you can see how nested namespaces are used with the `reverse` method and `{% url %}` tag using a `:` to separate namespaces.

In 99% of Django urls you can use the `name` and `namespace` parameters just as they been described. However, the `namespace` parameter takes on special meaning when you deploy multiple instances of the same Django app in the same project.

Since Django apps are self-contained units with url definitions, it raises an edge case even if Django apps use url namespaces. What happens if a Django app uses namespace X, but you want to deploy the app two or three times in the same project? How do you reference urls in each app, given they're all written to use namespace X? This is where the term *instance* namespace and the `app_name` attribute come into the picture.

Let's walk through a scenario that uses multiple instances of the same Django app to illustrate this edge case associated with url namespaces. Let's say you develop a Django app called banners to display advertisements. The banners app is built in such a way that it has to run on different urls (e.g., `/coffeebanners/`,`/teabanners/`,`/foodbanners/`) to simplify the selection of banners. In essence, you are required to run multiple instances of the banners app in the same project, each one on different urls.

So what's the problem of multiple app instances and url naming? It has to do with using named urls that need to change dynamically based on the current app instance. This issue is easiest to understand with an example, so let's jump to the example in Listing 2-18.

Listing 2-18. Django urls.py with multiple instances of the same app

```
# Main urls.py
from django.conf.urls import include, url

urlpatterns = [
    url(r'^$',TemplateView.as_view(template_name='homepage.html'),name="homepage"),
    url(r'^coffeebanners/',include('coffeehouse.banners.urls',namespace="coffee-banners")),
    url(r'^teabanners/',include('coffeehouse.banners.urls',namespace="tea-banners")),
    url(r'^foodbanners/',include('coffeehouse.banners.urls',namespace="food-banners")),
]
```

```
# Banners urls.py
from django.conf.urls import url
from . import views

urlpatterns = [
    url(r'^$',views.index,name="index"),
]

# Definition in view method
from django.http import HttpResponsePermanentRedirect
from django.core.urlresolvers import reverse

def method(request):
    ....
    return HttpResponsePermanentRedirect(reverse('coffee-banners:index'))
    return HttpResponsePermanentRedirect(reverse('tea-banners:index'))
    return HttpResponsePermanentRedirect(reverse('food-banners:index'))

# Definition in template
<a href="{% url 'coffee-banners:index' %}">Coffee banners</a>
<a href="{% url 'tea-banners:index' %}">Tea banners</a>
<a href="{% url 'food-banners:index' %}">Food banners</a>
```

In Listing 2-18 you can see we have three urls that point to the same `coffeehouse.banners.urls` file and each has its own unique namespace. Next, let's take a look at the various `reverse` method and `{% url %}` tag examples in Listing 2-18.

Both the reverse method and `{% url %}` tag examples in Listing 2-18 resolve to the three different url names using the `<namespace>:<name>` syntax. So you can effectively deploy multiple instances of the same Django app using just `namespace` and `name`.

However, by relying on just `namespace` and `name` the resolved url names cannot adapt dynamically to the different app instances, which is an edge case associated with *internal* app logic that must be included to support multiple instances of a Django app. Now let's take a look at both a view and template scenario that illustrates this scenario and how the `app_name` attribute solves this problem.

Suppose inside the banners app you want to redirect control to the app's main index url (e.g., due to an exception). Now put on an app designer hat, how would you resolve this problem? As an app designer you don't even know about the coffee-banners, tea-banners or food-banners namespaces, as these are deployment namespaces. How would you internally integrate a redirect in the app that adapts to multiple instances of the app being deployed? This is the purpose of the `app_name` parameter.

Listing 2-19 illustrates how to leverage the `app_name` attribute to dynamically determine where to make a redirect.

Listing 2-19. Django redirect that leverages app_name to determine url

```
# Main urls.py
from django.conf.urls import include, url

urlpatterns = [
    url(r'^$',TemplateView.as_view(template_name='homepage.html'),name="homepage"),
    url(r'^coffeebanners/',include('coffeehouse.banners.urls',namespace="coffee-banners")),
    url(r'^teabanners/',include('coffeehouse.banners.urls',namespace="tea-banners")),
    url(r'^foodbanners/',include('coffeehouse.banners.urls',namespace="food-banners")),
]
```

```
# Banners urls.py
from django.conf.urls import url
from . import views

app_name = 'banners_adverts'
urlpatterns = [
    url(r'^$',views.index,name="index"),
]

# Logic inside Banners app
from django.http import HttpResponsePermanentRedirect
from django.core.urlresolvers import reverse

def method(request):
    ....
    try:
       ...
    except:
       return HttpResponsePermanentRedirect(reverse('banners_adverts:index'))
```

Notice the `urls.py` file in Listing 2-19 of the banners app sets the app_name attribute before declaring the `urlpatterns` value. Next, notice the `reverse` method in Listing 2-19 uses the `banners_adverts:index` value, where `banners_adverts` represents the app_name. This is an important convention, because Django relies on the same syntax to search for app_name or namespace matches.

So to what url do you think `banners_adverts:index` resolves to? It all depends on where the navigation takes place, it's dynamic! If a user is navigating through the coffee-banners app instance (i.e., url `coffeebanners`) then Django resolves `banners_adverts:index` to the coffee-banners instance index, if a user is navigating through the tea-banners app instance (i.e., url `teabanners`) then Django resolves `banners_adverts:index` to the tea-banners instance index, and so on for any other number of instances. In case a user is navigating outside of a banners app instance (i.e., there is no app instance) then Django defaults to resolving `banners_adverts:index` to the last defined instance in `urls.py`, which would be food-banners.

In this manner and based on where the request path instance a user is coming from (e.g., if the user is on a path with `/coffeebanners/` or `/teabanners/`), the reverse method resolves `banners_adverts:index` dynamically to one of the three url app instances vs. hard-coding specific url namespaces as shown in Listing 2-18.

Now let's assume the banners app has an *internal* template with a link to the app's main `index` url. Similarly, how would you generate this link in the template to take into account the possibility of multiple app instances? Relying on the same app_name parameter solves this problem for the template link illustrated in Listing 2-20.

Listing 2-20. Django template link that leverages app_name to determine url

```
# template banners/index.html
<a href="{% url 'banners_adverts:index' %}">{% url 'banners_adverts:index' %}</a>
```

Notice the `{% url %}` tag in Listing 2-20 points to `banners_adverts:index`. The resolution process for the `banners_adverts:index` is the same outlined in the previous method example that uses the `reverse` method.

If a user is navigating through the coffee-banners app instance (i.e., url `coffeebanners`) then Django resolves `banners_adverts:index` to the coffee-banners instance index, if a user is navigating through the tea-banners app instance (i.e., url `teabanners`) then Django resolves `banners_adverts:index` to the tea-banners instance index, and so on for any other number of instances. In case a user is navigating outside of a banners app instance (i.e., there is no app instance) then Django defaults to resolving `banners_adverts:index` to the last defined instance in `urls.py` that would be `food-banners`.

As you can see, the app_name attribute's purpose is to give Django app designers an internal mechanism by which to integrate logic for named urls that dynamically adapt to multiple instances of the same app. For this reason, it's not as widely used for url naming and can be generally foregone in most cases in favor of just using the namespace and name attributes.

View Method Requests

So far you've worked with Django view methods and their input - a `request` object and parameters - as well as their output, consisting of generating a direct response or relying on a template to generate a response. However, now it's time to take a deeper look at what's available in view method requests and the various alternatives to generate view method responses.

The `request` reference you've placed unquestionably in view methods up to this point, is an instance of the `django.http.request.HttpRequest` class.[3] This `request` object contains information set by entities present before a view method: a user's web browser, the web server that runs the application, or a Django middleware class configured on the application.

The following list shows some of the most common attributes and methods available in a `request` reference:

- `request.method`.- Contains the HTTP method used for the request (e.g., GET, POST).
- `request.GET` or `request.POST`.- Contains parameters added as part of a GET or POST request, respectively. Parameters are enclosed as a `django.http.request.QueryDict`[4] instance.
  - `request.POST.get('name',default=None)`.- Gets the value of the name parameter in a POST request or gets None if the parameter is not present. Note `default` can be overridden with a custom value.
  - `request.GET.getlist('drink',default=None)`.- Gets a list of values for the `drink` parameter in a GET request or gets an empty list None if the parameter is not present. Note `default` can be overridden with a custom value.
- `request.META`.- Contains HTTP headers added by browsers or a web server as part of the request. Parameters are enclosed in a standard Python dictionary where keys are the HTTP header names - in uppercase and underscore (e.g., `Content-Length` as key `CONTENT_LENGTH`).
  - `request.META['REMOTE_ADDR']`.- Gets a user's remote IP address.
- `request.user`.- Contains information about a Django user (e.g., username, email) linked to the request. Note `user` refers to the user in the `django.contrib.auth` package and is set via Django middleware, described later in this chapter.

As you can attest from this brief list, the `request` reference contains a lot of actionable information to fulfill business logic (e.g., you can respond with certain content based on geolocation information from a user's IP address). There are well over 50 `request` options available between `django.http.request.HttpRequest` and `django.http.request.QueryDict` attributes and methods, all of which are explained in parts of the book where they're pertinent - however you can review the full extent of `request` options in the footnote links in the previous page.

---

[3]https://docs.djangoproject.com/en/1.11/_modules/django/http/request/#HttpRequest
[4]https://docs.djangoproject.com/en/1.11/_modules/django/http/request/#QueryDict

Once you're done extracting information from a request reference and doing related business logic with it (e.g., querying a database, fetching data from a third-party REST service), you then need to set up data in a view method to send it out as part of a response.

To set up data in a Django view method, you first need to declare it or extract it inside the method body. You can declare strings, numbers, lists, tuples, dictionaries, or any other Python data structure.

Once you declare or extract the data inside a view method, you create a dictionary to make the data accessible on Django templates. The dictionary keys represent the reference names for the template, while the values are the data structures themselves. Listing 2-21 illustrates a view method that declares multiple data structures and passes them to a Django template.

Listing 2-21. Set up dictionary in Django view method for access in template

```
from django.shortcuts import render

def detail(request,store_id='1',location=None):
    # Create fixed data structures to pass to template
    # data could equally come from database queries
    # web services or social APIs
    STORE_NAME = 'Downtown'
    store_address = {'street':'Main #385','city':'San Diego','state':'CA'}
    store_amenities = ['WiFi','A/C']
    store_menu = ((0,''),(1,'Drinks'),(2,'Food'))
    values_for_template = {'store_name':STORE_NAME, 'store_address':store_address, 'store_
amenities':store_amenities, 'store_menu':store_menu}
    return render(request,'stores/detail.html', values_for_template)
```

Notice in Listing 2-21 how the render method includes the `values_for_template` dictionary. In previous examples, the `render` method just included the `request` object and a template to handle the request. In Listing 2-21, a dictionary is passed as the last `render` argument. By specifying a dictionary as the last argument, the dictionary becomes available to the template - which in this case is `stores/detail.html`.

■ **Tip** If you plan to access the same data on multiple templates, instead of declaring it on multiple views, you can use a context processor to declare it once and make it accessible on all project templates. The next chapter on Django templates discusses this topic.

The dictionary in Listing 2-21 contains keys and values that are data structures declared in the method body. The dictionary keys become references to access the values inside Django templates.

OUTPUT VIEW METHOD DICTIONARY IN DJANGO TEMPLATES

Although the next chapter covers Django templates in depth, the following snippet shows how to output the dictionary values in Listing 2-21 using the {{}} syntax.

```
<h4>{{store_name}} store</h4>
<p>{{store_address.street}}</p>
<p>{{store_address.city}},{{store_address.state}}</p>
<hr/>
<p>We offer: {{store_amenities.0}} and {{store_amenities.1}}</p>
<p>Menu includes : {{store_menu.1.1}} and {{store_menu.2.1}}</p>
```

The first declaration `{{store_name}}` uses the stand-alone key to display the `Downtown` value. The other access declarations use dot(.) notation because the values themselves are composite data structures.

The `store_address` key contains a dictionary, so to access the internal dictionary values you use the internal dictionary key separated by a dot(.). `store_address.street` displays the street value, `store_address.city` displays the city value, and `store_address.state` displays the state value.

The store_amenities key contains a list that uses a similar dot(.) notation to access internal values. However, since Python lists don't have keys you use the list index number. store_amenities.0 displays the first item in list store_amenities and store_amenities.1 displays the second item in list store_amenities.

The `store_menu` key contains a tuple of tuples that also requires a number on account of the lack of keys. `{{store_menu.1.1}}` displays the second tuple value of the second tuple value of `store_menu` and `{{store_menu.2.1}}` displays the second tuple value of the third tuple of `store_menu`.

View Method Responses

The `render()` method to generate view method responses you've used up to this point is actually a shortcut. You can see toward the top of Listing 2-21, the `render()` method is part of the `django.shortcuts` package.

This means there are other alternatives to the `render()` method to generate a view response, albeit the `render()` method is the most common technique. For starters, there are three similar variations to generate view method responses with data backed by a template, as illustrated in Listing 2-22.

Listing 2-22. Django view method response alternatives

```
# Option 1)
from django.shortcuts import render

def detail(request,store_id='1',location=None):
    ...
    return render(request,'stores/detail.html', values_for_template)

# Option 2)
from django.template.response import TemplateResponse

def detail(request,store_id='1',location=None):
    ...
    return TemplateResponse(request, 'stores/detail.html', values_for_template)

# Option 3)
from django.http import HttpResponse
from django.template import loader, Context

def detail(request,store_id='1',location=None):
     ...
     response = HttpResponse()
     t = loader.get_template('stores/detail.html')
     c = Context(values_for_template)
     return response.write(t.render(c))
```

The first option in Listing 2-22 is the `django.shortcuts.render()` method that shows three arguments to generate a response: the (required) `request` reference, a (required) template route and an (optional) dictionary - also known as the context - with data to pass to the template.

There are three more (optional) arguments for the `render()` method that are not shown in Listing 2-22: `content_type` that sets the HTTP `Content-Type` header for the response and which defaults to `DEFAULT_CONTENT_TYPE` parameter in `settings.py`, which in itself defaults to `text/html`; `status` that sets the HTTP `Status` code for the response that defaults to `200`; and `using` to specify the template engine - either `jinja2` or `django` - to generate the response. The next section on HTTP handling for the `render()` method describes how to use `content_type & status`, while Chapters 3 and 4 talk about Django and Jinja template engines.

The second option in Listing 2-22 is the `django.template.response.TemplateResponse()` class, which in terms of input is nearly identical to the `render()` method. The difference between the two variations is that `TemplateResponse()` can alter a response once a view method is finished (e.g., via middleware), where as the `render()` method is considered the last step in the life cycle after a view method finishes. You should use `TemplateResponse()` when you foresee the need to modify view method responses in multiple view methods after they finish their work, a technique that's discussed in a later section in this chapter on view method middleware.

There are four more (optional) arguments for the `TemplateResponse()` class that are not shown in Listing 2-22: `content_type` that defaults to `text/html`; `status` that defaults to `200`; `charset` that sets the response encoding from the HTTP `Content-Type` header or `DEFAULT_CHARSET` in `settings.py` that in itself defaults to `utf-8`; and `using` to indicate the template engine - either `jinja2` or `django` - to generate the response.

The third option in Listing 2-22 represents the longest, albeit the most flexible response creation process. This process first creates a raw `HTTPResponse` instance, then loads a template with the `django.template.loader.get_template()` method, creates a `Context()` class to load values into the template, and finally writes a rendered template with its context to the `HTTPResponse` instance. Although this is the longest of the three options, it's the preferred choice when a view method response requires advanced options. The upcoming section on built-in response shortcuts for inline and streamed content, has more details on `HTTPResponse` response types.

Response Options for HTTP Status and Content-Type Headers

Browsers set HTTP headers in requests to tell applications to take into account certain characteristics for processing. Similarly, applications set HTTP headers in responses to tell browsers to take into account certain characteristics for the content being sent out. Among the most important HTTP headers set by applications like Django are `Status` and `Content-Type`.

The HTTP `Status` header is a three-digit code number to indicate the response status for a given request. Examples of `Status` values are `200`, which is the standard response for successful HTTP requests and `404`, which is used to indicate a requested resource could not be found. The HTTP `Content-Type` header is a MIME (Multipurpose Internet Mail Extensions) type string to indicate the type of content in a response. Examples of `Content-Type` values are `text/html`, which is the standard for an HTML content response and `image/gif`, which is used to indicate a response is a GIF image.

By default and unless there's an error, all Django view methods that create a response with `django.shortcuts.render()`, a `TemplateResponse()` class, or `HttpResponse()` class - illustrated in Listing 2-22 - create a response with the HTTP `Status` value set to `200` and the HTTP `Content-Type` set to `text/html`. Although these default values are the most common, if you want to send a different kind of response (e.g., an error or non-HTML content) it's necessary to alter these values.

Overriding HTTP `Status` and `Content-Type` header values for any of the three options in Listing 2-22 is as simple as providing the additional arguments `status` and/or `content_type`. Listing 2-23 illustrates various examples of this process.

Listing 2-23. HTTP Content-type and HTTP Status for Django view method responses

```
from django.shortcuts import render

# No method body(s) and only render() example provided for simplicity

# Returns content type text/plain, with default HTTP 200
return render(request,'stores/menu.csv', values_for_template, content_type='text/plain')

# Returns HTTP 404, wtih default text/html
# NOTE: Django has a built-in shortcut & template 404 response, described in the next
section
return render(request,'custom/notfound.html',status=404)

# Returns HTTP 500, wtih default text/html
# NOTE: Django has a built-in shortcut & template 500 response, described in the next
section
return render(request,'custom/internalerror.html',status=500)

# Returns content type application/json, with default HTTP 200
# NOTE: Django has a built-in shortcut JSON response, described in the next section
return render(request,'stores/menu.json', values_for_template, content_type='application/json')
```

The first example in Listing 2-23 is designed to return a response with plain text content. Notice the `render` method `content_type` argument. The second and third examples in Listing 2-23 set the HTTP `Status` code to 404 and 500. Because the HTTP Status 404 code is used for resources that are not found, the `render` method uses a special template for this purpose. Similarly, because the HTTP `Status` 500 code is used to indicate an error, the render method also uses a special template for this purpose.,

---

■ **Tip** Django has built-in shortcuts and templates to deal with HTTP `Status` codes 404 and 500, as well as a JSON short-cut response, all of which are described in the next section and that you can use instead of the examples in Listing 2-23.

The fourth and last example in Listing 2-23 is designed to return a response with JavaScript Object Notation(JSON) content. The HTTP `Content-Type application/json` is a common requirement for requests made by browsers that consume JavaScript data via Asynchronous JavaScript (AJAX).

Built-In Response Shortcuts and Templates for Common HTTP Status: 404 (Not Found), 500 (Internal Server Error), 400 (Bad Request), and 403 (Forbidden)

Although Django automatically triggers an HTTP 404 `Status` (Not Found) response when a page is not found and also triggers an HTTP 500 `Status` (Internal Server Error) response when an unhandled exception is thrown in a view, it has built-in shortcuts and templates that are meant to be used explicitly in Django views when you know end users should get them. Table 2-3 illustrates the different shortcuts to trigger certain HTTP status responses.

Table 2-3. Django shortcut exceptions to trigger HTTP statuses

HTTP status code	Python code sample
404 (Not Found)	from django.http import Http404 raise Http404
500 (Internal Server Error)	raise Exception
400 (Bad Request)	from django.core.exceptions import SuspiciousOperation raise SuspiciousOperation
403 (Forbidden)	from django.core.exceptions import PermissionDenied raise PermissionDenied

**Django automatically handles not found pages raising HTTP 404 and unhandled exceptions raising HTTP 500*

As you can see in the examples in Table 2-3, the shortcut syntax is straightforward. For example, you can make evaluations in a Django view like `if article_id < 100:` or `if unpayed_subscription:` and based on the result throw exceptions from Table 2-3 so end users get the proper HTTP status response.

So what is the actual content sent in a response besides the HTTP status when an exception from Table 2-3 is triggered? The default for HTTP 400 (Bad Request) and HTTP 403 (Forbidden) is a single line HTML page that says "`Bad Request (400)`" and "`403 Forbidden`", respectively. For HTTP 404 (Not Found) and HTTP 500 (Internal Server Error), it depends on the `DEBUG` value in `settings.py`.

If a Django project has `DEBUG=True` in `settings.py`, HTTP 404 (Not Found) generates a page with the available urls - as illustrated in Figure 2-1 - and HTTP 500 (Internal Server Error) generates a page with the detailed error - as illustrated in Figure 2-2. If a Django project has `DEBUG=False` in `settings.py`, HTTP 404 (Not Found) generates a single line HTML page that says "`Not Found. The requested URL <url_location> was not found on this server.`" and HTTP 500 (Internal Server Error) generates a single line HTML page that says "`A server error occurred. Please contact the administrator`".

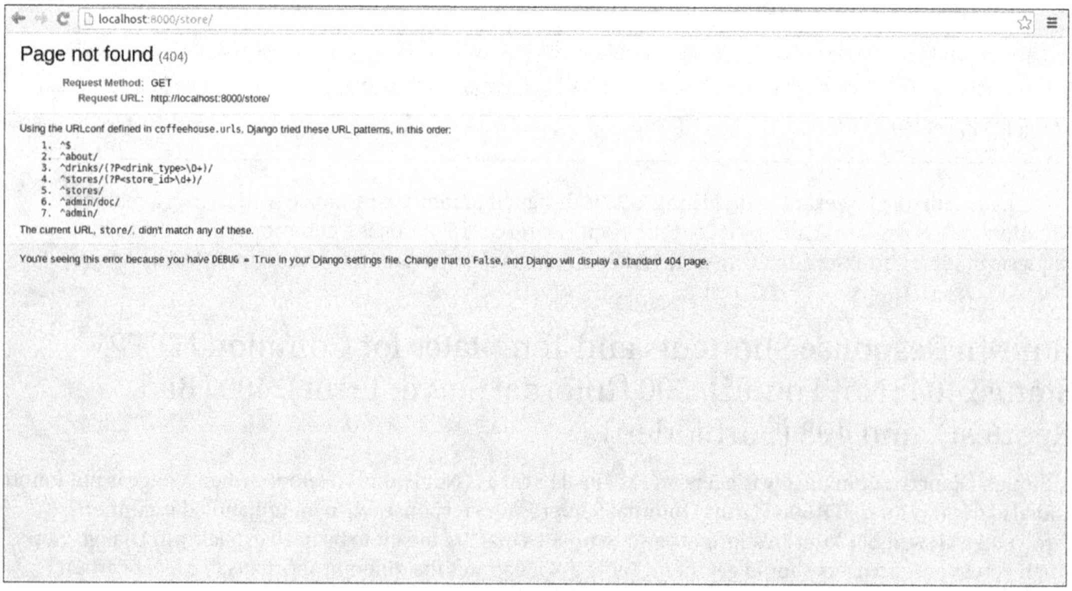

***Figure 2-1.** HTTP 404 for Django project when DEBUG=True*

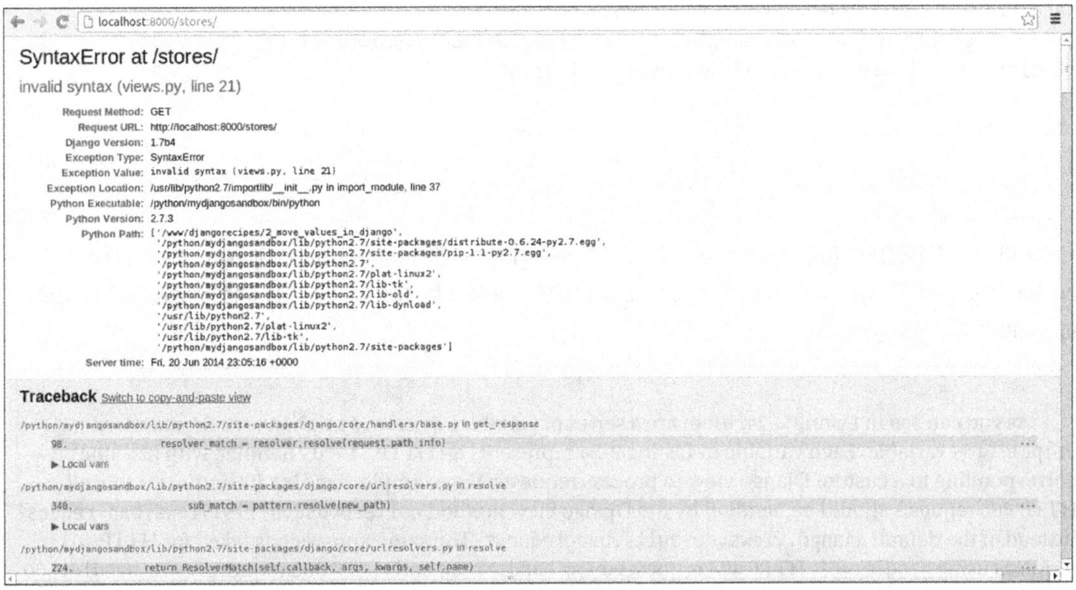

Figure 2-2. *HTTP 500 for Django project when DEBUG=True*

It's also possible to override the default response page for all the previous HTTP codes with custom templates. To use a custom response page, you need to create a template with the desired HTTP code and `.html` extension. For example, for HTTP 403 you would create the `403.html` template and for HTTP 500 you would create the `500.html` template. All these custom HTTP response templates need to be placed in a folder defined in the `DIRS` list of the `TEMPLATES` variable so Django finds them before it uses the default HTTP response templates.

■ **Caution** Custom 404.html and 500.html pages only work when DEBUG=False.

If `DEBUG=True`, it doesn't matter if you have `404.html` or `500.html` templates in the right location, Django uses the default response behavior illustrated in Figure 2-1 and Figure 2-2, respectively. You need to set `DEBUG=False` for the custom `404.html` and `500.html` templates to work.

On certain occasions, using custom HTTP response templates may not be enough. For example, if you want to add context data to a custom template that handles an HTTP response, you need to customize the built-in Django HTTP view methods themselves, because there's no other way to pass data into this type of template. To customize the built-in Django HTTP view methods you need to declare special handlers in a project's `urls.py` file. Listing 2-24 illustrates the `urls.py` file with custom handlers for Django's built-in HTTP `Status` view methods.

Listing 2-24. Override built-in Django HTTP Status view methods in urls.py

```
# Overrides the default 400 handler django.views.defaults.bad_request
handler400 = 'coffeehouse.utils.views.bad_request'
# Overrides the default 403 handler django.views.defaults.permission_denied
handler403 = 'coffeehouse.utils.views.permission_denied'
# Overrides the default 404 handler django.views.defaults.page_not_found
```

```
handler404 = 'coffeehouse.utils.views.page_not_found'
# Overrides the default 500 handler django.views.defaults.server_error
handler500 = 'coffeehouse.utils.views.server_error'

urlpatterns = [....
]
```

■ **Caution** If DEBUG=True, the handler404 and handler500 handlers won't work, Django keeps using the built-in Django HTTP view methods. You need to set DEBUG=False for the handler404 and handler500 handlers to work.

As you can see in Listing 2-24, there are a series of variables in `urls.py` right above the standard `urlpatterns` variable. Each variable in Listing 2-24 represents an HTTP `Status` handler, with its value corresponding to a custom Django view to process requests. For example, `handler400` indicates that all HTTP 400 requests should be handled by the Django view method `coffeehouse.utils.views.bad_request` instead of the default `django.views.defaults.bad_request`. The same approach is taken for HTTP 403 requests using `handler403`, HTTP 404 requests using `handler404` and HTTP 500 requests using `handler500`.

As far as the actual structure of custom Django view methods is concerned, they are identical to any other Django view method. Listing 2-26 shows the structure of the custom view methods used in Listing 2-25.

Listing 2-25. Custom views to override built-in Django HTTP view methods

```
from django.shortcuts import render

def page_not_found(request):
    # Dict to pass to template, data could come from DB query
    values_for_template = {}
    return render(request,'404.html',values_for_template,status=404)

def server_error(request):
    # Dict to pass to template, data could come from DB query
    values_for_template = {}
    return render(request,'500.html',values_for_template,status=500)

def bad_request(request):
    # Dict to pass to template, data could come from DB query
    values_for_template = {}
    return render(request,'400.html',values_for_template,status=400)

def permission_denied(request):
    # Dict to pass to template, data could come from DB query
    values_for_template = {}
    return render(request,'403.html',values_for_template,status=403)
```

As you can see in Listing 2-26, the custom HTTP view methods use the same `render` method from `django.shortcuts` as the previous view method examples. The methods point to a template named by the HTTP `Status` code, use a custom data dictionary that becomes accessible on the template and uses the `status` argument to indicate the HTTP status code.

Built-In Response Shortcuts for Inline and Streamed Content

All the prior view response examples have worked on the basis of content being structured through a template. However, there can be times when using a template to output a response is unnecessary (e.g., a one-line response that says "Nothing to see here").

Other times it makes no sense for a response to use a template, such is the case for HTTP 301 (Permanent Redirect) or HTTP 302 (Redirect) where the response just requires a redirection url. Table 2-4 illustrates the different shortcuts to trigger HTTP redirects.

***Table 2-4.** Django shortcuts for HTTP redirects*

HTTP status code	Python code sample
301 (Permanent Redirect)	from django.http import HttpResponsePermanentRedirect return HttpResponsePermanentRedirect("/")
302 (Redirect)	from django.http import HttpResponseRedirect return HttpResponseRedirect("/")

Both samples in Table 2-4 redirect to an application's home page (i.e., `"/"`). However, you can also set the redirection to any application url or even a full url on a different domain (e.g., `http://maps.google.com/`).

In addition to response redirection shortcuts, Django also offers a series of response shortcuts where you can add inline responses. Table 2-5 illustrates the various other shortcuts for HTTP status codes with inline content responses.

***Table 2-5.** Django shortcuts for inline and streaming content responses*

Purpose or HTTP Status code	Python code sample
304 (NOT MODIFIED)	from django.http import HttpResponseNotModified return HttpResponseNotModified()*
400 (BAD REQUEST)	from django.http import HttpResponseBadRequest return HttpResponseBadRequest("<h4>The request doesn't look right</h4>")
404 (NOT FOUND)	from django.http import HttpResponseNotFound return HttpResponseNotFound("<h4>Ups, we can't find that page</h4>")
403 (FORBIDDEN)	from django.http import HttpResponseForbidden return HttpResponseForbidden("Can't look at anything here",content_type="text/plain")
405 (METHOD NOT ALLOWED)	from django.http import HttpResponseNotAllowed return HttpResponseNotAllowed("<h4>Method not allowed</h4>")
410 (GONE)	from django.http import HttpResponseGone return HttpResponseGone("No longer here",content_type="text/plain")
500 (INTERNAL SERVER ERROR)	from django.http import HttpResponseServerError return HttpResponseServerError("<h4>Ups, that's a mistake on our part, sorry!</h4>")

(continued)

Table 2-5. *(continued)*

Purpose or HTTP Status code	Python code sample
Inline response that serializes data to JSON (Defaults to HTTP 200 and content type application/json)	from django.http import JsonResponse data_dict = {'name':'Downtown','address':'Main #385','city':'San Diego','state':'CA'} return JsonResponse(data_dict)
Inline response that stream data (Defaults to HTTP 200 and streaming content, which is an iterator of strings)	from django.http import StreamingHttpResponse return StreamingHttpResponse(large_data_structure)
Inline response that stream binary files (Defaults to HTTP 200 and streaming content)	from django.http import FileResponse return FileResponse(open('Report.pdf','rb'))
Inline response with any HTTP status code (Defaults to HTTP 200)	from django.http import HttpResponse return HttpResponse("<h4>Django inline response</h4>")

** The HTTP 304 status code indicates a "Not Modified" response, so you can't send content in the response, it should always be empty.*

As you can see in the samples in Table 2-5, there are multiple shortcuts to generate different HTTP Status responses with inline content and entirely forgo the need to use a template. In addition, you can see the shortcuts in Table 2-5 can also accept the `content_type` argument if the content is something other than HTML (i.e., `content_type=text/html`).

Since non-HTML responses have become quite common in web applications, you can see Table 2-5 also shows three Django built-in response shortcuts to output non-HTML content. The `JsonResponse` class is used to transform an inline response into JavaScript Object Notation (JSON). Because this response converts the payload to a JSON data structure, it automatically sets the content type to `application/json`. The `StreamingHttpResponse` class is designed to stream a response without the need to have the entire payload in-memory, a scenario that's helpful for large payload responses. The `FileResponse` class – a subclass of `StreamingHttpResponse` – is designed to stream binary data (e.g., PDF or image files).

This takes us to the last entry in Table 2-5, the `HttpResponse` class. As it turns out, all the shortcuts in Table 2-5 are customized subclasses of the `HttpResponse` class, which I initially described in Listing 2-22 as one of the most flexible techniques to create view responses.

The `HttpResponse` method is helpful to create responses for HTTP status codes that don't have direct shortcut methods (e.g., HTTP 408 [Request Timeout], HTTP 429 [Too Many Requests]) or to inclusively harness a template to generate inline responses as illustrated in Listing 2-26.

Listing 2-26. HttpResponse with template and custom CSV file download

```
from django.http import HttpResponse
from django.utils import timezone
from django.template import loader, Context

response = HttpResponse(content_type='text/csv')
response['Content-Disposition'] = 'attachment; filename=Users_%s.csv' % str(timezone.now().
today())
t = loader.get_template('dashboard/users_csvexport.html')
c = Context({'users': sorted_users,})
response.write(t.render(c))
return response
```

The HTTPResponse object in Listing 2-26 is generated with a text/csv content type to advise the requesting party (e.g., browser) that it's about to receive CSV content. Next, the Content-Disposition header also tells the requesting party (e.g., browser) to attempt to download the content as a file named Users_%s.csv where the %s is substituted with the current server date.

Next, using the loader module we use the get_template method to load the template users_csvexport.html that will have a CSV-like structure with data placeholders. Then we create a Context object to hold the data that will fill the template, which in this case it's just a single variable named users. Next, we call the template's render method with the context object in order to fill in the template's data placeholders with the data. Finally, the rendered template is written to the response object via the write method and the response object is returned.

The HttpResponse class offers over 20 options between attributes and methods,[5] in addition to the content_type and status parameters.

View Method Middleware

In most circumstances, data in requests and responses is added, removed, or updated in a piecemeal fashion in view methods. However, sometimes it's convenient to apply these changes on all requests and responses.

For example, if you want to access certain data on all view methods, it's easier to use a middleware class to make this data accessible across all requests. Just as if you want to enforce a security check on all responses, it's easier to do so globally with a middleware class.

Since middleware is a rather abstract concept, before I describe the structure of a Django middleware class, I'll walk you through the various built-in Django middleware classes so you can get a firmer understanding of where middleware is good design choice.

Built-In Middleware Classes

Django comes equipped with a series of middleware classes, some of which are enabled by default on all Django projects. If you open a Django project's settings.py file you'll notice the MIDDLEWARE variable whose default contents are shown in Listing 2-27.

Listing 2-27. Default Django middleware classes in MIDDLEWARE

```
MIDDLEWARE = [
    'django.middleware.security.SecurityMiddleware',
    'django.contrib.sessions.middleware.SessionMiddleware',
    'django.middleware.common.CommonMiddleware',
    'django.middleware.csrf.CsrfViewMiddleware',
    'django.contrib.auth.middleware.AuthenticationMiddleware',
    'django.contrib.messages.middleware.MessageMiddleware',
    'django.middleware.clickjacking.XFrameOptionsMiddleware',
]
```

As you can see in Listing 2-27, Django projects in their out-of-the-box state come enabled with seven middleware classes, so all requests and responses are set to run through these seven classes. If you plan to leverage Django's main features, I advise you not to remove any of these default middleware classes. However, you can leave the MIDDLEWARE variable empty if you wish; just be aware doing so may break certain Django functionalities.

---

[5]https://docs.djangoproject.com/en/1.11/ref/request-response/#django.http.HttpResponse

To give you a better understanding of what the Django middleware classes in Listing 2-27 do and help you make a more informed decision to disable them or not, Table 2-6 describes the functionality for each of these middleware classes.

Table 2-6. *Django default middleware classes and functionality*

Middleware class	Functionality
django.middleware.security.SecurityMiddleware	Provides security enhancements, such as: • SSL redirects based on the SECURE_SSL_REDIRECT and SECURE_SSL_HOST settings. • Strict transport security through a variety of settings.
django.contrib.sessions.middleware.SessionMiddleware	Enables session support.
django.middleware.common.CommonMiddleware	Provides a common set of features, such as: • Forbidding access to user agents in the DISALLOWED_USER_AGENTS setting, which can be a list of compiled regular expression objects. • Performing url rewriting based on the APPEND_SLASH and PREPEND_WWW settings in order to normalize urls. • Setting the HTTP Content-Length header for non-streaming responses.
django.middleware.csrf.CsrfViewMiddleware	Adds protection against Cross Site Request Forgeries by adding hidden form fields to POST forms and checking requests for the correct value.
django.contrib.auth.middleware.AuthenticationMiddleware	Adds the user attribute, representing the currently logged-in user, to every incoming HttpRequest object. NOTE: This middleware class depends on functionality from the middleware django.contrib.sessions.middleware. SessionMiddleware and must appear after it.
django.contrib.messages.middleware.MessageMiddleware	Enables cookie-based and session-based message support. NOTE: This middleware class depends on functionality from the middleware django.contrib.sessions.middleware.SessionMiddleware and must appear after it.
django.middleware.clickjacking.XFrameOptionsMiddleware	Provides clickjacking protection via the X-Frame-Options header. For more details on what is clickjacking see: `http://en.wikipedia.org/wiki/Clickjacking`.

As you can see in Table 2-6, although the purpose of the various default middleware classes varies considerably, their functionality applies to features that need to be applied across all requests or responses in a project.

Another important factor of the middleware classes in Table 2-6 is that some are dependent on others. For example, the `AuthenticationMiddleware` class is designed on the assumption it will have access to functionality provided by the `SessionMiddleware` class. Such dependencies are important because it makes the middleware class definition order relevant (i.e., certain middleware classes need to be defined before others in `MIDDLEWARE`), a topic I'll elaborate on more in the next section.

In addition to the default middleware classes presented in Table 2-6, Django also offers other middleware classes. Table 2-7 illustrates the remaining set of Django middleware classes you can leverage in your projects, which can be helpful so you don't have to write middleware classes from scratch.

***Table 2-7.** Other Django middleware classes and functionality*

Middleware class	Functionality
django.middleware.cache. UpdateCacheMiddleware	Response-phase cache middleware that updates the cache if the response is cacheable. NOTE: UpdateCacheMiddleware must be the first piece of middleware in MIDDLEWARE so that it'll get called last during the response phase.
django.middleware.cache. FetchFromCacheMiddleware	Request-phase cache middleware that fetches a page from the cache. NOTE: FetchFromCacheMiddleware must be the last piece of middleware in MIDDLEWARE so that it'll get called last during the request phase.
django.middleware.common. BrokenLinkEmailsMiddleware	Sends broken link notification emails to MANAGERS.
django.middleware. ExceptionMiddleware	Django uses this middleware regardless of whether or not you include it in MIDDLEWARE; however, you may want to subclass if your own middleware needs to transform the exceptions it handles into the appropriate responses.
django.middleware.gzip. GZipMiddleware	Compresses content for browsers that understand GZip compression. NOTE: GZipMiddleware should be placed before any other middleware that need to read or write the response body so that compression happens afterward. Compression is only done by this middleware if the request party sends gzip on the HTTP Accept-Encoding header and if content is larger than 200 bytes and the response hasn't set the HTTP Content-Encoding header.
django.middleware.http. ConditionalGetMiddleware	Handles conditional GET operations. If the response doesn't have an HTTP ETag header, one is added. If the response has an ETag or Last-Modified header, and the request has If-None-Match or If-Modified-Since, the response is replaced by an HttpNotModified.
django.middleware.locale. LocaleMiddleware	Parses a request and decides what translation object to install in the current thread context. This allows pages to be dynamically translated to the language the user desires.
django.contrib.sites.middleware. CurrentSiteMiddleware	Adds the site attribute representing the current site to every incoming HttpRequest object.
django.contrib.auth.middleware. PersistentRemoteUserMiddleware	Adds REMOTE_USER -- available in request.META -- via an external source (e.g., web server) for the purpose of Django authentication.
django.contrib.auth.middleware. RemoteUserMiddleware	Allows web-server-provided authentication. If request.user is not authenticated, this middleware attempts to authenticate the username passed in the REMOTE_USER request header. If authentication is successful, the user is automatically logged in to persist the user in the session.
django.contrib. flatpages.middleware. FlatpageFallbackMiddleware	Each time a Django application raises a 404 error, this middleware checks the flatpages database for the requested url as a last resort.
django.contrib. redirects.middleware. RedirectFallbackMiddleware	Each time a Django application raises a 404 error, this middleware checks the redirects database for the requested url as a last resort.

Now that you know about Django's built-in middleware classes and what they're used for, let's take a look at the structure of middleware classes and their execution process.

Middleware Structure and Execution Process

A Django middleware class has two required methods and three optional methods that execute at different points of the view request/response life cycle. Listing 2-28 illustrates a sample middleware class with its various parts.

Listing 2-28. Django middleware class structure

```
class CoffeehouseMiddleware(object):

    def __init__(self, get_response):
        self.get_response = get_response
        # One-time configuration and initialization on start-up

    def __call__(self, request):
        # Logic executed on a request before the view (and other middleware) is called.

        # get_response call triggers next phase
        response = self.get_response(request)

        # Logic executed on response after the view is called.

        # Return response to finish middleware sequence
        return response

    def process_view(self, request, view_func, view_args, view_kwargs):
        # Logic executed before a call to view
        # Gives access to the view itself & arguments

    def process_exception(self,request, exception):
        # Logic executed if an exception/error occurs in the view

    def process_template_response(self,request, response):
        # Logic executed after the view is called,
        # ONLY IF view response is TemplateResponse, see listing 2-22
```

In order for view methods to execute the Django middleware class in Listing 2-28, middleware classes must be added to the `MIDDLEWARE` variable in `settings.py`. So for example, if the `CoffeehouseMiddleware` class in Listing 2-28 is stored in a file/module named `middleware.py` under the `coffeehouse/utils/` project folders, you would add the `coffeehouse.utils.middleware.CoffeeMiddleware` statement to the list of `MIDDLEWARE` values in `settings.py`.

Next, I'll describe the two required methods in all Django middleware class shown in Listing 2-28:

- `__init__`.- Used in all Python classes to bootstrap object instances. The `__init__` method in Django middleware classes only gets called once, when the web server backing the Django application starts. The `__init__` method in Django middleware must declare a `get_response` input, which represents a reference to a prior middleware class response. The `get_response` input is assigned to an instance variable - also named `get_response` - which is later used in the main processing logic of the middleware class. The purpose of the `get_response` reference should become clearer shortly when I expand on the Django middleware execution process.

- `__call__`.- Used in all Python classes to call an object instance as a function. The `__call__` method in Django middleware classes is called on every application request. As you can see in Listing 2-28, the `__call__` method declares a `request` input that represents the same `HttpRequest` object used by view methods. The `__call__` method goes through three phases:
  - Before view method call.- Once the `__call__` method is triggered, you get the opportunity to alter the `request` reference *before* it's passed to a view method. If you want to add or modify something in `request` before it gets turned over to a view method, this is the phase to do it in.
  - Trigger view method call.- After you modify (or not) the original `request`, you must turn over control to the view method in order for it to run. This phase is triggered when you pass `request` to the `self.get_response` reference you set in the `__init__` method. This phase effectively says, "I'm done modifying the `request`, go ahead and turn it over to the view method so it can run."
  - Post view method call.- Once a view method finishes, the results are assigned to the `response` reference in `__call__`. In this phase, you have the opportunity to perform logic after a view method finishes. You exit this phase by simply returning the `response` reference from the view method (i.e., `return response`).

This is the core logic behind every Django middleware class performed by these two required methods. Now let's take a look at the three optional middleware class methods presented in Listing 2-28:

- `process_view`.- The required middleware methods - `__init__` and `__call__` - lack any knowledge about the view method they're working on. The `process_view` method gives you access to a view method and its argument *before* the view method is triggered. If present, the `process_view` middleware method is invoked right after `__call__` and before calling `self.get_response(request)`, which triggers the view method.
- `process_exception`.- If an error occurs in the logic of a view method, the `process_exception` middleware method is invoked to give you the opportunity to perform post-error clean-up logic.
- `process_template_response`.- After the self.get_response(request) is called and a view method finishes, it can be necessary to alter the response itself to perform additional logic on it (e.g., modify the context or template). If present, the `process_template_response` middleware method is invoked after a view method finishes to give you the opportunity to tinker with the response.

■ **Warning** The process_template_response middleware method is only triggered if a view method returns a TemplateResponse. If a view method generates a response with render() the process_template_response is not triggered. See Listing 2-22 for view method responses for more details.

In summary, the execution process for a single middleware class is the following:

1. `__init__` method triggered (On server startup).
2. `__call__` method triggered (On every request).
3. If declared, `process_view()` method triggered.
4. View method starts with `self.get_response(request)` statement in `__call__`.
5. If declared, `process_exception()` method triggered when exception occurs in view.
6. View method finishes.
7. If declared, `process_template_response()` triggered when view returns `TemplateResponse`.

Although it's important to understand the execution process of a single middleware class, a more important aspect is to understand the execution process of multiple middleware classes. As I mentioned at the outset of this section, Django projects are enabled with seven middleware classes shown in Listing 2-27, so the execution of multiple middleware classes is more the norm rather than the exception.

Django middleware classes are executed back to back, but the view method represents an inflection point in their execution order. The execution order for the default middleware classes in Listing 2-27 is the following:

```
Server start-up

__init__ on django.middleware.security.SecurityMiddleware called
__init__ on django.contrib.sessions.middleware.SessionMiddleware called
__init__ on django.middleware.common.CommonMiddleware called
__init__ on django.middleware.csrf.CsrfViewMiddleware called
__init__ on django.contrib.auth.middleware.AuthenticationMiddleware called
__init__ on django.contrib.messages.middleware.MessageMiddleware called
__init__ on django.middleware.clickjacking.XframeOptionsMiddleware called

request for index() view method

__call__ on django.middleware.security.SecurityMiddleware called
process_view on django.middleware.security.SecurityMiddleware called (if declared)
__call__ on django.contrib.sessions.middleware.SessionMiddleware called
process_view on django.contrib.sessions.middleware.SessionMiddleware called (if declared)
__call__ on django.middleware.common.CommonMiddleware called
process_view on django.middleware.common.CommonMiddleware called (if declared)
__call__ on django.middleware.csrf.CsrfViewMiddleware called
process_view on django.middleware.csrf.CsrfViewMiddleware called (if declared)
__call__ on django.contrib.auth.middleware.AuthenticationMiddleware called
process_view on django.contrib.auth.middleware.AuthenticationMiddleware called (if declared)
__call__ on django.contrib.messages.middleware.MessageMiddleware called
process_view on django.contrib.messages.middleware.MessageMiddleware called (if declared)
__call__ on django.middleware.clickjacking.XframeOptionsMiddleware called
process_view on django.middleware.clickjacking.XframeOptionsMiddleware called (if declared)

start index() view method logic

if an exception occurs in index() view
process_exception on django.middleware.clickjacking.XframeOptionsMiddleware called (if declared)
process_exception on django.contrib.messages.middleware.MessageMiddleware called (if declared)
```

```
process_exception on django.contrib.auth.middleware.AuthenticationMiddleware called(if
declared)
process_exception on django.middleware.csrf.CsrfViewMiddleware called (if declared)
process_exception on django.middleware.common.CommonMiddleware called (if declared)
process_exception on django.contrib.sessions.middleware.SessionMiddleware called (if declared)
process_exception on django.middleware.security.SecurityMiddleware called (if declared)

if index() view returns TemplateResponse
process_template_response on django.middleware.clickjacking.XframeOptionsMiddleware called
(if declared)
process_template_response on django.contrib.messages.middleware.MessageMiddleware called (if
declared)
process_template_response on django.contrib.auth.middleware.AuthenticationMiddleware
called(if declared)
process_template_response on django.middleware.csrf.CsrfViewMiddleware called (if declared)
process_template_response on django.middleware.common.CommonMiddleware called (if declared)
process_template_response on django.contrib.sessions.middleware.SessionMiddleware called (if
declared)
process_template_response on django.middleware.security.SecurityMiddleware called (if declared)
```

Notice the execution order for middleware classes prior to entering the execution of the view method, follows the declared order (i.e., first declared runs first, last declared last). But once the view method is executed, the middleware execution order is inverted (i.e., last declared runs first, first declared last).

This behavior is similar to a corkscrew, where to get to the center (view method), you move in one direction (1 to 7) and to move out you go in the opposite direction (7 to 1). Therefore the middleware methods `process_exception` and `process_template_response` execute in the opposite order of `__init__`, `__call__` and `process_view`.

Visually the execution process for the default Django middleware classes in Listing 2-27 is illustrated in Figure 2-3.

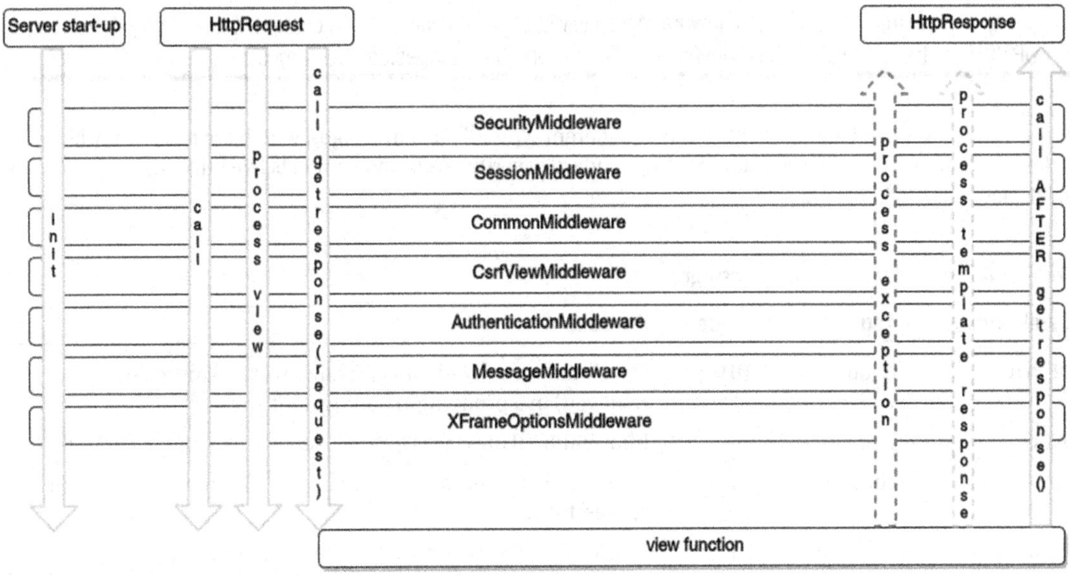

Figure 2-3. Django middleware execution process

Middleware Flash Messages in View Methods

Flash messages are typically used when users perform an action (e.g., submit a form) and it's necessary to tell them if the action was successful or if there was some kind of error. Other times flash messages are used as one-time notifications on web pages to tell users about certain events (e.g., site maintenance or special discounts). Figure 2-4 shows a set of sample flash messages.

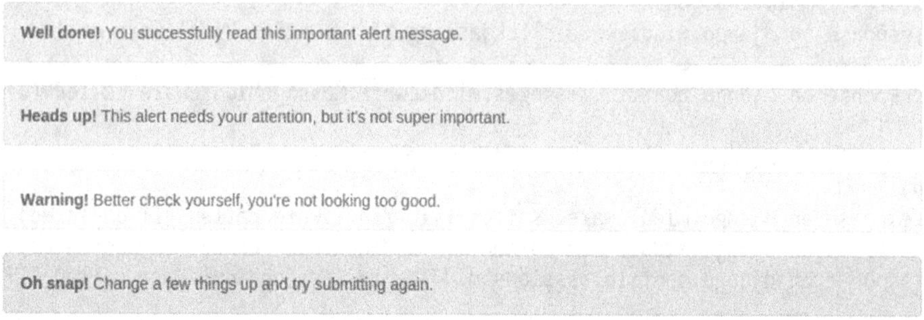

Well done! You successfully read this important alert message.
Heads up! This alert needs your attention, but it's not super important.
Warning! Better check yourself, you're not looking too good.
Oh snap! Change a few things up and try submitting again.

Figure 2-4. *Web page flash messages*

DJANGO FLASH MESSAGES REQUIRE A DJANGO APP, MIDDLEWARE, AND A TEMPLATE CONTEXT PROCESSOR

By default, all Django projects are enabled to support flash messages. However, if you tweaked your project's settings.py file you may have inadvertently disabled flash messages.

In order for Django flash messages to work you must ensure the following values are set in settings.py: The variable INSTALLED_APPS has the django.contrib.messages value, the variable MIDDLEWARE has the django.contrib.messages.middleware.MessageMiddleware value, and the context_processors list in OPTIONS of the TEMPLATES variable has the django.contrib.messages.context_processors.messages value.

As you can see in Figure 2-4 there can be different types of flash messages, which are technically known as levels. Django follows the standard Syslog standard severity levels and supports five built-in message levels described in Table 2-8.

Table 2-8. *Django built-in flash messages*

Level Constant	Tag	Value	Purpose
DEBUG	debug	10	Development-related messages that will be ignored (or removed) in a production deployment.
INFO	info	20	Informational messages for the user.
SUCCESS	success	25	An action was successful, for example, "Contact info was sent successfully."
WARNING	warning	30	A failure did not occur but may be imminent.
ERROR	error	40	An action was not successful or some other failure occurred.

Add Flash Messages

Django flash messages are managed on a per request basis and are added in view methods, as this is the best place to determine whether flash messages are warranted. To add messages you use the `django.contrib.messages` package.

There are two techniques to add flash messages with the `django.contrib.messages` package: one is the generic `add_message()` method, and the other is shortcuts methods for the different levels described in Table 2-8. Listing 2-29 illustrates the different techniques.

Listing 2-29. Techniques to add Django flash messages

```
from django.contrib import messages

# Generic add_message method
messages.add_message(request, messages.DEBUG, 'The following SQL statements were executed: 
%s' % sqlqueries) # Debug messages ignored by default
messages.add_message(request, messages.INFO, 'All items on this page have free shipping.')
messages.add_message(request, messages.SUCCESS, 'Email sent successfully.')
messages.add_message(request, messages.WARNING, 'You will need to change your password in 
one week.')
messages.add_message(request, messages.ERROR, 'We could not process your request at this 
time.')

# Shortcut level methods
messages.debug(request, 'The following SQL statements were executed: %s' % sqlqueries) # 
Debug messages ignored by default
messages.info(request, 'All items on this page have free shipping.')
messages.success(request, 'Email sent successfully.')
messages.warning(request, 'You will need to change your password in one week.')
messages.error(request, 'We could not process your request at this time.')
```

The first set of samples in Listing 2-29 uses the `add_message()` method, where as the second set uses shortcut level methods. Both sets of samples in Listing 2-29 produce the same results.

If you look closely at Listing 2-29 you'll notice both `DEBUG` level messages have the end-of-line comment `# Ignored by default`. The Django messages framework by default processes all messages above the `INFO` level (inclusive), which means `DEBUG` messages - being a lower-level message threshold, as described in Table 2-8 - are ignored even though they might be defined.

You can change the default Django message level threshold to include all message levels or inclusively reduce the default `INFO` threshold. The default message level threshold can be changed in one of two ways: globally (i.e., for the entire project) in `settings.py` with the `MESSAGE_LEVEL` variable as illustrated in Listing 2-30 or on a per request basis with the `set_level` method of the `django.contrib.messages` package as illustrated in Listing 2-31.

Listing 2-30. Set default Django message level globally in settings.py

```
# Reduce threshold to DEBUG level in settings.py
from django.contrib.messages import constants as message_constants
MESSAGE_LEVEL = message_constants.DEBUG

# Increase threshold to WARNING level in setting.py
from django.contrib.messages import constants as message_constants
MESSAGE_LEVEL = message_constants.WARNING
```

Listing 2-31. Set default Django message level on a per request basis

```
# Reduce threshold to DEBUG level per request
from django.contrib import messages
messages.set_level(request, messages.DEBUG)

# Increase threshold to WARNING level per request
from django.contrib import messages
messages.set_level(request, messages.WARNING)
```

The first `MESSAGE_LEVEL` definition in Listing 2-30 changes the default message level to `DEBUG`, which means all message level definitions get processed, since `DEBUG` is the lowest threshold. The second `MESSAGE_LEVEL` definition in Listing 2-30 changes the default message level to `WARNING`, which means message levels higher than `WARNING` (inclusive) are processed (i.e., `WARNING` and `ERROR`).

The first `set_level` definition in Listing 2-31 changes the default request message level to `DEBUG`, which means all message level definitions get processed, since `DEBUG` is the lowest threshold. The second `set_level` definition in Listing 2-31 changes the default message level to `WARNING`, which means message levels higher than `WARNING` (inclusive) are processed (i.e., `WARNING` and `ERROR`).

If you define both default message level mechanisms at once, the default request message level takes precedence over the default global message level definition (e.g., if you define `messages.set_level(request, messages.WARNING)`, message levels above `WARNING` (inclusive) are processed, even if the global `MESSAGE_LEVEL` variable is set to `MESSAGE_LEVEL = message_constants.DEBUG` to include all messages.

In addition to setting up flash messages and knowing about the built-in threshold mechanism that ignores messages from a certain level, it's also important you realize the message definitions in Listing 2-29 assume the Django messages framework prerequisites are declared in `settings.py` – as described in the sidebar at the beginning of this section.

Because you can end up distributing a Django project to a third party and have no control over the final deployment `settings.py` file, the Django messages framework offers the ability to silently ignore message definitions in case the necessary prerequisites aren't declared in `settings.py`. To silently ignore message definitions if prerequisites aren't declared, you can add the `fail_silently=True` attribute to either technique that adds messages, as illustrated in Listing 2-32.

Listing 2-32. Use of the fail_silently=True attribute to ignore errors in case Django messages framework not installed

```
from django.contrib import messages

# Generic add_message method, with fail_silently=True
messages.add_message(request, messages.INFO, 'All items on this page have free
shipping.',fail_silently=True)

# Shortcut level method, with fail_silently=True
messages.info(request, 'All items on this page have free shipping.',fail_silently=True)
```

Now that you know how to add messages and the important aspects to keep in mind when adding messages, let's take a look at how to access messages.

Access Flash Messages

The most common place you'll access Django flash messages is in Django templates to display to end users. As a shortcut and thanks to the context processor `django.contrib.messages.context_processors.messages` Django flash messages are available on all templates through the `messages` variable. But before we get to an actual template sample, let's take a quick look at the structure of Django flash messages.

When you add a Django flash message with one of the techniques described in the previous section, Django creates an instance of the `storage.base.Message` class. Table 2-9 describes the structure of the `storage.base.Message` class.

Table 2-9. *Django storage.base.Message structure*

Attribute	Description	Example
message	The actual text of the message.	All items on this page have free shipping.
level	An integer describing the type of the message (see Value column in Table 2-8).	20
tags	A string combining all the message tags (extra_tags and level_tag) separated by spaces.	info
extra_tags	A string containing custom tags for this message, separated by spaces.	Empty, by default.
level_tag	The string representation of the level.	info

As you can see in Table 2-9, there are several attributes that you can leverage to display in Django templates. Listing 2-33 shows the boilerplate template code you can use to display all flash messages set in a request.

Listing 2-33. Boilerplate code to use in Django template to display Django flash messages

```
{% if messages %}
<ul class="messages">
    {% for msg in messages %}
    <li>
        <div class="alert alert-{{msg.level_tag}}" role="alert">
        {{msg.message}}
        </div>
    </li>
    {% endfor %}
</ul>
{% endif %}
```

Listing 2-33 starts by checking if the `messages` variable exists - which contains all flash messages - if it does, then an HTML list is started with `<ul>`. Next, a loop is made over all the elements in `messages`, where each of these elements corresponds to a `storage.base.Message` instance. For each of these elements, a list and section tag - `<li>` and `<div>` - are created to output the `level_tag` attribute as a CSS class and the message attribute as the `<div>` content.

You can modify the boilerplate code in Listing 2-33 as you see necessary, for example, to include conditionals and output certain message levels or leverage some of the other `storage.base.Message` attributes, among other things.

■ **Note** The HTML code in Listing 2-33 uses the CSS class class="alert alert-{{msg.level_tag}}" that gets rendered into class="alert alert-info" or class="alert alert-success", depending on the level_tag attribute.These CSS classes are part of the CSS bootstrap framework. In this manner, you can quickly format flash messages to look like those presented in Figure 2-2.

Although you'll commonly access Django flash messages in Django templates, this doesn't mean you can't access them elsewhere, such as view methods. You can also gain access to Django flash messages in a request through the `get_messages()` method of the `django.contrib.messages` package. Listing 2-34 illustrates a code snippet with the use of the `get_messages()` method.

Listing 2-34. Use of get_messages() method to access Django flash messages

```
from django.contrib import messages

the_req_messages = messages.get_messages(request)
for msg in the_req_messages:
    do_something_with_the_flash_message(msg)
```

In Listing 2-34 the `get_messages()` method receives the `request` as input and assigns the result to `the_req_messages` variable. Next, a loop is made over all the elements in `the_req_messages`, where each of these elements corresponds to a `storage.base.Message` instance. For each of these elements, a call is made to the method `do_something_with_the_flash_message` to do something with each flash message.

An important aspect to understand when accessing Django flash messages is the duration of the messages themselves. Django flash messages are marked to be cleared when an iteration occurs on the main messages instance and cleared when the response is processed.

For access in Django templates, this means that if you fail to make an iteration in a Django template like the one in Listing 2-33 and flash messages are in the request, it can lead to stale or phantom messages appearing elsewhere until an iteration is made and a response is processed. For access in Django view methods (i.e., using `get_messages()`), this has no impact because even though you may make an iteration over the main messages instance - therefore, marking messages to be cleared - a response is not processed in a Django view method, so messages are never cleared, just marked to be cleared.

Class-Based Views

In Chapter 1 and at the start of this chapter - in Listing 2-1 - you saw how to define a Django url and make it operate with a Django template without the need of a view method. This was possible due to the `django.views.generic.TemplateView` class, which is called a class-based view.

Unlike Django view methods backed by standard Python methods that use a Django `HttpRequest` input parameter and output a Django `HttpResponse`, class-based views offer their functionality through full-fledged Python classes. This, in turn, allows Django views to operate with object-oriented programming (OOP) principles (e.g., encapsulation, polymorphism, and inheritance) leading to greater reusability and shorter implementation times.

Although Django class-based views represent a more powerful approach to create Django views, they are simply an alternative to the view methods you've used up to this point. If you want to quickly execute business logic on Django requests you can keep using view methods, but for more demanding view requirements (e.g., form processing, boilerplate model queries) class-based views can save you considerable time.

Built-In Class-Based Views

The functionality provided by the `django.views.generic.TemplateView` class-based view is really a time saver. While it would have been possible to configure a url to execute on an empty view method and then send control to a template, the `TemplateView` class allows this process to be done in one line.

In addition to the `TemplateView` class-based view, Django offers many other built-in class-based views to shorten the creation process for common Django view operations using OOP-like principles. Table 2-10 illustrates Django's built-in classes for views.

Table 2-10. *Built-in classes for views*

Class	Description
django.views.generic.View	Parent class of all class-based views, providing core functionality.
django.views.generic.TemplateView	Allows a url to return the contents of a template, without the need of a view.
django.views.generic.RedirectView	Allows a url to perform a redirect, without the need of a view.
django.views.generic.ArchiveIndexView django.views.generic.YearArchiveView django.views.generic.MonthArchiveView django.views.generic.WeekArchiveView django.views.generic.DayArchiveView django.views.generic.TodayArchiveView django.views.generic.DateDetailView	Allows a view to return date-based object results, without the need to explicitly perform Django model queries.
django.views.generic.CreateView django.views.generic.DetailView django.views.generic.UpdateView django.views.generic.DeleteView django.views.generic.ListView django.views.generic.FormView	Allows a view to execute Create-Read-Update-Delete (CRUD) operations , without the need to explicitly perform Django model queries.

In the upcoming and final section of this chapter, I'll explain the classes in the top half of Table 2-10 so you can gain a better understanding of the structure and execution process of Django class-based views. The class-based views in the bottom half of Table 2-10 that involve Django models are described in a separate chapter on Django models.

Class-Based View Structure and Execution

To create a class-based view you need to create a class that inherits from one of the classes in Table 2-10. Listing 2-35 shows a class-based view with this inheritance technique, as well as the corresponding url definition to execute a class-based view.

Listing 2-35. Class-based view inherited from TemplateView with url definition

```
# views.py
from django.views.generic import TemplateView

class AboutIndex(TemplateView):
      template_name = 'index.html'
```

```
    def get_context_data(self, **kwargs):
       # **kwargs contains keyword context initialization values (if any)
       # Call base implementation to get a context
       context = super(AboutIndex, self).get_context_data(**kwargs)
       # Add context data to pass to template
       context['aboutdata'] = 'Custom data'
       return context

#urls.py
from coffeehouse.about.views import AboutIndex

urlpatterns = [
    url(r'^about/index/',AboutIndex.as_view(),{'onsale':True}),
]
```

I chose to create a view that inherits from `TemplateView` first because of its simplicity and because you already know the purpose of this class. The example in Listing 2-35 and the first example in this chapter from Listing 2-1 produce nearly identical outcomes.

The difference is, Listing 2-1 declares a `TemplateView` class instance directly as part of the url (e.g., `TemplateView.as_view(template_name='index.html'))`), where as Listing 2-35 declares an instance of a `TemplateView` subclass named `AboutIndex`. Comparing the two approaches, you can get the initial feel for the OOP behavior of class-based views.

The first part in Listing 2-35 declares the `AboutIndex` class-based view, which inherits its behavior from the `TemplateView` class. Notice the class declares the `template_name` attribute and the `get_context_data()` method.

The `template_name` value in the `AboutIndex` class acts as a default template for the class-based view. But in OOP fashion, this same value can be overridden by providing a value at instance creation (e.g., `AboutIndex.as_view(template_name='other.html')` to use the `other.html` template).

The `get_context_data` method in the `AboutIndex` class allows you to add context data to the class-view template. Notice the signature of the `get_context_data` method uses `**kwargs` to gain access to context initialization values (e.g., declared in the url or parent class-views) and invokes a parent's class `get_context_data` method using the Python `super()` method per standard OOP Python practice. Next, the `get_context_data` method adds the additional context data with the `aboutdata` key and returns the modified `context` reference.

In the second part of Listing 2-35, you can see how the `AboutIndex` class-based view is first imported into a `urls.py` file and then hooked up to a url definition. Notice how the class-based view is declared on the `url` definition using the `as_view()` method. In addition, notice how the url definition declares the url extra option `{'onsale':True}` that gets passed as context data to the class-based view (i.e., in the `**kwargs` of the `get_context_data` method).

■ **Tip** All class-based views use the as_view() method to integrate into url definitions.

Now that you have a basic understanding of Django class-based views, Listing 2-36 shows another class-based view with different implementation details.

Listing 2-36. Class-based view inherited from View with multiple HTTP handling

```
# views.py
from django.views.generic import View
from django.http import HttpResponse
from django.shortcuts import render
```

```
class ContactPage(View):
    mytemplate = 'contact.html'
    unsupported = 'Unsupported operation'

    def get(self, request):
        return render(request, self.mytemplate)

    def post(self, request):
        return HttpResponse(self.unsupported)

#urls.py
from coffeehouse.contact.views import ContactPage

urlpatterns = [
    url(r'^contact/$',ContactPage.as_view()),
]
```

The first difference in Listing 2-36 is the class-based view inherits its behavior from the general purpose `django.views.generic.View` class. As outlined in Table 2-10, the `View` class provides the core functionality for all class-based views. So in fact, the `TemplateView` class used in Listing 2-35 is a subclass of `View`, meaning class-based views that use `TemplateView` have access to the same functionalities of class-based views that use `View`.

The reason you would chose one class over another to implement class-based views is rooted in OOP polymorphism principles. For example, in OOP you can have a class hierarchy Drink→ Coffee → Latte, where a Drink class offers generic functionalities available to Drink, Coffee, and Latte instances; a Coffee class offers more specific functionalities applicable to Coffee and Latter instances; and a Latte class offers the most specific functionalities applicable to only Latte instances.

Therefore if you know beforehand you need a class-based view to relinquish control to a template without applying elaborate business logic or custom request and response handling, the `TemplateView` class offers the quickest path to a solution vs. the more generic `View` class. Expanding on this same principle, once you start working with Django models and views, you'll come to realize some of the more specialized class-based views in Table 2-10 also offer quicker solutions than creating a class-based view that inherits from the general purpose `View` class. Now that you know the reason why you would chose a `View` class-based view over a more specialized class, let's break down the functionality in Listing 2-36.

Notice the class-based view `ContactPage` declares two attributes: `mytemplate` and `unsupported`. These are generic class attributes and I used the `mytemplate` name to illustrate there's no relation to the `template_name` attribute used in Listing 2-35 and `TemplateView` class-based views. Class-based views derived from a `TemplateView` *expect* a `template_name` value and automatically use this template to generate a response. However, class-based views derived from a `View` class don't expect a specific template, but instead expect you to implement how to generate a response, which is where the `get` and `post` methods in Listing 2-36 come into play.

The `get` method is used to handle HTTP GET requests on the view, while the `post` method is used to HTTP POST requests on the view. This offers a much more modular approach to handle different HTTP operations vs. standard view methods that require explicitly inspecting a request and creating conditionals to handle different HTTP operations. For the moment, don't worry about HTTP GET and HTTP POST view handling; this is explored in greater detail in Django forms where the topic is of greater relevance.

Next, notice both the `get` and `post` methods declare a `request` input, which represents a Django `HttpRequest` instance just like standard view methods. In both cases, the methods immediately return a response, but it's possible to inspect a request value or execute any business logic before generating a response, just like it can be done in standard view methods.

The `get` method generates a response with the `django.shortcuts.render` method and the `post` method generates a response with the `HttpResponse` class, both of which are the same techniques used to generate responses in standard view methods . The only minor difference in Listing 2-36 is both the `render` method and `HttpResponse` class use instance attributes (e.g., `self.mytemplate`, `self.unsupported`) to generate the response, but other than this, you're free to return a Django `HttpResponse` with any of the variations already explained in this chapter (e.g., Listing 2-22 response alternatives, Table 2-5 shortcut responses).

Finally, the last part in Listing 2-36 shows how the `ContactPage` class-based view is imported into a `urls.py` file and later hooked up to a url using the `as_view()` method.

To close out the discussion on class-based views and this chapter, we come to the `django.views.generic.RedirectView` class. Similar to the `TemplateView` class-based view that allows you to quickly generate a response without a view method, the `RedirectView` class-based view allows you to quickly generate an HTTP redirect – like the ones described in Table 2-4 – without the need of a view method.

The `RedirectView` class supports four attributes described in the following list:

- `permanent`.- Defaults to `False` to perform a non-permanent redirect supported by the `HttpResponseRedirect` class described in Table 2-4. If set to `True`, a permanent redirect is made with the `HttpResponsePermanentRedirect` class described in Table 2-4.
- `url`.- Defaults to `None`. Defines a url value to perform the redirect.
- `pattern_name`.- Defaults to `None`. Defines a url name to generate a redirect url via the `reverse` method. Note the `reverse` method is explained in the url naming and namespace section earlier in this chapter.
- `query_string`.- Defaults to `False` to append a query string to a redirect url. If provided, the `query_string` value to the redirect url.

And with this we conclude our exploration into Django views and urls. In the next two chapters, you'll learn about Django templates and Jinja templates.

CHAPTER 3

Django Templates

Django templates define the layout and final formatting sent to end users after a view method is finished processing a request. In this chapter, you'll learn the syntax used by Django templates, the configuration options available for Django templates, as well as the various Django template constructs (e.g., filters, tags, context processors) that allow you to create elaborate layouts and apply formatting to the content presented to end users.

Django Template Syntax

Although there are over 100 built-in constructs that help you build Django templates - all of which you'll learn as this chapter progresses - to start out, these are the most important syntax elements you need to recognize:

- `{{output_variable}}`.- Values surrounded by double curly braces at the start and end represent output for variables. Variables are passed by Django views, url options, or context processors into templates. In a template, you can use `{{}}` to output the contents of a variable, as well as use Python's dot notation to output deeper elements of a variable (e.g., fields, keys, methods). For example, `{{store.name}}` tells a Django template to output the `store` variable's `name`, where `store` can be an `object` and `name` a field or `store` can be a dictionary and `name` a key.
- `{% tag %}`.- Values surrounded by curly braces wrapped with percentage signs are called tags. Django tags offer complex formatting logic wrapped in a simple syntax representation.
- `variable|filter`.- Values declared after a vertical bar | are called filters. Django filters offer a way to apply formatting logic to individual variables.

Any other syntax in Django templates besides these three variations is treated 'as is'. This means that if a template declares the Hypertext Markup Language(HTML) heading `<h1>Welcome!</h1>`, a user will get a large HTML heading. It's that simple.

But let's take a look at one not so obvious Django template syntax behavior that's important you understand right away, since it's a recurring theme in practically everything associated with Django templates.

D. Rubio, *Beginning Django*, https://doi.org/10.1007/978-1-4842-2787-9_3

Auto-Escaping: HTML and Erring on the Safe Side

Django projects operate on the Web, so by default all templates are assumed to produce HTML. While this is a reasonable assumption, it isn't, until you face one of two things:

- You can't ensure Django templates produce valid HTML and in fact may produce dangerous markup.
- You want Django templates to produce non-HTML content, such as Comma Separated Values (CSV), eXtensible Markup Language (XML), or JavaScript Object Notation (JSON).

So how could you possibly introduce invalid HTML or even dangerous content into Django templates? Well it's the Internet, its content from other users or providers that can end up in your Django templates that can cause problems (e.g., data submitted by users, third-party services, content from databases).

The issue isn't content you place directly in Django templates - that's given to be valid since you type it in - the issue is dynamic content placed through variables, tags, filters, and context processors, which has the potential to come from anywhere. Let's analyze this further with the following variables:

```
store_legend = "<b>Open since 1965!</b>"
js_user_date = "<script>var user_date = new Date()</script>"
```

If variables with this content make it to Django templates and you attempt to output them, they are output *verbatim*. The store_legend won't be output as an HTML bold statement, but rather a statement surrounded by <b> and </b>. Similarly, the js_user_date won't produce a JavaScript variable with a user browser local date, but rather output the <script> statement literally.

This happens because by default Django auto-escapes content present in dynamic constructs (i.e., variables, tags, filters, and context processors). Table 3-1 illustrates the characters Django auto-escapes by default.

Table 3-1. *Characters Django auto-escapes by default*

Original character	Escaped to
<	<
>	>
'(single quote)	'
" (double quote)	"
&	&

As you can see in Table 3-1, Django auto-escaping consists of converting potentially conflicting and even dangerous characters - in the context of HTML - to equivalent visual representations also known as escape characters.[1]

This is done because malicious users or unchecked sources can easily produce content with the characters on the left column of Table 3-1, which can mangle a user interface or execute malicious JavaScript code. So Django errs on the safe side and auto-escapes the characters in Table 3-1 to equivalent visual representations. While you can certainly disable the auto-escaping of characters from Table 3-1, this has to be done explicitly, since it represents a security risk.

[1]https://en.wikipedia.org/wiki/Escape_character

While auto-escaping is a good security precaution for HTML output, this takes us to the second point in assuming Django always produces HTML. What happens if a Django template has to output CSV, JSON, or XML content, where characters like < , >, ' (single quote), " (double quote), and &, have special meaning to content consumers and can't use equivalent visual representations? In such cases, you'll also to need to explicitly disable the default auto-escaping behavior enforced by Django.

So whether you want to output actual HTML through variables in Django templates or output CSV, JSON, or XML without Django applying an HTML security practice to this content, you'll need to deal with Django auto-escaping.

There are various ways to control auto-escaping in Django templates (e.g., globally, individual variables, individual filters), which you'll learn as you progress through this chapter. But auto-escaping is a constant theme in Django templates, along with these related terms:

- *Safe*.- If a Django template construct is marked as *safe*, it means no characters from Table 3-1 are escaped. In other words, *safe* equals "I know what I'm doing" output the content 'as is'.
- *Escape*.- If a Django template construct is marked to be *escaped*, it means characters from Table 3-1 are escaped. In other words, *escape* equals "Ensure no potentially dangerous HTML characters are output, use equivalent visual representations."
- *Auto-escape on/ Auto-escape off (safe)*.- If a Django template uses *auto-escape on*, it means Django template constructs in this scope should escape characters from Table 3-1. If a Django template uses *auto-escape off*, it means Django template constructs in this scope should be output 'as is' and not escape characters from Table 3-1.

And with this we finish the conversation on this rather dry, yet important topic of Django auto-escaping. Next, let's explore the various configuration options for Django templates.

Django Template Configuration

By default, Django templates are enabled on all Django projects due to the `TEMPLATES` variable in `settings.py`. Listing 3-1 illustrates the default `TEMPLATES` value in Django projects.

Listing 3-1. Default Django template configuration in settings.py

```
TEMPLATES = [
    {
        'BACKEND': 'django.template.backends.django.DjangoTemplates',
        'DIRS': [],
        'APP_DIRS': True,
        'OPTIONS': {
            'context_processors': [
                'django.template.context_processors.debug',
                'django.template.context_processors.request',
                'django.contrib.auth.context_processors.auth',
                'django.contrib.messages.context_processors.messages',
            ],
        },
    },
]
```

The BACKEND variable indicates the project uses Django templates. The DIRS and APP_DIRS variables tell Django where to locate Django templates and are explained in the next section. The context_processors field inside OPTIONS tells Django which context processors to enable for a Django project. In short, a context processor offers the ability to share data across all Django templates, without the need to define it in a piecemeal fashion in Django views.

Later sections in this chapter describe what data is provided by default Django context processors and how to write your own context processors to share custom data on all Django templates.

Template Search Paths

Django determines where to look for templates based on the values in the DIRS and APP_DIRS variables. As you can see in Listing 3-1, Django defaults to an empty DIRS value and sets the APP_DIRS variable to True.

The APP_DIRS variable set to True tells Django to look for templates in Django app subfolders named templates - if you've never heard of the Django app concept, look over Chapter 1, which describes this concept.

The APP_DIRS behavior is helpful to contain an app's templates to an app's structure, but be aware the template search path is not aware of an app's namespace. For example, if you have two apps that both rely on a template named index.html and both app's have a method in views.py that returns control to the index.html template(e.g., render(request,'index.html')), both apps will use the index.html from the top-most declared app in INSTALLED_APPS, so only one app will use the expected index.html.

The first set of folders illustrated in Listing 3-2 shows two Django apps with this type of potential template layout conflict.

Listing 3-2. Django apps with templates dirs with potential conflict and namespace qualification

```
# Templates directly under templates folder can cause loading conflicts
+---+-<PROJECT_DIR_project_name_conflict>
    |
    +-__init__.py
    +-settings.py
    +-urls.py
    +-wsgi.py
    |
    +-about(app)-+
    |            +-__init__.py
    |            +-models.py
    |            +-tests.py
    |            +-views.py
    |            +-templates-+
    |                        |
    |                        +-index.html
    +-stores(app)-+
                 +-__init__.py
                 +-models.py
                 +-tests.py
                 +-views.py
                 +-templates-+
                             |
                             +-index.html
```

```
# Templates classified with additional namespace avoid loading conflicts
+---+-<PROJECT_DIR_project_name_namespace>
    |
    +-__init__.py
    +-settings.py
    +-urls.py
    +-wsgi.py
    |
    +-about(app)-+
    |            +-__init__.py
    |            +-models.py
    |            +-tests.py
    |            +-views.py
    |            +-templates-+
    |                        |
    |                        +-about-+
    |                                |
    |                                +-index.html
    +-stores(app)-+
                  +-__init__.py
                  +-models.py
                  +-tests.py
                  +-views.py
                  +-templates-+
                              |
                              +-stores-+
                                       |
                                       +-index.html
```

To fix this potential template search conflict, the recommended practice is to add an additional subfolder to act as a namespace inside each templates directory, as illustrated in the second set of folders in Listing 3-2.

In this manner, you can redirect control to a template using this additional namespace subfolder to avoid any ambiguity. So to send control to the about/index.html template you would declare render(request,'about/index.html') and to send control to the stores/index.html you would declare render(request,'stores/index.html').

If you wish to disallow this behavior of allowing templates to be loaded from these internal app subfolders, you can do so by setting APP_DIRS to FALSE.

A more common approach to define Django templates is to have a single folder or various folders that live outside app structures to hold Django templates. In order for Django to find such templates, you use the DIRS variable as illustrated in Listing 3-3.

Listing 3-3. DIRS definition with relative path in settings.py

```
BASE_DIR = os.path.dirname(os.path.dirname(os.path.abspath(__file__)))
PROJECT_DIR = os.path.dirname(os.path.abspath(__file__))

TEMPLATES = [
    {
        'BACKEND': 'django.template.backends.django.DjangoTemplates',
        'DIRS': ['%s/templates/' % (PROJECT_DIR),
                 '%s/dev_templates/' % (PROJECT_DIR),],
        'APP_DIRS': True,
        'OPTIONS': {
```

```
            'context_processors': [
                'django.template.context_processors.debug',
                'django.template.context_processors.request',
                'django.contrib.auth.context_processors.auth',
                'django.contrib.messages.context_processors.messages',
            ],
        },
    },
]
```

As you can see in Listing 3-3, you can declare various directories inside the DIRS variable. Django looks for templates inside DIRS values and then in templates folder in apps - if APP_DIRS is TRUE - until it either finds a matching template or throws a TemplateDoesNotExist error.

Also note the DIRS values in Listing 3-3 rely on a path determined dynamically by the PROJECT_DIR variable. This approach is helpful when you deploy a Django project across different machines, because the path is relative to the top-level Django project directory (i.e., where the settings.py and main urls.py file are) and adjusts dynamically irrespective of where a Django project is installed (e.g., /var/www/, /opt/website/, C://website/).

Invalid Template Variables

By default, Django templates do not throw an error when they contain invalid variables. This is due to design choices associated with the Django admin that also uses Django templates.

While this is not a major issue in most cases, it can be frustrating for debugging tasks as Django doesn't inform you of misspelled or undefined variables. For example, you could type {{datee}} instead of {{date}} and Django ignores this by outputting an empty string '', you could also forget to pass a variable value to a template in the view method and Django also silently outputs an empty string '' even though you may have it defined in the template.

To enable Django to inform you when it encounters an invalid variable in Django templates, you can use the string_if_invalid option. The first configuration option for string_if_invalid shown in Listing 3-4 outputs a visible string instead of an empty string ''.

Listing 3-4. Output warning message for invalid template variables with string_if_invalid

```
BASE_DIR = os.path.dirname(os.path.dirname(os.path.abspath(__file__)))
PROJECT_DIR = os.path.dirname(os.path.abspath(__file__))

TEMPLATES = [
    {
        'BACKEND': 'django.template.backends.django.DjangoTemplates',
        'DIRS': ['%s/templates/' % (PROJECT_DIR),'%s/dev_templates/' % (PROJECT_DIR),],
        'APP_DIRS': True,
        'OPTIONS': {
            'string_if_invalid': "**** WARNING INVALID VARIABLE %s ****",
            'context_processors': [
                'django.template.context_processors.debug',
                'django.template.context_processors.request',
                'django.contrib.auth.context_processors.auth',
                'django.contrib.messages.context_processors.messages',
            ],
        },
    },
]
```

As you can see in Listing 3-4, `string_if_invalid` is assigned the string "`**** WARNING INVALID VARIABLE %s ****`". When Django encounters an invalid variable, it replaces the occurrence with this string, where the `%s` variable gets substituted with the invalid variable name, allowing you to easily locate where and what variables are invalid.

Another configuration option for the `string_if_invalid` option is to perform more complex logic when an invalid variable is encountered. For example, Listing 3-5 illustrates how you can raise an error so the template fails to render in case an invalid variable is found.

Listing 3-5. Error generation for invalid template variables with string_if_invalid

```
BASE_DIR = os.path.dirname(os.path.dirname(os.path.abspath(__file__)))
PROJECT_DIR = os.path.dirname(os.path.abspath(__file__))

class InvalidTemplateVariable(str):
    def __mod__(self,other):
        from django.template.base import TemplateSyntaxError
        raise TemplateSyntaxError("Invalid variable : '%s'" % other)

TEMPLATES = [
    {
        'BACKEND': 'django.template.backends.django.DjangoTemplates',
        'DIRS': ['%s/templates/' % (PROJECT_DIR),'%s/dev_templates/' % (PROJECT_DIR),],
        'APP_DIRS': True,
        'OPTIONS': {
            'string_if_invalid': InvalidTemplateVariable("%s"),
            'context_processors': [
                'django.template.context_processors.debug',
                'django.template.context_processors.request',
                'django.contrib.auth.context_processors.auth',
                'django.contrib.messages.context_processors.messages',
            ],
        },
    },
]
```

In Listing 3-5 `string_if_invalid` is assigned the `InvalidTemplateVariable` class that uses the `%s` input variable, which represents the invalid variable name - just like the previous example in Listing 3-4.

The `InvalidTemplateVariable` class is interesting because it inherits its behavior from the `str(string)` class and uses a Python `__mod__` (modulo) magic method implementation. While the `__mod__` (modulo) magic method is proper of number operations, in this case, it's useful because the passed in string uses the `%` (modulo) symbol, which makes the `__mod__` method run. Inside the `__mod__` method we just raise the `TemplateSyntaxError` error with the invalid variable name to halt the execution of the template.

■ **Caution** The Django admin might get mangled or broken with a custom `string_if_invalid` value.

The Django admin templates in particular rely heavily on the default `string_if_invalid` outputting empty strings `''`, due to the level of complexity in certain displays. In fact, this `string_if_invalid` default behavior is often considered a "feature," as much as it's considered a "bug" or "annoyance."

Therefore if you use one of the approaches in Listing 3-4 or Listing 3-5 to override `string_if_invalid`, be aware you will most likely mangle or brake Django admin pages. If you rely on the Django admin, you should only use these techniques to debug a project's templates.

Debug Output

When you run a Django project with the top-level `DEBUG=True` setting and an error occurs, Django templates output a very detailed page to make the debugging process easier – see Chapter 5 for more details on the `DEBUG` variable, specifically the section "Django `settings.py` for the Real World."

By default, Django templates reuse the top-level `DEBUG` variable value to configure template debug activity. Behind the scenes, this configuration is set through the debug field inside `OPTIONS` of the `TEMPLATES` variable. Figure 3-1 illustrates what an error page looks when `DEBUG=True`.

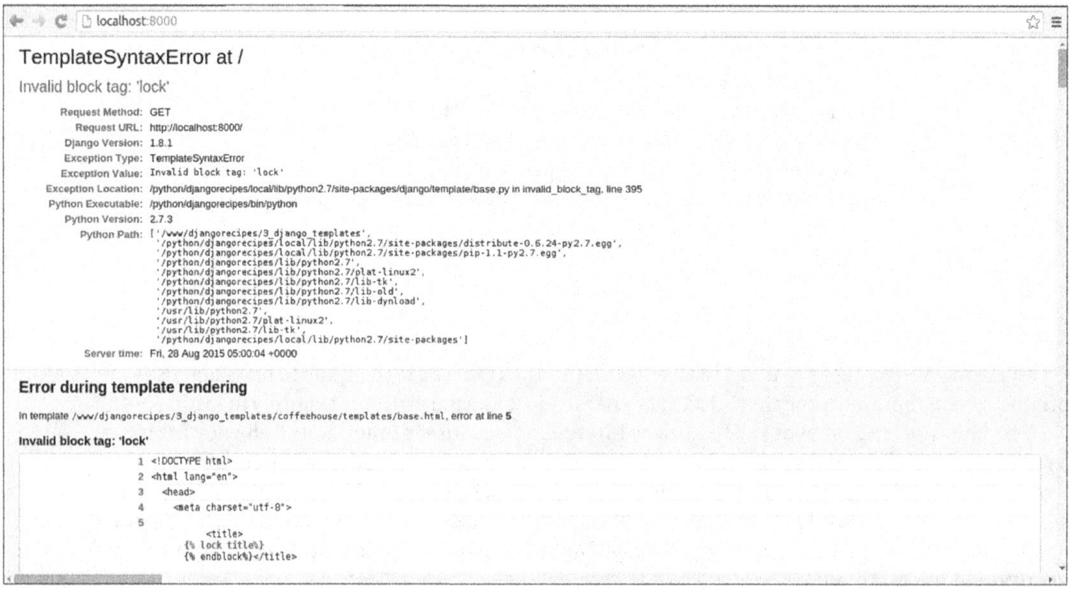

Figure 3-1. *Django error page when DEBUG=True automatically sets template OPTION to 'debug':True*

As you can see in Figure 3-1, Django prints the location of the template, as well as a snippet of the template itself to make it easier to locate an error. This template information is generated due to the `'debug':True` option, which is set based on the top-level `DEBUG` variable. However, you can explicitly set the debug option to `False` as illustrated in Listing 3-6, in which case the error page would result without any template details and just the traceback information, as illustrated in Figure 3-2.

Listing 3-6. Option with debug equals False omits template details

```
BASE_DIR = os.path.dirname(os.path.dirname(os.path.abspath(__file__)))
PROJECT_DIR = os.path.dirname(os.path.abspath(__file__))

TEMPLATES = [
    {
        'BACKEND': 'django.template.backends.django.DjangoTemplates',
        'DIRS': ['%s/templates/' % (PROJECT_DIR),'%s/dev_templates/' % (PROJECT_DIR),],
        'APP_DIRS': True,
        'OPTIONS': {
            'debug':False,
            'context_processors': [
                'django.template.context_processors.debug',
                'django.template.context_processors.request',
                'django.contrib.auth.context_processors.auth',
                'django.contrib.messages.context_processors.messages',
            ],
        },
    },
]
```

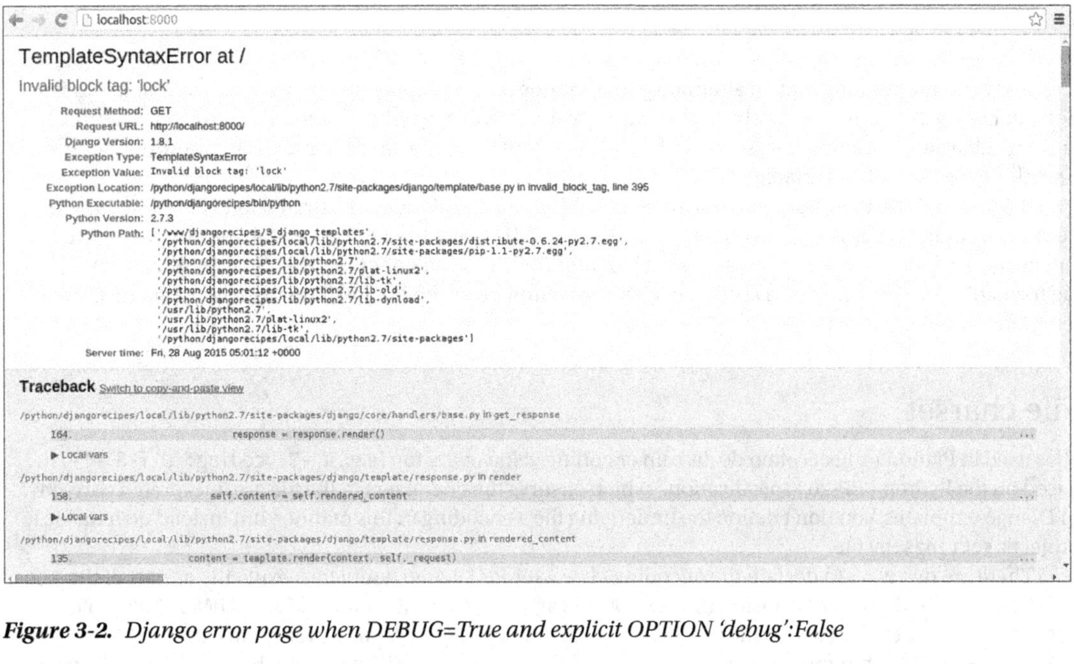

Figure 3-2. *Django error page when DEBUG=True and explicit OPTION 'debug':False*

Auto-Escape

By default, Django templates use the security practice to auto-escape certain characters - described in Table 3-1 - contained in dynamically generated constructs (e.g., variables, tags, filters). Auto-escaping converts characters that can potentially mangle a user interface or produce dangerous outcomes into safe representations, a process that was described in the first section of this chapter.

However, you can globally disable auto-escaping on all Django templates -- and knowingly render < as <, > as >, etc... -- with the autoescape field in OPTIONS as shown in Listing 3-7.

Listing 3-7. Option with auto-escape equals False omits auto-escaping on all Django templates

```
BASE_DIR = os.path.dirname(os.path.dirname(os.path.abspath(__file__)))
PROJECT_DIR = os.path.dirname(os.path.abspath(__file__))

TEMPLATES = [
    {
        'BACKEND': 'django.template.backends.django.DjangoTemplates',
        'DIRS': ['%s/templates/' % (PROJECT_DIR),'%s/dev_templates/' % (PROJECT_DIR),],
        'APP_DIRS': True,
        'OPTIONS': {
            'autoescape':False,
            'context_processors': [
                'django.template.context_processors.debug',
                'django.template.context_processors.request',
                'django.contrib.auth.context_processors.auth',
                'django.contrib.messages.context_processors.messages',
            ],
        },
    },
]
```

It's worth mentioning that an alternative to disabling auto-escaping on every Django template - as it's done in Listing 3-7 - is to selectively disable auto-escaping. You can either use the `{% autoescape off %}` tag to disable auto-escaping on a section of a Django template or the `safe` filter to disable auto-escaping on a single Django template variable.

If you do decide to disable auto-escaping on all Django templates as illustrated in Listing 3-7 - which I frankly wouldn't recommend if you plan to use just HTML, because of the potential security risk-- you can also granularly enable auto-escaping again if required. You can either use the `{% autoescape on %}` tag to enable auto-escaping on a section of a Django template or the `escape` filter to escape a single Django template variable.

File charset

Files used in Python projects often declare an encoding value at the top (e.g., `# -*- coding: utf-8 -*-`) based on the Python PEP-263 specification,[2] which ensures the characters in the file are interpreted correctly. In Django templates, you don't define the underlying file's encoding in this manner, but instead do it inside a project's `settings.py` file.

There are two ways to declare the encoding character for Django templates: explicitly as part of the `file_charset` field in `OPTIONS` inside the `TEMPLATES` variable or via the top-level `FILE_CHARSET` variable in `settings.py`. The explicit declaration in `file_charset` within `OPTIONS` takes precedence over the `FILE_CHARSET` assignment, but the value of `file_charset` defaults to `FILE_CHARSET`, which, in itself defaults to utf-8 (Unicode) encoding.

[2]https://www.python.org/dev/peps/pep-0263/

So by default, Django template encoding is assigned to utf-8 or Unicode, which is one of the most widely used encodings in software. Nevertheless, in the event you decide to incorporate data into Django templates that isn't utf-8 compatible (e.g., Spanish vowels with accents like á or é encoded as ISO-8859-1 or Kanji characters like 漢 or 字 encoded as JIS) you must define the `FILE_CHARSET` value in a project's `settings.py` file - or directly in the `file_charset` field in `OPTIONS` inside the `TEMPLATES` - so Django template data is interpreted correctly.

Django templates can be assigned any encoding value from Python's standard encoding values.[3]

Automatic Access to Custom Template tag/filter Modules

Django templates have access to a series of built-in tags and filters that don't require any setup steps. However, if you plan to use a third-party template tag/filter module or write your own template tag/filter module, then you need to set up access on each Django template with the `{% load %}` tag (e.g., `{% load really_useful_tags_and_filters %}`), a process that can get tiresome if you need to access a particular tag/filter on dozens or hundreds of templates.

To automatically gain access to third-party template tags/filters or your own template tags/filters as if they were built-in tags/filters (i.e., without requiring the `{% load %}` tag), you can use the `builtins` field in `OPTIONS` as illustrated in Listing 3-8.

Listing 3-8. Option with builtins to gain automatic access to tags/filters on all templates

```
BASE_DIR = os.path.dirname(os.path.dirname(os.path.abspath(__file__)))
PROJECT_DIR = os.path.dirname(os.path.abspath(__file__))

TEMPLATES = [
    {
        'BACKEND': 'django.template.backends.django.DjangoTemplates',
        'DIRS': ['%s/templates/' % (PROJECT_DIR),'%s/dev_templates/' % (PROJECT_DIR),],
        'APP_DIRS': True,
        'OPTIONS': {
            'context_processors': [
                'django.template.context_processors.debug',
                'django.template.context_processors.request',
                'django.contrib.auth.context_processors.auth',
                'django.contrib.messages.context_processors.messages',
            ],
            'builtins': [
                 'coffeehouse.builtins',
                 'thirdpartyapp.customtags.really_useful_tags_and_filters',
            ],
        },
    },
]
```

As you can see in Listing 3-8, the `builtins` field accepts a list of modules that includes tags/filters for built-in treatment. In this case, `coffeehouse.builtins` represents a `builtins.py` file - which includes the custom tags/filters - under a project named `coffeehouse`. And the `thirdpartyapp.customtags.really_useful_tags_and_filters` is a third-party package with tags/filters that we also want to access in Django templates without the need to use the `{% load %}` tag.

[3]https://docs.python.org/3/library/codecs.html#standard-encodings

Another default behavior of third-party template tag/filter modules and custom template tag/filter modules is they are required to use their original label/name for reference, while the latter also requires it to be placed inside a folder named `templatetags` in a registered Django app. These two default behaviors can be overridden with the `libraries` field in `OPTIONS` as illustrated in Listing 3-9.

Listing 3-9. Option with libraries to register tags/filters with alternative label/name and under any project directory

```
BASE_DIR = os.path.dirname(os.path.dirname(os.path.abspath(__file__)))
PROJECT_DIR = os.path.dirname(os.path.abspath(__file__))

TEMPLATES = [
    {
        'BACKEND': 'django.template.backends.django.DjangoTemplates',
        'DIRS': ['%s/templates/' % (PROJECT_DIR),'%s/dev_templates/' % (PROJECT_DIR),],
        'APP_DIRS': True,
        'OPTIONS': {
            'context_processors': [
                'django.template.context_processors.debug',
                'django.template.context_processors.request',
                'django.contrib.auth.context_processors.auth',
                'django.contrib.messages.context_processors.messages',
            ],
            'libraries': {
                 'coffeehouse_tags': 'coffeehouse.tags_filters.common',
            },
        },
    },
]
```

The libraries statement in Listing 3-9 `'coffeehouse_tags': 'coffeehouse.tags_filters.common'` tells Django to load the `common.py` file - that includes the custom tags/filters - from the `tags_filters` folder in the `coffeehouse` project and make it accessible to templates through the `coffeehouse_tags` reference (e.g., `{% load coffeehouse_tags %}`). With the approach in Listing 3-9, you can place custom tag/filter modules anywhere in a Django project, as well as assign custom tag/filter modules - or third-party tag/filter modules - an alternative reference value instead of their original label/name.

Template Loaders

Earlier in the section “Template Search Paths,” I described how Django searches for templates using the `DIRS` and `APP_DIRS` variables, which are part of Django's template configuration. However, I intentionally omitted a deeper aspect associated with this template search process: each search mechanism is backed by a template loader.

A template loader is a Python class that implements the actual logic required to search and load templates. Table 3-2 illustrates the built-in template loaders available in Django.

Table 3-2. Built-in Django template loaders

Template loader class	Description
django.template.loaders.filesystem.Loader	Searches and loads templates in directories declared in the DIRS variable. Enabled by default when DIRS is not empty.
django.template.loaders.app_directories.Loader	Searches and loads templates from subdirectories named templates in all apps declared in INSTALLED_APPS. Enabled by default when APP_DIRS is True.
django.template.loaders.cached.Loader	Searches for templates from an in-memory cache, after loading templates from a file-system or app directory loader.
django.template.loaders.locmem.Loader	Searches for templates from an in-memory cache, after loading templates from a Python dictionary.

As you can see, two of the Django template loaders in Table 3-2 are automatically set up by the presence of either the `DIRS` or `APP_DIRS` variables. Nevertheless, any of the template loaders in Table 3-2 can be set up explicitly using the `loaders` field in `OPTIONS` inside `TEMPLATES`.

Create Reusable Templates

Templates tend to have common sections that are equally used across multiple instances. For example, the header and footer sections on all templates rarely change, whether a project has 5 or 100 templates. Other template sections like menus and advertisements also fall into this category of content that's constant across multiple templates. All of this can lead to repetition over multiple templates, which can be avoided by creating reusable templates.

With reusable Django templates you can define common sections on separate templates and reuse them inside other templates. This process makes it easy to create and manage a project's templates because a single template update takes effect on all templates.

Reusable Django templates also allow you to define page blocks to override content on a page-by-page basis. This process makes a project's templates more modular because you define top-level blocks to establish the overall layout and define content on a page-by-page basis.

Lets take the first step toward building reusable Django templates exploring the Django built-in `{% block %}` tag. Listing 3-10 illustrates the first lines of a template called `base.html` with several `{% block %}` tags.

Listing 3-10. Django template with {% block %} tags

```
<!DOCTYPE html>
<html lang="en">
  <head>
    <meta charset="utf-8">
    <title>{% block title%}Default title{% endblock title %}</title>
    <meta name="description" content="{% block metadescription%}{% endblock metadescription %}">
    <meta name="keywords" content="{% block metakeywords%}{% endblock metakeywords %}">
```

Notice the syntax {% block <name>%}{% endblock <name> %} in Listing 3-10. Each {% block %} tag has a reference name. The reference name is used by other Django templates to override the content for each block.

For example, the {% block title %} tag within the HTML <title> tags defines a web page title. If another template reuses the template in Listing 3-10, it can define its own web page title by overriding the title block. If a block is not overridden on a template, the block receives the default content within the block. For the title block the default content is Default title, for the metadescription and metakeywords blocks the default content is an empty string.

The same mechanism illustrated in Listing 3-10 can be used to define any number of blocks (e.g., content, menu, header, footer). It's worth mentioning the <name> argument of {% endblock <name> %} is optional and it's valid to just use {% endblock %} to close a block statement; however, the former technique makes it clearer where a block statement ends, which is especially helpful when a template has multiple blocks.

Although it's possible to call the template in Listing 3-10 directly by a Django view method or url request, the purpose of this kind of template is to use it as a base template for other templates. To reuse a Django template you use the Django built-in {% extends %} tag.

The {% extends %} tag uses the syntax {% extends <name> %} to reuse the layout of another template. This means that in order to reuse the layout in Listing 3-10 defined in a file base.html, you use the syntax {% extends "base.html" %}. In addition, if you use the {% extends %} tag it has to be the first definition in Django template, as illustrated in Listing 3-11.

Listing 3-11. Django template with {% extends %} and {% block %} tag

```
{% extends "base.html" %}
{% block title %}Coffeehouse home page{% endblock title %}
```

■ **Tip** In an {% extend <name> %} tag statement, the <name> value can also use a relative path (e.g., "../base.html"), as well as a variable passed by a view that can be a string (e.g., "master.html") or Template object loaded in the view.

Notice in Listing 3-11 how the first template statement is {% extends "base.html" %}. In addition, notice how Listing 3-11 defines the {% block title %} tag with the content Coffeehouse home page. The block in Listing 3-11 overrides the title block from the base.html template. So where are the HTML <title> tags in Listing 3-11? There aren't any and you don't need them. Django automatically reuses the layout from the base.html template and substitutes the blocks content where necessary.

Django templates that reuse other templates tend to have limited layout elements (e.g., HTML tags) and more Django block statements to override content. This is beneficial because as I outlined previously, it lets you establish the overall layout once and define content on a page-by-page basis.

The reusability of Django templates can occur multiple times. For example, you can have templates A, B, and C, where B requires to reuse A, but C requires to reuse parts of B. The only difference is template C needs to use the {% extends "B" %} tag instead of the {% extends "A"%} tag. But since template B reuses A, template C also has access to the same elements in template A.

When reusing Django templates, it's also possible to access the block content from a parent template. Django exposes the block content from a parent template through the reference block.super. Listing 3-12 illustrates three templates that show this mechanism for a block containing web page paths or "breadcrumbs."

Listing 3-12. Django templates use of {{block.super}} with three reusable templates

```
# base.html template
<p>{% block breadcrumb %}Home{% endblock breadcrumb %}</p>

# index.html template
{% extends "base.html" %}
{% block breadcrumb %}Main{% endblock breadcrumb %}

# detail.html template
{% extends "index.html" %}
{% block breadcrumb %} {{block.super}} : Detail {% endblock breadcrumb %}
```

The `base.html` template in Listing 3-12 defines the `breadcrumb` block with a default value of `Home`. Next, the `index.html` template reuses the `base.html` template and overrides the `breadcrumb` block with a value of `Main`. Finally, the `detail.html` template reuses the `index.html` template and overrides the `breadcrumb` block value. However, notice the `{{block.super}}` statement in the final block override. Since `{{block.super}}` is inside the `breadcrumb` block, `{{block.super}}` tells Django to get the content from the parent template block.

Another reusability functionality in Django templates is the inclusion of a Django template inside another Django template. Django supports this functionality through the `{% include %}` tag.

The `{% include %}` tag expects a template argument - similar to the `{% extend %}` tag - which can be either a hard-coded string reference (e.g., `{% include "footer.html" %}`), a relative path to a template (e.g., `{% include "../header.html" %}`), or a variable passed by a view that can be a string or Template object loaded in the view.

Templates declared as part of `{% include %}` tags are made aware of context variables in the template that declares them. This means if template A uses the `{% include "footer.html" %}` tag, template A variables are automatically made available to the `footer.html` template.

Inclusively, it's possible to explicitly provide context variables to `{% include %}` statements using the `with` keyword. For example, the statement `{% include "footer.html" with year="2013" %}` makes the `year` variable accessible inside the `footer.html` template. The `{% include %}` tag also supports the ability to pass multiple variables using the `with` notation (e.g., `{% include "footer.html" with year="2013" copyright="Creative Commons" %}`).

Finally, if you want templates declared as part of `{% include %}` tags to have restricted access to context variables from the template that declares them, you can use the `only` keyword. For example, if template B uses the `{% include "footer.html" with year="2013" only %}` statement, the `footer.html` template only gets access to the year variable, irrespective of the variables available in template B. Similarly, the `{% include "footer.html" only %}` statement restricts the `footer.html` template to no variables, irrespective of the variables available in the template that uses the statement.

Built-In Context Processors

By default, Django templates are enabled to have access to various variables. This eliminates the need to constantly declare widely used variables in every single Django view methods or as url extra options. These variables are made available through template context processors.

Django template context processors are explicitly defined in a project's `settings.py` file, in the `TEMPLATES` variable inside the `OPTIONS` key. By default and as illustrated in Listing 3-1, Django projects are enabled with four context processors built in to Django. Next, I'll describe the data variables made available by each of these context processors.

Django debug context processor (django.template.context_processors.debug)

The Django debug context processor exposes variables that are helpful for debugging. This context processor makes the following variables available on all Django templates:

- `debug`.- Contains True or False, based on the `DEBUG` variable in the `settings.py` file.
- `sql_queries`.- Contains the database connection details (e.g., SQL statements) run by the backing method view.

■ **Note** The Django debug context processor displays variable values only if the requesting IP address is defined in the INTERNAL_IPS variable in settings.py. Even if the variables are declared in a template (e.g., {{debug}} or {{sql_queries}}) this restriction permits that only certain users view the debug messages in the template, while other users won't view anything.

For example, to view the debug and sql_queries values on your local workstation, add INTERNAL_IPS = ['127.0.0.1'] to the settings.py file. This tells Django to display these variables values for requests made from the IP address 127.0.0.1.

Django request context processor (django.template.context_processors.request)

The Django request context processor exposes variables related to a request (i.e., HTTP request). This context processor makes data available through a massive dictionary named `request`, which includes some of the following key-values:

- `request.GET`.- Contains a request's HTTP GET parameters.
- `request.POST`.- Contains a request's HTTP POST parameters.
- `request.COOKIES`.- Contains a request's HTTP COOKIES.
- `request.CONTENT_TYPE`.- Contains a request's HTTP Content-type header.
- `request.META`.- Contains a request's HTTP META data.
- `request.REMOTE_ADDR`.- Contains a request's HTTP remote address.

Django auth context processor (django.contrib.auth.context_processors.auth)

The Django auth context processor exposes variables related to authentication logic. This context processor makes the following variables accessible in Django templates:

- `user`.- Contains user data (e.g., id, name, email, anonymous user).
- `perms`.- Contains user app permissions (e.g., True, False or explicit app permissions a user has access to in a `django.contrib.auth.context_processors.PermWrapper` object).

Django messages context processor (django.contrib.messages.context_processors.messages)

The Django messages context processor exposes variables related to the Django messages framework, introduced in Chapter 2. Messages are added in Django view methods to the message framework, which are then exposed in Django templates. This context processor makes the following variables accessible in Django templates:

- `messages`.- Contains the messages added through the Django messages framework in Django view methods.
- `DEFAULT_MESSAGE_LEVELS`.- Contains a mapping of the message level names to their numeric value (e.g., `{'DEBUG': 10, 'INFO': 20, 'WARNING': 30, 'SUCCESS': 25, 'ERROR': 40}`).

Other Built-In Django Context Processors: i18n, media, static, tz, and CSRF context Processors

The previous context processors offer some of the most common data required across all Django project templates, which is why they're enabled by default. However, this doesn't mean they are the only built-in Django context processors. There are, in fact, five more built-in context processors you can use to access certain data from all Django templates.

Django i18n context processor (django.template.context_processors.i18n)

The Django i18n context processor exposes variables related to internationalization logic. This context processor makes the following variables accessible in Django templates:

- `LANGUAGES`.- Contains available languages for Django projects.
- `LANGUAGE_CODE`.-Contains the project language code, based on the `LANGUAGE_CODE` variable in the `settings.py` file.
- `LANGUAGE_BIDI`.- Contains the current project language direction. It's set to `False` for left-to-right languages (e.g., English, French, German) or `True` for right-to-left languages (e.g., Hebrew, Arabic).

Django media context processor (django.template.context_processors.media)

The Django media context processor exposes a variable related to media resources. This context processor makes the following variable accessible in Django templates:

- `MEDIA_URL`.- Contains the media url, based on the `MEDIA_URL` variable in the `settings.py` file.

Django static context processor (django.template.context_processors.static)

The Django static context processor exposes a variable related to static resources. This context processor makes the following variable accessible in Django templates:

- `STATIC_URL`.- Contains the static url, based on the `STATIC_URL` variable in the `settings.py` file.

■ **Tip** Even though the static context processor is accessible (i.e., it's not deprecated) its functionality is outdated and should be avoided. You should use the staticfiles app instead. More details are provided in Chapter 5 in the section on setting up static web page resources (Images, CSS, JavaScript).

Django tz context processor (django.template.context_processors.tz)

The Django tz context processor exposes a variable related to a project's time zone. This context processor makes the following variable accessible in Django templates:

- `TIME_ZONE`.- Contains a project's time zone, based on the `TIME_ZONE` variable in the `settings.py` file.

Django CSRF context Processor (django.template.context_processors.csrf)

The Cross Site Request Forgeries (CSRF) context processor adds the `csrf_token` variable to all requests. This variable is used by the `{% csrf_token %}` template tag to protect against Cross Site Request Forgeries.

Although you can gain access to the `csrf_token` variable value in any Django template, you will have little - if any - need to expose it directly, as it's used as a security mechanism to detect forged requests. Chapter 6, covering the topic of Django forms, describes what it is and how CSRF works with Django.

Due to the security significance of having the `csrf_token` variable available on all requests, the CSRF context processor is always enabled - irrespective of the `context_processors` list in `OPTIONS` - and cannot be disabled.

Custom Context Processors

When you set up data in view methods or url extra options, you do so to access the data on individual Django templates. Custom Django context processors allow you to set up data for access on all Django templates.

A Django custom context processor is structured just like a regular Python method with an `HttpRequest` object argument that returns a dictionary. The returning dictionary keys of the context processor represent template references and the dictionary values data objects (e.g., strings, lists, dictionaries) accessible in templates. Listing 3-13 illustrates a custom Django context processor method.

Listing 3-13. Custom Django context processor method

```
def onsale(request):
    # Create fixed data structures to pass to template
    # data could equally come from database queries
    # web services or social APIs
    sale_items = {'Monday':'Mocha 2x1','Tuesday':'Latte 2x1'}
    return {'SALE_ITEMS': sale_items}
```

As you can see in Listing 3-13, the `onsale` method has a `request` argument - representing an `HttpRequest` object - and returns a dictionary. The dictionary in this case has a single key called `SALE_ITEMS` and a value that is a hard-coded dictionary.

However, just as you can set up any type of data in a Django view method or url option to pass to a template, a custom Django context processor method can also access data from the request argument (e.g., cookie, remote IP address) or even query a database and make this data available to all templates.

The custom context processor method can be placed inside any project file or directory. The location and naming conventions are of little importance, because Django detects context processors through the `context_processors` variable in `OPTIONS` of the `TEMPLATES` variable in a project's `settings.py` file. I'll place the context processor method in Listing 3-13 in a file called `processors.py` in the `stores` app subdirectory.

Once you save the custom context processor method, you have to configure Django to locate it. Listing 3-14 shows the `context_processors` variable update to include the custom context processor method from Listing 3-13.

Listing 3-14. Django template context processor definitions in context_processors in OPTIONS of TEMPLATES

```
'OPTIONS': {
    'context_processors': [
        'coffeehouse.stores.processors.onsale',
        'django.template.context_processors.debug',
        'django.template.context_processors.request',
        'django.contrib.auth.context_processors.auth',
        'django.contrib.messages.context_processors.messages',
    ],
}
```

In Listing 3-14 you can see the `coffeehouse.stores.processors.onsale` declaration, where `coffeehouse.stores` represents the package.app name, `processors` is the file that contains the custom context processor (i.e., `processors.py` inside the stores app) and `onsale` is the actual method that contains the custom context processor logic.

Once you declare the context processors on you project's `settings.py` file, the custom dictionary with the `SALE_ITEMS` key from Listing 3-13 becomes available to all Django templates.

Built-In Django Filters

Django filters are designed to format template variables. The syntax to apply Django filters is the vertical bar character | also known as "pipe" in Unix environments (e.g., `{{variable|filter}}`). It's worth mentioning that it's possible to use multiple filters on the same variable (e.g., `{{variable|filter|filter}}`).

I'll classify each built-in Django filter into functional sections so it's easier to identify them. The functional classes I'll use are Dates, Strings, Lists, Numbers, Dictionaries, Spacing and special characters, Development, and Testing and Urls.

■ **Tip** You can apply Django filters to entire sections with the {% filter %} tag. If you have a group of variables in the same section and want to apply the same filter to all of them, it's easier to use the {% filter %} tag than to individually declare the filter on each variable. The next section in this chapter on Django built-in tags provides more details on the {% filter %} tag

---

Dates

- `date`.- The `date` filter formats Python `datetime` objects and only works if the variable is this type of Python object. The `date` filter uses a string to specify a format. For example, if a variable contains a `datetime` object with the date 01/01/2018, the filter statement `{{variable|date:"F jS o"}}` outputs January 1st 2018. The string syntax for the date filter is based on the characters described in Table 3-3.

■ **Tip** If you provide no string argument to the date filter (e.g., {{variable|date}}), it defaults to the "N j, Y" string, which comes from the default value of DATE_FORMAT.

■ **Note** The date filter can also accept predefined date variables {{variable|date:"DATE_FORMAT"}}, {{variable|date:"DATETIME_FORMAT"}}, {{variable|date:"SHORT_DATE_FORMAT" %} or {{variable|date: "SHORT_DATETIME_FORMAT"}}.

The predefined date variables in themselves are also composed of date strings based on the syntax in Table 3-3. For example DATE_FORMAT default's to "N j, Y" (e.g., Jan 1, 2018), DATETIME_FORMAT defaults to "N j, Y, P" (e.g., Jan 1, 2018, 12 a.m.), SHORT_DATE_FORMAT defaults to "m/d/Y" (e.g., 01/01/2018) and SHORT_DATETIME_FORMAT defaults to "m/d/Y P" (e.g., 01/01/2018 12 a.m.). Each date variable can be overridden with different date strings in a project's settings.py file.

Table 3-3. *Django date and time format characters*

Standards based characters	Description
c	Outputs ISO 8601 format (e.g., 2015-01-02T10:30:00.000123+02:00 or 2015-01-02T10:30:00.000123 if the datetime has no timezone [i.e.,naive datetime])
r	Outputs RFC 2822 formatted date (e.g., 'Thu, 21 Dec 2000 16:01:07 +0200')
U	Outputs seconds since Unix epoch date--January 1 1970 00:00:00 UTC
I (Uppercase i)	Outputs whether daylight savings time is in effect (e.g., '1' or '0')
Hour based characters	**Description**
a	Outputs 'a.m.' or 'p.m.'
A	Outputs 'AM' or 'PM'
f	Outputs time, 12-hour hours and minutes, with minutes left off if they're zero (e.g., '1', '1:30')
g	Outputs hour, 12-hour format without leading zeros (e.g.'1' to '12')
G	Outputs hour, 24-hour format without leading zeros (e.g., '0' to '23')
h	Outputs hour, 12-hour format (e.g., '01' to '12')
H	Outputs hour, 24-hour format (e.g., '00' to '23')
i	Outputs minutes (e.g., '00' to '59')
P	Outputs time, 12-hour hours, minutes and 'a.m.'/'p.m.', with minutes left off if they're zero and the special-case strings 'midnight' and 'noon' if appropriate (e.g., '1 a.m.', '1:30 p.m.', 'midnight', 'noon', '12:30 p.m.')
s	Outputs seconds, 2 digits with leading zeros (e.g., '00' to '59')
u	Outputs microseconds (e.g., 000000 to 999999)
Timezone characters	**Description**
e	Outputs timezone name. Can be in any format, or might return an empty string, depending on datetime definition (e.g., '', 'GMT', '-500', 'US/Eastern')

(*continued*)

Table 3-3. *(continued)*

Standards based characters	Description
O	Outputs difference in timezone to Greenwich time in hours (e.g., '+0200')
T	Outputs datetime time zone (e.g., 'EST', 'MDT')
Z	Outputs time zone offset in seconds. The offset for timezones west of UTC is always negative, and for those east of UTC is always positive (e.g., -43200 to 43200)
Day and week characters	**Description**
D	Outputs day of the week, textual, 3 letters (e.g., 'Thu','Fri')
l (Lowercase L)	Outputs day of the week, textual, long (e.g.,'Thursday','Friday')
S	Outputs English ordinal suffix for day of the month, 2 characters (e.g., 'st', 'nd', 'rd' or 'th')
w	Outputs day of the week, digits without leading zeros (e.g., '0' for Sunday to '6' for Saturday)
z	Outputs day of the year (e.g., 0 to 365)
W	Outputs the week number of the year, with weeks starting on Monday based on ISO-8601 (e.g., 1, 53)
o	Outputs week-numbering year, corresponding to the ISO-8601 week number (W)(e.g., '1999')
Month characters	**Description**
b	Outputs textual month, 3 letters, lowercase (e.g., 'jan','feb')
d	Outputs day of the month, 2 digits with leading zeros (e.g., '01' to '31')
j	Outputs day of the month without leading zeros (e.g., '1' to '31')
E	Outputs month, locale specific alternative representation usually used for long date representation (e.g., 'listopada' for Polish locale, as opposed to 'Listopad')
F	Outputs month, textual, long (e.g., 'January','February')
m	Outputs month, 2 digits with leading zeros (e.g., '01' to '12')
M	Outputs month, textual, 3 letters (e.g.'Jan','Feb')
n	Outputs month without leading zeros (e.g., '1' to '12')
N	Outputs month abbreviation in Associated Press style (e.g., 'Jan', 'Feb', 'March', 'May')
t	Outputs number of days in the given month (e.g., 28 to 31)
Year characters	**Description**
L	Outputs Boolean for whether it's a leap year (e.g., True or False)
y	Outputs year, 2 digits (e.g., '99')
Y	Outputs year, 4 digits (e.g., '1999')

To literally output a date character in a string statement you can use the backslash character (e.g., `{{variable|date:"jS \o\f F o"}}` outputs 1st of January 2018, note the escaped `\o\f`)

- time.- The time filter formats the time component of a Python datetime object. The time filter is similar to the date filter, which uses a string to specify a time format. For example, if a variable contains a datetime object with a time of noon the filter statement {{variable|time:"g:i"}} outputs 12:00. The time filter uses the same format characters illustrated in Table 3-3 related to the time of day.

■ **Tip** If you provide no string argument to the date filter (e.g., {{variable|time}}), it defaults to the "P" string, which comes from the default value of TIME_FORMAT.

■ **Note** The time filter can also accept a predefined time variable {{variable|date:"TIME FORMAT"}. The predefined time is also composed of a time string based on the syntax in Table 3-3. For example, TIME_FORMAT default's to "P" (e.g., 4 a.m.) and this can be overridden defining TIME_FORMAT in a project's settings.py file.

- timesince.- The timesince filter outputs the time that's passed between a datetime object and the current time. The timesince filter output is expressed in seconds, minutes, hours, days, or weeks. For example, if a variable contains the datetime object 01/01/2018 12:00pm and the current time is 01/01/2018 3:30pm the statement {{variable|timesince}} outputs 3 hours 30 minutes. The timesince filter can also calculate the time that's passed between two datetime object variables - instead of the default current time - by appending a second datetime object argument (e.g., {{variable|timesince:othervariable}}).
- timeuntil.- The timeuntil filter outputs the time that needs to elapse from the current time to a datetime object. The timeuntil filter output is expressed in seconds, minutes, hours, days, or weeks. For example, if a variable contains the datetime object 01/01/2018 10:00pm and the current time is 01/01/2018 9:00pm the statement {{variable|timeuntil}} outputs 1 hour. The timeuntil filter can also calculate the time that needs to elapse between two datetime object variables - instead of the default current time - by appending a second datetime object argument (e.g., {{variable|timeuntil:othervariable}}).

Strings, Lists, and Numbers

- add.- The add filter adds values. The add filter can add two variables or a hard-coded value and a variable. For example, if a variable contains 5 the filter statement {{variable|add:"3"}} outputs 8. If values can be coerced to integers - like the last example - the add filter performs a sum, if not the add filter concatenates. For a string variable that contains "Hello" the filter statement {{variable|add:" World"}} outputs Hello World. For a list variable that contains ['a','e','i'] and another list variable that contains ['o','u'] the filter statement {{variable|add:othervariable}} outputs ['a','e','i','o','u'].
- default.- The default filter is used to specify a default value if a variable is false, doesn't exist, or is empty. For example, if a variable doesn't exist in a template, contains False or is an empty string ('') the filter statement {{variable|default:"no value"}} outputs no value.

- `default_if_none`.- The default filter is used to specify a default value if a variable is `None`. For example, if a variable contains `None` the filter statement `{{variable|default_if_none:"No value"}}` outputs `No value`. Note if a variable contains an empty string (`''`) this is not considered `None` and the `default_if_none` filter does not output its argument value.
- `length`.- The `length` filter is used to obtain the length of a value. For example, if a variable contains the string `latte` the filter statement `{{variable|length}}` outputs 5. For a list variable that contains `['a','e','i']` the filter statement `{{variable|length}}` outputs 3.
- `length_is`.- The `length_is` filter is used to evaluate if the length of a value is the size of a given argument. For example, if a variable contains `latte` the tag and filter statement `{% if variable|length_is:"7" %}` evaluates to false. For a list variable that contains `['a','e','i']` the tag and filter statement `{% if variable|length_is:"3" %}` evaluates to true.
- `make_list`.- The `make_list` filter creates a list from a string or number. For example, for the filter and tag statement `{% with mycharlist="mocha"|make_list %}` the mycharlist variable is assigned the list ['m', 'o', 'c', 'h', 'a']. For an integer variable that contains 724 the filter and tag statement `{% with myintlist=variable|make_list %}` the myintlist is assigned the list ['7', '2', '4'].
- `yesno`.- The `yesno` filter maps the value of a variable from `True`,`False` and `None` to the strings yes,no,maybe. For example, if a variable evaluates to `True` the filter statement `{{variable|yesno}}` outputs yes, if the variable evaluates to `False` the same statement outputs no, and if the variable evaluates to `None` the same statement outputs maybe. The `yesno` filter also accepts custom messages as arguments. For example, if a variable evaluates to `True` the filter statement `{{variable|yesno:"yea,nay,novote"}}` outputs yea, if the variable evaluates to `False` the same statement outputs nay, and if the variable evaluates to `None` the same statement outputs novote.

Numbers

- `divisibleby`.- The `divisibleby` filter returns a Boolean value if a variable is divisible by a given value. For example, if a variable contains 20 the filter statement `{{variable|divisibleby:"5"}}` returns `True`.
- `filesizeformat`.-The `filesizeformat` filter converts a number of bytes into a friendly file size string. For example, if a variable contains 250 the filter statement `{{variable|filesizeformat}}` outputs 250 bytes, if it contains 2048 the output is 2 KB, if it contains 2000000000 the output is 1.9 GB.
- `floatformat`.- The `floatformat` filter rounds a floating-point number variable. The `floatformat` filter can accept a positive or negative integer argument to round a variable a specific number of decimals. If no argument is used, the `floatformat` filter rounds to one decimal place, as if the argument where -1. For example, if a variable contains 9.33253 the filter statement `{{variable|floatformat}}` outputs 9.3, for the same variable `{{variable|floatformat:3}}` outputs 9.333 and for `{{variable|floatformat:-3}}` the output is 9.333; if a variable contains 9.00000 the filter statement `{{variable|floatformat}}` outputs 9, `{{variable|floatformat:3}}` outputs 9.000 and `{{variable|floatformat:-3}}` outputs 9; and if a variable contains 9.37000 the filter statement `{{variable|floatformat}}` outputs 9.4, `{{variable|floatformat:3}}` outputs 9.370 and `{{variable|floatformat:-3}}` outputs 9.370.

- `get_digit`.- The `get_digit` filter outputs the digit of a number variable, where 1 is the last digit, 2 is the second to last digit, and so on. For example, if a variable contains 10257, the filter statement `{{variable|get_digit:"1"}}` outputs 7 and the filter statement `{{variable|get_digit:"3"}}` outputs 2. If the variable or argument is not an integer or if the argument is less than 1, the `get_digit` filter outputs the original variable value.
- `phone2numeric`.- The `phone2numeric` filter converts mnemonic letters in phone numbers to digits. For example, if a variable contains 1-800-DJANGO the filter statement `{{variable|phone2numeric}}` outputs 1-800-352646. A `phone2numeric` filter value doesn't necessarily need to process valid phone numbers, the filter simply converts letters to their equivalent telephone keypad numbers.

Strings

`capfirst`.- The `capfirst` filter capitalizes the first character of a string variable. For example, if a variable contains `hello world` the filter statement `{{variable|capfirst}}` outputs `Hello world`.

- `cut`.- The `cut` filter removes all values of a given argument from a string variable. For example, if a variable contains `mocha latte` the filter statement `{{variable|filter:"mocha"}}` outputs `latte`. For the same variable the filter statement is `{{variable|filter:" "}}` outputs `mochalatte`.
- `linenumbers`.- The `linenumbers` filter adds line numbers to each string value separated by a new line. Listing 3-15 illustrates an example of the `linenumbers` filter.

Listing 3-15. Django linenumbers filter

```
# Variable definition
Downtown
Uptown
Midtown

# Template definition with linenumbers filter
{{variable|linenumbers}}

# Output
1.Downtown
2.Uptown
3.Midtown
```

- `lower`.- The `lower` filter converts all values of a string variable to lowercase. For example, if a variable contains `Hello World` the filter statement `{{variable|lower}}` outputs `hello world`.
- `stringformat`.- The `stringformat` filter formats a value with Python string formatting syntax.[4] For example, if a variable contains 7 the filter statement `{{variable|stringformat:"03d"}}` outputs 007. Note the `stringformat` filter does not require the leading `%` used in Python string formatting syntax.

[4]https://docs.python.org/3/library/stdtypes.html#old-string-formatting

- pluralize.- The pluralize filter returns a plural suffix based on the value of an argument. For example, if the variable drink_count contains 1 the filter statement "You have {{drink_count}} drink{{pluralize|drink_count}}" outputs "You have 1 drink", if the variable contains 2 the same filter statement outputs "You have 2 drinks". By default, the pluralize filter uses the letter s which is the most common plural suffix. However, you can specify different singular and plural suffixes with additional arguments. For example, the filter statement "We have {{store_count}} business{{store_count|pluralize:"es"}}" outputs "We have 1 business" if store_count is 1 or "We have 5 businesses" if store_count is 5. Another example is the filter statement "We have {{resp_number}} responsibilit{{resp_number|pluralize:"y","ies"}}" that outputs "We have 1 responsibility" if resp_number is 1 or "We have 3 responsibilities" if resp_number is 3.

- slugify.- The slugify filter converts a string to an ASCII-type string. This means a string in converted to lowercase, removes non-word characters (alphanumerics and underscores), strips leading and trailing whitespace, as well as converts spaces to hyphens. For example, if a variable contains Welcome to the #1 Coffeehouse! the filter statement {{variable|slugify}} outputs welcome-to-the-1-coffeehouse. The slugify filter is typically used to normalize strings for urls and file paths.

- title.- The title filter converts all first character values of a string variable to uppercase. For example, if a variable contains hello world the filter statement {{variable|title}} outputs Hello World.

- truncatechars.- The truncatechars filter truncates a string to a given number of characters and appends an ellipsis sequence. For example, if a variable contains Coffeehouse started as a small store the filter statement {{variable|truncatechars:20}} outputs Coffeehouse started....

- truncatechars_html.- The truncatechars_html filter is similar to the truncatechars filter but is aware of HTML tags. This filter is designed for HTML content, so content isn't left with open HTML tags. For example, if a variable contains <b>Coffeehouse started as a small store</b> the filter statement {{variable|truncachars_html:20}} outputs <b>Coffeehouse start...</b>.

- truncatewords.- The truncatewords filter truncates a string to a given number of words and appends an ellipsis sequence. For example, if a variable contains Coffeehouse started as a small store the filter statement {{variable|truncatwords:3}} outputs Coffeehouse started as....

- truncatewords_html.- The truncatewords_html filter is similar to the truncatewords filter but is aware of HTML tags. This filter is designed for HTML content, so content isn't left with open HTML tags. For example, if a variable contains <b>Coffeehouse started as a small store</b> the filter statement {{variable|truncatwords_html:3}} outputs <b>Coffeehouse started as...</b>.

- upper.- The upper filter converts all values of a string variable to uppercase. For example, if a variable contains Hello World the filter statement {{variable|lower}} outputs HELLO WORLD.

- wordcount.- The wordcount filter counts the words in a string. For example, if a variable contains Coffeehouse started as a small store the filter statement {{variable|wordcount}} outputs 6.

Lists and Dictionaries

- `dictsort`.- The `dictsort` filter sorts a list of dictionaries and returns a new list sorted by a given key argument. For example, if a variable contains `[{'name':'Downtown','city':'San Diego'}, {'name':'Uptown','city':'San Diego'},{'name':'Midtown','city':'San Diego'}]` the filter and tag statement `{% with newdict=variable|dictsort:"name" %}` the `newdict` variable is assigned the list `[{'name':'Downtown','city':'San Diego'},{'name':'Midtown','city':'San Diego'},{'name':'Uptown','city':'San Diego'}]`. The `dictsort` filter can also operate on lists of tuples or lists by specify an index number (e.g., `{% with otherlist=listoftuples|dictsort:0 %}`) to sort by the first element of each tuple in the list).
- `dictsortreversed`.- The `dictsortreversed` filter sorts a list of dictionaries and returns a new list sorted in reverse by a given key argument. The `dictsortreversed` filter works like `dictsort` except it returns the list in reverse order.
- `join`.- The `join` filter joins a list with a string. The join filter works just like Python's `str.join(list)`. For example, for a list variable that contains ['a','e','i','o','u'] the filter statement `{{variable|join:"--"}}` outputs a--e--i--o--u.
- `first`.- The `first` filter returns the first item in a list. For example, for a list variable that contains ['a','e','i','o','u'] the filter statement `{{variable|first}}` outputs a.
- `last`.- The `last` filter returns the last item in a list. For example, for a list variable that contains ['a','e','i','o','u'] the filter statement `{{variable|last}}` outputs u.
- `random`.- The `random` filter returns a random item in a list. For example, for a list variable that contains ['a','e','i','o','u'] the filter statement `{{variable|random}}` could output a, e, i, o, or u.
- `slice`.- The `slice` filter returns the slice of a list. For example, for a list variable that contains ['a','e','i','o','u'] the filter statement `{{variable|slice:":3"}}` outputs ['a','e','i'].
- `unordered_list`.- The `unordered_list` outputs an HTML unordered list from a list variable. Listing 3-16 illustrates an example of the unordered_list filter.

Listing 3-16. Django unordered_list filter

```
# Variable definition
["Stores",["San Diego",["Downtown","Uptown","Midtown"]]]

# Template definition with linenumbers filter
{{variable|unordered_list}}

# Output
<li>Stores
   <ul>
       <li>San Diego
           <ul>
   <li>Downtown</li>
   <li>Uptown</li>
   <li>Midtown</li>
  </ul>
       </li>
   </ul>
</li>
```

■ **Caution** The first level of the unordered_list filter does not include opening or closing HTML <ul> tags

Spacing and Special Characters

- addslashes.- The addslashes filter adds slashes to all quotes (i.e., it escapes quotes). The addslashes filter is useful when Django templates are used to export data to other systems that require to escape quotes (e.g., CSV files). For example, if a variable contains Today's news the filter statement {{variable|addslashes}} outputs Today\'s news.
- center.- The center filter center aligns a value and pads it with additional whitespace characters until it reaches the given argument of characters. For example, if a variable contains mocha the filter statement {{variable|center:"15"}} outputs.
- "mocha". (i.e., 5 spaces to the left of mocha, 5 spaces for mocha, 5 spaces to the right of mocha.
- ljust.- The ljust filter left aligns a value and pads it with additional whitespace characters until it reaches the given argument of characters. For example, if a variable contains mocha the filter statement {{variable|ljust:"15"}} outputs.
- "mocha".(i.e., 5 spaces for mocha, 10 space padding).
- rjust.- The rjust filter right aligns a value and pads it with additional whitespace characters until it reaches the given argument of characters. For example, if a variable contains latte the filter statement {{variable|rjust:"10"}} outputs.
- "latte"."(i.e., 5 space padding, 5 spaces for latte).
- escape.- The escape filter escapes HTML characters from a value. Specifically with the escape filter: < is converted to < ,> is converted to > ,' (single quote) is converted to ' ," (double quote) is converted to " and & is converted to &amp.

■ **Tip** If you use the escape filter on contiguous variables, it's easier to wrap the variables with the {% autoescape %} tag to achieve the same results.

- escapejs.- The escapejs filter escapes characters into Unicode strings that are often used for JavaScript strings. Though the escapejs filter does not make a string HTML safe, it does protect against syntax errors when using templates to generate JavaScript/JSON. For example, if a variable contains "mocha\r\n \'price:2.25" the filter statement {{variable|escapejs}} outputs \u0022mocha\u000D\u000A \u0027price:2.25\u0022.
- force_escape.- The force_escape filter escapes HTML characters from a value just like the escape filter. The difference is force_escape is applied immediately and returns a new and escaped string. This is useful when you need multiple escaping or want to apply other filters to the escaped results. Normally, you'll use the escape filter.

- `linebreaks`.- The `linebreaks` filter replaces plain text line breaks with HTML tags, a single newline becomes an HTML line break (`<br/>`), and a new line followed by a blank line becomes a paragraph break (`</p>`). For example, if a variable contains `385 Main\nSan Diego, CA` the filter statement `{{variable|linebreaks}}` outputs `<p>385 Main<br/>San Diego, CA</p>`.
- `linebreaksbr`.- The `linebreaksbr` filter converts all text variable new lines to HTML line breaks (`<br/>`). For example, if a variable contains `385 Main\nSan Diego, CA` the filter statement `{{variable|linebreaksbr}}` outputs `385 Main<br/>San Diego, CA`.
- `striptags`.- The `striptags` filter removes all HTML tags from a value. For example, if a variable contains `<b>Coffee</b>house, the <i>best</i> <span>drinks</span>` the filter statement `{{variable|striptags}}` outputs `Coffeehouse, the best drinks`.

■ **Caution** The striptags filter uses very basic logic to strip HTML tags. This means there's a possibility a convoluted piece of HTML isn't fully stripped of tags. This is why content in variables passed through the striptags filter is automatically escaped and should never be marked as safe.

- `safe`.- The safe filter marks a string as not requiring HTML escaping.
- `safeseq`.- The `safeseq` applies the `safe` filter to each element of a list. It's useful in conjunction with other filters that operate on a list, such as the `join` filter (e.g., `{{stores|safeseq|join:", "}}`). You wouldn't use the `safe` filter directly on list variables, as it would first convert the variable to a string, rather than working with the individual elements of a list.
- `wordwrap`.- The `wordwrap` filter wraps words at a given character line length argument. Listing 3-17 illustrates an example of the `wordwrap` filter.

Listing 3-17. Django wordwrap filter

```
# Variable definition

Coffeehouse started as a small store

# Template definition with wordwrap filter for every 12 characters
{{variable|wordwrap:12}}

# Output
Coffeehouse
started as a
small store
```

Development and Testing

- `pprint`.- The `pprint` filter is a wrapper for Python's `pprint.pprint()`. The `pprint` filter is useful during development and testing because it outputs the formatted representation of an object.

Urls

- iriencode.- The iriencode filter converts an Internationalized Resource Identifier (IRI) to a string that is suitable for inclusion in a URL. This is necessary if you're trying to use strings containing non-ASCII characters in a URL. For example, if a variable contains ?type=cold&size=large the filter statement {{variable|iriencode}} outputs ?type=cold&size=large.
- urlencode.- The urlencode filter escapes a value for use in a URL. For example, if a variable contains http://localhost/drinks?type=cold&size=large the filter statement {{variable|urlencode}} outputs http%3A//localhost/drinks%3Ftype%3Dcold%26size%3Dlarge. The urlenconde filter assumes the / character is safe. The urlencode filter can accept an optional argument with the characters that should not be escaped. An empty string can be provided when all characters should be escaped (e.g., {{variable|urlencode:""}} outputs http%3A%2F%2Flocalhost%2Fdrinks%3Ftype%3Dcold%26size%3Dlarge).
- urlize.- The urlize filter converts text URLs or email addresses into clickable HTML links. This urlize filter works on links prefixed with http://, https://, or www.. Links generated by the urlize filter have a rel="nofollow" attribute added to them. For example, if a variable contains Visit http://localhost/drinks the filter statement {{variable|urlize}} outputs Visit <a href="http://localhost/drinks" rel="nofollow">http://localhost/drinks</a>; if a variables contains Contact support@coffeehouse.com the filter statement {{variable|urlize}} outputs Contact <a href="mailto:support@coffeehouse.com">support@coffeehouse.com</a>.
- urlizetrunc.- The urlizetrunc filter converts text URLs and emails into clickable HTML links - just like the urlize filter - except it truncates the url to a given number of characters that include an ellipsis sequence. For example, if a variable contains Visit http://localhost/drinks the filter statement {{variable|urlizetrunc:20}} outputs Visit <a href="http://localhost/drinks" rel="nofollow">http://localhost/...</a>.

■ **Caution** The urlize and urlizetrunc filters should only be applied to variables with plain text. If applied to variables with HTML links, the filter logic won't work as expected.

Built-In Django Tags

Django offers several built-in tags that offer immediate access to elaborate operations on Django templates. Unlike Django filters that operate on individual variables, tags are designed to produce results without a variable or operate across template sections.

I'll classify each of these built-in tags into functional sections so it's easier to identify them. The functional classes I'll use are Dates, forms, comparison operations, loops, Python and filter operations, spacing and special characters, template structures, development and testing, and urls.

Dates

- {% now %}.- The {% now %} tag offers access to the current system time. The {% now %} tag accepts a second argument to format the system date. For example, if the system date is 01/01/2015 for the statement {% now "F jS o" %} the tag output is January 1st 2015. The string syntax for the {% now %} tag is based on Django date characters described in Table 3-3. It's also possible to use the as keyword to reuse the value through a variable(e.g. {% now "Y" as current_year %} and later in the template declare Copyright {{current_year}}).

■ **Tip** The {% now %} tag can accept Django date variables: {% now "DATE_FORMAT" %}, {% now "DATETIME_FORMAT" %}, {% now "SHORT_DATE_FORMAT" %}, or {% now "SHORT_DATETIME_FORMAT"}.

The date variables in themselves are also composed of date strings. For example DATE_FORMAT default's to "N j, Y" (e.g., Jan 1, 2015), DATETIME_FORMAT defaults to "N j, Y, P" (e.g., Jan 1, 2015, 12 a.m.), SHORT_DATE_FORMAT defaults to "m/d/Y" (e.g., 01/01/2015) and SHORT_DATETIME_FORMAT defaults to "m/d/Y P" (e.g., 01/01/2015 12 a.m.). Each date variable can be overridden with different date strings in a project's settings.py file.

Forms

- {% csrf_token %}.- The {% csrf_token %} tag provides a string to prevent cross site scripting. The {% csrf_token %} tag is only intended to be used inside HTML <form> tags. The data output of the {% csrf_token %} tag allows Django to prevent request forgeries (e.g., HTTP POST requests) from form data submissions. More details about the {% csrf_token %} tag are provided in the Django form chapter.

Comparison Operations

- {% if %} with {% elif %} {% else %}.- The {% if %} tag is typically used in conjunction with the {% elif %} and {% else %} tags to evaluate more than one condition. An {% if %} tag with an argument variable evaluates to true if a variable exists and is not empty or if the variable holds a True Boolean value. Listing 3-18 illustrates a series of {% if %} tag examples.

Listing 3-18. Django {% if %} tag with {% elif %} and {% else %}

```
{% if drinks %}
  We have drinks!
{% endif %}
```

```
{% if drinks %}
      We have drinks
{% else %}
     No drinks,sorry
{% endif %}
```

```
{% if drinks %}
     We have drinks
{% elif drinks_on_sale %}
     We have drinks on sale!
{% else %}
   No drinks, sorry
{% endif %}
```

■ **Note** A variable must both exist and not be empty to evaluate to true. A variable that just exists and is empty evaluates to false.

- {% if %} with and, or and not operators.- The {% if %} tag also supports the and, or, and not operators to create more elaborate conditions. These operators allow you to compare if more than one variable is not empty (e.g., {% if drinks and drinks_on_sale %}), if one or another variable is not empty (e.g., {% if drinks or drinks_on_sale %}), or if a variable is empty (e.g., {% if not drinks %}).
- {% if %} with ==, !=, <, >, <= and >= operators.- The {% if %} tag also supports equal, not equal, larger than and less than operators to create conditions that compare variables to fixed strings or numbers. These operators allow you to compare if a variable equals a string or number (e.g., {% if drink == "mocha" %}), if a variable does not equal a variable or number (e.g., {% if store.id != 2 %}) or if a variable is greater than or lesser than a number (e.g., {% if store.id > 5 %}).
- {% firstof %}.- The {% firstof %} tag is a shorthand tag to output the first variable in a set of variables that's not empty. The same functionality of the {% firstof %} tag is achieved by nesting {% if %} tags. Listing 3-19 illustrates a sample of the {% firstof %} tag, as well as an equivalent set of nested {% if %} tags.

Listing 3-19. Django {% firstof %} tag and equivalent {% if %}{% elif %}{% else %} tags

```
# Firstof example
{% firstof var1 var2 var3 %}

# Equivalent of firstof example
{% if var1 %}
    {{var1|safe}}
{% elif var2 %}
    {{var2|safe}}
{% elif var3 %}
    {{var3|safe}}
{% endif %}

# Firstof example with a default value in case of no match (i.e, all variables are empty)
{% firstof var1 var2 var3 "All vars are empty" %}

# Assign the firstof result to another variable
{% firstof var1 var2 var3 as resultof %}
# resultof now contains result of firstof statement
```

- {% if <value> in %} and {% if <value> not in %}.- The {% if %} tag also supports the in and not in operators to verify the presence of a constant or variable. For example {% if "mocha" in drinks %} tests if the value "mocha" is in the drinks list variable or {% if 2 not in stores %} tests if the value 2 is not in the stores list variable. Although the in and not in operators are commonly used to test list variables, it's also possible to test the presence of characters on strings (e.g., {% if "m" in drink %}). In addition, it's also possible to compare if the value of one variable is present in another variable (e.g., {% if order_drink in drinks %}).
- {% if <value> is <value> %} and {% if <value> is not %}.- The {% if %} tag also supports the is and is not operators to make object-level comparisons. For example {% if target_drink is None %} tests if the value target_drink is a None object or {% if daily_special is not True %} tests if the value daily_special is not True.

- `{% if value|<filter> <condition> <value> %}`.- The `{% if %}` tag also supports applying filters directly on a value and then performing an evaluation. For example, `{% if target_drink_list|random == user_drink %}Congratulations your drink just got selected!{% endif %}` uses the `random` filter directly in a condition.

PARENTHESES ARE NOT ALLOWED IN IF TAGS: OPERATOR PRECEDENCE GOVERNS, USE NESTED IF TAGS TO ALTER PRECEDENCE

Comparison operators are often aggregated into single statements (e.g., if...<...or...>...and...==...) and follow a certain execution precedence. Django follows the same operator precedence as Python.[5] So, for example, the statement {% if drink in specials or drink == drink_of_the_day %} gets evaluated as ((drink in specials) or (drink == drink_of_the_day)), where the internal parentheses operations are run first, since in and == have higher precedence than or.

In Python you can alter this precedence by using explicit parentheses in comparison statements. However, Django does not support the use of parentheses in {% if %} tags, you must either rely on operator precedence or use nested {% if %} statements to declare the same logic produced by explicit parentheses.

Loops

- `{% for %}` and `{% for %}` with `{% empty %}`.- The `{% for %}` tag iterates over items on a dictionary, list, tuple, or string variable. The `{% for %}` tag syntax is `{% for <reference> in <variable> %}`, where `reference` is assigned a new value from variable on each iteration.

Depending on the nature of a variable there can be one or more references (e.g., for a list one reference `{% for item in list %}`, for a dictionary two references `{% for key,value in dict.items %}`).In addition, it's also possible to invert the loop sequence with the `reversed` keyword (e.g., `{% for item in list reversed %}`). The `{% for %}` tag also supports the `{% empty %}` tag which is processed in case there are no iterations in a loop (i.e., the main variable is empty). Listing 3-20 illustrates a `{% for %}` and a `{% for %}` and `{% empty %}` loop example.

Listing 3-20. Django {% for %} tag and {% for %} with {% empty %}

```
<ul>
{% for drink in drinks %}
 <li>{{ drink.name }}</li>

{% empty %}
 <li>No drinks, sorry</li>
{% endfor %}
</ul>
```

```
<ul>
 {% for storeid,store in stores %}
 <li><a href="/stores{{storeid}}/">{{store.name}}</a>
 </li>
 {% endfor %}
</ul>
```

---

[5]https://docs.python.org/3/reference/expressions.html#evaluation-order

The `{% for %}` tag also generates a series of variables to manage the iteration process, such as an iteration counter, a first iteration flag, and a last iteration flag. These variables can be useful when you want to create behaviors (e.g., formatting, additional processing) on a given iteration. Table 3-4 illustrates the `{% for %}` tag variables.

Table 3-4. *Django {% for %} tag variables*

Variable	Description
forloop.counter	The current iteration of the loop (1-indexed)
forloop.counter0	The current iteration of the loop (0-indexed)
forloop.revcounter	The number of iterations from the end of the loop (1-indexed)
forloop.revcounter0	The number of iterations from the end of the loop (0-indexed)
forloop.first	True if it's the first time through the loop
forloop.last	True if it's the last time through the loop
forloop.parentloop	For nested loops, this is the parent loop to the current one

- `{% ifchanged %}`.- The `{% ifchanged %}` tag is a special logical tag used inside `{% for %}` tags. Sometimes it's helpful to know if a loop reference has changed from one iteration to the other (e.g., to insert a new title). The argument for the `{% ifchanged %}` tag is the loop reference itself (e.g.`{% ifchanged drink %}{{drink}} section{% endifchanged %}`) or a part of the reference (e.g., `{% ifchanged store.name %} Available in {{store.name}}{% endifchanged %}`). The `{% ifchanged %}` tag also support the use of `{% else %}` tag (e.g., `{% ifchanged drink %}{{drink.name}}{% else %}Same old {{drink.name}} as before{% endifchanged %}`).
- `{% cycle %}`.- The `{% cycle %}` tag is used inside `{% for %}` tags to iterate over a given set of strings or variables. One of the primary uses of the `{% cycle %}` tag is to define CSS classes so each iteration receives a different CSS class. For example, if you want assign different CSS classes to a list so each line appears in different colors (e.g., white, gray, white, gray) you can use `<li class="{% cycle 'white' 'grey' %}">`, in this manner on each loop iteration the class value alternates between white and gray. The `{% cycle %}` tag can iterate sequentially over any number of strings or variables (e.g., `{% cycle var1 var2 'red' %}`).

By default, a `{% cycle %}` tag progresses through its values on the basis of its enclosing loop (i.e., one by one). But under certain circumstances, you may need to use a `{% cycle %}` tag outside of a loop or explicitly declare how a `{% cycle %}` tag advances. You can achieve this behavior by naming the `{% cycle %}` tag with the as keyword, as illustrated in Listing 3-21.

Listing 3-21. Django {% cycle %} with explicit control of progression

```
<li class="{% cycle 'disc' 'circle' 'square' as bullettype %}">...</li>
<li class="{{bullettype}}">...</li>
<li class="{{bullettype}}">...</li>
<li class="{% cycle bullettype %}">...</li>
<li class="{{bullettype}}">...</li>
<li class="{% cycle bullettype %}">...</li>
# Outputs
```

```
<li class="disc">...</li>
<li class="disc">...</li>
<li class="disc">...</li>
<li class="circle">...</li>
<li class="circle">...</li>
<li class="square">...</li>
```

As you can see in Listing 3-21, the `{% cycle %}` tag statement initially produces the first value and afterwards you can continue using the cycle reference name to output the same value. In order to advance to the next value in the cycle, you call the `{% cycle %}` once more with the cycle reference name. A minor side effect of the `{% cycle %}` tag is that it outputs its initial value where it's declared, something that can be problematic if you plan to use the cycle as a placeholder or in nested loops. To circumvent this side effect, you can use the `silent` keyword after the cycle reference name (e.g., `{% cycle 'disc' 'circle' 'square' as bullettype silent %}`).

- `{% resetcycle %}`.- The `{% resetcycle %}` tag is used is to reinitiate a `{% cycle %}` tag to its first element. A `{% cycle %}` tag always loops over its entire set of values before returning to its first one, something that can be problematic in the context of nested loops. For example, if you want to assign three color codes (e.g.`{% cycle 'red' 'orange' 'yellow' %}`) to nested groups, the first group can consist of two elements that use up the first two cycle values (e.g., 'red' 'orange'), which means the second group starts on the third color code (e.g., 'yellow'). In order for the second group to start with the first `{% cycle %}` element again, you can use the `{% resetcycle %}` tag after a nested loop iteration finishes so the `{% cycle %}` tag returns to its first element.

- `{% regroup %}`.- The `{% regroup %}` tag is used to rearrange the contents of a dictionary variable into different groups. The `{% regroup %}` tag avoids the need to create complex conditions inside a `{% for %}` tag to achieve the desired display. The `{% regroup %}` tag arranges the contents of a dictionary beforehand, making the `{% for %}` tag logic simpler. Listing 3-22 illustrates a dictionary with the use of the `{% regroup %}` tag along with its output.

Listing 3-22. Django {% for %} tag and {% regroup %}

```
# Dictionary definition
stores = [
    {'name': 'Downtown', 'street': '385 Main Street', 'city': 'San Diego'},
    {'name': 'Uptown', 'street': '231 Highland Avenue', 'city': 'San Diego'},
    {'name': 'Midtown', 'street': '85 Balboa Street', 'city': 'San Diego'},
    {'name': 'Downtown', 'street': '639 Spring Street', 'city': 'Los Angeles'},
    {'name': 'Midtown', 'street': '1407 Broadway Street', 'city': 'Los Angeles'},
    {'name': 'Downton', 'street': '50 1st Street', 'city': 'San Francisco'},
]

# Template definition with regroup and for tags
{% regroup stores by city as city_list %}

<ul>
{% for city in city_list %}
    <li>{{ city.grouper }}
    <ul>
        {% for item in city.list %}
```

```
        <li>{{ item.name }}: {{ item.street }}</li>
      {% endfor %}
    </ul>
    </li>
{% endfor %}
</ul>

# Output
San Diego
    Downtown : 385 Main Street
    Uptown : 231 Highland Avenue
    Midtown : 85 Balboa Street
Los Angeles
    Downtown: 639 Spring Street
    Midtown: 1407 Broadway Street
San Francisco
    Downtown: 50 1st Street
```

■ **Tip** The {% regroup %} tag can also use filters or properties to achieve grouping results. For example, the stores list in 3-22 is conveniently preordered by city making grouping by city automatic, but if the stores list were not preordered, you would need to sort the list by city first to avoid fragmented groups, you can use a dictsort filter directly (e.g., {% regroup stores|dictsort:'city' by city as city_list %}). Another possibility of the {% regroup %} tag is to use nested properties if the grouping object has them (e.g., if city had a state property {% regroup stores by city.state as state_list %}).

Python and Filter Operations

- `{% filter %}`.- The `{% filter %}` tag is used to apply Django filters to template sections. If you declare `{% filter lower %}` the lower filter is applied to all variables between this tag and the `{% endfilter %}` tag - note the filter `lower` converts all content to lowercase. It's also possible to apply multiple filters to the same section using the same pipe technique to chain filters to variables (e.g., `{% filter lower|center:"50" %}...variables to convert to lower case and center...{% endfilter %}`).
- `{% with %}`.- The `{% with %}` tag lets you define variables in the context of Django templates. It's useful when you need to create variables for values that aren't exposed by a Django view method or when a variable is tied to a heavyweight operation. It's also possible to define multiple variables in the same `{% with %}` tag (e.g., `{% with drinkwithtax=drink.cost*1.07 drinkpromo=drink.cost*0.85 %}`). Each variable defined in a `{% with %}` tag is made available to the template until the `{% endwith %}` tag is reached.

PYTHON LOGIC ONLY ALLOWED BEHIND THE SCENES IN CUSTOM DJANGO TAGS OR FILTERS

Django templates don't allow the inclusion of inline Python logic. In fact, the closest thing Django templates allow to inline Python logic is through the {% with %} tag, which isn't very sophisticated.

The only way to make custom Python logic work in Django templates is to embed the code inside a custom Django tag or filter. This way you can place a custom Django tag or filter on a template and the Python logic runs behind the scenes. The next section describes how to create custom Django filters.

Spacing and Special Characters

- `{% autoescape %}`.- The `{% autoescape %}` tag is used to escape HTML characters from a template section. The `{% autoescape %}` accepts one of two arguments on or `off`. With `{% autoescape on %}` all template content between this tag and the `{% endautoescape %}` tag is HTML escaped and with `{% autoescape off %}` all template content between this tag and the `{% endautoescape %}` tag is not escaped.

■ **Tip** If you want to enable or disable auto-escaping globally (i.e., on all templates), it's easier to disable it at the project level using the autoescape field in the OPTIONS variable in the TEMPLATES configuration, inside a project's settings.py file, as described in the first section of this chapter.

If you want to enable or disable auto-escaping on individual variables, you can either use the safe filter to disable auto-escaping on a single Django template variable or the escape filter to escape a single Django template variable.

- `{% spaceless %}`.- The `{% spaceless %}` tag removes whitespace between HTML tags, including tab characters and newlines. Therefore all HTML content contained within the `{% spaceless %}` and `{% endspaceless %}` becomes more compact. Note the `{% spaceless %}` tag only removes space between HTML tags, it does not remove space between text and HTML tags (e.g., `<p> <span> my span </span> </p>`, only the space between `<p> <span>` and `</span> </p>` tags is removed, the space between `<span>` tags that pads the `myspan` string remains).
- `{% templatetag %}`.- The `{% templatetag %}` tag is used to output reserved Django template characters. So if by any chance you want to display any of the characters `{%`, `%}`, `{{`, `}}`, `{`, `}`, `{#` or `#}` verbatim on a template you can. The `{% templatetag %}` is used in conjunction with one of eight arguments to represent Django template characters. `{% templatetag openblock %}` outputs `{%`, `{% templatetag closeblock %}` outputs `%}`, `{% templatetag openvariable %}` outputs `{{`, `{% templatetag closevariable %}` outputs `}}`, `{% templatetag openbrace %}` outputs `{`, `{% templatetag closebrace %}` outputs `}`, `{% templatetag opencomment %}` outputs `{#` and `{% templatetag closecomment %}` outputs `#}`. A simpler approach is to wrap reserved Django characters with the `{% verabtim %}` tag.

- {% verbatim %}.- The {% verbatim %} tag is used to isolate template content from being processed. Any content inside the {% verbatim %} tag and {% endverbatim %} tag is bypassed by Django. This means special characters like {{ , variable statements like {{drink}}, or JavaScript logic that uses special Django characters is ignored and rendered verbatim. If you need to output individual special characters use the {% templatetag %} tag.
- {% widthratio %}.- The {% widthratio %} tag is used to calculate the ratio of a value to a maximum value. The {% widthratio %} tag is helpful for displaying content that is fixed in width but requires to be scaled based on the amount of available space, such as the case with images and charts. For example, given the statement <img src="logo.gif" style="width:{% widthratio available_width image_width 100 %}%"/>, if the available_width is 75 and image_width is 150 it results in 0.50 multiplied by 100, which results in 50. This image's width ratio is calculated based on the available space and image size, in this case the statement is rendered as: <img src="logo.gif" style="width:50%"/>.
- {% lorem %}.- The {% lorem %} tag is used to display random Latin text, which is useful for filler on templates. The {% lorem %} tag supports up to three parameters {% lorem [count] [method] [random] %}. Where [count] is a number or variable with the number of paragraphs or words to generate, if not provided the default [count] is 1. Where [method] is either w for words, p for HTML paragraphs, or b for plain-text paragraph blocks, if not provided the default [method] is b. And where the word random (if given) outputs random Latin words, instead of a common pattern (e.g., Lorem ipsum dolor sit amet...).

Template Structures

- {% block %}.- The {% block %} tag is used to define page sections that can be overridden on different Django templates. See the previous section in this chapter on how to create reusable templates for examples of this tag.
- {% comment "Optional explanation" %}.- The {% comment %} tag is used to define comment sections on Django templates. Any content placed between the {% comment %} and {% endcomment %} tag is bypassed by Django and doesn't appear in the final rendered web page. Note the string argument in the opening {% comment %} tag is optional, but helps clear up the purpose of the comment.
- {# #}.- The {# #} syntax can be used for a single line comment on Django templates. Any content placed between {# and #} in a single line is bypassed by Django and doesn't appear in the final rendered web page. Note that if the comment spans multiple lines you should use the {% comment %} tag.
- {% extends %}.- The {% extends %} tag is used to reuse the layout of another Django template. See the previous section in this chapter on creating reusable templates for examples of this tag.
- {% include %}.- The {% include %} tag is used to embed a Django template on another Django template. See the previous section in this chapter on creating reusable templates for examples of this tag.
- {% load %}.- The {% load %} tag is used to load custom Django tags and filters. The {% load %} tag requires one or multiple arguments to be the names of the custom Django tags or filters. The next section of this chapter describes how to create custom filters and how to use the {% load %} tag.

■ **Tip** If you find yourself using the {% load %} tag on many templates, you may find it easier to register Django tags and filters with the builtins option in TEMPLATES so they become accessible on all templates as if they were built in. See the first section in this chapter on template configuration for more details.

Development and Testing

- `{% debug %}`.- The `{% debug %}` tag outputs debugging information that includes template variables and imported modules. The `{% debug %}` tag is useful during development and testing because it outputs 'behind the scenes' information used by Django templates.

Urls

- `{% url %}`.- The `{% url %}` tag is used to build urls from predefined values in a project's `urls.py` file. The `{% url %}` tag is useful because it avoids the need to hard-code urls on templates, instead it inserts urls based on names. The `{% url %}` tag accepts a url name as its first argument and url parameters as subsequent arguments.

For example, if a url points to `/drinks/index/` and is named `drinks_main`, you can use the `{% url %}` to reference this url (e.g., `<a href="{% url drinks_main %}"> Go to drinks home page </a>`); if a url points to `/stores/1/` and is named `stores_detail` you can use the `{% url %}` with an argument to reference this url (e.g., `<a href="{% url stores_detail store.id %}"> Go to {{store.name}} page </a>`).

The `{% url %}` tag also supports the as keyword to define the result as a variable. This allows the result to be used multiple times or at a point other than where the `{% url %}` tag is declared (e.g., `{% url drink_detail drink.name as drink_on_the_day%}`...later in the template `<a href="{{drink_of_the_day}}> Drink of the day </a>`). Chapter 2 describes this process to name Django url's for easier management and reverse matches in greater detail.

Custom Filters

On occasions, Django built-in filters fall short in terms of the logic or output they offer. In these circumstances, the solution is to write a custom filter to achieve the outcome you require.

The logic behind Django filters is entirely written in Python, so whatever is achievable with Python & Django (e.g., perform a database query, use a third-party REST service) can be integrated as part of the logic or output generated by a custom filter.

Structure

The simplest custom Django filter only requires you to create a standard Python method and decorate it with `@register.filter()` as illustrated in Listing 3-23.

Listing 3-23. Django custom filter with no arguments

```
from django import template
register = template.Library()

@register.filter()
def boldcoffee(value):
    '''Returns input wrapped in HTML  tags'''
    return '<b>%s</b>' % value
```

Listing 3-23 first imports the template package and creates a register reference to decorate the boldcoffee method and tells Django to create a custom filter out of it.

By default, a filter receives the same name as the decorated method. So in this case, the boldcoffee method creates a filter named boldcoffee. The method input value represents the input of the filter caller. In this case, the method simply returns the input value wrapped in HTML <b> tags, where the syntax used in the return statement is a standard Python string format operation.

To apply this custom filter in a Django template you use the syntax {{byline|boldcoffee}}. The byline variable is passed as the value argument to the filter method, so if the byline variable contains the text Open since 1965! the filter output is <b>Open since 1965!</b>.

Django custom filters also support the inclusion of arguments, as illustrated in Listing 3-24.

Listing 3-24. Django custom filter with arguments

```
@register.filter()
def coffee(value,arg="muted"):
    '''Returns input wrapped in HTML  tags with a CSS class'''
    '''Defaults to CSS class 'muted' from Bootstrap'''
    return '<span class="%s">%s</span>' % (arg,value)
```

The filter method in Listing 3-24 has two input arguments. The value argument that represents the variable on which the filter is applied and a second argument arg="muted" where "muted" represents a default value. If you look at the return statement you'll notice it uses the arg variable to define a class attribute and the value variable is used to define the content inside a <span> tag.

If you call the custom filter in Listing 3-24 with the same syntax as the first custom filter (e.g., {{byline|coffee}}) the output defaults to using "muted" for the arg variable and the final output is <span class="muted">Open since 1965!</span>.

However, you can also call the filter in Listing 3-24 using a parameter to override the arg variable. Filter parameters are appended with :. For example, the filter statement {{byline|coffee:"lead muted"}} assigns "lead muted". as the value for the arg variable and produces the output <span class="lead muted">Open since 1965!</span>.

Parameters provide more flexibility for custom filters because they can further influence the final output with data that's different than the main input.

■ **Tip** In case a filter requires two or more arguments, you can use a space-separated or CSV-type string parameter in the filter definition (e.g., byline|mymultifilter:"18,success,green,2em") and later parse the string inside the filter method to access each parameter.

Options: Naming, HTML, and What Comes In and Out

Although the two previous examples illustrate the core structure of custom filters, they are missing a series of options that make custom filters more flexible and powerful. Table 3-5 illustrates a series of custom filter options, along with their syntax and a description of what it is they do.

Table 3-5. *Custom filter options.*

Option syntax	Values	Description
@register.filter (**name=<method_name>**)	A sting to name the filter	Assigns a filter name different from the filter method name.
@register.filter(**is_safe=False**)	True/False	Defines how to treat a filter's return value (safe or with auto-escape).
@register.filter (**needs_autoescape=False**)	True/False	Defines the need to access the auto-escaping status of the caller (i.e., whether the filter is called in a template with or without auto-escaping).
@register.filter (**expects_localtime=False**)	True/False	If the filter is applied on a datetime value, it converts the value to the project timezone, before running the filter logic.
@register.filter() **@stringfilter**	N/A	Stand-alone decorator that casts input to string.

As you can see in Table 3-5, with the exception of one option, all custom filter options are offered by arguments of the `@register.filter()` decorator and include default values. So even if you declare an empty `@register.filter()` decorator, four out of five options in Table 3-5 operate with default values. Note it's possible to add multiple options to the `@register.filter()` decorator separated by commas (e.g., `@register.filter(name='myfilter',is_safe=True)`).

Let's talk about the `name` option in Table 3-5. By default and as you learned in the previous examples, custom filters receive the same name as the method they decorate (i.e., if the backing method of a custom filter is named `coffee`, the filter is also called `coffee`). The `name` option allows you to give a filter a different name than the backing method name. Note that if use the `name` option and try to call the filter with the method name, you'll get an error because the filter doesn't exist by method name anymore.

All custom filters operate on input provided by variables that can potentially be any Python type (string, integer, datetime, list, dictionary, etc.). This creates a multitude of possibilities that must be handled in the logic of a custom filter; otherwise errors are bound to be common (e.g., a call is made to a filter with an integer variable, but the internal filter logic is designed for string variables). To alleviate these potential input type issues, custom filters can use the last two options presented in Table 3-5.

The `expects_localtime` option in Table 3-5 is designed for filters that operate on `datetime` variables. If you expect a `datetime` input, you can set the `expects_localtime` to `True` and this makes the `datetime` input timezone aware based on your project settings.

The `@stringfilter` option in Table 3-5 – which is a stand-alone decorator, placed below the `@register.filter` decorator – is designed to cast a filter input variable to a string. This is helpful because it removes the need to perform input type checks and irrespective of what variable type a filter is called with (e.g., string, integer, list, or dictionary variable) the filter logic can ensure it will always gets a string.

A subtle but default behavior of custom filters is the output that is not considered safe, due to the `is_safe` option in Table 3-5 defaulting to `False`.

This default setting causes the custom filters from Listings 3-23 and 3-24 that contain HTML `<b>` or `<span>` tags to create verbatim output (i.e., you won't see the text rendered in bold, but rather `<b>Open since 1965!</b>` literally). Sometimes this is desired behavior, but sometimes it's not.

■ **Tip** To make a Django template render HTML characters after applying a custom filter with default settings, you can use the built-in `safe` filter (e.g., `{{byline|coffee|safe}}`) or surround the filter declaration with the built-in `{% autoescape %}` tag (e.g., `{% autoescape off %} {{byline|coffee}} {% endautoescape %}` tag). However, Django filters can also set the filter is_safe option to True to make the process automatic and avoid the need to use an extra filter or tag.

You can set the `is_safe` option in a custom filter to `True`, to ensure the custom filter output is rendered 'as is' (e.g., the <b> tag is rendered in bold) and HTML elements aren't escaped .

This filter design approach though makes one big assumption: a custom filter will always be called with variables containing safe content. What happens if the `byline` variable contains the text `Open since 1965 & serving > 1000 coffees day!`. The variable now contains the unsafe characters & and > , why are they unsafe? Because they have special meaning in HTML and have the potential to mangle a page layout if they're not escaped (e.g., the > might mean 'more than' in this context, but in HTML it also means a tag opening, which a browser can interpret as markup, in turn mangling the page because it's never closed).

To avoid this potential issue of marking unsafe input characters and marking them as safe on output, you need to rely on the calling template telling the filter if the input is safe or unsafe, which takes us to the last custom filter option in Table 3-5: `needs_autoescape`.

The `needs_autoescape` option – which defaults to False – is used to enable a filter to be informed of the underlying auto-escaping setting in the template where the filter is called. Listing 3-25 shows a filter that makes use of this option.

Listing 3-25. Django custom filter that detects autoescape setting

```
from django import template
from django.utils.html import escape
from django.utils.safestring import mark_safe

register = template.Library()

@register.filter(needs_autoescape=True)
def smartcoffee(value, autoescape=True):
    '''Returns input wrapped in HTML tags'''
    '''and also detects surrounding autoescape on filter (if any) and escapes '''
    if autoescape:
        value = escape(value)
    result = '<b>%s</b>' % value
    return mark_safe(result)
```

The `needs_autoescape` parameter and the `autoescape` keyword argument of the filter method allow the filter to know whether escaping is in effect when the filter is called. If auto-escaping is on, then the `value` is passed through the escape method to escape all characters. Whether or not the content of value is escaped, the filter passes the final result through the `mark_safe` method so the HTML <b> tag is interpreted as bold in the template.

This filter is more robust than a filter that uses the `is_safe=True` option - and marks everything as 'safe' - because it can deal with unsafe input, as long as the template user makes the appropriate use of auto-escape.

Installation and Access

Django custom filters can be stored in one of two locations:

- Inside apps .- Stored in .py files located inside Django apps in a folder called `templatetags`.
- Any project location.- Stored in .py files on any folder in a Django project, configured through the `libraries` field in `OPTIONS` of the `TEMPLATES` variable in `settings.py`.

Listing 3-26 illustrates a project directory structure that exemplifies these two locations to store custom filters.

Listing 3-26. Django custom filter directory structure

```
+-<PROJECT_DIR_project_name>
|
+-__init__.py
+-settings.py
+-urls.py
+-wsgi.py
|
+----common----+
|              |
|              +--coffeehouse_filters.py
|
+----<app_one>---+
|                |
|                +-__init__.py
|                +-models.py
|                +-tests.py
|                +-views.py
|                +-----------<templatetags>---+
|                                             |
|                                             +-__init__.py
|                                             +-store_format_tf.py
+----<app_two>---+
|                |
                 +-__init__.py
                 +-models.py
                 +-tests.py
                 +-views.py
                 +-----------<templatetags>---+
                                              |
                                             +-__init__.py
                                              +-tax_operations.py
```

Listing 3-26 shows two apps that contain Django custom filters in two different files - `store_formay.tf.py` and `tax_operations.py`. Keep in mind you need to create the `templatetags` folder manually inside a Django app folder and also create an `__init__.py` file so Python is able to import the modules from this folder. In addition, remember apps need to be defined in Django's `INSTALLED_APPS` variable inside `settings.py` for the custom filters to be loaded.

In Listing 3-26 there's another .py file - `coffeehouse_filters.py` - that also contains Django custom filters. This last custom filter file is different because it's located in a generic folder called `common`. In order for Django to locate a custom filter file in a generic location, you must declare it as part of the `libraries` field in `OPTIONS` of the `TEMPLATES` variable in `settings.py`. See the first section in this chapter for detailed instructions on using the libraries field.

Even though custom filters are generally placed into files and apps based on their functionality, this does not restrict the usage of custom filters to certain templates. You can use custom filters on any Django template irrespective of where custom filter are stored.

To make use of Django custom filters in Django templates you need to use of the `{% load %}` tag inside Django templates, as illustrated in Listing 3-27.

Listing 3-27. Configure Django template to load custom filters

```
{% load store_format_tf %}
{% load store_format_t tax_operations %}
{% load undercoffee from store_format_tf %}
```

As shown in Listing 3-27 there are various ways you can use the `{% load %}` tag. You can make all the filters present in a custom file available to a template - note the lack of .py in the `{% load %}` tag syntax - or inclusively multiple custom files at once. In addition, you can also selectively load certain filters using the Python-like syntax `load filter from custom_file`. Keep in mind the `{% load %}` tag should be declared at the top of the template.

■ **Tip** If you find yourself using the {% load %} tag extensively, you can make custom -filters available to all templates using the builtins field. The builtins field is part of OPTIONS in the TEMPLATES variable in settings.py. See the first section in this chapter on Django template configuration for detailed instructions on using the builtins field.

CHAPTER 4

Jinja Templates in Django

In addition to Django templates, the Django framework also supports Jinja templates. Jinja is a stand-alone template engine project[1] that's very similar to Django's built-in template system.

However, the adoption and growth behind Jinja templates in Django projects is in part due to the design limitations of Django templates, which have changed little to nothing since Django's creation.

Jinja Advantages and Disadvantages

In order for you to gain a high-level perspective of Jinja templates and learn if they're a good fit for your Django projects, I'll first enumerate some of the main advantages and disadvantages of Jinja templates. Let's start with the advantages:

- **Speed and performance.**- Jinja compiles template source code to Python byte-code when it's first loaded, so the template is only parsed once, resulting in better runtime performance. In addition, Jinja also supports the option of ahead-of-time compilation, which can also result in better performance.

  Although speed and performance are some of the most debatable advantages to Jinja templates, given the many factors affecting speed and performance benchmarks (e.g., database queries/load, server configuration). Generally speaking and all things being equal, a Jinja template that does exactly the same thing as a Django template, the Jinja version will be faster than the Django version.

Note It's only fair to mention Django templates also support custom loaders with caching to improve speed and performance – as described in the previous chapter – but this requires further configuration effort in Django.

- **Flexibility**.- Jinja templates are very flexible in terms of what they can contain, supporting concepts like macros and more Python-like constructs. While some of these practices are discouraged in web templates, you'll come to appreciate some of these features that are not available or severely constrained in Django templates.

[1] `http://jinja.pocoo.org/`

D. Rubio, *Beginning Django*, https://doi.org/10.1007/978-1-4842-2787-9_4

- **Similar to Django templates**.- Jinja is actually inspired by Django templates, so there's a lot of common ground between the two systems. Powerful features like template inheritance and blocks work in the same way, so there's a smaller learning curve to use Jinja in Django projects than you might realize. In addition, security features (e.g., auto-escaping) are also tightly integrated into Jinja, just like they are in Django templates.
- **Asynchronous execution**.- Templates can sometimes load a lot of data or use functions that take a long time to run, causing delays in templates that must 'wait' for backing tasks to finish (i.e., they're synchronous). Jinja templates support asynchronous execution, which allows backing tasks to run their course - without holding-back templates - and later reconvene with templates when finished. Note this feature requires the use of asynchronous generators,[2] which is only available in Python 3.6 or newer releases.

And now some Jinja template disadvantages:

- **Little to no third-party package support**.- Because official Django support for Jinja templates is relatively recent - since Django 1.8, the prior long-term-support(LTS) version to Django 1.11 on which this book is based on - almost all third-party packages (e.g., Django admin) are still designed with Django templates. This can make it difficult to have a pure Jinja template Django project and require that Jinja templates coexist alongside Django templates, which can in turn lead to difficulties and confusion when template customization is required.
- **New concepts**.- If you're accustomed to Django templates, some Jinja features require additional practice to understand and use correctly (e.g., Jinja macros, Jinja filters). Although this shouldn't be an issue if you're new to Django in general, as every concept is new and will require some practice.

Transition to Jinja Templates from Django Templates

If you're accustomed to using Django templates, this section describes the finer details you need to be aware of when using Jinja templates, such as what Django template knowledge you can leverage in Jinja templates, what works differently in Jinja templates compared to Django templates, and what are new things you need to learn that you'll come to appreciate in Jinja templates.

If you've never used Django templates, you can skip to the next section on Jinja template configuration in Django, as most of what follows is intended for experienced Django template users.

What Works the Same Way in Jinja and Django Templates

Just because Jinja is an entirely different template engine doesn't mean it's radically different from Django's built-in template engine. You can expect to use the same approach for Variables and blocks, conditionals and loops, comments, as well as spacing and special characters.

[2] `https://www.python.org/dev/peps/pep-0525/`

Variables and blocks

Curly braces `{}` are broadly used in Jinja templates just like they're used in Django templates. To output a variable in Jinja you use the same `{{myvariable}}` syntax. Similarly, you also name blocks to inherit snippets between templates with the `{% block footer %} {% endblock %}` syntax. In addition, Jinja also uses the same Django `{% extends "base.html" %}` syntax to create parent/child relationships between templates.

Conditionals and loops

Jinja uses the same Django syntax to create conditionals: `{% if variable %}{% elif othervariable %}{% else %}{% endif %}`. In addition, Jinja also uses the same for loop syntax as Django: `{% for item in listofitems %}{{item}}{% endfor %}`.

Comments

Jinja also uses the same comment tag as Django: `{# This is a template comment that isn't rendered #}`. However, note Jinja uses the `{# #}` tag for both single and multiline comments.

Spacing and special characters

Since Jinja templates were inspired from Django templates, Jinja uses a similar approach to dealing with spacing and special characters. For example, things like spacing filters (e.g., `center` and `wordwrap`) and special character handling (e.g., `safe` and `escape` filters) work the same way in Jinja templates as they do in Django templates.

What Works Differently in Jinja Templates Compared to Django Templates

However, not everything works the same way in Jinja templates; here are some Django template techniques you'll need to relearn to work with Jinja templates.

Filters

Although Jinja uses the same pipe | symbol to apply filters to variables, Jinja filters are technically classified into filters and tests. In Django templates there are just filters that perform tests (e.g., `divisibleby`), but in Jinja these type constructs are called tests and use the conditional syntax `{% if variable is test %}` instead of the standard pipe | symbol.

In addition, Jinja filters and tests are backed by standard methods. This has the advantage that passing arguments to Jinja filters and tests is as simple as a method call (e.g., `{{variable|filesizeformat(true)}}`) vs. the unintuitive Django filter argument syntax of using a colon and even requiring arguments to be parsed in custom Django filters (e.g., `{{variable|get_digit:"1"}}`).

It's also possible to create custom Jinja filters and tests - in addition to the built-in Jinja filters and tests that are similar to Django built-in filters. However, unlike Django filters that are loaded into templates via the `{% load %}` tag, Jinja custom filters and tests are registered globally and become accessible to all Jinja templates like Django context processors.

Context processors

Context processors give Django templates access to sets of variables across every template in a project, but in Jinja this functionality is called global variables. This is one area where you'll likely miss the Django template functionality of simply declaring context processors and getting access to sets of variables. However, it's relatively easy to create Jinja global variables to become accessible on all Jinja templates and act as Django context processors.

No date elements like the {% now %} tag and filters like time and timesince

Jinja in its out-of-the-box state provides no tags or filters to work with dates or times. Although Jinja does offer the `format` filter that works just like Python's standard method and can be used for date formatting, you'll need to write your own custom filters and tags to deal with date and time elements in a more advanced way.

{% comment %} tag not supported

Jinja uses the `{# #}` tag to define either single or multiline comments, so there's no support for the `{% comment %}`, which in Django templates is used for multiline comments.

{% load %} tag not supported

In Jinja the `{% load %}` tag to import custom tags and filters is not supported. In Jinja custom tags and filters are registered globally and automatically become accessible to all Jinja templates.

Use {{super()}} instead of {{block.super}}

In Django templates you use the syntax `{{ block.super }}` to access the contents of a parent template's block. In Jinja you must use the `{{super()}}` syntax to gain access to the contents of a parent template's block.

{% csrf_token %} tag not supported, instead use csrf_input or csrf_token variables

In Django templates when you create a form that has an HTTP POST action, you place the `{% csrf_token %}` tag in its body to generate a special token that avoids XSS('Cross-site scripting'). To replicate this behavior in Jinja you must use the `csrf_input` variable (e.g., `{{csrf_input}}` that generates a string like `<input type="hidden" name="csrfmiddlewaretoken" value="4565465747487">`) or use the `csrf_token` variable that contains the raw CSRF token (e.g., `4565465747487`).

{% for %} loop variables

In Django templates the context of `{% for %}` loops offers access to a series of variables (e.g., counter, first, and last iteration). Jinja templates offer a similar variable in the context of `{% for %}` but they are not identical.

{% empty %} tag not supported in loops, use the {% else %} tag

`{% for %}` loops in Django templates support the `{% empty %}` clause as a last argument to generate logic or a message when an iteration is empty. In Jinja `{% for %}` loops you can use the `{% else %}` clause as a last argument to generate logic or a message when an iteration is empty.

{% groupby %} tag not supported, use the groupby filter

Django templates support the `{% groupby %}` tag to rearrange dictionaries or objects based on different attributes. In Jinja you can achieve the same functionality, but you must do it through the `groupby` filter as described in the Jinja `groupby` filter.

{% cycle %} tag not supported, use the cycler function or the loop.cycle variable in {% for %} loops

Django templates support the `{% cycle %}` tag to cycle over a list of values. In Jinja this functionality is available in two forms. You can use the `cycler` method if you require the functionality outside of loops. Or you can use the `loop.cycle` function available in all `{% for %}` loops.

{% lorem %} tag not supported, use the lipsum Function

Django templates support the `{% lorem %}` tag to generate random Latin text as filler content. In Jinja you can achieve the same functionality with the `lipsum` function.

Other miscellaneous tags like {% static %}, {% trans %}, {% blocktrans %}, and {% url %} not supported

A series of Django template tags like `{% static %}` and `{% trans %}` are simply not available in Jinja. However, there are third-party projects that have ported these and many other Django template tags into Jinja extensions. A later section in this chapter on Jinja extensions discusses these options.

New Concepts and Features in Jinja Templates vs. Django Templates

Now that you know what Django template knowledge you can leverage and what techniques you'll need to relearn to effectively work with Jinja templates, let's take a look at some concepts that only apply to Jinja templates.

More useful built-in filters, tests, and more resemblance to a Python environment

Jinja templates offer a variety of built-in filters and tests that are sorely missing in Django templates. For example, for something as simple as checking variable types (e.g., string, number, iterable, etc.), Jinja offers a series of built-in tests for this purpose, where as in Django this requires creating custom filters.

Access and manipulation of complex data types (e.g., objects and dictionaries) is also vastly improved in Jinja templates vs. Django templates. For example, Jinja offers filters such as `reject`, `select`, and `map` to prune, filter, or alter data subsets on a template, a technique that although frowned upon by purists (i.e., those who stand by only manipulating data in views) are a very common requirement in real and time-constrained projects.

Jinja templates also support syntax that is more in line with a standard Python environment. For example, in Django something like accessing a dictionary key through a variable requires a custom filter, where as in Jinja templates this works with standard Python syntax (e.g., if you have the variables `stores={"key1":"value1", "key2":"value2"}`, and `var="key1"`, Django template can't do `stores.get(var)`, which is standard Python syntax, but in Jinja this works out of the box as expected of a Python environment).

Global functions

Jinja also supports a series of global functions. For example, Jinja offers the `range` function that works just like Python's standard function that is useful in loops (e.g., `{% for number in range(50 - coffeeshops|count) %}`). In addition, Jinja also offers the global functions `lipsum` to generate dummy placeholder content, `dict` to generate dictionaries, `cycler` to generate a cycle over elements, and `joiner` to join sections.

Flexible tag nesting, conditionals, and references

Jinja is very flexible in terms of nesting tags, particularly compared to what's permissible in Django templates. For example, in Jinja you can even conditionally apply the `{% extends %}` tag (e.g., `{% if user %}{% extends "base.html" %}{% else %}{% extends "signup_base.html" %}{% endif %}`) or also use variable reference names with inline conditions (e.g., `{% extends layout_template if layout_template is defined else 'master.html' %}`) - something that's not possible in Django templates.

Macros

In Jinja, macros allow you to define function-like snippets with complex layouts that can be called from any template with different instance values. Macros are particularly useful to limit the spread of complex layouts across templates. With macros you define a complex layout once (i.e., as a macro) and invoke it with different parameters to output the complex layout customized every single time, just as if were a function.

Flexible variable assignment in templates with less restrictive scope

In Jinja you can use the `{% set %}` tag to define variables to have a valid scope until the end of the template. Although Jinja also supports the `{% with %}` tag – just like the Django template version - the `{% with %}` tag can become cumbersome for multiple variable definitions because it requires closing the scope with `{% endwith %}` every time. The `{% set %}` is a good alternative for global template variables because you only require the initial definition and the scope propagates to the end of the template without having to worry about closing the scope.

Line statements

Jinja supports the definition of logical statements in what it calls line statements. By default, a line statement is preceded with the # symbol and can serve as an alternative to tag syntax. For example, the `{% for %}` tag statement `{% for item in items %}` can use the equivalent line statement `# for item in items`, just as the tag statement `{% endfor %}` can use the equivalent line statement `# endfor`. Line statements, more than anything, give templates a Python feel to them that can make complex logic easier to decipher vs. using tag statements that require the `{% %}` syntax.

Jinja Template Configuration in Django

The first step to use Jinja in Django is to install the core package with the command `pip install Jinja2`. Note the installation is for version 2 (i.e., Jinja2), which is the most recent version. While Jinja 1 is still available, Django does not offer built-in support for version 1, so place special attention to make sure you install version 2.

Next, you need to configure Jinja in a Django project inside the `settings.py` file. Listing 4-1 illustrates a basic Jinja configuration for Django.

Listing 4-1. Jinja configuration in Django settings.py

```
import os
BASE_DIR = os.path.dirname(os.path.dirname(os.path.abspath(__file__)))
PROJECT_DIR = os.path.dirname(os.path.abspath(__file__))

TEMPLATES = [
    {
        'BACKEND':'django.template.backends.jinja2.Jinja2',
        'DIRS': ['%s/jinjatemplates/'% (PROJECT_DIR),],
        'APP_DIRS': True,
        },
    {
        'BACKEND': 'django.template.backends.django.DjangoTemplates',
        'DIRS': [],
        'APP_DIRS': True,
        'OPTIONS': {
            'context_processors': [
                'django.template.context_processors.debug',
                'django.template.context_processors.request',
                'django.contrib.auth.context_processors.auth',
                'django.contrib.messages.context_processors.messages',
            ],
        },
    },
]
```

As you can see in Listing 4-1, there are two configurations declared in `TEMPLATES`, a dictionary for Jinja template configuration and another dictionary with the default Django template configuration. Since Django templates are still used by things like the Django admin and many third-party packages, I highly recommended you use the base configuration in Listing 4-1 since it keeps other things you don't have template control over from breaking.

The Jinja configuration in Listing 4-1 is one of the most basic possible. In this case, the `BACKEND` variable uses the `django.template.backends.jinja2.Jinja2` value to activate Jinja templates, and is followed immediately with the `DIRS` and `APP_DIRS` variables, which tell Django where to locate Jinja templates.

Template Search Paths

The `APP_DIRS` variable permits the lookup of templates inside special app subdirectories named `jinja2`. This is helpful if you wish to contain Jinja templates to apps, but be aware the template search path is not aware of app namespaces. For example, if you have two apps that both rely on a template named `index.html` - as illustrated in Listing 4-2 - and both apps have a method in `views.py` that returns control to the index.html template (e.g., render(request,'index.html')), both apps will use the index.html from the topmost declared app in INSTALLED_APPS, so one app won't use the expected index.html.

Listing 4-2. Django apps with jinja2 dirs with potential conflict and namespace qualification

```
# Templates directly under jinja2 folder can cause loading conflicts
+---+-<PROJECT_DIR_project_name_conflict>
    |
    +-__init__.py
    +-settings.py
    +-urls.py
    +-wsgi.py
    |
    +-about(app)-+
    |            +-__init__.py
    |            +-models.py
    |            +-tests.py
    |            +-views.py
    |            +-jinja2-+
    |                     |
    |                     +-index.html
    +-stores(app)-+
                 +-__init__.py
                 +-models.py
                 +-tests.py
                 +-views.py
                 +-jinja2-+
                          |
                          +-index.html

# Templates classified with additional namespace avoid loading conflicts
+---+-<PROJECT_DIR_project_name_namespace>
    |
    +-__init__.py
    +-settings.py
    +-urls.py
    +-wsgi.py
    |
    +-about(app)-+
    |            +-__init__.py
    |            +-models.py
    |            +-tests.py
    |            +-views.py
    |            +-jinja2-+
    |                     |
    |                     +-about-+
    |                             |
    |                             +-index.html
    +-stores(app)-+
                 +-__init__.py
                 +-models.py
                 +-tests.py
```

```
+-views.py
+-jinja2-+
         |
         +-stores-+
                  |
                  +-index.html
```

To fix this potential conflict, the recommended practice is to add an additional subfolder to act as a namespace inside each `jinja2` directory as illustrated in the second set of folders in Listing 4-2. In this manner, you can then redirect control to a template using this additional namespace subfolder to avoid any ambiguity. So to send control to the `about/index.html` template you would declare `render(request,'about/index.html')` and to send control to the `stores/index.html` you would declare `render(request,'about/index.html')`.

If you wish to disallow this behavior of allowing templates to be loaded from these internal app subfolders, you can do so by setting `APP_DIRS` to `FALSE`.

A more common approach for Jinja templates is to have a single folder or various folders - that live outside app structures - to hold Jinja templates. Django first looks for a matching Jinja template in the first `DIRS` value and then in `jinja2` folders in apps - if `APP_DIRS` is `TRUE` - until it either finds a matching template or throws a `TemplateDoesNotExist` error.

For the case illustrated in Listing 4-1, the only `DIRS` value relies on a directory named `jinjatemplates` relative to a path determined by the `PROJECT_DIR` variable. This variable technique is helpful when deploying a Django project across different machines, because the path is relative to the top-level Django project directory (i.e., where the `settings.py` and main `urls.py` file are) and adjusts dynamically irrespective of where a Django project is installed (e.g., `/var/www/`, `/opt/website`, `C://website/`).

Similar to the Django template `OPTIONS` variable, Jinja also supports a series of customizations through the `OPTIONS` variable. In the case of Jinja, the `OPTIONS` variable is a dictionary of key-values that correspond to Jinja environment initialization parameters.[3]

By default, Django internally sets a series of Jinja environment initialization parameters to align Jinja's template behavior with that of Django templates. However, you can easily override these settings with the `OPTIONS` variable. The next sections describe these important settings.

Auto-Escaping Behavior

Django enables Jinja template auto-escaping by default, a behavior that's actually disabled in the Jinja engine in its out-of-the-box state. The crux of auto-escaping is that, on the one hand it errs on the side of precaution and security - limiting the possibility to mangle output or introduce XSS (Cross-site scripting) vulnerabilities in HTML - but on the other hand, it also introduces extra processing in the template engine that can cause performance problems.

By default, Django templates auto-escape all output from template variables - < is converted to `<`, > is converted to `>`, ' (single quote) is converted to `'`, " (double quote) is converted to `"` and & is converted to `&amp` - unless you explicitly disable this behavior. Jinja in its out-of-the-box state doesn't auto-escape anything, and you need to explicitly tell it when you want to auto-escape something.

Because the Jinja template integration for Django was done by Django designers, Jinja auto-escaping is enabled, to err on the side of security, just like it's for Django templates. However, you can disable Jinja auto-escaping with the `autoescape` parameter in `OPTIONS` as illustrated in Listing 4-3.

---

[3]`http://jinja.pocoo.org/docs/dev/api/#jinja2.Environment`

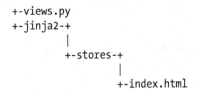

Listing 4-3. Jinja disable auto-escaping in Django

```
import os
BASE_DIR = os.path.dirname(os.path.dirname(os.path.abspath(__file__)))
PROJECT_DIR = os.path.dirname(os.path.abspath(__file__))

TEMPLATES = [
    {
        'BACKEND':'django.template.backends.jinja2.Jinja2',
        'DIRS': ['%s/jinjatemplates/'% (PROJECT_DIR),],
        'APP_DIRS': True,
        'OPTIONS': {
            'autoescape': False
        },
    }
]
```

As you can see in Listing 4-3, `autoescape` is assigned `False` and with this change Jinja templates behave just as Jinja designers intended (i.e., you need to explicitly check where auto-escaping is necessary vs. the Django template way to check where auto-escaping isn't necessary).

Auto-Reload Template Behavior and Caching

In its out-of-the-box state, Jinja's template loader checks every time a template is requested to see if the source has changed; if it has changed, Jinja reloads the template. This can be helpful in development where a template's source changes constantly, but can also translate into a performance hit in production where a template's source rarely changes and the check incurs a delay.

By default, the Django framework Jinja integration takes a sensible approach and enables Jinja template auto-reloading based on the `DEBUG` variable in `settings.py`. If `DEBUG=True` - a common setting in development - Jinja template auto-reloading is set to `True` and if `DEBUG=False` - a common setting in production - Jinja template auto-reloading is set to `False`. Nevertheless, you can explicitly set Jinja's auto-loading behavior with the `auto_reload` parameter in `OPTIONS`.

The Jinja engine by default also caches up to 400 templates. This means that when template 401 is loaded, Jinja cleans out the least recently used template, the latter of which must be reloaded from its origin again if required at a later time. The Jinja cache limit can be adjusted with the `cache_size` parameter in `OPTIONS` (e.g., `cache_size=1000`, to set a 1000 template cache). Setting `cache_size` to 0 (zero) disables caching and setting `cache_size` to -1 enables unlimited caching.

Another caching mechanism available in Jinja templates is byte-code caching. When you create Python source files (i.e., those with `.py` extensions), Python produces mirror-like files with `.pyc` extensions that contain byte-code. Generating these byte-code files takes time, but they're a natural part of Python's runtime process. Jinja templates being based on Python also need to be turned into byte-code, but it's a process you can customize with the `bytecode_cache` parameter in `OPTIONS`.

The `bytecode_cache` parameter can be assigned either a custom byte-cache[4] or one of Jinja's built-in byte-code caches, which include support for standard file-system caching or more specialized caching with memcached.

[4]`http://jinja.pocoo.org/docs/2.9/api/#bytecode-cache`

Invalid Template Variables

You can set various behaviors when an invalid variable is encountered in Jinja templates. Django sets Jinja with two default behaviors, one for when DEBUG=True - a common setting in development - and the other for when DEBUG=False - a common setting in production.

If DEBUG=True and an invalid variable is set in a Jinja template, Jinja uses the jinja2.DebugUndefined class to process it. The jinja2.DebugUndefined class outputs the variable verbatim for rendering (e.g., if the template has the {{foo}} statement and the variable doesn't exist in the context, Jinja outputs {{foo}}, making it easier to spot an invalid variable).

If DEBUG=False and an invalid variable is set in a Jinja template, Jinja uses the jinja2.Undefined class to process it. The jinja2.Undefined class outputs a blank space in the position of the variable for rendering (e.g., if the template has the {{bar}} statement and the variable doesn't exist in the context, Jinja outputs a blank space). It's worth mentioning this last behavior aligns with the default behavior of invalid variables in Django templates.

In addition to the jinja2.DebugUndefined and jinja2.Undefined classes, Jinja also supports the jinja2.StrictUndefined class. The jinja2.StrictUndefined class is used to generate an immediate error instead of proceeding with rendering, which is helpful for quicker diagnosis of invalid variables. However, be aware this last class changes its behavior based on the DEBUG variable; it either generates a stack error with the invalid variable name (i.e., when DEBUG=True) or it generates a standard HTTP 500 error page (i.e., when DEBUG=False).

Listing 4-4 illustrates how to configure a Jinja class to handle invalid variables through the OPTIONS parameter in settings.py.

Listing 4-4. Generate error for invalid variables in Jinja with jinja2.StrictUndefined

```
import os
BASE_DIR = os.path.dirname(os.path.dirname(os.path.abspath(__file__)))
PROJECT_DIR = os.path.dirname(os.path.abspath(__file__))

import jinja2

TEMPLATES = [
    {
        'BACKEND':'django.template.backends.jinja2.Jinja2',
        'DIRS': ['%s/jinjatemplates/'% (PROJECT_DIR),],
        'APP_DIRS': True,
        'OPTIONS': {
            'undefined':jinja2.StrictUndefined
        },
    }
]
```

As you can see in Listing 4-4, we first declare import jinja2 to gain access to Jinja's classes in settings.py. Next, we declare the undefined key inside the OPTIONS parameter and assign it the Jinja class to process invalid variables. In this case, we use the jinja2.StrictUndefined class to get errors when invalid templates variables are encountered, but you could equally use any of the other two Jinja classes to handle invalid variables (i.e., jinja2.DebugUndefined or jinja2.Undefined).

Template Loaders

Jinja template loaders are Python classes that implement the actual logic required to search and load templates. Earlier in the section "Template Search Paths," I described how Jinja searches for templates using the `DIRS` and `APP_DIRS` variables, which are part of Django's template configuration. However, I intentionally omitted a deeper aspect associated with this template search process: each search mechanism is backed by a template loader.

In most circumstances, you won't need to deal with Jinja template loaders, since Jinja loaders are taken care of in the background by simply relying on the `DIRS` and `APP_DIRS` variables. But if you need to load Jinja templates from somewhere else than these locations (e.g., from an in-memory structure or a database), you can specify template loaders with the `loader` key inside the `OPTIONS` parameter.

Like Django template loaders, Jinja also offers the ability to create custom template loaders,[5] in addition to using built-in Jinja template loaders similar to those offered by Django template (e.g., loading templates from a Python dictionary).

■ **Tip** You can set custom values for any Jinja environment *initialization* parameter[6] in OPTIONS. The prior sections are just four of the most common Jinja template parameters; later sections describe other available OPTIONS.

■ **Note** OPTIONS is only intended for Jinja environment *initialization* parameters; other Jinja environment settings require configuring a separate Jinja environment class (e.g., Jinja globals, Jinja custom filters and tests, and Jinja policies).

Create Reusable Jinja Templates

Templates tend to have common sections that are equally used across multiple instances. For example, the header and footer sections on all templates rarely change, whether a project has 5 or 100 templates. Other template sections like menus and advertisements also fall into this category of content that's constant across multiple templates. All of this can lead to repetition over multiple templates, which can be avoided by creating reusable templates.

With reusable Jinja templates you can define common sections on separate templates and reuse them inside other templates. This process makes it easy to create and manage a project's templates because a single template update takes effect on all templates.

Reusable Jinja templates also allow you to define page blocks to override content on a page-by-page basis. This process makes a project's templates more modular because you define top-level blocks to establish the overall layout and define content on a page-by-page basis.

[5] http://jinja.pocoo.org/docs/2.9/api/#loaders
[6] http://jinja.pocoo.org/docs/dev/api/#jinja2.Environment

Let's take the first step toward building reusable Jinja templates by exploring Jinja's built-in {% block %} tag. Listing 4-5 illustrates the first lines of a template called base.html with several {% block %} tags.

Listing 4-5. Jinja template with {% block %} tags

```
<!DOCTYPE html>
<html lang="en">
  <head>
    <meta charset="utf-8">
    <title>{% block title%}Default title{% endblock title %}</title>
    <meta name="description" content="{% block metadescription%}{% endblock metadescription %}">
    <meta name="keywords" content="{% block metakeywords%}{% endblock metakeywords %}">
```

Notice the syntax {% block <name>%}{% endblock <name>%} in Listing 4-5. Each {% block %} tag has a reference name. The reference name is used by other Jinja templates to override the content for each block. For example, the {% block title %} tag within the HTML <title> tags defines a web page title. If another template reuses the template in Listing 4-5, it can define its own web page title by overriding the title block. If a block is not overridden on a template, the block receives the default content within the block. For the title block the default content is Default title, for the metadescription and metakeywords blocks the default content is an empty string.

The same mechanism illustrated in Listing 4-5 can be used to define any number of blocks (e.g., content, menu, header, footer). It's worth mentioning the <name> argument of {% endblock <name> %} is optional and it's valid to just use {% endblock %} to close a block statement; however, the former technique makes it clearer where a block statement ends, which is especially helpful when a template has multiple blocks.

Although it's possible to call the template in Listing 4-5 directly by a Django view method or url request, the purpose of this kind of template is to use it as a base template for other templates. To reuse a Jinja template you use the Jinja built-in {% extends %} tag.

The {% extends %} tag uses the syntax {% extends <name> %} to reuse the layout of another template. This means that in order to reuse the layout in Listing 4-5 defined in a file base.html, you use the syntax {% extends "base.html" %}, as illustrated in Listing 4-6.

Listing 4-6. Jinja template with {% extends %} and {% block %} tag

```
{% if user %}{% extends "base.html" %}{% else %}{% extends "signup_base.html" %}{% endif %}
{% block title %}Coffeehouse home page{% endblock %}
```

Look how Listing 4-6 uses the {% extends "base.html" %} wrapped around the {% if user %} statement. If the user variable is defined, Jinja extends the base.html template; otherwise it extends the signup_base.html template. This conditional syntax is not possible in Django templates.

In addition, notice how Listing 4-6 defines the {% block title %} tag with the content Coffeehouse home page. The block in Listing 4-6 overrides the title block from the base.html template. So where are the HTML <title> tags in Listing 4-6? There aren't any and you don't need them. Jinja automatically reuses the layout from either the base.html or signup_base.html templates and substitutes the blocks' content where necessary.

Jinja templates that reuse other templates tend to have limited layout elements (e.g., HTML tags) and more Jinja block statements to override content. This is beneficial because, as I outlined previously, it lets you establish the overall layout once and define content on a page-by-page basis.

The reusability of Jinja templates can occur multiple times. For example, you can have templates A, B, and C, where B requires the reuse A, but C requires the reuse of parts of B. The only difference is template C needs to use the {% extends "B" %} tag instead of the {% extends "A"%} tag. But since template B reuses A, template C also has access to the same elements in template A.

When reusing Jinja templates, it's also possible to access the block content from a parent template. Jinja exposes the block content from a parent template through the `super()` method. Listing 4-7 illustrates three templates that show this mechanism for a block containing web page paths or 'breadcrumbs'.

Listing 4-7. Jinja templates use of super() with three reusable templates

```
# base.html template
<p>{% block breadcrumb %}Home{% endblock %}</p>

# index.html template
{% extends "base.html" %}
{% block breadcrumb %}Main{% endblock %}

# detail.html template
{% extends "index.html" %}
{% block breadcrumb %} {{super()}} : Detail {% endblock %}
```

The `base.html` template in Listing 4-7 defines the `breadcrumb` block with a default value of `Home`. Next, the `index.html` template reuses the `base.html` template and overrides the breadcrumb block with a value of `Main`. Finally, the `detail.html` template reuses the `index.html` template and overrides the `breadcrumb` block value. However, notice the `{{super()}}` statement in the final block override. Since `{{super()}}` is inside the `breadcrumb` block, `{{super()}}` tells Jinja to get the content from the parent template block.

Another reusability functionality supported by Jinja templates is the inclusion of a Jinja template inside another Jinja template. Jinja supports this functionality through the `{% include %}` tag.

By default, the `{% include %}` tag expects the name of a template. For example, `{% include "footer.html" %}` inserts the contents of the `footer.html` template in the position of the template where it's declared. The `{% include %}` tag also makes the underlying template aware of variables. This means the `footer.html` template can have variable definitions (e.g., `{{year}}`) and if the calling template has these variable definitions, the `{% include %}` tag automatically substitutes these values.

In addition, it's possible to provide a list of templates as a fallback mechanism. For example, `{% include ['special_sidebar.html', 'sidebar.html'] ignore missing %}` tells Jinja to first attempt to locate the `special_sidebar.html` template and if it isn't found to attempt to locate the `sidebar.html` template; if neither template is found the last argument `ignore missing` tells Jinja to render nothing. Note the `ignore missing` argument can also be used in individual statements (e.g., `{% include "footer.html" ignore missing %}`, as well as lists). In addition, if the `ignore missing` statement is not used and Jinja can't find a matching template declared in `{% include %}`, Jinja raises an exception.

The `{% macro %}` tag allows the definition of reusable content snippets across templates. For example, if you need to incorporate elaborate markup to display elements that have common characteristics, you can define the elaborate markup once in a `{% macro %}` statement and then reuse this `{% macro %}` to output the markup customized to each element instance.

Macros are helpful because if you decide to change the markup, you only need to change it in a single location and the changes propagate to other locations. Listing 4-8 illustrates the definition of a `{% macro %}` statement and its usage in templates.

Listing 4-8. Jinja {% macro %} definition and use of {% import %}

```
# base.html template
{% macro coffeestore(name, id='', address='', city='San Diego', state='CA', email=None) -%}
    <a id="{{id}}"></a>
    <h4>{{name}}</h4>
    <p>{{address}} {{city}},{{state}}</p>
    {% if email %}<p><a href='mailto:{{email}}'>{{email}}</a></p>{% endif %}
{%- endmacro %}
```

```
# index.html template calls inherited macro directly
{% extends "base.html" %}
{{coffeestore('Downtown',1,'Horton Plaza','San Diego','CA','downtown@coffeehouse.com')}}

# detail.html template with no extends, uses {% import %} to access macro in base.html
{% import 'base.html' as base %}
{{base.coffeestore('Downtown',1,'Horton Plaza','San Diego','CA','downtown@coffeehouse.com')}}

# otherdetail.html template with no extends, uses {% from import %} to access macro in base.html
{% from 'base.html' import coffeestore as mycoffeestoremacro %}
{{mycoffeestoremacro('Downtown',1,'Horton Plaza','San Diego','CA','downtown@coffeehouse.com')}}
```

The first thing that's done in Listing 4-8 is the `{% macro %}` definition declared in the `base.html` template. Notice that after the `{% macro` snippet, there's what appears to be a regular method named `coffeestore`, which corresponds to the name of the macro with six input arguments, five of which have default values. Next, inside the `{% macro %}` and `{% endmacro %}` statements you can see some elaborate HTML markup that makes use of the standard `{{ }}` syntax to output whatever variable values are passed on a given instance of the macro.

Since the `{% macro %}` in Listing 4-8 is defined inside the `base.html` template, any other template that uses the `base.html` template can access the macro and call the macro with an instance (e.g., `{{coffeestore ('Downtown',1,'Horton Plaza','San Diego','CA','downtown@coffeehouse.com')}}` - hard-coded values for simplicity) for Jinja to render the HTML markup customized with the instance values.

If you want to access a `{% macro %}` in other templates you have three alternatives that are also presented in Listing 4-8. If a template extends another template (e.g., `{% extends "base.html" %}`) then by default it will also gain access to the parent's template `{% macro %}` definitions. It's also possible to access another template's `{% macro %}` definitions with the `{% import %}` statement. For example, the statement `{% import 'base.html' as base %}` imports the `base.html` definitions into another template with the base namespace, in which case to invoke the `{% macro %}` called `coffeestore` you would use the `{{base.coffeestore(...}}` syntax. Finally, it's also possible to selectively import a `{% macro %}` definition with the `{% from import %}` statement. For example, the statement `{% from 'base.html' import coffeestore as mycoffeestoremacro %}` imports the `coffeestore` definition from the `base.html` template and places it under the `mycoffeestoremacro` name, in which case you would use the `{{mycoffeehousemacro(...}}` syntax to invoke the `{% macro %}`.

The `{% call %}` tag is another option that, used in conjunction with the `{% macro %}` tags, favors the reusability of macros themselves. The first usage scenario of the `{% call %}` tag is to invoke a `{% macro %}` that requires a placeholder for content that's defined until the invocation of the macro. Listing 4-9 illustrates this basic scenario of the `{% call %}` tag along with a `{% macro %}`.

Listing 4-9. Jinja {% call %} and {% macro %} use

```
# macro definition
{% macro contentlist(adcolumn_width=3,contentcolumn_width=6) -%}
  <div class="col-md-{{adcolumn_width}}">
   Sidebar ads
  </div>
  <div class="col-md-{{contentcolumn_width}}">
     {{ caller() }}
  </div>
  <div class="col-md-{{adcolumn_width}}">
   Sidebar ads
  </div>
{%- endmacro %}
```

```
# macro call/invocation
{% call contentlist() %}
  <ul>
    <li>This is my list</li>
  </ul>
{% endcall %}

# rendering
<div class="col-md-3">
    Sidebar ads
</div>
<div class="col-md-6">
  <ul>
    <li>This is my list</li>
  </ul>
</div>
<div class="col-md-3">
    Sidebar ads
</div>
```

In Listing 4-9 we first define a `{% macro %}` with a similar structure to that of Listing 4-8; however, notice inside the `{% macro %}` the `{{ caller() }}` statement. The `caller()` method inside `{% macro %}` serves as placeholder to be substituted by the calling entity.

Next, in Listing 4-9 you can see the `{% call %}` statement is declared with the macro call - in this case `contentlist()` - and the body of the `{% call %}` statement contains an HTML list. When Jinja executes the `{% call %}` statement, the `{% call %}` contents are placed in the location of the `{% macro %}` `{{caller()}}` declaration.

A more advanced scenario of the `{% call %}` tag with a `{% macro %}` is for the `caller()` statement to use references, a process that's more natural to data that's recursive in nature (i.e., a macro over a macro). Listing 4-10 illustrates this recursive scenario of the `{% call %}` tag along with a `{% macro %}`.

Listing 4-10. Jinja {% call %} and {% macro %} recursive calls

```
# macro definition
{% macro contentlist(itemlist,adcolumn_width=3,contentcolumn_width=6) -%}
   <div class="col-md-{{adcolumn_width}}">
    Sidebar ads
   </div>
   <div class="col-md-{{contentcolumn_width}}">
     {% for item in itemlist %}
      {{ caller(item) }}
     {% endfor %}
   </div>
   <div class="col-md-{{adcolumn_width}}">
    Sidebar ads
   </div>
{%- endmacro %}
```

```
# variable definition
{% set coffeestores=[{'id':0,'name':'Corporate','address':'624 Broadway','city':'San Diego',
'state':'CA','email':'corporate@coffeehouse.com'},{'id':1,'name':'Downtown','address':'Hort
on Plaza','city':'San Diego','state':'CA','email':'downtown@coffeehouse.com'},{'id':2,'name
':'Uptown','address':'1240 University Ave','city':'San Diego','state':'CA','email':'uptown@
coffeehouse.com'},{'id':3,'name':'Midtown','address':'784 W Washington St','city':'San Diego
','state':'CA','email':'midtown@coffeehouse.com'}] %}

# macro call/invocation
{% call(item) contentlist(coffeestores) %}
    <a id="{{item.id}}"></a>
    <h4>{{item.name}}</h4>
    <p>{{item.address}} {{item.city}},{{item.state}}</p>
    {% if item.email %}<p><a href='mailto:{{item.email}}'>{{item.email}}</a></p>{% endif %}
{% endcall %}

# rendering
<div class="col-md-3">
    Sidebar ads
</div>
<div class="col-md-6">
    <a id="0"></a>
    <h4>Corporate</h4>
    <p>624 Broadway San Diego,CA</p>
    <p><a href="mailto:corporate@coffeehouse.com">corporate@coffeehouse.com</a></p>

    <a id="1"></a>
    <h4>Downtown</h4>
    <p>Horton Plaza San Diego,CA</p>
    <p><a href="mailto:downtown@coffeehouse.com">downtown@coffeehouse.com</a></p>

    <a id="2"></a>
    <h4>Uptown</h4>
    <p>1240 University Ave San Diego,CA</p>
    <p><a href="mailto:uptown@coffeehouse.com">uptown@coffeehouse.com</a></p>

    <a id="3"></a>
    <h4>Midtown</h4>
    <p>784 W Washington St San Diego,CA</p>
    <p><a href="mailto:midtown@coffeehouse.com">midtown@coffeehouse.com</a></p>
</div>
<div class="col-md-3">
    Sidebar ads
</div>
```

As you can see in Listing 4-10, the `{% macro %}` definition now has an argument called `itemlist` on which it creates an iteration and for each item it invokes `{{caller(item)}}`. Also notice in Listing 4-10 the `{% call %}` statement is now `{% call(item) contentlist(coffeestores) %}`, where item represents the callback item sent from the macro and `contentlist(coffeestores)` is the actual call to the macro named `contentlist` along with its input `coffeestores` that's a list of dictionaries. When Jinja executes the `{% call %}` statement, the `{% call %}` contents are run recursively over each item, resulting in the output presented at the bottom of Listing 4-10.

■ **Tip** The built-in {% set %} statement – described in the Jinja built-in filters section – provides simpler reuse functionality for static content blocks compared to {% macro %} statements that use variables. (e.g., {% set advertisement %}<div class='banner'><img src=...></div>{% endset %} creates the advertisement variable that can output the contents between {% set %} and {% endset %} anywhere in a template).

Jinja Globals: Access Data on All Jinja Templates, Like Django Context Processors

Just like Django templates offer context processors to facilitate the access of data on all Django templates, Jinja also offers its own version of the same feature that is called *globals*. Jinja in its out-of-the-box state has no globals, but in its Django integrated mode includes three globals to mimic Django's most common context processors, these globals are `request`, `csrf_input`, and `csrf_token`.

This means you get access to three Django context processors like variables in all Jinja templates used in Django projects. However, to set up additional global variables you need to work with Jinja's environment.

To set up Jinja globals you need to access Jinja's environment, which is where globals are stored, in a variable properly called `globals`. By default, the Django-Jinja configuration uses Jinja's built-in `jinja2.Environment` environment. In order to access Jinja's environment in Django and set globals, the easiest path is to create your own Jinja environment and use it to initialize the Django-Jinja configuration. Listing 4-11 illustrates a custom Jinja environment class that sets the global variables named `static` and `url`.

Listing 4-11. Custom Jinja environment with global variable

```
from jinja2.environment import Environment
from django.contrib.staticfiles.storage import staticfiles_storage
from django.core.urlresolvers import reverse

class JinjaEnvironment(Environment):
    def __init__(self,**kwargs):
        super(JinjaEnvironment, self).__init__(**kwargs)
        self.globals['static'] = staticfiles_storage.url
        self.globals['reverse'] = reverse
```

As you can see in Listing 4-11, the custom `JinjaEnvironment` class is a subclass of the `jinja2.Environment` class; this is so the custom class inherits the bulk of its features from this base class provided by Jinja. Next, you can see we use the `__init__` method to initialize the base class.

Prior to exiting the initialization method of the class, you can also see we access the `globals` variable of the instance. `globals` is composed of a dictionary, where the key-values correspond to the Jinja template variable names and values, respectively. In this case, we create the static variable and assign it Django's `django.contrib.staticfiles.storage.staticfiles_storage.url` method. This gives the `static` global variable the same behavior as Django's staticfiles app, so that it's possible to declare static resources just like it's done in Django (e.g., Jinja can then do `<img src="{{ static('images/background.png') }}" alt="Background">`) - a topic that is described in greater detail in Chapter 5 on static resource management, but this is important to mention here due to the gap it fills in Jinja lacking functionality on this front.

The second global in Listing 4-11 creates the url variable and assigns it Django's `django.core.urlresolvers.reverse` method. This gives the `url` global variable the same behavior as Django's `{% url %}` tag, so that it's possible to resolve a URL based on a name - as described in Chapter 2 on Django url management and reverse matches - just like it's done in Django (e.g., Jinja can then do

`<a href="{{ url('homepage') }}">Go to homepage</a>`) - note this is another important gap to fill given Jinja's lack of functionality on this front.

Just as you can add these last two global variables to mimic the behavior of Django apps and tags that are missing in Jinja templates, you can add more globals in the same manner or increase the complexity of a Jinja global as needed.

Once the custom Jinja environment is ready, you need to set it up in Django's `settings.py` file so it's used to initialize Jinja. Listing 4-12 illustrates how to set up a custom Jinja environment in Django.

Listing 4-12. Configure custom Jinja environment in Django setttings.py

```
TEMPLATES = [
    {
        'BACKEND':'django.template.backends.jinja2.Jinja2',
        'DIRS': ['%s/templates/'% (PROJECT_DIR),],
        'APP_DIRS': True,
        'OPTIONS': {
            'environment': 'coffeehouse.jinja.env.JinjaEnvironment'
            }
        },
    ]
```

The Jinja environment is set through the `environment` key, as part of the `OPTIONS` variable. The value of the environment key is a string with dot notation that points to a custom Jinja environment class. In this case, you can see the value corresponds to `coffeehouse.jinja.env.JinjaEnvironment`, where `JinjaEnvironment` is the class, `env` is the file/module name, and `coffeehouse.jinja` is the directory path.

To better illustrate the location of the `env.py` file containing the custom Jinja environment, Listing 4-13 illustrates a directory structure with additional Django project files for reference.

Listing 4-13. Directory structure and location of custom Jinja environment

```
+---+-<PROJECT_DIR_coffeehouse>
    |
    +-__init__.py
    +-settings.py
    +-urls.py
    +-wsgi.py
    |
    +-jinja-+
            +-__init__.py
            +-env.py
```

Jinja Built-In Statements/Tags and Functions (Like Django Template Tags)

Jinja offers several built-in statements/tags that offer immediate access to elaborate operations on Jinja templates. I'll classify each of these built-in statements/tags and functions into sections so it's easier to identify them; note I'll add the reference (Function) to indicate it's referring to a Jinja function. The categories I'll use are Comparison operations, loops, Python and filter operations, spacing and special characters, and template structures.

Comparison Operations

- {% if %} with {% elif %} {% else %}.- The {% if %} statement is the primary building block to evaluate conditions. The {% if %} statement is typically used in conjunction with the {% elif %} and {% else %} statements to evaluate more than one condition. An {% if %} statement with an argument variable evaluates to true if a variable exists and is not empty or if the variable holds a True Boolean value. Listing 4-14 illustrates a series of {% if %} statement examples.

Listing 4-14. Jinja {% if %} statement with {% elif %} and {% else %}

```
{% if drinks %}
  We have drinks!
{% endif %}
```

```
{% if drinks %}
      We have drinks
{% else %}
     No drinks,sorry
{% endif %}
```

```
{% if drinks %}
    We have drinks
{% elif drinks_on_sale %}
    We have drinks on sale!
{% else %}
    No drinks, sorry
{% endif %}
```

■ **Note** A variable must both exist and not be empty to match a condition. A variable that just exists and is empty does not match a condition.

- {% if %} with and, or and not operators.- The {% if %} statement also supports the and, or, and not operators to create more elaborate conditions. These operators allow you to compare if more than one variable is not empty (e.g., {% if drinks and drinks_on_sale %}), if one or another variable is not empty (e.g., {% if drinks or drinks_on_sale %}) or if a variable is empty (e.g., {% if not drinks %}).
- {% if %} with ==, !=, <, >, <= and >= operators.- The {% if %} statement also supports equal, not equal, larger than, and less than operators to create conditions that compare variables to fixed strings or numbers. These operators allow you to compare if a variable equals a string or number (e.g., {% if drink == "mocha" %}), if a variable does not equal a variable or number (e.g.{% if store_id != 2 %}) or if a variable is greater than or lesser than a number (e.g., {% if store_id > 5 %}).
- {% if <value> in %} and {% if <value> not in %}.- The {% if %} statement also supports the in and not in operators to verify the presence of a constant or variable. For example, {% if "mocha" in drinks %} tests if the value "mocha" is in the drinks list variable or {% if 2 not in stores %} tests if the value 2 is not in the stores list variable. Although the in and not in operators are commonly used to test list variables, it's also possible to test the presence of characters on strings (e.g., {% if "m" in drink %}). In addition, it's also possible to compare if the value of one variable is present in another variable (e.g., {% if order_drink in drinks %}).

Loops

- {% for %} and {% for %} with {% else %}.- The {% for %} statement iterates over items on a dictionary, list, tuple, or string variable. The {% for %} statement syntax is {% for <reference> in <variable> %}, where <reference> is assigned a new value from <variable> on each iteration. Depending on the nature of a variable there can be one or more references (e.g., for a list one reference, for a dictionary two references).The {% for %} statement also supports the {% else %} statement which is processed in case there are no iterations in a loop (i.e., the main variable is empty). Listing 4-15 illustrates a {% for %} and a {% for %} and {% else %} loop example.

Listing 4-15. Jinja {% for %} statement and {% for %} with {% else %}

```
<ul>
{% for drink in drinks %}
 <li>{{ drink.name }}</li>

{% else %}
 <li>No drinks, sorry</li>
{% endfor %}
</ul>
```

```
<ul>
 {% for storeid,store in stores %}
   <li><a href="/stores/{{storeid}}/">{{store.name}}
   </a></li>
 {% endfor %}
</ul>
```

The {% for %} statement also generates a series of variables to manage the iteration process such as an iteration counter, a first iteration flag, and a last iteration flag. Table 4-1 illustrates the {% for %} statement variables.

Table 4-1. *Jinja {% for %} statement variables*

Variable	Description
loop.index	The current iteration of the loop (1-indexed).
loop.index0	The current iteration of the loop (0-indexed).
loop.revindex	The number of iterations from the end of the loop (1-indexed).
loop.revindex0	The number of iterations from the end of the loop (0-indexed).
loop.first	True if it's the first time through the loop.
loop.last	True if it's the last time through the loop.
loop.length	The number of items in the sequence.
loop.cycle	A helper function to cycle between a list of sequences.
loop.depth	Indicates how deep in a recursive loop the rendering currently is, starts at level 1
loop.depth0	Indicates how deep in a recursive loop the rendering currently is, starts at level 0.

NESTED JINJA LOOPS: USE REFERENCE VARIABLE AND CYCLE VARIABLE

On certain occasions you may need to nest multiple {% for %} statements and access parent loop items. In Django templates, this is easy because there's a variable for just this purpose. However, Jinja templates don't have this variable as you can see in Table 4-1. A solution in Jinja templates is to define a reference variable with {% set %} before entering the child loop to gain access to the parent loop, as illustrated in the following snippet.

```
<ul>
{% for chapter in chapters %}
  {% set chapterloop = loop %}
  {% for section in chapter %}
    <li> {{ chapterloop.index }}.{{ loop.index }}">{{ section }}</li>
  {% endfor %}
{% endfor %}
</ul>
```

Another nested loop feature in Jinja templates is cycle, which does not exist in Django templates (as a variable at least, it does exist as a tag). The primary use of cycle is to define CSS classes so that each iteration receives a different CSS class and upon rendering each iteration is displayed in a different color. The following snippet illustrates the use of the cycle variable.

```
{% for drink in drinks %}
 <li class="{{ loop.cycle('odd', 'even') }}">{{ drink.name }}</li>
{% endfor %}
```

Note cycle can iterate sequentially over any number of strings or variables (e.g., {{ `loop.cycle('red' 'white' 'blue')` }}).

- `{% for %}` with `if`.- The `{% for %}` statement also supports the inclusion of `if` statements to filter the iteration over a dictionary, list, tuple, or string variable. In this manner you can limit the iteration to elements that pass or fail a certain criteria. The `{% for %}` statement syntax with an `if` clause is `{% for <reference> in <variable> if <test_for_reference>%}` (e.g., `{% for drink in drinks if drink not in ['Cappuccino'] %}`)
- `{% for %}` with `recursive` keyword.- The `{% for %}` statement also supports recursion over nested dictionaries, lists, tuples, or string variables. Instead of creating multiple nested `{% for %}` statements, you can use recursion to reuse the same layout over each of the nested structures. Listing 4-16 illustrates a sample of a recursive loop in Jinja.

Listing 4-16. Jinja {% for %} statement with recursive keyword

```
# Dictionary definition
coffees={
    'espresso':
        {'nothing else':'Espresso',
```

```
            'water': 'Americano',
            'steamed milk': {'more steamed milk than milk foam': 'Latte',
                             'chocolate syrup': {'Whipped cream': 'Mocha'}
             },
             'more milk foam than steamed milk': 'Capuccino'
        }
}

# Template definition with for and recursive
{% for ingredient,result in coffees.iteritems() recursive %}
    <li>{{ ingredient }}
    {% if result is mapping %}
        <ul>{{ loop(result.iteritems()) }}</ul>
    {% else %}
         YOU GET:  {{ result }}
    {% endif %}</li>
{% endfor %}

# Output
espresso
     water YOU GET: Americano
     steamed milk
          more steamed milk than milk foam YOU GET: Latte
          chocolate syrup
               Whipped cream YOU GET: Mocha
     more milk foam than steamed milk YOU GET: Capuccino
     nothing else YOU GET: Espresso
```

- `{% break %}` and `{% continue %}`.- The `{% break %}` and `{% continue %}` statements are available inside `{% for %}` statements and allow you to break out of the loop or continue to the next iteration, just like the same keywords available in regular Python loops.

■ **Note** {% break %} and {% continue %} require enabling the built-in jinja2.ext.loopcontrols extension. See the second to last section in this chapter on how to enable Jinja extensions for more details.

- `range` (Function).- The `range` function works just like Python's standard function and is useful when you want to generate a loop over a given range of numbers from i to j-1. For example, `range(0,5)` generates the range `[0,1,2,3,4]`. In addition, the range function also supports overriding the step count --- which defaults to 1 --- in the third position (e.g., `range(0,11,2)` generates `[0,2,4,6,8,10]`).
- `cycler` (Function)).- The `cycler` function lets you cycle among a series of values. It works just like the `loop.cycle` variable available in `{% for %}` loops, except the `cycler` function can be used outside loops. The `cycler` function uses its `next()` method to advance one item, the `reset()` method to cycle to the first item and the current attribute to return the current item. Listing 4-17 illustrates a cycler method definition with CSS classes, which is then used over multiple `{% for %}` loops to define a list where each item is assigned a different CSS class based on the cycle iteration.

Listing 4-17. Jinja cycler function

```
{% set row_class = cycler('white','lightgrey','grey') %}

<ul>
{% for item in items %}
  <li class="{{ row_class.next() }}">{{ item }}</li>
{% endfor %}
{% for otheritem in moreitems %}
  <li class="{{ row_class.next() }}">{{ otheritem }}</li>
{% endfor %}

# Output
<ul>
  <li class="white">Item 1</li>
  <li class="lightgrey">Item 2 </li>
  <li class="grey">Item 3 </li>
  <li class="white">Item 4</li>
  <li class="lightgrey">Item 5</li>
  <li class="grey">Other item 1</li>
  <li class="white">Other item 2</li>
</ul>
```

- `joiner` (Function).- The `joiner` function lets you join a series of disparate sections and join them with a given separator, which defaults to a comma-space (", "). A characteristic of the joiner function is that it returns the separator string every time it's called, except the first time to give the correct appearance in case sections are dependent on a condition. Listing 4-18 illustrates a joiner method definition with a slash-space ("/ ") as its separator, which is then used to join a list of sections.

Listing 4-18. Jinja joiner function

```
{% set slash_joiner = joiner("/ ") %}

User: {% if username %} {{ slash_joiner() }}
    {{username}}
{% endif %}
{% if alias %} {{ slash_joiner() }}
    {{alias}}
{% endif %}
{% if nickname %} {{ slash_joiner() }}
    {{nickname}}
{% endif %}

# Output
# If all variables are defined
User: username / alias / nickname
# If only nickname is defined
User: nickname
# If only username and alias is defined
User: username / alias
# Etc, the joiner function avoids any unnecessary preceding slash because it doesn't print
anything the first time its called
```

Python and Filter Operations

- `{% set %}`.- The `{% set %}` statement lets you define variables in the context of Jinja templates. It's useful when you need to create variables for values that aren't exposed by a Django view method or when a variable is tied to a heavyweight operation. The following is a sample statement of this statement `{% set drinkwithtax=drink.cost*1.07 %}`. The scope of a variable defined in a `{% set %}` statement is from its declaration until the end of the template.

  The `{% set %}` statement can also define content blocks. For example, the statement `{% set advertisement %}<div class'banner'><img src=.....></div>{% endset %}`, creates the variable `advertisement` with the content enclosed between `{% set %}` and `{% endset %}` that can later be reused in other parts of a template (e.g., `{{advertisement}}`). The built-in `{% macro %}` statement - described in the template structures section - provide more advanced reuse functionality for content blocks.

- `{% do %}` (This statement requires enabling the built-in jinja2.ext.do extension; see the section Enable Jinja extensions for more details).- The `{% do %}` statement is an expression evaluator that works like the `{{ }}` variable syntax, except it doesn't produce output. For example, to increment the value of a variable or add a new element without producing any output, you can use the `{% do %}` statement (e.g.,`{% do itemlist.append('Forgot to add this other item') %}`).

■ **Note** {% break %} and {% continue %} require enabling the built-in jinja2.ext.loopcontrols extension. See the second to last section in this chapter on how to enable Jinja extensions for more details.

- `{% with %}`.- The `{% with %}` statement is similar to the `{% set %}` statement; the only difference is the `{% with %}` statement limits the scope of a variable with the `{% endwith %}` statement (e.g., `{% with myvar=1 %}...{% endwith %}` any elements declared in ... have access to the `myvar` variable). It's also valid to declare `{% set %}` statements within `{% with %}` and `{% endwith %}` statements to limit the scope of variables (e.g., `{% with %}{% set myvar=1 %}...{% endwith %}`).

■ **Note** {% with %} requires enabling the built-in jinja2.ext.with_ extension. See the second to last section in this chapter on how to enable Jinja extensions for more details.

- `{% filter %}`.- The `{% filter %}` statement is used to apply Jinja filters to template sections. By default, Jinja filters are applied individually to template variables, but sometimes it can be helpful to apply Jinja filters to entire template sections. For example, if you declare `{% filter lower %}` the `lower` filter is applied to all content between this statement and the `{% endfilter %}` statement - note the `lower` filter statement converts all content to lowercase; the next major section in this chapter describes Jinja's built-in filters.

- `dict` (Function).- The `dict` function offers an alternative to define dictionaries without literals (e.g., `{'id':1}` is equivalent to `dict(id=1)`).

Spacing and Special Characters

By default, Jinja keeps all spacing (e.g., tabs, spaces, newlines) unchanged from how they are defined in a template. Figure 4-1 illustrates the default rendering of a template snippet in Jinja.

```
<div>
    {% for drink in drinks %}
      {{drink}}
    {% endfor %}
</div>

<div>    {% if drinks_on_sale %} Drinks on sale! {% endif %}
```

```
<div>

        Espresso

        Capuccino

        Mocha

</div>
<div>     Drinks on sale!     </div>
```

Figure 4-1. *Default space rendering in Jinja template*

As you can see in Figure 4-1, the spacing before, after, and by the {% for %} and {% if %} statements themselves is generated as is. While this spacing is natural, it can be beneficial to create more compact outputs with templates that handle a lot of data. The minus sign - appended to either the start or end of a statement (e.g., {%- <statement> -%}) tells Jinja to strip the new line that follows it. This is best illustrated with the examples presented in Figure 4-2 and Figure 4-3.

```
<div>
    {% for drink in drinks -%}
      {{drink}}
    {% endfor %}
</div>

<div>    {% if drinks_on_sale -%} Drinks on sale! {% endif %}
```

```
<div>
    Espresso
    Capuccino
    Mocha

</div>
<div>    Drinks on sale!     </div>
```

Figure 4-2. *Space rendering in Jinja template with single -*

```
<div>
    {% for drink in drinks -%}
      {{drink}}
    {%- endfor %}
</div>

<div>    {% if drinks_on_sale -%} Drinks on sale! {%- endif %}
```

```
<div>
    EspressoCapuccinoMocha
</div>
<div>    Drinks on sale!    </div>
```

Figure 4-3. *Space rendering in Jinja template with double -*

As you can see in Figure 4-2, the - symbol before closing the `{% for %}` statement makes Jinja eliminate the new line after each iteration. In the case of the `{% if %}` statement also in Figure 4-2, the - symbol has no impact because there's no newline associated with the statement. In Figure 4-3 you can see there's an additional - symbol at the start of the `{% endfor %}` statement which makes Jinja eliminate the newline before the start of each iteration. In the case of the `{% if %}` statement also is Figure 4-3, the additional - symbol has no impact because there's no newline associated with the statement.

Because adding - symbols to every Jinja statement can become tiresome, you can configure Jinja so that by default it uses this behavior (i.e., just as if you added -). To alter Jinja's default spacing behavior, you can use two Jinja environment parameters : `trim_blocks` and `lstrip_blocks`, both of which default to `False`. Note that in Django you set up Jinja environment parameters as part of the `OPTIONS` variable in `settings.py`, as described in the prior section on setting up Jinja template configuration in Django.

Figure 4-4 illustrates the rendering of a code snippet when `trim_blocks` is set to `True`, whereas Figure 4-5 illustrates the rendering of a code snippet when both `trim_blocks` and `lstrip_blocks` are set to `True`.

```
<div>
    {% for drink in drinks %}
      {{drink}}
    {% endfor %}
</div>

<div>    {% if drinks_on_sale %} Drinks on sale! {% endif %}
```

```
<div>
          Espresso
          Capuccino
          Mocha
    </div>
<div>     Drinks on sale!     </div>
```

Figure 4-4. *Space rendering in Jinja template with trim_blocks*

```
<div>
    {% for drink in drinks %}
      {{drink}}
    {% endfor %}
</div>

<div>     {% if drinks_on_sale %} Drinks on sale! {% endif %}
```

```
<div>
        Espresso
        Capuccino
        Mocha
</div>
<div>       Drinks on sale!      </div>
```

Figure 4-5. *Space rendering in Jinja template with both trim_blocks and lstrip_blocks set to True*

As you can see in Figures 4-4 and 4-5, the rendering produced by changing the `trim_blocks` and `lstrip_blocks` Jinja environment variables is very similar to that of using - symbols to start and end Jinja statements. It's worth mentioning that if you set `lstrip_blocks` to `True` and want to omit its behavior for certain sections, you can do so by adding the plus sign + to either the start or end of a statement - just like you use the minus sign - to achieve its opposite behavior.

- `{% raw %}`.- The `{% raw %}` statement is used to output any Jinja reserved characters verbatim until the `{% endraw %}` statement is reached. The `{% raw %}` statement is ideal if you want to render large chunks of Jinja template code or if you have a lot of text that includes special Jinja template characters (e.g., {{, {%).

■ **Tip** You can output special Jinja template characters individually by quoting them as part of a hard-coded string variable (e.g., to output {{ use {{ '{{' }}) vs. using a {% raw %} statement.

- `{% autoescape %}`.- The `{% autoescape %}` statement lets you escape HTML characters from a template section, effectively overriding Django's Jinja default auto-escaping behavior. The `{% autoescape %}` accepts one of two arguments `true` or `false`. With `{% autoescape true %}` all template content between this statement and the `{% endautoescape %}` statement is HTML escaped, with `{% autoescape false %}` no template content between this statement and the `{% endautoescape %}` statement is HTML escaped.

■ **Note** {% autoescape %} requires enabling the built-in jinja2.ext.auto-escape extension. See the second to last section in this chapter on how to enable Jinja extensions for more details.

- `lipsum` (Function).- The `lipsum` function is used to display random Latin text, which is useful for filler on templates. The `lipsum` function is called with four parameters: `lipsum(n=5, html=True, min=20, max=100)`. Where `n` is a number of paragraphs to generate, if not provided the default `n` is `5`; `html` defaults to `True` to return HTML or you can set it to `False` to return regular text; and `min` and `max` represent the minimum and maximum number of random words per paragraph. To use the lipsum function you simply define a variable with it and the output to generate the random Latin text (e.g., `{% set latinblurb=lipsum() %}` and then `{{latinblurb}}` to output the random Latin text).

Template Structures

- `{% block %}`.- The `{% block %}` statement is used to define page sections that can be overridden on different Jinja templates. See the previous section on creating reusable Jinja templates for detailed examples of this statement.
- `{# #}`.- The `{# #}` statement is used to enclose comments on Jinja templates. Any content placed between {# and #} is bypassed by Jinja and doesn't appear in the final rendered web page.
- `{% extends %}`.- The `{% extends %}` statement is used to reuse the layout of another Jinja template. See the previous section on creating reusable Jinja templates for detailed examples of this statement.
- `{% include %}`.- The `{% include %}` statement is used to embed a Jinja template in another Jinja template. Note that by default, the `{% include %}` statement gets access to the current template instance values (i.e., its context). If you want to disable access to a template's context you can use the `{% import %}` statement or pass the keyword `without context` to the end of the `{% include %}` statement (e.g., `{% from 'footer.html' without context %}`). In addition, the `{% include %}` statement also accepts the `ignore missing` keyword, which tells Jinja to ignore the statement if the template to be included does not exist. See the previous section on creating reusable Jinja templates for detailed examples of this statement.
- `{% macro %}`.- The `{% macro %}` statement is a template function designed to output content. It's ideal for repetitive content snippets, where you define a `{% macro %}` statement once and execute it multiple times with different variables - like a function - on any template. See the previous section on creating reusable Jinja templates for detailed examples of this statement. It's also worth mentioning the built-in `{% set %}` statement - described in the Python and filter operations section - provides simpler reuse functionality for content blocks.
- `{% call %}`.- The `{% call %}` statement is used in conjunction with the `{% macro %}` statement to reference the `caller()` method within a `{% macro %}` statement. If you define a `{% macro %}` statement with a `caller()` reference as part of its content, you can rely on the `{% call %}` statement to invoke the `{% macro %}` and have the contents of the `{% call %}` statement substituted in place of the `caller()` method. See the previous section on creating reusable Jinja templates for detailed examples of this statement.

- `{% import %}` and `{% from ... import %}`.- The `{% import %}` statement is used to access elements from other templates. Similar to Python's standard import, you can also use the `from` and `as` keywords to limit or rename the elements imported into a template. Note that by default and due to its caching behavior, the `{% import %}` statement doesn't get access to the current template instance values (i.e., its context), it just gets access to globals (e.g., variables and macros). If you want to access a template's context you can use the `{% include %}` statement or pass the keyword `with context` to the end of the `{% import %}` statement to disable caching and access a template's context (e.g., `{% from 'footer.html' with context %}`). See the previous section on creating reusable Jinja templates for detailed examples of this statement.

Jinja Built-In Filters and Tests (Like Django Filters)

The Jinja documentation makes an explicit difference between what it calls filters and tests. The only difference is that Jinja tests are used to evaluate conditions and Jinja filters are used to format or transform values. In Django there is no such naming difference and an equivalent Jinja test in Django is simply called a Django filter.

The syntax to apply Jinja filters to template variables is the vertical bar character `|`, also called a 'pipe' in Unix environments (e.g., `{{variable|filter}}`). It's worth mentioning you can apply multiple filters to the same variable (e.g., `{{variable|filter|filter}}`). The syntax to apply Jinja tests uses the `is` keyword along with a regular conditional to evaluate the validity of a test (e.g., `{% if variable is divisibleby 10 %}do something{% endif %}`).

In the upcoming sections, I'll add the reference (Test) to indicate it's referring to a Jinja test vs. a Jinja filter. I'll also classify each Django built-in filter and test into functional sections so they are easier to identify. I'll define the broadest category 'Strings, lists, dictionaries, numbers and objects' for filters and tests that are applicable for most scenarios and then more specialized sections for each data type, including 'String and lists,' 'Dictionaries and objects,' Strings, Numbers, Spacing and special characters, Development and testing, and Urls.

Strings, Lists, Dictionaries, Numbers, and Objects

- `default` or `d`.- The `default` or `d` filter is used to specify a default value if a variable is undefined or is false (i.e., it doesn't exist or is empty). For example, the filter statement `{{variable|default("no value")}}` outputs `no value` only if the variable is undefined; otherwise it outputs the variable value. If in addition you want to provide a default value for a variable that evaluates to false, is None or is an empty string, you have to add `true` as a second filter parameter (e.g., `{{variable|default("no value",true)}}` outputs `no value` if the variable is undefined, false, is None, or is an empty string).

- `defined` (Test).- The `defined` test is used to check if a variable is defined, and if a variable is defined this tests return true. Listing 4-19 illustrates an example of the `defined` test.

Listing 4-19. Jinja defined test

```
{% if variable is defined %}
    value of variable: {{ variable }}
{% else %}
    variable is not defined
{% endif %}
```

- `none` (Test).- The `none` test is used to check if a variable is none, and if a variable is None this tests return true.
- `length` or `count`.- The `length` filter is used to obtain the length of a value. For example, if a variable contains `latte` the filter statement `{{variable|length}}` outputs 5. For a list variable that contains `['a','e','i']` the filter statement `{{variable|length}}` outputs 3.
- `equalto` (Test).- The `equalto` test checks if an object has the same value as another object. For example `{% if coffee.price is equalto 1.99 %} coffee prices equals 1.99 {% endif %}`. This works just like the ==, but is more helpful when used with other filters such as `selectattr` (e.g., `{{ users|selectattr("email", "equalto", "webmaster@coffeehouse.com") }}`, gets users with email `webmaster@coffeehouse.com`).
- `string` (Test).- The `string` test checks if a variable is a string (e.g., `{% if variable is string %}Yes, the variable is a string!{% endif %}`).
- `number` (Test).- The `number` test returns true if a variable is a number.
- `iterable` (Test).- The `iterable` test checks if it's possible to iterate over an object.
- `sequence` (Test).- The `sequence` test checks if the object is a sequence (e.g., a generator).
- `mapping` (Test).- The `mapping` test checks if the object is a mapping (e.g., a dictionary).
- `callable` (Test).- The callable test verifies if an object is callable. In Python a function, classes and object instances with a __call__ method are callables.
- `sameas` (Test).- The `sameas` test verifies if an object points to the same memory address than another object.

Strings and Lists

- `reverse`.- The reverse filter is used to get inverse representation of a value. For example, if a variable contains `latte` the filter statement `{{variable|reverse}}` generates `ettal`.
- `first`.- The `first` filter returns the first item in a list or string. For example, for a list variable that contains `['a','e','i','o','u']` the filter statement `{{variable|first}}` outputs a.
- `join`.- The `join` filter joins a list with a string. The `join` filter works just like Python's `str.join(list)`. For example, for a list variable that contains `['a','e','i','o','u']` the filter statement `{{variable|join("--)}}` outputs `a--e--i--o--u`. The `join` filter also supports joining certain attributes of an object (e.g., `{{ users|join(', ', attribute='username') }}`).

- `last`.- The `last` filter returns the last item in a list or string. For example, for a list variable that contains `['a','e','i','o','u']` the filter statement `{{variable|last}}` outputs `u`.
- `map`.- The `map` filter allows you to apply a filter or look up attributes, just like the standard Python `map` method. For example, if you have list of users but are only interested in outputting a list of usernames a map is helpful (e.g., `{{ users|map(attribute='username')|join(', ') }}`). In addition, it's also possible to invoke a filter by passing the name of the filter and the arguments afterwards (e.g., `{{ titles|map('lower')|join(', ') }}` applies the `lower` filter to all the elements in `titles` and then joins the items separated by a comma).
- `random`.- The `random` filter returns a random item in a list. For example, for a list variable that contains `['a','e','i','o','u']` the filter statement `{{variable|random}}` could output `a`, `e`, `i`, `o`, or `u`.
- `reject`.- The `reject` filter removes elements that pass a certain test - see bullets in this chapter section marked as (Test) for acceptable values. For example, for a list variable that contains `[1,2,3,4,5]` the loop statement with this filter `{% for var in variable|reject("odd") %}{{var}}{% endfor %}` - where odd is the Jinja test – rejects elements that are odd and thus its output is `2` and `4`.
- `select`.- The `select` filter selects elements that pass a certain test --see bullets in this chapter section marked as (Test) for acceptable values. For example, for a list variable that contains `[1,2,3,4,5]` the loop statement with this filter `{% for var in variable|select("odd") %}{{var}}{% endfor %}` -- where odd is the Jinja test – selects elements that are odd and thus its output is `1`, `3`, and `5`.
- `slice`.- The `slice` filter returns a slice of lists. For example, for a variable that contains `["Capuccino"]` the filter statement `{% for var in variable|slice(4) %}{{var}}{% endfor %}` outputs `['C', 'a', 'p'],['u', 'c'],['c', 'i'],['n', 'o']`. It's possible to use the `fill_with` as a second argument – which defaults to None – so all segments contain the same number of elements filled with a given value. For example, `{% for var in variable|slice(4,'FILLER') %}{{var}}{% endfor %}` outputs: `['C', 'a', 'p'],['u', 'c','FILLER'],['c', 'i','FILLER'], ['n', 'o','FILLER']`.
- `batch`.- The `batch` filter returns a batch of lists. For example, a variable that contains `["Capuccino"]` the filter statement `{% for var in variable|batch(4) %}{{var}}{% endfor %}` outputs `['C', 'a', 'p', 'u'],['c', 'c', 'i', 'n'],['o']`. It's possible to use the `fill_with` as a second argument – which defaults to None – so all segments contain the same number of elements filled with a given value. For example, `{% for var in variable|slice(4,'FILLER') %}{{var}}{% endfor %}` outputs: `['C', 'a', 'p', 'u'],['c', 'c', 'i', 'n'],['o','FILLER','FILLER','FILLER']`.
- `sort`.- The `sort` filter sorts elements by ascending order. For example, if a variable contains `['e','u','a','i','o']` the statement `{{variable|sort}}` outputs `['a','e','i','o','u']`. It's possible to indicate descending order by setting the first argument to true (e.g., `{{variable|sort(true)}}` outputs `['u','o','i','e','a']`). In addition, if a list is made up strings, a second argument can be used to indicate case sensitiveness - which is disabled by default - to perform the sort operation (e.g., `{{variable|sort(true,true)}}`). Finally, if a list is composed of objects, it's also possible to specify the sort operation on a given attribute (e.g., `variable|sort(attribute='date')` to sort the elements based on the `date` attribute).

Dictionaries and Objects

- `dictsort`.- The `dictsort` filter sorts a dictionary by key, case insensitive. For example, if a variable contains `{'name':'Downtown','city':'San Diego','state':'CA'}` the filter `{% with newdict=variable|dictsort %}` the `newdict` variable is assigned the dictionary `{'city':'San Diego','name':'Downtown','state':'CA'}`. In addition, the `dictsort` can accept two arguments, for case sensitive/insensitive order and sorting by key/value. The default behavior is case insensitive sort by key (e.g., `variable|dictsort`), to use case sensitive sort by key use true as the first argument (e.g., `variable|dictsort(true)`), to use sort by value is value as the second argument (e.g., `variable|dictsort(false,'value')` performs a case insensitive sort by value).

- `attr`.- The `attr` filter returns the attribute of an object (e.g., `{{coffeehouse.city}}` outputs the `city` attribute value of the `coffeehouse` object). Note the `attr` filter only attempts to look up an attribute and not an item (e.g., if `coffeehouse` is a dictionary and `city` is a key item it won't be found). Alternatively, you can just use the standard Python syntax `variable.name` - which first attempts to locate an attribute called `name` on `variable`, then the `name` item on `variable` or if nothing matches an undefined object is returned-- or `variable['name']` - which first attempts to locate the `name` item on `variable`, then an attribute called `name` on `variable` or if nothing matches an undefined object is returned.

- `rejectattr`.- The `rejectattr` filter removes objects that don't contain an attribute or objects for which a certain attribute doesn't pass a test - see bullets in this chapter section marked as (Test) for acceptable values. For example, `{% for ch in coffeehouses|rejectattr("closedon") %}` generates a loop for `coffeehouse` objects that don't have the `closedon` attribute or `{% for u in users|rejectattr("email", "none") %}` generates a loop for `user` objects that don't have `email` None - note the second argument none represents the test.

- `selectattr`.- The `selectattr` filter selects objects that contain an attribute or objects for which a certain attribute passes a test - see bullets in this chapter section marked as (Test) for acceptable values. For example, `{% for u in users|selectattr("superuser") %}` generates a loop for `user` objects that have the `superuser` attribute or `{% for u in users|selectattr("email", "none") %}` generates a loop for `user` objects that have `email` None - note the second argument none represents the test.

- groupby.- The groupby filter is used to rearrange the contents of a list of dictionaries or objects into different group object sequences by a common attribute. Listing 4-20 illustrates an example of the groupby filter.

Listing 4-20. Jinja groupby filter

```
# Dictionary definition
stores = [
    {'name': 'Downtown', 'street': '385 Main Street', 'city': 'San Diego'},
    {'name': 'Uptown', 'street': '231 Highland Avenue', 'city': 'San Diego'},
    {'name': 'Midtown', 'street': '85 Balboa Street', 'city': 'San Diego'},
    {'name': 'Downtown', 'street': '639 Spring Street', 'city': 'Los Angeles'},
    {'name': 'Midtown', 'street': '1407 Broadway Street', 'city': 'Los Angeles'},
    {'name': 'Downton', 'street': '50 1st Street', 'city': 'San Francisco'},
]
```

```
<ul>
{% for group in stores|groupby('city') %}
    <li>{{ group.grouper }}
    <ul>
        {% for item in group.list %}
          <li>{{ item.name }}: {{ item.street }}</li>
        {% endfor %}
    </ul>
    </li>
{% endfor %}
</ul>

# Output
Los Angeles
    Downtown: 639 Spring Street
    Midtown: 1407 Broadway Street
San Diego
    Downtown : 385 Main Street
    Uptown : 231 Highland Avenue
    Midtown : 85 Balboa Street
San Francisco
    Downtown: 50 1st Street

# Alternate shortcut syntax, produces same output
<ul>
{% for grouper, list in stores|groupby('city') %}
    <li>{{ grouper }}
    <ul>
        {% for item in list %}
          <li>{{ item.name }}: {{ item.street }}</li>
        {% endfor %}
    </ul>
    </li>
{% endfor %}
</ul>
```

- `tojson`.- The `tojson` filter outputs data structures to JavaScript Object Notation(JSON) (e.g.`{{variable|tojson}}`). The `tojson` filter accepts the `indent` argument - which is set to None - to generate pretty output by a given number of spaces (e.g., `{{variable|tojson(indent=2)}}`) generates output indented with two spaces).

Tip You can globally set options for the tojson filter through Jinja policies, described in the last section of this chapter.

Strings

- `capitalize`.- The `capitalize` filter capitalizes the first character of a string variable. For example, if a variable contains `hello world` the filter statement `{{variable|capitalize}}` outputs `Hello world`.
- `list`.- The `list` filter is used to return a list of characters. For example, if a variable contains `latte` the filter statement `{{variable|list}}` generates `['l','a','t','t','e']`.
- `lower`.- The `lower` filter converts all values of a string variable to lowercase. For example, if a variable contains `Hello World` the filter statement `{{variable|lower}}` outputs `hello world`.
- `lower` (Test).- The `lower` test returns true if a variable is lowercased. For example, `{% if variable is lower %}Yes, the variable is lowercase!{% endif %}` outputs the statement if `variable` is lowercased.
- `replace`.- The `replace` filter works just like Python's standard `replace` string. The first argument is the substring that should be replaced, the second is the replacement string. If the optional third argument amount is given, only this amount of occurrences are replaced. For example `{{ "Django 1.8"|replace("1.8", "1.9") }}` outputs `Django 1.9` and `{{"oooh Django!"|replace("o", "",2) }}` outputs `oh Django!`.
- `string`.- The `string` filter makes a string unicode if it isn't already.
- `title`.- The `title` filter converts all first character values of a string variable to uppercase. For example, if a variable contains `hello world` the filter statement `{{variable|title}}` outputs `Hello World`.
- `upper`.- The `upper` filter converts all values of a string variable to uppercase. For example, if a variable contains `Hello World` the filter statement `{{variable|upper}}` outputs `HELLO WORLD`.
- `upper` (Test).- The `upper` test returns true if a variable is uppercased. For example, `{% if variable is upper %}Yes, the variable is uppercase!{% endif %}` outputs the statement if `variable` is uppercase.
- `wordcount`.- The `wordcount` filter counts the words in a string. For example, if a variable contains `Coffeehouse started as a small store` the filter statement `{{variable|wordcount}}` outputs 6.

Numbers

- `abs`.- The `abs` return the absolute value of the number argument. For example, if a variable contains `-5` the filter statement `{{variable|abs}}` outputs `5`.
- `filesizeformat`.-The `filesizeformat` filter converts a number of bytes into a friendly file size string. For example, if a variable contains 250 the filter statement `{{variable|filesizeformat}}` outputs 250 Bytes, if it contains 2048 the output is 2 kB, if it contains 2000000000 the output is 2.0 GB. By default, decimal prefixes are used (e.g., Giga, Mega, Kilo), if you pass an additional Boolean parameter with true (e.g., `{{variable|filesizeformat(true)}}`) then binary prefixes are used (e.g., Gibi, Mebi, Kibi).

- float.- The float filter converts a value into a floating-point number. If the conversion doesn't work it returns 0.0 or a custom value argument (e.g., variable|float("It didn't work") returns "It didn't work" if variable can't be converted to a floating-point number).
- int.- The int filter converts a value into an integer. If the conversion doesn't work it returns 0 or a custom value specified as the first argument to the filter – just like the float filter. You can also override the default base 10 with a second filter argument, which handles input with prefixes such as 0b, 0o and 0x for bases 2, 8, and 16 respectively (e.g., {{'0b001111'|int(0,2)}} a base 2 number outputs 15.
- round.- The round filter rounds a number to a given precision, where the first argument is the precision - which defaults to 0 - and the second argument is a rounding method - which defaults to 'common' rounding either up or down. For example, {{ 33.55|round }} assumes 'common' rounding to output 34.0). In addition to 'common', it's also possible to use 'ceil' to always round up or 'floor' to always round down (e.g., {{ 33.55|round(1,'floor') }} outputs 33.5). Note that even if rounded to the default 0 precision, a float is returned. If you need an integer you can apply the int filter (e.g., {{ 33.55|round|int }} outputs 34).
- sum.- The sum filter returns the sum of a sequence of numbers, plus the value provided with the start parameter that defaults to 0. In addition, it's also possible to sum certain attributes of a list of objects {{ items|sum(attribute='price') }}.
- divisibleby (Test).- The divisibleby test checks if a variable is divisible by a given number. For example, if a variable contains 20 the filter statement {% if variable is divisibleby(5) %}Variable is divisible by 5!{% endif %} outputs the conditional statement.
- even (Test).- The even test checks if a number is even.
- odd (Test).- The odd test checks if a number is odd.

Spacing and Special Characters

- center.- The center filter center aligns a value and pads it with additional whitespace characters until it reaches the given argument of characters. For example, if a variable contains mocha the filter statement {{variable|center(width="15")}} outputs "   mocha   ".
- escape or e.- The escape or e filter escapes HTML characters from a value. Specifically with the escape filter: < is converted to <, > is converted to >, ' (single quote) is converted to ', " (double quote) is converted to ", and & is converted to &amp.
- escaped (Test).- The escaped test checks if a value is escaped.
- forceescape.- The forceescape filter escapes HTML characters from a value just like the escape filter. The difference between both filters is the forceescape filter is applied immediately and returns a new and escaped string. This is useful in the rare cases where you need multiple escaping or want to apply other filters to the escaped results. Normally, you'll use the escape filter.

- `format`.- The `format` filter is used to apply Python string formatting to a variable. For example, the statement `{{ "%s and %s"|format("Python", "Django!") }}` outputs `Python and Django!`.
- `indent`.- The `indent` filter is used to output a string with each line except the first one indented with four spaces. It's possible to change the number of spaces and the indentation of the first line with additional filter arguments (e.g., `{{ textvariable|indent(2, true) }}` the 2 indicates two spaces and `true` indicates to indent the first line.
- `safe`.- The `safe` filter marks a string as not requiring further HTML escaping. When this filter is used with an environment without automatic escaping it has no effect.
- `striptags`.- The `striptags` filter removes all HTML tags from a value. For example, if a variable contains `<b>Coffee</b>house, the <i>best</i> <span>drinks</span>` the filter statement `{{variable|striptags}}` outputs `Coffeehouse, the best drinks`.
- `trim`.- The `trim` filter is used to strip leading and trailing whitespace just like Python's string `strip()` method.
- `truncate`.- The `truncate` filter truncates a string to a given number of characters - defaulting to 255 characters - and appends an ellipsis sequence. For example, if a variable contains `Coffeehouse started as a small store` the filter statement `{{variable|truncate(20)}}` outputs `Coffeehouse ...`, keeping up until character number 20 and then discarding the last full word, finally adding the ellipsis. You can add `true` as a second argument so the string is cut at an exact length (e.g., `{{variable|truncate(20,true)}}` outputs `Coffeehouse start...` including the ellipsis characters). It's possible to provide a different symbol than an ellipsis passing a second parameter (e.g., `{{variable|truncate(20,true,"!!!")}}` would output !!! instead of an elipsis). And finally, the `truncate` filter accepts a fourth argument `leeway` to specify a string tolerance in characters - which defaults to 5 - to avoid truncating strings (e.g., this avoids truncating words with less than 5 characters).

■ **Tip** You can globally set the leeway value for the truncate filter through Jinja policies, described in the last section of this chapter.

- `wordwrap`.- The `wordwrap` filter wraps words at a given character line length argument. By default, the wrapping occurs after 79 characters, which can be overridden providing a first argument with the number of characters. If you set a second parameter to false, Jinja does not split words longer than the wrapping character length. In addition, wrapping generates a newline character as defined in the environment -- generally the \n character - but this can be changed by specifying the `wrapstring` keyword argument (e.g., `{{variable|wordwrap(40,true,'-')` uses a hyphen as the wrapping newline character). Listing 4-21 illustrates an example of the `wordwrap` filter.

Listing 4-21. Jinja wordwrap filter

```
# Variable definition
Coffeehouse started as a small store

# Template definition with wordwrap filter for every 12 characters
{{variable|wordwrap(12)}}

# Output
Coffeehouse
started as a
small store
```

- `xmlattr`.- The `xmlattr` filter is used to create an SGML/XML attribute string based on the items in a dictionary or object. Once you create a dictionary structure containing attribute names and reference values, you pass it through the `xmlattr` filter to generate the attribute string. By default, all values that are neither none or undefined are automatically escaped, but you can override this behavior by passing false as the first filter argument. Listing 4-22 illustrates an example of the `xmlattr` filter.

Listing 4-22. Django xmlattr filter

```
# Variable definition
{% set stores = [
    {'id':123,'name': 'Downtown', 'street': '385 Main Street', 'city': 'San Diego'},
    {'id':243,'name': 'Uptown', 'street': '231 Highland Avenue', 'city': 'San Diego'},
    {'id':357,'name': 'Midtown', 'street': '85 Balboa Street', 'city': 'San Diego'},
    {'id':478,'name': 'Downtown', 'street': '639 Spring Street', 'city': 'Los Angeles'},
    {'id':529,'name': 'Midtown', 'street': '1407 Broadway Street', 'city': 'Los Angeles'},
    {'id':653,'name': 'Downton', 'street': '50 1st Street', 'city': 'San Francisco'},
] %}

# Template definition
<ul>
{% for store in stores %}
  <li {{ {'id':'%d'|format(store.id),'class':'%s'|format(store.city|lower|replace(' ','-'))
}|xmlattr }}> {{store.city}} {{store.name}}</li>
{% endfor %}
</ul>

# Output
<ul>
  <li id="123" class="san-diego"> San Diego Downtown</li>
  <li id="243" class="san-diego"> San Diego Uptown</li>
  <li id="357" class="san-diego"> San Diego Midtown</li>
  <li id="478" class="los-angeles"> Los Angeles Downtown</li>
  <li id="529" class="los-angeles"> Los Angeles Midtown</li>
  <li id="653" class="san-francisco"> San Francisco Downton</li>
</ul>
```

Development and Testing

- pprint.- The pprint filter is a wrapper for Python's pprint.pprint(). The pprint filter is useful during development and testing because it outputs the formatted representation of an object. By default, the pprint filter is not verbose but you can make it verbose passing it the true argument (e.g., {{variable|pprint(true)}}).

Urls

- **urlencode.**- The urlencode filter escapes a value for use in a URL. For example, if a variable contains http://localhost/drinks?type=cold&size=large the filter statement {{variable|urlencode}} outputs http%3A//localhost/drinks%3Ftype%3Dcold%26size%3Dlarge.
- **urlize.**- The urlize filter converts text URLs into clickable HTML links. You can pass the filter an additional integer to shorten the visible url (e.g., {{ variable|urlize(40)}} links are shortened to 40 characters plus an ellipsis). It's also possible to add a second argument as a Boolean to make the urls "nofollow" (e.g., {{ variable|urlize(40, true)}} links are shortened to 40 characters and defined with rel="nofollow"). Finally, it's also possible to add the target argument to define a link target (e.g., {{ variable|urlize(40, target="_blank")}} links are shortened to 40 characters and open in a new window).

■ **Tip** You can globally set rel and target values for the the urlize filter through Jinja policies, described in the last section of this chapter.

Custom Filters and Tests in Jinja

Custom Jinja filters and tests are easy to create because they are backed by regular Python methods. For custom Jinja filters a method should return the desired formatted value, and for Jinja tests a method should contain the logic to return a Boolean value.

Structure

The backing method for a custom Jinja filter or test has arguments that correspond to the variable itself - as the first argument - and any remaining values passed by the filter or test as other method arguments (e.g., variable|mycustomfilter("<div>") backed by a method like def mycustomfilter(variable,htmltag="<p>"): -- note the htmltag argument has a default value in case the filter doesn't specify this value with a statement like variable|mycustomfilter).

The only Jinja specific logic you need to consider when creating backing Python methods is related to character safety in Jinja filters. By default, if a backing method for a Jinja filter returns a string, it's considered unsafe and is therefore escaped (e.g., if the result of the filter returns <div>, Jinja renders the result as <div>) - which is the same behavior enforced by custom Django filters.

To mark the result as a safe string, the backing Python method used by a Jinja filter must return a jinja2.Markup type, a process that's illustrated in one of the sample filters in Listing 4-23. Listing 4-23 illustrates various backing methods for custom Jinja filters and tests.

Listing 4-23. Backing Python methods for Jinja custom filters and tests.

```
import jinja2

def customcoffee(value,arg="muted"):
    return jinja2.Markup('%s' % (arg,value))

import math

def squarerootintext(value):
    return "The square root of %s is %s" % (value,math.sqrt(value))

def startswithvowel(value):
    if value.lower().startswith(("a", "e", "i", "o","u")):
        return True
    else:
        return False
```

The first method in Listing 4-23 returns the `value` argument wrapped in an HTML `<span>` tag and appends a CSS class with the `arg` argument - note the `arg` argument in the method definition defaults to the `muted` value in case no value is provided. And also notice the `customcoffee` method returns a `jinja2.Markup` type; this is done so Jinja renders the output as a safe string and interprets the `<span>` tag as HTML.

The second method in Listing 4-23 calculates the square root of a given value and returns the standard string `"The square root of %s is %s"` where the first `%s` represents the passed in `value` and the second `%s` the calculated square root. The third method in Listing 4-23 takes the `value` argument, transforms it to lowercase, and checks if `value` starts with a vowel; if it does it returns a Boolean True otherwise it returns a Boolean False.

Installation and Access

Once you create the backing methods for custom Jinja filters and tests, you need to declare them as part of the filters and/or tests variables on Jinja's environment configuration, which is described in the next section. Note that it's assumed the backing methods in Listing 4-23 are placed in a file/module named filters under the `coffeehouse.jinja` directory path.

To better illustrate the location of the `filters.py` file containing the custom Jinja extension, Listing 4-24 illustrates a directory structure with additional Django project files for reference.

Listing 4-24. Directory structure and location of custom Jinja filters and tests

```
+---+-<PROJECT_DIR_coffeehouse>
    |
    +-__init__.py
    +-settings.py
    +-urls.py
    +-wsgi.py
    |
    +-jinja-+
            +-__init__.py
            +-env.py
            +-filters.py
```

Jinja filters and tests are set up as part of Jinja's environment configuration. Listing 4-25 illustrates a custom Jinja environment definition that sets a series of custom Jinja filters through the variable named filters and tests.

Listing 4-25. Custom Jinja environment with custom filters and tests

```
from jinja2.environment import Environment
from coffeehouse.jinja.filters import customcoffee, squarerootintext, startswithvowel

class JinjaEnvironment(Environment):
    def __init__(self,**kwargs):
        super(JinjaEnvironment, self).__init__(**kwargs)
        self.filters['customcoffee'] = customcoffee
        self.filters['squarerootintext'] = squarerootintext
        self.filters['startswithvowel'] = startswithvowel
        self.tests['startswithvowel'] = startswithvowel
```

As you can see in Listing 4-25, each backing Python method is first imported into the custom Jinja environment. Next, to register custom Jinja filters you access `self.filters` and assign it a variable key name - corresponding to the filter name - along with the backing method for the filter. And to register custom Jinja tests you access `self.tests` and assign it a variable key name - corresponding to the test name - along with the backing method for the test.

An interesting aspect of Listing 4-25 is the registration of `startswithvowel` as both a filter and test, which means the same backing method - which returns True or False - can be used for both cases. This dual registration allows `startswithvowel` to either use a pipe (i.e., as a filter `{{variable|startwithvowel}}` to output True or False verbatim) or the `is` keyword in a conditional (i.e., as a test `{% if variable is startswithvowel %}variable starts with vowel{% endif %}`).

Once a custom Jinja environment is created, you need to set it up as part of Django's configuration in the `OPTIONS` variable of `settings.py`, as illustrated in Listing 4-26.

Listing 4-26. Configure custom Jinja environment in Django setttings.py

```
TEMPLATES = [
    {
        'BACKEND':'django.template.backends.jinja2.Jinja2',
        'DIRS': ['%s/templates/'% (PROJECT_DIR),],
        'APP_DIRS': True,
        'OPTIONS': {
            'environment': 'coffeehouse.jinja.env.JinjaEnvironment'
            }
        },
    ]
```

In this case, you can see in Listing 4-26 the environment value corresponds to `coffeehouse.jinja.env.JinjaEnvironment`, where `JinjaEnvironment` is the class - in Listing 4-25 - env is the file/module name and `coffeehouse.jinja` is the directory path. To better illustrate the location of the `env.py` file take a look at the directory structure in Listing 4-24.

Once you finish this last registration step, all the declared custom Jinja filters and tests become available on all Jinja templates just like the regular built-in filters and tags described in the previous section.

■ **Note** The custom Jinja environment in Listing 4-25 for custom Jinja filters and tests is the same technique used in Listing 4-11 to declare Jinja globals.

Jinja Extensions

A Jinja extension is to Jinja templates what a library is for programming languages: a reusable set of features contained in a specific format to not have to continuously 'reinvent the wheel.'

Jinja itself includes various extensions that need to be enabled to be used. In addition, there are also various third-party Jinja extensions that you can find helpful in certain situations (e.g., Jinja statements that emulate Django template tags). Table 4-2 contains a list of extensions including their technical name that's used to enable them.

Table 4-2. *Jinja extensions with description and technical name*

Extension functionality	Description	Technical name
{% break %} and {% continue %} statements	Offers the ability to break and continue in template loops, just like the standard break and continue Python keywords.	jinja2.ext.loopcontrols
{% do %} statement	Offers the ability to evaluate an expression without producing output.	jinja2.ext.do
{% with %} statement	Offers the ability to define variables and limit their scope.	jinja2.ext.with_
{% autoescape %} statement	Offers the ability to enable/disable the escape of HTML characters from a template section.	jinja2.ext.autoescape
{% csrf_token %}, {% trans %}, {% blocktrans %}, {% static %} and {% url %} statements	Offers the ability to use the equivalent functionality provided by Django tags with the same name.	*jdj_tags.extensions. DjangoCompat (For all tags) See extension documentation for more granular statement import names.

** All extensions with the exception of jdj_tags.extensions.DjangoCompat are part of Jinja itself, so they require no additional installation. To install jdj_tags.extensions.DjangoCompat use pip install jinja2-django-tags.*

As you can see in Table 4-2, the functionality provided by each extension varies and if you do an Internet search for 'Jinja2 extensions,' you are sure to find a few more options that can save you time and work on various fronts.

To create a custom Jinja extension you need to reuse the functionality provided by Jinja's `jinja2.ext.Extension` class, as well as use Jinja's API to create the custom logic you're pursuing. Once you create a custom Jinja extension and add it to your Django project, you must also enable it with the `extensions` key of the `OPTIONS` variable in `settings.py`.

Enable Jinja Extensions

Jinja extensions are set up as part of Jinja's environment configuration, which in Django is configured in the OPTIONS variable of settings.py, as described in the previous section on configuring Jinja templates in Django. Listing 4-27 illustrates a sample Django configuration that enables a series of Jinja extensions.

Listing 4-27. Jinja extension configuration in Django

```
TEMPLATES = [
    {
        'BACKEND':'django.template.backends.jinja2.Jinja2',
        'DIRS': ['%s/templates/'% (PROJECT_DIR),],
        'APP_DIRS': True,
        'OPTIONS': {
            'extensions': [
                'jinja2.ext.loopcontrols',
                'jdj_tags.extensions.DjangoCompat',
                'coffeehouse.jinja.extensions.DjangoNow',
                ],
        }
    }
]
```

As you can see in Listing 4-27, we use the Jinja extension's name - as described in Table 4-2 - and add it to a list that's assigned to the extensions key of the OPTIONS variable, which itself is part of Jinja's TEMPLATES Django configuration in settings.py. Note that the third extension coffeehouse.jinja.extensions.DjangoNow in Listing 4-27 is a custom Jinja extension that I'll create in the next and final section of this chapter.

This is all that's necessary to enable a Jinja extension across all Jinja templates. Now that you know how to enable Jinja extensions, the next section explores how to create custom Jinja extensions.

Create Jinja Extensions

Jinja has its own extension API, which is thoroughly documented[7] and tackles all the possible cases you may need an extension for. I won't attempt to use all of the API's functionality, because it would be nearly impossible to do so in a single example; instead I'll focus on creating a practical extension and in the process illustrate the layout and deployment process for a custom Jinja extension.

In Django templates when you want to output the current date or time, there's a tag named {% now %} for just this purpose; Jinja has no such statement, so I'll create a Jinja extension to mimic the same behavior as the Django template {% now %} tag. The Jinja {% now %} statement will function just like the Django template version and accept a format string, as well as the possibility to use the as keyword to define a variable with the value.

Listing 4-28 illustrates the source code for the custom Jinja extension that produces a Jinja {% now %} statement.

[7]http://jinja.pocoo.org/docs/2.9/extensions/

Listing 4-28. Jinja custom extension for Jinja {% now %} statement

```
from jinja2 import lexer, nodes
from jinja2.ext import Extension
from django.utils import timezone
from django.template.defaultfilters import date
from django.conf import settings
from datetime import datetime

class DjangoNow(Extension):
    tags = set(['now'])

    def _now(self, date_format):
        tzinfo = timezone.get_current_timezone() if settings.USE_TZ else None
        formatted = date(datetime.now(tz=tzinfo),date_format)
        return formatted

    def parse(self, parser):
        lineno = next(parser.stream).lineno
        token = parser.stream.expect(lexer.TOKEN_STRING)
        date_format = nodes.Const(token.value)
        call = self.call_method('_now', [date_format], lineno=lineno)
        token = parser.stream.current
        if token.test('name:as'):
            next(parser.stream)
            as_var = parser.stream.expect(lexer.TOKEN_NAME)
            as_var = nodes.Name(as_var.value, 'store', lineno=as_var.lineno)
            return nodes.Assign(as_var, call, lineno=lineno)
        else:
            return nodes.Output([call], lineno=lineno)
```

After the various import statements in Listing 4-28, you can see we create the `DjangoNow` class that inherits its behavior from the `jinja2.ext.Extension` class, the last of which is part of Jinja and used for all custom extensions. Next, you can see we define the tags field with the `set(['now'])` value, which is necessary to set up the statement/tag name. If you wanted the custom statement/tag to be called `{% mytimer %}` then you would declare `tags = set(['mytimer'])`.

Next in Listing 4-28 you can see the `_now` and `parse` methods. The `_now` method performs the actual current date or time calculation and checks the Django project's timezone configuration in `settings.py` - a process that's just like Django's `{% now %}` tag. The `parse` method represents the entry point that executes the custom `{% now %}` statement/tag, where it uses the Jinja extension API to analyze the input and depending on the `{% now %}` declaration (e.g.`{% now "F jS o" %}`, `{% now "F jS o" as today %}`) executes the `_now` method and returns a result.

Once you create the custom Jinja extension, you need to declare it as part of the `extensions` variable on Jinja's environment configuration, as illustrated in Listing 4-27.

To better illustrate the location of the `extensions.py` file containing the custom Jinja extension, Listing 4-29 illustrates a directory structure with additional Django project files for reference.

Listing 4-29. Directory structure and location of custom Jinja extension

```
+---+-<PROJECT_DIR_coffeehouse>
    |
    +-__init__.py
    +-settings.py
    +-urls.py
    +-wsgi.py
    |
    +-jinja-+
            +-__init__.py
            +-extensions.py
```

Note that based on the statement to import the custom Jinja extension in Listing 4-27 - `coffeehouse.jinja.extensions.DjangoNow` - it's assumed the `DjangoNow` class in Listing 4-28 is placed in a file/module named `extensions.py` under the `coffeehouse.jinja` directory path.

Jinja Policies

Jinja policies are used to set the global behavior of Jinja built-in filters and other template constructs. Jinja policies are set in Jinja environments – just like Jinja globals in Listing 4-11 or custom Jinja filters and tests in Listing 4-25.

For example, you can use Jinja policies to alter the way the `json` or `urlize` built-in filters operate by default. Listing 4-30 illustrates a custom Jinja environment that alters the Jinja built-in `truncate` filter and sets the `leeway` option to `0`.

Listing 4-30. Custom Jinja environment with policies

```
from jinja2.environment import Environment
from coffeehouse.jinja.filters import customcoffee, squarerootintext, startswithvowel

class JinjaEnvironment(Environment):
    def __init__(self,**kwargs):
        super(JinjaEnvironment, self).__init__(**kwargs)
        self.policies['truncate.leeway'] = 0
```

As you can see in Listing 4-30, to register Jinja policies you access `self.policies` and assign it the policy key name[8] – in this case corresponding to `truncate.leeway` - along with the policy value – in this case corresponding to `0`. By setting the Jinja policy in Listing 4-30, anytime you use the `truncate` filter in Jinja templates, the `leeway` is set to `0`, instead of the default `5`.

[8] http://jinja.pocoo.org/docs/2.9/api/#policies

CHAPTER 5

Django Application Management

Django, like all modern application development frameworks, requires that you eventually manage tasks to support the core operation of a project. This can range from efficiently setting up a Django application to run in the real world, to managing an application's static resources (e.g., CSS, JavaScript, image files).

In addition, other routine application management tasks can include the following: establishing a logging strategy to enforce problem detection, setting up email delivery for application users and/or administrators, as well as debugging tasks to inspect the outcome of complex operations. In this chapter, you'll learn about these and other common topics associated with Django application management.

Django settings.py for the Real World

The `settings.py` is the central configuration for all Django projects. In previous chapters you already worked with a series of variables in this file to configure things like Django applications, databases, templates, and middleware, among other things.

Although the `settings.py` file uses reasonable default values for practically all variables, when a Django application transitions into the real world, you need to take into account a series of adjustments, to efficiently run the Django application, offer end users a streamlined experience, and keep potential rogue attackers in check.

Switch DEBUG to False

One of the first things that's necessary to launch a Django application into the real world is to change the `DEBUG` variable to `False`. I've briefly mentioned in previous chapters how Django's behavior changes when switching `DEBUG=False` to `DEBUG=True`. All these behavioral changes associated with the `DEBUG` variable are intended to enhance project security. Table 5-1 illustrates the differences between having a project run with `DEBUG=False` and `DEBUG=True`.

D. Rubio, *Beginning Django*, https://doi.org/10.1007/978-1-4842-2787-9_5

Table 5-1. Django behavior differences between DEBUG=True and DEBUG=False

Functionality	DEBUG=True behavior	DEBUG=False behavior
Error handling and notification	Displays full stack of errors on request pages for quick analysis.	Displays default 'vanilla' or custom error pages without any stack details to limit security threats or embarrassments. Emails project administrators of errors. (See the 'Define administrators for ADMINS and MANAGERS' section in this section for more details on email notifications.)
Static resources	Set up by default on a project's /static/ URL for simplicity.	Disables automatic setup to avoid security vulnerabilities and requires consolidation in a separate directory to run static resources on a separate web server. (See the Set up static web page resources - Images, CSS, JavaScript - in the next section.)
Host/site qualifier	Requests for all hosts/ sites are accepted for processing.	It's necessary to qualify for which hosts/sites a project can handle requests. If a site/host is not qualified, all requests are denied. (See the 'Define ALLOWED_HOSTS' section in this section for more details.)

As you can see in Table 5-1, the changes enforced by changing `DEBUG=True` to `DEBUG=False` are intended for publicly accessible applications (i.e., production environments). You may not like the hassle of adapting to these changes, but they are enforced to maintain a heightened level of security on all Django projects that run in the real world.

Define ALLOWED_HOSTS

By default, the `ALLOWED_HOSTS` variable in `settings.py` is empty. The purpose of `ALLOWED_HOSTS` is to validate a request's HTTP `Host` header. Validation is done to prevent rogue users from sending fake HTTP `Host` headers that can potentially poison caches and password reset emails with links to malicious hosts. Since this issue can only present itself under an uncontrolled user environment (i.e., public/production servers), this validation is only done when `DEBUG=False`.

If you switch to `DEBUG=False` and `ALLOWED_HOSTS` is left empty, Django refuses to serve requests and instead responds with HTTP 400 bad request pages, since it can't validate incoming HTTP `Host` headers. Listing 5-1 illustrates a sample definition of `ALLOWED_HOSTS`.

Listing 5-1. Django ALLOWED_HOSTS definition

```
ALLOWED_HOSTS = [
    '.coffeehouse.com',
    '.bestcoffeehouse.com',
]
```

As you can see in Listing 5-1, the `ALLOWED_HOSTS` value is a list of strings. In this case it defines t wo host domains that allow `bestcoffeehouse.com` to act as an alias of `coffeehouse.com`. The leading .(dot) for each domain indicates a subdomain is also an allowed host domain (e.g., `static.coffeehouse.com` or `shop.coffeehouse.com` is valid for `.coffeehouse.com`).

If you wanted to accept a single and fully qualified domain (FQDN), you would define `ALLOWED_HOSTS=['www.coffeehouse.com']`, which would only accept requests with an HTTP `Host` `www.coffeehouse.com`. In a similar fashion, if you wanted to accept any HTTP host - effectively bypassing the verification - you would define `ALLOWED_HOSTS=['*']`, which indicates a wildcard.

Be Careful with the SECRET_KEY Value

The `SECRET_KEY` value in `settings.py` is another security-related variable like `ALLOWED_HOSTS`. However, unlike `ALLOWED_HOSTS`, `SECRET_KEY` is assigned a default value and a very long value at that (e.g., `'oubrz5ado &%+t(qu^fqo_#uhn7*+q*#9b3gje0-yj7^#g#ronn'`).

The purpose of the `SECRET_KEY` value is to digitally sign certain data structures that are sensitive to tampering. Specifically, Django by default uses the `SECRET_KEY` on sensitive data structures like session identifiers, cookies, and password reset tokens. But you can rely on the `SECRET_KEY` value to cryptographically protect any sensitive data structure in a Django project.[1]

The one thing the default data structures signed with the `SECRET_KEY` have in common is they're sent to users on the wider Internet and are then sent back to the application to trigger actions on behalf of users. It's in this scenario we enter into a trust issue. Can the data sent back to the application be trusted? What if a malicious user attempts to simulate another user's cookie or session data to hijack his access? This is what digitally signed data prevents.

Before Django sends any of these sensitive data structures to users on the Internet, it signs them with a project's `SECRET_KEY`. When the data structures come back to fulfill an action, Django rechecks these sensitive data structures against the `SECRET_KEY` again. If there was any tampering on the data structures, the signature check fails and Django halts the process.

The only remote possibility a rogue user has to successfully pull an attack of this kind is if the `SECRET_KEY` is compromised - since an attacker can potentially create an altered data structure that matches a project's `SECRET_KEY`. Therefore you should be careful about exposing your project's `SECRET_KEY`. If you suspect for any reason a project's `SECRET_KEY` has been compromised, you should replace it immediately - only a few ephemeral data structures (i.e., sessions, cookies) become invalid with this change, until users re-log in again and the new `SECRET_KEY` is used to regenerate these data structures.

Define Administrators for ADMINS and MANAGERS

Once a Django project is made accessible to end users, you'll want some way to receive notifications of important events related to security or other critical factors. Django has two sets of administrative groups defined in `settings.py`: `ADMINS` and `MANAGERS`. By default, both `ADMINS` and `MANAGERS` are empty. The values assigned to both variables need to be tuples, where the first value of the tuple is a name and the second part of the tuple is an email. Listing 5-2 shows a sample definition of `ADMINS` and `MANAGERS`.

Listing 5-2. Django ADMINS and MANAGERS definition

```
ADMINS = (('Webmaster','webmaster@coffeehouse.com'),('Administrator','admin@coffeehouse.com'))

MANAGERS = ADMINS
```

As you can see in Listing 5-2, the `ADMINS` variable is assigned two tuples with different administrators. Next, you can see the `ADMINS` value is assigned to the `MANAGERS` variable. You can, of course, define different values for `MANAGERS` using the same syntax as `ADMINS`, but in this case I just gave both variables the same values for simplicity.

[1]https://docs.djangoproject.com/en/1.11/topics/signing/

The purpose of having these two administrative groups in `settings.py` is for Django to send email notifications of project events. By default, these events are limited and happen under certain circumstances. After all, you don't want to send administrators 10 email notifications every minute, 24/7.

By default, `ADMINS` are sent email notifications of errors associated with the `django.request` or `django.security` packages, if and only if `DEBUG=False`. This is a pretty narrow criteria, as it's intended to notify only the most serious errors - for requests and security - and only for production environments, which is when `DEBUG=False`. For no other events or conditions are the `ADMINS` notified by email.

By default, `MANAGERS` are sent email notifications of broken links (i.e., HTTP 404 page requests), if and only if `DEBUG=False` and the Django middleware `django.middleware.common.BrokenLinkEmailsMiddleware` is enabled. Because HTTP 404 page requests aren't a serious problem, by default `BrokenLinkEmailsMiddleware` is disabled. This is an even narrower criteria than for `ADMINS`, because irrespective of a project being in development (`DEBUG=True`) or production (`DEBUG=False`), the `BrokenLinkEmailsMiddleware` class needs to be added to `MIDDLEWARE` variable in `settings.py` for `MANAGERS` to get notifications. For no other events or conditions are the `MANAGERS` notified by email.

Now that you know the purpose of `ADMINS` and `MANAGERS`, add users and emails as you see fit to your project. Remember you can always leverage the values in `ADMINS` and `MANAGERS` for other custom logic in a Django project (e.g., notify administrators of user signups).

MODIFY LOGGING TO STOP EMAIL NOTIFICATIONS TO ADMINS

By default, users in ADMINS start receiving error emails as soon as you switch to DEBUG=False - this is unlike MANAGERS, which will never receive emails unless you add the BrokenLinkEmailsMiddleware to MIDDLEWARE_CLASSES.

To stop email notifications to ADMINS even when DEBUG=False, you can modify Django's logging settings, which are described in the logging section in this chapter. You can also leave ADMINS undefined so no emails are sent out, but that leaves your project with no ADMINS definitions that may be useful for other purposes.

Use Dynamic Absolute Paths

There are some Django variables in `settings.py` that rely on directory locations, such is the case for `STATIC_ROOT`, which defines a consolidation directory for a project's static files or the `DIRS` list of the `TEMPLATES` variable that defines the location of a project's templates, among other variables.

The problem with variables that rely on directory locations is that if you run the project on different servers or share it with other users, it can be difficult to keep track or reserve the same directories across a series of environments. To solve this issue you can define variables to dynamically determine the absolute paths of a project. Listing 5-3 illustrates a Django project directory structure, deployed to the `/www/` system directory.

Listing 5-3. Django project structure deployed to /www/

```
+-/www/+
       |
       +--STORE--+
                 |
                 +---manage.py
                 |
                 +---coffeestatic--+
                 |                 |
```

```
|                              +-(Consolidated static resources)
|
+---coffeehouse--+
                 |
                 +-__init__.py
                 +-settings.py
                 +-urls.py
                 +-wsgi.py
                 |
                 +---templates---+
                                 +-app_base_template.html
                                 +-app_header_template.html
                                 +-app_footer_template.html
```

Typically a Django `settings.py` file would define the values for `STATIC_ROOT` and `DIRS` in `TEMPLATES` as illustrated in Listing 5-4.

Listing 5-4. Django settings.py with absolute path values

```
# Other configuration variables omitted for brevity
STATIC_ROOT = '/www/STORE/coffeestatic/'

# Other configuration variables omitted for brevity
TEMPLATES = [
{
'BACKEND': 'django.template.backends.django.DjangoTemplates',
'DIRS': ['/www/STORE/coffeehouse/templates/',],
}
]
```

The issue with the setup in Listing 5-4 is it will require editing if you deploy the Django application to a server where the `/www/` directory isn't available (e.g., due to restrictions or a Windows OS where directories start with a leading letter C:/).

An easier approach illustrated in Listing 5-5 is to define variables to dynamically determine the absolute paths of a project.

Listing 5-5. Django settings.py with dynamically determined absolute path

```
import os
BASE_DIR = os.path.dirname(os.path.dirname(os.path.abspath(__file__)))
PROJECT_DIR = os.path.dirname(os.path.abspath(__file__))

# Other configuration variables omitted for brevity
STATIC_ROOT = '%s/coffeestatic/' % (BASE_DIR)

# Other configuration variables omitted for brevity
TEMPLATES = [
{
'BACKEND': 'django.template.backends.django.DjangoTemplates',
'DIRS': ['%s/templates/'% (PROJECT_DIR),],
}
]
```

The variables defined at the top of Listing 5-5 rely on the Python os module to dynamically determine the absolute system path relative to the settings.py file. The PROJECT_DIR=os.path.dirname(os.path.abspath(__file__)) statement gets translated into the /www/STORE/coffeehouse/ value, which is the absolute system directory of files like settings.py. And to access the parent of /www/STORE/coffeehouse/ you simply wrap the same statement with another call to os.path.dirname and define the BASE_DIR variable so it gets translated into the /www/STORE/ value.

The remaining statements in Listing 5-5 use standard Python string substitution to use the PROJECT_DIR and BASE_DIR to set the absolute paths in the STATIC_ROOT and TEMPLATE_DIRS variables. In this manner you don't need to hard-code the absolute paths for any Django configuration variable; the variables automatically adjust to any absolute directory irrespective of the application deployment directory.

Use Multiple Environments or Configuration Files for Django

In every Django project you'll eventually come to the realization that you have to split settings.py into multiple environments or files. This will be either because the values in settings.py need to change between development and production servers, there are multiple people working on the same project with different requirements (e.g., Windows and Linux), or you need to keep sensitive settings.py information (e.g., passwords) in a local file that's not shared with others.

In Django there is no best or standard way to split settings.py into multiple environments or files. In fact, there are many techniques and libraries to make a Django project run with a split settings.py file. Next, I'll present the three most popular options I've used in my projects. Depending on your needs you may feel more comfortable using one option over another or inclusively mixing two or all three of these techniques to achieve an end solution.

Option 1) Multiple environments in the same settings.py file with a control variable

The settings.py file is treated as an ordinary Python file, so there's no limitation to using Python libraries or conditionals to obtain certain behaviors. This means you can easily introduce a control variable based on a fixed value (e.g., server host name) to conditionally set up certain variable values.

For example, changing the DATABASES variable - because passwords and the database name change between development and production - changing the EMAIL_BACKEND variable - since you don't need to send actual emails in development as you do in production - or changing the CACHES variable - since you don't need a cache to speed up performance in development as you need in production.

Listing 5-6 illustrates the setup of a control variable called DJANGO_HOST based on Python's socket module; the variable is then used to load different sets of Django variables based on a server's host name.

Listing 5-6. Django settings.py with control variable with host name to load different sets of variables

```
# Import socket to read host name
import socket
# If the host name starts with 'live', DJANGO_HOST = "production"
if socket.gethostname().startswith('live'):
    DJANGO_HOST = "production"
# Else if host name starts with 'test', set DJANGO_HOST = "test"
elif socket.gethostname().startswith('test'):
    DJANGO_HOST = "testing"
else:
# If host doesn't match, assume it's a development server, set DJANGO_HOST = "development"
    DJANGO_HOST = "development"
```

```
# Define general behavior variables for DJANGO_HOST and all others
if DJANGO_HOST == "production":
    DEBUG = False
    STATIC_URL = 'http://static.coffeehouse.com/'
else:
    DEBUG = True
    STATIC_URL = '/static/'

# Define DATABASES variable for DJANGO_HOST and all others
if DJANGO_HOST == "production":
   # Use mysql for live host
   DATABASES = {
    'default': {
        'NAME': 'housecoffee',
        'ENGINE': 'django.db.backends.mysql',
        'USER': 'coffee',
        'PASSWORD': 'secretpass'
    }
  }
else:
   # Use sqlite for non live host
   DATABASES = {
    'default': {
        'ENGINE': 'django.db.backends.sqlite3',
        'NAME': os.path.join(BASE_DIR, 'coffee.sqlite3'),
    }
  }

# Define EMAIL_BACKEND variable for DJANGO_HOST
if DJANGO_HOST == "production":
    # Output to SMTP server on DJANGO_HOST production
    EMAIL_BACKEND = 'django.core.mail.backends.smtp.EmailBackend'
elif DJANGO_HOST == "testing":
    # Nullify output on DJANGO_HOST test
    EMAIL_BACKEND = 'django.core.mail.backends.dummy.EmailBackend'
else:
    # Output to console for all others
    EMAIL_BACKEND = 'django.core.mail.backends.console.EmailBackend'

# Define CACHES variable for DJANGO_HOST production and all other hosts
if DJANGO_HOST == "production":
   # Set cache
   CACHES = {
        'default': {
            'BACKEND': 'django.core.cache.backends.memcached.MemcachedCache',
            'LOCATION': '127.0.0.1:11211',
            'TIMEOUT':'1800',
            }
        }
   CACHE_MIDDLEWARE_SECONDS = 1800
```

```
else:
   # No cache for all other hosts
   pass
```

The first line in Listing 5-6 imports the Python socket module to gain access to the host name. Next, a series of conditionals are declared using socket.gethostname() to determine the value of the control variable DJANGO_HOST. If the host name starts with the letters live the DJANGO_HOST variable is set to "production", if the host name starts with test then DJANGO_HOST is set to "testing", and if the host name starts with neither of the previous options then DJANGO_HOST is set to "development".

In this scenario, the string method startswith is used to determine how to set the control variable based on the host name. However, you can just as easily use any other Python library or even criteria (e.g., IP address) to set the control variable. In addition, since the control variable is based on a string, you can introduce as many configuration variations as needed. In this case we use three different variations to set settings.py variables - "production","testing" and "development" - but you could easily define five or a dozen variations if you require such an amount of different setups.

Option 2) Multiple environment files using configparser

Another variation to split settings.py is to rely on Python's built-in configparser module. configparser allows Django to read configuration variables from files that use a data structure similar to the one used in Microsoft Windows INI files. Listing 5-7 illustrates a sample configparser file.

Listing 5-7. Python configparser sample file production.cfg

```
[general]
DEBUG: false
STATIC_URL: http://static.coffeehouse.com/

[databases]
NAME: housecoffee
ENGINE: django.db.backends.mysql
USER: coffee
PASSWORD: secretpass

[security]
SECRET_KEY: %%ea)cjy@v9(7!b(20gl+4-6iur28dy=tc4f$-zbm-v=!t
```

As you can see in Listing 5-7, the format for a configparser file is structured in various sections declared between brackets (e.g., [general], [databases]) and below each section are the different keys and values. The variables in Listing 5-7 represents a production environment placed in a file named production.cfg. I chose the .cfg extension for this file, but you can use the .config or .ini extensions if you like; the extension is irrelevant to Python - the only thing that matters is the data format in the file itself.

Similar to the contents in production.cfg, you can create other files with different variables for other environments (e.g., testing.cfg, development.cfg). Once you have the configparser file or files, then you can import them into a Django settings.py. Listing 5-8 shows a sample settings.py that uses values from a configparser file.

Listing 5-8. Django settings.py with configparser import

```
import os

BASE_DIR = os.path.dirname(os.path.dirname(os.path.abspath(__file__)))
PROJECT_DIR = os.path.dirname(os.path.abspath(__file__))

# Access configparser to load variable values
from django.utils.six.moves import configparser
config = configparser.SafeConfigParser(allow_no_value=True)

# Import socket to read host name
import socket
# If the host name starts with 'live', load configparser from "production.cfg"
if socket.gethostname().startswith('live'):
    config.read('%s/production.cfg' % (PROJECT_DIR))
# Else if host name starts with 'test', load configparser from "testing.cfg"
elif socket.gethostname().startswith('test'):
    config.read('%s/testing.cfg' % (PROJECT_DIR))
else:
# If host doesn't match, assume it's a development server, load configparser from
"development.cfg"
    config.read('%s/development.cfg' % (PROJECT_DIR))

DEBUG = config.get('general', 'DEBUG')
STATIC_URL = config.get('general', 'STATIC_URL')

DATABASES = {
    'default': {
        'NAME': config.get('databases', 'NAME'),
        'ENGINE': config.get('databases', 'ENGINE'),
        'USER': config.get('databases', 'USER'),
        'PASSWORD': config.get('databases', 'PASSWORD')
    }
  }

SECRET_KEY = config.get('security', 'SECRET_KEY')
```

■ **Note** The configuration in Listing 5-8 assumes the host name starts with the name live in order to load configparser production.cfg in Listing 5-7. Adjust conditionals at the start of Listing 5-8 to match the host name and load the appropriate configparser file.

As you can see in Listing 5-8, configparser is loaded into Django via `django.utils.six.moves`, which is a utility to allow cross-imports between Python 2 and Python 3. In Python 2 the configparser package is actually named `ConfigParser`, but this utility allows us to use the same import statement using either Python 2 or Python 3. After the import, we use the `SafeConfigParser` class with the argument `allow_no_value=True` to allow processing of empty values in configparser keys.

Then we rely on the same prior technique using Python's socket module to gain access to the host name and determine which configparser file to load. The configparser file is loaded using the read method of the SafeConfigParser instance. At this juncture all configparser variables are loaded and ready for access. The remainder of Listing 5-8 shows a series of standard Django settings.py variables that are assigned their value using the get method of the SafeConfigParser instance, where the first argument is the configparser section and the second argument is the key variable.

So there you have another option on how to split the variables in settings.py into multiple environments. Like I mentioned at the start, there's no best or standard way of doing this. Some people like configparser better because it splits values into separate files and avoids the many conditionals of option 1, but other people can hate configparser because of the need to deal with the special syntax and separate files. Choose whatever feels best for your project.

Option 3) Multiple settings.py files with different names for each environment

Finally, another option to split Django variables into multiple environments is to create multiple settings.py files with different names. By default, Django looks for configuration variables in the settings.py file in a project's base directory.

However, it's possible to tell Django to load a configuration file with a different name. Django uses the operating system (OS) variable DJANGO_SETTINGS_MODULE for this purpose. By default, Django sets this OS variable to <project_name>.settings in the manage.py file located in the base directory of any Django project. And since the manage.py file is used to bootstrap Django applications, the DJANGO_SETTINGS_MODULE value in this file guarantees configuration variables are always loaded from the settings.py file inside the <project_name> subdirectory.

So let's suppose you create different settings.py files for a Django application - placed in the same directory as settings.py - named production.py, testing.py, and development.py. You have two options to load these different files.

One option is to change the DJANGO_SETTINGS_MODULE definition in a project's manage.py file to the file with the desired configuration (e.g., os.environ.setdefault("DJANGO_SETTINGS_MODULE", "coffeehouse.production") to load the production.py configuration file). However, hard-coding this value is inflexible because you would need to constantly change the value in manage.py based on the desired configuration. Here you could use a control variable in manage.py to dynamically determine the DJANGO_SETTINGS_MODULE value based on a host name - similar to the process described in the previous option 1 for settings.py.

Another possibility to set DJANGO_SETTINGS_MODULE without altering manage.py is to define DJANGO_SETTINGS_MODULE at the OS level so it overrides the definition in manage.py. Listing 5-9 illustrates how to set the DJANGO_SETTINGS_MODULE variable on a Linux/Unix OS so that application variables in the testing.py file are used instead of the settings.py file.

Listing 5-9. Override DJANGO_SETTINGS_MODULE to load application variables from a file called testing.py and not the default settings.py

```
$ export DJANGO_SETTINGS_MODULE=coffeehouse.load_testing
$ python manage.py runserver
Validating models...

0 errors found
Django version 1.11, using settings 'coffeehouse.load_testing'
Development server is running at http://127.0.0.1:8000/
Quit the server with CONTROL-C.
```

In Listing 5-9 we use the standard Linux/Unix syntax `export variable_name=variable_value` to set an environment variable. Once this is done, notice the Django application that uses the development server displays the startup message "`using settings 'coffeehouse.load_testing'`".

If you plan to override the `DJANGO_SETTINGS_MODULE` at the OS level to load different Django application variables, be aware that by default OS variables aren't permanent or inherited. This means you may need to define the `DJANGO_SETTINGS_MODULE` for every shell from which you start Django and also define it as a local variable for runtime environments (e.g., Apache).

Set Up Static Web Page Resources - Images, CSS, JavaScript

The setup process for static resources in Django projects varies considerably if a project runs with `DEBUG=True` or `DEBUG=False`. This means static resource deployment depends on whether you're doing work on a development environment - where you generally use `DEBUG=True` - or on a production environment - where you generally use `DEBUG=False`.

Considering you'll always start a Django project in a development environment and later migrate to a production environment, I'll describe the development set up process first and later describe the production setup process.

Set Up Static Resources in a Development Environment (DEBUG=False)

By default when `DEBUG=False`, Django automatically sets up static resources from two major locations. The first location is `static` folders in all Django apps and the second location is folders declared in the `STATICFILES_DIR` variable in `settings.py`.

Although you'll need to manually create the `static` folder inside Django apps, it's this easy to set up static resources in a project. Because Django sets up all the `static` folders for every project app, it's a recommended practice to further add a subdirectory to the `static` folder (e.g., `<app_folder>/static/<app_name>/<static_files_here>`) to qualify static resources and avoid potential naming conflicts. Listing 5-10 illustrates a sample directory structure for static resources.

Listing 5-10. Django app structure with static directories

```
+-<BASE_DIR_project_name>
|
+-manage.py
|
+-bootstrap-3.1.1-dist+
|                    +-bootstrap.min.js
|
+-jquery-1-11-1-dist+
|                  +jquery.min.js
|
+-jquery-ui-1.10.4+
|                +jquery-ui.min.js
|
+-website-static-default+
|                      +-favicon.ico
|                      +-robots.txt
|
|
```

```
+---+-<PROJECT_DIR_project_name>
    |
    +-__init__.py
    +-settings.py
    +-urls.py
    +-wsgi.py
    |
    +-about(app)-+
    |            +-__init__.py
    |            +-models.py
    |            +-tests.py
    |            +-views.py
    |            +-static-+
    |                     |
    |                     +-about-+
    |                             +-img-+
    |                             |     +-logo.png
    |                             |
    |                             +-css-+
    |                                   +-custom.css
    +-stores(app)-+
                 +-__init__.py
                 +-models.py
                 +-tests.py
                 +-views.py
                 +-static-+
                          |
                          +-stores-+
                                   +-img-+
                                   |     +-coffee.gif
                                   |
                                   +-css-+
                                         +-custom.css
```

As illustrated in Listing 5-10, all Django app directories have a `static` subdirectory that contains static resources. Anything under these static subdirectories is set up for access.

Also notice in Listing 5-10 the importance of the app name subdirectory within the `static` subdirectories that acts as a namespace. If static resources were placed directly below the `static` folder in all apps, in this scenario it would lead to two identical file paths named `/static/css/custom.css`, In which case a call to load this static resource would lead to a conflict. Technically, Django always uses the first file it finds, but will the first one be the right one? By using an app name subdirectory inside `static` it avoids any potential conflict, with one static resource set up at `/static/about/css/custom.css` and the other at `/static/stores/css/custom.css`.

Because there can be static resources that don't necessarily belong to a specific project app, Django also supports the ability to set up static resources stored on any subdirectory.

If you look again at Listing 5-10 in between the `BASE_DIR` and `PROJECT_DIR`, you'll see there are various subfolders that contain popular static resource libraries - `jquery`, `jquery-ui` and `bootstrap`-- as well as a subfolder `website-static-default` with a web site's standard static resources – `robots.txt & favicon.ico`.

In order to set up these additional static resources, you define the location of these directories in the `STATICFILES_DIR` variable in `settings.py`. Listing 5-11 illustrates an example of a `STATICFILES_DIR` definition.

Listing 5-11. Django STATICFILES_DIR definition with namespaces in settings.py

```
BASE_DIR = os.path.dirname(os.path.dirname(os.path.abspath(__file__)))

STATICFILES_DIRS = ('%s/website-static-default/'% (BASE_DIR),
                    ('bootstrap','%s/bootstrap-3.1.1-dist/'% (BASE_DIR)),
                    ('jquery','%s/jquery-1-11-1-dist/'% (BASE_DIR)),
                    ('jquery-ui','%s/jquery-ui-1.10.4/'% (BASE_DIR)),)
```

As you can see in Listing 5-11, `STATICFILES_DIRS` accepts a list of directories. In this case, all directories are under a Django project's `BASE_DIR`, so it's using the `BASE_DIR` variable that dynamically determines the parent directory. Another aspect of the directory list in Listing 5-11 is you can optionally declare a namespace, similar to the approach used in an app's `static` subdirectories.

The first directory definition in Listing 5-11 is a simple string (i.e., it has no namespace), which means the static resources in `website-static-default` is set up with a direct access pattern. The remaining directory definitions are tuples and not strings. By using a tuple, it defines the first part of the tuple as the namespace and the second part as the directory with the static resources. Definitions with a namespace mean that all static resources under a given directory will use a prefix namespace in their access pattern (e.g., to access static resources on `bootstrap-3.1.1-dist` the access pattern should be prefixed with `bootstrap`).

Now that you know where and how to set up all static resources, let's take a quick look at how Django *visualizes* these static resources to understand what the final access patterns for static resources look like. Listing 5-12 shows a *visualization* of the static resources presented in the previous listings.

Listing 5-12. Django visualization of static resources in apps and STATICFILES_DIRS

```
+-favicon.ico
+-robots.txt
|
+-jquery+
|       +jquery.min.js
|
+-jquery-ui+
|          +jquery-ui.min.js
|
+-bootstrap+
|          +-bootstrap.css
|
+-about-+
|       +-img-+
|       |     +-logo.png
|       |
|       +-css-+
|             +-custom.css
|
+-stores-+
         +-img-+
         |     +-coffee.gif
         |
         +-css-+
               +-custom.css
```

The files `favicon.ico` and `robots.txt` in Listing 5-12 are in the top level of the visualization because their source directory - `website-static-default` - was defined without a namespace in `STATICFILES_DIRS`.

The remainder of the static resources are all grouped in subfolders because we either defined a namespace for them in `STATICFILES_DIRS` or defined a subfolder as a namespace within an app's `static` subdirectory.

Now that you understand how Django visualizes static resources as a group and how this determines the final access pattern for static resources, let's turn our attention to the `STATIC_URL` variable in `settings.py`.

The `STATIC_URL` is used to define a URL entry point into Django's visualization of static resources presented in Listing 5-12. By default, `STATIC_URL` is assigned the `/static/` value. This means that if `STATIC_URL='/static/'`, the static resource `robots.txt` becomes accessible at the URL `/static/robots.txt`, just like `stores/img/coffee.gif` becomes accessible at the URL `/static/stores/img/coffee.gif`.

This means you access static resources on the `/static/` URL, or on a different URL if you change the `STATIC_URL` value. However, don't go and hard-code these static resources paths on templates! (e.g., `<img src="/static/stores/img/coffee.gif"/>`). You should use a variable so the final path is determined dynamically in case `STATIC_URL` changes. The next section describes how to do this in Django templates.

■ **Caution** Automatic access to static resources only works with Django's built-in web server and when DEBUG=True.

The previous setup process for static resources has a little 'behind the scenes' help from Django. It only works with Django's built-in web server (i.e., `python manage.py runserver`) and only if `DEBUG=True`. As soon as you change to a different web server or switch `DEBUG=False` even using Django's built-in web server, no static resource will be available as visualized in Listing 5-12.

The primary reason behind this behavior is because reserving and dispatching static resources from an application's main web server/URL structure (e.g., `/static/`) is very inefficient. So this just works as a convenience in development using Django's built-in web server and when `DEBUG=True`. Of course, you can assign a full URL domain to `STATIC_URL` (e.g., `http://static.coffeehouse.com/`) but this assumes you've already set up the project's static resources on a production-like environment, something that I'll discuss shortly once I describe how to access static resources in Django and Jinja templates.

Access Static Resources in Django Templates

The recommended approach to reference static resources in Django templates is through staticfiles app via the `{% static %}` tag. Listing 5-13 illustrates various examples of the staticfiles app syntax.

Listing 5-13. Django {% static %} tag to reference static resources

```
{% load static %}

# For static resource at about/img/logo.png
<img src="{% static 'about/img/logo.gif' %}">

# For static resource at bootstrap/bootstrap.css
<link href="{% static 'bootstrap/bootstrap.css' %}" rel="stylesheet">

# For static resource at jquery/jquery.min.js
<script src="{% static 'jquery/jquery.min.js' %}"></script>
```

First it's important to note the `{% load static %}` tag in Listing 5-13 is available through the staticfiles app, which is installed by default on all Django projects in the `INSTALLED_APPS` variable. If for some reason you modified the default values in `INSTALLED_APPS`, make sure you have the `django.contrib.staticfiles` value in the `INSTALLED_APPS` variable or none of what follows will work.

As you can see in Listing 5-13, at the top of the template you always declare the `{% load static %}` statement. Once this is done, a template can use the `{% static %}` tag to generate dynamic paths for static resources. In most circumstances, the `{% static %}` tag relies on the `STATIC_URL` variable in `settings.py` to generate an appropriate path to the static resources.

For more advanced cases, the `{% static %}` tag uses a combination of the same `STATIC_URL` variable and the backing storage technology (e.g., CDN-'Content Delivery Network') configuration to generate an appropriate path to the static resources.

For example, notice in Listing 5-13 how the `{% static %}` tag is always followed by a file path identical to the Django visualization of static resources in Listing 5-12. Due to the `STATIC_URL` variable having a value of `/static/`, it means the `{% static %}` statements in Listing 5-13 get substituted with this value (e.g., `{% static 'bootstrap/bootstrap.css' %}` becomes `/static/bootstrap/bootstrap.css`).

The cases where the `{% static %}` tag gets substituted for something different than the `STATIC_URL` variable are when a Django project uses a nonstandard back end to serve static resources - this last scenario is briefly discussed in the sidebar below.

WHY USE THE STATICFILES {% STATIC %} TAG VS. USING THE STATIC_URL VARIABLE DIRECTLY IN TEMPLATES?

In the early versions of Django, Django templates used the STATIC_URL variable directly in templates (e.g., <img src="{{STATIC_URL}}about/img/logo.gif">). A trace of this remains in the fact that you can still gain access to the STATIC_URL variable on all Django templates via the django.template.context_processors.static context processor.

However, with the underlying technology to serve static resources becoming more sophisticated, the STATIC_URL variable by itself proves insufficient. For example, static-serving technologies like CDNs or Amazon S3 often use special tokens to enforce authentication or caching strategies. This means a statement like <img src="{{STATIC_URL}}about/img/logo.gif"> needs to be converted into something like <img src="`http://cdnprovider.com/about/img/logo.gif?token=e354534566`"> or <img src="`http://staticresources.com/about/img/logo32AzTB9r5.gif`">. And while it's possible to change the STATIC_URL variable to a full domain, what becomes difficult is to modify the static resource's path itself.

Rewriting a static resource's path with a tag like {% static %} is easy. Because {% static %} can take a static resource's base string (e.g., about/img/logo.gif) and dynamically produce a full path with the STATIC_URL variable and any special tokens required by the underlying static-serving technology. This process is achieved by using a custom storage class – designed for the static-serving technology.

Granted not all projects require the use of advanced static-serving technologies. But by using the {% static %} tag of the staticfiles app to declare static resources in Django templates, you ensure a Django project is capable of using any static-serving technology, from the most basic to the most advanced.

Access Static Resources in Jinja Templates

Jinja templates offer an alternative to Django's own templates, as described in the previous chapter. But unlike Django templates, you'll have to follow a different setup to use something like Django's `{% static %}` tag from the staticfiles app in Jinja templates.

To be able to use the same staticfiles app / `{% static %}` tag behavior in Jinja templates, you'll need to set up a global variable named static that hooks into this functionality. In the previous chapter on Jinja template, the section "Set Up Data for Access on All Jinja Templates in Django (like Django Context Processors)" describes how to create a global variable with this functionality.

Set Up Static Resources in a Production Environment (DEBUG=True)

When you switch your Django project's `DEBUG` variable to `True` or change to a different web server (e.g., Apache, Nginx), you'll be surprised that none of the static resources in your project appear anymore. Don't be alarmed, this is by design. It isn't too difficult to set up Django to serve static resources when `DEBUG=True` with Django's built-in web server or if you switch to a third-party web server.

■ **Tip** You can access static resources to make Django's built-in web server serve static resources as if DEBUG=False when it's actually set to DEBUG=True. Run the web server with the --insecure flag: python manage.py runserver –insecure.

■ **Caution** Although the previous workaround is available, I recommend you don't use it, in case the flag name itself --insecure wasn't enough to keep you from using it.

Django's built-in web server (i.e., `python manage.py runserver`) is really a convenience tool to get up and running quickly, which as part of this convenience also serves static resources when `DEBUG=False`.

However, it really is wasteful to allow the same web server process to handle both dynamic content (Django web pages) and static resources (Images, CSS, JavaScript). The recommended approach is to use a separate web server entirely to serve static resources, which is why Django goes to the extent of breaking this convenience in its built-in web server when switching the `DEBUG=True`.

The first thing you need to do when `DEBUG=True` is create a directory to hold a copy of all the static resources Django visualizes as static resources. Previously you learned that when `DEBUG=False`, Django visualizes static resources from several locations and subdirectories in a single tree - illustrated in Listing 5-12. It's precisely this single tree Django visualizes that you need to create a copy of to run on a production environment.

You'll need to define the `STATIC_ROOT` variable in `settings.py`. The value you assign to `STATIC_ROOT` should be a directory and it will be where Django copies all of your project's static resources - identical to how Django visualizes them when `DEBUG=True` as illustrated in Listing 5-12. Note this directory should be empty, as it's overwritten constantly each time you perform a syncing process. The location of this directory could be anywhere on your system depending on your needs. For simplicity, I'll keep the `STATIC_ROOT` directory under the Django project's `BASE_DIR` as `STATIC_ROOT = '%s/coffeestatic/'% (BASE_DIR)`.

To trigger the syncing process (i.e., copy all static resources to `STATIC_ROOT`), you'll need to use the `collectstatic` command available in the `manage.py` script. Listing 5-14 illustrates the sample output of the syncing process.

Listing 5-14. Django collectstatic command to copy all static resources

```
[user@coffeehouse ~]$ python manage.py collectstatic

You have requested to collect static files at the destination
location as specified in your settings:

    /www/STORE/coffeestatic

This will overwrite existing files!
Are you sure you want to do this?

Type 'yes' to continue, or 'no' to cancel: yes
yes
Copying '/www/STORE/website-static-default/sitemap.xml'
Copying '/www/STORE/website-static-default/robots.txt'
Copying '/www/STORE/website-static-default/favicon.ico'
....
....
....
Copying '/www/STORE/coffeehouse/about/static/css/custom.css'

732 static files copied to '/www/STORE/coffeestatic'.
```

Once you collect all your project's static resources in a single folder - in this case `/www/STORE/coffeestatic` - they're ready to be set up on a production server (e.g., Apache, Nginx, or AWS S3). Keep in mind the directory/file structure generated by `collectstatic` is identical to the one visualized by Django in the previous section illustrated in Listing 5-12.

The final step you need to do is update the `STATIC_URL` value in `settings.py` to reflect the new location of the static resources. For example, if you mount the `/www/STORE/coffeestatic/` directory on Apache or Nginx under the `http://static.coffeehouse.com/` domain, you would set `STATIC_URL='http://static.coffeehouse.com'`. Similarly, if you copy the static resources in `/www/STORE/coffeestatic/` to an Amazon AWS S3 bucket named `http://coffeehouse.s3.amazonaws.com`, you would set `STATIC_URL='http://coffeehouse.s3.amazonaws.com'`

Once you make this last change, all the statements in your Django templates that use the `{% static %}` tag get updated with this new full-domain URL, in which case a resource like `/www/STORE/coffeestatic/bootstrap/bootstrap.css` becomes available at `http://static.coffeehouse.com/bootstrap/bootstrap.css` or `http://coffeehouse.s3.amazonaws.com/bootstrap/bootstrap.css`.

Django Logging

Logging is one of the most useful and also one of the most underused application management practices. If you're still not using logging in your Django projects or are using Python `print()` statements to gain insight into what an application is doing, you're missing out on a great of functionalities. Up next, you'll learn about Python core logging concepts, how to set up Django custom logging, and how to use a monitoring service to track log messages.

Python Core Logging Concepts

Django is built on top of Python's logging package. The Python logging package provides a robust and flexible way to set up application logging. In case you've never used Python's logging package, I'll provide a brief overview of its core concepts. There are four core concepts in Python logging:

- Loggers.- Provide the initial entry point to group log messages. Generally, each Python module (i.e., .py file) has a single logger to assign its log messages. However, it's also possible to define multiple loggers in the same module (e.g., one logger for business logic, another logger for database logic, etc.). In addition, it's also possible to use the same logger across multiple Python modules or .py files.
- Handlers.- Are used to redirect log messages (created by loggers) to a destination. Destinations can include flat files, a server's console, an email or SMS messages, among other destinations. It's possible to use the same handler in multiple loggers, just as it's possible for a logger to use multiple handlers.
- Filters.- Offer a way to apply rules on log messages. For example, you can use a filter to send log messages generated by the same logger to different handlers.
- Formatters.- Are used to specify the final format for log messages.

With this brief overview of Python logging concepts, let's jump straight into exploring Django's default logging functionality.

Django Default Logging

The logging configuration for Django projects is defined in the `LOGGING` variable in `settings.py`. For the moment, don't even bother opening your project's `settings.py` file because you won't see `LOGGING` in it. This variable isn't hard-coded when you create a project, but it does have some logging values in effect if it isn't declared. Listing 5-15 shows the default `LOGGING` values if it isn't declared in `settings.py`.

Listing 5-15. Default LOGGING in Django projects

```
LOGGING = {
    'version': 1,
    'disable_existing_loggers': False,
    'filters': {
        'require_debug_false': {
            '()': 'django.utils.log.RequireDebugFalse',
        },
        'require_debug_true': {
            '()': 'django.utils.log.RequireDebugTrue',
        },
    },
    'handlers': {
        'console': {
            'level': 'INFO',
            'filters': ['require_debug_true'],
            'class': 'logging.StreamHandler',
        },
        'null': {
            'class': 'logging.NullHandler',
        },
```

```
        'mail_admins': {
            'level': 'ERROR',
            'filters': ['require_debug_false'],
            'class': 'django.utils.log.AdminEmailHandler'
        }
    },
    'loggers': {
        'django': {
            'handlers': ['console'],
        },
        'django.request': {
            'handlers': ['mail_admins'],
            'level': 'ERROR',
            'propagate': False,
        },
        'django.security': {
            'handlers': ['mail_admins'],
            'level': 'ERROR',
            'propagate': False,
        },
        'py.warnings': {
            'handlers': ['console'],
        },
    }
}
```

In summary, the default Django logging settings illustrated in Listing 5-15 have the following logging behaviors:

- Console logging or the `console` handler is only done when `DEBUG=True`, for log messages worse than `INFO` (inclusive) and only for the Python package `django` - and its children (e.g., `django.request`, `django.contrib`) - as well as the Python package `py.warnings`.
- Admin logging or the `mail_admins` handler - which sends emails to `ADMINS` – is only done when `DEBUG=False`, for log messages worse than `ERROR` (inclusive), and only for the Python packages `django.request` and `django.security`.

Let's first break down the `handlers` section in Listing 5-14. Handlers define locations to send log messages and there are three in Listing 5-14: `console`, `null` and `mail_admins`. The handler names by themselves do nothing - they are simply reference names - the relevant actions are defined in the associated properties dictionary. All the handlers have a `class` property that defines the backing Python class that does the actual work.

The `console` handler is assigned the `logging.StreamHandler` class that is part of the core Python logging package. This class sends logging output to streams such as standard input and standard error, and as the handler name suggests, this is technically the system console or screen where Django runs.

The `null` handler is assigned the `logging.NullHandler` class, which is also part of the core Python logging package and which generates no output.

The `mail_admins` handler is assigned the `django.utils.log.AdminEmailHandler` class, which is a Django custom handler utility that sends logging output as an email to people defined as `ADMINS` in `settings.py` - see the previous section on setting up `settings.py` for the real world for more information on the `ADMINS` variable.

Another property in handlers is `level`, which defines the threshold level at which the handler must accept log messages. There are five threshold levels for Python logging, from worst to least worst they are `CRITICAL`, `ERROR`, `WARNING`, `INFO`, and `DEBUG`. The `INFO` level for the `console` handler indicates that all log messages worse or equal to `INFO` - which is every level, except `DEBUG` - should be processed by the handler, a reasonable setting as the console can handle many messages. The `ERROR` level for the `mail_admins` handler indicates that only messages worse or equal to `ERROR` - which is just `CRITICAL` - should be processed by the handler, a reasonable setting as only the two worst types of error messages should trigger emails to administrators.

The other property in handlers is `filters`, which defines an additional layer to restrict log messages for a handler. Handlers can accept multiple filters, which is why the `filters` property accepts a Python list. The `console` handler has a single filter `require_debug_true` and the `mail_admins` handler has a single filter `require_debug_false`.

Filters are defined in their own block as you can observe in Listing 5-15. The `require_debug_false` filter is backed by the `django.utils.log.RequireDebugFalse` class, which checks if a Django project has `DEBUG=False`, whereas the `require_debug_true` filter is backed by the `django.utils.log.RequireDebugTrue` class, which checks if a project has `DEBUG=True`. This means the `console` handler only accepts log messages if a Django project has `DEBUG=True` and the `mail_admins` handler only accepts log messages if a Django project has `DEBUG=False`.

Now that you understand handlers and filters, let's take a look at the `loggers` section. Logger definitions generally map directly to Python packages and have parent-child relationships. For example, Python modules (i.e., `.py` files) that belong to a package named `coffeehouse` generally have a logger named `coffeehouse` and Python modules that belong to the package `coffeehouse.about` generally have a logger named `coffeehouse.about`. The dot notation in logger names also represents a parent-child relationship, so the `coffeehouse.about` logger is considered the child of the `coffeehouse` logger.

In Listing 5-15 there are four loggers: `django`, `django.request`, `django.security`, and `py.warnings`. The `django` logger indicates that all log messages associated with it and its children be processed by the `console` handler.

The `django.request` logger indicates that all log messages associated with it and its children be processed by the `mail_admins` handler. The `django.request` logger also has the `'level':'ERROR'` property to provide the threshold level at which the logger should accept log messages - a property that overrides the `handler` level property. And in addition, the `django.request` logger also has the `'propagate':'False'` statement to indicate the logger should not propagate messages to parent loggers (e.g., `django` is the parent of `django.request`).

Next, we have the `django.security` logger that is identical in functionality to the `django.request` logger. And the `py.warnings` that indicate that all log messages associated with it and its children be processed by the `console` handler.

Finally, there are the first two lines in Listing 5-15 that are associated with Python logging in general. The `version` key identifies the configuration version as `1`, which at present is the only Python logging version. And the `disable_existing_loggers` key is used to disable all existing Python loggers. If `disable_existing_loggers` is `False` it keeps the preexisting logger values and if it's set to `True` it disables all preexisting loggers values. Note that even if you use `'disable_existing_loggers': False` in your own `LOGGING` variable you can redefine/override some or all of the preexisting logger values.

Now that you have a firm understanding of what Django logging does in its default state, I'll describe how to create log messages in a Django project and then describe how to create custom `LOGGING` configurations.

Create Log Messages

At the top of any Python module or `.py` file you can create loggers by using the `getLogger` method of the Python `logging` package. The `getLogger` method receives the name of the logger as its input parameter. Listing 5-16 illustrates the creation of two logger instances using `__name__` and the hard-coded `dba` name.

Listing 5-16. Define loggers in a Python module

```
# Python logging package
import logging

# Standard instance of a logger with __name__
stdlogger = logging.getLogger(__name__)

# Custom instance logging with explicit name
dbalogger = logging.getLogger('dba')
```

The Python `__name__` syntax used for `getLogger` in Listing 5-16 automatically assigns the package name as the logger name. This means that if the logger is defined in a module under the application directory `coffeehouse/about/views.py`, the logger receives the name `coffeehouse.about.views`. So by relying on the `__name__` syntax, loggers are automatically created based on the origin of the log message.

Don't worry about having dozens or hundreds of loggers in a Django project for each module or `.py` file. As described in the past section, Python logging works with inheritance, so you can define a single handler for a parent logger (e.g., `coffeehouse`) that handles all children loggers (e.g., `coffeehouse.about`, `coffeehouse.about.views`,`coffeehouse.drinks`, `coffeehouse.drinks.models`).

Sometimes it's convenient to define a logger with an explicit name to classify certain types of messages. In Listing 5-16 you can see a logger named `dba` that's used for messages related to databases issues. This way database administrators can consult their own logging stream without the need to see log messages from other parts of the application.

Once you have loggers in a module or `.py` file, you can define log messages with one of several methods depending on the severity of a message that needs to be reported. These methods are illustrated in the following list:

- <logger_name>.critical().- Most severe logging level. Use it to report potentially catastrophic application events (e.g., something that can halt or crash an application).
- <logger_name>.error().- Second most severe logging level. Use it to report important events (e.g., unexpected behaviors or conditions that cause end users to see an error).
- <logger_name>.warning().- Mid-level logging level. Use it to report relatively important events (e.g., unexpected behaviors or conditions that shouldn't happen, yet don't cause end users to notice the issue).
- <logger_name>.info().- Informative logging level. Use it to report informative events in an application (e.g., application milestones or user activity).
- <logger_name>.debug().- Debug logging level. Use it to report step-by-step logic that can be difficult to write (e.g., complex business logic or database queries).
- <logger_name>.log().- Use it to manually emit log messages with a specific log level.
- <logger_name>.exception().- Use it to create an error level logging message, wrapped with the current exception stack.

What methods you use to log messages across your project depends entirely up to you. As far as the logging levels are concerned, just try to be consistent with the selection criteria. You can always adjust the runtime logging level to deactivate log messages of a certain level.

In addition, I would also recommend you use the most descriptive log messages possible to maximize the benefits of logging. Listing 5-17 illustrates a series of examples using several logging methods and messages.

Listing 5-17. Define log messages in a Python module

```
# Python logging package
import logging

# Standard instance of a logger with __name__
stdlogger = logging.getLogger(__name__)

# Custom instance logging with explicit name
dbalogger = logging.getLogger('dba')

def index(request):
    stdlogger.debug("Entering index method")

def contactform(request):
    stdlogger.info("Call to contactform method")

    try:
         stdlogger.debug("Entering store_id conditional block")
         # Logic to handle store_id
    except Exception, e:
         stdlogger.exception(e)

    stdlogger.info("Starting search on DB")
    try:
         stdlogger.info("About to search db")
         # Loging to search db
    except Exception, e:
         stdlogger.error("Error in searchdb method")
         dbalogger.error("Error in searchdb method, stack %s" % (e))
```

As you can see in Listing 5-17, there are various log messages of different levels using both loggers described in Listing 5-16. The log messages are spread out depending on their level in either the method body or inside try/except blocks.

If you place the loggers and logging statements like the ones in Listing 5-17 in a Django project, you'll see that logging-wise nothing happens! In fact, what you'll see in the console are messages in the form `'No handlers could be found for logger ...<logger_name>'`.

This is because by default Django doesn't know anything about your loggers! It only knows about the default loggers described in Listing 5-15. In the next section, I'll describe how to create a custom `LOGGING` configuration so you can see your project log messages.

Custom Logging

Since there are four different components you can mix and match in Django logging (i.e., loggers, handlers, filters, and formatters), there is an almost endless amount of variations to create custom logging configurations.

In the following sections, I'll describe some of the most common custom logging configuration for Django projects, which include overriding default Django logging behaviors (e.g., not sending emails), customizing the format of log messages, and sending logging output to different loggers (e.g., files).

Listing 5-18 illustrates a custom LOGGING configuration you would place in a project's settings.py file, covering these common requirements. The sections that follow explain each configuration option.

Listing 5-18. Custom LOGGING Django configuration

```
LOGGING = {
    'version': 1,
    'disable_existing_loggers': True,
    'filters': {
        'require_debug_false': {
            '()': 'django.utils.log.RequireDebugFalse',
        },
        'require_debug_true': {
            '()': 'django.utils.log.RequireDebugTrue',
        },
    },
    'formatters': {
        'simple': {
            'format': '[%(asctime)s] %(levelname)s %(message)s',
            'datefmt': '%Y-%m-%d %H:%M:%S'
        },
        'verbose': {
            'format': '[%(asctime)s] %(levelname)s [%(name)s.%(funcName)s:%(lineno)d]
            %(message)s',
            'datefmt': '%Y-%m-%d %H:%M:%S'
        },
    },
    'handlers': {
        'console': {
            'level': 'DEBUG',
            'filters': ['require_debug_true'],
            'class': 'logging.StreamHandler',
            'formatter': 'simple'
        },
        'development_logfile': {
            'level': 'DEBUG',
            'filters': ['require_debug_true'],
            'class': 'logging.FileHandler',
            'filename': '/tmp/django_dev.log',
            'formatter': 'verbose'
        },
        'production_logfile': {
            'level': 'ERROR',
            'filters': ['require_debug_false'],
```

```
            'class': 'logging.handlers.RotatingFileHandler',
            'filename': '/var/log/django/django_production.log',
            'maxBytes' : 1024*1024*100, # 100MB
            'backupCount' : 5,
            'formatter': 'simple'
        },
        'dba_logfile': {
            'level': 'DEBUG',
            'filters': ['require_debug_false','require_debug_true'],
            'class': 'logging.handlers.WatchedFileHandler',
            'filename': '/var/log/dba/django_dba.log',
            'formatter': 'simple'
        },
    },
    'root': {
        'level': 'DEBUG',
        'handlers': ['console'],
    },
    'loggers': {
        'coffeehouse': {
            'handlers': ['development_logfile','production_logfile'],
         },
        'dba': {
            'handlers': ['dba_logfile'],
        },
        'django': {
            'handlers': ['development_logfile','production_logfile'],
        },
        'py.warnings': {
            'handlers': ['development_logfile'],
        },
    }
}
```

Caution When using logging files, ensure the destination folder exists (e.g., /var/log/dba/) and the owner of the Django process has file access permissions.

Disable default Django logging configuration

The `'disable_existing_loggers':True` statement at the top of Listing 5-18 disables Django's default logging configuration from Listing 5-15. This guarantees no default logging behavior is applied to a Django project.

An alternative to disabling Django's default logging behavior is to override the default logging definitions on an individual basis, as any explicit `LOGGING` configuration in `settings.py` takes precedence over Django defaults even when `'disable_existing_loggers':False`. For example, to apply a different behavior to the `console` logger (e.g., output messages for debug level, instead of default `info` level) you can define a handler in `settings.py` for `console` with a debug level - as shown in Listing 5-18.

However, if you want to ensure no default logging configuration inadvertently ends up in a Django project, you must set `'disable_existing_loggers'` to `True`. Because Listing 5-18 sets `'disable_existing_` loggers':True, notice the same default filters from Listing 5-15 are re-declared, since the default filters are lost on account of 'disable_existing_loggers':True.

Logging formatters: Message output

By default, Django doesn't define a logging formatters section as you can confirm in Listing 5-15. However, Listing 5-18 declares a formatters section to generate log messages with either a simpler or more verbose output.

By default, all Python log messages follow the format %(levelname)s:%(name)s:%(message)s, which means "Output the log message level, followed by the name of the logger and the log message itself."

However, there is a lot more information available through Python logging that can make log messages more comprehensive. As you can see in Listing 5-18, the simple and verbose formatters use a special syntax and a series of fields that are different from the default. Table 5-2 illustrates the different Python formatter fields including their syntax and meaning.

***Table 5-2.** Python logging formatter fields*

Field syntax	Description
%(name)s	Name of the logger (logging channel)
%(levelno)s	Numeric logging level for the message (DEBUG, INFO,WARNING, ERROR, CRITICAL)
%(levelname)s	Text logging level for the message ("DEBUG", "INFO","WARNING", "ERROR", "CRITICAL")
%(pathname)s	Full pathname of the source file where the logging call was issued (if available)
%(filename)s	Filename portion of pathname
%(module)s	Module (name portion of filename)
%(lineno)d	Source line number where the logging call was issued (if available)
%(funcName)s	Function name
%(created)f	Time when the log record was created (time.time() return value)
%(asctime)s	Textual time when the log record was created
%(msecs)d	Millisecond portion of the creation time
%(relativeCreated)d	Time in milliseconds when the log record was created,relative to the time the logging module was loaded (typically at application startup time)
%(thread)d	Thread ID (if available)
%(threadName)s	Thread name (if available)
%(process)d	Process ID (if available)
%(message)s	The result of record.getMessage(), computed just as the record is emitted

You can add or remove fields to the format field for each formatter based on the fields in Yable 5-2. Besides the format field for each formatter, there's also a datefmt field that allows you to customize the output of the %(asctime)s format field in formatter(e.g., with the datefmt field set to %Y-%m-%d %H:%M:%S, if a logging message occurs on midnight New Year's 2018, %(asctime) outputs 2018-01-01 00:00:00).

■ **Note** The syntax for the `datefmt` field follows Python's strftime() format.[2]

Logging handlers: Locations, classes, filters, and logging thresholds

The first handler in Listing 5-18 is the `console` handler, which provides custom behavior over the default `console` handler Listing 5-15. The `console` handler in Listing 5-18 raises the log level to the `DEBUG` level to process all log messages irrespective of their level. In addition, the `console` handler uses the custom `simple` formatter - described in the past section - and uses the same default `console` filters and class, which tells Django to process log messages when `DEBUG=True` (i.e., `'filters': ['require_debug_true']`) and send logging output to a stream (i.e., `'class': 'logging.StreamHandler'`).

In Listing 5-18, you can also see there are three different `class` values for each of the remaining handlers: `logging.FileHandler`, which sends log messages to a standard file; `logging.handlers.RotatingFileHandler`, which sends log messages to files that change based on a given threshold size; and `logging.handlers.WatchedFileHandler`, which sends log messages to a file that's managed by a third-party utility (e.g., logrotate).

The `development_logfile` handler is configured to work for log messages worse than `DEBUG` (inclusive) - which is technically all log messages - and only when `DEBUG=True` due to the `require_debug_true` filter. In addition, the `development_logfile` handler is set to use the custom `verbose` formatter and send output to the `/tmp/django_dev.log` file.

The `production_logfile` handler is configured to work for log messages worse than `ERROR` (inclusive) - which is just `ERROR` and `CRITICAL` log messages - and only when `DEBUG=False` due to the `require_debug_false` filter. In addition, the handler uses the custom `simple` formatter and is set to send output to the file `/var/log/django_production.log`. The log file is rotated every time a log file reaches 100 MB (i.e., `maxBytes`) and old log files are backed up to `backupCount` by appending a number (e.g., `django_production.log.1`,`django_production.log.2`).

The `dba_logfile` is configured to work for log messages worse than `DEBUG` (inclusive) - which is technically all log messages - and when `DEBUG=True` or `DEBUG=False` due to the `require_debug_true` and `require_debug_false` filters. In addition, the handler uses the custom `simple` formatter and is set to send output to the file `/var/log/django_dba.log`.

The `dba_logfile` handler is managed by the `WatchedFileHandler` class, which has a little more functionality than the basic `FileHandler` class used by the `development_logfile` handler. The `WatchedFileHandler` class is designed to check if a file changes, if it changes a file is reopened; this in turn allows a log file to be managed/changed by a Linux log utility like logrotate. The benefit of a log utility like logrotate is that it allows Django to use more elaborate log file features (e.g., compression, date rotation). Note that if you don't use a third-party utility like logrotate to manage a logfile that uses `WatchedFileHandler`, a log file grows indefinitely.

■ **Caution/Tip** The RotatingFileHandler logging handler class in Listing 5-18 is not safe for multi-process applications. Use the ConcurrentLogHandler logging handler class[3] to run on multi-process applications.

[2] `https://docs.python.org/3/library/time.html#time.strftime`

[3] `https://pypi.python.org/pypi/ConcurrentLogHandler/0.9.1`

■ **Tip** The core Python logging package includes many other logging handler classes to process messages with things like Unix syslog, Email (SMTP), and HTTP.[4]

Logging loggers: Python packages to use logging

The `loggers` section in Listing 5-18 defines the handlers to attach to Python packages - technically the attachment is done to logger names, but I used this term since loggers are generally named after Python packages. I'll provide an exception to this 'Python package=logger name' shortly so you can gain a better understanding of this concept.

The first logger `coffeehouse` tells Django to attach all the log messages for itself and its children (e.g., `coffeehouse.about`, `coffeehouse.about.views` and `coffeehouse.drinks`) to the `development_logfile` and `production_logfile` handlers. By assigning two handlers, log messages from the `coffeehouse` logger (and its children) are sent to two places.

Recall that by using Python's `__name__` syntax to define loggers - see Listing 5-16 and 5-17 - the name of the loggers end up being based on the Python package structure.

Next, you can see the `dba` logger links all its log messages to the `dba_logfile` handler. In this case, it's an exception to the rule that loggers are named after Python packages. As you can see in Listing 5-17, a logger can be purposely named `dba` and forgo using `__name__` or another convention related to Python packages.

Next, the `django` and `py.warnings` loggers are re-declared to obtain some of Django's default behavior, given Listing 5-18 uses `'disable_existing_loggers': True`. The `django` logger links all its log messages to the `development_logfile` and `production_logfile` handlers, since we want log messages associated with the `django` package/logger and its children (e.g., `django.request`, `django.security`) to go to two log files.

Notice Listing 5-18 doesn't declare explicit loggers for `django.request` and `django.security` unlike the Django default's in Listing 5-15. Because the `django` logger automatically handles its children and we don't need different handlers for each logger - like the default logging behavior - Listing 5-18 just declares the `django` logger.

At the end of Listing 5-18, the `py.warnings` logger links all its log messages to the `development_logfile` handler, to avoid any trace of `py.warnings` log messages in production logs.

Finally, there's the `root` key in Listing 5-18, which although declared outside of the `loggers` section, is actually the *root* logger for all loggers. The `root` key tells Django to process messages from all loggers - whether declared or undeclared in the configuration - and handle them in a given in way. In this case, `root` tells Django that all log messages - since the `DEBUG` level includes all messages - generated by any logger (`coffeehouse, dba, django, py.warnings` or any other) be processed by the `console` handler.

Disable email to ADMINS on errors

You may be surprised Listing 5-18 makes no use of the `mail_admins` handler defined by default in Listing 5-15. As I mentioned in the previous section on Django default logging, the `mail_admins` handler sends an email error notification for log messages generated by `django.request` or `django.security` packages/loggers.

While this can seem like an amazing feature at first - avoiding the hassle of looking through log files - once a project starts to grow it can become extremely inconvenient. The problem with the default logging email error notification mechanism or `mail_admins` handler is it sends out an email *every single* time an error associated with `django.request` or `django.security` packages/loggers is triggered.

[4]`https://docs.python.org/3/library/logging.handlers.html`

If you have 100 visitors per hour on a Django site and all of them hit the same error, it means 100 email notifications are sent in the same hour. If you have 3 people in `ADMINS`, then it means at least 300 email notifications per hour. All this can add up quickly, so a couple of different errors and a few thousand visitors a day can lead to email overload. So as convenient as it can appear to get email log error notifications, you should turn this feature off.

I recommend you stick to the old method on inspecting log files on a constant basis or if you require the same real-time log error notifications provided by email, that you instead use a dedicated reporting system such as Sentry, which is described in the next section.

Logging with Sentry

As powerful a discovery mechanism as logging is, inspecting and making sense of log messages can be an arduous task. Django and Python projects are no different in this area. As it was shown in the previous section, relying on core logging packages still results in log messages being sent to either the application console or files, where making sense of log messages (e.g., the most relevant or common log message) can lead to hours of analysis.

Enter *Sentry*, a reporting and aggregation application. Sentry facilitates the inspection of log messages through a web-based interface, where you can quickly determine the most relevant and common log messages.

To use Sentry you need to follow two steps: set up Sentry to receive your project log messages, and set up your Django project to send log messages to Sentry.

WHY SENTRY?

Although there are alternatives that offer similar log monitoring functionalities as Sentry (e.g., OverOps, Airbrake, Raygun), what sets Sentry apart is that it's built as a Django application!

Even though Sentry has evolved considerably to the point it's now a very complex Django application, the fact that Sentry is an open source project based on Django, makes it an almost natural option to monitor Django projects, since you can install and extend it using your Django knowledge – albeit there are software-as-service Sentry alternatives.

Set up Sentry the application

You can set up Sentry in two ways: install it yourself or use a software-as-service Sentry provider.

Sentry is a Django open source project, so the full source code is freely available to anyone.[5] But before you go straight to download Sentry and proceed with the installation,[6] beware Sentry has grown considerably from its Django roots. Sentry now requires a Docker environment, the relational Postgres database, and the NoSQL Redis database. Unfortunately, Sentry evolved to support a wide variety of programming languages and platforms, to the point it grew in complexity and is no longer a simple Django app installation. So if you install Sentry from scratch, expect to invest a couple of hours setting it up.

[5] `https://github.com/getsentry/sentry`
[6] `https://docs.sentry.io/server/installation/`

■ **Tip** Earlier Sentry releases (e.g., v. 5.0[7]) don't have such strict dependencies and can run like basic Django applications (e.g., any Django relational database, no Docker, no NoSQL database). They represent a good option for simple Sentry installations, albeit they require dated Django versions (e.g., v. Django 1.4).

The Sentry creators and maintainers run the software-as-a-service: `https://sentry.io`. The Sentry software-as-a-service offers three different plans: a hobbyist plan that's free for up to 10,000 events per month and is designed for one user; a professional plan that's $12 (USD) a month, which starts at 50,000 events per month and is designed for unlimited users; and an enterprise plan with custom pricing for millions of events and unlimited users.

Since you can set up Sentry for free in a few minutes with just your email - and no credit card - the Sentry software-as-a-service from `https://sentry.io` is a good option to try out Sentry. And even after trying it out, at a cost of $12 (USD) per month for 50,000 events and $0.00034 per additional event, it represents a good value - considering an application that generates 50,000 events per month should have a considerable audience to justify the price.

Once you create a sentry.io account you'll enter into the main dashboard. Create a new Django project. Take note of the client key or DSN, which is a long url that contains the @sentry.io snippet in it - this is required to configure Django projects to send log messages to this particular Sentry Django project. If you missed the project client key or DSN, click on the top right 'Project Settings' button illustrated in Figure 5-1, and select the bottom left option 'Client Keys (DSN)' to consult the value.

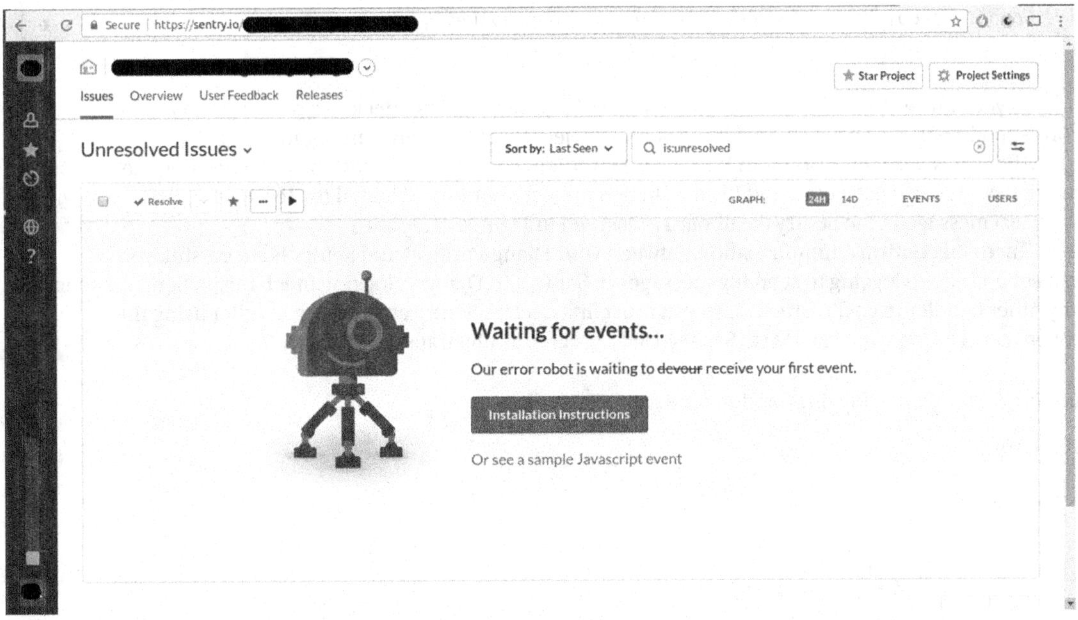

Figure 5-1. *Sentry SaaS project dashboard*

---

[7] `https://github.com/getsentry/sentry/releases/tag/5.0.21`

As you can see in Figure 5-1, the Sentry SaaS project dashboard acts as a central repository to consult all project logging activity. In Figure 5-1 you can also see the various action buttons, which allow log messages to be sorted, searched, charted, as well as managed by different users. All of this creates a very efficient environment in which to analyze any Django logging activity in real time.

Once you have Sentry set up, you can configure a Django project to send log messages to a Django project.

Set up a Django application to use Sentry

To use Sentry in a Django project you require a package called Raven to establish communication between the two parties. Simply do `pip install raven` to install the latest Raven version.

Once you install Raven, you must declare it in the `INSTALLED_APPS` list of your project's `settings.py` file as illustrated in Listing 5-19. In addition, it's also necessary to configure Raven to communicate with a specific Sentry project via a DSN value, through the `RAVEN_CONFIG` variable also shown in Listing 5-19.

Listing 5-19. Django project configuration to communicate with Sentry via Raven

```
INSTALLED_APPS = [
    ...
    'raven.contrib.django.raven_compat',
    ...
]

RAVEN_CONFIG = {
    'dsn': '<your_dsn_value>@sentry.io/<your_dsn_value>',
}
```

As you can see in Listing 5-19, the `RAVEN_CONFIG` variable should declare a `dsn` key with a value corresponding to the DSN value from the Sentry project that's to receive the log messages.

After you set up this minimum Raven configuration, you can send a test message running the `python manage.py raven test` command from a Django project's command line. If the test is successful, you will see a test message in the Sentry dashboard presented in Figure 5-1.

Once you confirm communication between your Django project and Sentry is successful, you can set up Django logging to send log messages to Sentry. To Django's logging mechanism, Sentry is seen as any other handler (e.g., file, stream), so you must first declare Sentry as a logging handler using the `raven.contrib.django.handlers.SentryHandler` class, as illustrated in Listing 5-20.

Listing 5-20. Django logging handler for Sentry/Raven

```
LOGGING = {
...
 'handlers': {
        ....
         'sentry': {
             'level': 'ERROR',
             'class': 'raven.contrib.django.handlers.SentryHandler',
        },
        ...
  }
```

The `sentry` handler in Listing 5-20 tells Django to handle log messages with an `ERROR` level through Sentry. Once you have a Sentry handler, the last step is to use the `sentry` handler on loggers to assign which packages/loggers get processed through Sentry (e.g., `django.request` or `root` logger, as described in the earlier "Logging Loggers" section).

Django Email Service

Email has become a staple of practically all applications that live on the Web. Whether an application requires sending email for signup purposes, notifications, or confirming a purchase, it's hard to imagine a web application that doesn't require some kind of email functionality.

For Django projects, there are two main aspects associated with setting up email. The first step is setting up the connection to an email server and the second is the composition of emails.

Set Up a Default Connection to an Email Server

Django supports connections to any email server and also offers various options to simulate email server connections. Email simulation is particularly powerful during development and testing where sending out real emails is unnecessary. The setup for an email server in Django is done in `settings.py`. Depending on the email server connection, you may need to set up several variables in `settings.py`. Table 5-3 illustrates various email server options for Django.

Table 5-3. *Django email server configurations*

Django email backend	Configuration	Description / Notes
For development (DEBUG=True)		
Console Email	EMAIL_BACKEND='django.core.mail.backends.console.EmailBackend'	Sends all email output to the console where Django is running.
File Email	EMAIL_BACKEND='django.core.mail.backends.filebased.EmailBackend' EMAIL_FILE_PATH='/tmp/django-email-dev'	Sends all email output to a flat file specified in EMAIL_FILE_PATH.
In memory Email	EMAIL_BACKEND='django.core.mail.backends.locmem.EmailBackend'	Sends all email output to an in memory attribute available at django.core.mail.outbox.
Nullify Email	EMAIL_BACKEND='django.core.mail.backends.dummy.EmailBackend'	Does nothing with all email output.
Python Email Server Simulator	EMAIL_BACKEND='django.core.mail.backends.smtp.EmailBackend' EMAIL_HOST=127.0.0.1 EMAIL_PORT=2525 Also needed is the Python command line email server: python -m smtpd -n -c DebuggingServer localhost:2525	Sends all email output to a Python email server set up via command line. This is similar to the Console Email option, because the Python email server outputs content to the console.

(continued)

Table 5-3. (*continued*)

Django email backend	Configuration	Description / Notes
For production (DEBUG=False)		
SMTP Email Server (Standard)	EMAIL_BACKEND='django.core.mail.backends.smtp.EmailBackend' [1]EMAIL_HOST=127.0.0.1 [1]EMAIL_PORT=25 [2]EMAIL_HOST_USER=<smtp_user> [2]EMAIL_HOST_PASSWORD=<smtp_user_pwd>	Sends all email output to a SMTP email server.
SMTP Email Server ([*]Secure-TLS)	EMAIL_BACKEND='django.core.mail.backends.smtp.EmailBackend' [1]EMAIL_HOST=127.0.0.1 [1]EMAIL_PORT=587 [2]EMAIL_HOST_USER=<smtp_user> [2]EMAIL_HOST_PASSWORD=<smtp_user_pwd> EMAIL_USE_TLS=True	Sends all email output to a secure SMTP (TLS) email server.
SMTP Email Server ([*]Secure-SSL)	EMAIL_BACKEND='django.core.mail.backends.smtp.EmailBackend' [1]EMAIL_HOST=127.0.0.1 [1]EMAIL_PORT=465 [2]EMAIL_HOST_USER=<smtp_user> [2]EMAIL_HOST_PASSWORD=<smtp_user_pwd> EMAIL_USE_SSL=True	Sends all email output to a secure SMTP (SSL) email server.

[1] *If the SMTP email server is running on a network or a different port than the default, adjust EMAIL_HOST and EMAIL_PORT accordingly.*
[2] *In today's email, spam-infested Internet, nearly all SMTP email servers require authentication to send email. If your SMTP server doesn't require authentication you can omit EMAIL_HOST_USER and EMAIL_HOST_PASSWORD.*
[*] *The terms SSL and TLS are often used interchangeably or in conjunction with each other (TLS/SSL). There are differences, though, in terms of their underlying protocol. From a Django setup prescriptive, you only need to ensure what type of secure email server you connect to, as they operate differently and on different ports.*

Whichever email connection you set up from Table 5-3 in `settings.py` is considered a Django project's default and is used when doing any email-related task - unless you specify otherwise when doing an email task.

Set Up a Default Connection to Third-Party Email Providers

The previous section provided the most generic approach to set up a default connection to an email server in Django. However, with the complexities involved in running email servers in today's world - namely, spam filtering and security issues - it can be easier and more practical to use a third-party service to relay email from a Django project to the outside world.

Although you can use the previous section's configurations to connect to any third-party email service, there can be certain subtleties to set up configurations to third-party email services. In this section I'll provide the Django configuration details for what I consider three of the most popular third-party email services.

DJANGO WITH EXIM, POSTFIX, OR SENDMAIL

Although you can set up Django to deliver email to a local email application (i.e., running on 127.0.0.1) such as Exim, Postfix, or Sendmail, which then deliver email to third-party providers. I personally would not recommend this alternative as it adds another component to set up, maintain, and worry about. Not to mention this is beyond the scope of Django, as it involves setting up different email apps with third-party email services.

This following section describes how to set up Django to connect directly with third-party email providers.

Email with Google Gmail/Google Apps

Google offers the ability to send out email through Gmail or Google Apps, the last of which is a Gmail version for custom domains (e.g., coffeehouse.com). Once you have a Gmail or Google Apps account, you'll need to set up the account's username/password credentials in `settings.py`.

You will not be able to use Google's email services without hard-coding your account credentials somewhere in your app. If you are weary of hard-coding the username/password credentials in `settings.py`, I suggest you create a separate account for this purpose to limit vulnerabilities, look into using multiple environments or configuration files for Django to keep the username/password in a different file, or set up a local email server with the credentials as described in the previous sidebar.

Listing 5-21 illustrates the configuration needed to set up Django to send email via a Gmail or Google Apps account.

Listing 5-21. Django email configuration for Gmail or Google Apps account

```
EMAIL_BACKEND='django.core.mail.backends.smtp.EmailBackend'
EMAIL_HOST='smtp.gmail.com'
EMAIL_PORT=587
EMAIL_HOST_USER='username@gmail.com/OR/username@coffeehouse.com'
EMAIL_HOST_PASSWORD='password'
EMAIL_USE_TLS=True
```

As you can see in Listing 5-21, the configuration parameters are pretty similar to those described in Table 5-3. This is all you need to set up a default email connection to Gmail or Google Apps in Django.

■ **Caution** Beware of sending too much email with Google. Since Google's email service is free, it's not designed for relaying too many email messages. If your Django app sends out a couple of email messages every hour you probably won't have a problem, but if your app sends out email messages every second or hundreds of email messages in the span of a few minutes, the account is likely to be blocked. If the account is blocked, you will either need to wait a few hours or manually log into the account (i.e., via a browser) for it to be unblocked. If the account is constantly blocked due to the email volume you send out, you should try another email service provider.

■ **Note** Google overwrites the From: email field with the Google account value, unless it's added as an alias. Django allows you to set an email's From: field to any value you want and defaults to the EMAIL_HOST_USER value in settings.py. However, to avoid spoofing, Google overwrites this field to the Google account email if the From: email value is not an alias in the Gmail or Google App account. This means if you send an email message in Django with From: support@coffeehouse.com and this email is not set up as an alias in the Gmail or Google App account, the final email appears with From: set to the Google account's main email.

Email with Amazon Simple Email Service (SES)

SES is another email service offered by AWS, which is run by Amazon.com. Unlike Google's email service, SES is a paid service with an average cost of 0.0001 cents per email (10 cents per 1000 emails). The easiest way to set up Django with SES is through the Python library boto and a custom Django email back end called django-ses.

Listing 5-22 illustrates the pip requirements to install boto, which is a library to integrate multiple AWS services using Python and django-ses, which is an open source project specifically designed to run SES with Django.

Listing 5-22. Python pip requirements for Amazon.com SES with Django

```
pip install boto
pip install django-ses
```

Once you install the Python packages in Listing 5-22 using pip, you can proceed to configure SES in `settings.py`. Listing 5-23 illustrates the necessary variables to set up Django to use SES.

Listing 5-23. Django email configuration for Amazon.com SES

```
EMAIL_BACKEND = 'django_ses.SESBackend'
AWS_ACCESS_KEY_ID = 'FZINISSZ3542DPIO32CQ'
AWS_SECRET_ACCESS_KEY = '3Nto4vknl+xeZR+1tF3L645EUyOS+zZy/uPJ1rN'
```

As you can see in Listing 5-23, the variable `EMAIL_BACKEND` is set to the custom class `django_ses.SESBackend`, which provides all the necessary hooks to connect to SES.

To connect to SES you'll also need to provide the variables `AWS_ACCESS_KEY_ID` and `AWS_SECRET_ACCESS_KEY`, which are access credentials related to your AWS account. These last values are provided in your AWS account..[8]

This is all you need to set up a default email connection to Amazon Simple Email Service (SES). There's no need to set up any other variable in `settings.py`, such as `EMAIL_HOST` or `EMAIL_HOST_USER` - everything is taken care of by the custom email back end.

Email with SparkPost

SparkPost is another third-party email service used by large companies like Twitter, Oracle, and PayPal. Pricing wise SparkPost is a mix between the two previous services; it's a free service for the first 100,000 emails per month, but after this volume it's a paid service with an average cost of .0002 cents per email (20 cents per next 1000 emails per month) and lower per email rates once you send 1 million emails a month.

The easiest way to set up Django with SparkPost is directly in `settings.py`. Listing 5-24 illustrates the necessary variables to set up Django to use SparkPost.

[8] `http://docs.aws.amazon.com/general/latest/gr/aws-sec-cred-types.html#access-keys-and-secret-access-keys`

Listing 5-24. Django email configuration for SparkPost

```
EMAIL_BACKEND='django.core.mail.backends.smtp.EmailBackend'
EMAIL_HOST = 'smtp.sparkpostmail.com'
EMAIL_PORT = 587
EMAIL_HOST_USER = 'SMTP_Injection'
EMAIL_HOST_PASSWORD = '<sparkpost_api_key>'
EMAIL_USE_TLS = True
```

As you can see in Listing 5-24, the configuration parameters are pretty similar to those described in Table 5-3 for a standard email connection. Just notice that in addition to the `EMAIL_HOST_USER` value being `SMTP_Injection` – a SparkPost requirement – you'll also need to assign a SparkPost API key to the `EMAIL_HOST_PASSWORD`. The SparkPost API key is created in your SparkPost account.[9]

Now that you understand the various ways to set up an email connection in a Django project, let's explore the actual composition of emails.

Built-In Helpers to Send Email

There can be many options and steps involved in sending an email. To simplify this process, Django offers four shortcut methods you can leverage anywhere in an application (e.g., when a signup is made, when a purchase is made, when a critical error occurs). Table 5-4 illustrates the various email shortcut methods.

Table 5-4. *Django email shortcut methods*

Shortcut method and description	Shortcut method with all arguments*	Argument descriptions and notes
send_mail is the most common option to send email.	send_mail(subject, message, from_email=settings.DEFAULT_FROM_EMAIL, recipient_list, fail_silently=False, auth_user=None, auth_password=None, connection=None, html_message=None)	subject.- Email subject string. message.- Email message string. from_email.- Email From: field. If not provided it's set to DEFAULT_FROM_EMAIL from settings.py that by default is webmaster@localhost. recipient_list.- Email recipients as a list of strings. fail_silently.- Offers the ability to bypass errors if email cannot be sent. By default set to False, which means any error when attempting to send email raises an smtplib.SMTPException exception. auth_user.- Authentication user for the SMTP server. If provided it overrides the variable EMAIL_HOST_USER in settings.py. auth_password.- Authentication password for the SMTP server. If provided it overrides the variable EMAIL_HOST_PASSWORD in settings.py. connection.- Django emails back end to send the mail. If provided it overrides the variable EMAIL_BACKEND in settings.py. See Table 5-3 for options. html_message.- An HTML string to send an HTML and text email message. If provided, the resulting email is a multipart/alternative email with message as the text/plain content type and html_message as the text/html content type.

(continued)

[9]`https://support.sparkpost.com/customer/portal/articles/1933377-create-api-keys`

Table 5-4. *(continued)*

Shortcut method and description	Shortcut method with all arguments*	Argument descriptions and notes
send_mass_mail is more efficient than the send_mail method. This is the preferred choice when sending multiple emails because it opens a single connection to the email server and sends all messages contained in a tuple. Note however send_mass_mail does not support HTML messages like send_mail.	send_mass_mail(datatuple, fail_silently=False, auth_user=None, auth_password=None, connection=None)	datatuple.- Is a tuple that contains tuples representing an email structure in the form (subject, message, from_email=settings.DEFAULT_FROM_EMAIL, recipient_list).
mail_admins sends email to all users defined in the ADMINS variable in settings.py.	mail_admins(subject, message, fail_silently=False, connection=None, html_message=None)	Email is sent with a From: field set to the variable SERVER_EMAIL in settings.py that by default is root@localhost. The email subject is prefixed with the variable EMAIL_SUBJECT_PREFIX in settings.py which by default is '[Django]'.
mail_managers sends email to all users defined in the MANAGERS variable in settings.py.	mail_managers(subject, message, fail_silently=False, connection=None, html_message=None)	Email is sent with a From: field set to the variable SERVER_EMAIL in settings.py which by default is root@localhost. The email subject is prefixed with the variable EMAIL_SUBJECT_PREFIX in settings.py which by default is '[Django]'.

** Method arguments without a default value (e.g. subject,message) must always be provided. Method arguments with a default value (e.g. fail_silently=False, connection=None) are optional.*

■ **Note** If you start to get emails with error messages once a project goes into production (i.e.DEBUG=False), it's because the mail_admins shortcut is automatically hooked-up for this purpose. This is due to the way Django's default logging works. To disable this behavior you will either need to clear all values from ADMINS in settings.py or override the default logging behavior as described in the previous section on logging.

Custom Email: Attachments, Headers, CC, BCC, and More with EmailMessage

Although the previous email shortcut methods can be used under most circumstances, they do not support things like attachments, CC, BCC, or other email headers. If you want total control for sending email messages in Django, the previous shortcut methods won't work.

Used 'under-the-hood' by the previous Django shortcut methods and offering the utmost flexibility for sending email in Django is the Django `EmailMessage` class. The various parameters and methods supported by the `EmailMessage` class are described in Table 5-5.

***Table 5-5.** Django EmailMessage class parameters and methods*

Parameter and/or method	Description
subject	The subject line of the email.
body	The body text as a plain text message.
from_email	The sender's address. Both plain email (e.g., `webmaster@coffeehouse.com`) and full name with email (e.g., `Webmaster <webmaster@coffeehouse.com>`) format are acceptable. If omitted, the DEFAULT_FROM_EMAIL value from settings.py is used.
to	A list or tuple of recipient addresses.
cc	A list or tuple of recipient addresses used in the the email CC header when sending the email.
bcc	A list or tuple of addresses used as the email BCC header when sending the email.
connection	An email back-end instance. Use this parameter if you want to use the same connection for multiple messages. If omitted, a new connection is created when send() is called.
attachments	A list of attachments to put on the message. These can be either email.MIMEBase.MIMEBase instances, or (filename, content, mimetype) triples.
headers	A dictionary of extra headers to put on the message. The keys are the header name, values are the header values. It's up to the caller to ensure header names and values are in the correct format for an email message. The corresponding attribute is extra_headers.
send(fail_silently=False)	Sends the message. If a connection was specified when the email was constructed, that connection is used. Otherwise, an instance of the default backend is instantiated and used. If the keyword argument fail_silently is True, exceptions raised while sending the message are omitted. An empty list of recipients does not raise an exception.
message()	Useful when extending the EmailMessage class to override and put the content you want into the MIME object. Constructs a django.core.mail.SafeMIMEText object (a subclass of Python's email.MIMEText.MIMEText class) or a django.core.mail.SafeMIMEMultipart object holding the message to be sent.
recipients()	Useful when extending the EmailMessage class because the SMTP server needs to be told the full list of recipients when the message is sent. It returns a list of all the recipients of the message, whether they're recorded in the to, cc, or bcc attributes.

(*continued*)

Table 5-5. *(continued)*

Parameter and/or method	Description
attach()	Creates a file attachment and adds it to the message. There are two ways to call attach(). You can pass it a single argument that is an email.MIMEBase. MIMEBase instance that gets inserted directly into the resulting message or you can passs it three arguments: filename, content, and mimetype (e.g., message.attach('menu.png', img_data, 'image/png'), where filename is the name of the file attachment as it will appear in the email, content is the data that will be contained inside the attachment, and mimetype is the optional MIME type for the attachment. If you omit mimetype, the MIME content type is guessed from the filename of the attachment.
attach_file()	Creates an attachment using a file from the filesystem. It can be called with the path of the file to attach (e.g., message.attach_file('/images/menu.png') and optionally with the MIME type to use for the attachment (e.g., message. attach_file('/images/menu.png','image/png'). If the MIME type is omitted, it's guessed from the filename.

With a clear idea of the functionalities provided by the `EmailMessage` classs in Table 5-5, let's take a look at some typical cases where you would use the EmailMessage class to send email.

Listing 5-25 provides a basic email example that uses options like CC, BCC. and the Reply-To header, which aren't support via the Django email shortcuts from the last section.

Listing 5-25. Send basic email with EmailMessage class

```
from django.core.mail.message import EmailMessage

# Build message
email = EmailMessage(subject='Coffeehouse specials', body='We would like to let you know
about this week\'s specials....', from_email='stores@coffeehouse.com',
            to=['ilovecoffee@hotmail.com', 'officemgr@startups.com'], bcc=['marketing@
            coffeehouse.com'], cc=['ceo@coffeehouse.com']
            headers = {'Reply-To': 'support@coffeehouse.com'})

# Send message with built-in send() method
email.send()
```

As you can see in Listing 5-25, the EmailMessage instance is created specifying its various class parameters. Once this is done, you just call the `send()` method to send the email. It's as simple as that. Because no connection values are provided in the `EmailMessage` instance in Listing 5-25, Django uses the default back-end connection defined in `settings.py`.

One drawback of the `EmailMessage` `send()` method is that it opens a connection to the email server every time it's called. This can be inefficient if you send hundreds or thousands of emails at once. In the spirit of the `send_mass_mail()` shortcut method from the last section, it's also possible to open a single connection to the email server and send multiple emails with `EmailMessage`. Listing 5-26 shows how to use a single connection and send multiple emails with `EmailMessage`.

Listing 5-26. Send multiple emails in a single connection with EmailMessage class

```
from django.core import mail
connection = mail.get_connection()

# Manually open the connection
connection.open()

# Build message
email = EmailMessage(subject='Coffeehouse specials', body='We would like to let you know
about this week\'s specials....', from_email='stores@coffeehouse.com',
            to=['ilovecoffee@hotmail.com', 'officemgr@startups.com'],
            bcc=['marketing@coffeehouse.com'], cc=['ceo@coffeehouse.com']
            headers = {'Reply-To': 'support@coffeehouse.com'})
# Build message
email2 = EmailMessage(subject='Coffeehouse coupons', body='New coupons for our best
customers....', from_email='stores@coffeehouse.com',
            to=['officemgr@startups.com','food@momandpopshop.com'],
            bcc=['marketing@coffeehouse.com'], cc=['ceo@coffeehouse.com']
            headers = {'Reply-To': 'support@coffeehouse.com'})

# Send the two emails in a single call
connection.send_messages([email, email2])
# The connection was already open so send_messages() doesn't close it.
# We need to manually close the connection.
connection.close()
```

In Listing 5-26 the first step is to create a connection to the email server using `mail.get_connection()` and then open the connection with the `open()` method. Next, you create the various `EmailMessage` instances. Once the email instances are prepared, you call the connection's `send_messages()` method with an argument list corresponding to each of the `EmailMessage` instances. Finally, once the emails are sent, you call the connection's `close()` method to drop the connection to the email server.

Another common email scenario is to send HTML emails. Django provides the `EmailMultiAlternatives` class for this purpose, which is a subclass of the `EmailMessage` class. By being a subclass, it means you can leverage the same functionalities as `EmailMessage` (e.g., CC, BCC), but you don't need to do a lot of work as the subclass `EmailMultiAlternatives` is specifically designed to handle a multiple types of messages. Listing 5-27 illustrates how to use the `EmailMultiAlternatives` class.

Listing 5-27. Send HTML (w/text) emails with EmailMultiAlternatives, a subclass of the EmailMessage class

```
from django.core.mail import EmailMultiAlternatives

subject, from_email, to = 'Important support message', 'support@coffeehouse.com', 'ceo@
coffeehouse.com'
text_content = 'This is an important message.'
html_content = '
This is an important message.
```

```
'
msg = EmailMultiAlternatives(subject=subject, body=text_content, from_email=from_email,
to=[to])
msg.attach_alternative(html_content, "text/html")
msg.send()
```

Listing 5-27 first defines all the email fields, which include the text and HTML version of the email. Note that having a text and HTML version of the email content is common practice, since there's no guarantee end users will allow or can read HTML email, so a text version is provided as a backup. Next, you define an instance of the `EmailMultiAlternatives` class; notice the parameters are inline with those of the `EmailMessage` class.

Next, in Listing 5-27 you can see a call to the `attach_alternative` method, which is specific to the `EmailMultiAlternatives` class. The first argument to this method is the HTML content and the second is the content type that corresponds to `text/html`. Finally, Listing 5-27 calls the `send()` method - part of the `EmailMessage` class, but which is also automatically part of to `EmailMultiAlternatives` since it's a subclass - to send the actual email.

In controlled environments (e.g., corporate email) where it can be guaranteed that all end users are capable of viewing HTML email, it can be practical to just send an HTML version of an email and bypass the text version altogether. Under these circumstances, you can actually use the `EmailMesssage` class directly with a minor tweak. Listing 5-28 illustrates how to send just HTML email with the `EmailMessage` class.

Listing 5-28. Send HTML emails with EmailMessage class

```
subject, from_email, to = 'Important support message', 'support@coffeehouse.com', 'ceo@
coffeehouse.com'
html_content = '
This is an important message.

'
msg = EmailMessage(subject=subject, body=html_content, from_email=from_email, to=[to])
msg.content_subtype = "html"  # Main content is now text/html
msg.send()
```

Listing 5-28 looks like a standard `EmailMessage` process definition; however, line four - `msg.content_subtype` - is what makes Listing 5-28 different. If the HTML content were sent without line setting `msg.content_subtype`, end users would receive a verbatim version of the HTML content (i.e., without the HTML tags rendered). This is because by default the `EmailMessage` class specifies the content type as text. In order to switch the default content type of an `EmailMessage` instance, in line four a call is made to set the `content_subtype` to `html`. With this change the email content type is set to HTML and end users are capable of viewing the content rendered as HTML.

BEWARE OF JUST SENDING HTML EMAIL VERSIONS TO THE PUBLIC

Although sending an HTML email version is quicker than sending a text and HTML email version, this can be problematic if you can't determine where end users read their email. There are certain users that for security reasons disable the ability to view HTML emails, as well as certain email products that can't or aren't very good at rendering HTML emails. So if you just send an HTML email version, there can be a subset of end users that won't be able to see the email content.

For this reason if you send email to end users where you can't control their environment (i.e., email reader), it is best you send a text and HTML email version - as illustrated in Listing 5-27 - than sending an HTML email version illustrated in Listing 5-28.

Another common practice when sending emails is to attach files. Listing 5-29 illustrates how to attach a PDF to an email.

Listing 5-29. Send email with PDF attachment with EmailMessage class

```
from django.core.mail.message import EmailMessage

# Build message
email = EmailMessage(subject='Coffeehouse sales report', body='Attached is sales
report....', from_email='stores@coffeehouse.com',
            to=['ceo@coffeehouse.com', 'marketing@coffeehouse.com']
            headers = {'Reply-To': 'sales@coffeehouse.com'})
# Open PDF file
attachment = open('SalesReport.pdf', 'rb')
# Attach PDF file
email.attach('SalesReport.pdf',attachment.read(),'application/pdf')

# Send message with built-in send() method
email.send()
```

As you can see in Listing 5-29, after creating an `EmailMessage` instance you just open the PDF file using Python's standard `open()` method. Next, you use the `attach()` method from the `EmailMessage` that takes three arguments: the file name, the file contents, and the file content type or MIME type. Finally, a call is made to the `send()` method to send the email.

Debug Django Applications

The first steps to correct unexpected behavior in an application are generally to review what you believe are the problematic sections of source code and the corresponding logs. Sometimes though these reviews are fruitless, either because an application has grown in complexity or the unexpected behavior is originating in a not so obvious location.

Under these circumstances, the next step is to start a debugging process with the help of tools to make it easier to detect and fix the problem. In the upcoming sections, I'll describe some of the most popular tools to debug Django applications.

Django Shell: Python manage.py Shell

Just like Python's CLI ('Command Line Interface') shell where you can evaluate expressions (e.g., 1+3, mystring = 'django'), Django offers its own shell version through the `python manage.py shell` command - where `manage.py` is the top-level file in every Django project.

Django's shell is helpful because it automatically loads a project's dependencies and apps, so you're able to evaluate expressions related to your Django project (e.g., queries, methods) without having to go through a tedious setup process. Listing 5-30 illustrates a series of sample expressions run from Django's shell.

Listing 5-30. Django shell sample expressions

```
[user@coffeehouse ~]$ python manage.py shell
Python 2.7.3
[GCC 4.6.3] on linux2
Type "help", "copyright", "credits" or "license" for more information.
(InteractiveConsole)
>>> from coffeehouse.items.models import *
>>> Drink.objects.filter(item__price__lt=2).filter(caffeine__lt=100).count()
2
>>> from django.test import Client
>>> c = Client()
>>> response = c.get('/stores/1/')
>>> response.content
'<!DOCTYPE html>\n<html....
....
....
<\html>
>>> c.get('/stores/5/')
Not Found: /stores/5/
<HttpResponseNotFound status_code=404, "text/html">
```

The first snippet in Listing 5-30 uses the `from import` syntax to gain access to a Django project's model classes, after which queries are made on the models to validate results. Note there's no need to import additional libraries or define database connections; all dependencies and configurations are loaded from the Django project itself.

The second snippet in Listing 5-30 uses Django's test library to simulate a client/browser request to the `/stores/1/` and `/stores/5/` URLs, after which you can inspect the content response or the HTTP status code (e.g., 404 Not Found). Here again note there's no need to start a web server or open a browser; you can quickly validate a Django project's URLs and its responses from the Django shell.

Django Debug Toolbar

The Django debug toolbar offers a more visual experience to debug Django applications compared to the Django shell. The Django debug toolbar offers per page information through a sliding sidebar related to things like resource usage (i.e., time), Django settings, HTTP headers, SQL queries, cache, and logging, among other things. Figures 5-2 and 5-3 illustrate a collapsed and non-collapsed screenshot of the Django debug toolbar.

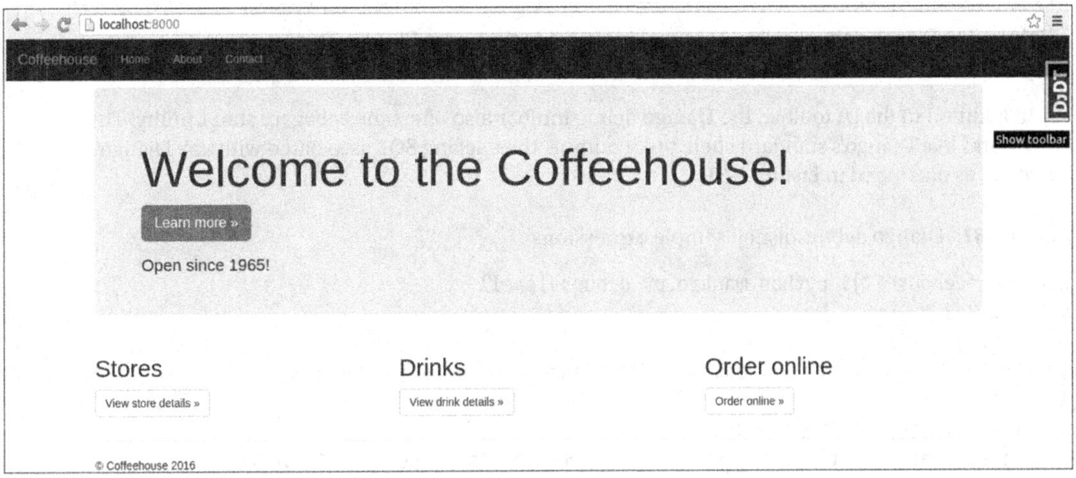

Figure 5-2. Django debug toolbar hidden

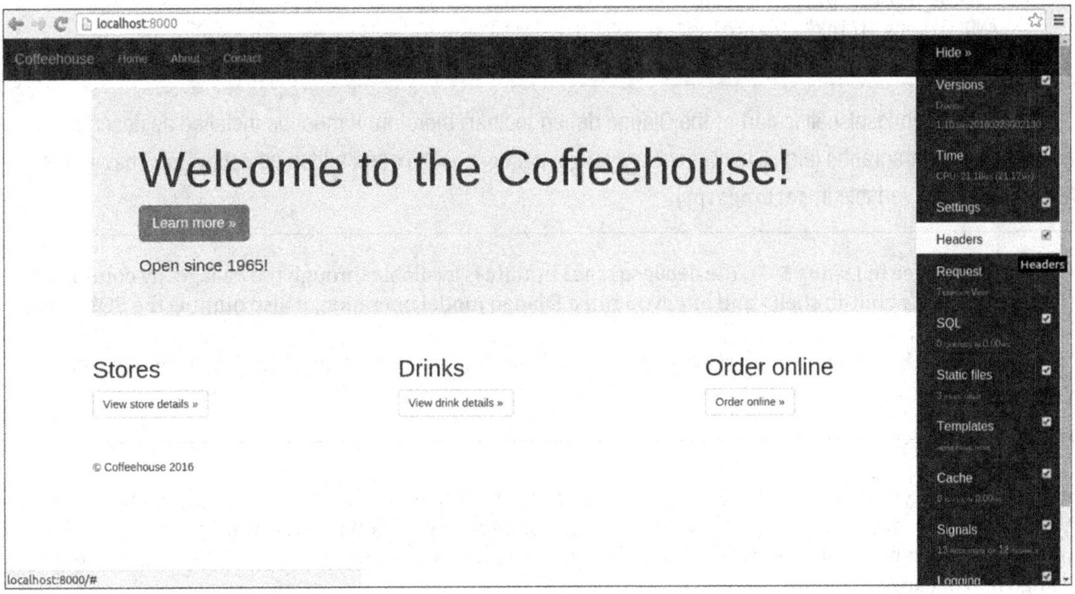

Figure 5-3. Django debug toolbar collapsed

As you can see in Figure 5-2, the Django debug toolbar is accessible through a small tab in the top right-hand side of every Django project page. Figure 5-3 illustrates a collapsed version of the Django debug toolbar where you can see its various sections; clicking on any of the sections further brings up a pop-window with detailed information about each section.

You can install the Django debug toolbar with the `pip install django-debug-toolbar` command. Once you install the `django-debug-toolbar`, you'll also need to add the `debug_toolbar` line to the `INSTALLED_APPS` variable in `settings.py` so Django enables the toolbar.

■ **Note** The Django debug toolbar only works when a project uses DEBUG=True.

In addition to the UI toolbar, the Django debug toolbar also offers the debugsqlshell utility. This utility works like Django's standard shell, but it outputs the backing SQL associated with any Django model operation, as illustrated in Listing 5-31.

Listing 5-31. Django debugsqlshell sample expressions

```
[user@coffeehouse ~]$ python manage.py debugsqlshell
Python 2.7.3
[GCC 4.6.3] on linux2
Type "help", "copyright", "credits" or "license" for more information.
(InteractiveConsole)
>>> from coffeehouse.items.models import *
>>> Drink.objects.filter(item__price__lt=2).filter(caffeine__lt=100).count()
SELECT COUNT(*) AS "__count"
FROM "items_drink"
INNER JOIN "items_item" ON ("items_drink"."item_id" = "items_item"."id")
WHERE ("items_item"."price" < 2.0
       AND "items_drink"."caffeine" < 100) [0.54ms]
```

■ **Note** The debugsqlshell is part of the Django debug toolbar; therefore it must be installed as described in the previous paragraphs (e.g., `pip install django-debug-toolbar` and added as `debug_toolbar` to the `INSTALLED_APPS` variable in `settings.py`).

As you can see in Listing 5-31, the `debugsqlshell` utility is available through the `manage.py` command - just like Django's built-in shell - and after you run a Django model operation, it also outputs the SQL query for the operation.

For detailed information on customizing the Django debug toolbar, see its official documentation.[10]

Django pdb

pdb - short for "Python Debugger" - is a Python core package designed to interactively debug source code. With Python pdb you can inspect the line-by- line execution of any Python application. To simplify the process of Python pdb in the context of Django applications (e.g., debug request methods) you can use the Django pdb package.

To install Python pdb run `pip install django-pdb` and then add `django_pdb` to the `INSTALLED_APPS` variable in `settings.py` in the first position - the position is important so other Django apps don't override Django pdb's behaviors (e.g., override runserver and test commands). Be aware the Django pdb package only works when `DEBUG=True`.

There are various way to run pdb with Django; the easiest is to append the ?pdb parameter to any Django URL you want to analyze with pdb. For example, Listing 5-32 shows a debugging sequence for the `http://localhost:8000/drinks/mocha/?pdb` URL.

[10]`http://django-debug-toolbar.readthedocs.org/`

Listing 5-32. Django pdb sequence

```
[user@coffeehouse ~]$ python manage.py runserver
INFO "GET /drinks/mocha/ HTTP/1.1" 200 11716
GET /drinks/mocha/?pdb
function "detail" in drinks/views.py:8
args: ()
kwargs: {'drink_type': u'mocha'}
()
> /python/djangodev/local/lib/python2.7/site-packages/django/core/handlers/base.py(79)make_
view_atomic()
-> non_atomic_requests = getattr(view, '_non_atomic_requests', set())
(Pdb) n
> /python/djangodev/local/lib/python2.7/site-packages/django/core/handlers/base.py(80)make_
view_atomic()
-> for db in connections.all():
...
...
...
--Call--
> /www/code/djangorecipes/5_django_settings/coffeehouse/drinks/views.py(8)detail()
-> def detail(request,drink_type):
(Pdb)
> /www/code/djangorecipes/5_django_settings/coffeehouse/drinks/views.py(9)detail()
(Pdb) c
```

You can see Listing 5-32 starts with Django's built-in web server and immediately receives and dispatches a response to the regular URL `/drinks/mocha/`. Up to this point everything is standard; however, notice the next request to the URL `/drinks/mocha/?pdb` and the verbose output that follows.

The verbose output tells you where the request enters the application, including arguments, as well as the initial entry point into Django's core framework in the `django.core.handlers.base.py` package.

After the initial verbose output, the execution stops at the first `(Pdb)` instance. At this juncture you've hit a breakpoint, so the console running `runserver` and the requesting client (i.e., browser) freeze until you provide additional input on the console. In Listing 5-32 you can see the letter `n` for next is introduced and the execution moves forward to another line, after which you'll be presented with another `(Pdb)` prompt or breakpoint. At this point, you can just press the `Enter` key to re-invoke the previous command (i.e., `n`) and move forward.

If you want to advance without hitting another breakpoint, you can type `c` for continue so the execution continues normally, without pausing again.

As you can see, the power of pdb with Django lies in the fact that you can walk through the execution cycle of any section in a very granular way, in addition to having the ability to analyze and set variables interactively. Table 5-6 describes the most basic commands related to pdb.

Table 5-6. *Python pdb commands used at (Pdb) prompt*

Pdb Command	Description
(Enter) (key)	Re-executes the previous command.
n	Moves execution to the next breakpoint.
c	Continues execution with no more breakpoints.
q	Quits the execution immediately.
p <variable(s)>	Print variable(s).
l (L lowercase)	Displays a list of source code at the current breakpoint, 11 lines worth: the breakpoint line, 5 lines prior, and 5 lines after. Helpful to provide context.
s	Enters a subroutine. In a non-method related breakpoint, s and n both move to the next breakpoint. In a method related breakpoint, s enters the method or subroutine.
r	Breaks out of a subroutine. Used after s to return to the main routine.

In addition to appending the `?pdb` parameter to a URL to enter pdb in a Django application, there are two more alternatives. You can append the `--pdb` flag to `runserver` to enter pdb on every request made to the application (e.g., `python manage.py runserver --pdb`). And you can also use the `--pm` flag to enter pdb only when an exception is raised in a view (e.g., `python manage.py runserver -pm`).

For additional information on pdb itself, consult the official Python documentation at `https://docs.python.org/3/library/pdb.html`. And for additional information on Django pdb, consult the project's documentation at `https://github.com/tomchristie/django-pdb`.

Django Extensions

Django extensions are a collection of tools designed for Django projects. As its name implies, it offers extensions for a wide array of areas where Django's standard tools level off in functionality. For debugging purposes, Django extensions offers two tools that I believe are the most important to explore: runserver_plus and runprofileserver.

To use Django extensions you'll first need to install it with `pip install django-extensions` and then add `django_extensions` to `INSTALLED_APPS` in `settings.py`. Once you set up Django extensions, its various tools become available through the `python manage.py` command just like Django's standard tools.

The Django extensions `runserver_plus` command offers interactive and enhanced debugging for Django projects. To use `runserver_plus` you'll first need to install the Werkzeug utility - `pip install Werkzeug`. Once you install Werkzeug, simply start a Django application with `python manage.py runserver_plus` instead of Django's standard `python manage.py runserver`. At first glance the `runserver_plus` command works just like Django's `runserver`; however, if you happen to hit an exception you'll see error pages like the ones in Figures 5-4 and 5-5.

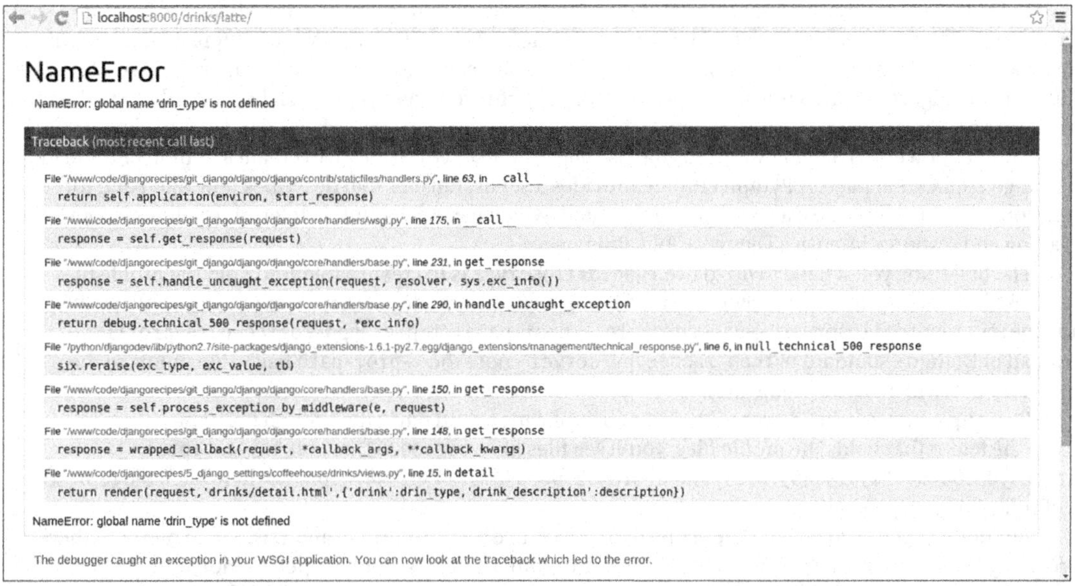

Figure 5-4. *Django extensions runserver_plus*

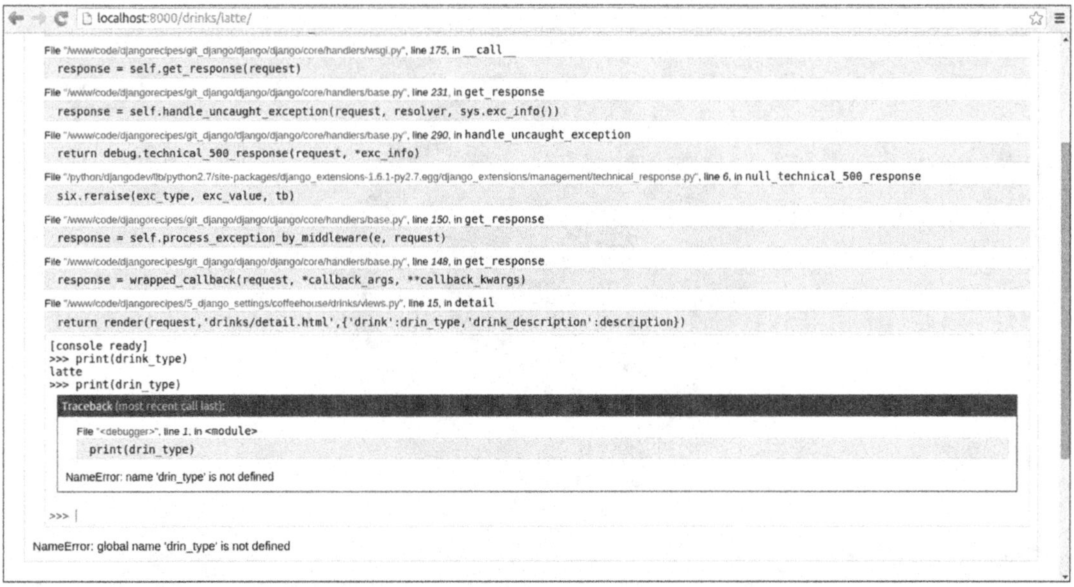

Figure 5-5. *Django extensions runserver_plus with interactive console*

In Figure 5-4 you can see a slightly different Django exception page vs. Django's default exception page. This different layout is generated by Werkzeug, but the layout itself isn't what's interesting about this approach: if you hover over any section of the stack trace you can start an interactive debugging session, as illustrated in Figure 5-5. This is a much simpler and powerful debugging approach because it's done directly in a browser!

Another powerful Django extensions tool is `runprofileserver`, which can create a Python cProfile for a Django application page. A Python cProfile provides a set of statistics that describes how often and for how long the various parts of a program are executed, which can be helpful to determine solutions for slow loading and resource intensive Django application pages.

The first thing you'll need to do to use `runprofileserver` is to create a folder to hold the profile files (e.g., `mkdir /tmp/django-coffeehouse-profiles/`). Next, simply start a Django application with `python manage.py runprofileserver --use-cprofile --prof-path=/tmp/django-coffeehouse-profiles/` instead of Django's standard `python manage.py server` - note the `--prof-path` flag value points to the directory that will hold the profile files.

Open up a browser, head over to the Django application. and navigate through it. If you open the folder that holds the profile files, you'll see files like `root.000037ms.1459139463.prof`, `stores.000061ms.1459139465.prof`, and `stores.2.000050ms.1459139470.prof`, where each file represents a cProfile for each page hit.

Although it would go beyond the scope of the book to dive into cProfile analysis, not to mention there are many tools available for this purpose, if you want a quick and easy tool to open Python cProfile files, I would suggest SnakeViz. Just do `pip install snakeviz` and then run `snakeviz <file_name>`. Once you run `snakeviz` on a file, you'll see Python cProfile details like the ones illustrated in Figures 5-6 and 5-7.

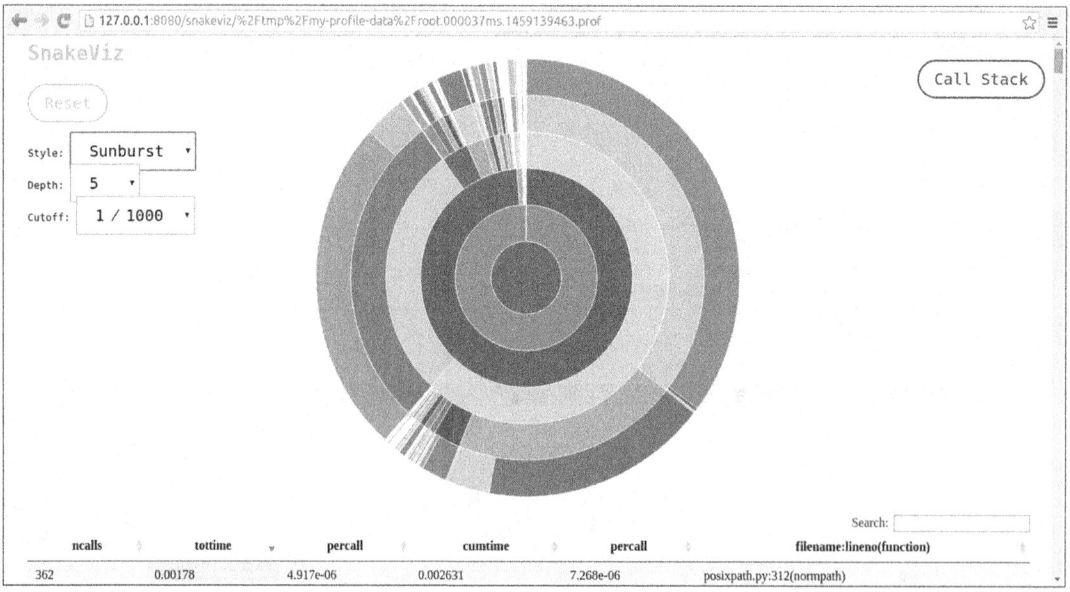

Figure 5-6. *SnakeViz cProfile image*

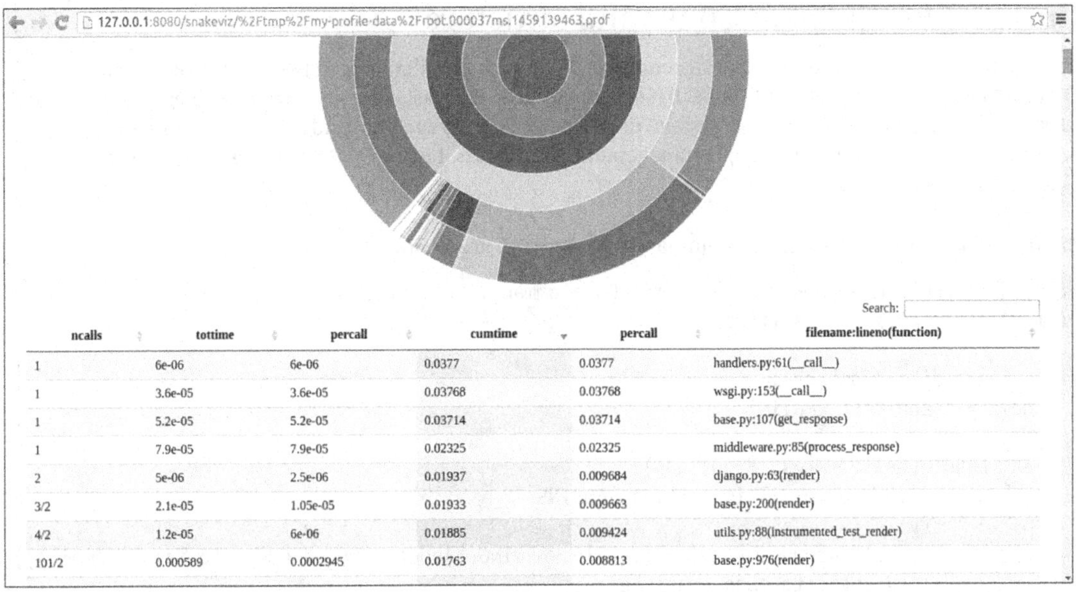

Figure 5-7. *SnakeViz cProfile listing sorted by run time*

As I mentioned at the start, Django extensions provide many tools in addition to `runserver_plus` and `runprofileserver`, which I believe are the most appropriate for debugging tasks. Nevertheless, I would recommend you review the Django extensions documentation available at `https://django-extensions.readthedocs.org/en/latest/` to explore other tools that might be of use in your own projects (e.g., the show_urls tool displays a Django project's url routes and the graph_models tools generates graphs for a Django project's models).

Django Management Commands

Throughout the previous chapters - including this one - you've relied on management commands invoked through the `manage.py` script included in all Django projects. For example, to start the development server of a Django project you've used the `runserver` command (e.g., `python manage.py runserver`), and to consolidate a project's static resources you've used the `collectstatic` command (e.g., `python manage.py collectstatic`).

Django management commands are included as part of Django apps and are designed to fulfill repetitive or complex tasks through a one keyword command line instruction. Every Django management command is backed by a script that contains the step-by-step Python logic to fulfill its duties. So when you type `python manage.py runserver`, behind the scenes Django triggers a much more complex Python routine.

If you type `python manage.py` (i.e., without a command) on a Django project, you'll see a list of Django management commands classified by app (e.g., `auth`, `django`, `staticfiles`). From this list you can gain insight into the various management commands available on all your Django apps.

I'll describe the purpose of Django management commands associated with core or third-party Django apps as they come up in the book, just as I've done up to this point (e.g., static file management commands in static file topics, model management commands in model topics).

What I'll do next is describe how to create custom management commands in your Django apps, so you can simplify the execution of routine or complex tasks through a single instruction.

Custom Management Command Structure

Custom management commands are structured as Python classes that inherit their behavior from the Django `django.core.management.base.BaseCommand` class. This last class provides the necessary structure to execute any Python logic (e.g., file system, database, or Django specific) and at the same time process arguments typically used with Django management commands. Listing 5-33 illustrates one of the most Django management commands possible.

Listing 5-33. Django management command class with no arguments

```
from django.core.management.base import BaseCommand, CommandError
from django.conf import settings

class Command(BaseCommand):
    help = 'Send test emails'

    def handle(self, *args, **options):
        for admin_name,email in settings.ADMINS:
            try:
                self.stdout.write(self.style.WARNING("About to send email to %s" % (email)))
                # Logic to send email here
                # Any other Python logic can also go here
               self.stdout.write(self.style.SUCCESS('Successfully sent email to "%s"' % email))
                raise Exception
            except Exception:
                raise CommandError('Failed to send test email')
```

Notice in Listing 5-33, the management command class must be named `Command` and inherit its behavior from the Django `BaseCommand` class. Next, there's a `help` attribute to describe the purpose of the management command. If you type `python manage.py help <task_file_name>` or `python manage.py <task_file_name> --help` Django outputs the value of the `help` attribute.

The `handle` method contains the core command logic and is automatically run when invoking the command. Notice the handle method declares three input argument: `self` to reference the class instance; `*args` to reference arguments of the method itself; and `**options` to reference arguments passed as part of the management command. The task logic in Listing 5-33 only uses the `self` reference. The other task management example - in Listing 5-34 - illustrates how to use arguments.

The task logic in Listing 5-33 is limited to looping over the `ADMINS` value in `settings.py` and outputting the task results. However, there's no limit to the logic you can execute inside the handle method, so long as it's valid Python.

Although standard Python try/except blocks work as expected inside Django management tasks, there are two syntax particularities you need to be aware of when creating Django management tasks: outputting messages and error handling.

To send output messages while executing task logic - success or informative - you can see Listing 5-33 uses the `self.stdout.write` reference, which represents the standard output channel where management tasks run. In addition, you can see `self.stdout.write` uses both the `self.style.WARNING` and `self.style.SUCCESS` to declare the actual messages to output. The wrapping of messages inside `self.style.*` is optional, but outputs colored formatted messages (e.g., SUCCESS in green font, WARNING in yellow font) in accordance with Django syntax coloring roles.[11]

[11] `https://docs.djangoproject.com/en/1.11/ref/django-admin/#syntax-coloring`

To send error messages while executing task logic, you can use the `self.stderr.write` reference, which represents the standard error channel where management tasks run. And to terminate the execution of a management task due to an error, you can `raise` the `django.core.management.base.CommandError` exception - as it's done in Listing 5-33 - which accepts an error message, which gets sent to the `self.stderr.write` channel.

In most circumstances, it's rare to have a fixed Django management command like the one in Listing 5-33 that uses no arguments to alter its logical workflow. For example, the Django `runserver` command accepts argument like `addrport` and `--nothreading` to influence how a web server is launched.

Django management commands can use two types of arguments: positional arguments - where the order in which they're declared gives them their meaning; or named arguments - which are preceded by names with two dashes -- (a.k.a.flags) to give them their meaning.

Although the `**options` argument of the `handle()` method - as shown in Listing 5-33 - provides access to a management command's arguments to alter the logical workflow, in order to use arguments in a custom Django management command, you must also declare the `add_arguments()` method.

The `add_arguments()` method must define a management task's arguments, including their type - positional or named - default value, choice values, and help message, among other things. In essence, the `add_arguments()` method works as a pre-processor to command arguments, which are then made available in the `**options` argument of the `handle()` method.

The `parser` reference of the `add_arguments(self,parser)` signature is an argument parser based on the standard Python argparse package[12] designed to easily process command-line arguments for Python scripts.

To add command arguments inside the `add_arguments()` method you do so via the `parser.add_argument()` method, as illustrated in Listing 5-34.

Listing 5-34. Django management task class with arguments

```
from django.core.management.base import BaseCommand, CommandError
from django.conf import settings

class Command(BaseCommand):
    help = 'Clean up stores'

    def add_arguments(self, parser):
        # Positional arguments are standalone name
        parser.add_argument('store_id')

        # Named (optional) arguments start with --
        parser.add_argument(
            '--delete',
            default=False,
            help='Delete store instead of cleaning it up',
        )

    def handle(self, *args, **options):
        # Access arguments inside **options dictionary
        #options={'store_id': '1', 'settings': None, 'pythonpath': None,
        #         'verbosity': 1, 'traceback': False, 'no_color': False, 'delete': False}
```

[12]https://docs.python.org/3/library/argparse.html

The management command in Listing 5-34 declares both a positional and a named argument. Notice both arguments are added with the `parser.add_argument()` method. The difference being, named arguments use leading dashes - and If omitted an argument is assumed to be positional.

Positional arguments by definition are required. So in the case of Listing 5-34, the `store_id` argument is expected (e.g., `python manage.py cleanupstores 1`, where `1` is the `store_id`), otherwise Django throws a 'too few arguments' error.

Named arguments are always optional. And because named arguments are optional, you can see in Listing 5-34 the `--delete` argument declares a `default=False` value, ensuring the argument always receives a default value to run the logic inside the `handle()` method.

The `--delete` argument in Listing 5-34 also uses the `help` attribute to define a descriptive text about the purpose of the argument. In addition to `default` and `help`, the `parser.add_argument()` method supports a wide variety of attributes, based on the Python argparse package - see the previous footnote to consult some of the arguments support by this method.

Finally, you can see in Listing 5-34 the `handle()` method gets access to the command arguments via the `**options` dictionary, where the values can then be used toward the structuring of the command logic. Note the additional arguments available in `**options` - `settings`, `pythonpath`,etc. - are inherited by default due to the `BaseCommand` class.

Custom Management Command Installation

All Django management tasks are placed inside individual Python files (i.e., one command per file) and stored inside an app directory structure under the `/management/commands/` folder. Listing 5-35 shows the folder structure for a couple of apps with custom management tasks.

Listing 5-35. Django management task folder structure and location

```
+-<BASE_DIR_project_name>
|
+-manage.py
|
|
+---+-<PROJECT_DIR_project_name>
    |
    +-__init__.py
    +-settings.py
    +-urls.py
    +-wsgi.py
    |
    +-about(app)-+
    |            +-__init__.py
    |            +-models.py
    |            +-tests.py
    |            +-views.py
    |            +-management-+
    |                         +-__init__.py
    |                         +-commands-+
    |                                    +-__init__.py
    |                                    |
    |                                    |
    |                                    +-sendtestemails.py
    |
```

```
+-stores(app)-+
              +-__init__.py
              +-models.py
              +-tests.py
              +-views.py
              +-management-+
                           +-__init__.py
                           +-commands-+
                                      +-__init__.py
                                      |
                                      |
                                      +-cleanupstores.py
                                      +-updatemenus.py
```

As you can see in Listing 5-35, the about app has a single management command inside the /management/commands/ folder and the stores app has two management commands nested inside its own /management/commands/ folder.

■ **Caution** To ensure the visibility of an app's management commands, don't forget to add the empty __init__.py files to the /management/ and /commands/ folders as shown in Listing 5-35 and declare the apps as part of INSTALLED_APPS in a project's settings.py file.

Management Command Automation

Django management commands are typically run from the command line, requiring human intervention. However, there can be times when it's helpful or necessary to automate the execution of management commands from other locations (e.g., a Django view method or shell).

For example, if a user uploads an image in a Django application and you want the image to become publicly accessible, you'll need to run the collectstatic command so the image makes its way to the public and consolidation location (STATIC_ROOT). Similarly, you may want to run a cleanupprofile command every time a user logs in.

To automate the execution of management commands, Django offers the django.core.management.call_command() method. Listing 5-36 illustrates the various ways in which you can use the call_command() method.

Listing 5-36. Django management automation with call_command()

```
from django.core import management

# Option 1, no arguments
management.call_command('sendtestemails')

# Option 2, no pause to wait for input
management.call_command('collectstatic', interactive=False)
```

```
# Option 3, command input with Command()
from django.core.management.commands import loaddata
management.call_command(loaddata.Command(), 'stores', verbosity=0)

# Option 4, positional and named command arguments
management.call_command('cleanupdatastores', 1, delete=True)
```

The first option in Listing 5-35 executes a management without any arguments. The second option in Listing 5-35 uses the `interactive=False` argument to indicate the command must not pause for user input (e.g., `collectstatic` always asks if you're sure if you want to overwrite preexisting files, the `interactive=False` argument avoids this pause and need for input).

The third option in Listing 5-35 invokes the management command by first importing it and then invoking its `Command()` class directly vs. using the command string value. And finally, the fourth option - just like the third - in Listing 5-35, uses a positional argument - declared as a stand-alone value (e.g., `'stores'`, `1`) and a named argument - declared as a `key=value` (e.g., `verbosity=0`, `delete=True`).

CHAPTER 6

Django Forms

Forms are the standard way that users input or edit data in web applications. At their lowest level, forms are made up of HTML tags with special meaning. While you can directly add HTML form tags to Django or Jinja templates, you really want to avoid this and use Django's built-in form support to make form processing easier.

In this chapter you'll learn how to structure Django forms and the workflow that forms undergo. You'll also learn the various field types and widgets supported by Django forms, how to validate form data and manage its errors, as well as how to lay out forms and their errors in templates.

Once you have a firm understanding of the basics behind Django forms, you'll learn how to create custom form fields and widgets. Finally, you'll learn more complex Django form processing techniques, such as partial form processing, form processing with AJAX, how to process files sent through Django forms, and how to process multiple forms on the same page with Django formsets.

Django Form Structure and Workflow

Django has a special forms package that offers a comprehensive way to work with forms. Among this package's features are the ability to define form functionality in a single location, data validation, and tight integration with Django models, among other things. Let's take a first look at a stand-alone Django form class in Listing 6-1 that is used to back a contact form.

Listing 6-1. Django form class definition

```
# forms.py in app named 'contact'
from django import forms

class ContactForm(forms.Form):
      name = forms.CharField(required=False)
      email = forms.EmailField(label='Your email')
      comment = forms.CharField(widget=forms.Textarea)
```

Note There's no specific location Django expects forms to be in. You can equally place Django form classes in their own file inside an app (e.g., forms.py) or place them inside other app files (e.g., models.py, views.py). You can later import Django form classes to where they're needed, just like Django views or Python packages.

D. Rubio, *Beginning Django*, https://doi.org/10.1007/978-1-4842-2787-9_6

The first important aspect to note in Listing 6-1 is a Django form definition is a subclass of the `forms.Form` class, so it automatically has all the base functionality of this parent class. Next, you can see the form class has three attributes, two of the type `forms.CharField` and one of the type `forms.EmailField`. These form field definitions restrict input to certain characteristics.

For example, `forms.CharField` indicates the input should be a set of characters and `forms.EmailField` indicates the input should be an email. In addition, you can see each form field includes properties (e.g., `required`) to further restrict the type of input. For the moment this should be enough detail about Django form field type;, the next section on Django form field types goes into greater detail on just this topic.

Next, let's integrate the Django form in Listing 6-1 to a Django view method so it can then be passed and rendered in a Django template. Listing 6-2 illustrates the initial iteration of this view method.

Listing 6-2. Django view method that uses a Django form

```
# views.py in app named 'contact'
from django.shortcuts import render
from .forms import ContactForm

def contact(request):
    form = ContactForm()
    return render(request,'about/contact.html',{'form':form})
```

The view method in Listing 6-2 first instantiates the `ContactForm` form class and assigns it to the `form` reference. This `form` reference is then passed as an argument to be made available inside the `about/contact.html` template.

Next, inside the Django template you can output a Django form as a regular variable. Listing 6-3 illustrates how the Django form is rendered if you use the standard template syntax `{{form.as_table}}`.

Listing 6-3. Django form instance rendered in template as HTML

```
<tr><th><label for="id_name">Name:</label></th><td><input id="id_name" name="name"
type="text" /></td></tr>
<tr><th><label for="id_email">Your email:</label></th><td><input id="id_email" required
name="email" type="email" /></td></tr>
<tr><th><label for="id_comment">Comment:</label></th><td><textarea cols="40" id="id_comment"
required name="comment" rows="10">
</textarea></td></tr>
```

In Listing 6-3 you can see how the Django form is translated into HTML tags! Notice how the Django form produces the appropriate HTML `<input>` tags for each form field (e.g., `forms.EmailField(label='Your email')` creates the specified `<label>` and an HTML 5 `type="email"` to enforce client-side validation of an email). In addition, notice the name field lacks the HTML 5 `required` attribute due to the `required=False` statement used in the form field in Listing 6-1.

If you look closely at Listing 6-3, the HTML output for the Django form instance are just inner HTML table tags (i.e., `<tr>`,`<th>`,`<td>`). The output is missing an HTML `<table>` wrapper tag and supporting HTML form tags (i.e., `<form>` tag and `action` attribute to indicate where to send the form, as well as a `submit` button). This means you'll need to add the missing HTML form tags to the template to create a working web form - a process that's described shortly in Listing 6-4.

In addition, if you don't want to output the entire form fields surrounded by HTML table elements like Listing 6-3, there are many other syntax variations to output form fields granularly and stripped of HTML tags. In this case, the `{{form.as_table}}` reference in the template is used to simplify things, but the upcoming section "Set Up the Layout for Django Forms in Templates" in this chapter elaborates on the different syntax variations to output Django forms in templates.

Next, let's take a look at Figure 6-1, which shows a Django form's workflow to better illustrate how Django forms work from start to finish.

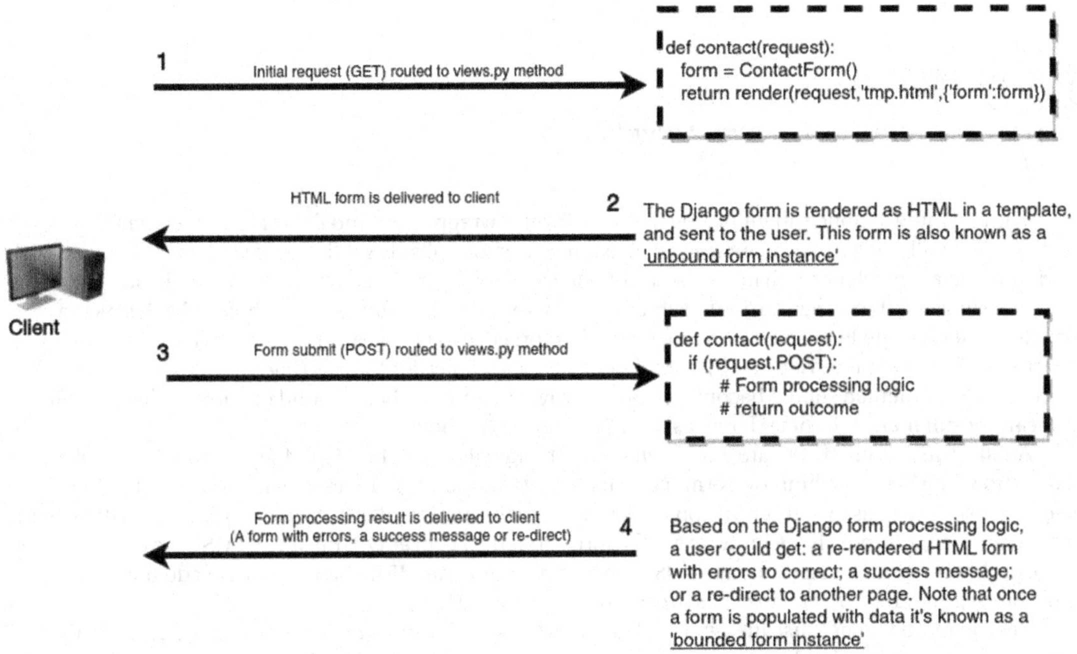

Figure 6-1. *Django forms workflow*

The first two steps of the workflow in Figure 6-1 is what I've described up to this point. It consists of a user hitting a URL that's processed by a view method that returns an empty form based on the Django form class definition. Listing 6-3 shows the raw HTML output of the Django form, but as I already mentioned, the form is missing elements in order to become a functional web form; next I'll describe the elements you need to add to get a functional web form.

Functional Web Form Syntax for Django Forms

So far you've learned how a Django form class definition can quickly be turned into an HTML form. But this automatic HTML generation is only part of the benefit of using Django form class definitions; you can also validate form values and present errors to end users much more quickly.

To perform these last actions, it's first necessary to have a functional web form. Listing 6-4 illustrates the template syntax to create a functional web form from a Django form.

Listing 6-4. Django form template declaration for functional web form

```
<form method="POST">
  {% csrf_token %}

<table>
{{form.as_table}}
</table>
<input type="submit" value="Submit form">
</form>
```

The first thing to notice about Listing 6-4 is the form is wrapped around the HTML `<form>` tag that is standard for all web forms. The reason Django forces you to explicitly set the `<form>` tag is because its attributes dictate much of a web form's behavior and can vary depending on the purpose of the form.

In Listing 6-4, the `method` attribute tells a web browser that when the form is submitted it POSTs the data to the server. The POST method value is standard practice in web forms that process user data - an alternative method option value is GET, but it's not a typical choice for transferring user-provided data. The use of the POST method should become clearer shortly, but for more background on form `method` attributes, you can consult many Internet references on HTTP request methods.[1]

Another important `<form>` attribute - which is actually missing in Listing 6-4 - is `action`, which tells a web browser where to submit the form (i.e., what URL is tasked with processing the form). In this case, because Listing 6-4 has no `action` attribute, a browser's behavior is to POST the data to the same URL where it's currently on, meaning if the browser got the form from the `/contact/` URL, it will POST the data to the same `/contact/` URL. If you wanted to POST the form to a separate URL, then you would add the action attribute (e.g., `action="/urltoprocessform/"`) to the `<form>` tag.

Keep in mind that because the same URL delivers the initial form - via a GET request - and must also process the form data - via a POST request - the backing view method of the URL must be designed to handle both cases. I'll describe a modified version of Listing 6-2 – which just handles the GET request case – to also handle the POST case in the next section.

The `{% csrf_token %}` statement in Listing 6-4 is a Django tag. `{% csrf_token %}` is a special tag reserved for cases when a web form is submitted via POST and processed by Django. The csrf initials mean Cross-Site Request Forgery, which is a default security mechanism enforced by Django. While it's possible to disable CSRF and not include the `{% csrf_token %}` Django tag in forms, I would advise against it and recommend you keep adding the `{% csrf_token %}` Django tag to all forms with POST, as CSRF works as a safeguard and mostly behind the scenes. The last subsection in this first section describes the reasoning behind CSRF and how it works in Django in greater detail.

Next in Listing 6-4 is the `{{form.as_table}}` snippet wrapped in an `<table>` tag, which represents the Django form instance and outputs the HTML output illustrated in Listing 6-3. Finally, there's the `<input type="submit">` tag, which generates the form's submit button - that when clicked on by a user submits the form - and the closing `</form>` tag.

Django View Method to Process Form (POST Handling)

Once you have a functional web form in Django, it's necessary to create a view method to process it. In the previous section, I mentioned how the same URL and, by extension, view method, would both handle generating the blank HTML form, as well as process the HTML form with data. Listing 6-5 illustrates a modified version of the view method in Listing 6-2 that does exactly this.

[1] `https://en.wikipedia.org/wiki/Hypertext_Transfer_Protocol#Request_methods`

Listing 6-5. Django view method that sends and processes Django form

```
from django.shortcuts import render
from django.http import HttpResponseRedirect
from .forms import ContactForm

def contact(request):
    if request.method == 'POST':
        # POST, generate form with data from the request
        form = ContactForm(request.POST)
        # check if it's valid:
        if form.is_valid():
            # process data, insert into DB, generate email,etc
            # redirect to a new URL:
            return HttpResponseRedirect('/about/contact/thankyou')
    else:
        # GET, generate blank form
        form = ContactForm()
    return render(request,'about/contact.html',{'form':form})
```

The most important construct in the view method of Listing 6-5 is the if/else condition that checks the `request` method type. If the request method type is POST (i.e., data submission or step 3 in Figure 6-1), the form's data is processed, but if the `request` method type is anything else (i.e., initial request or step 1 in Figure 6-1) an empty form is generated to produce the same behavior as Listing 6-2. Notice the last line in Listing 6-5 is a `return` statement that assigns the form instance - whether empty (a.k.a. *unbound*) or populated (a.k.a. *bound*) - and returns it to a template for rendering.

Now let's take a closer look at the POST logic in Listing 6-5. If the `request` method type is POST it means there's incoming user data, so we access the incoming data with the `request.POST` reference and initialize the Django form with it. But notice how there's no need to access individual form fields or make piecemeal assignments - although you could if you wanted to and this process is described in a later section in this chapter – using `request.POST` as the argument of a Django form class is sufficient to populate a Django form instance with user data; it's that simple! It's worth mentioning that a Django form instance created in this manner (i.e., with user-provided data) is known as a *bound* form instance.

At this point, we still don't know if a user-provided valid data with respect to a Django form's field definitions (e.g., if values are text or a valid email). To validate a form's data, you must use the `is_valid()` helper method on the bound form instance. If `form.is_valid()` is `True` the data is processed and subsequent action is taken; in Listing 6-5 this additional action consists of redirecting control to the `/about/contact/thankyou` URL. If `form.is_valid()` is `False` it means the form data has errors, after which point control falls to the last `return` statement that now passes a bound form instance to render the template. By using a bound form instance in this last case, the user gets a rendered form filled with his initial data submission and errors so he's able to correct the data without reintroducing values from scratch.

I purposely didn't mention anymore details about the `is_valid()` helper method or error message displays, because Django form processing can get a little complex. The subsequent section "Django Form Processing: Initialization, Field Access, Validation, and Error Handling" covers all you need to know about Django form processing so it doesn't interfere in this introductory section.

CSRF: What Is It and How Does It Work with Django?

CSRF or Cross-Site Request Forgery is a technique used by cyber-criminals to force users into executing unwanted actions on a web application. When users interact with web forms, they make all kinds of state-changing tasks that range from making orders (e.g., products, money transfers) to changing their data (e.g. name, email, address). Most users tend to feel a heightened sense of security when they interact with web forms because they see an HTTPS/SSL security symbol or they've used a username/password prior to interacting with a web form, all of which leads to a feeling there's no way a cyber-criminal could eavesdrop, guess, or interfere with their actions.

A CSRF attack relies for the most part on social engineering and lax application security on a web application, so the attack vector is open irrespective of other security measures (e.g., HTTPS/SSL, strong password). Figure 6-2 illustrates a CSRF vulnerable scenario on a web application.

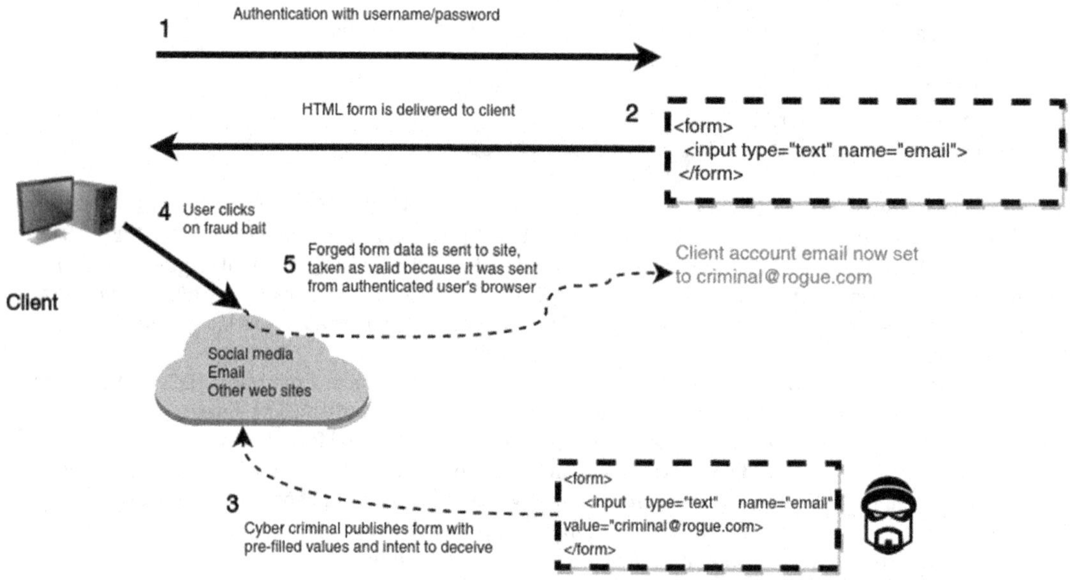

Figure 6-2. *Web application with no CSRF protection*

After user "X" interacts with web application "A" (e.g., making an order, updating his email) he simply navigates away and goes to other sites. Like most web applications, web application "A" maintains valid user sessions for hours or days, in case users come back and decide to do other things without having to sign in again. Meanwhile, a cyber-criminal has also used site "A" and knows exactly where and how all of its web forms work (e.g., URLs, input parameters such as email, credit card).

Next, a cyber-criminal creates links or pages that mimic the submission of web forms on web application "A." For example, this could be a form that changes a user's email in order to overtake an account or transfers money from a user's account to steal funds. The cyber-criminal then seeds the Internet with these links or pages through email, social media, or other web sites with enticing or frightening headlines: "Get a $100 coupon from site 'A'", "Urgent: Change your password on site 'A' because of a security risk.' In reality, these links or pages don't do what they advertise, but instead in a single click mimic web form submissions from site "A" (e.g., change a user's email or transfer funds).

Now let's turn our attention to unsuspecting user "X" that visited site "A" hours or days earlier. He catches a glimpse of these last advertisements and thinks "Wow, I can't pass this up." Thinking what harm can a click do, he clicks on the bogus advertisement, the user is then sent to a legitimate site 'A' page as a façade or the click 'appears' to have done nothing. User "X" thinks nothing of it and goes back to some other task. If site 'A' did not have web forms with CSRF protection, then user "X" just inadvertently - in a single click - performed an action on site "A" he wasn't aware of.

As you can see, in order to perform a CSRF attack, all that's needed is for a user to have an active session on a given site and a cyber-criminal crafty enough to trick a user into clicking on a link or page that performs actions on said site. Hence the term's name: "Cross-Site," because the request doesn't come from the original site, and "Request Forgery" because it's a forged request by a cyber-criminal.

To protect against web form CSRF attacks, it's isn't sufficient for web applications to trust authenticated users, because as I've just described, authenticated users could have inadvertently triggered actions they weren't aware of. Web forms must be equipped with a unique identifier - often called a CSRF token - that's unique to a user and has an expiration time, similar to a session identifier. In this manner, if a request is made by an authenticated user to a site, only requests that match his CSRF token are considered valid and all other requests are discarded, as illustrated in Figure 6-3.

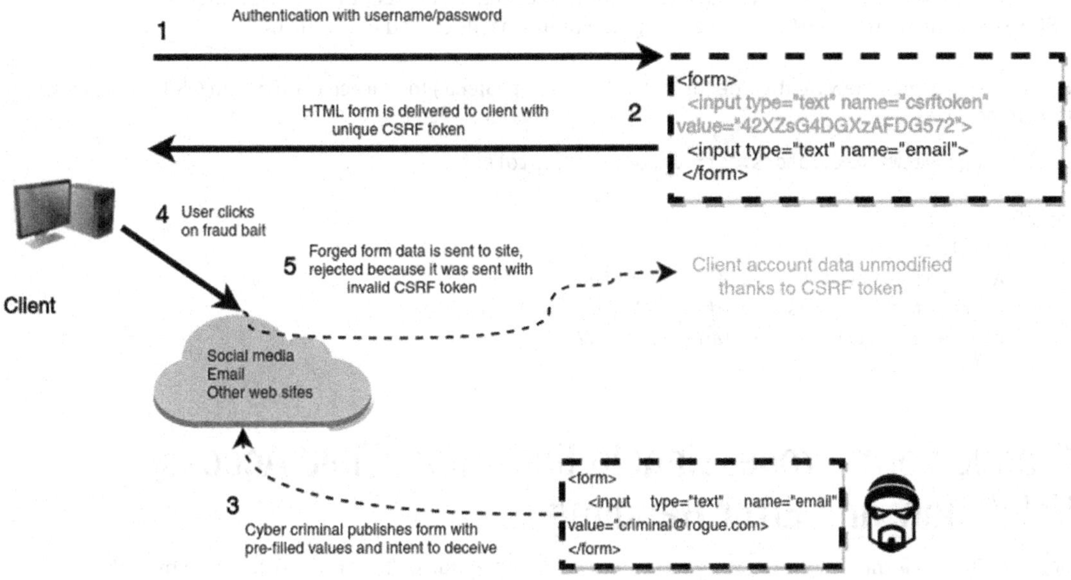

Figure 6-3. *Web application with CSRF protection*

As you can see in Figure 6-3, the inclusion of a CSRF token in a web form makes it very difficult to forge a user's request.

In Django, a CSRF token is generated in web forms with the `{% csrf token %}` tag that generates an HTML tag in the form `<input type="hidden" name="csrfmiddlewaretoken" value="32_character_string">`, where the 32-character string value varies by user. In this manner, if a Django application makes a POST request - like those made by web forms - it will only accept the request if the CSRF token is present and valid for a given user; otherwise it will generate a '403 Forbidden' page error.

Be aware CSRF is enabled by default on all Django applications thanks to its out-of-the-box middleware settings that include the `django.middleware.csrf.CsrfViewMiddleware` class charged with enforcing CSRF functionality. If you wish to disable the CSRF support in a Django application completely, you can just remove the `django.middleware.csrf.CsrfViewMiddleware` class from the `MIDDLEWARE` variable in `settings.py`.

If you wish to enable or disable CSRF on certain web forms, you can selectively use the `@csrf_exempt()` and `@csrf_protect` decorators on the view methods that process a web form's POST request.

To enable CSRF on all web forms and disable CSRF behavior on certain web forms, keep the `django.middleware.csrf.CsrfViewMiddleware` class in `MIDDLEWARE` and decorate the view methods you don't want as CSRF validation on with the `@csrf_exempt()` decorator, as illustrated in Listing 6-6.

Listing 6-6. Django view method decorated with @csrf_exempt() to bypass CSRF enforcement

```
from django.views.decorators.csrf import csrf_exempt

@csrf_exempt
def contact(request):
    # Any POST-processing inside view method
    # ignores if there is or isn't a CSRF token
```

To disable CSRF on all web forms and enable CSRF behavior on certain web forms, remove the `django.middleware.csrf.CsrfViewMiddleware` class from `MIDDLEWARE` and decorate the view methods you want CSRF validation on with the `@csrf_protect()` decorator, as illustrated in Listing 6-7.

Listing 6-7. Django view method decorated with @csrf_protect() to enforce CSRF when CSRF is disabled at the project level

```
from django.views.decorators.csrf import csrf_protect

@csrf_protect
def contact(request):
    # Any POST processing inside view method
    # checks for the presence of a CSRF token
    # even when CsrfViewMiddleware is removed
```

Django Form Processing: Initialization, Field Access, Validation, and Error Handling

Because Django form processing can have a great deal of variations, I'll start the discussion from the same form and view method explained in the previous section, now consolidated in Listing 6-8.

Listing 6-8. Django form class with backing processing view method

```
from django import forms
from django.shortcuts import render

class ContactForm(forms.Form):
      name = forms.CharField(required=False)
      email = forms.EmailField(label='Your email')
      comment = forms.CharField(widget=forms.Textarea)

def contact(request):
    if request.method == 'POST':
        # POST, generate form with data from the request
        form = ContactForm(request.POST)
```

```
        # Reference is now a bound instance with user data sent in POST
        # process data, insert into DB, generate email, redirect to a new URL,etc
    else:
        # GET, generate blank form
        form = ContactForm()
        # Reference is now an unbound (empty) form
    # Reference form instance (bound/unbound) is sent to template for rendering
    return render(request,'about/contact.html',{'form':form})
```

Initialize Forms: Initial for Fields and Forms, __init__ method, label_suffix, auto_id, field_order, and use_required_attribute

When users request a page backed by a Django form they're sent an empty form (a.k.a. *unbound* form) - represented by the GET section and `ContactForm()` instance in Listing 6-8. Although the form is always empty from a user data perspective, the form can contain data from as part of its initialization sequence (e.g., a pre-filled form with a user's email or name).

To perform this kind of Django form initialization you have three options. The first technique consists of initializing the form with a dictionary of values via the `initial` argument directly on the form instance declared in the view method. Listing 6-9 shows this technique.

Listing 6-9. Django form instance with initial argument declared in view method

```
def contact(request):
        ....
        ....
    else:
        # GET, generate blank form
        form = ContactForm(initial={'email':'johndoe@coffeehouse.com','name':'John Doe'})
        # Form is now initialized for first presentation to display these values
    # Reference form instance (bound/unbound) is sent to template for rendering
    return render(request,'about/contact.html',{'form':form})
```

The `ContactForm()` now uses `initial={'email':'johndoe@coffeehouse.com','name':'John Doe'}` to generate a pre-filled form instance with values for the email and name fields so end users don't have to go to the trouble of typing these values from scratch themselves.

The technique in Listing 6-9 is intended for one-time or instance-specific initialization values. If you want to constantly provide the same value for a given form field, a more suitable technique is to use the same `initial` argument directly on a form field, as show in Listing 6-10.

Listing 6-10. Django form fields with initial argument

```
from django import forms

class ContactForm(forms.Form):
      name = forms.CharField(required=False,initial='Please provide your name')
      email = forms.EmailField(label='Your email', initial='We need your email')
      comment = forms.CharField(widget=forms.Textarea)
```

```
def contact(request):
        ....
        ....
    else:
        # GET, generate blank form
        form = ContactForm()
        # Form is now initialized for first presentation and is filled with initial values
          in form definition
    # Reference form instance (bound/unbound) is sent to template for rendering
    return render(request,'about/contact.html',{'form':form})
```

Notice in Listing 6-10 how it's now the form fields in the form class equipped with the `initial` argument. It's worth mentioning that if you use the `initial` argument on both the form instance and form fields, form instance values take precedence over any form field (e.g., if you combine the statements from Listing 6-9 and Listing 6-10, the form will always be pre-filled with `email='johndoe@coffeehouse.com'` and `name='John Doe'` from Listing 6-9).

One of the drawbacks of using the `initial` argument in form fields like Listing 6-10 is that values can't change dynamically at runtime (i.e., you can't personalize the `initial` values based on who calls the form like Listing 6-9). To solve this and provide the utmost flexibility for the most complex form initialization scenarios is a third technique using the `__init__` method of a form class illustrated in Listing 6-11.

Listing 6-11. Django form initialized with __init__ method

```
from django import forms

class ContactForm(forms.Form):
      name = forms.CharField(required=False)
      email = forms.EmailField(label='Your email')
      comment = forms.CharField(widget=forms.Textarea)

      def __init__(self, *args, **kwargs):
            # Get 'initial' argument if any
            initial_arguments = kwargs.get('initial', None)
            updated_initial = {}
            if initial_arguments:
                  # We have initial arguments, fetch 'user' placeholder variable if any
                  user = initial_arguments.get('user',None)
                  # Now update the form's initial values if user
                  if user:
                        updated_initial['name'] = getattr(user, 'first_name', None)
                        updated_initial['email'] = getattr(user, 'email', None)
            # You can also initialize form fields with hardcoded values
            # or perform complex DB logic here to then perform initialization
            updated_initial['comment'] = 'Please provide a comment'
            # Finally update the kwargs initial reference
            kwargs.update(initial=updated_initial)
            super(ContactForm, self).__init__(*args, **kwargs)

def contact(request):
        ....
        ....
    else:
```

```
        # GET, generate blank form
        form = ContactForm(initial={'user':request.user,'otherstuff':'otherstuff'})
        # Form is now initialized via the form's __init__ method
    # Reference form instance (bound/unbound) is sent to template for rendering
    return render(request,'about/contact.html',{'form':form})
```

The first important aspect in Listing 6-11 is how the form is initialized in the view method; notice it uses the same `initial` argument but the dictionary values are now `{'user':request.user,'otherstuff':'otherstuff'}`. Do these values look strange? The form doesn't even have fields named `user` or `otherstuff`, so what's happening?

These last values are perfectly valid and in other circumstances would be ignored because the Django form does indeed have no fields by these names, but since we'll be manipulating the guts of form initialization process in the `__init__` method, we can access these placeholder values for indirect initialization purposes. More importantly, using these placeholder values illustrates how it's possible to use context data or unrelated form data to initialize Django form fields.

Next, let's turn our attention to the Django form's `__init__` method, which is invoked when you create a form instance. The `__init__` method's arguments `*args`, `**kwargs` are standard Python syntax - if you've never seen this last syntax check out the appendix on Python Basics: Methods: Default, Optional, *args & **kwargs Arguments.

The first step in `__init__` checks for an initial value and creates a reference to hold the new values to initialize the form. If an `initial` value is present, a check is made for a `user` value to use these values for the form's actual `name` and `email` fields. Next, irrespective of any passed in values, a direct assignment is made on the form's `comment` field.

Finally, the form's `initial` reference is updated with a new set of values that reflect the form's actual fields, leading to the form's initialization using data outside the context of a form (e.g., request data, database query, etc.). As a last step in the `__init__` method, a call is made to the `super()` method so that the base/parent class initialization process takes place.

ALWAYS USE THE INITIAL ARGUMENT OR __INIT__ METHOD TO POPULATE FORMS WITH INITIALIZATION DATA AND KEEP THEM UNBOUND.

It's important to note all the previous initialization techniques keep a form unbound, which is a term used to describe form instances that haven't been populated with user data. The term bound is reserved for when a form's field values are populated with user data. This subtle difference between bound and unbound is really important when you enter the validation phase of Django forms described in the next section.

This also means the syntax ContactForm(initial={'email':'johndoe@coffeehouse.com','name':'John Doe'}) is not equivalent to ContactForm({'email':'johndoe@coffeehouse.com','name':'John Doe'}). The first variation uses the initial argument to create an unbound form instance, while the second variation creates a bound form instance by passing the values directly without any argument.

In addition to initializing the first set of data loaded on a Django form, there are four other initialization options for Django forms that influence a form's layout in templates: `label_suffix`, `auto_id`, `field_order`, and `use_required_attribute`.

When you generate the output for a Django form in a template - a topic that's described in detail later in this chapter in "Set Up the Layout for Django Forms in Templates" - form fields are generally accompanied by what's called a field label, which is another name for a human-friendly descriptor. For example, if you have fields called name and email, their default labels are Your name and Your email, respectively. To separate field labels from a field's HTML markup (e.g., <input type="text">) Django defines a label suffix, which defaults to : (the colon symbol) to produce output with the pattern <field_label>:<input type="<field_type>">. Through the label_suffix you can define a custom label suffix symbol to separate every form field from its label. So, for example, the ContactForm(label_suffix='...') syntax outputs every form field label separated by ... (e.g., Your email...<input type="text">).

■ **Tip** Individual form fields can also use the label_suffix attribute; see the Django form field types section. If label_suffix is declared in both a form field and form initialization, the former takes precedence.

Another initialization option for Django forms is auto_id that automatically generates an id and label for every form field. By default, a Django form is always set to auto_id=True so you'll always get auto-generated HTML ids and labels when outputting a form with form.as_table(), as illustrated in the first part of Listing 6-12.

Listing 6-12. Django form with automatic ids (default auto_id=True option) and no automatic ids auto_id=False option

```
<!-- Option 1, default auto_id=True -->
<tr><th><label for="id_name">Name:</label></th><td><input id="id_name" name="name"
type="text" /></td></tr>
<tr><th><label for="id_email">Your email:</label></th><td><input id="id_email" name="email"
type="email" /></td></tr>
<tr><th><label for="id_comment">Comment:</label></th><td><textarea cols="40" id="id_comment"
name="comment" rows="10">
</textarea></td></tr>

<!-- Option 2 auto_id=False -->
<tr><th>Name:</th><td><input name="name" type="text" /></td></tr>
<tr><th>Your email:</th><td><input name="email" type="email" /></td></tr>
<tr><th>Comment:</th><td><textarea cols="40" name="comment" rows="10">\r\n</textarea>
</td></tr>
```

Notice how the field labels in the top output of Listing 6-12 are wrapped around <label for="id_field_name"> <label> and the fields HTML tags include the id="id_field_name" attribute. In most cases this is a desirable output as it allows fields to be easily referenced for purposes of attaching JavaScript events or CSS classes. However, for other circumstances auto_id=True can produce very verbose output and inclusively conflicting HTML tags (e.g., if you have two form instances of the same type on the same page, there will be two identical ids).

To turn off the auto-generation of ids and labels you can initialize a form with the auto_id=False option. For example, the ContactForm(auto_id=False) syntax generates the output presented in the second half of Listing 6-12.

Another initialization option for unbound form instances that influences a form's layout is the field_order option. By default, form fields are output in the order they're declared, so the form definition in Listing 6-10 follows the output order: name, email, comment. You can override this default field output by using the field_order option, which accepts a list of field names with the desired output order. The field_order option can be declared as part of the initialization process or inclusively as if it were a form field.

For example, the ContactForm(field_order=['email','comment','name']) syntax ensures the email field is output first, followed by comment and name. It's worth mentioning the field_order option can accept an incomplete field list, such as ContactForm(field_order=['email']), which outputs the email field followed by the remaining form fields in their declared order, in this case name and then comment. If you're constantly setting field_order to initialize a form's field order, a quicker solution is to set a default field_order as part of the form itself:

```
class ContactForm(forms.Form):
      name = forms.CharField(required=False)
      email = forms.EmailField(label='Your email')
      comment = forms.CharField(widget=forms.Textarea)
      field_order = ['email','comment','name'] # Sets order email,comment,name
```

If you declare field_order as part of the form itself, on initialization, the initialization field_order takes precedence. The upcoming section "Set Up the Layout for Django Forms in Templates" contains more details on the practical use of field_order in templates.

Finally, the use_required_attribute option allows you to set the overall use of the HTML 5 required attribute. By default use_required_attribute=True, which means all required form fields are output with the HTML 5 required attribute, ensuring browsers enforces these form fields are always provided. You can disable the use of this HTML 5 client-side validation required attribute by initializing a form with use_required_attribute=False. Note that setting use_required_attribute=False does not influence the Django server-side validation of a form field (e.g., if a form field is required, Django server-side validation still catches fields that aren't provided, irrespective of the use_required_attribute option).

Accessing Form Values: request.POST and cleaned_data

Once a user fills out a Django form, the form is sent back to the server to be processed and performs an action with the user data (e.g., creates an order, send an email, saves the data to the database) - a step that is represented in the POST section in Listing 6-8.

One of the key advantages of Django form processing is you can use the request.POST variable to create a bound form instance. But although the request.POST variable is the initial access point to populate a Django form with user data, you shouldn't use this data beyond initializing a form instance, as the data in request.POST is too raw for direct access.

For example, in request.POST you still don't know if the user-provided data is valid. In addition, the data in request.POST is still treated as strings, so if your Django form happens to have an IntegerField() or DateField() it still needs to be converted manually to the expected data type (e.g., '6' to 6 integer, '2017-01-01' to 2017-01-01 datetime), which is just unnecessary work that another another part of Django forms deals with.

Once you have a bound form generated with the request.POST variable, you can then access each of the form's field values through the cleaned_data dictionary. For example, if the bound form has a form field called name you can use the syntax form.cleaned_data['name'] to access the user-provided name value. More importantly, if the form field is an IntegerField() named age the syntax form.cleaned_data['age'] produces an integer value, a formatting behavior that also applies to other form fields with non-string data types (e.g. DateField()).

■ **Caution** You can't access cleaned_data until is_valid() is called on the form.

By design, it isn't possible to access a form instance's cleaned_data dictionary unless you first call the is_valid() method. If you try to access cleaned_data before calling is_valid() you'll get the error AttributeError: 'form_reference' object has no attribute 'cleaned_data'.

If you think about this for a second it's good practice, after all, why would you want to access data that hasn't been validated? The next section describes the is_valid() method.

Validating Form Values: is_valid(), validators, clean_<field>(), and clean()

The `is_valid()` method is one of the more important parts of Django form processing. Once you create a bound form with `request.POST`, you call the `is_valid()` method on the instance to determine if the included values comply with a form's field definitions (e.g., if an `EmailField()` value is a valid email). Although the `is_valid()` method returns a Boolean `True` or `False` value, it has two important side effects:

Calling `is_valid()` also creates the `cleaned_data` dictionary on the form instance to hold the form field values that passed validation rules.

- Calling `is_valid()` also creates the `errors` dictionary on the form instance to hold the form errors for each of the fields that didn't pass the validation rules.

Listing 6-13 illustrates a modified version of Listing 6-8 with the `is_valid()` method.

Listing 6-13. Django form is_valid() method for form processing

```
from django.http import HttpResponseRedirect

def contact(request):
    if request.method == 'POST':
        # POST, generate form with data from the request
        form = ContactForm(request.POST)
        # Reference is now a bound instance with user data sent in POST
        # Call is_valid() to validate data and create cleaned_data and errors dict
        if form.is_valid():
           # Form data is valid, you can now access validated values in the cleaned_data dict
           # e.g. form.cleaned_data['email']
           # process data, insert into DB, generate email
           # Redirect to a new URL
           return HttpResponseRedirect('/about/contact/thankyou')
        else:
           pass # Not needed
           # is_valid() method created errors dict, so form reference now contains errors
           # this form reference drops to the last return statement where errors
           # can then be presented accessing form.errors in a template
    else:
        # GET, generate blank form
        form = ContactForm()
        # Reference is now an unbound (empty) form
    # Reference form instance (bound/unbound) is sent to template for rendering
    return render(request,'about/contact.html',{'form':form})
```

Notice in Listing 6-13 that right after a bound form instance is created, a call is made to the `is_valid()` method. If all the form field values comply against the form field data types, we enter a conditional where it's possible to access the form values through the `cleaned_data` dictionary, perform whatever business logic is necessary, and relinquish control to another page, which in Listing 6-13 is to perform redirect.

If any of the form field values fails to pass a rule, then `is_valid()` returns `False` and in the process creates an `errors` dictionary with details about the values that failed to pass their rules. Because of this last automatic creation of `errors`, all that's needed after `is_valid()` returns `False` is to return the same form instance in order to display the `errors` dictionary to an end user so he can correct his mistakes.

But as important as the is_valid() method is to Django form processing, its validation is just done against a form field's data type. For example, is_valid() can validate if a value is left empty, if a value matches a given number range, or even if a value is a valid date: in essence anything supported by Django form field types.

But what if you want to perform more sophisticated validation after is_valid() ? Like checking a value against a database before deeming it valid or checking two values against one another (e.g., a provided zip code value against a provided city value). While you can add these validation checks directly after the is_valid() call, Django offers three more efficient ways to enforce advanced rules by adding them to the form field or form class definition.

If you want a reusable validation mechanism you can use across multiple Django form fields, the best choice is a validator assigned through a form field's validators option. The validators form field option expects a list of methods designed to raise a forms.ValidationError error in case a value doesn't comply with expected rules. Listing 6-14 illustrates a Django form with one of its fields using a custom validator method via the validators option.

Listing 6-14. Django form field validators option with custom validator method for form processing

```
from django import forms
import re

def validate_comment_word_count(value):
      count = len(value.split())
      if count < 30:
            raise forms.ValidationError(('Please provide at least a 30 word message,
            %(count)s words is not descriptive enough'), params={'count': count},)

class ContactForm(forms.Form):
      name = forms.CharField(required=False)
      email = forms.EmailField(label='Your email')
      comment = forms.CharField(widget=forms.Textarea,validators=[validate_comment_word_count])
```

The first section in Listing 6-14 shows the custom validate_command_word_count()method, which (rudimentarly) checks if message has at least 30 words. If the method's input is not at least 30 words, Django's forms.ValidationError error is raised to indicate a rule violation.

In the bottom half of Listing 6-14 you can see a modified ContactForm where the comment field uses the validators=[validate_csv] option. This tells Django that after is_valid() is run and all the form fields have been checked for errors against their data types, it should also run the validate_comment_word_count validator method against the value provided for the comment field. If the comment value does not comply with this rule, then a ValidatioError error is raised, which is added to the form errors dictionary - the same one described in the past section that is used to check field values against their data types.

As you can see from the example in Listing 6-14, you can equally reuse the custom validate_comment_word_count() method on any other form field in the same form or in another Django form through the validators option. In addition, you can also apply multiple validators to a field since the validators option accepts a list of validators. Finally, it's worth mentioning the django.core.validators package contains a series of validators you can also reuse[2] and which are used behind by the scenes by certain form field data types.

In addition to the form field validators option, it's also possible to add validation form rules through the clean_<field>() and clean() methods, which are created as part of a Django form class - just like __init__() described earlier. Just like methods specified in the form field validators option, clean_<field>() and clean() methods are automatically invoked when the is_valid() method is run. Listing 6-15 illustrates the use of two clean_<field>() methods.

---

[2]https://docs.djangoproject.com/en/1.11/ref/validators/#built-in-validators

Listing 6-15. Django form field validation with clean_<field>() methods

```
from django import forms

class ContactForm(forms.Form):
      name = forms.CharField(required=False)
      email = forms.EmailField(label='Your email')
      comment = forms.CharField(widget=forms.Textarea)

      def clean_name(self):
          # Get the field value from cleaned_data dict
          value = self.cleaned_data['name']
          # Check if the value is all upper case
          if value.isupper():
             # Value is all upper case, raise an error
             raise forms.ValidationError("Please don't use all upper case for your name, use
             lower case",code='uppercase')
          # Always return value
          return value

      def clean_email(self):
          # Get the field value from cleaned_data dict
          value = self.cleaned_data['email']
          # Check if the value end in @hotmail.com
          if value.endswith('@hotmail.com'):
             # Value ends in @hotmail.com, raise an error
             raise forms.ValidationError("Please don't use a hotmail email, we simply don't
             like it",code='hotmail')
          # Always return value
          return value
```

In Listing 6-15 there are two `clean_<field>()` methods to add validation rules for the name and `email` fields. Django automatically searches for form methods prefixed with `clean_` and attempts to match a form's field names to the remaining name, to enforce validation on the field in question. This means you can have as many `clean_<field>()` methods as form fields.

The logic inside each `clean_<field>()` method follows a similar pattern to `validators` methods. First you extract a field's value from the form's `cleaned_data` dictionary via the `self` reference that represents the form instance. Next, you run whatever rule or logic you want against the field value, and if you deem the value doesn't comply you raise a `forms.ValidationError`, which adds the error to the form instance. Finally, and this is only different to `validators` methods, you must return the field value irrespective of raising an error or changing its value.

Sometimes it's necessary to apply a rule that doesn't necessarily belong to a specific field, in which case the generic `clean()` method is the preferred approach vs. a `clean_<field>()` method. Listing 6-16 illustrates the use of the `clean()` method.

Listing 6-16. Django form field validation with clean() method

```
from django import forms

class ContactForm(forms.Form):
      name = forms.CharField(required=False)
      email = forms.EmailField(label='Your email')
      comment = forms.CharField(widget=forms.Textarea)
```

```
    def clean(self):
        # Call clean() method to ensure base class validation
        super(ContactForm, self).clean()

        # Get the field values from cleaned_data dict
        name = self.cleaned_data.get('name','')
        email = self.cleaned_data.get('email','')

        # Check if the name is part of the email
        if name.lower() not in email:
           # Name is not in email, raise an error
           raise forms.ValidationError("Please provide an email that contains your name,
           or viceversa")
```

In Listing 6-16 you can see a similar approach to the previous `clean_<field>()` methods in Listing 6-15. But because the `clean()` method is a class-wide method and you're overriding it yourself, it differs from `clean_<field>()` methods in that you must first explicitly call the `clean()` method of the base/parent form class (i.e., `super(...).clean()`) to ensure the base class validation is applied. Form field value extraction is also done through the `cleaned_data` data dictionary, as is the validation logic and raising of `forms.ValidationError` to indicate a rule violation. Finally, the `clean()` method differs from `clean_<field>()` methods in that it doesn't return a value.

Functionally the `clean()` method is different because it's called after all the methods in the `validators` options and `clean_<field>()` methods, a behavior that's important because all these methods rely on data in the `cleaned_data` dictionary. This means if a `validators` or `clean_<field>()` method raises a `ValidationError` error it won't return any value and the `cleaned_data` dictionary won't contain a value for this field. So by the time the `clean()` method is run, the `cleaned_data` dictionary may not necessarily have all the form field values if one was short-circuited in a `validators` or `clean_<field>()` method, which is the reason why the `clean()` method uses the safer dictionary access syntax `cleaned_data.get('<field>','')` to assign a default value in case the `cleaned_data` dictionary doesn't have a given field.

Another important behavioral difference between the `clean()` method, `clean_<field>()` and `validators` methods is how they treat `forms.ValidationError`. When a `forms.ValidationError` is raised in a `validators` or `clean_<field>()` method, the error is assigned to the `<field>` in question in the form's `errors` dictionary - which is important for display purposes. But when a `forms.ValidationError` is raised in the `clean()` method, the error is assigned to a special placeholder field named `__all__` - also known as "non-field errors" - which is also placed in the form's `errors` dictionary.

If you want to assign an error in the `clean()` method to a specific form field you can use the `add_error()` method as illustrated in Listing 6-17.

Listing 6-17. Django form field error assignment with add_error() in clean() method

```
def clean(self):
    # Call clean() method to ensure base class validation
    super(ContactForm, self).clean()

    # Get the field values from cleaned_data dict
    name = self.cleaned_data.get('name','')

    # Check if the name is part of the email
    if name.lower() not in email:
       # Name is not in email, raise an error
       message = "Please provide an email that contains your name, or viceversa"
       self.add_error('name', message)
       self.add_error('email', forms.ValidationError(message))
       self.add_error(None, message)
```

Notice how Listing 6-17 uses the add_error() method on the form instance instead of the raise forms.ValidationError() syntax. The add_error() method accepts two arguments: the first one the form field name on which to assign the error and the second can be either an error message string or an instance of the ValidationError class.

The first two add_error() methods in Listing 6-17 assign the error to the name and email fields, respectively. And the third add_error() method with the None key assigns the error to the __all__ placeholder making it equivalent to raise forms.ValidationError() from Listing 6-16.

Error Form Values: Errors

Form errors as its been described in the previous sections are automatically added to a form instance in the errors dictionary after calling the is_valid() method. Inclusively, it's possible to access the errors dictionary directly without calling the is_valid() method, unlike the cleaned_data dictionary.

The errors dictionary is important because all form errors end up on it. Whether the errors are raised because a value doesn't comply with a form field data type or with raise forms.ValidationError() in the clean() method, clean_<field>() methods, validators methods or the add_error() method in the clean() method, all errors end up in a form's errors dictionary.

The errors dictionary follows the pattern {'<field_name>':'<error_message>'} that makes it easy to identify form errors in either a view method or in a template for display purposes. The only exception to this last pattern occurs when a form error isn't field specific (e.g., such as those created in the clean() method) in which case a form error is assigned to a special key named __all__, errors which are also called non-field errors.

Although you can access the errors dictionary as any other Python dictionary, Django provides a series of methods described in Table 6-1 to make working with errors much easier.

Table 6-1. *Django form errors methods*

Method	Description
form.errors	Gives you access to the raw errors dictionary.
form.errors.as_data()	Outputs a dictionary with the original ValidationError instances. For example, if errors outputs {'email':['This field is required']}, then errors.as_data() outputs {'email':[ValidationError(['This field is required'])]}.
form.errors.as_json (escape_html=False)	Outputs a JSON structure with the contents of the errors dictionary. For example, if errors outputs {'email':['This field is required']}, then errors.as_json() outputs {'email':[{'message':'This field is required','code':'required'}]}. Note that by default as_json() does not escape its output, if you want errors to be escaped use the escape_html flag (e.g., as_json(escape_html=True)).
form.add_error field,message)	Associates an error message to a given form field. Although typically used in the clean() method, it can be used in a view method if necessary. Note that if field is not specified the error message goes on to form part of the __all__ placeholder key in errors which are deemed non-field errors.
form.has_error (field, code=None)	Returns a True or False value if a given field has an error. Note that by default has_error returns True if any error type is associated with a field. To perform the evaluation against a particular error type you can use the code keyword (e.g., form.has_error('email',code='required')). To check if a form has non-field errors you can use NON_FIELD_ERRORS as the field value.
form.non_field_errors()	Returns a list of non-form errors associated with a form (i.e., the __all__ placeholder key). These errors are typically created in the clean() clean method via ValidationError or add_error(None,'message').

You may have noticed the `ValidationError` class instances created in all the previous examples use different arguments, meaning there are multiple ways to create `ValidationError` instances. For example, some `ValidationError` instances use a simple string, but it's also possible to create a `ValidationError` instance with a list of `ValidationError` instances, as well as specify a `code` attribute to further classify an error type. Listing 6-18 illustrates a series of `ValidationError` class instances using these variations.

Listing 6-18. Django form ValidationError instance creation

```
from django import forms

# Placed inside def clean_email(self):
raise forms.ValidationError("Please don't use a hotmail email, we simply don't like
it",code='hotmail')

# Placed inside def clean(self):
raise forms.ValidationError([
     forms.ValidationError("Please provide an email that matches your name, or
     viceversa",code='custom'),
     forms.ValidationError("Please provide your professional email, %(value)s doesn't look
     professional ",code='required',params={'value':self.cleaned_data.get('email') })
```

The `ValidationError` instance variations presented in Listing 6-18 are all optional, but can become powerful when it comes time to display or filter error messages on a template, a process that's described in detail in the "Set Up the Layout for Django Forms in Templates" section later in this chapter.

Django Form Field Types: Widgets, Options, and Validations

Because of the uncontrolled nature of the Internet - with its many types of devices, browsers, and user-experience levels - it creates all kinds of demands on web forms regarding the types of data they must handle, as well as endless variations of how data must be sanitized to comply with the original purpose of a web form.

When you create web forms for Django applications you rely on Django form classes, which are composed of form fields. Each Django form field is important because it dictates a small piece of functionality that eventually composes the bulk of a web form's overall behavior.

Django form fields define two types of functionality, a form field's HTML markup and its server-side validation facilities. For example, a Django form field translates into the actual HTML form markup (e.g., an `<input>`, `<select>` or `<textarea>` tag), the HTML markup attributes (e.g., length, whether a field can be left blank, or if a field must be disabled), as well as the necessary hooks to easily perform server-side validation on a form field's data.

Django form fields define these two types of web form functionality out of necessity. Although browsers have progressed tremendously with technologies like HTML5 to provide out-of-the-box form field validation through the HTML markup itself - without JavaScript - a browser is still in full control of an end user that with sufficient knowledge can bypass and feed whatever data he wants to a form. Therefore, it's standard practice to further inspect form field data once it's submitted by users to see if it complies with a form's rules, a process that's made very easy thanks to the use of Django form fields.

Table 6-2 illustrates the various Django forms fields, including their type, the HTML they produce, their default widget, and their validation behavior.

Table 6-2. *Django form field types, generated HTML, default widget, and validation behavior*

Field type	Django form field type	HTML output	Default Django widget	Validation behavior
Boolean	forms.BooleanField()	<input type='checkbox' ...>	forms.widgets. CheckboxInput()	Generates HTML check box input markup to obtain a Boolean True or False value; returns False when the check box is unchecked, True when the check box is checked.
Boolean	forms.NullBooleanField()	<select><option value="1" selected="selected">Unknown </option><option value="2">Yes </option><option value="3">No </option></select>	forms.widgets. NullBooleanSelect()	Works just like BooleanField but also allows "Unknown" value; returns None when the Unknown(1) value is selected, True when the Yes(2) value is selected and False when the No(3) value is selected.
Text	forms.CharField()	<input type="text" ...>	forms.widgets.TextInput()	Generates HTML text input markup.
Text (Specialized)	forms.EmailField()	<input type="email" ...>	forms.widgets.EmailInput()	Generates HTML email input markup. Note this HTML5 markup is for client-side email validation and only works if a browser supports HTML5. If a browser doesn't support HTML5, then it treats this markup as a regular text input. Django server-side form validation is done for email irrespective of HTML5 support.
Text (Specialized)	forms. GenericIPAddressField()	<input type="text" ...>	forms.widgets.TextInput()	Works just like CharField, but server-side Django validates the (text) value can be converted to an IPv4 or IPv6 address (e.g., 192.46.3.2, 2001:0db8:85a3:0000:0000:8a2e:0370:7334).

Text (Specialized)	forms.RegexField (regex='regular_ expression')	<input type="text" ...>	forms.widgets.TextInput()	Works just like CharField, but server-side Django validates the (text) value complies with the regular expression defined in regex. Note regex can be either a string that represents a regular expression (e.g., \.com$ for a string that ends in .com) or a compiled Python regular expression from Python's re package (e.g., re.compile ('\.com$')).
Text (Specialized)	forms.SlugField()	<input type="text" ...>	forms.widgets.TextInput()	Works just like CharField, but server-side Django validates the (text) value can be converted to slug. In Django a 'slug' is a value that contains only lowercase letters, numbers, underscores and hyphens, which is typically used to sanitize URLs and file names (e.g., the slug representation of 'What is a Slug?! A sanitized-string' is what-is-a-slug-a-sanitized-string.

(*continued*)

Table 6-2. *(continued)*

Field type	Django form field type	HTML output	Default Django widget	Validation behavior
Text (Specialized)	forms.URLField()	<input type="url" ...>	forms.widgets.URLInput()	Generates HTML url input markup. Note this HTML5 markup is for client-side url validation and only works if the browser supports HTML5. If a browser doesn't support HTML5 then it treats this markup as regular text input. Django server-side form validation is done for a url irrespective of HTML5 support.
Text (Specialized)	forms.UUIDField()	<input type="text" ...>	forms.widgets.TextInput()	Works just like CharField, but server-side Django validates the (text) value is convertable to a UUID (Universally unique identifier).
Text (Specialized)	forms.ComboField(fields=[field_type1,field_type1])	<input type="text" ...>	forms.widgets.TextInput()	Works just like CharField, but server-side Django enforces the data pass rules for a list of Django form fields (e.g., ComboField(fields=[CharField(max_length=50), SlugField()]) enforces the data be a slug field with a maximum length of 50 characters).

Text (Specialized)	forms.MultiValueField (fields=[field_type1, field_type1])	*Varies depending on field list (e.g. for three CharField : <input type="text" ...><input type="text" ...><input type="text" ...>; for two CharField: <input type="text" ...><input type="text" ...>*	forms.widgets.TextInput()	Designed to create custom form fields made up of multiple preexisting form fields (e.g., Social Security form field made up of three CharField()). It requires a subclass implementation (e.g., class SocialSecurity Field(MultiValueField):) to include the base form fields and validation logic of the new field.
Text (Specialized) / Files	forms.FilePathField (path='directory')	<select ><option value="directory/file_1">file_1</option><option value="directory/file_2">file_2 </option><option value="directory/file_2">file_2 </option></select>	forms.widgets.Select()	Generates an HTML select list from files located on a server-side path directory. Note value is composed of path+filename and just displays filename.
Files	forms.FileField()	<input type="file" ...>	forms.widgets. ClearableFileInput()	Generates HTML file input markup so an end user is able to select a file through his web browser. In addition, it provides various utilities to handle post-processing of files.
Files (Specialized)	forms.ImageField()	<input type="file" ...>	forms.widgets. ClearableFileInput()	Generates HTML file input markup so an end user is able to select an image file through his web browser. Works just like FileField but provides additional utilities to handle post-processing of images using the Pillow package. Note this field forces you to install Pillow (e.g., pip install Pillow).

(*continued*)

Table 6-2. (*continued*)

Field type	Django form field type	HTML output	Default Django widget	Validation behavior
Date/time	forms.DateField()	<input type="text" ...>	forms.widgets.DateInput()	Works just like CharField, but server-side Django validates the (text) value can be converted to a datetime.date, datetime.datetime, or string formatted in a particular date format (e.g. 2017-12-25, 11/25/17).
Date/time	forms.TimeField()	<input type="text" ...>	forms.widgets.TextInput()	Works just like CharField, but server-side Django validates the (text) value can be converted to a datetime. time or string formatted in a particular time format (e.g., 15:40:33, 17:44).
Date/time	forms.DateTimeField()	<input type="text" ...>	forms.widgets. DateTimeInput()	Works just like CharField, but server-side Django validates the (text) value can be converted to a datetime. datetime, datetime.date, or string formatted in a particular datetime format (e.g. 2017-12-25 14:30:59, 11/25/17 14:30).
Date/time	forms.DurationField()	<input type="text" ...>	forms.widgets.TextInput()	Works just like CharField, but server-side Django validates the (text) value can be converted to a timedelta. Note Django uses the django.utils. dateparse.parse_duration() method as a helper, which means the string must match the format DD HH:MM:SS. uuuuuu (e.g., 2 1:10:20 for a timedelta of 2 days, 1 hour, 10 minutes, 20 seconds).

Date/time	forms.SplitDateTimeField()	<input type="text" name="_0" ...> <input type="text" name="_1" ...>	forms.widgets.SplitDateTimeWidget	Works similar to DateTimeField but generates two separate text inputs for date and time, unlike DateTimeField which expects a single string with date and time. Validation-wise Django enforces the date input can be converted to a datetime.date and the time input can be converted to a datetime.time.
Number	forms.IntegerField()	<input type="number" ...>	forms.widgets.NumberInput()	Generates an HTML number input markup. Note this HTML5 markup is for client-side number validation and only works if the browser supports HTML5. If a browser doesn't support HTML5 then it treats this markup as a regular text input. Django server-side form validation is done for an integer number irrespective of HTML5 support.
Number	forms.DecimalField()	<input type="number" ...>	forms.widgets.NumberInput()	Generates an HTML number input markup. Note this HTML5 markup is for client-side number validation and only works if a browser supports HTML5. If a browser doesn't support HTML5 then it treats this markup as a regular text input. Django server-side form validation is done for a decimal number irrespective of HTML5 support.

(continued)

Table 6-2. *(continued)*

Field type	Django form field type	HTML output	Default Django widget	Validation behavior
Number	forms.FloatField()	<input type="number" ...>	forms.widgets.NumberInput()	Generates an HTML number input markup. Note this HTML5 markup is for client-side number validation and only works if a browser supports HTML5. If a browser doesn't support HTML5 then it treats this markup as a regular text input. Django server-side form validation is done for a float number irrespective of HTML5 support.
Predefined values	forms.ChoiceField (choices=tuple_of_tuples)	<select><option value="tuple1_1" selected="selected">tuple1_2 </option><option value="tuple_2_1">tuple_2_2 </option><option value="tuple_3_1">tuple_3_2 </option></select>	forms.widgets.Select()	Generates an HTML select list from a tuple of tuples defined through choices (e.g., ((1,'United States'),(2,'Canada'),(3,'Mexico'))). Note with ChoiceField if no value is selected an empty string '' is passed for post-processing and if a value like '2' is selected a literal string is passed for post-processing, irrespective of the original data representation. See TypeChoiceField or clean form methods to override these last behaviors for empty values and string handling.

Predefined values	forms.TypeChoiceField (choices=tuple_of_tuples, coerce=coerce_function, empty_value=None)	<select><option value="tuple1_1" selected="selected">tuple1_2 </option><option value="tuple_2_1">tuple_2_2 </option><option value="tuple_3_1">tuple_3_2 </option></select>	forms.widgets.Select()	Works just like ChoiceField but provides extra post-processing functionality with the coerce and empty_value arguments. For example, with TypeChoiceField you can define a different default value with the empty_value arguement (e.g.empty_value=None) and you can define a coercion method with the coerce argument so the selected value is converted from its string representation (e.g., with coerce=int a value like '2' gets converted to 2 (integer) through the built-in int function).
Predefined values	forms.MultipleChoiceField (choices=tuple_of_tuples)	<select multiple='multiple'><option value="tuple1_1" selected="selected">tuple1_2 </option><option value="tuple_2_1">tuple_2_2 </option><option value="tuple_3_1">tuple_3_2 </option></select>	forms.widgets.SelectMultiple()	Generates an HTML select list for multiple values from tuple of tuples defined through choices (e.g., ((1,'United States'),(2,'Canada'),(3,'Mexico'))). It works just like ChoiceField but allows multiple values to be selected, which become available as a list in post-processing.

(continued)

Table 6-2. *(continued)*

Field type	Django form field type	HTML output	Default Django widget	Validation behavior
Predefined values	forms.TypedMultipleChoiceField(choices= tuple_of_tuples, coerce=coerce_function, empty_value=None)	<select multiple='multiple'><option value="tuple1_1" selected="selected">tuple1_2 </option><option value="tuple_2_1">tuple_2_2 </option><option value="tuple_3_1">tuple_3_2 </option></select>	forms.widgets.Select()	Works just like MultipleChoiceField but provides extra post-processing functionality with the coerce and empty_value arguments. For example, with TypedMultipleChoiceField you can define a different default value with the empty_value argument (e.g., empty_value=None) and you can define a coercion method with the coerce argument so the selected value is converted from its string representation (e.g., with coerce=int a value like '2' gets converted to 2 (integer) through the built-in int function).

As you can see in Table 6-2, the Django form fields provided out-of-the-box support for the generation of practically every HTML form input in existence, as well as provided the necessary server-side validation for a wide array of data types. For example, you can use the `CharField()` form field type to capture standard text or the more specialized `EmailField()` form field type to ensure the captured value is a valid email. Just as you can use `ChoiceField()` to generate a form list with predefined values or `DateField()` to enforce a form value is a valid date.

The Relationship between Widgets and Form Fields

In Table 6-2 you can see that besides the actual Django form field syntax (e.g., `forms.CharField()`, `forms.ImageField()`) each form field is associated with a default *widget*. Django widgets for the most part go unnoticed and are often mixed together with the functionality of a form field itself (e.g., if you want an HTML text input `<input type="text"..>` you use `forms.CharField()`). However, when you require changes to the HTML produced by a form field or the way a form field's data is initially processed, you'll need to work with widgets.

To make matters a little more confusing, there are many options you specify on form fields that end up being used as part of a widget. For example, the form field `forms.CharField(max_length=25)` tells Django to limit a value to a maximum of 25 characters upon processing, but this same `max_length` option is passed to the `forms.widgets.TextInput()` widget to generate the HTML `<input type="text" maxlength="25"...>` to enforce the same rule on the browser via the HTML `maxlength="25"` attribute. So in this case, you can actually change the HTML output through a form field option, without even knowing about widgets!

So do you really need to work with widgets to change the HTML produced by a form field? The answer is it depends. A lot of form fields options are automatically passed to a widget behind the scenes in effect altering the generated HTML, but make no mistake about it, it's a widget that's tasked with generating the HTML and not a form field. For cases when a form field's options can't achieve a desired HTML output, then it becomes necessary to change a form field's widget to achieve a custom HTML output.

In upcoming sections in this chapter, I'll expand on the topic of Django widgets and describe how to override and customize a Django form field's default widget. Now that you know about the existence of Django widgets and their relationship with Django form fields, I'll continue on the topic of Django form fields and explain the various Django form field options and their validation behavior.

DJANGO 'HIDDEN' BUILT-IN WIDGETS

Table 6-2 shows all the built-in form fields in Django, which can mislead you to believe the same table also shows all Django built-in form widgets. This is not the case. The widget column in Table 6-2 only shows the default widgets assigned to all built-in form fields. There are a few more Django built-in widgets you can use that are also included in the forms.widgets. package:

- PasswordInput.- Widget for password field (e.g., displays **** as a user types text). Also supports re-display of a field value after validation error.
- HiddenInput.- Widget for hidden field (e.g., <input type='hidden'...>.
- MultipleHiddenInput.- Like HiddenInput but for multiple values (i.e., a list).
- Textarea.- Widget for text area field (e.g., <textarea></textarea>).

RadioSelect.- Like the Select widget, but generates a list of radio buttons (e.g., <ul><li><input type="radio"></li>.. </ul>).

CheckboxSelectMultiple.- Like the SelectMultiple widget, but generates a list of check boxes (e.g., <ul><li><input type="checkbox"></li>.. </ul>).

TimeInput.- Like the DateTimeInput widget, but for time input only (e.g., 13:54, 13:54:59).

SelectDateWidget.- Widget to generate three Select widgets for date (e.g., select widget for day, select widget for month, select widget for year).

SplitHiddenDateTimeWidget.- Like the SplitDateTimeWidget widget, but uses Hidden input for date and time.

FileInput.- Like the ClearableFileInput widget, but without a check box input to clear the field's value.

Future sections in this chapter that describe a form field's widget argument and how to customize Django widgets, provide more context on how and when to use these additional built-in widgets.

Empty, Default, and Predetermined Values: Required, Initial, and Choices

By default, all Django form fields are marked as required, which means every field must contain a value to pass validation. The `required` argument is valid on all Django form fields described in Table 6-2 and in addition to enforcing a value is not empty on the server-side, the HTML 5 `required` attribute is also assigned to a form field so a user's browser also enforces validation.

■ **Tip** You can initialize a form with use_required_field=False to forgo the use of the HTML 5 required attribute. See the previous subsection entitled "Initialize Forms."

If you want to allow a field value to be left empty - `None` or empty string `''` -- then a field must be assigned the `required=False` argument.

You can also assign a default value to a field through the `initial` argument. The initial argument is equally valid across all Django form fields described in Table 6-2 and is described in detail in the previous subsection "Initialize forms."

For cases in which you don't want to allow a user the ability to introduce open-ended values for a field you can restrict a field's values to a predetermined set of values through the `choices` argument. If you want to use the `choices` attribute you must use a form field data type designed to generate an HTML `<select>` list such as `forms.ChoiceField()`, `forms.MultipleChoiceField`, or `forms.FielPathField()`. The `choices` argument cannot be used on data types like `forms.CharField()` designed for open-ended input.

Limiting Text Values: max_length, min_length, strip, and Validators

Form field data types that accept text such as `CharField()`, `EmailField()`, and others described in Table 6-2, can accept both the `max_length` and `min_length` arguments to restrict a field's value to a maximum and minimum character length, respectively.

The `strip` argument is used to apply Python's `strip()` method - which strips all trailing and leading whitespace - to a field's value. The `strip` argument can only be used on two Django field data types, `CharField()` that defaults to `strip=True`, and `RegexField()` that defaults to `strip=False`.

To apply more advanced limitation rules on fields that accept text values, see the previous subsection on "Validating Form Values," which describes `validators` and other techniques to limit field values.

Limiting Number Values: max_value, min_value, max_digits, decimal_places, and Validators

Form field data types that accept numbers such as `IntegerField()`, `DecimalField()`, and `FloatField()` can accept both the `max_value` and `min_value` arguments to restrict the upper and lower bounds of a field's number value, respectively.

In addition, the `DecimalField()` data type, which accepts more elaborate number types, can use the `max_digits` argument to restrict the maximum number of digits in a value or the `decimal_places` argument to specify the maximum number of decimal places in a value.

To apply more advanced limitation rules on fields that accept number values, see the previous subsection on "Validating Form Values," which describes `validators` and other techniques to limit field values.

Error Messages: error_messages

Every Django field data type has built-in error messages. For example, when a field data type is `required` and no value is added by a user, Django assigns the error message `This field is required` to the field, as part of a form's `errors` dictionary. Similarly, if a field data type uses the `max_length` argument and the value provided by a user exceeds this threshold, Django creates the error message `Ensure this value has at most X characters (it has X)`.

As described earlier in Listing 6-18, Django error messages are typically given a message error code in addition to the error message itself. And it's these message error codes that are used to assign custom messages via the `error_messages` argument.

The `error_messages` argument expects a dictionary where each key is the message error code and its value a custom error message. For example, to provide a custom message for the `required` code you would use the syntax `forms.CharField(error_messages={"required":"Please, pretty please provide a comment"})`.Similarly, if you expect a form field to violate its `max_length` value, you would assign a custom error message through the `max_length` code (e.g., `error_messages={"max_length":"This value exceeds its max length value"}`).

Error codes generally map directly to the rule they violate (e.g., if a `forms.IntegerField` violates its `max_value`, Django uses the `max_value` code to assign a default error message, which you can override by using this code). However, there are over two dozen built-in error message codes (e.g., `'missing'`, `'contradiction'`), some of which are not too obvious. For example, a `forms.ImageField` can generate the error message `'Upload a valid image. The file you uploaded was either not an image or a corrupted image.'`, which uses the `'invalid_image'` error code, meaning that to override this default error message you would need to know the error code beforehand to declare it as part of `error_messages`.

For the most part, customizing error messages for some of the more esoteric error codes is rarely needed. But if you're having trouble customizing error messages for a given field because you can't determine its error code, a little logging debugging on a form errors dictionary (e.g., `form.errors.as_json()` or some of the other methods in Table 6-1) can quickly net you a form's error codes to override the messages with the `error_messages` argument.

Field Layout Values: label, label_suffix, help_text

When you output a form field in a template besides the essential HTML form field markup (e.g., <input type="text">) it's almost always accompanied by a human-friendly descriptor to indicate what a field is for (e.g., Email: <input type="text">). This human-friendly descriptor is called a label and by default in Django it's assigned the same value as the field name.

To customize a form field's label you can use the label argument. For example, to provide a more descriptive label for a field named email you can use the syntax email = EmailField(label="Please provide your email"). By default, all labels on a form are accompanied by the : symbol, which functions as a suffix. You can further customize the output of field labels with the label_suffix argument on individual form fields or the form instance itself.

For example, the syntax email = EmailField(label_suffix='-->') overrides the default suffix label on the email field for the --> symbol.

■ **Tip** The label_suffix can also be used to initialize a form (e.g., form = ContactForm(label_suffix='-->')) so all fields receive a label suffix, instead of doing it field by field. See the "Initialize Forms" section earlier for more details.

In certain circumstances it can be helpful to add more explicit instructions to a form field; for such cases you can use the help_text argument. Depending on the template layout you use, the help_text value is added right next to the HTML form field markup.

For example, the syntax comment = CharField(help_text="Please be as specific as possible to receive a quick response") generates the given html_text value right next to the comment input field (e.g., Please be as specific as possible to receive a quick response <input type="text">). The next section "Set Up the Layout for Django Forms in Templates" goes into greater detail on the use of help_text and other form layout properties.

Set Up the Layout for Django Forms in Templates

When you pass a Django form - unbound or bound - to a template there are many options to generate its layout. You can use one of Django's pre-built HTML helpers to quickly generate a form's output or granularly output each field to create an advanced form layout (e.g., responsive design[3]).In addition, there can also be many ways to output form errors (e.g., besides the fields themselves or at the top of a form). Up next, I'll describe the various options to output Django forms in templates.

Listing 6-19 shows the Django form I'll use throughout the remaining layout sections - which is the same form used throughout this chapter.

Listing 6-19. Django form class definition

```
from django import forms

class ContactForm(forms.Form):
      name = forms.CharField(required=False)
      email = forms.EmailField(label='Your email')
      comment = forms.CharField(widget=forms.Textarea)
```

---

[3]https://en.wikipedia.org/wiki/Responsive_web_design

Output Form Fields: form.as_table, form.as_p, form.as_ul, and Granularly by Field

Django forms offer three helper methods to simplify the output of all form fields. The syntax `form.as_table` outputs a form's fields to accommodate an HTML `<table>` as illustrated in Listing 6-20. The syntax `form.as_p` outputs a form's fields with HTML `<p>` tags as illustrated in Listing 6-21. Where as the syntax `form.as_ul` outputs a form's fields to accommodate an HTML `<ul>` list tag, as illustrated in Listing 6-22.

■ **Caution** If you use form.as_table, form.as_p, form.as_ul you must declare opening/closing HTML tags, a wrapping <form> tag, a Django {% csrf_token %} tag and an <input type="submit"> button, as described in the initial section of this chapter "Functional web form syntax for Django forms".

Listing 6-20. Django form output with form.as_table

```
<tr>
    <th><label for="id_name">Name:</label></th>
    <td><input id="id_name" name="name" type="text" /></td>
</tr>\n
<tr>
    <th><label for="id_email">Your email:</label></th>
    <td><input id="id_email" name="email" type="email" required/></td>
</tr>\n
<tr>
    <th><label for="id_comment">Comment:</label></th>
    <td><textarea cols="40" id="id_comment" name="comment" rows="10" required>\r\n</
    textarea></td>
</tr>
```

Listing 6-21. Django form output with form.as_p

```
<p>
    <label for="id_name">Name:</label> <input id="id_name" name="name" type="text" />
</p>\n
<p>
    <label for="id_email">Your email:</label> <input id="id_email" name="email" type="email"
    required/>
</p>\n
<p>
    <label for="id_comment">Comment:</label> <textarea cols="40" id="id_comment"
    name="comment" rows="10" required>\r\n</textarea>
</p>'
```

Listing 6-22. Django form output with form.as_ul

```
<li>
    <label for="id_name">Name:</label> <input id="id_name" name="name" type="text" />
</li>\n
<li>
```

```
    <label for="id_email">Your email:</label> <input id="id_email" name="email" type="email"
    required/>
</li>\n
    <li><label for="id_comment">Comment:</label> <textarea cols="40" id="id_comment"
    name="comment" rows="10" required>\r\n</textarea>
</li>
```

■ **Tip** The form.as_table, form.as_p & form.as_ul output can be made less verbose - omitting label tags and id attributes - by initializing the form with auto_id=False. In addition, you can also change the symbol that separates label names (by default :) with another symbol by initializing the form with the label_suffix variable. It's also possible to use the field_order option to alter the output field order.

Under certain circumstances, none of the previous helper methods may be sufficient to achieve certain form layouts. For example, to create a responsive design you'll need to output each field manually to accommodate specific layout requirements (e.g., Bootstrap CSS grid columns). To achieve the custom output of fields, every form instance permits access to its fields through the form.<field_name> syntax using the attributes in Table 6-3.

Table 6-3. *Django form field attributes accessible in templates*

Attribute name	Description
{{form.<field_name>}} (i.e. No attribute, just the field name by itself)	Outputs the HTML form tag - technically known as the Django widget - associated with the field (e.g., <input type="text">.)
{{form.<field_name>.name}}	Outputs the name of a field, as defined in the form class.
{{form.<field_name>.value}}	Outputs the value of the field assigned with initial or user-provided data. Useful if you need to separately output the HTML form tag's value attribute (e.g., for <input type="text" name="name" value="John Doe">, {{form.name.value}} outputs John Doe).
{{form.<field_name>.label}}	Outputs the label of a field, which by default uses the syntax "Your <field_name>" (e.g., for the email field, {{form.email.label}} outputs Your email).
{{form.<field_name>.id_for_label}}	Outputs the label id of a field, which by default uses the syntax id_<field_name> (e.g., for the email field, {{form.email.id_for_label}} outputs id_email).
{{form.<field_name>.auto_id}}	Outputs the auto id of a field, which by default uses the syntax id_<field_name> (e.g., for the email field, {{form.email.auto_id}} outputs id_email).
{{form.<field_name>.label_tag}}	Helper method to output the HTML <label> tag along with id_for_label and label(e.g., for the email field, {{form.email.label_tag}} outputs <label for="id_email">Your email:</label>).
{{form.<field_name>.help_text}}	Outputs the help text associated with a field.
{{form.<field_name>.errors}}	Outputs the errors associated with a field.
{{form.<field_name>.css_classes}}	Outputs the CSS classes associated with a field.

(continued)

Table 6-3. (*continued*)

Attribute name	Description
{{form.<field_name>.as_hidden}}	Outputs the HTML of a field as a hidden HTML field (e.g., <input type="hidden" >).
{{form.<field_name>.is_hidden}}	Boolean result of a field's hidden status.
{{form.<field_name>.as_text}}	Outputs the HTML of a field as a text HTML field (e.g., <input type="text">).
{{form.<field_name>.as_textarea}}	Outputs the HTML of a field as a textarea HTML field (e.g., <textarea></textarea>).
{{form.<field_name>.as_widget}}	Outputs the Django widget associated with a field; technically produces the same output as calling the stand-alone field with the syntax {{form.<field_name>}} - shown at the top of this table.

■ **Tip** You can override the default output for `{{form.<field_name>.label}}`, the suffix for `{{form.<field_name>.label_tag}}`, and the default output for `{{form.<field_name>.help_text}}` in Table 6-4, by using the `label`, `label_suffix`, and `help_text` options on form fields. This process is described in the previous section on "Django Form Field Types: Widgets, Options, and Validations."

As you can see in Table 6-4, there are many field attributes available to customize the layout of a form. Just be careful that if you output form fields granularly you don't miss a field, because if you do miss a field, the most likely outcome is Django won't be able to process the form as it won't receive values from missing fields.

Listing 6-23 illustrates a standard `{% for %}` loop that ensures you don't miss any field and provides more flexibility than the previous `form.as_table`, `form.as_p & form.as_ul` methods.

Listing 6-23. Django form {% for %} loop over all fields

```
{% for field in form %}
    <div class="row">
       <div class="col-md-2">
        {{ field.label_tag }}
        {% if field.help_text %}
          <sup>{{ field.help_text }}</sup>
        {% endif %}
        {{ field.errors }}
       </div><div class="col-md-10 pull-left">
         {{ field }}
       </div>
    </div>
 {% endfor %}
```

In Listing 6-23, a loop is created over the `form` reference to ensure no fields are missed. If you want to avoid presenting a field in certain form layouts, then I recommend you use the `{{field.as_hidden}}` vs. `{{field}}`, as this ensures the field still forms part of the form for validation purposes and is simply hidden from a user - more details about this scenario are provided in the upcoming section on advanced form processing and partial forms.

Output Field Order: field_order and order_fields

If you use any of the techniques presented in Listings 6-20, 6-21, 6-22, or 6-23, the form fields are output in the same order as they're declared in the form class in Listing 6-19 (i.e., name, email, comment). However, you can use several techniques to alter the order in which form fields are output.

The first and obvious approach is to change the form field order directly in the form class definition. Because this last technique requires altering a form's source code, Django also offers the `field_order` option. The `field_order` option accepts a list of form field names in the order you want them output (e.g., `field_order=['email','name','comment']` outputs the `email` field first, followed by `name` and `comment`). The `field_order` option is flexible enough that you can provide a partial list of form fields (e.g., `field_order=['email']` outputs the email field first and the remaining form fields in their declared order) as well as declare nonexistent field names that are ignored and is helpful when using form inheritance.

The `field_order` option can be declared in two locations. First, it can be declared as part of a form class definition, as illustrated in Listing 6-24.

Listing 6-24. Django form field_order option to enforce field order

```
from django import forms

class ContactForm(forms.Form):
      name = forms.CharField(required=False)
      email = forms.EmailField(label='Your email')
      comment = forms.CharField(widget=forms.Textarea)
      field_order = ['email','comment','name']
```

As you can see in Listing 6-24, `field_order` is declared as any other form field and assigned a list of field names to ensure the fields are output in the order: email, comment, and name. It's also possible to use the `field_order` option as part of a form's initialization processes - described in detail in the form processing section. It's worth mentioning that if you use the `field_order` option on both the class definition - as shown in Listing 6-24 - and form instance initialization, the latter value takes precedence over the former.

In addition to the `field_order` option, Django also offers `order_fields` that also expects a list of field names to alter a form's output field order. But unlike the `field_order` option that must be declared in a form class or as part of the initialization of a form instance, `order_fields` can be called directly on a form instance, which makes it a good option to use in a view method or template (e.g., `form.order_fields(['email'])`).

Output CSS Classes, Styles, and Field Attributes: error_css_class, required_css_class, Widget, Customization, and Various Form Field Options

By default, when you output form fields and labels there are no CSS classes or styles associated with them. Django offers several mechanisms to associate CSS classes with form fields. The first two approaches are the `error_css_class` and `required_css_class` fields, which are declared directly in a Django form, as illustrated in Listing 6-25.

Listing 6-25. Django form error_css_class and required_css_class fields to apply CSS formatting

```
from django import forms

class ContactForm(forms.Form):
      name = forms.CharField(required=False)
      email = forms.EmailField(label='Your email')
      comment = forms.CharField(widget=forms.Textarea)
      error_css_class = 'error'
      required_css_class = 'bold'
```

As you can see in Listing 6-25, the `error_css_class` and `required_css_class` fields are added just like regular form fields. When a field associated with a form instance of this kind is rendered on a template, Django adds the error CSS class to all fields marked with an error and adds the bold CSS class to all fields marked as required.

For example, all form fields are treated as required except when they explicitly use `required=False`. This means if you output an unbound form instance from Listing 6-25 using `form.as_p`, the comment field is output as `<p class="bold">Comment: <textarea cols="40" name="comment" rows="10" required>\r\n </textarea></p>` -- note the `class` in the `<p>` tag. Similarly, if a field associated with a bound form instance from Listing 6-25 raises an error, Django adds the `error` CSS class to the field (e.g., if the email field value is not valid, the email field is output as `<p class="bold error">Your email: <input name="email" type="email" value="aninvalidemail" required /></p>`, note the bold CSS class remains because the form field is also required).

As helpful as the `error_css_class` and `required_css_class` fields are, they still offer limited CSS formatting functionality. To gain full control over CSS class output, you'll need to either use some of the more granular output options for fields in Table 6-4 or customize a form field's widget as illustrated in Listing 6-26.

Listing 6-26. Django form with inline widget definition to add custom CSS class

```
from django import forms

class ContactForm(forms.Form):
      name = forms.CharField(required=False)
      email = forms.EmailField(label='Your email', widget=forms.TextInput(attrs={'class' :
      'myemailclass'}))
      comment = forms.CharField(widget=forms.Textarea)
```

Notice in Listing 6-26 how the email field is declared with the `widget=forms.TextInput(attrs={'class' : 'myemailclass'})` argument. This last statement tells Django that when it outputs the `email` field, it use the custom `forms.TextInput` widget, which declares the CSS `class` attribute with the `myemailclass` value.

By using the form definition in Listing 6-26, the `email` field is output as `<input class="myemailclass" type="text"...>`. If you don't know what a Django widget is, see the earlier section entitled "The Relationship between Widgets and Form Fields."

The approach presented in Listing 6-26 is a powerful technique, because just as you can declare the CSS `class` attribute, you can also declare any other form field HTML attribute. For example, if you wanted to declare custom HTML attributes - such as those used by frameworks like jQuery or Bootstrap -- you can easily use this same technique (e.g., `widget=forms.TextInput(attrs={'role' : 'dialog'})` would output `<input role="dialog" type="text"...>`).

However, a word of caution now that you know how easy it is to output any HTML attribute alongside a Django form field. Be aware that nearly all Django form field data types come with built-in options that get translated into HTML attributes. For example, the `forms.CharField(max_length=25)` statement gets output to `<input type="text" maxlength="25"...>`, which means the form field `max_length` option automatically generates the HTML `maxlength="25"` attribute. So be careful to start adding HTML attributes indiscriminately using the approach in Listing 6-26, as they may already be supported through built-in data type options. See the previous section on "Django Form Field Types: Widgets, Options and Validations" for more details on these built-in data type options.

Output Form Field Errors: form.<field_name>.errors, form.errors, form.non_field_errors

Just as form fields can be output in different ways, form field errors can also be output in different ways. Toward the end of the first section in Listing 6-23, you can see how we use the `{{field.errors}}` syntax to output errors associated with a particular field. However, an important thing to keep in mind when outputting a field's `errors` value in this manner is the output is generated as an HTML formatted list:

```
<ul class="errorlist">
    <li>Name is required.</li>
</ul>
```

As you can see in Listing 6-27, the `{{fields.errors}}` value is list with the `errorlist` CSS class - which allows you to provide CSS behaviors like a background color or borders - and the values are pre-wrapped as list elements.

If you want to strip these wrapping HTML list tags to gain more control over the error layout (e.g., creating a responsive design or CSV list) you can do so creating a loop on each `field.errors` as illustrated in Listing 6-27.

Listing 6-27. Django loop over form.<field_name>.errors

```
{% for field in form %}
   <div class="row">
     <div class="col-md-2">
       {{ field.label_tag }}
       {% if field.help_text %}
         <sup>{{ field.help_text }}</sup>
         {% endif %}
         {% for error in field.errors %}
          <div class="row">
            <div class="alert alert-danger">{{error}}</div>
          </div>
         {% endfor %}
      </div><div class="col-md-10 pull-left">
        {{ field }}
      </div>
   </div>
 {% endfor %}
```

You can see in Listing 6-27 that inside the loop for each field, another loop is made on the `field.errors` reference to granularly output and assign custom markup to each field error.

As granular as the error output in Listing 6-27 is, this type of layout assumes you want to display a form's error messages besides each field, in addition to requiring a loop over a form's fields. But what if you want to display a form's errors at the top or besides the main form? Or if you want to keep using Django's shortcut methods (i.e., `form.as_table`, `form.as_p` & `form.as_ul`) and still display errors?

Besides the `form.<field_name>.errors` syntax in Listing 6-27 to access field errors, Django also can output form's errors with the `errors` and `non_field_errors` dictionaries as illustrated in Listing 6-28.

Listing 6-28. Django form.errors and form.non_field_errors with custom HTML output

```
<!-- Field errors -->
 {% if form.errors %}
  <div class="row">
    {% for field_with_error,error_messages in form.errors.items %}
        <div class="alert alert-danger">{{field_with_error}}  {{error_messages}}</div>
    {% endfor %}
  </div>
  {% endif %}

<!-- Non-field errors -->
 {% if form.non_field_errors %}
  <div class="row">
    {% for error in form.non_field_errors %}
    <div class="alert alert-danger">{{error}}</div>
    {% endfor %}
  </div>
  {% endif %}
```

As you can see in Listing 6-28, the `form.errors` dictionary provides an aggregated version of all the `form.<field_name>.errors`, where each dictionary key represents the form field name and the value is a list of error messages with error code (e.g., `required`) to further filter the error list. If you want to output every form error at the top of a form/page, require error filtering by code type or want to keep using Django's shortcut output form methods (e.g., `form.as_table`) and obtain form errors, then using `form.errors` on a template is the way to go.

In addition, notice toward the top of Listing 6-28 the loop over the `form.non_field_errors` dictionary. The `form.non_field_errors` contains errors that don't belong to a specific form field – as discussed earlier in the "Error Form Values: Errors" section and the special error placeholder field named `__all__`. Because non-field errors don't apply to a specific form field, it's common to output these type of errors at the top of a form accessing the `non_field_errors` dictionary.

Be aware that if you use `form.errors` or `form.non_field_errors` to output errors, by default the error reference – `{{error_messages}}` and `{{error}}` in Listing 6-28 – are wrapped as an HTML formatted list (e.g., `<ul class="errorlist"><li>...</li></ul>`) but you can add an additional for loop to the error list - as in Listing 6-27 - to create a custom HTML error layout.

Finally, it's worth mentioning there are a series of auxiliary methods designed to facilitate error output (e.g., in JSON format); Table 6-1 in the Django form processing section describes these methods.

Django Custom Form Fields and Widgets

In Table 6-2 you saw the wide variety of built-in Django form fields, from basic text and number types, to more specialized text types (e.g., CSV, predefined options), including file and directory types. But as extensive as these built-in form fields are, in certain circumstances it can be necessary to build custom form fields.

Similarly, in Table 6-2 you learned how all Django forms fields are linked to Django widgets that define the HTML produced by a form field. While in previous sections (e.g., Listings 6-25 and 6-26) you learned how it's possible to use a form field's `widget` property to override its default widget with custom properties (e.g., a CSS `class` attribute) or assign it a different widget altogether (e.g., a `forms.Textarea` widget to a `forms.CharField` field), in certain circumstances, playing around with Django's built-in widgets (i.e., adding attributes or switching one built-in widget for another) can be insufficient for complex HTML form inputs.

Up next, you'll learn how to customize both Django form fields and widgets.

CUSTOMIZE DJANGO FORM FIELDS, WIDGETS, OR BOTH?

As you've learned throughout this chapter, there's a fuzzy relationship between a form field and a form widget, which can make it hard to determine which one to customize when built-in options become insufficient.

As a rule of thumb, if you need to constantly change a form field's data or validation logic, you should use a custom form field. If you need to constantly change a form field's HTML output (e.g., form tags, CSS classes, JavaScript events), you should use a custom widget.

Create Custom Form Fields

The good news about creating custom form fields is you don't have to write everything from scratch, compared to other custom Django constructs (e.g., a custom template filter or context processor). Since Django's built-in form fields are subclasses that inherit their behavior from the `forms.Form` class, you can further subclass a built-in form field into a more specialized form field. Therefore, a custom form field can start with a basic set of functionalities present in a built-in form field, which you can then customize as required.

For example, if you find yourself creating forms with the built-in `forms.FileField` and constantly customizing it in a certain way (e.g., for certain file sizes or types), you can create a custom form field (e.g., `PdfFileField`, `MySpecialFileField`) that inherits the behavior from `forms.FileField`, customize it, and use the custom form field directly in your forms.

Listing 6-29 illustrates a custom form field that inherits its behavior from the built-in `forms.ChoiceField` form field.

Listing 6-29. Django custom form field inherits behavior from forms.ChoiceField

```
class GenderField(forms.ChoiceField):
    def __init__(self, *args, **kwargs):
        super(GenderField, self).__init__(*args, **kwargs)
        self.error_messages = {"required":"Please select a gender, it's required"}
        self.choices = ((None,'Select gender'),('M','Male'),('F','Female'))
```

As you can see in Listing 6-29, the `GenderField` class inherits its behavior from the built-in `forms.ChoiceField` field class, giving it automatic access to the same behaviors and features as this latter class. Next, the `__init__` method - used to initialize instances of the class - a call to `super()` is made to ensure the initialization process of the parent class (i.e., `forms.ChoiceField`) is made and immediately after values are assigned to the `error_messages` and `choices` fields.

The error_messages and choices fields in Listing 6-29 might look familiar because they're arguments typically used in the built-in forms.ChoiceField and are part of Django's standard form field arguments described earlier in this chapter. You can similarly add any other argument supported by form fields (e.g., self.required, self.widget) so the custom form field is created with behaviors set by form field arguments.

Once you have a custom form field like the one in Listing 6-29, you can use it to declare a form field in a Django form class (e.g., gender = <pkg_location>.GenderField() vs. gender = forms.ChoiceField(error_messages={...},choices=...)). As you can see, custom form fields are a great choice if you're doing repetitive customizations on built-in form fields.

Customize Built-In Widgets

In Listings 6-25 and 6-26 you already explored some customizations associated with Django's built-in widgets. For example, in Listing 6-25 you saw how it's possible to customize the default built-in widget assigned to form fields, while in Listing 6-26 you saw how it's possible to add custom attributes to built-in widgets. In this section you'll learn how to globally customize built-in widgets.

Looking back at Table 6-2, you can see, for example, the forms.widget.TextInput() widget produces an HTML output like <input type="text" ...> and similarly all the other widgets in Table 6-2 produce their own specific HTML output.

Given the high expectations set forth by many front-end designs, producing this type of basic boilerplate HTML output can be a non-starter for a lot of Django projects. For example, if you want to tightly integrate JavaScript jQuery or ReactJS logic into HTML forms, customizing the default HTML produced by Django's built-in widgets can be a necessity. In these circumstances, the ideal approach is to produce custom HTML for Django's built-in widgets, forgoing the use of the default markup defined by Django in its out-of-the-box state.

The first thing you need to know about customizing Django's built-in widgets is where Django keeps its default built-in widgets. Django builds the HTML output for its built-in widgets from the Django templates located inside the django/forms/templates/django/forms/widgets/ directory in the main Django distribution (e.g., if your Python installation is located at /python/coffeehouse/lib/python3.5/site-packages/, append this directory path to locate the widget templates).

If you look inside this last directory, you'll find templates (e.g., input.html, radio.html) for each built-in Django widget. Be aware all these widgets templates don't use plain HTML, but instead use Django template syntax (e.g., {% include %} tags, {% if %} conditionals) to favor code reuse. If you're unfamiliar with Django template syntax, look over Chapter 3.

Now, while you could directly modify the templates in this location to alter the HTML output produced by each widget, don't do this. The recommended approach to customize the output for each built-in widget is to include custom built-in widgets on a project basis. Therefore the first step to customize Django's built-in widgets is to build custom built-in widgets and make them part of a Django project.

■ **Tip** Copy all the built-in widgets in the Django distribution (i.e., the templates inside django/forms/templates/django/forms/widgets/) to your project and modify them as needed.

Since built-in widgets are Django templates, and they need to be placed in a project directory where they can be discovered. This means custom built-in widgets must be placed in a project directory that's part of the DIRS list declared in the TEMPLATES variable in settings.py. In most cases, a project declares a directory named templates - as part of DIRS - that also contains a project's templates - but you can use any directory so long as it's declared as part of DIRS - see the section "Template Search Paths" in Chapter 3 for more details on DIRS.

Besides using a directory that's part of the DIRS list to locate widget templates, Django also expects to locate custom built-in widgets in the same path it uses for its default built-in widgets (i.e., those included in the Django distribution).

Therefore, if you have a project directory named templates as part of the DIRS list, inside this templates directory you'll need to create the same directory path django/forms/widgets/ and inside this last widgets subdirectory place the custom built-in widgets (e.g., to customize the built-in input.html widget located in the Django distribution at django/forms/templates/django/forms/widgets/input.html you would create a project version at <project_dir>/templates/django/forms/widgets/input.html, this way the latter input.html template takes precedence over the default built-in distribution template).

Once you have the custom built-in widgets set up in your project, you need to make two configuration changes to your project's settings.py. The first configuration requires you add the FORM_RENDERER variable, as follows:

```
FORM_RENDERER = 'django.forms.renderers.TemplatesSetting'
```

By default, Django built-in widgets are loaded through a stand-alone Django template renderer – django.forms.renderers.DjangoTemplates – which is unrelated to a project's main TEMPLATES configuration containing the DIRS list with a project's templates. Because you now placed custom built-in widgets inside a directory declared as part of the DIRS list, you need to configure Django to use a project's main TEMPLATES configuration as part of the form-rendering process. By setting the FORM_RENDERER variable to django.forms.renderers.TemplatesSetting, Django also inspects paths in the DIRS list of the main TEMPLATES configuration for built-in widgets. The last subsection on widgets provides additional details on the FORM_RENDERER variable.

Finally, because you're overriding the django.forms package in a project to get custom built-in widgets, you must also declare the django.forms package as part of the INSTALLED_APPS list in settings.py.

Create Custom Form Widgets

Custom form widgets are used for cases where you need to keep Django's built-in widget functionality as is, but still need to customize the HTML output produced by widgets.

■ **Tip** Before creating custom form widgets, look closely at the built-in widgets in Table 6-2 and the widgets in the sidebar "Django Hidden Built-In Widgets." You may be able to find what you're looking for without the need to create custom widgets.

Similar to custom form fields, custom form widgets have the advantage of being class based and can therefore inherit their behavior from built-in widgets. For example, if you find yourself constantly customizing the built-in forms.widgets.TextInput widget in a certain way (e.g., HTML attributes or JavaScript events), you can create a custom widget (e.g., CustomerWidget, EmployeeWidget) that inherits its behavior from forms.widgets.TextInput, customize it, and use the custom widget directly in form fields.

For example, let's say you're constantly modifying Django text widgets to include the HTML 5 placeholder attribute – used to give end users a hint about the purpose of an input form field and which goes away when a user focuses on a field. Listing 6-30 illustrates a custom form widget that generates the HTML 5 placeholder attribute based on the field name attribute assigned to a widget.

Listing 6-30. Django custom form widget inherits behavior from forms.widgets.Input

```
class PlaceholderInput(forms.widgets.Input):
      template_name = 'about/placeholder.html'
      input_type = 'text'
      def get_context(self, name, value, attrs):
            context = super(PlaceholderInput, self).get_context(name, value, attrs)
            context['widget']['attrs']['maxlength'] = 50
            context['widget']['attrs']['placeholder'] = name.title()
            return context
```

■ **Note** The `forms.widgets.Input` widget is a more general purpose widget than `forms.widgets.TextInput` and does not include text input behaviors; hence it's often the preferred choice to build custom widgets due to its basic feature set. It's worth mentioning `forms.widgets.Input` is the parent widget of `forms.widgets.TextInput`, `forms.widgets.NumberInput`, `forms.widgets.EmailInput` and other input widgets described in Table 6-2.

As you can see in Listing 6-30, the `PlaceholderInput` class inherits its behavior from the built-in `forms.widgets.Input` widget class, giving it access to the same behaviors and features as this latter class.

Next are two class fields. The `template_name` field defines the backing template for the custom widget which points to `'about/placeholder.html'` - note that if you omit the `template_name` field, the parent class template is used (i.e., for the `forms.widgets.Input` widget the template is `django/forms/widgets/input.html`). The `input_type` field is a requirement for `forms.widgets.Input` subclasses and is used to assign the HTML input type attribute, values can include: `text`, `number`, `email`, `url`, `password`, or any other valid HTML input type value.

Inside the custom widget class is the `get_context()` method, which is used to set the context for the backing widget template - just like standard Django templates. In this case, a call is made to `super()` to ensure the context for the parent widget class template (i.e., `forms.widgets.Input`) is set and immediately after a pair of attributes - `maxlength` and `placeholder` - are set on the widget context in the `['widget']['attrs']` dictionary for use inside the widget template. Note the value for `maxlength` is fixed and the value for `placeholder` is taken from the field `name` attribute and converted to a title with Python's standard `title` method. Finally, the `get_context()` method returns the updated `context` reference to pass it to the widget template.

Now let's take a look at the widget template `'about/placeholder.html'` in Listing 6-31.

Listing 6-31. Django custom form widget inherits behavior from forms.widgets.Input

```
# about/placeholder.html
<input type="{{ widget.type }}" name="{{ widget.name }}"{% if widget.value != None %}
value="{{ widget.value }}"{% endif %}{% include "django/forms/widgets/attrs.html" %} />

# django/forms/widgets/attrs.html
{% for name, value in widget.attrs.items %}{% if value is not False %} {{ name }}{% if value
is not True %}="{{ value }}"{% endif %}{% endif %}{% endfor %}
```

You can see in Listing 6-31 the HTML `input` tag is generated with values from the `widget` dictionary set through the `get_context` method. The values for `widget.type`, `widget.name`, and `widget.value` are all set behind the scenes in the parent class (i.e., `forms.widgets.Input`). In addition, notice the HTML `input` tag uses the built-in widget template `django/forms/widgets/attrs.html` shown at the bottom of Listing 6-31.

This last widget template loops over all the elements in the `widgets.attrs` context dictionary and generates the `input` attributes. Since the `widgets.attrs` context dictionary is modified in Listing 6-30 to include the `maxlength` and `placeholder` attributes, the `input` tag is generated with these additional attributes (e.g., `<input type="text" name="email" maxlength="50" placeholder="Email">`).

Now let's take a step back to discuss the location of the `'about/placeholder.html'` widget template. By default, Django custom widgets are only searched for inside the `templates` folders in all Django apps defined in `INSTALLED_APPS`. This means that in order for Django to find the custom `'about/placeholder.html'` widget template, it must be placed inside any project app's `templates` folder (e.g., given a project app named `about`, the custom widget should be located under `templates/about/placeholder.html`, where the `templates` folder is at the same level of an app's `models.py` and `views.py` files). It's possible to define custom widgets on a global directory, but I'll discuss this in the last subsection on widgets.

Finally, once you define the custom widget in the right location, you can use it as part of a Django form field (e.g., `email=forms.EmailField(widget=<pkg_location>.PlaceholderInput)`) to generate an HTML `input` tag with a default `placeholder` attribute.

Custom Form Widget Configuration Options

In the previous two sections on customizing form widgets, I didn't mention a variety of configuration options in order to avoid getting sidetracked from the main task at hand. But now that you know how to customize Django's built-in widgets and how to create custom form widgets, I can provide you with these additional details.

The first topic is related to finding and loading custom widget templates. Django defines a form renderer through the `FORM_RENDERER` variable in `settings.py`. Table 6-4 describes the three different values supported by the `FORM_RENDERER` variable.

Table 6-4. *FORM_RENDERER values that influence finding and loading custom widget templates*

Form renderer class	Description
django.forms.renderers.DjangoTemplates **(Default)**	Searches and loads widget templates from the built-in django/forms/templates/ directory (i.e., the distribution). Searches and loads widget templates from all the templates directories inside apps declared in INSTALLED_APPS.
django.forms.renderers.JinjaTemplates	Searches and loads widget templates from the built-in django/forms/jinja2/ directory (i.e., the distribution). Searches and loads widget templates from all the jinja2 directories inside apps declared in INSTALLED_APPS.
django.forms.renderers.TemplatesSetting	Searches and loads widget templates based on a project's TEMPLATES configuration (e.g., its DIRS values). NOTE: This renderer requires you declare the django.forms package as part of INSTALLED_APPS.

As you can see in Table 6-4, there's even a Jinja template renderer to allow you to customize widgets backed by Jinja templates, in addition to other renderers used in the previous sections.

In Listing 6-30 you learned how custom widget classes use fields (e.g., `template_name`, `input_type`) to specify certain behaviors. Fields in widgets classes are highly dependent on the parent widget class. For example, although `template_name` is valid for all built-in widgets, more specialized built-in widgets can accept additional fields. If in doubt, consult the fields supported for the built-in widget[4] used as a widget's parent class.

In Listing 6-30 you also learned how to access and modify a widget's template context through the `get_context()` method. Although in Listing 6-30 you only added a couple of widget attributes to the `context['widget']['attrs']` dictionary, the parent `context['widget']` dictionary is a large data structure that stores all data associated with a widget, where you can inclusively update a widget's field values. The following snippet illustrates the contents of the `context['widget']` for a form field using the `PlaceholderInput` widget class from Listing 6-30.

```
{'widget': {'attrs': {'placeholder': 'Email', 'maxlength': 50}, 'name': 'email', 'is_
hidden': False, 'type': 'text', 'value': None, 'template_name': 'about/placeholder.html',
'required': True}}
```

As you can see, in addition to the HTML input attributes stored under the `attrs` key, there are other `widget` field keys (e.g., `name`, `is_hidden`) that are made available in a template to render the final output. This also means there's nothing limiting you from adding custom data keys to the `context['widget']` dictionary inside the `get_context()` method to integrate them as part of the final template layout (e.g., `'react':{<react_data>}`, `'jquery':{<jquery_data>})`.

Django Advanced Form Processing: Partial Forms, AJAX, and Files

In most cases, Django form processing adheres to the steps and code sequences outlined in the first section of this chapter, shown in Figure 6-1. However, Django form processing can require small adjustments for certain scenarios, like those involving partial form processing, AJAX forms, and file uploads.

Partial Forms

On occasions you may find yourself with the need to use a partial form based on a preexisting Django form. For example, you get a request to add a similar form to the `ContactForm` used up to this point - in Listing 6-25 - but without requiring the `name` and `email` fields. Since the `ContactForm` is tried and tested, including the necessary post-processing logic (e.g., adding the form data to a CRM [Customer Relationship Management] system), it's a worthwhile idea to reuse the `ContactForm` class. But how do you go about using a Django form partially?

The first alternative to achieve partial forms is to hide the unneeded form fields from a user, allowing the original form class to remain intact while not requiring a new subclass. This is the least invasive approach, but you need to be careful with two aspects. The first aspect is the form template layout, shown in Listing 6-32.

Listing 6-32. Django form with fields marked as hidden

```
<form method="POST">
  {% csrf_token %}
    <div class="row">
      <div class="col-md-2">
        {{ form.comment.label_tag }}
          {% if form.comment.help_text %}
```

[4]https://docs.djangoproject.com/en/1.11/ref/forms/widgets/#built-in-widgets

```
            <sup>{{ form.comment.help_text }}</sup>
            {% endif %}
            {% for error in form.comment.errors %}
             <div class="row">
               <div class="alert alert-danger">{{error}}</div>
             </div>
            {% endfor %}
        </div><div class="col-md-10 pull-left">
          {{ form.comment }}
        </div>
    </div>
    {{form.name.as_hiddden}}
    {{form.email.as_hidden}}
<input type="submit" value="Submit form" class="btn btn-primary">
</form>
```

First notice in Listing 6-32 the form fields are output individually and do not use a shortcut method (e.g., `form.as_table`) or loop like some of the previous form layout examples. The reason is, the last `form` fields are explicitly output as hidden through the `as_hidden` method - described earlier in Table 6-4. The `as_hidden` method generates a form field as a hidden HTML input (e.g., `<input type="hidden"...>`), irrespective of its form field data type. This mechanism effectively hides fields from end users, but keeps the fields as part of the form.

Why is it important to keep fields as part of the form and not just remove them? *Validation.* Remember the form instance hasn't changed, only the requirements; you may not need the `name` and `email` data on this template page, but the form instance and validation logic doesn't know that. All of which takes us to the second aspect you need to take care of: required values.

If you publish the template in Listing 6-32 without taking care of this second aspect, you might be surprised when you realize the form never passes validation! Why? The underlying `ContactForm` class treats the `email` field as required, therefore it must be given a value, but since the field is now hidden from an end user, you must take care of giving the `email` field a value yourself - note the `name` field doesn't present this problem because it's configured with `required=False`. Therefore, in order for the template in Listing 6-32 to work, the form must be initialized with a value like the following snippet:

```
form = ContactForm(initial={'email':'anonymous@gmail.com'})
```

By initializing the form in this manner, the email form field is given this initial value as a hidden input. So once a user submits the form, the email value is transferred back to Django as part of the form, where validation passes since the post-processing logic gets all its expected values. Of course, if a form's fields are all optional (i.e., they're marked with `required=False`), this initialization process is unnecessary, since the validation won't be expecting any value anyway.

A second alternative to achieve partial forms is to create a subclass from a form class and delete the unneeded fields. This is a little more straightforward approach, but it does require creating a form subclass, which may be overkill for certain scenarios. Listing 6-33 shows how to subclass a Django form class and remove some of its parent's fields.

Listing 6-33. Django form subclass with removed parent fields

```
from coffeehouse.about.forms import ContactForm

class ContactCommentOnlyForm(ContactForm):
    def __init__(self, *args, **kwargs):
        super(ContactCommentOnlyForm, self).__init__(*args, **kwargs)
        del self.fields['name']
        del self.fields['email']
```

As you can see in Listing 6-33, the ContactCommentOnlyForm form inherits its behavior from the ContactForm class. Next, inside the form class __init__ method, a call is made to the parent's __init__ class via super() and two calls are made on self.fields using Python's del to remove both the name and email fields from this form subclass.

Once you have the form subclass from Listing 6-33, you can generate an unbound instance form in a view method and pass it to a template for rendering. Since this last subclass removes the name and email fields, upon validation you won't face previously described problem of missing values for hidden fields, since the ContactCommentOnlyForm form now only has a single field.

AJAX Form Submission

AJAX is a technique where JavaScript on a web page communicates with a server-side application, re-renders the web page with the result of this communication, all without a web page transition. Django forms are often designed to submit their data via AJAX to create a smoother workflow (i.e., without changing the original web page with a web form)

The workflow for a form that uses AJAX as far as the initial form delivery is concerned - steps 1 an 2 in Figure 6-1 - is identical to that of a regular Django non-AJAX form: you create an unbound form instance in a view method, which is passed to a template for rendering into a web page that's delivered to an end user.

The first difference in Django forms that submit their data via AJAX, is the web page on which the unbound form is delivered, must also contain the necessary JavaScript logic to send the form data to the server-side application and also process the server-side response. Listing 6-34 illustrates this JavaScript logic using the jQuery library to submit a Django form via AJAX.

Listing 6-34. JavaScript jQuery logic to submit Django form via AJAX

```
# NOTE: The following is only the Django (HTML) template with AJAX logic
# See Listing 6-35 for AJAX processing views.py and urls.py
<h4>Feedback</h4>
<div class="row">
  <div id="feedbackmessage"</div>
</div>
<form method="POST" id="feedbackform" action="{% url 'stores:feedback' %}">
  {% csrf_token %}
    <div class="row">
      <div class="col-md-12 pull-left">
         {{ form.comment }}
       </div>
    </div>
    {{form.name.as_hiddden}}
    {{form.email.as_hidden}}
<input type="submit" value="Submit feedback" class="btn btn-primary">
</form>

<script>
$(document).ready(function() {
    $("#feedbackform").submit(function(event) {
       event.preventDefault();
       $.ajax({ data: $(this).serialize(),
                type: $(this).attr('method'),
                url: $(this).attr('action'),
                success: function(response) {
```

```
                console.log(response);
                if(response['success']) {
                    $("#feedbackmessage").html("<div class='alert alert-success'>
                    Succesfully sent feedback, thank you!</div>");
                    $("#feedbackform").addClass("hidden");
                }
                if(response['error']) {
                    $("#feedbackmessage").html("<div class='alert alert-danger'>" +
                    response['error']['comment'] +"</div>");
                }
            },
            error: function (request, status, error) {
                console.log(request.responseText);
            }
        });
    });
})
</script>
```

The first part of Listing 6-34 is a standard Django form layout. However, notice the `<form>` tag includes the `action` attribute. In previous Django forms, the `action` attribute was not used because the serving url - GET request - and processing url - POST request - was the same one. In Listing 6-34, the `action` attribute explicitly tells the browser the url where it should send the POST request - in this case `{% url 'stores:feedback' %}` is a Django template tag that gets translated into a url (e.g., `/stores/feedback/`). Different urls are necessary in this case, because Django view methods that handle AJAX requests/responses are different from Django view methods that handle standard web requests/responses.

Now let's turn our attention to the bottom half of Listing 6-34 and the JavaScript logic enclosed in `<script>` tags. In brief - as it would go beyond the scope of our discussion to describe jQuery syntax - the web page awaits a click on the `#feedbackform` form's submit button. Once this click is detected, an AJAX POST request using the form's data is sent to the url defined in the form's `action` attribute. Upon completion of the AJAX request (i.e., when the server side sends a response back), the response - in JSON format - is analyzed. If the AJAX response contains a `success` message, the message is output at the top of the form and the form is hidden to avoid multiple submissions. If the AJAX response contains an `error` message, the message is output at the top of the form.

Now that you know how Django form data is submitted to the server side via AJAX, Listing 6-35 illustrates the Django view method necessary to handle this AJAX request payload.

Listing 6-35. Django view method to process Django form via AJAX

```
# urls.py (Main)
urlpatterns = [
    url(r'^stores/',include('coffeehouse.stores.urls',namespace="stores"))
]

# urls.py (App stores)
urlpatterns = [
    url(r'^$',views.index,name="index"),
    url(r'^feedback/$',views.feedback,name="feedback"),
]

# views.py (App stores)
from django.http import HttpResponse, JsonResponse
from coffeehouse.about.forms import ContactForm
```

```
def feedback(request):
    if request.POST:
        form = ContactForm(request.POST)
        if form.is_valid():
            return JsonResponse({'success':True})
        else:
            return JsonResponse({'error':form.errors})
    return HttpResponse("Hello from feedback!")
```

The first important point about the view method in Listing 6-35 is that it only handles POST requests. Notice that in case the `if request.POST:` statement isn't true, the view method always responds with the `Hello from feedback!` string.

Next, inside the `request.POST` segment, the process starts out pretty similar to a standard Django form processing sequence (i.e., a bound form instance is created and a call is made to the form's `is_valid()` method to validate the user-provided data). However, notice the responses for both valid and invalid form data use `JsonResponse()`. Since the AJAX form submission operates in a JavaScript context, the JSON format response is a common format to use to send a response back to the browser.

If you turn your attention back to Listing 6-34, you can see the JavaScript logic is designed to handle and output either JSON response (`success` or `error`) returned by the view method in Listing 6-35.

Files in Forms

Django offers a couple of form fields to capture files through forms - `forms.ImageField()` and `forms.ImageField()` described in Table 6-2. However, although these form fields generate the necessary HTML and validation logic to enforce files are submitted via forms, there are a couple of subtleties related to processing files in forms.

The first issue is the HTML `<form>` tag for forms that transfer files must explicitly set the encoding type to `enctype="multipart/form-data"`, in addition to using `method=POST`. The second issue is the contents of files are placed in the Django `request` object under the special `FILES` dictionary key. Listing 6-36 illustrates a form with file fields, its corresponding view method, and its template layout.

Listing 6-36. Django form with file fields, corresponding view method, and template layout

```
# forms.py
from django import forms

class SharingForm(forms.Form):
    # NOTE: forms.PhotoField requires Python PIL & other operating system libraries,
    #       so generic FileField is used instead
    video = forms.FileField()
    photo = forms.FileField(widget=forms.ClearableFileInput(attrs={'multiple': True}))

# views.py
def index(request):
    if request.method == 'POST':
        # POST, generate form with data from the request
        form = SharingForm(request.POST,request.FILES)
        # check if it's valid:
        if form.is_valid():
            # Process file data in request.FILES
            # Process data, insert into DB, generate email,etc
```

```
            # redirect to a new URL:
            return HttpResponseRedirect('/about/contact/thankyou')
    else:
        # GET, generate blank form
        form = SharingForm()
    return render(request,'social/index.html',{'form':form})

# social/index.html
<form method="post" enctype="multipart/form-data">
  {% csrf_token %}
  <ul>
    {{form.as_ul}}
  </ul>
    <input type="submit" value="Submit photo" class="btn btn-primary">
</form>
```

Notice how the HTML `<form>` tag declares the required attributes and in addition notice how the `request.FILES` reference is used to create a bound form – along with the standard `request.POST`. The remaining form structures in Listing 6-36 are identical to regular non-file forms (e.g., unbound form creation, call to `is_valid()`).

But similar to regular Django form processing, once a form is valid – if `is_valid()` returns `True` – you'll want do something with the contents of the form data; therefore in this case, you'll need to access `request.FILES` to do something with the files uploaded by a user.

But before describing how to process the contents of files in `request.FILES` it's important you understand the possible contents of the `request.FILES` dictionary:

```
Option 1) request.FILES = {'photo': [<InMemoryUploadedFile>,<TemporaryUploadedFile>],
                           'video': [<InMemoryUploadedFile>]}
Option 2) request.FILES = {'photo': [<TemporaryUploadedFile>],'video':
                           [<InMemoryUploadedFile>]}
```

The `request.FILES` dictionary contains keys corresponding to file field names. In this case, you can see the `photo` and `video` keys correspond to the form fields names declared in Listing 6-36 that represent files. Next, notice the value for each key is a list, irrespective if the file form field can accept multiple files – like `photo` due to the overridden widget with the `'multiple': True` attribute – or a single file – in the case of `video`.

Now let's analyze the contents of the lists assigned to each file form field key. Each of the list elements represents an uploaded file. But notice how the files are represented by either the `InMemoryUploadedFile` or `TemporaryUploadedFile` class – both of which are subclasses of the `django.core.files.uploadedfile.UploadedFile` class. The reason uploaded files are represented by either an `InMemoryUploadedFile` or `TemporaryUploadedFile` instance class, is dependent on the size of an uploaded file.

As it turns out, before you even decide how to handle uploaded files, Django must decide what to do and where to place uploaded files. To do this, Django relies on upload handlers. By default and unless explicitly overridden in the `FILE_UPLOAD_HANDLERS` variable in `settings.py`, Django uses the following two file upload handlers:

```
FILE_UPLOAD_HANDLERS= [
    'django.core.files.uploadhandler.MemoryFileUploadHandler',
    'django.core.files.uploadhandler.TemporaryFileUploadHandler',
]
```

By default, if a file is less than 2.5 MB, Django uses `MemoryFileUploadHandler` to place the contents of an uploaded file into memory; if a file is larger than 2.5 MB, Django uses `TemporaryFileUploadHandler` to place the contents of an uploaded file in a temporary file (e.g., `/tmp/Af534.upload`).

You can define FILE_UPLOAD_HANDLERS in settings.py to only include the file upload handler you desire (e.g., if you wish to save memory resources remove MemoryFileUploadHandler). However, note a file upload handler must *always* be active in order for file uploads to work. If you don't like the behavior of Django's built-in file upload handlers, then you'll need to write your own file upload handler.[5]

In addition to defining FILE_UPLOAD_HANDLERS in settings.py, there are two other parameters you can declare in settings.py to influence the behavior of file upload handlers. The FILE_UPLOAD_MAX_MEMORY_SIZE variable sets the threshold size at which files are held in memory vs. handled as temporary files, defaulting to 2621440 bytes (or 2.5 MB). And the FILE_UPLOAD_TEMP_DIR variable sets the directory to which temporary uploaded files must be saved, defaulting to None, meaning an operating system's temporary file directory is used (e.g., on Linux OS /tmp/).

Now that you know where and how Django stores uploaded files even before you decide how to handle them, let's take a look at how to process the contents of request.FILES. Listing 6-37 shows the continuation of Listing 6-36 with the relevant snippets necessary to process uploaded files.

Listing 6-37. Django form file processing with save procedure to MEDIA_ROOT

```
# views.py
from django.conf import settings

def save_uploaded_file_to_media_root(f):
    with open('%s%s' % (settings.MEDIA_ROOT,f.name), 'wb+') as destination:
        for chunk in f.chunks():
            destination.write(chunk)

def index(request):
    if request.method == 'POST':
        # POST, generate form with data from the request
        form = SharingForm(request.POST,request.FILES)
        # check if it's valid:
        if form.is_valid():
            for field in request.FILES.keys():
                for formfile in request.FILES.getlist(field):
                    save_uploaded_file_to_media_root(formfile)
            return HttpResponseRedirect('/about/contact/thankyou')
    else:
        # GET, generate blank form
        form = SharingForm()
    return render(request,'social/index.html',{'form':form})
```

After the form is_valid() method, you know each of the keys in the request.FILES dictionary are file form fields, so a loop is created to get each file field (i.e., video, photo). Next, using the getlist() method of the request.FILES dictionary, you obtain the list of file instances (i.e., InMemoryUploadedFile,TemporaryUploadedFile) for each file field and loop over each element to get file instances. Finally, you execute the save_uploaded_file_to_media_root() method on each file instance.

Each file instance – represented as the formfile reference in Listing 6-37 – is either a InMemoryUploadedFile or TemporaryUploadedFile instance type. But as I mentioned earlier, these classes are derived from the parent class django.core.files.uploadedfile.UploadedFile, which means file instances are also UploadedFile instances.

[5]https://docs.djangoproject.com/en/1.11/ref/files/uploads/#custom-upload-handlers

By design, the Django `django.core.files.uploadedfile.UploadedFile` class has a series of methods and fields, specifically made to easily handle the contents of uploaded files, some of which include the following:

`<file_instance>.name`.- Outputs the name of the file, as was on a user's computer.

- `<file_instance>.size`.- Outputs the size of the file, in bytes.
- `<file_instance>.content_type`.- Outputs the HTTP Content-Type header assigned to the file (e.g., text/html, application/zip).
- `<file_instance>.chunks()`.- A generator method to efficiently output contents of a file in chunks.

With the use of these `UploadedFile` fields and methods, you can see toward the top of Listing 6-37 the `save_uploaded_file_to_media_root()` method logic includes saving the uploaded file with its original name – using Python's standard `with...open` syntax – and then using the `chunks()` method to efficiently write all the pieces of the uploaded file to the file system.

■ **Note** The uploaded files in Listing 6-37 are saved under the settings.MEDIA_ROOT folder. Although you can save files to any location you want, the standard practice for user uploaded files in Django is to save them under the MEDIA_ROOT folder defined in settings.py.

Django Formsets

Because Django forms represent the primary means by which users introduce data into Django projects, it's not uncommon for Django forms to be used as a data-capturing mechanism. This, however, can lead to an efficiency problem, relying on one Django form per web page. Django formsets allow you to integrate multiple forms of the same type into a template – with all the necessary validation and layout facilities – to simplify data capturing by means of multiple forms.

The good news is that all you've learned about Django forms up to this point – form fields, validation workflow, template layouts, widgets, and all the other topics – applies equally to Django formsets. This means the learning curve for formsets is rather simple, albeit you will have to learn some new concepts.

Formset initialization.- Although formsets are initialized as a group of regular Django forms, formset initialization requires parameters specific to formsets.

- Formset management form.- To keep track of multiple Django forms on the same page, formsets also use a special form called a 'management form'.

Let's assume you're in the process of adding online ordering capabilities to your coffehouse application. You already have a drink form so users can place an order for a drink, but want to add the ability for users to order multiple drinks, so you need multiple drink forms on the same page or a drink formset.

Listing 6-38 illustrates the stand-alone `DrinkForm` class, the corresponding view method that generates an empty formset, and the template layout used to display the formset.

Listing 6-38. Django formset factory initialization and template layout

```
# forms.py
from django import forms

DRINKS = ((None,'Please select a drink type'),(1,'Mocha'),(2,'Espresso'),(3,'Latte'))
SIZES = ((None,'Please select a drink size'),('s','Small'),('m','Medium'),('l','Large'))
```

```
class DrinkForm(forms.Form):
    name = forms.ChoiceField(choices=DRINKS,initial=0)
    size = forms.ChoiceField(choices=SIZES,initial=0)
    amount = forms.ChoiceField(choices=[(None,'Amount of drinks')]+[(i, i) for i in
    range(1,10)])

# views.py
from django.forms import formset_factory

def index(request):
    DrinkFormSet = formset_factory(DrinkForm, extra=2, max_num=20)
    if request.method == 'POST':
        # TODO
    else:
        formset = DrinkFormSet(initial=[{'name': 1,'size': 'm','amount':1}])
    return render(request,'online/index.html',{'formset':formset})

# online/index.html
<form method="post">
        {% csrf_token %}
    {{ formset.management_form }}
    <table>
        {% for form in formset %}
        <tr><td><ul class="list-inline">{{ form.as_ul }}</ul></td></tr>
        {% endfor %}
    </table>
    <input type="submit" value="Submit order" class="btn btn-primary">
</form>
```

The DrinkForm class in Listing 6-38 uses standard Django form syntax, so there's nothing new there. However, the index view method starts by using the django.forms.formset_factory method. The formset_factory is used to generate a FormSet class from a given form class. In this case, notice the formset_factory uses the DrinkForm argument - representing the form class - to generate a DrinkForm formset. I'll provide details about the additional formset_factory arguments shortly.

Next, in Listing 6-38 you can see an unbound DrinkFormSet() instance is created with an initial value - similar to how stand-alone unbound forms are created and use the initial argument. However, notice the initial value is a list, unlike a stand-alone dictionary used in standard forms. Because a formset is a group of forms, a formset's initial value is a group of dictionaries, where each dictionary represents the initial values for each form. In the case of Listing 6-38, one of the formset's forms is set to initialize with the {'name': 1,'size': 'm','amount':1} values.

Toward the bottom of Listing 6-38 you can see the template for the formset. The first difference between a stand-alone form template, is the {{ formset.management_form }} statement to output the management form. The second difference is the loop over the formset reference outputs the various forms. In this case, each formset form is output in its entirety with {{form.as_ul}} as a inline form, but you can equally use any Django form template layout technique to output each form instance in a custom manner (e.g., remove field id values).

Formset Factory

The `formset_factory()` method used in Listing 6-38 is one of the centerpieces to working with formsets. Although the example in Listing 6-38 only uses three arguments, the `formset_factory()` method can accept up to nine arguments. The following snippet illustrates the names and default values for each argument in the `formset_factory()` method.

```
formset_factory(form, formset=BaseFormSet, extra=1, can_order=False, can_delete=False,
                max_num=None, min_num=None, validate_max=False, validate_min=False)
```

As you can confirm in this snippet, the only required argument (i.e., that doesn't have a default value) for the `formset_factory()` method is `form`. The meaning for each argument is the following:

`form`.- Defines the form class on which to create a formset.

`formset`.- Defines the formset base class, defaults to `django.forms.formsets.BaseFormSet`. Changes when you require a custom formset for cases like custom formset validation.

`extra`.- Defines the amount of empty forms added to a formset. If a formset's forms are all empty (i.e., they're not initialized) a formset contains an `extra` number of forms. If a formset's forms contain data (i.e., they're initialized) a formset contains the number of initialized forms + `extra` (empty forms).

`can_order`.- Adds the ORDER field (as a `forms.IntegerField`) to every form in a formset, with the purpose to alter the form order in a formset. Defaults to `False`.

`can_delete`.- Adds the DELETE field (as a `forms.BooleanField`) to every form in a formset, with the purpose to mark a form in a formset for deletion. Defaults to `False`.

`max_num`.- Defines the maximum number of forms to display in a formset. Defaults to `None`, to indicate up to 1000 forms instances be displayed.

`min_num`.- Defines the minimum number of forms to display in a formset. Defaults to `None`, to indicate a minimum 0 form instances be displayed.

`validate_max`.- Used in conjunction with `max_num` to ensure validation is enforced and the form instances never exceed `max_num`. Defaults to `False`.

`validate_min`.- Used in conjunction with `min_num` to ensure validation is enforced and the form instances are never less than `min_num`. Defaults to `False`.

Now that you're aware of the various `formset_factory()` method options, let's turn out attention back to the method used in Listing 6-38:

```
formset_factory(DrinkForm, extra=2, max_num=20)
```

This `formset_factory` method creates a formset with the `DrinkForm` class; the `extra=2` indicates to always include 2 empty `DrinkForm` instances; this means that because the formset was initialized with one `DrinkForm` instance in Listing 6-38, the total number of forms in the formset will be one, plus two empty forms on account of `extra=2`; the `max_num=20` argument indicates the formset should contain a maximum 20 `DrinkForm` instances.

Formset Management Form and Formset Processing

To understand the purpose of a formset's management form, it's easiest to look at what this form contains. Listing 6-39 illustrates the contents of the formset management form based on the example from Listing 6-38.

Listing 6-39. Django formset management form contents and fields

```
<input type="hidden" name="form-TOTAL_FORMS" value="3" id="id_form-TOTAL_FORMS" />
<input type="hidden" name="form-INITIAL_FORMS" value="1" id="id_form-INITIAL_FORMS" />
<input type="hidden" name="form-MIN_NUM_FORMS" value="0" id="id_form-MIN_NUM_FORMS" />
<input type="hidden" name="form-MAX_NUM_FORMS" value="20" id="id_form-MAX_NUM_FORMS" />
```

As you can see in Listing 6-39, the contents of a formset management form (i.e., the {{formset.management_form}} statement from Listing 6-38) are four hidden input variables. The form-TOTAL_FORMS field indicates the total amount of forms in a formset; the form-INITIAL_FORMS fields indicates the total amount of initialized forms in a formset; the form-MIN_NUM_FORMS field indicates the minimum number of forms in a formset; and the form-MAX_NUM_FORMS field indicates the maximum number of forms in the formset.

At first glance the variables in Listing 6-39 can appear unimportant, but they provide an important role in formsets once the various forms in a formset enter the processing and rendering phase. To better illustrate the relevance of these formset management fields, let's modify the formset in Listing 6-38 to allow users to add more drink forms so they can grow their order as needed.

Listing 6-40. Django formset designed to add extra forms by user

```
#views.py
def index(request):
    extra_forms = 2
    DrinkFormSet = formset_factory(DrinkForm, extra=extra_forms, max_num=20)
    if request.method == 'POST':
        if 'additems' in request.POST and request.POST['additems'] == 'true':
            formset_dictionary_copy = request.POST.copy()
            formset_dictionary_copy['form-TOTAL_FORMS'] = int(formset_dictionary_copy
            ['form-TOTAL_FORMS']) + extra_forms
            formset = DrinkFormSet(formset_dictionary_copy)
        else:
            formset = DrinkFormSet(request.POST)
            if formset.is_valid():
                return HttpResponseRedirect('/about/contact/thankyou')
    else:
        formset = DrinkFormSet(initial=[{'name': 1,'size': 'm','amount':1}])
    return render(request,'online/index.html',{'formset':formset})

# online/index.html
<form method="post">
        {% csrf_token %}
    {{ formset.management_form }}
    <table>
        {% for form in formset %}
        <tr><td>{{ form }}</td></tr>
        {% endfor %}
    </table>
    <input type="hidden" value="false" name="additems" id="additems">
    <button class="btn btn-primary" id="additemsbutton">Add items to order</button>
    <input type="submit" value="Submit order" class="btn btn-primary">
</form>

<script>
$(document).ready(function() {
        $("#additemsbutton").on('click',function(event) {
         $("#additems").val("true");
        });
});
</script>
```

The first important modification in Listing 6-40 comes in the formset template. Notice how the form declares a hidden input field named `additems` set to `false`, as well as a button that when clicked changes the value of this hidden input field to `true`. This mechanism is a simple control variable to keep track when a user wants to add more items to an order (i.e., add more drink forms to the formset).

Now let's turn to the view method in Listing 6-40 that processes the formset. First, notice the formset uses the `extra_forms` variable set to two to define a formset's `extra` value, so the initial formset factory contain two extra forms, just like in Listing 6-38.

Next comes the `request.POST` processing formset section that has two possible outcomes. If `request.POST` contains the `additems` field and it's set to `true`, it indicates a user clicked on the button to add more forms to the formset. If `request.POST` does not contain the `additems` field or it's set to false, it indicates the user clicked on the standard submit button, so a bound formset set is created and a call to `is_valid()` is made on the formset. Now, let's break down the logic behind each possible outcome.

When a user adds more forms to the formset, a copy of the `request.POST` is made - the `copy()` method is necessary because `request.POST` is immutable. Next, the formset's management form field `form-TOTAL_FORMS` is modified to reflect additional forms by adding the `extra_forms` variables. Finally, the `DrinkFormSet` is re-bound with this new modified `request.POST` dictionary - with an altered `form-TOTAL_FORMS`. When the re-bound formset is sent back to a user, the formset will now contain two additional empty forms due to simply modifying the `form-TOTAL_FORMS` management formset field.

If the formset falls to the standard POST processing and validation section in Listing 6-40, here is what happens. First, a bound formset is created using `request.POST` - just like it's done with regular bound forms - next, the `is_valid()` method is called on the formset - also just like it's done in regular bound forms. If `is_valid()` returns true (i.e., there are no errors in the formset or individual forms) a redirect is made to the success page. If `is_valid()` returns false (i.e., there are errors in the formset or individual forms) an `errors` dictionary is attached to the formset reference and control falls to the last line - `return render(request,'online/index.html',{'formset':formset})` - which sends the `formset` instance with errors for display on the template - a process that again is almost identical to standard form validation and error management.

As you can see, with this minor modification to one of the fields in a Django formset's management form, it's possible to dynamically alter the amount of forms in a formset. Note that in most cases, it isn't necessary to manipulate a formset's management form fields directly, more often Django uses these values behind the scenes to keep track of processing and rendering tasks. Albeit once you create more advanced formset behavior (e.g., ordering forms, deleting forms), the remaining management formsets fields take on an equally important role and may need to be manipulated directly.

Formset Custom Validation and Formset Errors

All the forms in a formset are validated against the form validation rules explained in the previous section (e.g., `validators`, `clean_<field>()` methods). However, sometimes it can be necessary enforce inter-form rules in a formset, in which case you'll need to build a custom formset class like the one illustrated in Listing 6-41.

Listing 6-41. Django custom formset with custom validation

```
from django.forms import BaseFormSet

class BaseDrinkFormSet(BaseFormSet):
    def clean(self):
        # Check errors dictionary first, if there are any error, no point in validating
        further
        if any(self.errors):
            return
        name_size_tuples = []
```

```
        for form in self.forms:
            name_size = (form.cleaned_data['name'],form.cleaned_data['size'])
            if name_size in name_size_tuples:
                raise forms.ValidationError("Ups! You have multiple %s %s items in your
                order, keep one and increase the amount" % (dict(SIZES)
                [name_size[1]],dict(DRINKS)[int(name_size[0])]))
            name_size_tuples.append(name_size)
```

First, notice the class in Listing 6-41 inherits its behavior from the `django.forms.BaseFormSet` class, giving it all the basic functionalities of a Django formset. Next, the custom formset class defines a `clean()` method, which serves the same purpose of the `clean()` method in a standard Django forms: to enforce validation rules on the whole (i.e., formset) and not its individual parts (i.e., forms). The validation logic inside the `clean()` method enforces that if two forms from the formset have the same `name` and `size`, an error is raised.

Notice in Listing 6-41 how the validation error creation also uses the same `forms.ValidationError()` class used in standard forms. In the event the `clean()` method raises a validation error, the error is assigned to a special field called `non_form_errors` in a formset's `errors` dictionary. Listing 6-42 shows an updated version of the formset template in Listing 6-38 illustrating how to out a formset's non-form errors.

Listing 6-42. Django custom formset to display non_form_errors

```
<form method="post">
          {% csrf_token %}
    {{ formset.management_form }}
    {% if formset.non_form_errors %}
      <div class="alert alertdanger">{{formset.non_form_errors}}</div>
    {% endif %}
     {{ formset.management_form }}
    <table>
        {% for form in formset %}
        <tr><td><ul class="list-inline">{{ form.as_ul }}</ul></td></tr>
        {% endfor %}
    </table>
</form>
```

You can see below the `{{formset.management_form}}` statement in Listing 6-42 a conditional loop is made to output any errors placed in the `non_forms_errors` key of the formset's `errors` dictionary. Although different in name, the purpose of the `formset.non_form_errors` is the same as the `form.non_field_errors` for regular Django forms, to display errors not associated with a specific part. Because formsets use form constructs the error variable is called `non_forms_errors` and because forms use field constructs the variable is called `non_field_errors`.

Note that if any errors are present in a formset's forms, they are placed in a form's `error` dictionary just like they are in regular forms, so you can use the techniques outlined in Listing 6-28 to customize the output of individual form errors in a formset.

DJANGO FORM TOOLS AND DJANGO CRISPY FORMS

In addition to the Django built-in form functionalities you've learned in this chapter, there are a couple of third-party Django apps worth mentioning that are designed to solve more advanced Django form problems.

The Django form tools package[6] supports the creation of form review processes and form wizards. A form review process forces a preview after a Django form's data has been validated, a procedure that's helpful when you want end users to double-check their form data before the form life cycle ends (e.g., reservation or purchase order). A form wizard consists of grouping forms in different pages as part of a sequence (e.g., signup or questionnaire). The benefit of the Django form tools package is it implements all the 'lower level' logic needed to support these types of Django form workflows.

Django crispy forms[7] is another third-party Django app focused on advanced form layouts. Django crispy forms is a popular choice for Django forms integrated with the Bootstrap library and forms requiring sophisticated widget and template layouts (e.g., inline and horizontal forms).

[6] https://django-formtools.readthedocs.io/
[7] http://django-crispy-forms.readthedocs.io/

CHAPTER 7

■ ■ ■

Django Models

The typical way for Django applications to interact with data is through Django models. A Django model is an object-oriented Python class that represents the characteristics of an entity. For example, an entity can be a person, a company, a product, or some other concept used by an application.

Because data is at the center of modern applications and the Django framework enforces the DRY (Don't Repeat Yourself) principle, Django models often serve as the building blocks for Django projects. Once you have a set of Django models representing an application's entities, Django models can also serve as the basis to simplify the creation of other Django constructs that operate with data (e.g., forms, class-based views, REST services, Django admin pages), hence the importance of Django models as a whole.

In this chapter you'll learn about the core behaviors of Django models, including how to create models and how to use migrations, which are central to working effectively with models. Next, you'll learn about the default behaviors of Django models and how to override them with custom behaviors. In addition, you'll learn about the different data types available to create Django models, the different relationships available for Django models, and how to manage database transactions with Django models.

Next, you'll learn more about migration files, including the various ways to create migration files, how to rename migration files, how to squash multiple migration files into a single migration file, the meaning behind each migration file element so you can edit migration files with confidence, and the procedure to roll back migration files.

In addition, you'll learn about the various Django tools designed to ease the work between Django models and databases, such backing up and loading model data with fixture files, including how to load initial data into Django models. Next, you'll learn about Django signals that support the software observer pattern in Django models. Finally, you'll finish the chapter learning how to declare Django models outside of their default location, as well as how to configure multiple databases and use them with Django models.

This chapter assumes you've already set up a database for a Django project. If you haven't set up a database, see Chapter 1 on setting up a database for a Django project.

Django Models and the Migrations Workflow

Django's primary storage technology is relational (i.e., out of the box it can connect to SQLite, Postgres, MySQL, or Oracle), so a Django model is designed to map directly to a relational database table. This means instances of a Django model are stored as rows of a relational table named after the model.

For example, for a Django model class named `Store`, by default Django performs database CRUD (Create, Read, Update, and Delete) operations on a database table called `<app_name>_store`, where each of the model's `Store` instances represent database rows and a model's fields (e.g., `name`, `address`, `city`, `state`) map to database table columns.

© Daniel Rubio 2017
D. Rubio, *Beginning Django*, https://doi.org/10.1007/978-1-4842-2787-9_7

Because Django models revolve around data, they are prone to change. For example, a Django model named `Store` can suddenly require the modification of its original fields due to business requirements (e.g., the addition of a new field like `email` or the removal of a field that's no longer needed like `telephone`). Maintaining these Django models changes throughout time is also an important aspect of Django models and is managed through the use migration files.

Create Django Models

Django models are stored in `models.py` files located inside Django apps. As soon as you create a Django app, an empty `models.py` file is added to the app for future use. If you're unfamiliar with the term Django app, see the Chapter 1 section on setting up content. Listing 7-1 illustrates a sample Django model definition.

■ **Tip** Remember the book's code is at `https://github.com/drubio/beginningdjango`, if you find it easier to follow along with a pre-typed and structured application.

Listing 7-1. Django model class definition in models.py

```
from __future__ import unicode_literals
from django.utils.encoding import python_2_unicode_compatible

from django.db import models

@python_2_unicode_compatible
class Store(models.Model):
    #id = models.AutoField(primary_key=True)# Added by default, not required explicitly
    name = models.CharField(max_length=30)
    address = models.CharField(max_length=30)
    city = models.CharField(max_length=30)
    state = models.CharField(max_length=2)
    #objects = models.Manager()# Added by default, to required explicitly
    def __str__(self):
        return "%s (%s,%s)" % (self.name, self.city, self.state)
```

The first two lines in Listing 7-1 import the functionality required to run Python classes in Django using both Python 2 and Python 3. If your Django project will just run on Python 3, you can omit these import statements. The third line in Listing 7-1 imports the `django.db.models` package, which is necessary to access Django model functionality in the class definition. Next, you can see the class `Store(models.Model)` statement. The `@python_2_unicode_compatible` annotation is required to run the class on Python 2, but if you just use Python 3 you can omit this annotation.

After the main class definition in Listing 7-1, you can see four fields with the `models.CharField` data type that qualify the fields as character strings. Further restricting the acceptable values for each field is the `max_length` argument for `models.CharField` (e.g., `max_length=30` indicates the maximum length for the character field is 30 characters).

For the moment, don't worry about the `models.CharField` field definitions. There are many other data types and arguments supported by Django's `models` package, I'll describe all of these options in the next section on Django model data types.

In addition, notice the Django model in Listing 7-1 has the `id` and `objects` fields. In this case, I commented them out with # because you don't need to explicitly declare them; both are automatically added to all Django models, but I put them there so you know they exist.

The id field is a Django AutoField data type, which behind the scenes creates an integer table column that increments automatically. For example, when you create the first Store record, the id field is set to 1 by the database, for the second Store record the database sets the id field to 2, and so on. The intent of the id field is to make record searches easier and more efficient. Because the id represents a unique number to identify a record, it's used as a reference, which is also used as a database table's primary key and as an index to speed up record access. While you can override various behaviors of this default id field (e.g., change the field name), I'll leave the details of this for a later section.

The objects field is Django model's default model manager, charged with managing all the query operations associated with a Django model. Future sections in this chapter and the following chapter describe the use of Django model managers.

■ **Tip** If you want to know more about the id field added by default to all Django models, Table 7-1 describes the AutoField data type, which is the basis for the id field; the section "Django Model Data Types" later in this chapter describes the purpose of the primary_key attribute used by the id field; and the save() method described in the "Model Methods" section later in this chapter describes the practical aspects of the id field.

Finally, in Listing 7-1 you can see the class method definition for __str__ that is a standard Python method - part of what are called 'magic methods' - that are helpful when attempting to view or print instances of Django models. The __str__ method defines a human readable representation of a class instance (e.g., a Store model instance based on Listing 7-1 is output by its name, city, and state field values).

Django model definitions even when placed in an app's models.py file still aren't discoverable by Django. In order for Django to discover model definitions in models.py files, it's necessary to declare apps as part of the INSTALLED_APPS variable in settings.py. Listing 7-2 illustrates an INSTALLED_APPS definition to discover Django models in the coffeehouse.stores app.

Listing 7-2. Add app to INSTALLED_APPS in Django settings.py to detect models.py definitions

```
INSTALLED_APPS = (
    'django.contrib.admin',
    'django.contrib.auth',
    'django.contrib.contenttypes',
    'django.contrib.sessions',
    'django.contrib.messages',
    'django.contrib.staticfiles',
    'coffeehouse.stores',
)
```

As you can see in Listing 7-2, in addition to the default apps declared in INSTALLED_APPS the coffeehouse.stores app is added at the end. This tells Django to inspect the models.py file in the coffeehouse.stores app to take into account any Django model definitions in it.

After the previous steps, an app's Django model definitions in models.py are ready for use. In the next section, I'll describe Django model migrations and the workflow associated with models in models.py files.

Migrations and the Django Model Workflow

Let's start with an illustration of how the Django models workflow operates with migrations thrown into the mix. Figure 7-1 shows the Django models workflow with migrations.

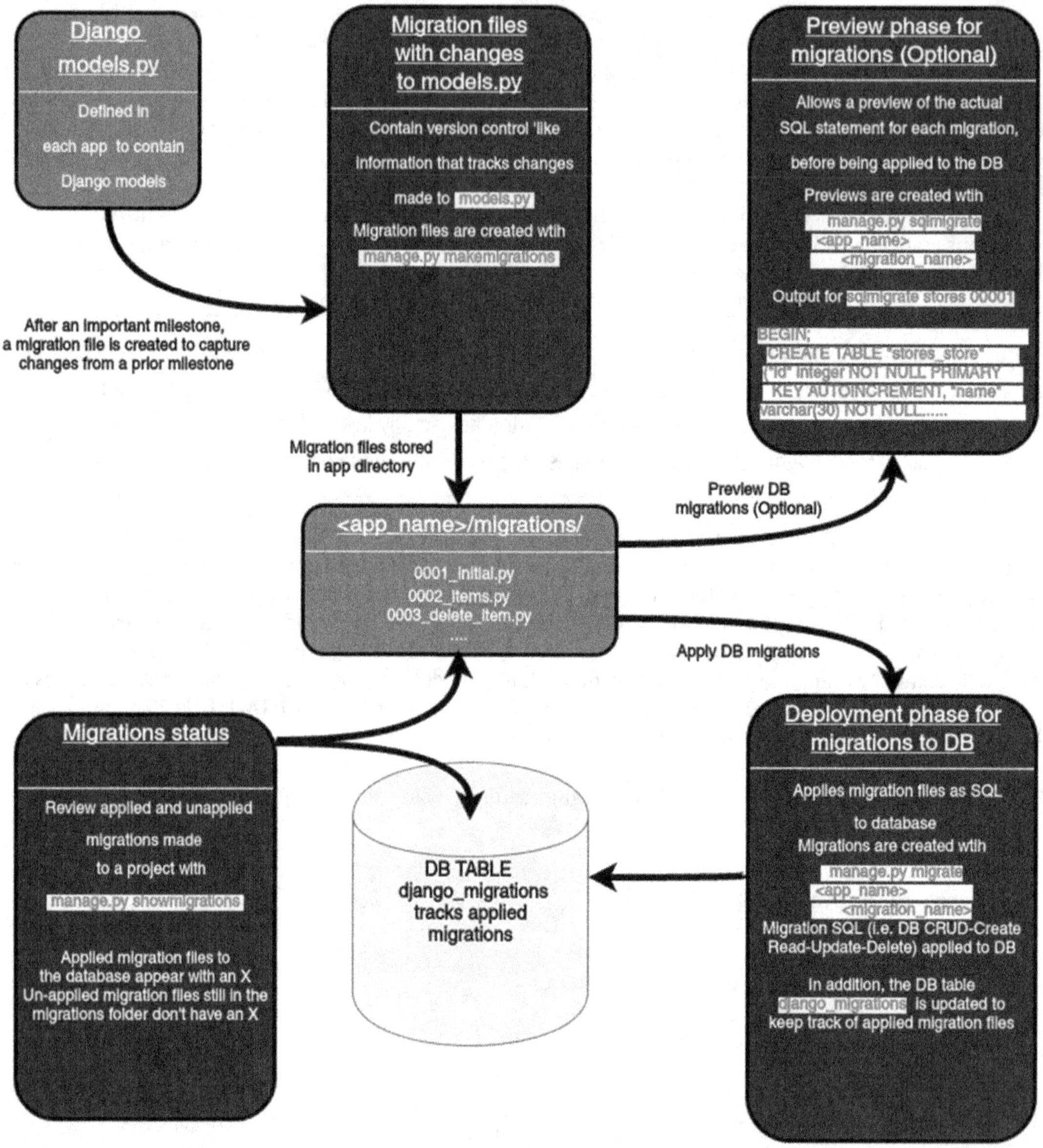

Figure 7-1. *Django workflow for models with migrations*

Illustrated on the top-left side of Figure 7-1, the workflow starts when you add or modify Django models on a `models.py` file. Once you deem the changes made to a `models.py` file are considerable or want them reflected on a database, you need to create a migration file. Migration files provide a step-by-step snapshot of the changes made to a `models.py` file, whether you add, remove, or modify content from the `models.py` file.

In order to create migration files you use the `makemigrations` management command. When you run this command, Django scans the `models.py` files for all Django apps declared in `INSTALLED_APPS`, and if Django detects a change to a `models.py` file, it creates a new migration file for the app. This process functions like a version control system, where migration files reflect changes made to `models.py` from a prior a migration file, and the entire series of migration files tells the whole evolution of an app's `models.py` file.

As you can see in Figure 7-1, migration files are stored in a `/migrations/` subdirectory inside an app, alongside the `models.py` file they track. And by default, migration files use the naming convention `<number_shortdescription>` so it's easy to track in what order they were created and what it is they contain.

Next, let's run `makemigrations` on the Django model you created in the last section. Listing 7-3 illustrates this sequence and adds the `stores` argument to limit the migration process to the `stores` app - if you run `makemigrations` without any argument, Django inspects the `models.py` for every app in defined in the `INSTALLED_APPS` variable in `settings.py`.

***Listing** 7-3.* Django makemigrations command to create migration file for changes made to models.py

```
[user@coffeehouse ~]$ python manage.py makemigrations stores
Migrations for 'stores':
  0001_initial.py:
    - Create model Store
```

After running `makemigrations stores` in Listing 7-3, you can see the migration file `0001_initial.py`. The file is given this name because it's the first migration parting from an empty `models.py`. Future changes to the `models.py` generate migration files named `0002.`,`0003...`

Turning our attention back the workflow in Figure 7-1, migration files by themselves are just a first step in the Django models workflow. Next, you can either preview or apply these migration files so the models become part of a database.

To preview the actual SQL statements for a migration before they're applied to a database, you run the `sqlmigrate <app_name> <migration_name>` command. Listing 7-4 illustrates the `sqlmigrate` sequence for the migration file from the last step.

***Listing** 7-4.* Django sqlmigrate command to preview SQL generated by migration file

```
[user@coffeehouse ~]$ python manage.py sqlmigrate stores 0001
BEGIN;
CREATE TABLE "stores_store" ("id" integer NOT NULL PRIMARY KEY AUTOINCREMENT, "name"
varchar(30) NOT NULL, "address" varchar(30) NOT NULL, "city" varchar(30) NOT NULL, "state"
varchar(2) NOT NULL);

COMMIT;
```

As you can see in Listing 7-4, the migration file `0001_initial.py` for the `stores` app is set to run an SQL statement that creates a database table named `stores_store` with field names that correspond to the Django model from Listing 7-1.

■ **Tip** You can change a Django model's default database table name with the db_table Meta class option; the 'Model Meta Class' section describes this in detail.

Previewing the SQL statements generated by a migration file might not seem too exciting at this stage, but it can be very helpful in other circumstances. For example, if you make complex changes to a Django model or your database is relatively large, it's beneficial to preview the SQL before applying the migration file directly to a database.

Finally, the last step in the workflow for Django models is to apply the migration files to a database with the migrate command. Listing 7-5 illustrates this sequence and adds the `stores` argument to limit the process to the stores app - if you run `migrate` without any argument, Django processes the migration files for every app in a project.

Listing 7-5. Django migrate command to execute migration files on database

```
[user@coffeehouse ~]$ python manage.py migrate stores
Operations to perform:
  Apply all migrations: stores
Running migrations:
  Applying stores.0001_initial... OK
```

In Listing 7-5 the `stores.0001_initial` migration is run against the database. This means the SQL presented in Listing 7-4 is executed against the database.

■ **Caution** Be careful manipulating the database directly without applying the same changes via Django migrations, as this can lead to inconsistencies and errors.

■ **Tip** If you don't want a Django model to use migrations, you can use the managed Meta class option; see the "Django Meta Class" section for details.

To keep track of applied migrations, on the bottom-left side of Figure 7-1 you can see the use of the `showmigrations` management command. The `showmigrations` command outputs a list of project migrations, with an X besides those migration files that have been applied to a database. It's worth mentioning the `showmigrations` command obtains its data by inspecting migration files in `migration` folders and the `django_migrations` database table that keeps track of applied migrations.

Django Model Data Types

Data needs to conform to certain rules for it to be useful in any application. If it weren't for rules, then you can easily end up with ZIP code numbers where you expect address information or extensive text where you expect a maximum 10-character input. Django models can use several data types to enforce model data fit certain rules (e.g., text, number, email).

It's important to understand Django model data types operate on two layers: at the database layer and the Django/Python layer. When you define a Django model with its data types and create its initial migration, Django generates and executes a model's DDL (Data definition language) to create a database table, and this DDL contains rules that reflect a Django model's fields (e.g., a Django `IntegerField` model field gets translated into an `INTEGER` DB column to enforce integer values). This means that if you change this type of Django model field (e.g., changing an integer field to a text field), it requires generating a new migration in order for the database table to also reflect any new rule.

In addition to this rule enforcement created at the outset by a Django model at the database layer, Django model fields also enforce data rules at the Django/Python layer (i.e., prior to inserting/updating data in the database). For example, Django model field parameters like `choices` enforce a field's values conform to a set of choices; this type of rule is enforced when you attempt to create, save, or update Django model records and is done irrespective of the database table rules. This means you can simply change a Django model field associated with this type of rule and not have to create a new migration to alter the underlying database table - in this case, changing the Python code is enough to change validation behavior.

Always keep this subtly in mind for Django model field data types: some Django model changes require creating a migration, while others can simply take effect changing the Django model field code. Table 7-1 illustrates the various Django model fields and the DDL they produce for all of the four main relational database supported by Django: SQLite, MySQL, PostgreSQL, and Oracle.

Table 7-1. Django model data types and generated DDL by database

Data type	Django model type	Database DDL				Description - Validation - Notes
		SQLite	MySQL	PostgreSQL	Oracle	
Binary	models.BinaryField()	BLOB NOT NULL	longblob NOT NULL	bytea NOT NULL	BLOB NULL	Creates a blob field to store binary data (e.g., images, audio or other multimedia objects).
Boolean	models.BooleanField()	bool NOT NULL	bool NOT NULL	boolean NOT NULL	NUMBER(1) NOT NULL CHECK ("VAR" IN (0,1))	Creates a Boolean field to store True/False (or 0/1) values.
Boolean	models.NullBooleanField()	bool NULL	bool NULL	boolean NULL	NUMBER(1) NULL CHECK (("VAR" IN (0,1)) OR ("VAR" IS NULL))	Works just like BooleanField but also allows NULL values.
Date/time	models.DateField()	date NOT NULL	date NOT NULL	date NOT NULL	DATE NOT NULL	Creates a date field to store dates.
Date/time	models.TimeField()	time NOT NULL	time NOT NULL	time NOT NULL	TIMESTAMP NOT NULL	Creates a time field to store times.
Date/time	models.DateTimeField()	datetime NOT NULL	datetime NOT NULL	timestamp with time zone NOT NULL	TIMESTAMP NOT NULL	Creates a datetime field to store dates with times.
Date/time	models.DurationField()	bigint NOT NULL	bigint NOT NULL	interval NOT NULL	INTERVAL DAY(9) TO SECOND(6) NOT NULL	Creates a field to store periods of time.
Number	models.AutoField()	integer NOT NULL AUTOINCREMENT	integer AUTO_INCREMENT NOT NULL	serial NOT NULL	NUMBER(11) NOT NULL & also creates a SEQUENCE and TRIGGER to increase the field	Creates an integer that autoincrements, primarily used for custom primary keys.

(*continued*)

Table 7-1. (*continued*)

Data type	Django model type	Database DDL				Description - Validation - Notes
		SQLite	MySQL	PostgreSQL	Oracle	
Number	models.BigInteger Field()	bigint NOT NULL	bigint NOT NULL	bigint NOT NULL	NUMBER(19) NOT NULL	Create a big integer to fit numbers between -9223372036854775808 to 9223372036854775807. This range may vary depending on the DB brand.
Number	models.DecimalField(decimal_places=X, max_digits=Y)	decimal NOT NULL	numeric(X, Y) NOT NULL	numeric(X, Y) NOT NULL	NUMBER(10, 3) NOT NULL	Enforces a number have a maximum X digits and Y decimal points. Creates a decimal field to store decimal numbers. Note both X and Y arguments are required, where the X argument represents the maximum number of digits to store and the Y argument represents the number of decimal places to store.
Number	models.FloatField()	real NOT NULL	double precision NOT NULL	double precision NOT NULL	DOUBLE PRECISION NOT NULL	Creates a column to store floating-point numbers.
Number	models.IntegerField()	integer NOT NULL	integer NOT NULL	integer NOT NULL	NUMBER(11) NOT NULL	Creates a column to store integer numbers.
Number	models. PositiveIntegerField()	integer unsigned NOT NULL	integer UNSIGNED NOT NULL	integer NOT NULL CHECK ("VAR" >= 0)	NUMBER(11) NOT NULL CHECK ("VAR" >= 0)	Enforces values from 0 to 2147483647. Works just like IntegerField but limits values to positive numbers.

Number	models.PositiveSmall IntegerField()	smallint unsigned NOT NULL	smallint UNSIGNED NOT NULL	smallint NOT NULL CHECK ("VAR" >= 0)	NUMBER(11) NOT NULL CHECK ("VAR" >= 0)	Enforces values from 0 to 32767. Works just like IntegerField and the specialized PositiveIntegerField but limits numbers to a smaller positive range.
Number	options.Small IntegerField()	smallint NOT NULL	smallint NOT NULL	smallint NOT NULL	NUMBER(11) NOT NULL	Enforces a number is in the range from -32768 to 32767. Works just like IntegerField but in a smaller integer range.
Text	models.CharField(max_length=N)	varchar(N) NOT NULL	varchar(50) NOT NULL	varchar(50) NOT NULL	NVARCHAR2(50) NULL	Creates a text column, where the max_length argument is required to specify the maximum length in characters.
Text	models.TextField()	text NOT NULL	longtext NOT NULL	text NOT NULL	NCLOB NULL	Creates a text field to store text.
Text (Specialized)	models. CommaSeparated IntegerField(max_length=50)	varchar(N) NOT NULL	varchar(N) NOT NULL	varchar(N) NOT NULL	NVARCHAR2(N) NULL	Enforces the string a CSV of integers. Works just like CharField except Django enforces the string be a comma separated value of integers prior to interacting with the database (e.g., 3,54, 54,664,65).

(*continued*)

Table 7-1. *(continued)*

Data type	Django model type	Database DDL				Description - Validation - Notes
		SQLite	MySQL	PostgreSQL	Oracle	
Text (Specialized)	models.EmailField()	varchar(254) NOT NULL	varchar(254) NOT NULL	varchar(254) NOT NULL	NVARCHAR2(254) NULL	Enforces the text is a valid email with the internal Django EmailValidator to determine what is and isn't a valid. Works just like CharField defaulting to a max_length of 254 characters and also enforces the string is a valid email.
Text (Specialized)	models.FileField()	varchar(100) NOT NULL	varchar(100) NOT NULL	varchar(100) NOT NULL	NVARCHAR2(100) NULL	Enforces and provides various utilities to handle files (e.g., opening/closing file, upload location,etc.). Works just like CharField defaulting to a max_length of 100 characters and also enforces the string is a valid file.
Text (Specialized)	models. FilePathField()	varchar(100) NOT NULL	varchar(100) NOT NULL	varchar(100) NOT NULL	NVARCHAR2(100) NULL	Enforces and provides various utilities to limit choices of filenames in certain filesystem directories. Works just like CharField defaulting to a max_length of 100 characters and also enforces the string is a valid file in a filesystem directory.

Text (Specialized)	models.ImageField()	varchar(100) NOT NULL	varchar(100) NOT NULL	varchar(100) NOT NULL	NVARCHAR2(100) NULL	Enforces and provides various utilities to handle image files (e.g. getting the height & width). Works just like CharField and the specialized FileField defaulting to a max_length of 100 characters and also enforces the string is a valid image. Note this field requires the presence of the Pillow Python library (e.g., pip install Pillow).
Text (Specialized)	models.GenericIPAddressField()	char(39) NOT NULL	char(39) NOT NULL	inet NOT NULL	VARCHAR2(39) NULL	Enforces and provides various utilities to only accept valid IPv4 or IPv6 addresses (e.g., 198.10.22.64 and FE80::0202:B3FF.:FE1E:8329, as well as utilities like unpack_ipv4 and protocol). Works just like CharField defaulting to a max_length of 39 characters and enforces the string is a valid IP address.

(continued)

Table 7-1. (*continued*)

Data type	Django model type	Database DDL				Description - Validation - Notes
		SQLite	MySQL	PostgreSQL	Oracle	
Text (Specialized)	models.SlugField()	varchar(50) NOT NULL	varchar(50) NOT NULL	varchar(50) NOT NULL	NVARCHAR2(50) NULL	Enforces a string is a slug string, which is a string that only contains letters, numbers, underscores or hyphens. Works just like CharField defaulting to a max_length of 50 characters and ensure the provided string is a slug - a concept that's typically used to cleanse URL strings that contain spaces and other potentially invalid character like letter with accents.
Text (Specialized)	models.URLField()	varchar(200) NOT NULL	varchar(200) NOT NULL	varchar(200) NOT NULL	NVARCHAR2(200) NULL	Enforces the provided text value is a valid URL. Works just like CharField defaulting to a max_length of 200 characters and enforces the string is a valid URL.
Text (Specialized)	models.UUIDField()	char(32) NOT NULL	char(32) NOT NULL	uuid NOT NULL	VARCHAR2(32) NOT NULL	Enforces the provided text is a Universally unique identifiers (UUID) Works just like CharField defaulting to a max_length of 32 characters and enforces the value is a UUID.

ORACLE NOT NULL CONSIDERED HARMFUL

If you look closely at some of the DDL generated for the different Django model fields in Table 7-1 (e.g., models.CharField(), models.FileField()), you'll notice Oracle generates DB columns with the NULL constraint, whereas the other three database brands generate DB columns with the NOT NULL constraint; this is neither a typo or a bug, it's by design due to the way Oracle works.

Even though Oracle does support the NOT NULL constraint as the other database brands do, Oracle comes with the side effect that it also treats empty strings '' as NOT NULL values. This means that if Django attempts to store an empty string '' (e.g., on a CharField() or FieldField()) in an Oracle database, the operation would be rejected if the NOT NULL constraint were present - an operation that's perfectly valid in other databases even with the NOT NULL constraint. So to maintain uniformity across databases and to avoid this Oracle specific edge-case, Django opts to not use the NOT NULL constraint for certain scenarios.

Note this is a well-known Oracle 'feature' or 'quirk' - depending on your perspective - that's been known for years: how to insert an empty string (zero-length) in a non-nullable column? A: You can't. Oracle states this fact in their docs and also mentions this behavior may change in the future to become standard compliant (ANSI), but as of the latest version Oracle 12c, this behavior remains the same. I'll provide some Django-specific details related to working with NULL, NOT NULL, and empty string '' issues in the next section.

As you can see in Table 7-1, Django model fields produce slightly different DDL depending on the database brand, albeit the end behavior for all back ends maps as close as possible to one another, with Django/Python rule enforcement filling in the gaps.

For example, for a Django model field like `models.DurationField()`, SQLite and MySQL use the `bigint` data type, whereas PostgreSQL and Oracle use the more specialized `interval` data type. Similarly for Django model fields like `models.CommaSeparatedIntegerField()` and `models.EmailField()`, at the database level these are represented as basic character `varchar` data types - or `NVARCHAR2` in Oracle - and it's Django/Python that enforces that the text representation is a valid CSV of integers or email, respectively.

With knowledge of the initial DDL generated by each Django model field, in the next sections I'll present the various Django model field options and their behavior associated with the original DDL and Django/Python validation.

Limiting Values: max_length, min_value, max_value, max_digits, and decimal_places

Limiting values to a certain range is one of the most basic options in Django model fields. For text-based data types the `max_length` option enforces values don't surpass a certain number of characters. In Table 7-1 you can see the `CharField` data type requires you specify the `max_length` option and for more specialized text-based data types (e.g., `EmailField`) Django assigns a default `max_length` option value, which you can override with an explicit `max_length` value.

For fields that use the `IntegerField` data type, Django offers the `min_value` and `max_value` options to restrict a value to lower/upper bounds (e.g., `IntegerField(min_value=0,max_value=1000)` limits values to a 0 to 1000 range). Similarly, for fields with the `DecimalField` data type, Django requires you specify the `max_digits` and `decimal_places` options to enforce a value's maximum number of digits and decimal points, respectively.

Empty, Null and Not Null Values: Blank and Null

By default, all Django model fields are assigned a `NOT NULL` restriction at the database level; if you look at Table 7-1 again you can confirm this by the generated DDL - the only exception is for certain fields on Oracle databases, which is explained in the sidebar below Table 7-1.

This means that when you create/update a record with a `NOT NULL` field on it, a value must be provided for the field or otherwise the database rejects the operation. On certain occasions though, it can be necessary to allow empty field values or as they're known in the database world `NULL` values. To allow Django model fields to support `NULL` values at the database level, you must declare the `null=True` field option (e.g., `IntegerField(null=True)` allows an integer field to be left empty and generates DDL with `NULL` instead of the default `NOT NULL`).

In addition to the `null` option that's enforced at the database level and which defaults to `null=False`, Django also supports the `blank` option. The `blank` option also defaults to `blank=False` on all fields and is used to enforce Django/Python validation through *forms* that work on Django models (e.g., creating a Django model record through a form in the Django admin or a custom Django form). If a Django model field is declared with `blank=True`, Django permits the field to be left blank in a form, otherwise (i.e., if `blank=True` isn't explicitly declared in a model field) Django rejects the form and forces an end user to provide a value for the field.

Since the use of `null` and `blank` options can be one of the most confusing topics in Django model field options, Table 7-2 presents a matrix with different model definitions and operations to better illustrate this behavior.

Table 7-2. *Django model validation for blank and null field options*

Model definition

```
class Person(models.Model):
    first_name = models.CharField(max_length=30)
    middle_name = models.CharField(max_length=30)
    last_name = models.CharField(max_length=30)
```

Blank and null field combinations	Default (blank=False, null=False) middle_name = models.CharField(max_length=30)	null=True (with default blank=False) middle_name = models.CharField (max_length=30,**null=True**)	blank=True (with default null=True) middle_name= models.CharField (max_length=30, **blank=True**)	null=True and blank=True models.CharField(max_length=30,**null=True,blank=True**)
Person.objects.create(first_name='Johann', **middle_name=None**, last_name='Bach')	None is treated as NULL and so middle_name can't be NULL.	middle_name can be NULL due to null=True	None is treated as NULL and so middle_name can't be NULL, blank=True is for forms.	middle_name can be NULL due to null=True
Person.objects.create(first_name='Johann', last_name='Bach')	Unspecified middle_name defaults to an empty string '' and operation succeeds as '' is treated as not null.	Unspecified middle_name defaults to an empty string '' and operation succeeds as '' is treated as not null.	Unspecified middle_name defaults to an empty string '' and operation succeeds as '' is treated as not null.	Unspecified middle_name defaults to an empty string '' and operation succeeds as '' is treated as not null.
Person.objects.create(first_name='Johann', **middle_name=''**, last_name='Bach')	Explicit empty string '' is treated as not null and operation succeeds.	Explicit empty string '' is treated as not null and operation succeeds.	Explicit empty string '' is treated as not null and operation succeeds.	Explicit empty string '' is treated as not null and operation succeeds.
Form validation with empty middle_name in Django admin or regular Django form.	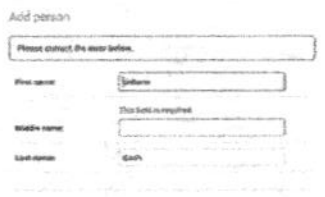 Validation error due to empty middle_name.	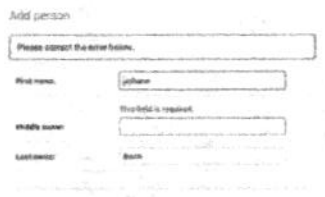 Validation error due to empty middle_name.	 Record creation valid even with empty middle_name due to blank=True.	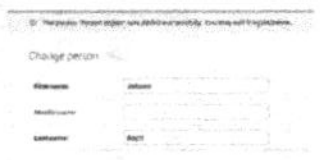 Record creation valid even with empty middle_name due to blank=True.

■ **Tip** The next chapter covers Django model forms and their validation.

Predetermined Values: default, auto_now, auto_now_add, and choices

Sometimes it's helpful to assign predetermined values to Django model fields. For example, to avoid empty strings when no value is provided - as illustrated in some of the cases in Table 7-2 - you can use the `default` option on a Django model field (e.g., provide a default id, city, or date). In most circumstances you assign a `default` option as a hard-coded value or a method reference. Listing 7-6 illustrates an example of the `default` option using both approaches.

Listing 7-6. Django model default option use

```
def default_city():
    return "San Diego"

class Store(models.Model):
    name = models.CharField(max_length=30)
    address = models.CharField(max_length=30)
    city = models.CharField(max_length=30,default=default_city)
    state = models.CharField(max_length=2,default='CA')
```

As you can see in Listing 7-6 we have two Django model fields that use the `default` option. First the `city` field relies on the `default=default_city` value – note the lack of parentheses in the syntax, which makes it a reference to the function – that tells Django to call the `default_city` method to populate the field every time a new record is created.

It's worth mentioning the method is placed outside the Django model class vs. declaring it in the same class body; this is to allow serialization and support of Django model migrations in Python 2 projects.[1] Next in Listing 7-6 you can see the `state` field uses the `default='CA'` value, which tells Django to use the hard-coded CA string to populate the field when a new record is created.

The enforcement of default options is done entirely by Django/Python (i.e., the database DDL is unaware of any default values). This means that when you work with a model like the one in Listing 7-6, Django/Python intervenes to provide default values. For example, if you create a Django model instance as `Person.objects.create(name='Downtown',address='Main Street #5')`, the `city` and `state` values are filled by Django/Python to create the record. Similarly, if you go to the Django admin and attempt to create an instance of the model in Listing 7-6, the `city` and `state` form fields are pre-filled with the default values.

Even though the `default` option works just as described for text fields, as well as number and Boolean fields, it has particular behaviors for date fields - specifically `models.DateField()` and `models.DateTimeField()` - that are important to explore, so let's do that and while on the topic of dates also learn about the `auto_now` and `auto_now_add` options related to date and time model fields.

[1]https://docs.djangoproject.com/en/1.11/topics/migrations/#serializing-values

Listing 7-7. Django model default options for dates and times, as well as auto_now and auto_now_add use

```
from datetime import date
from django.utils import timezone

class Store(models.Model):
    name = models.CharField(max_length=30)
    address = models.CharField(max_length=30)
    date = models.DateField(default=date.today)
    datetime = models.DateTimeField(default=timezone.now)
    date_lastupdated = models.DateField(auto_now=True)
    date_added = models.DateField(auto_now_add=True)
    timestamp_lastupdated = models.DateTimeField(auto_now=True)
    timestamp_added = models.DateTimeField(auto_now_add=True)
```

Listing 7-7 illustrates a modified version of the `Store` model from Listing 7-6 with a series of date field variations. The first two additional fields `date` and `datetime` use a `DateField` with a default value using Python's standard `datetime` library and a `DateTimeField` with a default value using Django's `django.utils.timezone` module, respectively - the sidebar contains more details on why the `django.utils.timezone` module was used to create a date time value.

In this case, if you create a `Store` record based on the model in Listing 7-7, Django/Python fills in the values for the `date` and `datetime` fields based on the backing library's functionality. Similarly, if you go to the Django admin and attempt to create an instance of the model in Listing 7-7, the `date` and `datetime` form fields are pre-filled with the default values for the current date and date with time, respectively.

DON'T ADD () PARENTHESES TO METHODS IN DEFAULT VALUES

If you look closely at the default values from previous listings, notice they lack () in their syntax, which creates an important behavior. By omitting the () syntax, Python assign a reference to a method and evaluates the expression until runtime, but if you use the () syntax (e.g., default=timezone.now()) Python evaluates the expression at compile time. For functions that return fixed values this is a non-issue, but for functions that return dynamically calculated values (e.g., dates) this is critical; otherwise you get a single value calculated at compile time (e.g., the date or datetime field would contain the same value calculated at compile time for all records).

DON'T USE THE BASIC DATETIME.NOW FOR DATETIMEFIELD FIELDS

Django is time-zone aware by default - due to the USE_TZ = True in settings.py. This means that when you handle dates with times (e.g., in DateTimeField model fields) you must provide time-zone aware dates. This is why in Listing 7-7 the models.DateTimeField(default=timezone.now) statement uses Django's django.utils.timezone module, which generates time-zone aware dates.

In Listing 7-7 there's an additional pair of DateField and DateTimeField fields that use the auto_now=True and auto_now_add=True options. Both of these options work like the default option - in the sense they add a default date or date & time - but have a slightly different behavior. The first important difference is that while the default option can be used with several types of fields, the auto_now and auto_now_add options are designed for DateField and DateTimeField fields.

Values for fields that use either the auto_now and auto_now_add options are generated when a record is created. Values for fields that use the auto_now option are updated every time a record is changed, while values for fields that use the auto_now_add option remain frozen for the lifetime of the record. By default, DateField fields that use either the auto_now or auto_now_add options generate their value from datetime.date.today(), whereas DateTimeField fields that use either auto_now or auto_now_add options generate their value from django.utils.timezone.now().

Unlike fields with the default option where you can provide a value for the field, fields with the auto_now and auto_now_add options can't be overridden. This means that even if you create or update a record and provide a value for a field with an auto_now or auto_now_add option, the value is ignored. Similarly, in the Django admin by default fields that use the auto_now and auto_now_add option are not displayed because their value can't be modified. Finally, it's worth mentioning the auto_now, auto_now_add and default options are mutually exclusive (i.e., you can't use more than one option in a field or it will result in an error).

As you can see, the auto_now option is ideal to track a record's last-modified date, the auto_now_add is ideal to track a record's creation date, and the default option works as a general purpose modifiable date on a form field.

Another scenario for predetermined values is to restrict a Django model field to a list of values with the choices option to limit open-ended values and reduce disparate data and errors (e.g., a list of states ["CA","AR"], instead of letting users introduce Ca, Cali, ar, or Arizona). Listing 7-8 illustrates an example of a Django model field that uses the choices option.

Listing 7-8. Django model choices option

```
ITEM_SIZES = (
            ('S','Small'),
            ('M','Medium'),
            ('L','Large'),
            ('P','Portion'),
            )

class Menu(models.Model):
    name = models.CharField(max_length=30)

class Item(models.Model):
    menu = models.ForeignKey(Menu, on_delete=models.CASCADE)
    name = models.CharField(max_length=30)
    description = models.CharField(max_length=100)
    size = models.CharField(choices=ITEM_SIZES,max_length=1)
```

The first thing you need to use the choices option is create a list of values as a tuple of tuples as illustrated in Listing 7-8. The ITEMS_SIZES tuple has four tuples, where the first tuple element represents a key to use in the database (e.g., S,M) and the second tuple element represents a human-friendly representation of the first tuple element (e.g., Small, Medium).

Next, in Listing 7-8 you can see the size field is assigned the choices=ITEM_SIZES value that tells Django to use the keys from ITEM_SIZES as potential values. Note that in this case the keys to use in the database are all one-character text values (e.g., S,M) that correspond to the CharField(max_length=1) data type, but you can also use numbers or Boolean values as keys so long as they match the target field data type.

■ **Tip** The next chapter covers Django form models with the choices option.

Unique values: unique, unique_for_date, unique_for_month and unique_for_year

It's possible to enforce a field value to be unique across all records. For example, in Listing 7-7 if you change `name=models.CharField(max_length=30)` to `name=models.CharField(max_length=30, unique=True)` it tells Django to ensure all `Store` records have a unique name value.

The `unique` option is enforced by Django at the database layer (i.e., by adding a DDL `UNIQUE` SQL constraint), as well as the Django/Python layer. In addition, the `unique` option is valid on all field types except `ManyToManyField`, `OneToOneField`, and `FileField`.

To enforce uniqueness of a field along with a `DateField` or `DateTimeField` value, Django offers the `unique_for_date`, `unique_for_month`, and `unique_for_year` options. For example, in Listing 7-7 to enforce the name field value be unique with a date of the `date_lastupdated` field you can use the `name = models.CharField(max_length=30, unique_for_date="date_lastupdated")` statement that tells Django to allow only one record with the same name and `date_lastupdated` (e.g., you can't have two records with `name="Downtown"` and `date_lastupdated="2018-01-01"`, but two records with `name="Downtown"` and different `date_lastupdated` values are allowed).

The `unique_for_month` and `unique_for_year` options provide wider ranges to enforce validation. For example, the `name = models.CharField(max_length=30, unique_for_month="date_lastupdated")` statement tells Django to only allow one record with the same name and `date_lastupdated` value for the same month and the `name = models.CharField(max_length=30, unique_for_year="date_lastupdated")` statement tells Django to only allow one record with the same name and `date_lastupdated` value for the same year.

Due to the more complex requirements of the `unique_for_date`, `unique_for_month`, and `unique_for_year` options, the enforcement of these options is done at the Django/Python layer. In addition, due to the nature of the validation process these options are only valid for `DateField` and `DateTimeField` fields, noting that for `DateTimeField` cases only the date portion of the value is used.

Form Values: Editable, help_text, verbose_name, and error_messages

When Django models are used in the context of forms, form fields backed by Django model fields can be influenced through various model options. The following options are identical to the form options you learned in the previous chapter on Django forms, except these options are assigned as part of model fields to influence forms fields.

By default, all Django model fields presented in forms are editable, but you can change this behavior by using the `editable=False` option. Setting a model field with `editable=False` tells Django to omit it completely in a form (e.g., in the Django admin) and as a consequence any validation associated with the form field is also bypassed.

The `help_text` option allows the inclusion of additional text alongside a form field. Listing 7-9 illustrates the use of the `help_text` option.

Listing 7-9. Django model help_text option

```
ITEM_SIZES = (
            ('S','Small'),
            ('M','Medium'),
            ('L','Large'),
            ('P','Portion'),
            )
```

```
class Menu(models.Model):
    name = models.CharField(max_length=30)

class Item(models.Model):
    menu = models.ForeignKey(Menu, on_delete=models.CASCADE)
    name = models.CharField(max_length=30)
    description = models.CharField(max_length=100,help_text="Ensure you provide some
    description of the ingredients")
    size = models.CharField(choices=ITEM_SIZES,max_length=1)
    calories = models.IntegerField(help_text="Calorie count should reflect <b>size</b> of
    the item")
```

In Listing 7-9 you can see there are two fields with the help_text option. When a Django form based on this Django model is rendered in a template, the help_text defined in the model goes on to form part of the final form layout.

By default, a Django model field name is used to generate the header of a Django form field using a capitalized version of the model field name. (e.g., Name, Description). You can configure more verbose form field headers with the verbose_name option (e.g., models.CharField (max_length=30,verbose_name="ITEM NAME"), outputs the ITEM NAME header for the form field.

If you attempt to save or update a Django model in a form and any of the values don't comply with the underlying field types, Django generates default error messages for the non-compliant values. These error messages while helpful are generic in nature, so it's possible to customize these error messages for each field with the error_messages option. The error_messages option accepts a dictionary of key-values, where keys represent error codes and values error messages. See the previous chapter on Django forms for detailed examples on the structure of the error_messages dictionary.

■ **Tip** Chapter 9 covers Django model forms in greater detail.

Database Definition Language (DDL) Values: db_column, db_index, db_tablespace, primary_key

By default, Django generates a database table's column names based on a Django model's field names. For example, if a Django model field is named menu, Django generates a DB column named menu. It's possible to override this behavior using the db_column option (e.g., name = models.CharField(max_length=30, db_column="my_custom_name"). Django generates the DDL with the my_custom_name column name).

Another database-related option for Django models is the db_index option that tells Django to generate a database index for the field (e.g., size = models.CharField(choices=ITEM_SIZES,max_length=1,db_index=True) generates a database index for the size field). Be aware that under the following circumstances Django automatically creates a database index, so db_index=True for the following scenarios is redundant:

- If a field uses the unique=True option, Django automatically creates an index for the field. You can disable this behavior setting db_index=False.
- If a field is a ForeignKey data type, Django automatically creates an index for the field. You can disable this behavior setting db_index=False.

■ **Tip** The meta indexes option can also define indexes for a single or multiple fields. See the following section on "Meta Class Options" for more details.

If you use a PostgreSQL or Oracle database, it's possible to specify a DB tablespace for a field's index through the `db_tablespace` name. By default, Django uses a project's `DEFAULT_INDEX_TABLESPACE` value in `settings.py` to determine a tablespace, but if a field uses the `db_tablespace` this value takes precedence. If a database brand doesn't support tablespaces (e.g., MySQL or SQLite) this option is ignored.

Finally, the `primary_key` option allows you to define a primary key for a model. By default, if no Django model field is set with the `primary_key=True` statement, Django automatically creates an `AutoField` data type named `id` to hold the primary key (e.g., `id = models.AutoField(primary_key=True)`). The typical use case for the `primary_key` option is for fields that are references to other fields (e.g., `OneToOneField`) or if you want a custom primary key due to design constraints.

Built-In and Custom Validators: Validators

In addition to the data enforcement options for Django models described in previous sections (e.g., `unique`, `default`), Django models also offer enforcement of values through the `validators` option, which allow more advanced validation logic through built-in or custom methods.

Django model offers a series of built-in validator methods in the `django.core.validators` package that are used by model data types. For example, the `models.EmailField` data type relies on `django.core.validators.EmailValidator` to validate email values, just as the `models.IntegerField` data type uses the `MinValueValidator` and `MaxValueValidator` validators to enforce the `min_value` and `max_value` options, respectively.

In addition to Django built-in validator methods, you can also create custom validator methods. The only requirements to create custom validator methods are for a method to accept a model field's input and to throw a `django.core.exceptions.ValidatorError` in case the value doesn't comply with the expected rules. Listing 7-10 illustrates a model that uses both a built-in validator and a custom validator.

Listing 7-10. Django model field validators option with built-in and custom validator

```
ITEM_SIZES = (
            ('S','Small'),
            ('M','Medium'),
            ('L','Large'),
            ('P','Portion'),
            )

# Import built-in validator
from  django.core.validators import MinLengthValidator

# Create custom validator
from django.core.exceptions import ValidationError

def calorie_watcher(value):
    if value > 5000:
        raise ValidationError(
            ('Whoa! calories are %(value)s ? We try to serve healthy food, try something
            less than 5000!'),
            params={'value': value},
        )
    if value < 0:
        raise ValidationError(
            ('Strange calories are %(value)s ? This can\'t be, value must be greater than 0'),
            params={'value': value},
        )
```

```
class Menu(models.Model):
    name = models.CharField(max_length=30)

class Item(models.Model):
    menu = models.ForeignKey(Menu, on_delete=models.CASCADE)
    name = models.CharField(max_length=30,validators=[MinLengthValidator(5)])
    description = models.CharField(max_length=100)
    size = models.CharField(choices=ITEM_SIZES,max_length=1)
    calories = models.IntegerField(validators=[calorie_watcher])
```

The first validators option in Listing 7-10 uses the built-in MinLengthValidator validator class to enforce the values for the name field contain at least 5 characters. The second validators option in Listing 7-10 uses the custom calorie_watcher validator method to enforce the values for the calories field fit a certain range and uses custom messages in case this range is not met. It's worth mentioning that it's possible to use multiple validator methods on a single field with a list syntax (e.g., validators=[MinLengthValidators(5), MaxLengthValidators(100)]).

Django Model Default and Custom Behaviors

When you create a Django model class it always inherits its behavior from the django.db.models.Model class, as illustrated back in Listing 7-1. This Django class provides a Django model with a great deal of functionality, which includes basic operations via methods like save() and delete(), as well as naming conventions and query behaviors for the model.

In most circumstances, the default behaviors provided by the django.db.models.Model class are sufficient, but in other cases you'll want to provide custom behavior. Next, I'll enumerate a Django model's functionalities provided via the django.db.models.Model class.

Model Methods

All Django models inherit a series of methods for operations that include saving, deleting, validating, loading, and applying custom logic to model data. In the next sections I'll describe the default behavior for each of these methods and how to customize their behavior.

save() method

The save() method offers one of the most common operations for Django models: to save (i.e., create or update) a record to a database. Once you create or have a reference to a Django model instance, you call the save() method to create/update the instance on a database. Listing 7-11 illustrates this process.

Listing 7-11. Django model use of the save() method

```
# Import Django model class
from coffeehouse.stores.models import Store

# Create a model Store instance
store_corporate = Store(name='Corporate',address='624 Broadway',city='San Diego',state='CA',
email='corporate@coffeehouse.com')

# Invoke the save() method to create/save the record
# No record id reference, so a create operation is made and the reference is updated with id
store_corporate.save()

# Change field on instance
store_corporate.city='625 Broadway'

# Invoke the save() method to update/save the record
# Record has id reference from prior save() call, so operation is update
store_corporate.save()
```

In Listing 7-11 two calls are made to the `save()` method on the same reference; the first one creates a record on the database and the second one updates the record on the database.

Can you tell how Django knows when to create and when to update a record with the same `save()` method? It's not in plain sight so don't worry if you can't spot it.

In the first section of this chapter when you created a Django model, I mentioned Django automatically adds an `id` field as a primary key to all Django models, in order to make searching for records easier and more efficient. The presence of this `id` primary key is what Django uses to determine if the `save()` method performs a create or update operation.

Although there's no trace of an explicit `id` primary key-value in Listing 7-11, a model instance gets an `id` value after Django creates an instance. The first time the `save()` method is invoked in Listing 7-11, Django attempts to create a new record because it can't find an `id` primary key-value on the instance. However, if the creation operation is successful, the database assigns the record an `id` primary key-value that's returned to Django, which updates the reference with this `id` primary key-value.

On subsequent calls made to the `save()` method on the same model reference, Django detects the presence of the `id` primary key-value and performs an update operation based on this `id` primary key-value. In case you're wondering, if you add an explicit `id` primary key-value to a record reference, Django also performs an update because that's the flag it looks for to determine whether to create or update a record, so be aware placing an explicit `id` primary key updates/overwrites the database record associated with the given `id` primary key.

Now that you have a firm understanding of the default behaviors of a Django model's `save()` method, I'll describe the various options available for the `save()` method. The `save()` method accepts a series of arguments to override its default behavior; Table 7-3 illustrates these arguments, their behavior, and their default value.

Table 7-3. *Django model save() method arguments*

Argument	Default	Description
force_insert	force_insert=False	Explicitly tells Django to force a create operation on a record (e.g., .save(force_insert=True). This is rarely used but can be helpful for cases when you don't or can't rely on Django detecting a create operation (i.e., via the id primary key).
force_update	force_update=False	Explicitly tells Django to force an update operation on a record (e.g., .save(force_update=True). This is rarely used but can be helpful for cases when you don't or can't rely on Django detecting an update operation (i.e., via the id primary key).
using	using=DEFAULT_DB_ALIAS, where DEFAULT_DB_ALIAS is a constant with a value of default	Allows save() to perform the operation against a database that's not the default value in settings.py (e.g.. .save(using='oracle') performs the operation against the oracle database, where oracle is a key in the DATABASES variable in settings.py) See the later section in the chapter on multiple databases.
update_fields	update_fields=None	Accepts a list of fields to update (e.g., .save(update_fields=['name']) only updates a record's name value). Helpful when you have large models and want to do a more efficient/granular update, because by default Django updates all model fields.
commit	commit=True	Ensures a record is saved to the database. In certain circumstances (e.g., model forms or relationship operations) commit is set to False to create a model instance without saving it. This allows additional operations (on forms, relationships) to be made and based on their outcome, determine to make a standard save() call to write the record to the database.

The option you're likely to use the most from Table 7-3 is `update_fields`, since it produces a performance boost by selectively choosing which fields to update. However, Table 7-3 gives you the full series of options in case you hit an edge-case with the `save()` method.

Finally, to close our discussion on the `save()` method, it's possible to define an implementation of the `save()` method on a Django model to execute custom logic when the method is called. Listing 7-12 illustrates this process.

Listing 7-12. Django model with custom save() method

```
class Store(models.Model):
    name = models.CharField(max_length=30)
    address = models.CharField(max_length=30)
    city = models.CharField(max_length=30)
    state = models.CharField(max_length=2)

    def save(self, *args, **kwargs):
        # Do custom logic here (e.g. validation, logging, call third party service)
        # Run default save() method
        super(Store,self).save(*args, **kwargs)
```

Notice the save() method in Listing 7-12 is declared inline with a Django model's fields. In this case, when a call is made to save() on a reference for this type of model (e.g., downtown.save()) Django attempts to run the model's custom save() method. This is helpful in circumstances where you want to perform other actions (e.g., log a message, call a third-party service) when a model instance is created or updated. The last snippet in the custom save() method super(Store,self).save(*args, **kwargs) tells Django to run the base save() method from django.db.models.Model.

■ **Tip** See the Django signals section later in this chapter to execute logic before or after a model's save() method is run.

---

delete() method

The delete() method is used to eliminate a record from the database through a reference. For example, if in Listing 7-11 you call store_corporate.delete() - where store_corporate is the record reference - Django removes the record from the database. Under the hood, the delete() method relies on the id primary key to remove the record, so it's a requirement for a reference to have the id value to invoke the delete() method.

When the delete() method is called on a reference, its id primary key-value is removed but the record's remaining values remain in memory. In addition, the delete() method responds with the amount of deleted records (e.g., (4, {u'stores.Store_amenities': 3, u'stores.Store': 1}), indicates 4 overall records were deleted, with 1 Store record and 3 stores.Store_amenities – the stores.Store represents a relationship on the main Store model.

Similar to the save() method, the delete() method also supports two arguments: using=DEFAULT_DB_ALIAS and keep_parents=False. The using argument allows you to specify an alternate database to perform the delete() operation on - see Table 7-3 for more details on this type of argument and the multiple database section later in this chapter. And the keep_parents arguments is useful when the delete() operation takes place on a model with a relationship and you wish to keep the parent model's data intact - or removed, which is the default. More details on the use of keep_parents are given in the Django model relationships section later in this chapter.

And finally, it's also possible to define a custom delete() method on a Django model class - just like save() in Listing 7-12-- to execute custom logic (e.g., create an audit trail) when a record is removed.

■ **Tip** See the Django signals section later in this chapter to execute logic before or after a model's delete() method is run.

Validation methods: clean_fields(), clean(), validate_unique() and full_clean()

When you create or update a Django model instance with the save() method, Django enforces that the instance values comply with those of the model definition. For example, if you use the model field name = models.CharField(max_length=30) Django enforces the name value is a text field with at most 30 characters.

The most important part to understand about Django model instance validation is that it's done on two layers: at the database layer and the Django/Python layer, both of which are enforced via the model data types you learned about in the previous section.

Let's analyze the database layer validation layer first. Once you have a Django model and create its initial migration - as described in the first section of this chapter on "Migrations and the Django Model Workflow" - Django generates the database DDL (Data definition language) to create a database table in accordance with the model definition (e.g., the Django model field CharField(max_length=30) generates a `varchar(30) NOT NULL` database column type). Therefore due to this initial database DDL, all Django model values that don't comply with validation rules are guaranteed to be rejected at the database layer where it's the database that performs the validation.

Now let's analyze the Django/Python validation layer. Although the Django model data types for fields (e.g., `CharField(max_length=30)`) can give the impression they act on model instances automatically, the Django/Python validation layer requires you to execute validation methods on the model instance to enforce validation. If you don't use these validation methods - which are the topic of this section - the database validation layer is the only enforcer of model field data types.

Although relying on validation at the database layer is perfectly acceptable, using model validation at the Django/Python layer has the advantage of supporting more complex validation rules, as well as reducing database load for operations that will end up being rejected by a database. However, unlike database layer validation, which is automatically done after a Django model's first migration, Django/Python layer validation requires you use some of the following model methods.

Let's first explore the Django model validation `clean_fields()` method. Listing 7-13 illustrates a model definition, followed by a call sequence that uses the `clean_fields()` method.

Listing 7-13. Django model use of validation clean_fields() method

```
class Store(models.Model):
    name = models.CharField(max_length=30)
    address = models.CharField(max_length=30,unique=True)
    city = models.CharField(max_length=30)
    state = models.CharField(max_length=2)

# Create a model Store instance, that violates the max_length rule
store_corporate = Store(name='This is a very long name for the Corporate store that exceeds
the 30 character limit',address='624 Broadway',city='San Diego',state='AZ',email='corporate@
coffeehouse.com')

# No error yet

# You could call save() and let the database reject the instance...
# But you can also validate at the Django/Python level with the clean_fields() method
store_corporate.clean_fields()
Traceback (most recent call last):
    raise ValidationError(errors)
ValidationError: {'name': [u'Ensure this value has at most 30 characters (it has 84).']}
```

First off, notice the model's name field in Listing 7-13 uses the `max_length=30` option to enforce that values of this kind are capped to 30 characters. After the model definition, you can see the `store_corporate` instance breaks this rule with a value greater than 30 characters, which means Django doesn't detect broken model rules at instance creation.

While you can attempt to call `save()` on this last instance and let the database reject the operation via its DDL, you can call the `clean_fields()` method on the instance to tell Django to check the values of the instance against the model date types and raise an error.

Also notice the output of the `clean_fields()` method in Listing 7-8 is a `ValidatioError` data type with a dictionary. This last dictionary follows the key-value pattern `'<model_field>'-'[<error_message_list>]'`, making it easy to identify multiple validation errors and reuse this data for other purposes (e.g., logging, presenting the error in a template).

While the `clean_fields()` method validates model values individually against their data types, the `clean()` method can be used to enforce more elaborate rules (e.g., relationships or specific values). Unlike the `clean_fields()` method you can invoke directly, you must define an implementation of the `clean()` method with validation logic, as illustrated in Listing 7-14.

Listing 7-14. Django model use of validation clean() method

```
class Store(models.Model):
    name = models.CharField(max_length=30)
    address = models.CharField(max_length=30,unique=True)
    city = models.CharField(max_length=30)
    state = models.CharField(max_length=2)
    def clean(self):
        # Don't allow 'San Diego' city entries that have state different than 'CA'
        if self.city == 'San Diego' and self.state != 'CA':
            raise ValidationError('Wait San Diego is CA!, are you sure there is another San
            Diego in %s ?' % self.state)

# Create a model Store instance, that violates city/state rule
store_corporate = Store(name='Corporate',address='624 Broadway',city='San Diego',state='AZ',
email='corporate@coffeehouse.com')

# To enforce more complex rules call the clean() method implemented on a model
store_corporate.clean()
Traceback (most recent call last):
    raise ValidationError('Wait San Diego is in CA!, are you sure there is another San Diego
    in %s ?' % (self.state))
ValidationError: [u'Wait San Diego is in CA!, are you sure there is another San Diego in AZ ?']
```

Notice in Listing 7-14 the Django model class defines the `clean()` method that enforces that if an instance city value is `San Diego` its state must be `CA`, and if this condition is not met, a `ValidationError` error is raised. Next, when the `clean()` method is invoked on an instance that violates this rule, a `ValidationError` error is raised just like the `clean_fields()` method.

Another Django validation mechanism you can use is the `clean_unique()` method to enforce no two instances have the same value for a field that uses unique options. Listing 7-15 illustrates the use the `clean_unique()` method.

■ **Note** The previous section on Django model data types describes Django's various unique values options for model fields: unique, unique_for_date, unique_for_month, and unique_for_year.

Listing 7-15. Django model use of validation clean_unique() method with unique* fields

```
class Store(models.Model):
    name = models.CharField(max_length=30)
    address = models.CharField(max_length=30,unique=True)
    city = models.CharField(max_length=30)
    state = models.CharField(max_length=2)
```

```
# Create a model Store instance
store_corporate = Store(name='Downtown',address='624 Broadway',city='San Diego',state='AZ',
                  email='corporate@coffeehouse.com')

# Save instance
store_corporate.save()

# Create another instance to violate uniqueness of address field
store_uptown = Store(name='Uptown',address='624 Broadway', city='San Diego',state='CA')

# You could call save() and let the database reject the instance...
# But you can also validate at the Django/Python level with the validate_unique() method
store_uptown.validate_unique()
Traceback (most recent call last):
    raise ValidationError(errors)
ValidationError: {'address': [u'Store with this Address already exists.']}
```

Look at how the address field of the Store model in Listing 7-15 uses unique=True, which tells Django not to allow two Store instances with the same address value. Next, we create a Store instance with address='624 Broadway' and save it to the database. Right after, we create another Store instance with the same address='624 Broadway' value, but because the address model field has the unique option this new instance is in violation of the rule.

Therefore when you call the validate_unique() method on the store_uptown reference, Django raises a ValidationError exception indicating there's already a Store record with the same address in the database. Note that even if you didn't call the validate_unique() method, the database would end up rejecting the duplicate record since the unique=True produces the necessary DDL to enforce unique address values.

In addition to the clean_unique function performing validation on fields marked with unique options, the clean_unique method also enforces validation for the unique_together option declared in a model's Meta class. This variation is illustrated in Listing 7-16.

Listing 7-16. Django model use of validation clean_unique() method with Meta unique_together

```
class Store(models.Model):
    name = models.CharField(max_length=30)
    address = models.CharField(max_length=30,unique=True)
    city = models.CharField(max_length=30)
    state = models.CharField(max_length=2)
    email = models.EmailField()
    class Meta:
        unique_together = ("name", "email")

# Create instance to show use of validate_unique() via Meta option
store_downtown_horton = Store(name='Downtown',address'Horton Plaza',city='San Diego',
                        state='CA',email='downtown@coffeehouse.com')
# Save intance to DB
store_downtown_horton.save()

# Create additional instance that violated unique_together rule in Meta class
store_downtown_fv = Store(name='Downtown',address'Fashion Valley',city='San Diego',
                    state='CA',email='downtown@coffeehouse.com')
```

```
# You could call save() and let the database reject the instance but lets use validate_unique
store_downtown_fv.validate_unique()
Traceback (most recent call last):
ValidationError: {'__all__': [u'Store with this Name and Email already exists.']}
```

Notice how the class in Listing 7-16 declares the `Meta` class followed by `unique_together = ("name", "email")`, which tells Django not to allow two `Store` instances with the same `name` and `email` value.

Next, two `Store` records are created with the same `name` and `email` value. Because this is in violation of the Django model meta option `unique_together = ("name", "email")`, after you save the first record `store_downtown_horton` and call the `validate_unique()` method on the second record `store_downtown_fv`, Django raises a `ValidationError` exception indicating there's already a `Store` record with the same `name` and `email` values in the database. Toward the end of this section I'll describe a Django model's Meta class options in greater detail.

Finally, the last validation method available on all Django models is the `full_clean()` method, which is a shortcut to run the `clean_fields()`, `clean()` and `validate_unique()` methods - in that order.

Data loading methods: Refresh_from_db(), from_db(), and get_deferred_fields() methods

The `refresh_from_db()` method is a helpful aid if you want to update a preexisting model instance with data from the database, either because the database was updated by another process or you accidentally (or purposely) changed the model instance and want it to reflect the data in database once again. Using the `refresh_from_db()` method is as simple as executing it on a model reference (e.g., `downtown.refresh_from_db()` updates the `downtown` instance from values in the database).

Although the `refresh_from_db()` method is generally called without arguments, it does support two optional arguments. The `using` argument can be used to specify an alternate database from which to perform the refresh operation, a mechanism that works just like the option used in the `save()` and `delete()` methods and is described in Table 7-3. The `fields` argument can be used to selectively refresh certain model fields; if no fields argument list is provided then the `refresh_from_db()` method refreshes all model fields.

In most circumstances, the initial loading mechanism for Django model instances is reasonable and sufficient. However, if you want to customize the default loading mechanism you can define the `from_db()` method. Unlike the `refresh_from_db()` method, which can be called on a model instance, the `from_db()` method cannot be called directly and is intended to be part of a model class to be called every time a model instance is created from database data. So what is a good reason for the `from_db` method? If you want to defer loading model data.

For example, if you start to work with large Django models (e.g., more than 10 fields) you can quickly notice a performance hit by accessing large amounts of data at once. To minimize this performance hit, you can create a `from_db` method to defer the loading of model field data, instead of having Django load the full field data set at once which it does by default.

Complementing the functionality of deferred model fields is the `get_deferred_fields()` method, which returns a list of model fields that have been deferred from loading. Although the `from_db()` and `get_deferred_fields()` methods don't have as many usage scenarios as the `refresh_from_db()` method, you may encounter a need for these two model methods once you work with larger and more complex models. The next chapter's section on CRUD operations describes the use of these methods in greater detail.

Custom methods

All the methods I've described up to this point come from Django's `django.db.models.Model` class. While it's important to learn how to use these methods and provide your own implementation for them, this doesn't necessarily mean a Django model class is restricted to using just these methods. You can use your own custom model class methods, as illustrated in Listing 7-17.

Listing 7-17. Django model with custom method

```
class Store(models.Model):
    name = models.CharField(max_length=30)
    address = models.CharField(max_length=30)
    city = models.CharField(max_length=30)
    state = models.CharField(max_length=2)

    def latitude_longitude(self):
        # Call remote service to get latitude & longitude
        latitude, longitude = geocoding_method(self.address, self.city, self.state)
        return latitude, longitude
```

The `latitude_longitude` method in Listing 7-17 gives the Django model the ability to offer a common calculation on the model instance. For example, for a Store instance called `downtown` you could call `downtown.latitude_longitude()` to get a result based on the instance's `address`, `city`, and `state` values aided by a remote service. This type of custom method is helpful because it favors encapsulation, keeping the logic that operates on a Django model where it belongs - in the model class itself.

Model Manager Field: Objects

The `objects` field - technically known as the default Django model manager - is available on all Django models and is charged with managing all query operations related to Django model instances. This means that when you perform Django model query operations (e.g., create, read, update, or delete) you'll end up using a Django model's `objects` field or model manager.

A Django model's `objects` reference is used directly on a model class and not an instance of a model. For example, to read a `Store` model record with id=1 you would use the `Store.objects.get(id=1)` syntax and to delete all `Store` model records you would use the `Store.objects.all().delete()` syntax.

The `objects` field of a model manager is not explicitly declared as part of Django model - just as it was described in Listing 7-1 alongside a Django model's `id` field - but it's nevertheless present on all Django models. You can, however, customize the default model manager to use another field name (e.g., if you require a Django model field named `objects`, you can customize the model manager to be named `mgr`). Listing 7-18 illustrates a model class that renames the default model manager to use the `mgr` reference name.

Listing 7-18. Django default model manager renamed

```
class Store(models.Model):
    name = models.CharField(max_length=30)
    address = models.CharField(max_length=30)
    city = models.CharField(max_length=30)
    state = models.CharField(max_length=2)
    mgr = models.Manager()
```

As you can see in Listing 7-18, you explicitly declare a model field with `models.Manager()` to mark another field as the default model manager. If you override the default manager in this way, you would use the `Store.mgr.get(id=1)` syntax to read a record with `id=1` or the `Store.mgr.all().delete()` syntax to delete all store records vs. the default model manager `objects` syntax.

■ **Note** The next chapter on Django model queries is dedicated to exploring the functional aspects of the default model manager or `objects` reference, including CRUD operations with multiple records and some of the subtle behaviors associated with `QuerySet` classes, as well as model managers.

Model Meta Class and Options

In the previous section on model validation methods - in Listing 7-16 - I made use of the `Meta` class on a Django model to enforce the uniqueness of model field values. In this section I'll expand on the purpose and options available for a Django model's Meta class.

The `Meta` class in a Django model is intended to define behaviors for a Django model as a whole, unlike Django model data types (e.g., `models.CharField`), which define granular behaviors on Django model fields (e.g., a model field data can be 30 or 50 characters in length).

The Django `Meta` class and its options are always declared after a Django model's data types, as illustrated in Listing 7-19.

Listing 7-19. Django model with Meta class and ordering option

```
class Store(models.Model):
    name = models.CharField(max_length=30)
    address = models.CharField(max_length=30)
    city = models.CharField(max_length=30)
    state = models.CharField(max_length=2)

    class Meta:
        ordering = ['-state']
```

In Listing 7-19 you can see the `class Meta:` statement declares the `ordering = ['-state']` option. In this case, the `ordering` option tells Django that when a query is made on the model it orders the results by the `state` field in descending order. The `ordering` meta option is helpful because it overrides the default model query order - which is by a model's `id` - and it avoids the need to constantly and explicitly declare a model query's sort order.

Now that you have a basic understanding of a Django model's `Meta` class, in the upcoming sections I'll classify the various Meta options by category so you can easily identify them and use them appropriately.

Database Definition Language (DDL) table options: db_table, db_tablespace, managed, required_db_vendor, required_db_features and unique_together

By default, the database table name for a Django model is based on the app name and model, with all lowercase letters and separated by an underscore. For example, for an app named `stores`, a model class named `Amenity` uses the `stores_amenity` database table by default. You can define a different database table name for a Django model with the meta `db_table` option.

By default, if a Django project's backing database brand (e.g., Oracle) supports the concept of a tablespace, Django uses the DEFAULT_TABLESPACE variable in settings.py as the default tablespace. It's possible to specify an alternative tablespace for a Django model through the meta db_tablespace option. Note that if a Django project's backing database doesn't support the concept of a tablespace, this option is ignored.

All Django models are subject to the life cycle described earlier in the Django models workflow in Figure 7-1. As part of this life cycle, Django manages the DDL that creates and/or destroys the backing database table for every Django model. If you want to disable Django executing a model's default DDL against a database, you can do so with meta managed=False option. The managed=False option is useful when a model's backing database table is created by some other means and you don't want Django to interfere with the management of this table.

Because Django can work with different database back ends (e.g., MySQL, Oracle, PostgreSQL) you can have situations where certain model definitions are designed to work with features that are not available on all database back ends. To ensure a Django model is deployed against a certain database back end, you can use two Meta class options.

The required_db_vendor option accepts the values sqlite, postgresql, mysql, and oracle to ensure a project's underlying database connection is for a given vendor; if the connection does not match the specified vendor, the model is not migrated against the database.

The required_db_features option is used to ensure a backing database connection is enabled with a given list of features, and if the connection does not have the specified feature list enabled, the model is not migrated against the database.

Django defines over 75 database features in django.db.backends.base.features.py. Once a connection is made to a database, you can get its supported Django features with:

```
from django.db import connection
dir(connection.features)
```

The previous snippet outputs the features supported by a database connected to a Django project. Most Django database features are supported across all brands, so the required_db_features option only requires you to declare esoteric database features to ensure the underlying Django database can support a given model (e.g., gis_enabled ensures a database supports Django's Geographic Information Systems model feature, can_share_in_memory_db is a feature supported by SQLite but not MySQL, is_sql_auto_is_null_enabled is a feature supported in MySQL but not SQLite).

The unique_together option enforces no two model records have the same pair of values. For example, unique_together('city','state') ensures only one record has a city/state value (e.g., San Diego,CA) and rejects all other attempts to create a record with the same city/state value. The unique_together option creates the DDL to enforce this rule at the database level. The unique_together option also supports the ability to specify multiple unique field pairs through a list of tuples (e.g., unique_together(('city','state'),('city','zipcode')) enforces both city/state and city/zipcode fields are unique together).

Database Definition Language (DDL) index options: Indexes and index_together

Indexes play an important role in the efficient lookup of relational database records. In very simple terms, indexes are special structures that contain certain record column values that ensure queries are made faster than doing queries on the full record values in the main database table.

The Django meta class offers two options to generate the necessary DDL (e.g., CREATE INDEX...) to create database indexes against Django model fields: indexes and index_together.

■ **Tip** By default fields marked as primary keys and unique don't require explicit creation of indexes. See the previous section on "db_index," "primary_key" in model data types.

The index meta options accepts a list of `models.Index` references. A `model.Index` reference accepts a `fields` value - which in itself is a list of model fields on which to create an index - and an optional `name` value - which is a string to name the index. Listing 7-20 illustrates the use of the `index` meta option.

Listing 7-20. Django model with meta class and index option

```
class Store(models.Model):
    name = models.CharField(max_length=30)
    address = models.CharField(max_length=30)
    city = models.CharField(max_length=30)
    state = models.CharField(max_length=2)

    class Meta:
        indexes = [
            models.Index(fields=['city','state']),
            models.Index(fields=['city'],name='city_idx')
        ]
```

As you can see in Listing 7-20, the `Store` model defines two indexes. A two-field index for the `city` and `state` fields, as well as an index for the `city` field named `city_idx`. If no `name` value is provided for an index, Django automatically gives the index a name.

■ **Tip** By default Django creates B*tree indexes for all relational database brands. However, if you're using PostgreSQL, Django also supports Brin and Gin indexes.[2]

The `index_together` meta option allows you to define a multi-field index on a Django model, just like the `model.Index` reference in the indexes meta options. The only difference being the `index_together` option is a top-level option of the Meta class (e.g., `index_together=['city','state']` is equivalent to the first index in Listing 7-20).

Naming convention options: verbose_name, verbose_name_plural, label, label_lower, and app_label

By default, Django models are referenced by their class name. In most cases, relying on this name is a non-issue - like the class `Store` in Listing 7-20, a `Store` is a store anyway you see it. But on other occasions, a model class name can use an acronym or abbreviation that while reasonable for development purposes, is inexpressive for others (e.g., on a user interface(UI) element like a template or the Django admin).

---

[2]`https://docs.djangoproject.com/en/1.11/ref/contrib/postgres/indexes/#module-django.contrib.postgres.indexes`

Django models can use both the verbose_name and verbose_name_plural meta class options to assign more explicit model names. For example, if a model class is named SSN, you can declare the meta class option verbose_name='Social Security Number' to use this last value on UIs that rely on model instances. By default, when referring to multiple instances of a Django model class, Django pluralizes a model class by appending an s (e.g., Store becomes Stores). The verbose_name_plural meta class option allows you to define a custom plural value when the letter s is not applicable (e.g., the model class Strawberry with verbose_name_plural='Strawberries' becomes Strawberries in a plural context, instead of the default and incorrect Straberrys).

To access a Django model meta class verbose_name and verbose_name_plural values, you can use the syntax <class_name>._meta.verbose_name and <class_name>._meta.verbose_name_plural.

■ **Tip** If you want to assign a verbose name value to individual model fields, see the verbose_name in the previous section on Django model data types.

A Django model label refers to the combination of an <app_name>.<model_class>, which can sometimes be necessary when models are used as part of forms or UI components. The Django model meta class offers the label and label_lower read-only attributes - by read-only it means the attribute values can't be set (i.e., like other meta attributes such as verbose_name) but only read as part of the meta class. For example, if a Store model is defined inside the stores app, the statement Store._meta.label outputs stores.Store. And the label_lower attribute outputs a lowercase label value, including classes that use camel case[3] (e.g., for the model class StoreFront in the stores app, StoreFront._meta.label outputs stores.StoreFront. and Store._meta.label_lower outputs stores.storefront).

A Django app is an integral part of all Django models since it defines among other things, a model's default database table prefix, where a model's migrations are placed and a model's default reference label. The meta class app_label attribute allows you to assign an explicit app name to a Django model. The Django meta app_label takes precedence over the default app model naming mechanism. One of the last sections in this chapter on placing Django models outside of models.py contains more details on the meta app_label option.

Inheritance Meta options: Abstract and proxy

The meta abstract option allows a Django model to function as a base class that doesn't have a backing database table, but serves as a foundation for other Django model classes. Listing 7-21 illustrates a set of Django models that use the abstract option.

Listing 7-21. Django model abstract option

```
from django.db import models

class Item(models.Model):
    name = models.CharField(max_length=30)
    description = models.CharField(max_length=100)
    class Meta:
        abstract = True

class Drink(Item):
    mililiters = models.IntegerField()
```

---

[3]https://en.wikipedia.org/wiki/Camel_case

The Item model class in Listing 7-21 is abstract, which means it behaves like other abstract classes across programming languages.[4] For Django model classes, it means no database table is created for this type model, nor is it possible to create an instance out of it. However, it's possible to use an abstract model as the basis for other Django models.

In Listing 7-21 you can see the Drink model class inherits its behavior from the Item class (vs. the standard Django models.Model class). Notice the Drink class declares the additional mililiters field, but since it inherits its behavior from the Item class, the Drink class also gains the model Item class fields (i.e., the Drink class becomes a three-field model, with a database table with three columns - name, description, and mililiters).

The meta proxy option is also designed for Django model inheritance scenarios. But unlike the abstract option where parent classes are declared abstract and children inherit their behavior, the proxy option is designed to give child classes access to a parent class without the child becoming a full-fledged model class. Classes marked with the meta proxy option enable them to perform operations on a parent class and its database table, without having a database table of their own.

For example, a Store model class can have multiple model proxies (e.g., FranchiseStore, Employee OwnedStore) where each proxy class defines its own operations made against Store models, while not replicating Store data into a separate table. Django model proxies are ideal to shield a parent class against model changes (e.g., custom model managers or custom operations) while still retaining access to the database table of the parent class.

Query Meta options: Ordering, order_with_respect_to, get_latest_by, default_manager_name, base_manager_name, default_related_name, and select_on_save

When you make Django model queries - which are explained in full in the next chapter - there are many kinds of default behaviors associated with their operations. If you want to use non-default query behaviors, you can explicitly create queries with explicit arguments. However, creating explicit queries over and over can get tiresome; you can instead rely on the meta options explained in this section to assign a model's default query behaviors.

The ordering meta option is used to define the default ordering for a list of model instances. Although you can use the order_by() method to define the order for a group of model instances (e.g., Store.objects.all().order_by('-name'), to get all Store objects in descending order by name), you can use the ordering meta option (e.g., ordering=[-name] on the Store model) to ensure a list of model instances is always sorted without needing the order_by() method (e.g., Store.objects.all() uses the ordering meta option to determine query order).

The order_with_respect_to meta option is also used to define default sorting query behavior, but in the context of model relationships. If you perform a query on a model that has a relationship and you want to establish the default ordering on a field in the related model, you can use the order_with_respect_to meta option.

The get_latest_by meta option is used to specify a default model field for queries that use the latest() and earliest() methods. Both the latest() and earliest() methods specify a field by which to get the latest or earliest model record (e.g., Receipt.objects.latest('date') to get the latest Receipt model instance by date). You can use the get_latest_by meta option so queries made with, the latest() and earliest() methods don't require an argument.

[4]https://en.wikipedia.org/wiki/Abstract_type

All models rely on the `objects` field as their default model manager, as described in the earlier "Model Manager Field" section. The `default_manager_name` meta option is used in cases where a model has multiple model managers and you must specify a default manager. The `base_manager_name` meta option is used to specify a base model manager - which defaults to `django.db.models.Manager` - for cases in which a base model manager isn't appropriate. The next chapter describes the use custom model managers and these meta options in greater detail.

The `default_related_name` meta option is used to define the reverse name for a field that serves as a related object. This reverse name concept is explained in greater detail in the model relationships section later in this chapter.

The `select_on_save` meta option is a Django legacy option, which tells Django to use the pre-1.6 Django version of a model's `save()` method algorithm. This algorithm has a distinct behavior than the `save()` method behavior explained earlier in this chapter.

Permission Meta options: default_permissions and permissions

All Django models are given a set of permissions to manipulate object model instances. These permissions are an integral part of Django's built-in user management system, which is used extensively by the Django admin and can be integrated as part of the general permission workflow of a Django project.

By default, all Django models are given permissions to add, change, and delete object instances through the meta `default_permissions` set to `('add','change','delete')` - who can actually add, change, and delete instances is covered in the chapter on Django user management and the Django admin. You can declare an explicit meta `default_permissions` value on a model class to rescind one if its default permissions (e.g., an empty tuple `()` if you don't want to assign permissions or `('add','change')` to deny a model class the delete permission).

The `permissions` meta attribute is designed to assign custom permissions to a Django model. For example, you can assign custom permissions to a Django model to allow tasks that are different than the generic add, change, delete operations (e.g., `can_do_refunds` on a Store model). The `permissions` meta attribute accepts a list of tuple permissions, where each tuple is composed of a reference permission code and a verbose permission description (e.g., `(('can_do_refunds','Can refund customers'),) )`. A later chapter on Django user management covers the topic of custom permissions.

Relationships in Django Models

Django models operate by default on relational database systems (RDBMS) and thus they also support relationships among one another. In the simplest terms, database relationships are used to associate records on the basis of a key or id, resulting in improved data maintenance, query performance, and less duplicate data, among other things.

Django models support the same three relationships supported by relational database systems: one to many, many to manym and one to one.

One to Many Relationships in Django Models

A one to many relationship implies that one model record can have many other model records associated with itself. For example, a Menu model record can have many Item model records associated with it and yet an Item belongs to a single Menu record. To define a one to many relationship in Django models you use the ForeignKey data type on the model that has the many records (e.g., on the Item model). Listing 7-22 illustrates a sample of a one to many Django relationship.

Listing 7-22. One to many Django model relationship

```
from django.db import models

class Menu(models.Model):
    name = models.CharField(max_length=30)

class Item(models.Model):
    menu = models.ForeignKey(Menu)
    name = models.CharField(max_length=30)
    description = models.CharField(max_length=100)
```

The first Django model in Listing 7-22 is Menu and has the name field (e.g., Menu instances can be Breakfast, Lunch, Drinks, etc.). Next, in Listing 7-22 is the Item Django model, which has a menu field, that itself has the models.ForeignKey(Menu) definition. The models.ForeignKey() definition creates the one to many relationship, where the first argument Menu indicates the relationship model.

In addition to the database level benefits of creating a one to many relationship (e.g., improved data maintenance), Django models also provide an API to simplify the access of data related to this kind of relationship, which is explained in the next chapter on CRUD records across Django model relationships.

Many to Many Relationships in Django Models

A many to many relationship implies that many records can have many other records associated among one another. For example, Store model records can have many Amenity records, just as Amenity records can belong to many Store records. To define a many to many relationship in Django models you use the ManyToManyField data type. Listing 7-23 illustrates a sample of a many to many Django relationship.

Listing 7-23. Many to many Django model relationship

```
from django.db import models

class Amenity(models.Model):
    name = models.CharField(max_length=30)
    description = models.CharField(max_length=100)

class Store(models.Model):
    name = models.CharField(max_length=30)
    address = models.CharField(max_length=30)
    city = models.CharField(max_length=30)
    state = models.CharField(max_length=2)
    email = models.EmailField()
    amenities = models.ManyToManyField(Amenity,blank=True)
```

The first Django model in Listing 7-23 is `Amenity` and has the `name` and `description` fields. Next, in Listing 7-23 is the `Store` Django model that has the `amenities` field, that itself has the `models.ManyToManyField(Amenity,blank=True)` definition. The `models.ManyToManyField()` definition creates the many to many relationship via a *junction table,*[5] where the first argument `Amenity` indicates the relationship model and the optional `blank=True` argument allows a `Store` record to be created without the need of an `amenities` value.

In this case, the junction table created by Django is used to hold the relationships between the `Amenity` and Store records through their respective keys. Although you don't need to manipulate the junction table directly, for reference purposes, Django uses the syntax <model_name>_<model_field_with_ManyToManyField> to name it (e.g., For `Store` model records stored in the `stores_store` table and `Amenity` model records stored in the `stores_amenity table`, the junction table is `stores_store_amenities`).

In addition to the database level benefits of creating a many to many relationship (e.g., improved data maintenance), Django models also provide an API to simplify the access of data related to this kind of relationship, which is explained in the next chapter on CRUD records across Django model relationships.

One to One Relationships in Django Models

A one to one relationship implies that one record is associated with another record. If you're familiar with object-oriented programming, a one to one relationship in RDBMS is similar to object-oriented inheritance that uses the *is a* rule (e.g., a Car object *is a* Vehicle object).

For example, generic `Item` model records can have a one to one relationship to `Drink` model records, where the latter records hold information specific to drinks (e.g., caffeine content) and the former records hold generic information about items (e.g., price). To define a one to one relationship in Django models you use the `OneToOneField` data type. Listing 7-24 illustrates a sample of a one to one Django relationship.

Listing 7-24. One to one Django model relationship

```
from django.db import models

class Menu(models.Model):
    name = models.CharField(max_length=30)

class Item(models.Model):
    menu = models.ForeignKey(Menu)
    name = models.CharField(max_length=30)
    description = models.CharField(max_length=100)
    calories = models.IntegerField()
    price = models.FloatField()

class Drink(models.Model):
    item = models.OneToOneField(Item,on_delete=models.CASCADE,primary_key=True)
    caffeine = models.IntegerField()
```

The first Django model in Listing 7-24 is Item, which is similar to the one presented in Listing 7-22, except the version in Listing 7-24 has the additional `calories` and `price` fields. Next, in Listing 7-24 is the `Drink` model, which has the `item` field, that itself has the `models.OneToOneField(Amenity,on_delete=models.CASCADE,primary_key=True)` definition.

[5]https://en.wikipedia.org/wiki/Associative_entity

The models.OneToOneField() definition creates the one to one relationship, where the first argument Item indicates the relationship model. The second argument on_delete=models.CASCADE tells Django that in case the relationship record is deleted (i.e., the Item,) its other record (i.e., the Drink) will also be deleted; this last argument prevents orphaned data. Finally, the primary_key=True tells Django to use the relationship id (i.e., Drink.id) as the primary key instead of using a separate and default column id, a technique that makes it easier to track relationships.

In addition to the database level benefits of creating a one to one relationship (e.g., improved data maintenance), Django models also provide an API to simplify the access of data related to this kind of relationship, which is explained in the next chapter on CRUD records across Django model relationships.

Options for Relationship Model Data Types

Previously you explored Django data types and the many options to customize how they handle data, such as limiting values, allowing empty and null values, establishing predetermined values, and enforcing DDL rules. In this section you'll learn about the options available for Django relationship model data types.

■ **Note** Options described in the general purpose model data type section (e.g., blank, unique) are applicable to relationship model data types unless noted.

Data integrity options: on_delete

All model relationships create dependencies between one another, so an important behavior to define is what happens to the other party when one party is removed. The on_delete option is designed for this purpose, to determine what to do with records on the other side of a relationship when one side is removed.

For example, if an Item model has a menu ForeignKey() field pointing to a Menu model (i.e., like Listing 7-22, a one to many relationship: an Item always belong to one Menu, and a Menu has many Items), what happens to Item model records if their related Menu model instance is deleted? Are the Item model records also deleted?

The on_delete option is available for all three relationship model data types and supports the following values:

- on_delete=models.CASCADE (Default).- Automatically deletes related records when the related instance is removed (e.g. if the Menu *Breakfast* instance is deleted, all Item records referencing the Menu *Breakfast* instance are also deleted).
- on_delete=models.PROTECT.- Prevents a related instance from being removed (e.g. if the menu field on Item uses ForeignKey(Menu,on_delete=models.PROTECT), any attempt to remove Menu instances referenced by Item instances are blocked).
- on_delete=models.SET_NULL.- Assigns NULL to related records when the related instance is removed, note this requires the field to also use the null=True option (e.g. if the Menu *Breakfast* instance is deleted, all Item records referencing the Menu *Breakfast* instance are assigned NULL to their menu field value).
- on_delete=models.SET_DEFAULT.- Assigns a default value to related records when the related instance is removed, note this requires the field to also use a default option value (e.g., if the Menu *Breakfast* instance is deleted, all Item records referencing the Menu *Breakfast* instance are assigned a default Menu instance to their menu field value).

- `on_delete=models.SET`.- Assigns a value set through a callable to related records when the related instance is removed (e.g., if the `Menu` *Breakfast* instance is deleted, all `Item` records referencing the `Menu` *Breakfast* instance are assigned an instance to their `menu` field value set through a callable function).
- `on_delete=models.DO_NOTHING`.- No action is taken when related records are removed. This is generally a bad relational database practice, so by default, databases will generate an error since you're leaving orphaned records with no value, null or otherwise. If you use this value, you must ensure the database table does not enforce referential integrity.

Reference options: Self, literal strings, and parent_link

Model relationships sometimes have recursive relationships. This is a common scenario in one to many relationship models with parent-child relationships. For example, a `Category` model can have a `parent` field that in itself is another `Category` model or a `Person` model can have a `relatives` field that in itself are other `Person` models. To define this type of relationship you must use the `'self'` keyword to reference the same model, as shown in Listing 7-25.

Listing 7-25. One to many Django model relationship with self-referencing model

```
from django.db import models

class Category(models.Model):
    menu = models.ForeignKey('self')

class Person(models.Model):
    relatives = models.ManyToManyField('self')
```

Although model relationship data types typically express their relationships through model object references (e.g., `models.ForeignKey(Menu)`), it's also valid to use literal strings to reference models (e.g., `models.ForeignKey('Menu')`). This technique is helpful when the model definition order does not allow you to reference model objects that are not yet in scope and is a technique often referred to as model 'lazy-loading'.

The `parent_link=True` option is an exclusive option for one to one relationships (i.e., the `models.OneToOneField` data type) used when inheriting model classes, to help indicate the child class field should be used as a link to the parent class.

Reverse relationships: related_name, related_query_name, and symmetrical

When you use relationship model data types, Django automatically establishes the reverse relationship between data types with the `_set` reference. This mechanism is illustrated in Listing 7-26.

Listing 7-26. One to many Django model relationship with reverse relationship references

```
from django.db import models

class Menu(models.Model):
    name = models.CharField(max_length=30)

class Item(models.Model):
    menu = models.ForeignKey(Menu, on_delete=models.CASCADE)
```

```
    name = models.CharField(max_length=30)
    description = models.CharField(max_length=100)
    price = models.FloatField(blank=True,null=True)

breakfast = Menu.objects.get(name='Breakfast')
# Direct access
all_items_with_breakfast_menu = Item.objects.filter(menu=breakfast)

# Reverse access through instance
same_all_items_with_breakfast_menu = breakfast.item_set.all()
```

As you can see in Listing 7-26, there are two routes between a Django relationship. The direct route involves using the model with the relationship definition; in this case, Item gets all the Item records with a Menu *Breakfast* instance. To do this, you use Item and filter on the menu ForeignKey reference (e.g., Item.objects.filter(menu=breakfast)).

But it's also possible to use a Menu instance (e.g., breakfast in Listing 7-26) and get all Item records with a menu instance; this is called a reverse relationship or path. As you can see in Listing 7-26, the reverse relationship uses the <model_instance>.<related_model>_set syntax (e.g., breakfast.item_set.all() to get all Item records with a the breakfast instance).Now that you know what a reverse relationship is, let's explore the options associated with this term.

The related_name option allows you to customize the name or disable a reverse model relationship. Renaming a reverse relationship provides more intuitive syntax over the _set syntax from Listing 7-26, whereas disabling a reverse relationship is helpful when a related model is used in other contexts and blocking access to a reverse relationship is required for accessibility reasons.

For example, in Listing 7-26 the reverse relationship uses the breakfast.item_set.all() syntax, but if you change the field to models.ForeignKey(...related_name='menus'), you can use the reverse relationship breakfast.menus.all() syntax. To disable a reverse relationship you can use the + (plus sign) on the related_name value (e.g., models.ForeignKey(...related_name='+')).

Reverse relationships are also available as part of queries, as illustrated in Listing 7-27.

Listing 7-27. One to many Django model relationship with reverse relationship queries

```
# Based on models from listing 7-26

# Direct access, Item records with price higher than 1
Items.objects.filter(price__gt=1)

# Reverse access query, Menu records with Item price higher than 1
Menu.objects.filter(item__price__gt=1)
```

Notice how the Menu query in Listing 7-27 uses the item reference to filter all Menu records via its Item relationship. By default, reverse relationship queries use the name of the model, so in this case, the related Menu model is Item; therefore the query field is item. However, if you define the related_name option on a field this value takes precedence. For example, with models.ForeignKey(...related_name='menus') the reverse query in Listing 7-27 becomes Menu.objects.filter(menus__price__gt=1), all of which takes us to the related_query_name option.

The related_query_name option is used to override the related_name option value for cases where you want the reverse query to have a different field value. For example, with models.ForeignKey(...related_name='menus',related_query_name='onlyitemswith') the reverse relationship reference for menus in Listing 7-26 would still work, but the reverse relationship query from Listing 7-27 would change to Menu.objects.filter(onlyitemswith__price__gt=1).

Covering an edge-case for many to many relationships is the symmetrical option. If you create a many to many relationships that references itself - as illustrated in Listing 7-25 with the 'self' syntax - Django assumes the relationship is symmetrical (e.g., all Person instances are relatives and therefore requires no reverse relationships since it would be redundant) thus self-referencing many to many relationships forgo adding a _set reverse relationship to the field. You can use symmetrical=False to force Django to maintain the reverse relationship.

■ **Tip** The next chapter covers Django model relationship queries in greater detail.

Database options: to_field, db_constraint, swappable, through, through_fields, and db_table

By default, Django model relationships are established on the primary key of a model, which, in itself, defaults to a model's id field. For example, the field menu = models.ForeignKey(Menu) stores the id from a Menu instance as the relationship reference. You can override this default behavior with the to_field option and specify a different field on which to establish the relationship reference. Note that if you assign a to_field value, this field must be set with unique=True.

By default, Django follows relational database conventions and constrains relationships at the database level. The db_constraint option - which defaults to True - allows you to bypass this constraint by assigning it a False value. Setting db_constraint=False should only by used when you know beforehand the data relationships in a database is broken and doesn't require constraint checking at database level.

The swappable option is intended to influence migrations for models that contain relationships and are swappable with other models. Unless you implement a very sophisticated model hierarchy with model swapping features, this option is primarily intended for Django's built-in User model, which uses a relationship and is often swapped out for custom user models. The chapter on user management contains more details on this option.

Specific to many to many model relationships (i.e., the models.ManyToManyField data type) the through, through_fields & db_table options, influence the junction table used in these types of relationships. If you want to change the default name for a many to many junction table, you can use the db_table option to specify a custom junction table name.

By default, a junction table for a many to many relationship stores a minimum amount of information: an id for the relationship and the id's for each of the model relationships. It's possible to specify a separate model to operate as a junction table and store additional information about the many to many relationship (e.g., through=MyCustomModel uses the MyCustomTable model as the many to many junction table). If you define a through option, then it's also necessary to use the through_fields to tell Django which fields in the new model are used to store references for the model relationships.

Form values: limit_choices_to

When Django models with relationships are used in the context of forms, it can be useful and even necessary to delimit the amount of displayed relationships. For example, if you use an Item model with a relationship to a Menu model, displaying the entire set of Item records as forms (e.g., in the Django admin) can be impractical if you have hundreds of Item records.

The limit_choices_to can be used on a relationship model type to filter the amount of displayed records in forms. The limit_choices_to can declare an inline reference field filter (e.g., limit_choices_to={'in_stock':True}) or a callable that performs more complex logic (e.g., limit_choices_to=my_complex_method_limit_picker).

■ **Tip** The next chapter covers Django model forms in greater detail.

Django Model Transactions

Transactions play an important role in the integrity of model data operations. When you set up a database for a Django project back in Chapter 1, among the many default options described in Table 1-3, were the following transaction-related settings:

```
AUTOCOMMIT = True
ATOMIC_REQUESTS = False
```

The `AUTOCOMMIT` option set to `True` ensures all operations that alter data (i.e., Create, Update, and Delete) run in their own transaction, and depending on the outcome, are automatically committed to a database if successful or rolled back if they fail. The `AUTOCOMMIT=True` settings fits the expectations of most applications, as it cuts down on the need to explicitly mark operations final and provides reasonable behaviors (i.e., if the data operation is successful it's made final [a.k.a. commit], if not, then it's reverted [a.k.a. rolled back]).

However, there are occasions when grouping operations that alter data into larger transactions - all-or-nothing tasks - is a necessity.

■ **Tip** If you set AUTOCOMMIT = False you'll need to explicitly declare commits. A more practical choice is to leave the default AUTOCOMMIT = True and declare larger transactions explicitly on a case-by-case basis.

Transaction per Request: ATOMIC_REQUESTS and Decorators

Django supports the `ATOMIC_REQUESTS` option that is disabled by default. The `ATOMIC_REQUEST` is used to open a transaction on every request made to a Django application. By setting `ATOMIC_REQUEST=True`, it ensures the data operations included in a request (i.e., view method) are committed only if a response is successful.

Django atomic requests are helpful when you want the logic in a view method to be an all-or-nothing task. For example, if a view method executes fives subtasks associated with data (e.g., credit card verification procedure, sending an email), it can be helpful to ensure that only if all subtasks are successful the data operations be considered final, and if only one subtasks fails, then all subtasks are rolled back as if nothing had happened.

Since `ATOMIC_REQUEST=True` opens a transaction for every request made on a Django application, it can cause a performance impact on high-traffic applications. Due to this factor, it's also possible to selectively disable atomic requests on certain requests when `ATOMIC_REQUEST=True` or inclusively selectively enable atomic requests on certain requests when `ATOMIC_REQUEST=False`. Listing 7-28 illustrates how to selectively activate and deactivate atomic requests.

Listing 7-28. Selectively activate and deactivate atomic requests with @non_atomic_requests and @atomic

```
from django.db import transaction

# When ATOMIC_REQUESTS=True you can individually disable atomic requests

@transaction.non_atomic_requests
def index(request):
    # Data operations with transactions commit/rollback individually
```

```
    # Failure of one operation does not influence other
    data_operation_1()
    data_operation_2()
    data_operation_3()

# When ATOMIC_REQUESTS=False you can individually enable atomic requests

@transaction.atomic
def detail(request):
    # Start transaction.
    # Failure of any operation, rollbacks other operations
    data_operation_1()
    data_operation_2()
    data_operation_3()
    # Commit transaction if all operation successful
```

As you can see in Listing 7-28, if you decide to use ATOMIC_REQUESTS=True, you can disable transactions per request on a view method with the `@transaction.non_atomic_requests` decorator from the `django.db.transaction` package. If you decide to keep the default `ATOMIC_REQUESTS=False`, you can enable transactions per request on a view method with the `@transaction.atomic` decorator from the same `django.db.transaction` package.

Context Manager and Callbacks: atomic() and on_commit()

In addition to the `AUTOCOMMIT` and `ATOMIC_REQUEST` transaction configurations, as well as the view method transaction decorators, it's possible to manage transactions at an intermediate scope. That is, coarser transactions than individual data operations (e.g., `save()`), but finer transactions than atomic requests (i.e., view methods).

The Python `with` keyword can invoke a context manager[6] charged with managing transactions. Context managers for transactions use the same `django.db.transaction.atomic()` method - used as a decorator in Listing 7-28 - but inside the body of a method, as illustrated in Listing 7-29.

Listing 7-29. Transactions with context managers

```
from django.db import transaction

def login(request):
    # With AUTO_COMMIT=True and ATOMIC_REQUEST=False
    # Data operation runs in its own transaction due to AUTO_COMMIT=True
    data_operation_standalone()

    # Open new transaction with context manager
    with transaction.atomic():
        # Start transaction.
        # Failure of any operation, rollbacks other operations
```

[6]https://docs.python.org/3/reference/datamodel.html#context-managers

```
        data_operation_1()
        data_operation_2()
        data_operation_3()
        # Commit transaction if all operation successful

    # Data operation runs in its own transaction due to AUTO_COMMIT=True
    data_operation_standalone2()
```

As you can see in Listing 7-29, it's possible to generate a transaction inside a method without influencing its entire scope vs. atomic requests which run on the entire view method scope. In addition, Django transactions also support *callbacks*, where by you can run a task once a transaction is successful (i.e., it's committed).

Callbacks are supported through the `on_commit()` method, which is also part the `django.db.transaction` package. The syntax for the `on_commit()` method is the following:

```
transaction.on_commit(only_after_success_operation)

transaction.on_commit(lambda: only_after_success_with_args('success'))
```

The argument to `on_commit()` method can be either a non-argument function to run after a successful transaction or a function wrapped in a `lambda` statement if the function to run after a successful transaction requires arguments.

The `transaction.on_commit()` method is triggered once the transaction in which the method was declared is successful. If the transaction running at the point where the `transaction.on_commit()` method is declared fails, the `on_commit()` callback is never called. If there's no transaction running at the point where the `transaction.on_commit()` method is declared, the `on_commit()` callback is trigged immediately.

■ **Tip** Use commit=False on a model's save() method – described in Table 7-3 – to avoid a transaction (i.e., write operation) and still create a model object in memory.

Django Model Migrations

At the start of this chapter you learned how Django models are closely tied to the migrations. Recapping, the migrations consists of registering the evolution of Django models in an app's `models.py` file into 'migration files,' with the purpose of later reviewing and applying these `models.py` changes to a database.

In essence, migration files serve as a buffer between a database and the changes made to a Django project's models defined in `models.py` files. With data being such a delicate piece of a project, migration files provide highly desirable functionalities, such as the ability to preview database change before they're committed (e.g., `sqlmigrate` in Listing 7-4) and also the ability to go back to a certain point in time in a `models.py` file state, reverting what are generally complex DDL structure changes.

Migration File Creation

The `manage.py makemigrations` command is the entry point to create migration files. If you execute this command without arguments, Django inspects all the `models.py` files for apps declared in the `INSTALLED_APPS` variable and creates a migration file for apps whose `models.py` contents has changed from prior migrations. Table 7-4 describes the most common `makemigrations` arguments and their purpose.

Table 7-4. Django most-used makemigrations arguments

Argument	Description
<app_name>	Indicates a specific app's models.py file (e.g., manage.py makemigrations stores, only inspects/creates migrations for the models.py in the stores app).
--dry-run	Simulates migration creation without creating the actual migration files.
--empty	Creates an empty migration file, irrespective of the models.py file being changed or not.
--name 'my_migration_file'	Creates a migration file a custom name, instead of the default 'auto_<current_date'>. Note the leading serial number used for migration files (e.g., 0001, 0002) is not customized, as this is a best practice to identify migration order.
--merge	Creates a merged migration from two conflicting migration files. Required when multiple serial number files are present in the same app (e.g., 0002_unique_constraints.py, 0002_field_update.py), generally due to multiple people creating a duplicate serial numbers (e.g., when you try to make a migration in these circumstances, Django throws the error 'Conflicting migrations detected', suggesting you use -merge to fix the problem).

As you can see in Table 7-4, the `makemigrations` command offers multiple ways to create migration files. You can create empty migration files, you can simulate the creation of migration files to inspect changes first, and you can also create migration files with a specific name, among other things.

■ **Tip** Remember you can use the sqlmigrate command to preview the SQL generated by a migration file and the migrate command to apply the migration file to a database. See the first section in this chapter for additional examples of model migration commands.

Migration File Renaming

Migration files are not set in stone, so it's possible to rename migration files. What steps you need to take to rename a migration file, depend on whether a migration has been applied to a database or not. To determine the state of a migration file with respect to a database, execute the `python manage.py showmigrations`, and if a migration file has an X beside it, it means it has been applied to the database.

For migrations that haven't been applied to the database, you can rename a migration file directly in the `migrations` folder to a more descriptive name. At this point, the migration file is just a representation of model changes that no one else knows about, so you can even delete the migration file if needed.

■ **Caution** Migration files should always maintain the serial number prefix (e.g., 0001, 0002) since it reduces confusion regarding migration file order.

For migrations that have been applied to a database you have two alternatives. The first option is to rename the migration file, alter the database table that holds the migration activity to reflect this new name, and update other migration file dependencies (if any) to also reflect this new name. Once you rename the migration file inside the `migrations` folder, access the `django_migrations` database table, and look for the record with the old migration file name and update it to the reflect the new migration name. Next, if there's a newer migration file than the one you're renaming, the newer migration file will have a `dependencies` statement - described in the migration file structure section - that must be updated with the new name.

The second alternative is to roll back to a migration prior to the migration file you want to rename, at which point you can simply rename the migration file - as an unapplied database migration file - and then reapply the migration process back to the most recent migration file. An upcoming section describes migration file rollback in greater detail.

Migration File Squashing

A `models.py` files that undergoes many changes can generate dozens or even hundreds of migrations files. In these circumstances, it's possible to squash multiple migration files into a single migration file to simplify file migration management. Note the term 'squash' is used vs. the more technically accurate term 'merge', because migration file merging refers to conflicting migration files, see the --merge option in Table 7-4.

The `manage.py squashmigrations` command is designed to squash multiple migration files, and its syntax is the following:

```
manage.py squashmigrations <app_name> <squash_up_to_migration_file_serial_number>
```

As you can see, the `squashmigrations` command requires you specify both the app on which you want to squash migration files, as well as the migration serial number up to which you want to squash (e.g., `squashmigrations stores 0004`, generates a single migration file for the `stores` app from the migration files 0001, 0002, 0003,and 0004).

The `squashmigrations` command also supports an additional positional argument to change the start of the squashing process from the default 0001 (e.g., `squashmigrations stores 0002 0004`, generates a single migration file from the migration files 0002, 0003, and 0004)

Like all file merging mechanisms, there's always a possibility `squashmigrations` may not be able to produce automatic results, in which case it generates the message 'Manual porting required', where it's necessary to manually edit the squashed migration file (e.g., just like it can happen with other file merging conflict operations in platforms like git).

Squashed migration files follow the naming convention:

```
<initial_serial_number>_squashed_<up_to_serial_number>_<date>.py
```

You can rename squashed migration file just like regular migration files; just follow the same steps described in the previous section, depending on whether the squashed migration file has been applied to a database or not.

Squashed migration files take over the duties of un-squashed migration files. You can keep the old (un-squashed) migration files as long as you want, but they only continue to serve a purpose until the squashed migration file is applied to a database. Behind the scenes, squashed migration files use the `replaces` migration field - described in the next section - to indicate which migration files it replaces. Therefore once you apply a squashed migration file to a database, the migration files in `replaces` are ignored.

Migration File Structure

Although migration files are automatically created based on the changes made to `models.py` files vs. the prior migration files belonging to the same `models.py` files, this doesn't mean you can't or won't have to change the internal structure of migration files. Listing 7-30 illustrates the basic structure of a Django migration file.

Listing 7-30. Django migration file basic structure

```
from django.db import migrations, models

class Migration(migrations.Migration):

    initial = True

    replaces = [
    ]

    dependencies = [
    ]

    operations = [
    ]
```

First, notice in Listing 7-30 all migration files include a class named `Migration` that inherits its behavior from `django.db.migrations.Migration`. This allows migrations to automatically receive a series of default behaviors, similar to how Django model classes inherit their behavior from the `django.db.models.Model` class.

Inside each `Migration` class are a series of fields that determine the actions of the migration file. The `initial` field is a Boolean value present on the initial migration file for every app (i.e., migration files with the `0001` serial number). The `replaces` field is a list field used by squashed migration files to declare which migration files it replaces, a value that is automatically populated when you create a squashing migration file.

The `dependencies` and `operations` fields are by far the two most common fields in migrations files. Although they're automatically populated once a migration file is created – just like other migration file fields – these two fields are the ones you're most likely to change if you require adjusting the logic executed by a migration file.

The `dependencies` field is a list of tuples with the `('<app_name>','<migration_file>')` syntax, where each tuple represents a migration dependency. For example, by default the second migration file for an app named about contains the following `dependencies` value:

```
dependencies = [
    ('about', '0001_initial'),
]
```

This tells Django the migration file depends on the execution of the migration file `0001_initial` in the `about` app, ensuring this last migration file is run first.

The most common scenario for editing the `dependencies` field is to add inter-app migration file dependencies. For example, if the `online` app depends on data from the `stores` app created by its `0002_data_population` migration file, you can add a dependency tuple to the `online` app's first migration file to ensure it's run after the `stores` migration files (e.g., `('stores', '0002_data_population')`).

■ **Tip** To reference the first migration file in an app you can use the __first__ reference (e.g., ('stores', '__first__')), to reference the last migration file in an app you can use the __latest__ reference (e.g., ('stores', '__latest__')).

The `operations` field declares a list of migration operations.[7] Migration operations include all database-related tasks performed by migrations. If you were wondering how Django generates the DDL to create, delete, alter, or rename the database table behind a model, it's all based on migration operations.

For most cases, Django generates the migration operations based on the changes made to models in a `models.py` file. For example, if you add a new model, the next migration file includes a `django.db.migrations.operations.CreateModel()` migration operation; if you rename a model in the `models.py`, the next migration file includes a `RenameModel()` operation from the same `django.db.migrations.operations` package; this same mechanism occurs when you change a model field (`AlterModel()`), add an index (`AddIndex()`) and perform all the other modifications possible to models in a `models.py` file.

The most common scenario for editing the `operations` field in a migration file is to add non-DDL operations (e.g., SQL DML- Data Manipulation Language) which can't be reflected as part of model changes. For example, you can insert SQL queries as part of a migration file through the `RunSQL` migration operation and you can also run Python logic as part of a migration file through the `RunPython` migration operation. The section "Django Model Initial Data Setup" describes how to use the `RunSQL` and `RunPython` migration operations.

Migration File Rollback

Reverting a database to a previous state of a Django model can be done by rolling back migration files. Reverting a database to a previous migration file is as simple as passing an additional argument to the same `migrate` command that applies migration files. For example, the `migrate stores 0001` statement tells Django to migrate the `stores` app to the `0001` migration file, if the app's database state is in a more recent migration file (e.g., `0004`), Django rolls back migration files until the database reflects the `0001` migration file.

But as simple as the migration file rollback command is, the actual rollback process is anything but simple. Since migration files can contain multiple DDL and DML operations - as described in the previous section - there are certain migration operations that are considered *irreversible*. This means once a migration is applied, Django can't determine with certainty how to undo it.

When a rollback is attempted on a migration with an irreversible operation, Django throws the error `django.db.migrations.exceptions.IrreversibleError`. Of course, irreversible does not mean impossible, but it does mean additional work to make a migration file reversible.

Most irreversible migration operations happen on DDL migration operations (e.g., `RunSQL, RunPython`) where you execute certain logic as part of the migration file. To make these types of migration operations reversible, you must equally provide the logic to revert the logic applied as part of the migration file. The section "Django Model Initial Data Setup" describes how to create reverse operations for the `RunSQL` and `RunPython` migration operations.

Django Model Database Tasks

Django is equipped to execute database-level tasks on Django models that are often done by database tools. A Django project's `manage.py` command offers several management subcommands for tasks like backing up, loading, and deleting data from database tables linked to Django models, as well as re-creating Django models from database tables and issuing interactive commands to a database.

---

[7]`https://docs.djangoproject.com/en/1.11/ref/migration-operations/`

Backup Data: Fixtures, dumpdata, loaddata, and inspectdb

The dumpdata and loaddata commands are Django's data backup and loading tools, similar to native tools included in databases (e.g., MySQL mysqldump, Postgres pg_dump).

Django uses the term *fixture* to refer to the data structures created and used by the dumpdata and loaddata commands. Because Django fixtures are designed for Django model instance data, their structure is based on formats that better describe this type of data. By default, Django fixtures use the JSON (JavaScript Object Notation) format, but it's also possible to create fixtures in XML and YAML.

The dumpdata command outputs database table data linked Django models. It accepts a wide array of options, the most common of which are described in the following examples:

- manage.py dumpdata > all_model_data.json.- Outputs data for all project models and places it in the all_model_data.json file.
- manage.py dumpdata stores --format xml.- Outputs data for all models in the stores app in XML.
- manage.py dumpdata about.contact --indent=2.- Outputs data for the Contact model in the about app with two space indentation -- the indentation makes the output more readable.
- manage.py dumpdata items.menu -pk=1,2,3 --format yaml.- Outputs the Menu model records with primary keys (i.e., id values) 1,2,3 from the items app in a YAML format.

■ **Note** To output YAML you need the PyYAML package (e.g., pip install PyYAML).

The manage.py loaddata command is designed to load fixture files produced by dumpdata. This means invoking loaddata is as simple as executing manage.py loaddata <fixture_file_name>. The loaddata command can accept relative or absolute paths to fixture files, but in addition, it also searches for fixture files in the fixtures folder inside apps. The next section on "Django Model Initial Data Setup" describes the procedure to use fixtures in apps.

The most important variation for the manage.py loaddata command are that it can accept multiple fixture files as arguments (e.g., loaddata <fixture_1>, <fixture_2>, <fixture_3>), which is necessary if fixture files have interdependencies; and it can restrict the searching/loading of fixtures to certain apps (e.g., manage.py loaddata menu --app items, searches/loads a fixture file named menu, but only inside the items app, specifically inside its fixtures folder).

The manage.py inspectdb is a reverse-engineering process that outputs Django models generated from database tables. Note the manage.py inspectdb outputs a single stream of model classes, so it requires rearranging the output if the model classes are to be placed in different models.py files.

Delete Data: Flush, sqlflush, and sqlsequencereset

Django also offers the flush and sqlflush commands to delete the contents of database tables linked to Django models. The manage.py flush command triggers the actual deleting process, whereas manage.py sqlflush outputs the SQL required to delete all data in Django model database tables (i.e., the logic triggered by flush).

The manage.py sqlsequenereset command outputs the required SQL to reset logic used by database sequences of a given app (e.g., manage.py sqlsequencereset stores to output the SQL necessary to reset the sequences used by models in the stores app). Sequences are used by databases to give automatically incrementing values to certain Django models fields (e.g., id field), and this command is used to fix issues when sequence values become out of sync.

Interact with Data: dbshell

Sometimes the need to connect directly to a database linked to a Django project can become inevitable in order to perform a complex task or query. The `manage.py dbshell` command is designed to connect to a Django project's database using the credentials in a Django projects `settings.py` file, in turn, avoiding the need to type in credentials to access a database.

Depending on the database brand you're using, the `dbshell` command opens an interactive command-line shell to the built-in tool for each database brand: for PostgreSQL to the `dpsql` environment, for MySQL to the `mysql` environment, for SQLite to the `sqlite3` environment, and for Oracle to the `sqlplus` environment.

Django Model Initial Data Setup

On many occasions it can be helpful or necessary to load a set of predefined data records on a Django model. Django allows you to load predefined records by either hard-coding them in Python; using a standard SQL script with SQL statements; or using a fixture file, which is a Django export/import format described in the previous section.

The first step to load a set of predefined data records is to generate an empty migration file to handle the actual data loading process. Listing 7-31 illustrates how to generate an empty migration file.

Listing 7-31. Create empty Django migration file to load initial data for Django model

```
[user@coffeehouse ~]$ python manage.py makemigrations --empty stores
Migrations for 'stores':
  0002_auto_20180124_0507.py:
```

As you can see in Listing 7-31, Django creates the empty migration file `0002_auto_20180124_0507.py` for the stores app. At this point, you can easily rename the migration file as described in the previous section. Once you have an empty Django migration, let's explore the different ways to modify it to set up initial data for a Django model.

Hard-code predefined records in Python migration file

The simplest approach to set up initial data is to hard-code the set of predefined data records and make it part of the migration file itself. Listing 7-32 illustrates a modified migration file with hard-coded model objects to load into a database.

Listing 7-32. Load initial data with hard-coded data in Django migration file

```
# -*- coding: utf-8 -*-
from __future__ import unicode_literals

from django.db import models, migrations

def load_stores(apps, schema_editor):
    Store = apps.get_model("stores", "Store")
    store_corporate = Store(id=0,name='Corporate',address='624 Broadway',city='San Diego',
                        state='CA',email='corporate@coffeehouse.com')
    store_corporate.save()
    store_downtown = Store(id=1,name='Downtown',address='Horton Plaza',city='San Diego',
                        state='CA',email='downtown@coffeehouse.com')
```

```
    store_downtown.save()
    store_uptown = Store(id=2,name='Uptown',address='1240 University Ave',city='San
                   Diego',state='CA',email='uptown@coffeehouse.com')
    store_uptown.save()
    store_midtown = Store(id=3,name='Midtown',address='784 W Washington St',city='San
                    Diego',state='CA',email='midtown@coffeehouse.com')
    store_midtown.save()

def delete_stores(apps, schema_editor):
    Store = apps.get_model("stores", "Store")
    Store.objects.all().delete()

class Migration(migrations.Migration):

    dependencies = [
        ('stores', '0001_initial'),
    ]

    operations = [
        migrations.RunPython(load_stores,delete_stores),
    ]
```

The first thing that's added to the empty migration file is the `migrations.RunPython(load_stores,delete_stored)` line in the `operations[]` list. The `RunPython` method runs Python code and its first argument indicates to run the `load_stores` method, the second argument - which is optional - is called the reverse code and is run when rolling back migrations - which is mentioned in the previous section on "Migration File Rollback."

The `load_stores` method in Listing 7-32 contains the hard-coded data records. This method first gets a reference of the `Store` model and then creates three different instances, which are then saved to the database. The `delete_stores` method does the opposite of the `load_stores` method - as its purpose is to roll back the applied data - deleting `Store` instances.

Once you make the additions illustrated in Listing 7-32 to an empty migration file, you just need to trigger the migration with the `migrate` command to load data into the database.

SQL script with SQL statements

On other occasions you may already have a set of predefined records in an SQL script to populate a database table. Listing 7-33 illustrates a sample SQL script to populate the table associated with the `Store` model.

Listing 7-33. SQL script with SQL statements

```
INSERT INTO stores_store (id,name,address,city,state,email) VALUES (0,'Corporate','624
Broadway','San Diego','CA','corporate@coffeehouse.com');
INSERT INTO stores_store (id,name,address,city,state,email) VALUES (1,'Downtown','Horton
Plaza','San Diego','CA','downtown@coffeehouse.com');
INSERT INTO stores_store (id,name,address,city,state,email) VALUES (2,'Uptown','1240
University Ave','San Diego','CA','uptown@coffeehouse.com');
INSERT INTO stores_store (id,name,address,city,state,email) VALUES (3,'Midtown','784 W
Washington St','San Diego','CA','midtown@coffeehouse.com');
```

By convention, Django names SQL scripts after the Django model its storing data for and places the SQL scripts in a subfolder named `sql` inside the app where the models are. For example, the contents of Listing 7-33 are for the `Store` model in the `stores` app and therefore would be placed in the project folder `stores/sql/store.sql`. Once you have an SQL script inside a Django project's directory structure, you can set it up as the initial data for a Django model. Listing 7-34 illustrates a modified migration file to load data from the SQL script in Listing 7-33 into a database.

Listing 7-34. Load initial data with SQL script in Django migration file

```
# -*- coding: utf-8 -*-
from __future__ import unicode_literals

from django.db import models, migrations

def load_stores_from_sql():
    from coffeehouse.settings import PROJECT_DIR
    import os
    sql_statements = open(os.path.join(PROJECT_DIR,'stores/sql/store.sql'), 'r').read()
    return sql_statements

def delete_stores_with_sql():
    return 'DELETE from stores_store;'

class Migration(migrations.Migration):

    dependencies = [
        ('stores', '0001_initial'),
    ]

    operations = [
        migrations.RunSQL(load_stores_from_sql(), delete_stores_with_sql()),
    ]
```

■ **Note** The RunSQL method used to load SQL statements relies on the sqlparse package. So if you plan to use this functionality you need to install this package (e.g., pip install sqlparse).

The first thing that's added to the empty migration file is the `migrations.RunSQL(load_stores_from_sql(),delete_stores_with_sql())` line in the `operations[]` list. The `RunSQL` method runs SQL statements, and its first argument indicates to run the `load_stores` method, the second argument - which is optional - is called the reverse code and is run when rolling back migrations - described in the previous section on "Migration File Rollback."

The `load_stores_from_sql` method in Listing 7-34 reads the contents of the SQL script from a relative path in the main project directory at `stores/sql/store.sql` and returns the SQL statements in the file. In this case, the relative path is provided by the `PROJECT_DIR` variable defined in a Django project's `settings.py` file and the SQL script is read using Python's standard open method. The `delete_stores_from_sql` method does the opposite of the `load_stores_from_sql` method - as its purpose is to roll back the applied data - deleting `Store` instances.

Once you make the additions illustrated in Listing 7-34 to an empty migration file, you just need to trigger the migration with the `migrate` command to load data into the database.

Django fixture file

Another alternative to load initial data in a Django model is through a fixture file. A fixture file is a Django-specific format used to manage the data export/import of Django models, described in the previous section on Django model database tasks. Listing 7-35 illustrates a JSON fixture file to populate the table associated with the Store model.

Listing 7-35. Django fixture file with JSON structure

```
[{
  "fields": {
    "city": "San Diego",
    "state": "CA",
    "email": "corporate@coffeehouse.com",
    "name": "Corporate",
    "address": "624 Broadway"
  },
  "model": "stores.store",
  "pk": 0
},
{
  "fields": {
    "city": "San Diego",
    "state": "CA",
    "email": "downtown@coffeehouse.com",
    "name": "Downtown",
    "address": "Horton Plaza"
  },
  "model": "stores.store",
  "pk": 1
}]
```

■ **Tip** Use dumpdata to generate fixture files, as described in the section "Model Database Tasks."

By convention, Django names fixture files after the Django model its stores data for and place fixture files in a subfolder named `fixtures` inside the app where a model is located. For example, the contents of Listing 7-35 are for the `Store` model in the `stores` app; therefore they're placed in the project folder `stores/fixtures/store.json`. Once you have a fixture file inside a Django project's directory structure, you can take the next step to set it up as the initial data for a Django model.

Listing 7-36 illustrates a modified migration file to load data from the fixture file in Listing 7-35 into a database.

Listing 7-36. Load initial data from Django fixture file in Django migration file

```
# -*- coding: utf-8 -*-
from __future__ import unicode_literals

from django.db import models, migrations
```

```
def load_stores_from_fixture(apps, schema_editor):
    from django.core.management import call_command
    call_command("loaddata", "store")

def delete_stores(apps, schema_editor):
    Store = apps.get_model("stores", "Store")
    Store.objects.all().delete()

class Migration(migrations.Migration):

    dependencies = [
        ('stores', '0001_initial'),
    ]

    operations = [
        migrations.RunPython(load_stores_from_fixture,delete_stores),
    ]
```

The first thing that's added to the empty migration file is the `migrations.RunPython(load_stores_from_fixture,,delete_stores)` line in the `operations[]` list. The `RunPython` method runs Python code as previously described in Listing 7-32.

The `load_stores_from_fixture` method in Listing 7-36 uses the `call_command` method to load the fixture file by simulating the command-line execution of the `manage.py loaddata` command. The `loaddata` command requires an additional argument to search for the fixture file in a specific app. In this case, the argument `store` tells Django to look for a fixture files named `store` in all the `fixtures` subdirectories for all apps. Note the `RunPython()` also uses a reverse code aegument - as it was done in Listing 7-32 - to be able to roll back the loading of fixture data.

Once you make the additions illustrated in Listing 7-36 to an empty migration file, you just need to trigger the migration with the `migrate` command to load data into the database.

Django Model Signals

As you've learned throughout this chapter, Django models have a series of methods you can override to provide custom functionalities. For example, you can create a custom `save()` or `__init__` method, so Django executes custom logic when saving or initializing a Django model instance, respectively.

While this ability provides a wide array of possibilities to execute custom logic at certain points in the life cycle of a Django model instance (e.g., create an audit trail if the `delete()` method is called on an instance), there are cases that require executing custom logic when an event happens in the life cycle of *another* model instance. For example, updating an `Item` model's `stock` value when an `Order` model instance is saved or generating a `Customer` model instance each time a `Contact` model instance is updated.

These scenarios create an interesting implementation problem. One approach is to interconnect the logic between two model classes to fulfill this type of logic (e.g., every time an `Order` object is saved, update related `Item` objects). This last approach though can become overly complex with more demanding requirements, because dependent classes need to be updated to perform actions on behalf of other classes. This type problem only grows in complexity once you confront the need to execute actions on classes you have no control over (e.g., how do you trigger a custom action when an instance of the built-in `django.contrib.auth.User` model class is saved?).

It turns out this scenario to trigger actions on behalf of other classes is so common in software, there's a name for it: the observer pattern.[8] The Django framework supports the observer pattern through Django signals.

In the simplest terms, signals are emitted by Django models into the project environment, just like airplanes emit signals into the environment. Similarly, all you need to intercept signals is create the appropriate receiver to intercept such signals (e.g., a receiver to detect the save signal for all project models, a receiver to detect the delete signal for a specific model) and execute whatever custom logic it is you need to run whenever the signal surfaces.

Built-In Django Model Signals

By default, all Django models emit signals for their most important workflow events. This is a very important fact for the sole reason it provides a noninvasive way to link into the events of *any* Django model. Note the emphasis on *any* Django model, meaning your project models, third-party app models and even Django built-in models, this is possible because signals are baked into the core `django.db.models.Model` class used by all Django models. Table 7-5 illustrates the various signals built in to Django models.

■ **Tip** Django also offers built-in signals for requests, responses, pre and post migrate events, and testing events. See built-in signal reference.[9]

Now that you know there are always a series of signals emitted by all of your Django project models, let's see how to get notified of signals, in order to execute custom logic when the signal occurs.

Listen for Django Model Signals

Listening for Django model signals - and Django signals in general - follows a straightforward syntax using the `@receiver` decorator from the `django.dispatch` package, as shown in Listing 7-37.

Listing 7-37. Basic syntax to listen for Django signals

```
from django.dispatch import receiver

@receiver(<signal_to_listen_for_from_django_core_signals>,sender=<model_class_to_listen_to>)
def method_with_logic_to_run_when_signal_is_emitted(sender, **kwargs):
      # Logic when signal is emitted
      # Access sender & kwargs to get info on model that emitted signal
```

As you can in Listing 7-37, you enclose the logic you want to execute on a signal in a Python method that follows the input signature of the signal callback; this in turn allows you to access information about the model that emitted the signal. For most signals, the input signature `sender, **kwargs` fits, but this can change depending on the signal - see the footnote reference on signals for details on the input arguments used by each signal.

---

[8]`https://en.wikipedia.org/wiki/Observer_pattern`
[9]`https://docs.djangoproject.com/en/1.11/ref/signals/`

Once you have a method to run on a signal emission, the method must be decorated with the `@receiver` annotation, which generally uses two arguments: a signal to listen for – those described in Table 7-5 – which is a required argument and the optional `sender` argument to specify which model class to listen into for the signal. If you want to listen for the same signal emitted by all your project's models – a rare case – you can omit the `sender` argument.

Table 7-5. *Built-in Django model signals*

Signal(s)	Signal class	Description
pre_init post_init	django.db.models.signals.pre_init django.db.models.signals.post_init	Signal emitted at the beginning and end of the model's __init__() method.
pre_save post_save	django.db.models.signals.pre_save django.db.models.signals.post_save	Signal emitted at the beginning and end of the model's __save__() method.
pre_delete post_delete	django.db.models.signals.pre_delete django.db.models.signals.post_delete	Signal emitted at the beginning and end of the model's __delete__() method.
m2m_changed	django.db.models.signals.m2m_changed	Signal emitted when a ManyToManyField is changed on a model instance.
class_prepared	django.db.models.signals.class_prepared	Signal emmited when a model has been defined and registered with Django's model system. Used internally by Django, but rarely used for other circumstances.

Now that you have a basic understanding of the syntax used to listen for Django signals, let's explore the placement and configuration of signals in a Django project.

The recommended practice is to place signals in a file called `signals.py` under an app's main folder (i.e., alongside `models.py`, `views.py`). This keeps signals in an obvious location, but more importantly it avoids any potential interference (e.g., loading issues, circular references) given signals can contain logic related to models and views. Listing 7-38 illustrates the contents of the `signals.py` file for an app named `items`.

Listing 7-38. Listen for Django pre_save signal on Item model in signals.py

```
from django.dispatch import receiver

from django.db.models.signals import pre_save
from django.dispatch import receiver

import logging

stdlogger = logging.getLogger(__name__)

@receiver(pre_save, sender='items.Item')
def run_before_saving(sender, **kwargs):
    stdlogger.info("Start pre_save Item in signals.py under items app")
    stdlogger.info("sender %s" % (sender))
    stdlogger.info("kwargs %s" % str(kwargs))
```

First, notice the signal listening method in Listing 7-38 uses the `@receiver` decorator to listen for the `pre_save` signal on the `Item` model. This means that every time an `Item` model instance is about to be saved, the method `run_before_saving` is triggered. In this case, a few log messages are generated, but the method can execute any logic depending on requirements.

■ **Tip** The sender argument in Listing 7-38 uses a string model reference instead of a standard class import reference. This ensures models in signals are lazy-loaded avoiding potential import conflicts between models and signals.

Once you have a `signals.py` file with all of its signal listening methods, you must tell Django to inspect this file to load the signal logic. The recommended practice is to do this with an `import` statement in the `apps.py` file, which is also part of an app's structure. Listing 7-39 illustrates a modified version of the default `apps.py` to inspect the `signals.py` file.

Listing 7-39. Django apps.py with custom ready() method to load signals.py

```
from django.apps import AppConfig

class ItemsConfig(AppConfig):
    name = 'coffeehouse.items'

    def ready(self):
        import coffeehouse.items.signals
```

In Listing 7-39 you can see the `apps.py` file contains the `ready()` method. The `ready()` method, as its name implies, is executed once the app is ready to be accessed. Inside `ready()` there's an `import` statement for the `signals` module in the same app (i.e., Listing 7-38), which in turn makes Django load the signal listening methods in Listing 7-38.

In addition to this change to the `apps.py` file to load signals, it's also necessary to ensure the `apps.py` file itself is loaded by Django. For this requirement there are two options illustrated in Listing 7-40.

Listing 7-40. Django configuration options to load apps.py

```
Option 1) Declare apps.py class as part of INSTALLED_APPS
# settings.py
INSTALLED_APPS = [
    'coffeehouse.items.apps.ItemsConfig',
     ...
]

Option 2) Declare default_app_config inside the __init__ file of the app

#/coffeehouse/items/__init__.py
default_app_config = 'coffeehouse.items.apps.ItemsConfig'
```

The first option in Listing 7-40 consists of explicitly declaring an app's configuration class as part of `INSTALLED_APPS` – in this case `coffeehouse.items.apps.ItemsConfig` – instead of the stand-alone package app statement (e.g., `coffeehouse.items`). This last variation ensures the custom `ready()` method is called as part of the initialization procedure.

The second option in Listing 7-40 consists of adding the `default_app_config` value to the `__init__` file of an app (i.e., the one besides the `apps.py`, `models.py` and `views.py`) and declaring the app's configuration class, in this case `coffeehouse.items.apps.ItemsConfig`.

The first option in Listing 7-40 is newer and supported since the introduction of the app configuration in Django 1.9, the second is equally valid and was used prior to introduction of athe pp configuration.

Emit Custom Signals in Django Model Signals

In addition to the Django built-in signals presented in Table 7-5, it's also possible to create custom signals. Custom signals are helpful when you want to execute actions pegged to important events in the workflow of your own models (e.g., when a store closes, when an order is created), whereas Django built-in signals let you listen to important Django model workflow signals (e.g., before and after a model instance is saved or deleted).

The first step to create custom signals is to generate a signal instance with the `django.dispatch.Signal` class. The `Signal` class only requires the `providing_args` argument, which is a list of arguments that both signal emitters and receivers expect the `Signal` to have. The following snippet illustrates two custom `Signal` instances:

```
from django.dispatch import Signal

order_complete = Signal(providng_args=["customer","barista"])

store_closed = Signal(providing_args=["employee"])
```

Once you have a custom `Signal` instance, the next step is to add a signal emission method to trigger a `Signal` instance. For Django models, the standard location is to emit signals as part of a class method, as illustrated in Listing 7-41.

Listing 7-41. Django model emitting custom signal

```
from django.db import models
from coffeehouse.stores.signals import store_closed

class Store(models.Model):
    name = models.CharField(max_length=30)
    address = models.CharField(max_length=30,unique=True)
    ...
    def closing(self,employee):
        store_closed.send(sender=self.__class__, employee=employee)
```

As you can see in Listing 7-41, the `Store` model defines a method called `closing()` that accepts an employee input. Inside this `closing()` method, a signal is emitted to the custom `Signal` class named `store_closed` using the `send()` method – inherited through `Signal` – which uses the arguments expected by the custom `Signal` class.

Next, when you have a reference to a `Store` model instance and call the `closing()` method on any store instance (e.g., `downtown_store.closing(employee=request.user)`) a custom `store_closed` signal is emitted. And who receives this signal? Anyone who is listening for it, just like built-in Django signals. The following snippet illustrates a signal listening method for the custom `store_closed` signal:

```
@receiver(store_closed)
def run_when_store_is_closed(sender,**kwargs):
    stdlogger.info("Start store_closed Store in signals.py under stores app")
    stdlogger.info("sender %s" % (sender))
    stdlogger.info("kwargs %s" % str(kwargs))
```

This last listening signal method is almost identical to the ones used to listen for built-in Django signals – presented in the past section in Listing 7-38. In this case, the only argument to the `@receiver` decorator corresponds to the signal name `store_closed`, which indicates the method is listening for this signal. Since the custom `store_closed` signal is produced in a limited location (i.e., in a single model method) – unlike built-in signals that are produced by all models – the `@receiver` decorator forgoes adding the optional `sender` argument.

Django Models Outside of models.py

By default, Django models are placed in `models.py` files inside apps. However, this single file can outgrow the needs of large apps that require storing dozens or hundreds of models. There are three techniques you can use to deallocate Django models from `models.py` files inside apps.

Django Models Inside Apps in the Models Folder

The first technique to store Django models outside of `models.py` files is to create a folder named `models` - inside the same app - declare class models in stand-alone files in this folder and import the classes through this new folder's `__init__` file. Listing 7-42 shows an app folder layout for this type of model deployment.

Listing 7-42. Django apps with models stored under models directory

```
+---+
    |
    +-stores(app)-+
                  +-__init__.py
                  +-models.py
                  +-tests.py
                  +-views.py
                  +-apps.py
                  +-models-+
                           |
                           +-__init__.py
                           +-menus.py
                           +-equipment.py
                           +-personnel.py
```

Notice in Listing 7-42 that alongside the standard `models.py` file is a `models` folder. Next, inside the `models` folder are multiple `.py` files with Django models declared as they would typically be done inside `models.py`. You can have as many models as needed in each `.py` file and as many `.py` files as you deem necessary (e.g., one model per file).

However, the `__init__` file inside this new `models` folder does require additional attention. While `__init__` files are typically left empty, in this case, the `__init__` file must make a relative import for each of the models - inside `.py` files - to make them visible to the app. For example, if the `menus.py` file contains the `Breakfast` model class, the `__init__` file must declare the line `from .menus import Breakfast`. This one-line syntax - `from .<file> import <model_class>` - must be used in `__init__.py` for every model declared in `.py` files inside the `models` folder.

With this layout you're able to place Django models outside of a single `models.py` file, but the following points apply to this first technique to relocate Django models:

- <u>The subfolder must be named</u> `models`.- Because the `models.py` file is inspected by default (as the Python path `<app>.models`), it requires an identically named Python path `<app>.models` to detect models - with the `__init__` file doing the rest of the import work. So beware any other folder name different than `models` won't work with this configuration - the next technique to configure models outside `models.py` a solution to using a different folder name.

- Declaring an app as part of INSTALLED_APPS is sufficient, so long as the __init__ file performs the correct relative imports.- So long as an app is declared as part of INSTALLED_APPS in settings.py, it's sufficient for Django to detect any models declared inside the models folder as described in Listing 7-42. Just take care of relatively importing all models in the __init__.py file.
- The app name for every model is determined automatically.- Since the models folder is nested inside an app, all the models inside this folder receive the app name configured in the apps.py file for the app. Although you can use the meta class app_label option to explicitly assign an app to a model - as described earlier in the Meta Class Options section - it's redundant in this case because the models receive the same app name they're in, including the placement of their migrations files.
- The models are accessible as if they were in models.py .- Athough the models are placed in different files, the Python access path remains t app.models, so the models are accessible as if they were in models.py (e.g., to access the Breakfast model class inside the menus.py file, you would still use from <app>.models import Breakfast from other parts of an application).

Django Models Inside Apps in Custom Folders

A second technique to declare models outside models.py files is to use custom folders inside an app. This requires using the main models.py file as the import mechanism and also requires using longer access paths for models. Listing 7-43 shows an app folder layout with custom folders for models.

Listing 7-43. Django apps with models stored under custom directories

```
+---+
    |
    +-stores(app)-+
                  +-__init__.py
                  +-models.py
                  +-tests.py
                  +-views.py
                  +-apps.py
                  +-menus+
                  |       +-__init__.py
                  |       +-breakfast.py
                  |
                  +-equipment+
                             +-__init__.py
                             +-kitchen.py
```

As you can Listing 7-43 the app now has multiple subfolders, where each folder contains multiple .py files with Django models declared as they would typically be done inside models.py. (i.e., breakfast.py and kitchen.py in Listing 7-43 contain model classes).

Since Django only looks for models under the Python path <app>.models, you must declare a relative import in the main models.py file - for each of the models inside subfolders - to make them visible to the app. For example, if the Breakfast model class is inside the menus subfolder file and breakfast.py file, the main models.py file must declare the line from .menus.breakfast import Breakfast. This one-line syntax - from .<sub_folder>.<file> import <model_class> - must be used in models.py for every model declared in subfolders inside an app.

Because the models.py file uses a relative import path to the models themselves, this alters the standard Django Python path to access models - from <app>.models... - and requires a longer path: from <app>.models.<sub_folder>.<file>.... Other than this change in import paths, the remaining configuration options for models have no change in behavior (i.e., INSTALLED_APPS, model app name).

Django Models Outside Apps and Model Assignment to Other Apps

A third technique available for Django models is to declare them completely outside of apps or inclusively assign Django models to a different app than the one in which they're declared. So what does it means to 'assign models to an app'? It means just that, you can *declare* models outside of apps or in a given app, but change the app a model *belongs* to.

Although I don't recommend this technique because it can lead to confusion, it does provide a different solution that I'll describe for the sake of completeness.

This technique requires you provide models an explicit app name through the meta class app_label option so they're assigned to an app. When Django detects a model it declares the meta app_label option, this takes the highest precedent to assign a model its app name. So even if a model is declared inside a random folder named common or an app named items, if a model's meta app_label value is set to stores, the model is assigned to the stores app, irrespective of its location.

The confusing aspect of using the app_label option is due to the influence an app name has on Django models. For example, an app name is used to give a model's database table name prefix and it's also used to determine the location of a model's migration files. So if you define a model inside a folder named common with the meta class app_label='stores', the model will end up belonging to the stores app - along with its migration files and a prefix table app name stores - even though it's declared in the common folder.

This last technique although flexible, as I've just explained, can also lead to unintuitive outcomes in the naming and placement of Django model constructs.

Django Models and Multiple Databases

Back in Chapter 1, when you set up a database for a Django project, you used the DATABASES variable in settings.py to define the type and connection parameters to perform all database-related operations in a Django application. Since this variable is plural, it means you can declare multiple databases in a Django project, as illustrated in Listing 7-44.

Listing 7-44. Django multiple DATABASES definitions in settings.py

```
DATABASES = {
    'default': {
        ...
    },
    'devops': {
        ...
    },
    'analytics': {
        ...
    }
    'warehouse': {
        ...
    }
}
```

Listing 7-44 shows four different databases for a Django project, where the ... notation is the position in which each database's connection parameters are declared (e.g., `ENGINE`, `NAME`, and all those other described in Table 1-3).

The most important aspect in Listing 7-44 is the `default` key, which represents the database on which all Django project database-related operations are made, unless otherwise specified. In the upcoming sections, I'll describe how to tell Django to perform data operations on different databases than the `default`.

■ **Tip** If you want Django to do operations by default on a different database than `default`, you can declare the `DEFAULT_DB_ALIAS` value in `settings.py`. (e.g., `DEFAULT_DB_ALIAS='analytics'`, tells Django to perform all database-related operation on the database assigned to the `analytics` handle, unless explicitly told otherwise).

Now that you know how to declare multiple databases in a Django project and the importance of the `default` database, let's explore how to execute instructions on multiple databases from within a Django project.

Multiple Databases for Django Models: using

All Django model operations described in this chapter and the upcoming chapter are designed to run against the database defined in the `default` handle in `DATABASES`, or if provided, the `DEFAULT_DB_ALIAS` database handle. However, with multiple databases it's possible to selectively execute operations against different databases, overriding the default database.

Django models support the `using` keyword to indicate against which database to execute operations. There are two variations of the `using` keyword:

- The `using` option.- Django model methods such as `save()` and `delete()` support the `using` option to indicate against which database to save or delete records. For example, `store.save(using='analytics')` tells Django to save the store records to the `analytics` database handle, overriding the default database value.
- The `using` method.- The default Django model manager `objects` supports the `using()` method to indicate against which database to perform a query. For example, `Item.objects.using('warehouse').all()` tells Django to get all `Item` records from the `warehouse` database handle, overriding the default database value.

Multiple Databases for Django Tools: --database

In addition to Django models having the ability to selectively execute operations against different databases, Django tools that perform database-related tasks also have the ability to specify a different database than the `default` database handle.

For example, `manage.py` commands such as `migrate`, `dumpdata`, `loaddata` and others described in this chapter support the `--database` flag to execute their logic against a different database than the `default` database handle. For example, `mange.py migrate --database devops` tells Django to perform the migration process on the `devops` database, overriding the default database value.

Multiple Database Routers: DATABASE_ROUTERS setting

Although the `using` and `--database` options offer a solution to work with multiple databases in a Django project, they both require spreading out the multi-database logic to different parts of an application (e.g., models and scripts). Django database routers offer the ability to centralize multi-database logic, so that based on the model or type of database operation, the logic is executed against a different database than the default.

Django database routers are standard Python classes that implement up to four different methods illustrated in Table 7-6.

Table 7-6. *Django database router methods*

Method	Description
db_for_read(model, **hints)	Suggests the database to use for read operations of a model.
db_for_write(model, **hints)	Suggests the database to use for write operations of a model.
allow_relation(obj1, obj2, **hints)	Suggests whether to (allow/prevent/no opinion) on relationship operations between obj1 and obj2.
allow_migrate(db, app_label, model_name=None, **hints)	Suggests the database to use for migration operations.

***Hints are additional information provided to each router method to further determine which database to use each routing case, in addition to the other input parameters.*

Armed with this basic knowledge of methods used by Django database routers, let's create a custom router that stores Django models associated with core Django apps (e.g., users, admin, sessions) in one database and other Django project models in another database. Listing 7-45 illustrates a Django database router that performs this logic.

Listing 7-45. Django database router to store core app models in devops database and all other models in default database

```
class DatabaseForDevOps(object):

    def db_for_read(self, model, **hints):
        if model._meta.app_label in ['auth','admin','sessions','contenttypes']:
            return 'devops'
        # Returning None is no opinion, defer to other routers or default database
        return None

    def db_for_write(self, model, **hints):
        if model._meta.app_label in ['auth','admin','sessions','contenttypes']:
            return 'devops'
         # Returning None is no opinion, defer to other routers or default database
        return None

    def allow_relation(self, obj1, obj2, **hints):
        # Allow relations between two models that are both Django core app models
        if obj1._meta.app_label in ['auth','admin','sessions','contenttypes'] and obj2._
        meta.app_label in ['auth','admin','sessions','contenttypes']:
            return True
        # If neither object is in a Django core app model (defer to other routers or default
        database)
        elif obj1._meta.app_label not in ['auth','admin','sessions','contenttypes'] or
        obj2._meta.app_label not in ['auth','admin','sessions','contenttypes']:
            return None
        return None
```

```
    def allow_migrate(self, db, app_label, model_name=None, **hints):
        if db == 'devops':
            # Migrate Django core app models if current database is devops
            if app_label in ['auth','admin','sessions','contenttypes']:
                return True
            else:
                # Non Django core app models should not be migrated if database is devops
                return False
        # Other database should not migrate Django core app models
        elif app_label in ['auth','admin','sessions','contenttypes']:
            return False
        # Otherwise no opinion, defer to other routers or default database
        return None
```

The first two methods in Listing 7-45 - `db_for_read()` and `db_for_write()` - tell Django how to proceed with the read and write operations of models. In this case, both methods check the model `app_name`, if the `app_name` is either `auth`, `admin`, `sessions` or `contenttypes` - all of which are Django core apps - the methods return the `'devops'` value, which represents a database handle, as described in Listing 7-44. This logic tells Django to perform all read and write operations for these type of models on the `devops` database. If a model does not match any of the cited `app_name` values, notice both methods return `None`, which is an indication the router class has no opinion on how to handle the model and passes control to another router class or the default database to determine where to perform a model's read/write operations.

Here it's worth mentioning you can use multiple Django database routers, with their configuration order defining their precedence. If one Django database router cannot determine or does not define a specific database on which to execute an operation or model, it moves on to the next database router, and this process continues until all database routers are run out and the operation or model defaults to using the `default` database. This behavior has the advantage that database routers don't have to declare database routing paths for every single model and operation in a project; it's sufficient to declare routing rules for certain models or operations, and let Django use the default database as a back stop.

Turning our attention back to Listing 7-45, the `allow_relation()` method is used to determine how to route model operations when a model contains related models. For example, if a model contains a `ForeignKey` field or `ManyToManyField` field, this relationship can cross over into another app, which in turn influences where a database table can reside. In the case of Listing 7-45, the `allow_relation()` method indicates to allow relationship operations if the related model objects belong to either the `auth`, `admin`, `sessions`, or `contenttypes` apps.

Finally, the `allow_migrate()` in Listing 7-45 is used to define against which database migrations operations are run. In this case, it indicates that if a migrate operation is done against the `devops` database, it only migrates models belonging to either the `auth`, `admin`, `sessions`, or `contenttypes` apps and it should ignore all other model migrations (i.e., the `devops` database should only contain model tables related to the `auth`, `admin`, `sessions`, or `contenttypes` apps). The second part in `allow_migrate()` indicates that for any other database that's not `devops`, it should ignore model migrations for the `auth`, `admin`, `sessions`, or `contenttypes` apps (i.e., the `default` database will not contain tables related to the `auth`, `admin`, `sessions`, or `contenttypes` apps).

Once you have a database router class like the one in Listing 7-45, you must declare it as part of the `DATABASE_ROUTERS` value list in `settings.py`. Assuming the database router class in Listing 7-45 is located in the folder `/coffeehouse/common/` in the `routers.py` file, then `DATABASE_ROUTERS = ['coffeehouse.common.routers.DatabaseForDevOps']`.

As I already mentioned, the `DATABASE_ROUTERS` value can be a list of database routers for which all models pass through to determine on which database to perform their operations, and if the `DATABASE_ROUTERS` list is exhausted, then the default database is used.

Once you finish setting up the database router configuration, you must run the migrate operation on both of your project databases. Once this is done, all read and write operations related to Django core app models will be done on the devops database and all other project models will be done on the `default` database.

■ **Caution** The manage.py migrate command only performs migrations against the default database. This means that if you need to perform migrations against other databases – such as with this database router configuration example – you must explicitly run the migrate with the --database flag to create migrations for all non-default databases.

CHAPTER 8

Django Model Queries and Managers

As you learned in the previous chapter, Django models encapsulate data through classes, enforce data validation, are used to interact with a Django project's relational database, and have a myriad of options to guarantee and customize how data operates in Django projects.

In this chapter we'll build on the previous Django model concepts and learn about a Django model queries and managers. We'll start with an in-depth look at Django model CRUD (Create-Read-Update-Delete) operations, including single, multiple, and relationship queries, covering their speed and efficiency implications. Next, you'll learn about the many SQL query variations supported by Django models, including field lookups to produce SQL WHERE statements; models methods to produce SQL statements like DISTINCT and ORDER; as well as query expressions to execute SQL aggregation operations, database functions, and subqueries.

Next, you'll learn how to create raw (open-ended) SQL queries when Django's built-in SQL facilities prove to be insufficient. Finally, you'll learn how to create and configure custom model managers in Django models.

CRUD Single Records in Django Models

Working with single records is one of the most common tasks you'll do with Django models. Next, I'll structure the following sections into the classical web application CRUD operations and describe the various techniques for each case so you can get a better grasp of what to use under different circumstances.

Note that although the following sections concentrate on the actual CRUD operation and its behaviors, sometimes I'll inevitably introduce more advanced query concepts in the examples (e.g., field lookups), which are described in detail in later sections of the chapter.

Create a Single Record with save() or create()

To create a single record on a Django model, you just need to make an instance of a model and invoke the `save()` method on it. Listing 8-1 illustrates the process to create a single record for a model called `Store`.

Tip Consult the book's accompanying source code to run the exercises, in order to reduce typing and automatically access test data.

D. Rubio, *Beginning Django*, https://doi.org/10.1007/978-1-4842-2787-9_8

Listing 8-1. Create a single record with model save() method

```
# Import Django model class
from coffeehouse.stores.models import Store

# Create a model Store instance
store_corporate = Store(name='Corporate',address='624 Broadway',state='CA',email='corporate@
coffeehouse.com')
# Assign attribute value to instance with Python dotted notation
store_corporate.city = 'San Diego'
# Invoke the save() method to create the record
store_corporate.save() # If successful, record reference has id
store_corporate.id
```

As you can see in Listing 8-1, you can declare all the instance attributes in a single step or you can use Python's dotted notation to assign attribute values one by one on the reference itself. Once the instance is ready, call the `save()` method on it to create the record in the database. There are two important behaviors to be aware of when you invoke the `save()` method:

- By default, all Django models are assigned an auto-incrementing primary key named `id`, created when you initiate a model's database table - see the previous chapter's section on "Django Models and the Migrations Workflow" for more details. This means the database assigns an `id` value to a record - unless you explicitly provide an `id` value to the instance - that gets passed back to the reference.
- The creation of a record is rejected if it violates any database or Django validation rule created by the Django model. This means that if a new instance doesn't comply with any of these validation rules, `save()` generates an error. See the previous chapter's section on "Django Models Data Types" for more details on rule validation.

These are the two most important points when you use the `save()` method to create a record. For the full set of options and subtleties associated with a Django model `save()` method, see the previous chapter's Table 7-3 and the section on "Model Methods."

After a successful call to the `save()` method in Listing 8-1, you can see the object reference is assigned the `id` attribute - created by the database - which serves to directly link it to a database record that can later be updated and/or deleted.

The `create()` method offers a shorter route alternative to create a record. Listing 8-2 illustrates the equivalent record creation in Listing 8-1 using the `create()` method.

Listing 8-2. Create a single record with create() method

```
# Import Django model class
from coffeehouse.stores.models import Store

# Create a model Store instance which is saved automatically
store_corporate = Store.objects.create(name='Corporate',address='624 Broadway',city='San Diego',
state='CA',email='corporate@coffeehouse') # If successful, record reference has id
store_corporate.id
```

You can see in Listing 8-2 that the `create()` method is invoked on a Django model class through the model's default `objects` model manager. The `create()` method accepts arguments that represent the model instance field values. The execution of `create()` returns an object reference to the created record including an `id` value just like the `save()` method.

Behind the scenes, the `create()` method actually uses the same `save()` method, but it uses the model manager to allow the creation of a record in a single line.

Read a Single Record with get() or get_or_create()

To read a single database record you can use the `get()` method - which is part of a model's default `objects` model manager - and which accepts any model field to qualify a record. Listing 8-3 illustrates a basic example of the `get()` Django model method.

Listing 8-3. Read model record with get() method

```
# Import Django model class
from coffeehouse.stores.models import Store

# Get the store with the name "Downtown" or equivalent SQL: 'SELECT....WHERE
name = "Downtown"
downtown_store = Store.objects.get(name="Downtown")

# Define uptown_email for the query
uptown_email = "uptown@coffeehouse.com"
# Get the store with the email value uptown_email or equivalent SQL: 'SELECT....WHERE
email = "uptown@coffeehouse.com"'
uptown_email_store = Store.objects.get(email=uptown_email)

# Once the get() method runs, you can access an object's attributes
# either in logging statements, functions or templates
downtown_store.address
downtown_store.email

# Note you can access the object without attributes.
# If the Django model has a __str__/ method definition, the output is based on this method
# If the Django model has no __str__ method definition, the output is just <object>
print(uptown_email_store)
```

As you can see in Listing 8-3, the `get()` method uses a Django model attribute as its argument to retrieve a specific record. The first example gets the `Store` record with `name=Downtown` and the second example gets the `Store` record with `email=uptown@coffeehouse.com`. Once the record is assigned to a variable, you can access its contents or attributes using Python's dotted notation.

■ **Tip** In addition to single fields – name="Downtown" or email="uptown@..." – the get() method also accepts multiple fields to produce an *and* query (e.g., get(email="uptown@...",name="Downtown") to get a record were both email and name match). In addition, Django also offers *field lookup* to create finer single record queries (e.g., get(name__contains="Downtown") to produce a substring query). See the later section in the chapter on queries classified by SQL keyword.

It's that simple to use a Django model's get() method. However, the get() method has some behaviors you should be aware of:

- With get() the query has to match one and only one record. If there are no matching records you will get a <model>.DoesNotExist error. If there are multiple matching records you will get a MultipleObjectsReturned error.
- get() calls hit the database immediately and every time. This means there's no caching on Django's part for identical or multiple calls.

Knowing these get() limitations, let's explore how to tackle the first scenario that involves a record that doesn't exist. A common occurrence when attempting to read a single record that doesn't exist is to get it and if it doesn't exist just create it. Listing 8-4 illustrates how to use the get_or_create() method for this purpose.

Listing 8-4. Read or create model record with get_or_create() method

```
# Import Django model class
from coffeehouse.items.models import Menu

# Get or create a menu instance with name="Breakfast"
menu_target, created = Menu.objects.get_or_create(name="Breakfast")
```

As you can see in Listing 8-4, the get_or_create() method - also part of a model's default objects model manager - is invoked on a Django model class using a model's attributes as its arguments to get or create a record in one step. The get_or_create() method returns a pair of results, the model instance - whether created or read - as well as a Boolean indicating whether a model instance was created or read (i.e., True if created, False if read).

The get_or_create() method is a shortcut that uses both the get() and the create() methods - the last of which uses the save() method behind the scenes, as you learned in the previous section. The difference being, the get_or_create() method automatically handles the error condition when get() finds no matches. Listing 8-5 illustrates how the get_or_create() method functions behind the scenes, which you can also use if you prefer to handle get() errors method explicitly.

Listing 8-5. Replicate get_or_create() method with explicit try/except block and save method

```
from django.core.exceptions import ObjectDoesNotExist
from coffeehouse.items.models import Menu

try:
     menu_target = Menu.objects.get(name="Dinner")
     # If get() throws an error you need to handle it.
     # You can use either the generic ObjectDoesNotExist or
     # <model>.DoesNotExist which inherits from
     # django.core.exceptions.ObjectDoesNotExist, so you can target multiple
     # DoesNotExist exceptions
except Menu.DoesNotExist: # or the generic "except ObjectDoesNotExist:"
     menu_target = Menu(name="Dinner")
     menu_target.save()
```

As you can see in Listing 8-5, it's necessary to write more code (e.g., error handling, get and save calls) when you know there's a possibility a record doesn't exist and you want to create it anyways. So the get_or_create() method becomes a helpful shortcut in this scenario.

Now let's take a look the second `get()` limitation, which involves getting multiple records on a query. By design, the `get()` method throws a `MultipleObjectsReturned` error if more than one record matches a query. This behavior is an actual feature, because there are circumstances when you want to ensure a query only returns one record and be informed otherwise (e.g., a query for a user or product where duplicates are considered erroneous).

If there's a possibility for a query to return one or multiple records, then you'll need to forgo the use of `get()` method and use either a model manager's `filter()` or `exclude()` methods. Both the `filter()` or `exclude()` methods produce a multirecord data structure called a `QuerySet`, which can be reduced to a single record with an additional `QuerySet` method (e.g., `Item.objects.filter(name__contains='Salad').first()` to get the first `Item` record whose name contains the Salad substring).

Since a Django model's `filter()` or `exclude()` methods are designed for multiple record queries, these methods along with `QuerySet` behaviors are described in detail in the later section on CRUD operations for multiple records. Additional `QuerySet` methods like `first()` are also described in the later section on model queries classified by SQL keyword.

Update a Single Record with save(), update(), update_or_create(), or refresh_from_db()

If you already have a reference to a model record, an update is as simple as updating its attributes using Python's dotted notation and calling the `save()` method on it. Listing 8-6 illustrates this process.

Listing 8-6. Update model record with the save() method

```
# Import Django model class
from coffeehouse.stores.models import Store

# Get the store with the name "Downtown" or equivalent SQL: 'SELECT....WHERE name = "Downtown"

downtown_store = Store.objects.get(name="Downtown")

# Update the name value
downtown_store.name = "Downtown (Madison)"

# Call save() with the update_fields arg and a list of record fields to update selectively
downtown_store.save(update_fields=['name'])

# Or you can call save() without any argument and all record fields are updated
downtown_store.save()
```

In Listing 8-6, you can see the `save()` method is called in two ways. You can use the `update_fields` argument with a list of fields to update certain fields and get a performance boost in large models. Or the other alternative is to use `save()` without any argument, in which case Django updates all fields.

If you don't yet have a reference to the record to update, it's slightly inefficient to first get it (i.e., issue a SELECT query) and then update it with the `save()` method. In addition, doing the update process in separate steps can lead to race conditions. For example, if another user fetches the same data at the same time and also does an update, you'll both race to save it, but whose update is definitive and whose is overwritten? Because no party is aware the other is working on the same data, you need a way to indicate - technically known as lock or isolate - the data to avoid race conditions.

For such cases you can use the update() method - part of a model's default objects model manager - which performs an update in a single operation and guarantees there are no race conditions. Listing 8-7 illustrates this process.

Listing 8-7. Update model record with the update() method

```
from coffeehouse.stores.models import Store

Store.objects.filter(id=1).update(name="Downtown (Madison)")

from coffeehouse.items.models import Item
from django.db.models import F

Item.objects.filter(id=3).update(stock=F('stock') +100)
```

The first example in Listing 8-7 uses the update() method to update the Store record with id=1 and set its name to Downtown (Madison). The second example in Listing 8-7 uses a Django F expression and the update() method to update the Item record with id=3 and set its stock value to the current stock value plus 100. For the moment, don't worry about Django F expressions - they're described later on for more elaborate queries - just realize Django F expressions allow you to reference model fields within a query - as an SQL expression - which is necessary in this case to perform the update in a single operation.

■ **Caution** The update() method can update a field across multiple records if you're not careful. The update() method is preceded by the objects.filter() method, which can return query results for multiple records. Notice in Listing 8-7 the query uses the id field to define the query, ensuring that only a single record matches the query, because id is the table's primary key. If the query definition in objects.filter() uses a less strict lookup (e.g., a string) you can inadvertently update more records than you expect.

Similar to the convenience get_or_create() method described in the previous section, Django also offers the convenience update_or_create() method. This method is helpful in cases where you want to perform an update and aren't sure if the record exists yet. Listing 8-8 illustrates this process.

Listing 8-8. Update or create model record with the update_or_create() method

```
# Import Django model class
from coffeehouse.stores.models import Store

values_to_update = {'email':'downtown@coffeehouse.com'}

# Update for record with name='Downtown' and city='San Diego' is found,
otherwise create record
obj_store, created = Store.objects.update_or_create(
    name='Downtown',city='San Diego', defaults=values_to_update)
```

The first thing that's done in Listing 8-8 is create a dictionary with field values to update. Next, you pass a query argument to `update_or_create` for a desired object (i.e., the one you wish to update or create), along with dictionary containing the field values to update.

For the case in Listing 8-8, if there's already a `Store` record with `name='Downtown'` and `city='San Diego'` the record's values in `values_to_update` are updated, if there is no matching `Store` record a new Store record with `name='Downtown'`, `city='San Diego'` along with the values in `values_to_update`. The `update_or_create` method returns an updated or created object, as well as a Boolean value to indicate if the record was newly created or not.

■ **Note** update_or_create only works on queries with single records. If there are multiple records that match the query in update_or_create() you'll get the error MultipleObjectsReturned just like the get() method.

If you change a model record inadvertently, you can reinstate its data from the database with the `refresh_from_db()` method, as illustrated in Listing 8-9.

Listing 8-9. Update model record from database with the refresh_from_db() method

```
from coffeehouse.stores.models import Store

store_corporate = Store.objects.get(id=1)
store_corporate.name = 'Not sure about this name'

# Update from db again
store_corporate.refresh_from_db()  # Model record name now reflects value in database again
store_corporate.name

# Multiple edits
store_corporate.name = 'New store name'
store_corporate.email = 'newemail@coffeehouse.com' store_corporate.address =
'To be confirmed'

# Update from db again, but only address field
# so store name and email remain with local values
store_corporate.refresh_from_db(fields=['address'])
```

As you can see in Listing 8-9, after changing the name field value on a model record, you can call the `refresh_from_db()` method on the reference to update the model record as it's in the database. The second example in Listing 8-9 uses the `refresh_from_db()` method with the `fields` argument, which tells Django to only update the model fields declared in the `fields` list, allowing any (local) edits made to other fields to remain unchanged.

Delete a Single Record with delete()

If you already have a reference to a record, deleting it is as simple as invoking the `delete()` method on it. Listing 8-10 illustrates this process.

Listing 8-10. Delete model record with the delete() method

```
# Import Django model class
from coffeehouse.stores.models import Store

# Get the store with the name "Downtown" or equivalent SQL: 'SELECT....WHERE
name = "Downtown"

downtown_store = Store.objects.get(name="Downtown")
# Call delete() to delete the record in the database
downtown_store.delete()
```

For cases where you don't yet have a reference to a record you want to delete, it can be slightly inefficient to first get it (i.e., issue a SELECT query) and then delete it with the `delete()` method. For such cases you can use the `delete()` method and append it to a query so everything is done in a single operation. Listing 8-11 illustrates this process.

Listing 8-11. Delete model record with the delete() method on query

```
from coffeehouse.items.models import Menu

Menu.objects.filter(id=1).delete()
```

Irrespective of the `delete()` method you use - directly on reference or through the `objects` model manager - a `delete()` method always returns a dictionary with the results of the delete operation. For example, if the delete operation in 8-11 is successful it returns `(1, {'items.Menu': 1})` indicating one record of the `items.Menu` type was deleted. If the delete operation in 8-10 is successful, it returns `(5, {'stores.Store_amenities': 4, 'stores.Store': 1})` indicating five overall records were deleted, four of the `stores.Store_amenities` type and one of the `stores.Store` - in this case multiple records are deleted because `stores.Store_amenities` is a model relationship in the `Store` model.

■ **Caution** The delete() method can delete multiple records if you're not careful. The delete() method is preceded by the objects.filter() method that can return query results with multiple records. Notice in Listing 8-11 the query uses an id field to define the query, ensuring that only a single record matches the query, because id is a table's primary key. If the query definition in objects.filter() uses a less strict lookup (e.g., a string) you can inadvertently delete more records than you expect.

CRUD Multiple Records in Django Models

In this section you'll learn how to work with multiple records in Django models. Although the process is just as easy as working with single records, working with multiple records can require multiple database calls, as well as caching techniques and bulk operations, all of which need to be taken into account to minimize execution times.

Create Multiple Records with bulk_create()

To create multiple records based on a Django model you can use the built-in bulk_create() method. The advantage of the bulk_create() method is that it creates all entries in a single query, so it's very efficient if you have a list of a dozen or a hundred entries you wish to create. Listing 8-12 illustrates the process to create multiple records for the Store model.

Listing 8-12. Create multiple records of a Django model with the bulk_create() method

```
# Import Django model class
from coffeehouse.stores.models import Store

# Create model Store instances
store_corporate = Store(name='Corporate',address='624 Broadway',city ='San Diego',state='CA',
email='corporate@coffeehouse.com')
store_downtown = Store(name='Downtown',address='Horton Plaza',city ='San Diego',state='CA',
email='downtown@coffeehouse.com')
store_uptown = Store(name='Uptown',address='240 University Ave',city ='San
Diego',state='CA',email='uptown@coffeehouse.com')
store_midtown = Store(name='Midtown',address='784 W Washington St',city ='San Diego',
state='CA',email='midtown@coffeehouse.com')

# Create store list
store_list = [store_corporate,store_downtown,store_uptown,store_midtown]

# Call bulk_create to create records in a single call
Store.objects.bulk_create(store_list)
```

In Listing 8-12 you can see the bulk_create() method accepts a list of model instances to create all records in one step. But as efficient as the bulk_create() method is, you should be aware it has certain limitations:

- It does not support pre-save and post-save model signals.- To speed things up and unlike the save() method to create single records, the bulk_create() method does not execute pre-save and post-save model signals. If you're unfamiliar with the model signal concept, pre-save and post-save model signals allow the execution of custom logic prior and after a model record is saved, a topic covered in the previous chapter.
- It does not support models that span multiple tables (i.e., have relationships among one another).- Because records are created in bulk, there is no way to obtain primary key references for the first type of created records, which are then used to create related child records. If a model spans multiple tables, then you must individually create each record using the save() method, which does support creating records that span multiple tables.

If you face these limitations for the bulk_create() method, the only alternative is to loop over each record and use the save() method to create each entry, as illustrated in Listing 8-13.

Listing 8-13. Create multiple records with the save() method

```
# Same store_list as Listing 8-12

# Loop over each store and invoke save() on each entry # save() method called on each list
member to create record
for store in store_list:
    store.save()
```

As I mentioned when I introduced the `bulk_create()` method, the process in Listing 8-13 can be highly inefficient if it's done for dozens or hundreds of records, but sometimes it's the only option to create multiple records in bulk. However, the speed issues related to Listing 8-13 can be improved if you manually deal with model transactions.

Listing 8-14 illustrates how to use the `save()` method and group the entire record creation process in a single transaction to speed up the bulk creation process.

Listing 8-14. Create multiple records with save() method in a single transaction

```
# Import Django model and transaction class
from coffeehouse.stores.models import Store
from django.db import transaction

# Create store list, with same references from Listing 8-12
first_store_list = [store_corporate,store_downtown]
second_store_list = [store_uptown,store_midtown]

# Trigger atomic transaction so loop is executed in a single transaction
with transaction.atomic():
    # Loop over each store and invoke save() on each entry
    for store in first_store_list:
        # save() method called on each member to create record
        store.save()

# Method decorated with @transaction.atomic to ensure logic is executed in single
transaction
@transaction.atomic
def bulk_store_creator(store_list):
    # Loop over each store and invoke save() on each entry
    for store in store_list:
        # save() method called on each member to create record
        store.save()

# Call bulk_store_creator with Store list
bulk_store_creator(second_store_list)
```

As you can see in Listing 8-14, there are two ways to create bulk operations in a single database transaction, both using the `django.db.transaction` package. The first instance uses the `with transaction.atomic():` statement, so any nested code within this statement is run in a single transaction. The second instance uses the `@transaction.atomic` method decorator, which ensures the method operations are run in a single transaction.

BE CAREFUL WITH EXPLICIT TRANSACTIONS

There's a reason Django's default database transaction mechanism creates transactions on every query: it's to err on the safe side and minimize the potential for data loss.

If you decide to use explicit transactions to improve performance – as illustrated in Listing 8-14 – be aware that either all or no records are created. Although this can be a desired behavior, for certain circumstances it might lead to unexpected results. Make sure you understand the implications of transactions on the data you're working with. The previous chapter contains a section discussing the topic of Django model transactions in greater detail.

Read Multiple Records with all(), filter(), exclude(), or in_bulk()

To read multiple records associated with a Django model you can use several methods, which include `all()`, `filter()`, `exclude()`, and `in_bulk()`. The purpose of the `all()` method should be self-explanatory: it retrieves all the records of a given model. The `filter()` method is used to restrict query results on a given model property, for example, `filter(state='CA')` is a query to get all model records with `state='CA'`. And the `exclude()` method is used to execute a query that excludes records on a given model property, for example, `exclude(state='AZ')` is a query to get all model records except those with `state='AZ'`.

It's also possible to chain `filter()` and `exclude()` methods to create more complex multiple record queries. For example, `filter(state='CA').exclude(city='San Diego')` is a query to get all model records with `state='CA'` and exclude those with `city='San Diego'`. Listing 8-15 illustrates more multiple record query examples.

Listing 8-15. Read multiple records with with all(), filter(), and exclude() methods

```
# Import Django model class
from coffeehouse.stores.models import Store

# Query with all() method or equivalent SQL: 'SELECT * FROM ...'
all_stores = Store.objects.all()

# Query with include() method or equivalent SQL: 'SELECT....WHERE city = "San Diego"'
san_diego_stores = Store.objects.filter(city='San Diego')

# Query with exclude() method or equivalent SQL: 'SELECT....WHERE NOT (city = "San Diego")'
non_san_diego_stores = Store.objects.exclude(city='San Diego')

# Query with include() and exclude() methods or equivalent SQL: 'SELECT....WHERE
STATE='CA' AND NOT (city = "San Diego")'
ca_stores_without_san_diego = Store.objects.filter(state='CA').exclude(city='San Diego')
```

APPEND .QUERY TO VIEW THE ACTUAL SQL

Sometimes it can be helpful or even necessary to view the actual SQL executed by a Django model query. You can do so by appending .query to a query, as illustrated in the following listing:

```
from coffeehouse.stores.models import Store

import logging
stdlogger = logging.getLogger(__name__)

# Get the Store records with city San Diego
san_diego_stores = Store.objects.filter(city='San Diego')
stdlogger.debug("Query %s" % str(san_diego_stores.query))
# You can also use print(san_diego_stores.query)
```

As you can see in the previous snippet, you can output the SQL query to a Python logger or use the 'quick & dirty' print statement. Note that .query only works with queries that output QuerySets, so it doesn't work with queries like with the get() method – more on QuerySets shortly. Chapter 5 describes other alternatives to inspect the SQL used by model queries (e.g., Django debug toolbar) and Chapter 3 shows how to output SQL queries in Django templates (e.g. Debug context processor sql_queries variable).

■ **Tip** In addition to single fields – city="San Diego" or state="CA" – the all(), filter(), and exclude() methods can also accept multiple fields to produce an *and* query (e.g., filter(city="San Diego", state="CA") to get records were both city and state match). See the later section in the chapter on queries classified by SQL keyword.

Besides the `all()`, `filter()`, and `exclude()` methods, Django models also support the `in_bulk()` method. The `in_bulk()` method is designed to efficiently read many records, just like the `bulk_create()` method - described in the past section - is used to efficiently create many records.

The `in_bulk()` method is more efficient to read many records vs. the `all()`, `filter()`,and `exclude()` methods, because all the latter methods produce a QuerySet and the former produces a standard Python dictionary. Listing 8-16 illustrates the use of the `in_bulk()` method.

Listing 8-16. Read multiple records with with in_bulk() method

```
# Import Django model class
from coffeehouse.stores.models import Store

# Query with in_bulk() all
Store.objects.in_bulk()
# Outputs: {1: <Store: Corporate (San Diego,CA)>, 2: <Store: Downtown (San Diego,CA)>,
3: <Store: Uptown (San Diego,CA)>, 4: <Store: Midtown (San Diego,CA)>}

# Compare in_bulk query to all() that produces QuerySet
Store.objects.all()
```

```
# Outputs: <QuerySet [<Store: Corporate (San Diego,CA)>, <Store: Downtown (San Diego,CA)>,
<Store: Uptown (San Diego,CA)>, <Store: Midtown (San Diego,CA)>]>

# Query to get single Store by id
Store.objects.in_bulk([1])
# Outputs: {1: <Store: Corporate (San Diego,CA)>}

# Query to get multiple Stores by id
Store.objects.in_bulk([2,3])
# Outputs: {2: <Store: Downtown (San Diego,CA)>, 3: <Store: Uptown (San Diego,CA)>}
```

The first example in Listing 8-16 uses the `in_bulk()` method without any arguments to produce a dictionary will the records of the Store model (i.e., just like the `all()` method). However, notice how the output of the `in_bulk()` method is a standard Python dictionary, where each key corresponds to the `id` value of the record.

The remaining examples in Listing 8-16 illustrate how the `in_bulk()` method can accept a list of values to specify which record id's should be read from the database. Here again, notice that although the behavior is similar to the `filter()` or `exclude()` methods, the output is a standard Python dictionary vs. a `QuerySet` data structure.

Now that you have a clear understanding of the various methods that can read multiple model records and how some methods produce a `QuerySet` and other don't, it begets the question, what is a `QuerySet` and why is it used in the first place? So before we move on to the next parts of this broader section - on how to do CRUD operations on multiple records - we'll take a brief detour to explore the `QuerySet` data type.

Understanding a QuerySet: Lazy Evaluation and Caching

The first important characteristic of a `QuerySet` data type is technically known as lazy evaluation. This means a `QuerySet` isn't executed against the database right away, it just waits until it's evaluated. In other words, the act of running a snippet like `Store.objects.all()` doesn't involve any database activity right away. Listing 8-17 illustrates how you can even chain query after query and still not trigger database activity.

Listing 8-17. Chained model methods to illustrate concept of QuerySet lazy evaluation

```
# Import Django model class
from coffeehouse.stores.models import Store

# Query with all() method
stores = Store.objects.all()
# Chain filter() method on query
stores = stores.filter(state='CA')
# Chain exclude() method on query
stores = stores.exclude(city='San Diego')
```

Notice the three different statements in Listing 8-17 that chain the `all()`, `filter()`, and `exclude()` methods. Although it can appear Listing 8-17 makes three database calls to get `Store` records with `state='CA'` and excludes those with `city='San Diego'`, there is no database activity!

This is how `QuerySet` data structures are designed to work. So when does a query made on a `QuerySet` data type hit the database? There are many triggers that make a `QuerySet` evaluate and invoke an actual database call. Table 8-1 illustrates the various triggers.

Table 8-1. *Django QuerySet evaluation triggers that invoke an actual database call*

Evaluation Trigger	Description	Example
Iteration	Creating a loop on a QuerySet triggers a database call.	for store in Store.objects.all():
Slicing with 'step' argument	Slicing a QuerySet with a third argument (a.k.a. 'step' or 'stride' argument) triggers a database call. NOTE: Slicing a Queryset with 1 or 2 arguments just creates another QuerySet.	# A list of every 5th record, for the first 100 records Store.objects.all()[:100:5] # This does NOT trigger a database hit, (2 arguments) # Records 50 to 100 Store.objects.all()[49:99] # All records starting from the 6th Store.objects.all()[5:] # This does NOT trigger a database hit (1 argument) Store.objects.all()[0] # First record
Pickling*	Pickling a QuerySet forces all the results to be loaded into memory prior to pickling.	import pickle stores = Store.objects.all() pickled_stores = pickle.dumps(stores)
repr() method	Calling repr() on a QuerySet triggers a database call. NOTE: This is for convenience in the Python interactive interpreter, so you can immediately see query results.	repr(Store.objects.all())

len() method	Calling len() on a QuerySet triggers a database call. NOTE: If you only want the number of records, it's more efficient to use the Django model count() method.	total_stores = len(Store.objects.all())
		#NOTE: The count() method is more efficient to get a total count
		efficient_total_stores = Store.objects.count()

list() method	Calling list() on a QuerySet triggers a database call.	store_list = list(Store.objects.all())

Boolean tests (bool(), or, and or if statements)	Making a Boolean test on a QuerySet triggers a database call. NOTE: If you only want to check if a record exists, it's more efficient to use the Django model exists() method.	# Check if there's a store with city='San Diego'
		if Store.objects.filter(city='San Diego'):
		# There is a store in 'San Diego'
		pass
		#NOTE: The exists() method is more efficient for a Boolean check
		san_diego_stores = Store.objects.exists(city='San Diego')

** Pickling is Python's standard mechanism for object serialization, a process that converts a Python object into a character stream. The character stream contains all the information necessary to reconstruct the object at a later time. Pickling in the context of Django queries is typically used for heavyweight queries in an attempt to save resources (e.g., make a heavyweight query, pickle it, and on subsequent occasions consult the pickled query). You can consider pickling Django queries a rudimentary form of caching.*

Now that you know the triggers that cause a QuerySet to make a call to a database, let's take a look at other important QuerySet subject: caching.

Every QuerySet contains a cache to minimize database access. The first time a QuerySet is evaluated and a database query takes place - see evaluation triggers in Table 8-1 - Django saves the results in the QuerySet's cache for later use.

A QuerySet's cache is most useful when an application has a recurring need to use the same data, as it leads to less hits on a database. However, leveraging a QuerySet's cache comes with a few subtleties tied to the evaluation of a QuerySet. A rule of thumb is to first evaluate a QuerySet you plan to use more than once and proceed to use its data to leverage the QuerySet cache. This is best explained with the examples presented in Listing 8-18.

Listing 8-18. QuerySet caching behavior

```
# Import Django model class
from coffeehouse.stores.models import Store

# CACHE USING SEQUENCE
# Query awaiting evaluation
lazy_stores = Store.objects.all()
# Iteration triggers evaluation and hits database
store_emails = [store.email for store in lazy_stores]
# Uses QuerySet cache from lazy_stores, since lazy_stores is evaluated in previous line
store_names = [store.name for store in lazy_stores]

# NON-CACHE SEQUENCE
# Iteration triggers evaluation and hits database
heavy_store_emails = [store.email for store in Store.objects.all()]
# Iteration triggers evaluation and hits database again, because it uses another
QuerySet ref
heavy_store_names = [store.name for store in Store.objects.all()]

# CACHE USING SEQUENCE
# Query wrapped as list() for immediate evaluation
stores = list(Store.objects.all())
# Uses QuerySet cache from stores
first_store  = stores[0]
# Uses QuerySet cache from stores
second_store = stores[1]
# Uses QuerySet cache from stores, set() is just used to eliminate duplicates
store_states = set([store.state for store in stores])
# Uses QuerySet cache from stores, set() is just used to eliminate duplicates
store_cities = set([store.city for store in stores])

# NON-CACHE SEQUENCE
# Query awaiting evaluation
all_stores = Store.objects.all()
# list() triggers evaluation and hits database
store_one = list(all_stores[0:1])
# list() triggers evaluation and hits database again, because partially evaluating a
QuerySet does not populate the cache
store_one_again = list(all_stores[0:1])
```

```
# CACHE USING SEQUENCE
# Query awaiting evaluation
coffee_stores = Store.objects.all()
# Iteration triggers evaluation and hits database
[store for store in coffee_stores]
# Uses QuerySet cache from coffee_stores, because it's evaluated fully in previous line
store_1 = coffee_stores[0]
# Uses QuerySet cache from coffee_stores, because it's already evaluated in full
store_1_again = coffee_stores[0]
```

As you can see in the examples in Listing 8-18, sequences that leverage a QuerySet's cache trigger the evaluation of the QuerySet right away and then use a reference to the evaluated QuerySet to access the cached data. Sequences that don't use a QuerySet cache either constantly create identical QuerySet statements or make the evaluation process late for each data assignment.

The only edge case for caching QuerySet's that doesn't fit the previous behavior is the second to last example in Listing 8-18. If you trigger a partial evaluation of QuerySet by slicing it (e.g., [0] or [1:5]) the cache is not populated. So to ensure a QuerySet cache is used, you must evaluate a QuerySet and then slice the results, as illustrated in the last example in Listing 8-18.

Read Performance Methods: defer(), only(), values(), values_list(), iterator(), exists(), and none()

Although QuerySet data structures represent a step forward toward dealing with multiple data records by integrating lazy evaluation and caching mechanisms, they don't cover the entire performance spectrum needed to deal with large data queries.

A common performance problem you'll face with large data queries is related to reading unnecessary record fields. Although selectively choosing which fields to read from a database record can be an afterthought in most circumstances, it can have an important impact for queries made on Django models with more than a couple of fields.

The first methods available to increase performance while reading model records are the defer() and only() methods, both of which are intended to delimit which fields to read in a query. The defer() and only() methods accept a list of fields to defer or load, respectively, and are complementary to one another depending on what you want to achieve. For example, if you want to defer loading the majority of model fields, it's simpler to specify which fields to load with only(), if you want to defer loading one or a few fields in a model you can specify the fields in the defer() method. Listing 8-19 illustrates the use of the defer() and only() methods.

Listing 8-19. Read performance with defer() and only() to selectively read record fields

```
from coffeehouse.stores.models import Store
from coffeehouse.items.models import Item

# Item names on the breakfast menu
breakfast_items = Item.objects.filter(menu__name='Breakfast').only('name')

# All Store records with no email
all_stores = Store.objects.defer('email').all()

# Confirm loaded fields on overall query
breakfast_items.query.get_loaded_field_names()
# Outputs: {<class 'coffeehouse.items.models.Item'>: {'id', 'name'}}
```

```
all_stores.query.get_loaded_field_names()
# Outputs: {<class 'coffeehouse.stores.models.Store'>: {'id', 'address', 'state', 'city', 'name'}}

# Confirm deferred fields on individual model records breakfast_items[0].get_deferred_fields()
# Outputs: {'calories', 'stock', 'price', 'menu_id', 'size', 'description'}
all_stores[1].get_deferred_fields()
# Outputs: {'email'}

# Access deferred fields, note each call on a deferred field implies a database hit
breakfast_items[0].price
breakfast_items[0].size
all_stores[1].email
```

As you can see in Listing 8-19, both the `defer()` and `only()` methods can be chained to a model manager (i.e., `objects`) either at the start or end of a query, as well as be used in conjunction with other methods like `all()` and `filter()`. In addition, notice how both methods can accept a list of fields to defer or load.

To verify which model fields have been deferred or loaded, Listing 8-19 illustrates two alternatives. The first technique consists of calling the `get_loaded_field_names()` on the query reference of a query statement to get a list of loaded fields. The second technique consists of calling the `get_deferred_fields()` method on a model instance to obtain a list of deferred fields.

So how do you obtain deferred fields? Easy, you cast call them. Toward the end of Listing 8-18, notice how even though the `breakfast_items` represents a query that only loads the `name` field, a call is made to the get the value of the `price` and `size` fields. Similarly, the `all_stores` reference in Listing 8-19 represents a query that defers the `email` field; nevertheless you can get a record's `email` field value by just calling it. Although this last technique requires an additional database hit to get the deferred field(s), it also illustrates how easy it is to get a record's entire fields even if they're deferred.

The `values()` and `values_list()` methods offer another alternative to delimit the fields fetched by a query. Unlike the `defer()` and `only()` methods that produce a `QuerySet` of model instances, the `values()` and `values_list()` methods produce `QuerySet` instances composed of plain dictionaries, tuples, or lists. This has the performance advantage of not creating full-fledged model instances, albeit this also has the disadvantage of not having access to full-fledged model instances.

The `values()` and `values_list()` methods accept a list of fields to load as part of a query, a process that's illustrated in Listing 8-20.

■ **Tip** You can use the values() and values_list() methods without any field argument to produce full model records as plain dictionaries, tuples, or lists.

Listing 8-20. Read performance with values() and values_list() to selectively read record fields

```
from coffeehouse.stores.models import Store
from coffeehouse.items.models import Item

# Item names on the breakfast menu
breakfast_items = Item.objects.filter(menu__name='Breakfast').values('name')
print(breakfast_items)
# Outputs: <QuerySet [{'name': 'Whole-Grain Oatmeal'}, {'name': 'Bacon, Egg & Cheese Biscuit'}]>
```

```
# All Store records with no email
all_stores = Store.objects.values_list('email','name','city').all()
print(all_stores)
# Outputs: <QuerySet [('corporate@coffeehouse.com', 'Corporate', 'San Diego'),
('downtown@coffeehouse.com', 'Downtown', 'San Diego'), ('uptown@coffeehouse.com',
'Uptown', 'San Diego'), ('midtown@coffeehouse.com', 'Midtown', 'San Diego')]>

all_stores_flat = Store.objects.values_list('email',flat=True).all()
print(all_stores_flat)
# Outputs: <QuerySet ['corporate@coffeehouse.com', 'downtown@coffeehouse.com', 'midtown@
coffeehouse.com', 'uptown@coffeehouse.com']>

# It isn't possible to access undeclared model fields with values() and values_list()
breakfast_items[0].price #ERROR
# Outputs AttributeError: 'dict' object has no attribute 'price'
```

The first variation in Listing 8-20 generates an Item QuerySet with the name field, which as you can see produces a list of dictionaries with only the name field and value. Next, a query is made to get the email, name, and city fields for all Store models using the values_list() method. Notice that unlike the values() method, the values_list() method produces a more compact structure in the form of a tuple. In Listing 8-20 you can also see the values_list() method accepts the optional flat=True argument to flatten the resulting tuple into a plain list.

Finally, toward the end of Listing 8-20 you can see that when using the values() and values_list() methods it isn't possible to obtain undeclared fields by just calling them, like it's possible with the defer() and only() methods. This behavior is due to the water-down QuerySet produced by the values() and values_list() methods, which aren't full-fledged model objects.

The iterator() method is yet another option available in Django models that creates an iterator over the results of a QuerySet. The iterator() method is ideal for large queries that are intended to be used once, as this lowers the required memory to store data, which is an inherent property of all Python iterators. Listing 8-21 illustrates a query that uses the iterator() method and appendix A describes the core concepts behind Python iterators.

Listing 8-21. Read performance with iterator(), exists(), and none()

```
from coffeehouse.stores.models import Store

# All Store with iterator()
stores_on_iterator = Store.objects.all().iterator()

print(stores_on_iterator)
# Outputs: <generator object __iter__ at 0x7f2864db8fc0>

# Advance through iterator with __next__()
stores_on_iterator.__next__()
# Outputs: <Store: Corporate (San Diego,CA)>

stores_on_iterator.__next__()
# Outputs: <Store: Downtown (San Diego,CA)>

# Check if Store object with id=5 exists
Store.objects.filter(id=5).exists()
# Outputs: False
```

```
# Create empty QuerySet on Store model
Store.objects.none()
# Outputs: <QuerySet []>
```

Another Django model read performance technique is the exists() method, which is illustrated in Listing 8-21 and is used to verify if a query returns data. Although the exists() method executes a query against the database, the query used by exists() is a simplified version compared to a standard query, in addition to the exists() method returning a Boolean True or False value compared to a full-fledged QuerySet. This makes the exists() method a good option for queries that operate on conditionals, where it's only necessary to verify if model records exists and the actual records data is unnecessary.

Finally, the Django model none() method - illustrated at the end of Listing 8-21 - is used to generate an empty QuerySet, specifically of a subclass named EmptyQuerySet. The none() method is helpful for cases where you knowingly need to assign an empty model QuerySet, such as edge cases related to Django model forms or Django templates, which expect a QuerySet instance in one way or another. In such cases, it becomes necessary to create a dummy QuerySet, instead of inefficiently creating QuerySet that return data and deleting its contents.

As you've learned in this subsection, in addition to the QuerySet data structure, Django also offers many methods specifically designed to efficiently read large or small amounts of records associated with Django models.

■ **Tip** Remember the in_bulk() method from the past section also provides read performance over the basic all(), filter(), and exclude() methods.

Update Multiple Records with update() or select_for_update()

In the section on single record CRUD operations, you explored how to update single records with the update() method; this same method can handle updating multiple records. This process is illustrated in Listing 8-22.

Listing 8-22. Update multiple records with the update() method

```
from coffeehouse.stores.models import Store

Store.objects.all().update(email="contact@coffeehouse.com")

from coffeehouse.items.models import Item
from django.db.models import F

Item.objects.all().update(stock=F('stock') +100)
```

The first example in Listing 8-22 uses the update() method to update all Store records and set their email value to contact@coffeehouse.com. The second example uses a Django F expression and the update() method to update all Drink records and set their stock value to the current stock value plus 100. Django F expressions allow you to reference model fields within a query, which is necessary in this case to perform the update in a single operation.

Although the update() method guarantees everything is done in a single operation to avoid race conditions, on certain occasions the update() method may not be enough to do complex updates. Offering another alternative to update multiple records is the select_for_update() method that locks rows on the given query until the update is marked as done. Listing 8-23 illustrates an example of the select_for_update() method.

SELECT_FOR_UPDATE() SUPPORT IS DATABASE DEPENDENT

Under the hood, the Django select_for_update() method is based on SQL's SELECT…FOR UPDATE syntax that is not supported by all databases. Postgres, Oracle, and MySQL databases support this functionality, but SQLite does not.

In addition, there's the special argument nowait (e.g., select_for_update(nowait=True) to make a query non-blocking). By default, if another transaction acquires a lock on one of the selected rows, the select_for_update() query blocks until the lock is released. If you use nowait, this allows a query to run right away and in case a conflicting lock is already acquired by another transaction the DatabaseError is raised when the QuerySet is evaluated. Be aware though, MySQL does not support the nowait argument and if used with MySQL, Django throws a DatabaseError.

Listing 8-23. Update multiple records with a Django model with the select_for_update() method

```
# Import Django model class
from coffeehouse.stores.models import Store
from django.db import transaction

# Trigger atomic transaction so loop is executed in a single transaction
with transaction.atomic():
    store_list = Store.objects.select_for_update().filter(state='CA')
    # Loop over each store to update and invoke save() on each entry
    for store in store_list:
        # Add complex update logic here for each store
        # save() method called on each member to update
        store.save()

# Method decorated with @transaction.atomic to ensure logic is executed in single
transaction
@transaction.atomic
def bulk_store_updae(store_list):
    store_list = Store.objects.select_for_update().exclude(state='CA')
    # Loop over each store and invoke save() on each entry
    for store in store_list:
        # Add complex update logic here for each store
        # save() method called on each member to update
        store.save()

# Call bulk_store_update to update store records
bulk_store_update(store_list_to_update)
```

Listing 8-23 shows two variations for `select_for_update()`, one using an explicit transaction and the other decorating a method to scope it inside a transaction. Both variations use the same logic; they first create a query with `select_for_update()`, then loop over the results to update each record and use `save()` to update individual records. In this manner the rows touched by the query remain locked to other changes until the transaction finishes.

Be aware that when using the `select_for_update()` it's absolutely necessary to use transactions using any of the techniques described in Listing 8-23. If you run the `select_for_update()` method in a database that supports it and you don't use transactions as illustrated in Listing 8-23 - maintaining Django's default auto-commit mode - Django throws a `TransactionManagementError` error because the rows cannot be locked as a group. Using the `select_for_update` method in a database that offers no support for it has no effect (i.e., you won't see an error).

Delete Multiple Records with delete()

To delete multiple records you use the `delete()` method and append it to a query. Listing 8-24 illustrates this process.

Listing 8-24. Delete model records with the delete() method

```
from coffeehouse.stores.models import Store

Store.objects.filter(city='San Diego').delete()
```

The example in Listing 8-24 uses the `delete()` method to delete the `Store` records with `city='San Diego'`.

CRUD Relationship Records Across Django Models

In the previous chapter, you learned how Django model relationships can help you improve data maintenance through special model data types (i.e., `ForgeignKey`, `ManyToManyField`, and `OneToOne`). CRUD operations made on Django model relationships also have a special syntax.

Although the same syntax from previous sections is applicable for *direct* operations made on Django model relationship data types, you can also make *reverse* operations on the model that's opposite to the Django model that defines the relationship data type.

■ **Note** Direct Django model operations operate through a Manager class, and reverse operations Django model operations are done through a RelatedManager class.

One to Many CRUD Operations

One to many relationships are established through `ForgeignKey` model data types. Listing 8-25 shows a one to many relationship between two models, including a series of direct query operations on the related model.

Listing 8-25. One to many ForeignKey direct query read operations

```
class Menu(models.Model):
    name = models.CharField(max_length=30)

class Item(models.Model):
    menu = models.ForeignKey(Menu, on_delete=models.CASCADE)
```

```
    name = models.CharField(max_length=30)
    description = models.CharField(max_length=100)

# Get the Menu of a given Item
Item.objects.get(name='Whole-Grain Oatmeal').menu.id

# Get the Menu id of a given Item
Item.objects.get(name='Whole-Grain Oatmeal').menu.name

# Get Item elements that belong to the Menu with name 'Drinks'
Item.objects.filter(menu__name='Drinks')
```

In Listing 8-25 you can see the Item model declares a ForeignKey relationship to the Menu model. Once an Item model is related to a Menu model in this way, it's possible to access a Menu model using Python's dot notation as shown in Listing 8-25 (e.g., menu.id and menu.name to get the id and name of the related Menu instance on the Item reference). Notice in Listing 8-25 it's also possible to create a query that references a related model using __ (two underscores) (a.k.a. "follow notation") to indicate a field in the related model.

The operations in Listing 8-25 use the same query syntax as non-relationship models, because the operations are created parting from the model that has the relationship data type. However, Django also supports CRUD operations initiated on models that don't have the relationship data type.

Listing 8-26 illustrates a series of CRUD actions made through an instance of the Menu model done against its related Item model. These tasks are called *reverse* operations, because the model holding the relationship - ForeignKey - is reached in reverse.

Listing 8-26. One to many ForeignKey reverse query read operations with _set syntax

```
from coffeehouse.items.models import Menu, Item

breakfast_menu = Menu.objects.get(name='Breakfast')

# Fetch all Item records for the Menu
breakfast_menu.item_set.all()

# Get the total Item count for the Menu
breakfast_menu.item_set.count()

# Fetch Item records that match a filter for the Menu
breakfast_menu.item_set.filter(name__startswith='Whole')
```

Listing 8-26 starts with a standard Django query for a Menu record. Although the Menu model lacks an explicit relationship to the Item model, the Item model does declare a relationship to a Menu model, and Django creates a reverse access pattern with the <one_model>.<many_model>_set syntax.

Therefore, parting from a Menu record, you can see it's possible to get all Item records that have a relationship with a Menu record using the menu_record.item_set.all() syntax. Similarly, as shown in the last example in Listing 8-26, it's possible to generate a query that filters a set of Item records parting from a Menu record using the same _set syntax.

■ **Tip** You can change the _set syntax to a more explicit name or disable this behavior altogether, with the related_name and related_query_name model field options. See the previous chapter section on "Options for Relationship Model Data Types" in the subsection "Reverse Relationship Options."

Just as the reverse _set syntax is used to perform read operations parting from models that don't have an explicit relationship field toward the model that has the relationship field, it's also possible to use the same _set syntax to execute other database operations (e.g., Create, Update, Delete), as illustrated in Listing 8-27.

Listing 8-27. One to many ForeignKey reverse query create, update, delete operations with _set syntax

```
from coffeehouse.items.models import Menu, Item

breakfast_menu = Menu.objects.get(name='Breakfast')

# Create an Item directly on the Menu
# NOTE: Django also supports the get_or_create() and update_or_create() operations
breakfast_menu.item_set.create(name='Bacon, Egg & Cheese Biscuit',description='A fresh
buttermilk biscuit...',calories=450)

# Create an Item separately and then add it to the Menu
new_menu_item = Item(name='Grilled Cheese',description='Flat bread or whole wheat
...',calories=500)
# Add item to menu using add()
# NOTE: bulk=False is necessary for new_menu_item to be saved by the Item model manager
first
# it isn't possible to call new_menu_item.save() directly because it lacks a menu instance
breakfast_menu.item_set.add(new_menu_item,bulk=False)

# Create copy of breakfast items for later
breakfast_items = [bi for bi in breakfast_menu.item_set.all()]

# Clear menu references from Item elements (i.e. reset the Item elements menu field to null)
# NOTE: This requires the ForeignKey definition to have null=True
# (e.g. models.ForeignKey(Menu, null=True)) so the key is allowed to be turned null
# otherwise the error 'RelatedManager' object has no attribute 'clear' is thrown
breakfast_menu.item_set.clear()

# Verify Item count is now 0
breakfast_menu.item_set.count()
0

# Reassign Item set from copy of breakfast items
breakfast_menu.item_set.set(breakfast_items)

# Verify Item count is now back to original count
breakfast_menu.item_set.count()
3

# Clear menu reference from single Item element (i.e. reset an Item element menu field to null)
# NOTE: This requires the ForeignKey definition to have null=True
# (e.g. models.ForeignKey(Menu, null=True)) so the key is allowed to be turned null
# otherwise the error 'RelatedManager' object has no attribute 'remove' is thrown
item_grilled_cheese = Item.objects.get(name='Grilled Cheese')
breakfast_menu.item_set.remove(item_grilled_cheese)
```

```
# Delete the Menu element along with its associated Item elements
# NOTE: This requires the ForeignKey definition to have blank=True and on_delete=models.
CASCADE (e.g. models.ForeignKey(Menu, blank=True, on_delete=models.CASCADE))
breakfast_menu.delete()
```

In Listing 8-27 you can see that after obtaining a reference to a Menu record, you can generate an Item record using the create() method directly on the _set reference. Listing 8-27 also illustrates how it's possible to first generate an Item record and later link it to a Menu record using the add() method that also works on the _set reference.

■ **Note** The add(), create(), remove(), clear(), and set() relationship methods all apply database changes immediately for all types of related fields. This means there's no need to call save() on either end of the relationship.

Next, Listing 8-27 is an example of the clear() relationship method. The clear() method is used to dissociate relationships, in the case of Listing 8-27, it sets the Menu reference for all Item records associated with a Menu named 'Breakfast' to NULL (i.e., it doesn't delete any data, it just removes the relationship reference). It's worth mentioning that in order to call the clear() method, a model field must be declared with the null=True option in order for the relationship reference to be set to NULL.

The add() relationship method in Listing 8-27 is used to associate a list of instances on a relationship. In the case of Listing 8-27, it reverts the logic made by the clear() method in the same listing. An important aspect of the add() relationship method is that behind the scenes it uses a model's standard update() method to add the relationship, and this in turn requires both model records to be previously saved before creating the relationship. You can bypass this limitation by using the bulk=False – used in Listing 8-27 – to delegate the save operation to the related manager and create the relationship without saving the related object beforehand.

The remove() relationship method works like the clear() relationship method, but is designed to dissociate relationships in a granular way. In the case of Listing 8-27, the remove() method sets the Menu reference for Item record named 'Grilled Cheese' to NULL (i.e., it doesn't delete any data, it just removes the relationship reference). Similar to the clear() relationship method, a model field must be declared with the null=True option in order for the relationship reference to be set to NULL.

Finally, Listing 8-27 illustrates how calling the delete() method on a model instance with a relationship deletes the instance on which it's called and also its related model instances. In the case of Listing 8-27, breakfast_menu.delete() deletes the Menu named 'Breakfast' and all the Item instances linked to it. Similar to the clear() and remove() relationship methods, the delete() relationship method requires a model field be declared with the on_delete=models.CASCADE option in order to automatically delete related models.

■ **Tip** See the previous chapter section on "Options for Relationship model Data Types" in the subsection "Data Integrity Options" for other on_delete options.

Many to Many CRUD Operations

In a similar fashion to one to many relationships, many to many relationships also support both direct and reverse CRUD operations. Listing 8-28 shows a many to many relationship between two models, including a series of direct query operations on the related model.

Listing 8-28. Many to many ManyToManyField direct query read operations

```
class Amenity(models.Model):
    name = models.CharField(max_length=30)
    description = models.CharField(max_length=100)

class Store(models.Model):
    name = models.CharField(max_length=30)
    address = models.CharField(max_length=30,unique=True)
    city = models.CharField(max_length=30)
    state = models.CharField(max_length=2)
    email = models.EmailField()
    amenities = models.ManyToManyField(Amenity,blank=True)

# Get the Amenity elements of a given Store
Store.objects.get(name='Downtown').amenities.all()

# Fetch store named Midtown
midtown_store = Store.objects.get(name='Midtown')

# Create and add Amenity element to Store
midtown_store.amenities.create(name='Laptop Lock',description='Ask our baristas...')

# Get all Store elements that have amenity id=3
Store.objects.filter(amenities__id=3)
```

In Listing 8-28 you can see the `Store` model declares a `ManyToManyField` relationship to the `Amenity` model. Once an `Store` model is related to an `Amenity` model in this way, it's possible to access the `Amenity` model using Python's dot notation as shown in Listing 8-28 (e.g., `amenities.all()` to get all related `Amenity` instance on the `Store` reference). In addition, Listing 8-28 also illustrates how it's possible to create `Amenity` instances using the `create()` method directly on the model `amenities` reference. Also notice in Listing 8-28 how it's possible to create a query that references a related model using __ (two underscores) (a.k.a. "follow notation") to indicate a field in the related model.

The operations in Listing 8-28 use the same query syntax as non-relationship models, because the operations are created parting from the model that has the relationship data type. However, Django also supports CRUD operations initiated on models that don't have the relationship data type.

Listing 8-29 illustrates a series of CRUD actions made through an instance of the `Amenity` model done against its related `Store` model. These tasks are called *reverse* operations, because the model holding the relationship - `ManyToManyField` - is reached in reverse.

Listing 8-29. Many to many ManyToManyField reverse query create, read, update, and delete operations with _set syntax

```
from coffeehouse.stores.models import Store, Amenity

wifi_amenity = Amenity.objects.get(name='WiFi')

# Fetch all Store records with Wifi Amenity
wifi_amenity.store_set.all()

# Get the total Store count for the Wifi Amenity
wifi_amenity.store_set.count()

# Fetch Store records that match a filter with the Wifi Amenity
wifi_amenity.store_set.filter(city__startswith='San Diego')

# Create a Store directly with the Wifi Amenity
# NOTE: Django also supports the get_or_create() and update_or_create() operations
wifi_amenity.store_set.create(name='Uptown',address='1240 University Ave...')

# Create a Store separately and then add the Wifi Amenity to it
new_store = Store(name='Midtown',address='844 W Washington St...')
new_store.save()
wifi_amenity.store_set.add(new_store)

# Create copy of breakfast items for later
wifi_stores = [ws for ws in wifi_amenity.store_set.all()]

# Clear all the Wifi amenity records in the junction table for all Store elements
wifi_amenity.store_set.clear()

# Verify Wifi count is now 0
wifi_amenity.store_set.count()
0

# Reassign Wifi set from copy of Store elements
wifi_amenity.store_set.set(wifi_stores)

# Verify Item count is now back to original count
wifi_amenity.store_set.count()
6

# Reassign Store set from copy of wifi stores
wifi_amenity.store_set.set(wifi_stores)

# Clear the Wifi amenity record from the junction table for a certain Store element
store_to_remove_amenity = Store.objects.get(name__startswith='844 W Washington St')
wifi_amenity.store_set.remove(store_to_remove_amenity)

# Delete the Wifi amenity element along with its associated junction table records for Store elements
wifi_amenity.delete()
```

In Listing 8-29 you can see the various examples of many to many Django model reverse query operations. Notice the similarities to the one to many relationship CRUD operation examples shown in Listings 8-26 and 8-27. Among the notable differences of calling relationship methods in one to many and many to many relationships, are the following:

- The `add()` and `remove()` relationship methods when applied on many to many models uses a model's standard `bulk_create()` and `delete()` methods to add and remove the relationship, respectively. This in turn means a model's standard `save()` method isn't called; therefore if either model's `save()` method executes custom logic, it will never run with the `add()` and `remove()` relationship methods. If you want to execute custom logic when a many to many relationship is created or removed, use the `m2m_changed` signal. See the previous chapter section on model signals for additional details.
- If you declare a custom junction table for a many to many model relationship, the `add()`, `create()`, `remove()`, and `set()` relationships methods are disabled. See the previous chapter section "Options for Relationship Model Data Types" in the subsection "Database Options" for how to use custom junction tables.

One to One CRUD Operations

CRUD operations on Django one to one relationships are much simpler than the previous relationship CRUD operations, simply because one to one relationships are inherently much simpler. In the previous chapter, you learned how one to one relationships resemble an inheritance hierarchy, where one model declares generic fields and a second (related) model inherits the fields of the former and adds more specialized fields.

This means one to one relationships just have direct query operations, as reverse operations don't make sense since models follow a hierarchy structure. Listing 8-30 shows a one to many relationship between two models, including a series of query operations on the related model.

Listing 8-30. One to one OneToOneField query operations

```
from coffeehouse.items.models import Item
# See Listing 8-25 for Item model definition

class Drink(models.Model):
    item = models.OneToOneField(Item,on_delete=models.CASCADE,primary_key=True)
    caffeine = models.IntegerField()

# Get Item instance named Mocha
mocha_item = Item.objects.get(name='Mocha')

# Access the Drink element and its fields through its base Item element
mocha_item.drink.caffeine

# Get Drink objects through Item with caffeine field less than 200
Item.objects.filter(drink__caffeine__lt=200)

# Delete the Item element and its associated Drink record
# NOTE: This deletes the associated Drink record due to the on_delete=models.CASCADE in the
OneToOneField definition
mocha_item.delete()
```

```
# Query a Drink through an Item property
Drink.objects.get(item__name='Latte')
```

As you can see in Listing 8-30, the operations for one to one Django model relationships are much simpler than the previous example, albeit the query operations still use the same dotted notation to move through the relationship models and fields as well as __ (two underscores) (a.k.a. "follow notation") to perform queries by field on the related model.

Read Performance Relationship Methods: select_related() and prefetch_related()

In these last Django model relationship CRUD operation sections — Listings 8-25 through 8-30 — you learned how easy it is to traverse from one model to another model via its relationship field to access other fields. For example, for a one to many relationship between an `Item` and `Menu` model, you can access the name field on a `Menu` record using the syntax `item.menu.name`; similarly for a many to many relationship between a `Store` and `Amenity` model, you can access the `name` field on an `Amenity` record using the syntax `store.amenities.all()[0].name`.

While this dot notation provides an effortless approach to access fields in related models - similar to how the `defer()` and `load()` methods allow effortless access to deferred data - this technique also generates additional database hits that can be prevented with the `select_related()` and `prefetch_related()` methods.

The `selected_related()` method accepts related model fields arguments that should be read as part of an initial query. Although this creates a more complex initial query, it avoids additional database hits on related model fields. Listing 8-31 illustrates an example of the `select_related()` method, along with a query that forgoes its use.

Listing 8-31. Django model select_related syntax and generated SQL

```
from coffeehouse.items.models import Item
# See Listing 8-25 for Item and Menu model definitions

# Inefficient access to related model
for item in Item.objects.all():
     item.menu # Each call to menu creates an additional database hit

# Efficient access to related model with selected_related()
for item in Item.objects.select_related('menu').all():
     item.menu # All menu data references have been fetched on initial query

# Raw SQL query with select_related
print(Item.objects.select_related('menu').all().query)
SELECT "items_item"."id", "items_item"."menu_id", "items_item"."name", "items_
item"."description", "items_item"."size", "items_item"."calories", "items_item"."price",
"items_item"."stock", "items_menu"."id", "items_menu"."name" FROM "items_item" LEFT OUTER
JOIN "items_menu" ON ("items_item"."menu_id" = "items_menu"."id")

# Raw SQL query without select_related
print(Item.objects.all().query)
SELECT "items_item"."id", "items_item"."menu_id", "items_item"."name", "items_
item"."description", "items_item"."size", "items_item"."calories", "items_item"."price",
"items_item"."stock" FROM "items_item"
```

In Listing 8-31 you can see there are two variations to access the related Menu model for all Item model records. The first variation uses the Item.objects.all() syntax to get all Item model records and then directly accesses the menu field to gain access to the corresponding Menu record. The problem with this approach is that getting the Menu record for each Item record generates an additional database hit, so if you have 100 Item records this implies an additional 100 database hits!

The second variation in Listing 8-31 adds the select_related('menu') method to the query, ensuring the related Menu record for each Item record is also fetched as part of the initial query. This technique guarantees that all relationship data is fetched in a single query.

In the bottom half of Listing 8-31 you can see the raw SQL generated when the select_related() method is used and omitted. When select_related() is used, a more complex LEFT OUTER JOIN query is used to ensure all related data is read in one step.

The prefetch_related() method solves the same problem as the select_related() method, but does so using a different technique. As you saw in Listing 8-31, the select_related() method fetches related model data in a single query by means of a database JOIN; however, the prefetch_related() method executes its join logic once the data is in Python.

Although a database JOIN solves a multi-query problem in a single query, it's a heavyweight operation that is often used sparingly. For this reason, the select_related() method is limited to single value relationships (i.e., ForeignKey and OneToOneField model fields), since multi-value relationships associated with a junction table (i.e., ManyToManyField) can produce an inordinate amount of data in a single query.

When a query uses the prefetch_related() method, Django first executes the primary query and later generates QuerySet instances for all the related models declared inside the prefetch_related() method. All of this happens in a single step, so by the time you attempt to access related model references, Django already has a pre-filled cache of related results, which it joins as Python data structures to produce the final results. Listing 8-32 illustrates an example of the prefetch_related() method.

Listing 8-32. Django model prefetch_related syntax and generated SQL

```
from coffeehouse.items.models import Item
from coffeehouse.stores.models import Store
# See Listing 8-25 for Item  model definitions
# See Listing 8-28 for Store  model definitions

# Efficient access to related model with prefetch_related()
for item in Item.objects.prefetch_related('menu').all():
     item.menu # All menu data references have been fetched on initial query

# Efficient access to many to many related model with prefetch_related()
# NOTE Store.objects.select_related('amenities').all() is invalid due to many to many model
for store in Store.objects.prefetch_related('amenities').all():
     store.amenities.all()

# Raw SQL query with prefetch_related
print(Item.objects.prefetch_related('menu').all().query)
SELECT "items_item"."id", "items_item"."menu_id", "items_item"."name", "items_
item"."description", "items_item"."size", "items_item"."calories", "items_item"."price",
"items_item"."stock" FROM "items_item"

# Raw SQL query with prefetch_related
print(Store.objects.prefetch_related('amenities').all().query)
SELECT "stores_store"."id", "stores_store"."name", "stores_store"."address", "stores_
store"."city", "stores_store"."state", "stores_store"."email" FROM "stores_store"
```

The first query in Listing 8-32 is equivalent to the query presented in Listing 8-31 that fetches the related `Menu` model for all `Item` model records, except that it uses the `prefetch_related()` method. The second query in Listing 8-32 is made on a many to many model relationship to fetch the related `amenities` model instances for all `Store` model records using the `prefetch_related()` method. It's worth mentioning this last query is only possible with the `prefetch_related()` method because it's a many to many model relationship.

Finally, in the bottom half of Listing 8-32, you can confirm the raw SQL produced by queries that use the `prefetch_related()` method appear as a plain SQL query (i.e., no JOIN). In this case, it's Django/Python itself that's charged with managing and creating the additional `QuerySet` data structures needed to efficiently read related model data.

■ **Tip** The prefetch_related() method can be further optimized with a Prefetch() object to further filter a prefetch operation or inclusively use selected_related.[1]

Model Queries by SQL Keyword

In the previous sections you learned how to query single, multiple and related records with Django model methods. However, the matching process was done for the most part on exact values. For example, a query for the `Store` record with `id=1` translated into the SQL `WHERE ID=1` or a query for all `Store` records with `state="CA"` translated into the SQL `WHERE STATE="CA"`.

In reality, exact SQL matching patterns are far from most real world scenarios that require finer grained SQL queries. In the following sub-sections, you'll learn about the various Django model query options classified by SQL keywords, this way you can easily identify the required Django syntax using the better known SQL keywords as identifiers.

WHERE Queries: Django Field Lookups

The SQL WHERE keyword is among the most used keywords in relational database queries, because it's used to delimit the amount of records in a query through a field value. Up to this point, you've mostly used the SQL WHERE keyword to create queries on exact values (e.g., `WHERE ID=1`); however, there are many other variations of the SQL WHERE keyword.

In Django models, variations of the SQL WHERE keyword are supported through field lookups, which are keywords appended to field filters using __ (two underscores) (a.k.a. "follow notation").

THE PK LOOKUP SHORTCUT

Django queries rely on model field names to classify queries. For example, the SQL WHERE ID=1 statement in a Django query is written as ...(id=1), and the SQL WHERE NAME="CA" statement in a Django query is written as ...(state="CA").

In addition, Django models can also use the pk shortcut – where pk="primary key" – to perform queries against a model's primary key. By default, a Django model's id field is the primary key, so id field and pk shortcut queries are considered equivalent (e.g., Store.objects.get(id=1) Store.objects.get(pk=1)).

A query with a pk lookup only has a different meaning than one with an id field, when a model defines a custom primary key model field.

---

[1] https://docs.djangoproject.com/en/1.11/ref/models/querysets/#prefetch-objects

=/EQUAL and !=/NOT EQUAL queries: exact, iexact

Equality or = queries is the default WHERE behavior used in Django models. There are two syntax variations for equality searches; one is a short-handed version and the other uses the `exact` field lookup, Listing 8-33 shows both approaches.

Listing 8-33. Django equality = or EQUAL query

```
from coffeehouse.stores.models import Store
from coffeehouse.items.models import Item

# Get the Store object with id=1
Store.objects.get(id__exact=1)

# Get the Store object with id=1 (Short-handed version)
Store.objects.get(id=1)

# Get the Drink objects with name="Mocha"
Item.objects.filter(name__exact="Mocha")

# Get the Drink objects with name="Mocha" (Short-handed version)
Item.objects.filter(name="Mocha")
```

As you can see in Listing 8-33, you can either use the `exact` field lookup to explicitly qualify the query or use the short-handed syntax `<field>=<value>`. Because exact WHERE queries are the most common, Django implies `exact` searches by default.

■ **Tip** You can do case insensitive equality queries with the iexact field lookup (e.g., match 'IF','if','If', or 'iF'). See LIKE and ILIKE queries section for details.

Inequality or != searches also have two syntax variations presented in Listing 8-34.

Listing 8-34. Django inequality != or NOT EQUAL query with exclude() and Q objects

```
from coffeehouse.stores.models import Store
from coffeehouse.items.models import Item
from django.db.models import Q

# Get the Store records that don't have state 'CA'
Store.objects.exclude(state='CA')

# Get the Store records that don't have state 'CA', using Q
Store.objects.filter(~Q(state="CA"))

# Get the Item records and exclude items that have more than 100 calories
Item.objects.exclude(calories__gt=100)

# Get the Item records and exclude those with 100 or more calories, using Q
Item.objects.filter(~Q(calories__gt=100))
```

As you can see in Listing 8-34, one syntax variation uses the `exclude()` method to exclude objects that match a given statement. Another alternative is to use a Django `Q` object to negate a query. In Listing 8-34 you can see the `Q` object `Q(state="CA")` that matches state values with `CA`, but because the `Q` object is preceded with ~(tilde symbol) it's a negation pattern (i.e., matches state values that aren't `CA`).

Both the `exclude()` and `Q` object syntax produce the same results. `Q` objects are mostly used in more complex queries, but in this case a negated `Q` object works just like `exclude()`.

AND queries

To create SQL WHERE queries with an AND statement you can add multiple statements to a query or use `Q` objects, as illustrated in Listing 8-35.

Listing 8-35. Django AND query

```
from coffeehouse.stores.models import Store
from django.db.models import Q

# Get the Store records that have state 'CA' AND city 'San Diego'
Store.objects.filter(state='CA', city='San Diego')

# Get the Store records that have state 'CA' AND city not 'San Diego'
Store.objects.filter(Q(state='CA') & ~Q(city='San Diego'))
```

The first example in Listing 8-35 adds multiple field values to the `filter()` method to produce a WHERE <field_1> AND <field_2> statement. The second example in Listing 8-35 also uses the `filter()` method, but uses two `Q` objects to produce a negation with the `AND` statement (i.e., WHERE <field_1> AND NOT <field2>) through the `&` operator.

■ **Tip** If you're looking for a broader AND query than the ones in Listing 8-35, for example, get Store objects with state 'CA' AND those with state 'AZ', look at either OR queries or IN queries.

If you're looking to combine two queries, for example, query1 AND query 2, look at the Merge queries section later in this same chapter.

OR queries: Q() objects

To create SQL WHERE queries with an OR statement you can use `Q` objects, as illustrated in Listing 8-36.

Listing 8-36. Django OR query

```
from coffeehouse.stores.models import Store
from coffeehouse.items.models import Item
from django.db.models import Q
```

```
# Get the Store records that have state 'CA' OR state='AZ'
Store.objects.filter(Q(state='CA') | Q(state='AZ'))

# Get the Item records with name "Mocha" or "Latte"
Item.objects.filter(Q(name="Mocha") | Q(name='Latte'))
```

Both examples in Listing 8-36 uses the | (pipe) operator between Q objects to produce a `WHERE <field1> OR <field2>` statement, similar to how the & operator is used for AND conditions.

IS and IS NOT queries: isnull

The SQL IS and IS NOT statements are typically used with WHERE in queries involving NULL values. And depending on the database brand, SQL IS and IS NOT can also be used in Boolean queries. To create SQL WHERE queries with an IS or IS NOT statement you can use a Python None data type with an equivalency test or the `isnull` field lookup, as illustrated in Listing 8-37.

Listing 8-37. Django IS and IS NOT queries

```
from coffeehouse.stores.models import Store
from coffeehouse.items.models import Drink
from django.db.models import Q

# Get the Store records that have email NULL
Store.objects.filter(email=None)

# Get the Store records that have email NULL
Store.objects.filter(email__isnull=True)

# Get the Store records that have email NOT NULL
Store.objects.filter(email__isnull=False)
```

The first example in Listing 8-37 attempts a query on Python's None value; in this case None gets translated to SQL's NULL (i.e., `IS NULL`). The second and third examples in Listing 8-37 use the `isnull` field lookup, to create `IS NULL` and `IS NOT NULL` queries, respectively.

IN queries: in

The SQL IN statement is used with WHERE clauses to generate queries that match a list of values. To create SQL WHERE queries with an IN statement you can use the `in` field lookup, as illustrated in Listing 8-38.

Listing 8-38. Django IN queries

```
from coffeehouse.stores.models import Store
from coffeehouse.items.models import Drink

# Get the Store records that have state 'CA' OR state='AZ'
Store.objects.filter(state__in=['CA','AZ'])

# Get the Item records with id 1,2 or 3
Item.objects.filter(id__in=[1,2,3])
```

As you can see in Listing 8-38, the Django `in` field lookup can be used to create a query for records that match a list values from any field (e.g., integers, strings).

LIKE and ILIKE queries: contains, icontains, startswith, istartswith, endswith, iendswith

The SQL LIKE and ILIKE queries are used with WHERE clauses to match string patterns, with the former being case sensitive and the latter case insensitive. Django offers three field lookups to generate SQL LIKE queries, depending on the string pattern you wish to match. Listing 8-39 illustrates how to generate three different SQL LIKE queries with Django field lookups.

Listing 8-39. Django LIKE queries

```
from coffeehouse.stores.models import Store
from coffeehouse.items.models import Item, Drink

# Get the Store records that contain a 'C' anywhere in state (LIKE '%C%')
Store.objects.filter(state__contains='C')

# Get the Store records that start with 'San' in city (LIKE 'San%')
Store.objects.filter(city__startswith='San')

# Get the Item records that end with 'e' in name (LIKE '%e')
Drink.objects.filter(item__name__endswith='e')
```

As you can see in Listing 8-39, the % symbol represents an SQL wildcard and is placed in different positions in the SQL LIKE pattern value depending on the Django field lookup: to generate an SQL query with the `LIKE '%PATTERN%'` you use the `contains` field lookup; to generate an SQL query with the `LIKE 'PATTERN%'` you used the `startswith` field lookup; and to generate an SQL query with the `LIKE '%PATTERN'` you use the `endswith` field lookup.

Django also supports the SQL ILIKE queries, which function as LIKE queries, but are case insensitive. Listing 8-40 illustrates how to create ILIKE queries with Django field lookups.

Listing 8-40. Django ILIKE queries

```
from coffeehouse.stores.models import Store
from coffeehouse.items.models import Item

# Get the Store recoeds that contain 'a' in state anywhere case insensitive (ILIKE '%a%')
Store.objects.filter(state__icontains='a')

# Get the Store records that start with 'san' in city case insensitive (ILIKE 'san%')
Store.objects.filter(city__istartswith='san')

# Get the Item records that end with 'a' in name case insensitive (ILIKE '%A')
Item.objects.filter(name__iendswith='A')

# Get the Store records that have state 'ca' case insensitive (ILIKE 'ca')
Store.objects.filter(state__iexact='ca')
```

The examples in Listing 8-40 are just like those in Listing 8-39, but the only difference is Django's field lookups are preceded with the letter i to indicate a case-insensitive ILIKE query.

It's worth mentioning the last example in Listing 8-40 is a case-insensitive version of =/EQUAL and !=/NOT EQUAL queries. However, because `iexact` uses ILIKE under the hood it's mentioned again in this section.

REGEXP queries: regex, iregex

Sometimes the patterns supported by SQL LIKE & ILIKE statements are too basic, in which case you can use an SQL REGEXP statement to define a complex pattern as a regular expression. Regular expressions are more powerful because they can define fragmented patterns, for example: a pattern that starts with sa followed by any letters, followed by a number; or a conditional pattern, such as pattern that starts with Los or ends in Angeles. Django supports the SQL REGEXP keyword through the `regex` field lookup and also supports case-insensitive regular expression queries through the `iregex` field lookup.

Although it would be beyond the scope of our discussion to describe the many regular expression syntax variations, a sample regular expression query to match `Store` records with a `city` that starts with `Los` or `San` would be: `Store.objects.filter(city__regex=r'^(Los|San) +')`.

Note the recommended practice to define patterns for `regex` or `iregex` field lookups is to use Python raw string literals. A Python raw string literal is a string preceded by `r` that conveniently expresses strings that would be modified by escape sequence processing (e.g., the raw string `r'\n'` is identical to the standard string `'\\n'`). This behavior is particularly helpful with regular expressions that rely heavily on escape characters. Appendix A describes the use of Python raw strings in greater detail.

>/GREATER THAN and </LESS THAN queries: gt, gte, lt, lte

SQL WHERE statements associated with numeric fields often use the mathematical operators >, >=, <, and <= to restrict queries to certain number ranges. Django models support the use of the mathematical operators >, >=, < and <= through the `gt`, `gte`, `lt`, and `lte` field lookups, respectively. Listing 8-41 illustrates the use of these field lookups in Django.

Listing 8-41. Django GREATER THAN and LESSER THAN queries

```
from coffeehouse.items.models import Item

# Get Item records with stock > 5
Item.objects.filter(stock__gt=5)

# Get Item records with stock > or equal 10
Item.objects.filter(stock__gte=10)

# Get Item records with stock < 100
Item.objects.filter(stock__lt=100)

# Get Item records with stock < or equal 50
Item.objects.filter(stock__lte=50)
```

Date and time queries: Range, date, year, month, day, week, week_day, time, hour, minute, second

Although SQL WHERE queries for date and time fields can be done with equality, greater than and lesser than symbols, writing SQL date and time queries can be time consuming due to their special characteristics. For example, to create an SQL query to get all records with a 2018 year timestamp, you need to create a query like `'WHERE date BETWEEN '2018-01-01' AND '2018-12-31'`. As you can see, syntax-wise these queries can become complex and error prone if you add the need to deal with things like timezones, months, and things like leap years.

To simplify the creation of SQL WHERE queries with date and time values, Django offers various field lookups, which are illustrated in Listing 8-42.

Listing 8-42. Django date and time queries with field lookups

```
from coffeehouse.online.models import Order
from django.utils.timezone import utc
import datetime

# Define custom dates
start_date = datetime.datetime(2017, 5, 10).replace(tzinfo=utc)
end_date = datetime.datetime(2018, 5, 21).replace(tzinfo=utc)

# Get Order recrods from custom dates, starting May 10 2017 to May 21 2018
Order.objects.filter(created__range=(start_date, end_date))

# Get Order records with exact start date
orders_2018 = Order.objects.filter(created__date=start_date)

# Get Order records with year 2018
Order.objects.filter(created__year=2018)

# Get Order records with month January, values can be 1 through 12 (1=January, 12=December).
Order.objects.filter(created__month=1)

# Get Order records with day 1, where values can be 1 through 31.
Order.objects.filter(created__day=1)

# Get Order records from January 1 2018
Order.objects.filter(created__year=2018,create__month=1,created__day=1)

# Get Order records that fall on week number 24 of the yr, where values can be 1 to 53.
Order.objects.filter(created__week=24)

# Get Order recrods that fall on Monday, where values can be 1 to 7 (1=Sunday, 7=Saturday).
Order.objects.filter(created__week_day=2)

# Get Order records made at 2:30pm using a time object
Order.objects.filter(created__time=datetime.time(14, 30))

# Get Order records made at 10am, where values can be 0 to 23 (0=12am, 23=11pm).
Order.objects.filter(date__hour=10)

# Get Order records made at the top of the hour, where values are 0 to 59.
Order.objects.filter(date__minute=0)

# Get Order records made the 30 second mark of every minute, where values are 0 to 59.
Order.objects.filter(date__second=30)
```

The first example in Listing 8-42 uses the `range` field lookup, which takes two Python `datetime.datetime` objects to define a date range for the query. Although `range` is the most flexible approach to create date and time queries, there are other field lookup alternatives that offer simpler syntax. The `date` field lookup allows you to create a query for an exact date.

The `year`, `month`, and `day` field lookups allow you to create queries that match records for a given year, month, or day, respectively. In addition, if you look at the middle of Listing 8-42, you'll notice it's also possible to create a query with multiple field lookups to match a combination of year, month, and day.

Finally, toward the bottom half of Listing 8-42 you can see the `week` and `week_day` field lookups can create a query for records that match a given week of the year or day of the week, respectively. In addition to the `time` field lookup designed to make a query based on a `datetime.time` object, as well as the `hour`, `minute`, and `second` field lookups designed to create queries for records that match a given hour, minute, or second, respectively.

■ **Tip** To make a query that only extracts dates and times from a record (and not the full record), look at the DISTINCT section under the date and time subsection.

CAN'T FIND AN SQL WHERE STATEMENT? CUSTOM LOOKUPS, EXTRA(), SUBQUERIES, OR RAW QUERY

Although Django provides an extensive list of field lookups to generate various SQL WHERE statements, this doesn't mean you will always find the necessary field lookup to generate a desired SQL WHERE statement. In such cases, you have the following alternatives:

- Create a custom lookup: Just like other Django custom constructs, you can create custom lookups with custom SQL WHERE statements.[2]
- Use the extra() method: The Django model extra() method can also be used to create a custom SQL WHERE statement.[3]
- Use a subquery: Subqueries allow the creation of WHERE statements dependent on the results of other queries. A later section in this chapter addresses how to crate SQL subqueries on Django models.
- Raw SQL query: You can create a raw (open-ended) SQL query with verbatim SQL WHERE statements. A later section in this chapter addresses how to execute raw SQL queries on Django models.

DISTINCT Queries

The SQL DISTINCT keyword is used to filter duplicate records and is supported in Django models through the `distinct()` method. By default, SQL DISTINCT and the Django `distinct()` method are applied against the contents of entire records. This means that unless a query limits its number of fields or a query spans multiple models, the `distinct()` method will never produce distinct results. Listing 8-43 illustrates several queries that use the `distinct()` method that better illustrate this behavior.

---

[2]https://docs.djangoproject.com/en/1.11/howto/custom-lookups/

[3]https://docs.djangoproject.com/en/1.11/ref/models/querysets/#extra

Listing 8-43. Django DISTINCT queries with distinct()

```
from coffeehouse.stores.models import Store

# Get all Store records number
Store.objects.all().count()
4

# Get all distinct Store record number
Store.objects.distinct().count()
4
 # Get distinct state Store record values
Store.objects.values('state').distinct().count()
1

# ONLY for PostgreSQL, distinct() can accept model fields to create DISTINCT ON query
Store.objects.distinct('state')
```

The first query in Listing 8-43 gets the total count for all `Store` records, whereas the second query gets the total count for distinct `Store` records. Notice how even though the second query uses the `distinct()` method, both counts are the same, since there's at least one field value (e.g., `id`) across all records that is distinct.

The third query in Listing 8-43 makes use of the `values()` method to restrict the query records to only the `state` field. Once this is done, the `distinct()` method is applied to the query followed by the `count()` method, to get the total number of distinct `state` values. By applying a selective query field method (e.g., `values()` or `values_list()`) prior to the distinct() method, the logic performed by the distinct() method produces a logical output.

The final example in Listing 8-43 passes a model field to the `distinct()` method to produce an SQL DISTINCT ON query. This last `distinct()` method syntax is only supported for PostgreSQL databases that understand the SQL DISTINCT ON statement.

Dates and times queries: dates() and datetimes()

In addition to the `distinct()` method, Django also offer two special methods designed to extract DISTINCT date and time values from records. The `dates()` and `datetimes()` methods generate a list of `datetime.date` or `datetime.datetime` objects (respectively) based on model record values that match distinct dates or times.

The `dates()` method accepts three arguments, two required and one optional. The first argument (required) is a date field on which to perform the DISTINCT query, the second argument (required) is the date component on which to perform the DISTINCT query, which can be `'year'`, `'month'`, or `'day'`. The third argument (optional) is the query order that defaults to `'ASC'` for ascending, but can also be for `'DESC'` descending.

The `datetimes()` method also accepts three arguments, two required and one optional. The first argument (required) is a date time field on which to perform the DISTINCT query, the second argument (required) is the date time component on which to perform the DISTINCT query, which can be `'year'`, `'month'`, `'day'`, `'hour'`, `'minute'`, or `'second'`. The third argument (optional) is the query order that defaults to `'ASC'` for ascending, but can also be for `'DESC'` descending.

Listing 8-44 illustrates a series of examples using the `dates()` and `datetimes()` methods.

Listing 8-44. Django DISTINCT date and time queries with dates and datetimes() methods

```
from coffeehouse.online.models import Order

# Get distinct years (as datetime.date) for Order objects
Order.objects.dates('created','year')
# Outputs: <QuerySet [datetime.date(2017, 1, 1),datetime.date(2018, 1, 1)]>

# Get distinct months (as datetime.date) for Order objects
Order.objects.dates('created','month')
# Outputs: <QuerySet [datetime.date(2017, 3, 1),datetime.date(2017, 6, 1),datetime.
date(2018, 2, 1)]>

# Get distinct days (as datetime.datetime) for Order objects
Order.objects.datetimes('created','day')
# Outputs: <QuerySet [datetime.datetime(2017, 6, 17, 0, 0, tzinfo=<UTC>)...]>

# Get distinct minutes (as datetime.datetime) for Order objects
Order.objects.datetimes('created','minute')
# Outputs: <QuerySet [datetime.datetime(2017, 6, 17, 3, 13, tzinfo=<UTC>)...]>
```

As you can see in Listing 8-44, the `dates()` method produces a list of `datetime.date` objects generated from a given date component across all model records, whereas the `datetimes()` method produces a list of `datetime.datetime` objects generated from a given date time component across all model records. Note the examples in Listing 8-44 apply the `dates()` and `datetimes()` methods to all model records, but it's valid to use these methods on any query (i.e., `filter()` or `exclude()`).

■ **Tip** You can also use an aggregation query to count distinct values. See the Aggregation queries section for additional details on this process.

ORDER Queries: order_by() and reverse()

SQL queries often use the ORDER keyword to tell the database engine to sort query results based on certain field or fields. This technique is helpful because it avoids the additional overhead of sorting records outside the database (i.e., in Python). Django models support the SQL ORDER statement through the `order_by()` method. The `order_by()` method accepts model fields as input to define the query order, a process that's illustrated in Listing 8-45.

Listing 8-45. Django ORDER queries

```
from coffeehouse.stores.models import Store

# Get Store records and order by city (ORDER BY city)
Store.objects.all().order_by('city')

# Get Store recrods, order by name descending, email ascending (ORDER BY name DESC, email ASC)
Store.objects.filter(city='San Diego').order_by('-name','email')
```

The first example in Listing 8-45 defines a query for all `Store` objects ordered by city. By default, `order_by` sets the order ascending (i.e., 'A' records first, 'Z' records last). The second example in Listing 8-45 defines a `Store` query but with multiple fields, so the query is first ordered by the first field and then with the second. In addition, the second example illustrates the use of the - (minus) symbol to override the default ascending order, `-name` indicates to order records by `name` but in descending order (i.e., 'Z' records first, 'A' records last).

■ **Tip** You can declare the ordering Meta option on a model to set its default query ordering behavior, instead of declaring the order_by() method. See the previous chapter's Query meta options section.

In addition to the `order_by()` method, Django models also support the `reverse()` method that inverts the results of a `QuerySet`. The `reverse()` method works just like Python's standard `reverse()` method that inverts the order of a list, except it's designed to operate on Django `QuerySet` data structures before the data is materialized.

LIMIT Queries

THE SQL LIMIT statement is used when you want to avoid reading an entire set of records in a query and instead limit the resulting records to a smaller set. The SQL LIMIT statement is helpful for cases when you purposely want to read query records gradually (e.g., large queries that are displayed on multiple pages, a.k.a. pagination) - or you want to sample a query (e.g., get the first, last, latest, or oldest record in a query).

Django models offer various mechanisms to generate LIMIT queries described in the next sections.

LIMIT and OFFSET queries: Python slice syntax

SQL LIMIT queries are often accompanied by the OFFSET statement, the last of which is used to extract records starting from a given point in the whole set of records. Django models support the creation of SQL queries with LIMIT and OFFSET statements using standard Python slice syntax (i.e., the same syntax used to split lists). Listing 8-46 illustrates how to generate LIMIT and OFFSET queries.

Listing 8-46. Django LIMIT and OFFSET queries with Python slice syntax

```
from coffeehouse.stores.models import Store
from coffeehouse.items.models import Item

# Get the first five (LIMIT=5) Store records that have state 'CA'
Store.objects.filter(state='CA')[:5]

# Get the second five (OFFSET=5,LIMIT=5) Item records (after the first 5)
Item.objects.all()[5:10]

# Get the first (LIMIT=1) Item object
Item.objects.all()[0]
```

As you can see in Listing 8-46, the technique to generate LIMIT and OFFSET queries is through Python's slice syntax applied directly to `QuerySet` data structures. In case you've never used Python's slice syntax, the technique is straightforward: The syntax `QuerySet[start:end]` gets items from `start` to `end-1` of a `QuerySet`, the syntax `QuerySet[start:]` gets items from `start` through the rest of a `QuerySet`,and the syntax `QuerySet[:end]` gets items from the beginning of a `QuerySet` through `end-1`.

Pseudo LIMIT 1 order queries: first() and last()

Under certain circumstances, the SQL LIMIT statement is used to get a single record that's the first or last record in a set of records. Django models support the first() and last() methods, which generate a LIMIT 1 query just as if you created a query with the slice syntax `[0]` - describe in Listing 8-46.

The `first()` and `last()` methods are typically preceded by the `order_by()` model method, in order to guarantee an expected record order and thus get the first or last record of said records. If the `first()` and `last()` methods are applied without the `order_by()` model method, then queries are applied against the default ordering mechanism - by the `id` field - and thus `first()` returns the record with the first `id` value and `last()` returns the record with the last `id` value.

For example, the query `Store.objects.filter(state='CA').first()` gets the first `Store` record with `state='CA'` with the lowest `id` (since order defaults to id), a query that's equivalent to `Store.objects.filter(state='CA')[0]`. The query `Item.objects.all().order_by('name').last()` gets the last Item record with the `name` that comes last in the alphabet (since order is specified by `name`), a query that's equivalent to `Item.objects.all().order_by('name').reverse()[0]`.

Pseudo LIMIT 1 date and time queries: latest() and earliest()

For SQL LIMIT queries associated with dates or times, Django offers the `latest()` and `earliest()` methods to obtain the most recently or first created model records (respectively) based on a date field. Both the `latest()` and `earliest()` methods accept a date field on which to perform a query and provide much shorter syntax to deal with LIMIT queries related to dates or times vs. the `first()` and `last()`. This is because `latest()` and `earliest()` methods automatically perform the `order_by()` operation on the field provided as an argument.

For example, `Order.objects.latest('created')` gets the most recent `Order` record based on the `created` field, whereas `Order.objects.earliest('created')` gets the oldest `Order` record based on the `created` field.

■ **Tip** Use the get_latest_by Meta option in a model to set a default field on which to execute the latest() and earliest() methods. See the previous chapter on Meta options for additional details.

Merge Queries

SQL queries often need to be merged to produce different sets of results, such as combining the records of multiple SQL queries or obtaining common records between multiple SQL queries. Django supports various ways to merge SQL queries, both as `QuerySet` data structures, as well as through SQL query statements like UNION, INTERSECT, and EXCEPT.

QuerySet merger: Pipe and itertools.chain

As you've learned throughout this chapter, Django models most often use `QuerySet` data structures to represent SQL queries. Such `QuerySet` data structures often require to be merged, to present a larger set of results and avoid having to perform new database queries. Listing 8-47 illustrates the two syntax variations available to merge `QuerySet` data structures.

Listing 8-47. Combine two Django queries with | (pipe) and itertools.chain

```
from coffeehouse.items.models import Item, Drink
from itertools import chain

menu_sandwich_items = Item.objects.filter(menu__name='Sandwiches')
menu_salads_items = Item.objects.filter(menu__name='Salads')
drinks = Drink.objects.all()

# A pipe applied to two QuerySets generates a larger QuerySet
lunch_items = menu_sandwich_items | menu_salads_items

# | can't be used to merge QuerySet's with different models # ERROR menu_sandwich_items | drinks

# itertools.chain generates a Python list and can merge different QuerySet model types
lunch_items_with_drinks = list(chain(menu_sandwich_items, drinks))
```

The first option in Listing 8-47 uses the | (pipe) operator to combine two `QuerySet` data structures. This technique produces yet another `QuerySet` data structure, but has the caveat of only working on `QuerySet`'s that use the same model (e.g., `Item`).

The second option in Listing 8-47 uses the Python `itertools` package to merge two `QuerySet` data structure with the `chain()` method. This technique produces a standard Python list - with the respective model objects - and is the more flexible option because it can combine `QuerySet` data structures even if they use different models (e.g., `Item` and `Drink`).

UNION queries: union()

The SQL UNION statement is used to merge two or more queries directly in the database. Unlike the previous merge query techniques - illustrated in Listing 8-47 - which take place in Django/Python, UNION queries are done entirely by the database engine. Django supports the SQL UNION statement through the `union()` method, as illustrated in Listing 8-48.

Listing 8-48. Merge Django queries with union()

```
from coffeehouse.items.models import Item

menu_breakfast_items = Item.objects.filter(menu__name='Breakfast')
menu_sandwich_items = Item.objects.filter(menu__name='Sandwiches')
menu_salads_items = Item.objects.filter(menu__name='Salads')

# All items merged with union()
all_items = menu_breakfast_items.union(menu_sandwich_items,menu_salads_items)
print(all_items.query)
SELECT "items_item"."id", "items_item"."menu_id" ... WHERE "items_menu"."name" = Breakfast UNION
SELECT "items_item"."id", "items_item"."menu_id" ... WHERE "items_menu"."name" =
Sandwiches UNION SELECT "items_item"."id", "items_item"."menu_id"... WHERE
"items_menu"."name" = Salads
```

Listing 8-48 first declares three standard SQL queries that produce `QuerySet` data structures. Next, notice how the `union()` method is linked to one of the queries and the remaining queries are passed as arguments. Finally, Listing 8-48 illustrates how the results of the `union()` method produce a query with multiple SQL UNION statements that merge the individual queries.

In addition to the `union()` method accepting different `QuerySet` instances as arguments, the `union()` method also accepts the optional keyword `all` argument that is set to `False`. By default, the `union()` method ignores duplicate values across `QuerySet` instances; however, you can set the `all` argument to `True` to tell Django to merge duplicate records (e.g., `menu_breakfast_items.union(menu_sandwich_items,menu_salads_items, all=True)`).

INTERSECT queries: intersection()

The SQL INTERSECT statement is used to obtain records that intersect (i.e., are present) across multiple queries. Django supports the SQL INTERSECT statement through the `intersection()` method, as illustrated in Listing 8-49.

Listing 8-49. Intersect (Common) Django query records with intersection()

```
from coffeehouse.items.models import Item

all_items = Item.objects.all()
menu_breakfast_items = Item.objects.filter(menu__name='Breakfast')

# Intersected (common) records merged with intersect()
intersection_items = all_items.intersection(menu_breakfast_items)
print(intersection_items.query)
SELECT "items_item"."id", "items_item"."menu_id", "items_item"."name"... INTERSECT
SELECT "items_item"."id", "items_item"."menu_id", "items_item"."name"... WHERE
"items_menu"."name" = Breakfast
```

Listing 8-49 first declares two standard SQL queries that produce `QuerySet` data structures. Next, notice how the `intersection()` method is linked to one of the queries and the remaining query is passed as an argument. Finally, Listing 8-49 illustrates how the results of the `intersection()` method produce a query with an SQL INTERSECTION statements to produce the common records across queries.

The `intersection()` method only accept `QuerySet` instances as arguments. In addition, be careful when declaring more than two `QuerySet` instances on an `intersection()` query, as only records that are present in all `QuerySet` instances form part of the final query result.

EXCEPT queries: difference()

The SQL EXCEPT statement is used to obtain records that are present in a query, but missing in other queries. Django supports the SQL EXCEPT statement through the `difference()` method, as illustrated in Listing 8-50.

Listing 8-50. Except Django query records with difference()

```
from coffeehouse.items.models import Item

all_items = Item.objects.all()
menu_breakfast_items = Item.objects.filter(menu__name='Breakfast')
menu_sandwich_items = Item.objects.filter(menu__name='Sandwiches')
menu_salads_items = Item.objects.filter(menu__name='Salads')
```

```
# Extract records in all_items, except those in:
#     menu_breakfast_items, menu_sandwich_items & menu_salads_items
ex_items = all_items.difference(menu_breakfast_items, menu_sandwich_items, menu_salads_
items)
print(ex_items.query)
SELECT "items_item"."id", "items_item"."menu_id", "items_item"."name"...EXCEPT
SELECT "items_item"."id", "items_item"."menu_id", "items_item"."name"... EXCEPT
SELECT "items_item"."id", "items_item"."menu_id", "items_item"."name", ... EXCEPT
SELECT "items_item"."id", "items_item"."menu_id", "items_item"."name" ... WHERE
"items_menu"."name" = Salads
```

Listing 8-50 first declares four standard SQL queries that produce QuerySet data structures. Next, notice how the difference() method is called on the all_items query and the remaining queries are passed as arguments to be excluded from the all_items query. Finally, Listing 8-50 illustrates how the results of the difference() method produce a query with multiple SQL EXCEPT statements that exclude query records from the parent query.

Aggregation Queries

SQL queries sometimes need to produce values derived from the core fields contained in Django models (e.g., mathematical calculations such as counts, averages, maximum or minimum values from sets of records). Storing this type of aggregate information as individual Django model fields is redundant - since it can be derived from core data - and calculating this data outside the context of a database is also wasteful (e.g., reading all records and producing the aggregate results in Python).

SQL offers the necessary statements for a database to solve this problem, through *aggregation functions*. An aggregation function forms part of an SQL query, which is executed by the database engine and returned as a stand-alone result - when used in conjunction with the aggregate() method - or as an additional field along with the resulting SQL response - when used in conjunction with the annotate() method. Django supports aggregation queries through a series of methods that include count(), aggregate(), and annotate(), as well as aggregation classes.

COUNT queries: count() method and Count() class

The SQL COUNT aggregation function is used in cases where you only need to get the number of records that match a certain criteria, rather than reading all records that make up a query. Queries that use SQL COUNT are also more efficient because it's the database engine that makes the calculation, instead of getting all the data and making the calculation in Python.

Django models supports the SQL COUNT aggregation function through the count() method and the aggregate Count class. Both variations are illustrated in Listing 8-51.

Listing 8-51. Django COUNT queries with aggregate(), annotate(), and Count()

```
from coffeehouse.stores.models import Store

from django.db.models import Count

# Get the number of stores (COUNT(*))
stores_count = Store.objects.all().count()
print(stores_count)
4
```

```
# Get the number of stores that have city 'San Diego' (COUNT(*))
stores_san_diego_count = Store.objects.filter(city='San Diego').count()

# Get the number of emails, NULL values are not counted (COUNT(email))
emails_count = Store.objects.aggregate(Count('email'))
print(emails_count)
{'email__count': 4}

# Get the number of emails, NULL values are not counted (COUNT(email)
AS "coffeehouse_store_emails_count")
emails_count_custom = Store.objects.aggregate(coffeehouse_store_emails_count=Count('email'))
print(emails_count_custom)
{'coffeehouse_store_emails_count': 4}

# Get number of distinct Amenities in all Stores, NULL values not counted (COUNT(DISTINCT name))
different_amenities_count = Store.objects.aggregate(Count('amenities',distinct=True))
print(different_amenities_count)
{'amenities__count': 5}

# Get number of Amenities per Store with annotate
stores_with_amenities_count = Store.objects.annotate(Count('amenities'))
# Get amenities count in individual Store
stores_With_amenities_count[0].amenities__count

# Get number of Amenities per Store with annotate and custom name
stores_amenities_count_custom = Store.objects.annotate(amenities_per_store=Count('amenities'))
stores_amenities_count_custom[0].amenities_per_store
```

The first two examples in Listing 8-51 append the count() method as the last part of a Django query to get a total count.

The third example in Listing 8-51 uses the aggregate() function and the aggregate Count class to get the total count of emails in Store records. Notice how a query with the aggregate() method produces a dictionary, where the key is the counted field - in this case email - suffixed with the __count to indicate aggregate class, and the dictionary value is the resulting count. The fourth example in Listing 8-51 is very similar to the third one, except it prefixes the aggregate Count class with a custom string to simulate the SQL AS keyword, so the resulting dictionary value uses the custom string coffeehouse_store_emails_count as the key result.

■ **Note** If no string is assigned to an aggregate class (e.g., Count) in a query, the resulting query output defaults to: <field>__<aggregate_class>.

The fifth example in Listing 8-51 illustrates how the aggregate Count class can accept the optional distinct=True argument to omit duplicate values in the count. In this case, a count is made for all amenities associated with Store records, but the count only reflects distinct amenities values.

Although the aggregate() method produces aggregation results, it's limited to only producing the aggregation result by itself, that is, it requires additional queries to get the core data from where the aggregation result was calculated. The annotate() method solves this problem, as shown in Listing 8-51.

The last two examples in Listing 8-51 use the annotate() method to add an additional field to a query's records to hold an aggregate result. The second to last example in Listing 8-51 adds the amenities__count field via the aggregate Count() class to all Store records. And the last example in Listing 8-51 assigns a custom string to the aggregate Count() class to create the custom amenities_per_store field to hold the amenities count for all Store records.

MAX, MIN, SUM, AVG, VARIANCE and STDDEV queries: Max(), Min(), Sum(), Avg(), Variance(), and StdDev() classes

In addition to the SQL COUNT aggregation function, SQL queries also support other aggregation functions for mathematical operations that are best done in the database. These SQL aggregation functions include MAX to get a maximum value from a set of records, MIN to get a minimum value from a set of records, SUM to a sum of values from a set of records, AVG to get the average from a set of records, VARIANCE to get the statistical variance of values from a set of records, and STDDEV to get the statistical deviation from a set of records.

Django models support all the previous SQL aggregation functions through the use of aggregation classes – just like Count() aggregation described in Listing 8-51. Therefore to make use of these additional SQL aggregation functions, you use a Django model's aggregate() or annotate() methods in conjunction with the relevant aggregation class, a processed that's illustrated in Listing 8-52.

Listing 8-52. Django MAX, MIN,SUM, AVG, VARIANCE and STDDEV queries with Max(), Min(), Sum(), Avg(), Variance() and StdDev() classes

```
from coffeehouse.items.models import Item
from django.db.models import Avg, Max, Min
from django.db.models import Sum
from django.db.models import Variance, StdDev

# Get the average, maximum and minimum number of stock for all Item records
avg_max_min_stock = Item.objects.aggregate(Avg('stock'), Max('stock'), Min('stock'))

print(avg_max_min_stock)
{'stock__avg': 29.0, 'stock__max': 36, 'stock__min': 27}

# Get the total stock for all Items
item_all_stock = Item.objects.aggregate(all_stock=Sum('stock'))
print(item_all_stock)
{'all_stock': 261}

# Get the variance and standard deviation for all Item records
# NOTE: Variance & StdDev return the population variance & standard deviation, respectively.
#       But it's also possible to return sample variance & standard deviation,
#       using the sample=True argument
item_statistics = Item.objects.aggregate(Variance('stock'), std_dev_stock= StdDev('stock'))
{'std_dev_stock': 5.3748, 'stock__variance': 28.8888}
```

As you can see in the first example in Listing 8-52, it's possible to define multiple aggregate classes to a single query as part of the aggregate() method, in this case the query gets the average, minimum, and maximum stock values across all Item records.

The second example in Listing 8-52 gets the sum of all `stock` values across all Item records by using the aggregate `Sum` class. Notice how it's possible in this second example to prefix the aggregate class with a custom string to act as an SQL AS keyword, in order for the query to output the results with a different value than the aggregate class name. Finally, the last example in Listing 8-52 calculates the variance and standard deviation for all `stock` values across all Item records.

▪ **Tip** If you want to perform more complex aggregation queries, such as multi-field math operations (e.g., multiplication), see the F expressions subsection.

If want to perform more complex aggregation queries, see the section on Model queries with raw (open-ended) SQL.

Expression and Function Queries

SQL queries irrespective of their many statements generally reference values provided by the calling environment. For example, when you create a query to get all `Store` records that have certain `state` values, Django/Python provides a value reference for the `state`, similarly, if you create a query to get all `Item` records that belong to a certain `Menu` model, Django/Python provides a value reference for the `Store`.

For certain SQL queries, though, it's necessary to use references that point toward data in the actual database. This is necessary because the results for certain SQL queries depend on the data present in the database, or because, manipulating the data outside the context of a database (i.e., Python) represents an additional effort that can easily be solved in SQL.

You already learned about this technique in the past section on Aggregation queries, where an SQL query can tell a database engine to calculate things like counts and averages, without the need to pull the data and do the operations outside the database (i.e., in Python). Aggregation queries rely on a special subset of expressions properly called *aggregation expressions*, but in this upcoming sections you'll learn how Django supports many other types of SQL expressions.

Another SQL technique designed in the same spirit of SQL expressions to favor the delegation of work to the database engine are SQL functions. SQL functions are intended to allow a database to alter the results of query (e.g., concatenate two fields or transform a field to upper/lowercase) and alleviate the need to such tasks in the calling party environment (i.e., Django/Python). In the upcoming section you'll also learn about different SQL functions supported by Django models.

SQL expression queries: F expressions

Django F expressions are among the most common type of SQL expressions you'll use in Django models. At the start of this chapter you were exposed to the utility of F expressions when you learned how it's possible to update a record in a single step, and let the database engine perform the logic without the need pull the record out of the database.

Through an F expression, it's possible to reference a model field in a query and let the database perform an operation on the model field value without the need to pull the data from the database. In turn, this not only provides a more succinct query syntax - a single update query, instead of two (one to read, one to update) - it also avoids 'race conditions'.[4]

[4]`https://en.wikipedia.org/wiki/Race_condition`

Listing 8-53 illustrates various ways that F expressions can be used on update queries.

Listing 8-53. Django F() expression update queries

```
from coffeehouse.items.models import Item
from django.db.models import F

# Get single item
egg_biscuit = Item.objects.get(id=2)
# Check stock
egg_biscuit.stock
2
# Add 10 to stock value with F() expression
egg_biscuit.stock = F('stock') + 10
# Trigger save() to apply F() expression
egg_biscuit.save()
# Check stock again
egg_biscuit.stock
<CombinedExpression: F(stock) + Value(10)>
# Ups, need to re-read/refresh from DB
egg_biscuit.refresh_from_db()
# Check stock again
egg_biscuit.stock
12

# Decrease stock value by 1 for Item records on the Breakfast menu
breakfast_items = Item.objects.filter(menu__name='Breakfast')
breakfast_items.update(stock=F('stock') - 1)

# Increase all Item records stock by 20
Item.objects.all().update(stock=F('stock') + 20)
```

The first example in Listing 8-53 reads a single model record and applies an `F()` expression to the `stock` field. Once the `F()` expression is applied, it's necessary to call the `save()` method on the record for the database to trigger the update. Next, notice that in order for the model record reference to reflect the results of the `F()` expression, you must reread the record from the database - in this case with the `refresh_from_db()` method - given the database is the only party aware of the result of the update operation.

Next in Listing 8-53, you can see how it's also possible to perform a subtraction operation on an `F()` expression, as well as apply an `F()` expression to all the records in a `QuerySet` through the `update()` method.

In addition to updating records without the need to extract data from the database, `F()` expressions can also be used in database read operations. `F()` expressions are helpful for read queries and aggregation queries where the results are best determined by the database engine, as shown in Listing 8-54.

Listing 8-54. Django F() expressions in read queries and aggregate queries

```
from django.db.models import  F, ExpressionWrapper, FloatField
from coffeehouse.items.models import Drink, Item

calories_dbl_caffeine_drinks = Drink.objects.filter(item__calories__gt=F('caffeine')*2)

items_with_assets = Item.objects.annotate(
                                 assets=ExpressionWrapper(F('stock')*F('price'),
                                 output_field=FloatField()))
```

Notice how the first query example in Listing 8-54 lacks any fixed values and is instead composed of references that are checked by the database engine to return records that match the condition. In this case, the query obtains all `Drink` records that have `calories` greater than two times their `caffeine` content, where its database engine - via the `F()` expression - is tasked with determining which `Drink` records comply with this rule.

The second example in Listing 8-54 creates an aggregate query from two `F()` expressions. In this case, a new field called `assets` is calculated with the `annotate()` method, by multiplying the value of a record's `stock` and `price` fields via `F()` expressions. Unlike the aggregation queries examples in the previous section, this aggregation has two important differences and arguments:

- `ExpressionWrapper`.- Because the aggregate query in Listing 8-54 is composed of multiple model fields, it's necessary to delimit its scope by wrapping the aggregate query in the `ExpressionWrapper` statement.
- `output_field`.- When an aggregate query is composed of multiple model fields and the data types differ, it's necessary to specify `output_field` with a model data type. In Listing 8-54, because `stock` is an `IntegerField` model field and `price` is a `FloatField` model field, the `output_field` tells Django to generate the aggregated `assets` field as a `FloatField`, thus avoiding data type ambiguity.

SQL function queries: Func expressions and Django database functions

Func expressions are another expression subset supported by Django models, which have the same purpose as other SQL expressions: to use the database to execute operations, instead of fetching data and later performing the operation outside the database (i.e., in Python).

Func expressions are used in Django to trigger the execution of database functions. Unlike F expressions that are used to perform basic operations against model fields, Func expressions are used to execute more sophisticated functions supported by databases and run them against models fields.

Listing 8-55 illustrates an example of a Func expression that calls an SQL function, as well as a couple of Django database functions that simulate SQL functions.

Listing 8-55. Django Func() expressions for SQL functions and Django SQL functions

```
from django.db.models import  F, Func, Value
from django.db.models.functions import Upper, Concat
from coffeehouse.stores.models import Store

# SQL Upper function call via Func expression and F expression
stores_w_upper_names = Store.objects.annotate(name_upper=Func(F('name'), function='Upper'))
stores_w_upper_names[0].name_upper
'CORPORATE'
stores_w_upper_names[0].name
'Corporate'

# Equivalent SQL Upper function call directly with Django SQL Upper function
stores_w_upper_names_function = Store.objects.annotate(name_upper=Upper('name'))
stores_w_upper_names_function[0].name_upper
'CORPORATE'

# SQL Concat function called directly with Django SQL Concat function
stores_w_full_address = Store.objects.annotate(full_address=
                                Concat('address',Value(' - '),'city',Value(' , '),'state'))
```

```
stores_w_full_address[0].full_address
'624 Broadway - San Diego, CA'
stores_w_full_address[0].city
'San Diego'
```

The first example in Listing 8-55 makes use of the Func() expression to generate the additional name_upper field via annotate(). The purpose of the additional name_upper field is to get the name of all Store records in an uppercase format, a process that fits perfectly with the SQL UPPER function. In the case of Listing 8-55, the Func() expression declares two arguments: an F expression to specify the model field on which to apply the function and the function argument to specify the SQL function to use. Once the query is created, you can see in Listing 8-55, each record has access to the additional name_upper field with an uppercase version of the name field, as well as access to the other model fields.

Although Func() expressions are the most flexible option to generate Django model queries with SQL expressions, Func() expressions can be verbose for default scenarios. Django offers a quicker alternative to generate SQL expressions via SQL functions that are of the django.db.models.functions package.

The second query in Listing 8-55 is equivalent to the first query, but notice this variation uses the Django database Upper() function as an argument of the annotate() method, similar to how Django aggregate classes are declared in annotate() statements.

The third example in Listing 8-55 generates the additional full_address field via annotate() and makes use of the Django database Concat() function. The purpose of the Concat() function is to concatenate the values of multiple model fields. In the case of Listing 8-55, the Concat() function concatenates the values of the Store model's address, city, and state. In order to leave spaces between the concatenated field values, the Concat() function uses the Django Value() expression to output verbatim separators and spaces. Once the query is created, you can see in Listing 8-55 that each record has access to the additional full_address field with a concatenated value of the address, city, and state fields, as well as access to the other model fields.

Django includes over a dozen database functions in the django.db.models.functions package[5] for strings, dates, and other data types you can leverage as SQL functions in queries.

SQL subqueries: Subquery expressions

SQL subqueries are queries that are nested inside other standard CRUD queries or inclusively other subqueries. Most SQL subqueries are used under two scenarios. The first scenario occurs when you need to create SQL queries with related fields that span multiple tables, yet the underlying tables don't have an explicit relationship between one another.

This first SQL subquery scenario is common for queries involving multiple Django models with missing relationship data types (i.e., OneToOneField, ForeignKey, and ManyToManyField). Listing 8-56 illustrates this SQL subquery scenario solved through the use of Subquery expressions.

Listing 8-56. Django Subquery expression with SQL subquery to get related model data

```
from django.db.models import OuterRef, Subquery

class Order(models.Model):
    created = models.DateTimeField(auto_now_add=True)
```

[5]https://docs.djangoproject.com/en/1.11/ref/models/database-functions/

```
class OrderItem(models.Model):
    item = models.IntegerField()
    amount = models.IntegerField()
    order = models.ForeignKey(Order)

# Get Items in order number 1
order_items = OrderItem.objects.filter(order__id=1)
# Get item
order_items[0].item
1
# Get item name ?

# OrderItem item field is IntegerField, lacks Item relationship
# Create sub-query to get Item records with id
item_subquery = Item.objects.filter(id=(OuterRef('id')))

# Annotate previous query with sub-query
order_items_w_name = order_items.annotate(item_name=Subquery(item_subquery.values('name')
[:1]))
# Output SQL to verify
print(order_items_w_name.query)
SELECT `online_orderitem`.`id`, `online_orderitem`.`item`,
    `online_orderitem`.`amount`, `online_orderitem`.`order_id`,
     (SELECT U0.`name` FROM `items_item` U0 WHERE U0.`id` = (online_orderitem.`id`) LIMIT 1)
     AS `item_name` FROM `online_orderitem` WHERE `online_orderitem`.`order_id` = 1
# Access item and item_name
order_items_w_name[0].item
1
order_items_w_name[0].item_name
'Whole-Grain Oatmeal'
```

The first lines in Listing 8-56 show the `Order` and `OrderItem` models, including a query that gets all the `OrderItem` records that belong to `Order` number 1. Next, you can see that although the `OrderItem` model has an `item` field, its value is an integer. This presents a problem because it isn't possible to obtain the `name` and other properties associated with an `item` field integer value, or in other words, the `OrderItem` records are missing a relationship to the Item model. This problem can be solved with a subquery.

Next in Listing 8-56, the `Item.objects.filter(id=(OuterRef('id')))` subquery is declared to get all the `Item` records by `id`, which is the value the main `OrderItem` expects to map to `item` values. The special `OuterRef` syntax work like an `F` expression to be evaluated until the parent query is resolved; after all, the `Item` records to get by `id` are dependent on the parent query (e.g., The subquery should only `Item` records by `id` for only those items in an `OrderItem` record).

Once the subquery is defined in Listing 8-56, it's linked via the `annotate()` method and the `Subquery()` expression to the initial `OrderItem` query. Next, you can see the SQL generated by the query contains a subquery referencing the `Item` model. Finally, Listing 8-56 illustrates the output of the additional `item_name` field on the `OrderItem` query that's generated via a subquery.

The second scenario involving subqueries is when an SQL query must generate a WHERE statement with values that are dependent on the results of another SQL query. This scenario is illustrated in Listing 8-57.

Listing 8-57. Django Subquery expression with SQL subquery in WHERE statement

```
# See Listing 8-56 for referenced model definitions
from coffeehouse.online.models import Order
from coffeehouse.items.models import Item
from django.db.models import OuterRef, Subquery

# Get Item records in lastest Order to replenish stock
most_recent_items_on_order = Order.objects.latest('created').orderitem_set.all()

# Get a list of Item records based on recent order using a sub-query
items_to_replenish = Item.objects.filter(id__in=Subquery(
                                    most_recent_items_on_order.values('item')))

print(items_to_replenish.query)
SELECT `items_item`.`id`, `items_item`.`menu_id`, `items_item`.`name`, `items_
item`.`description`, `items_item`.`size`, `items_item`.`calories`,
 `items_item`.`price`, `items_item`.`stock` FROM `items_item` WHERE `items_item`.`id`
  IN (SELECT U0.`item` FROM `online_orderitem` U0 WHERE U0.`order_id` = 1)
```

The first step in Listing 8-57 gets all `OrderItem` records from the latest `Order` record, with the purpose to detect which `Item` stock to replenish. However, because `OrderItem` records use a plain integer id to reference `Item` records, it's necessary to create a subquery that gets all `Item` records based on the `OrderItem` integer reference.

Next in Listing 8-57, a query is made for Item records whose id is contained in a subquery. In this case, a `Subquery` expression is used to point toward the `most_recent_items_on_order` query that only gets the `item` values (i.e., integer values) from the most recent `Order` record.

Finally, Listing 8-57 illustrates how the generated query uses a WHERE statement that makes use of a subquery.

JOIN QUERIES

The SQL JOIN keyword is used to produce queries from multiple database tables. Django supports JOIN queries for related models through the select_related() method, described earlier in the CRUD relationship records across Django models.

If you want to create a JOIN query between tables that don't have a Django model relationship, you can use a raw SQL query, described in the next section.

Model Queries with Raw (Open-Ended) SQL

As extensive as Django model queries are, there can be circumstances when neither of the options presented in previous sections is sufficient to execute certain CRUD operations. Under these circumstances, you must rely on raw (open-ended) SQL queries, which represent the most flexible approach to execute operations against databases connected to Django projects.

Django offers two ways to execute raw SQL queries. The first consists of using a model manager's `raw()` method that fits the resulting SQL query data into a Django model, which has the added advantage of raw SQL queries behaving as close as possible to native Django model queries. And a second approach consists of using a Python database connection - managed by Django - to fetch the SQL query data and process it with lower-level Python DB API functions (e.g., `cursor`).[6]

SQL Queries with a Model Manager's raw() Method

A model manager's `raw()` method should be your first option to execute raw SQL queries, since the results are structured as a `RawQuerySet` class instance, which is very similar to the `QuerySet` class instances produced by Django model queries you've used up to this point.

Thus a `RawQuerySet` class instance - just like a `QuerySet` class instance - offers an easy way to access records using a Django model's fields, the ability to defer the loading of model fields, as well as indexing and slicing. Listing 8-58 illustrates a series a raw SQL query performed with a model manager's `raw()` method.

Listing 8-58. Django model manager raw() method

```
from coffeehouse.items.models import Drink, Item

# Get all drink
all_drinks = Drink.objects.raw("SELECT * FROM items_drink")

# Confirm type
type(all_drinks)
# Outputs: <class 'django.db.models.query.RawQuerySet'>

# Get first drink with index 0
first_drink = all_drinks[0]

# Get Drink name (via item OneToOne relationship)
first_drink.item.name

# Use parameters to limit a raw SQL query
caffeine_limit = 100

# Create raw() query with params argument to pass dynamic arguments
drinks_low_caffeine = Drink.objects.raw("SELECT * FROM items_drink where caffeine <
%s",params=[caffeine_limit]);
```

The first snippet in Listing 8-58 uses the `Drink` model manager's `raw()` method to issue the `SELECT * FROM items_drink` query. It's worth mentioning this raw query produces the same results as the native Django query `Drink.objects.all()`, but unlike native queries that produce `QuerySet` data structures, notice how `raw()` method queries produce `RawQuerySet` data structure.

Because a `RawQuerySet` data structure is a subclass of `QuerySet`, Listing 8-58 shows how it's possible to use many of the same mechanisms as `QuerySet` data structures. For example, access to records is also done by index (e.g., [0] to get the first elements) and it's also possible to access related models using dot notation.

[6] `https://www.python.org/dev/peps/pep-0249/`

Finally, the last example in Listing 8-58 illustrates how to create raw SQL queries with dynamic arguments using the params argument. In all cases where you need to create raw() SQL queries that depend on dynamic values (e.g., provided by a user or another subroutine) you should always create the backing raw SQL query string with placeholders – %s – which then get substituted through the params argument. In the case of Listing 8-58, notice how the caffeine_limit variable is declared in params to later be substituted into the raw SQL query. The params argument ensures dynamic values are escaped from queries before being applied to the database, avoiding a potential SQL injection security attack.[7]

The raw() SQL example in Listing 8-58 is straightforward because the results of the query map directly to the intended model. In other words, the SELECT * FROM items_drink query produces the necessary results for Django to create Item records without additional help. Sometimes though, raw() SQL queries require additional configuration to be able to create the underlying model records.

For example, if you perform a raw SQL query on a legacy table or multiple tables, with the intention to use the raw() method of a certain model, you must ensure Django is able to interpret the results of raw SQL query to the model, by either using SQL AS statements in the raw SQL or relying on the raw() translations parameter. Listing 8-59 illustrates both techniques.

Listing 8-59. Django model manager raw() method with mapping, deferred fields, and aggregate queries

```
# Map results from legacy table into Item model
all_legacy_items = Item.objects.raw("SELECT product_name AS name, product_description AS
description from coffeehouse_products")

# Access legacy results as if they are standard Item model records
all_legacy_items[0].name

# Use explicit mapping argument instead of 'as' statements in SQL query
legacy_mapping = {'product_name':'name','product_description':'description'}

# Create raw() query with translations argument to map table results
all_legacy_items_with_mapping = Item.objects.raw("SELECT * from coffeehouse_products",
translations=legacy_mapping)

# Deferred model field loading, get item one with limited fields
item_one = Item.objects.raw("SELECT id,name from items_item where id=1")
# Acess model fields not referenced in the raw query, just like QuerySet defer()
item_one[0].calories
item_one[0].price

# Raw SQL query with aggregate function added as extra model field
items_with_inventory = Item.objects.raw("SELECT *, sum(price*stock) as assets from items_
item");
# Access extra field directly as part of the model
items_with_inventory[0].assets
```

The first example in Listing 8-59 declares a raw() method with multiple SQL AS statements, in this case, each of the AS clauses corresponds to an Item model field. In this manner, when Django inspects the results of the raw query, it knows how to map the results to Item instances, irrespective of the underlying database table column names.

[7]https://en.wikipedia.org/wiki/SQL_injection

The second example in Listing 8-59 declares a `raw()` method with the `translations` argument whose value is a Python dictionary that maps database table column names to Django model fields. In this case, when Django encounters an unknown database table column name in the raw query results, it uses the `translations` dictionary to determine how to map the results to Item instances.

The third example in Listing 8-59 illustrates how even when issuing a partial raw SQL query with the `raw()` method, Django is capable of fetching missing fields as if it were a native `QuerySet` data structure. Finally, the fourth example in Listing 8-59 illustrates how the `raw()` method is capable of handling extra fields declared as aggregation queries and how they become accessible as if they were added with the native model `aggregate()` method.

SQL Queries with Python's DB API

Although the Django model `raw()` method offers a great alternative to create raw SQL queries and have the ability to leverage native Django model features, there are circumstances where raw SQL queries with a model's `raw()` method won't work. Either because the results of a raw SQL query can't be mapped to a Django model, or because, you simply want access to the raw data without any Django model influence.

Under such circumstances, you'll need to use the second Django alternative to perform raw SQL queries, which consists of directly connecting to a database and explicitly extracting the results of a query. Although this second Django alternative is technically the most flexible to interact with a database, it also requires using lower-level calls from Python's DB API.

The only thing you can leverage from Django when performing raw SQL queries using this technique is the database connection defined in a Django project (i.e., the `DATABASES` variable in `settings.py`). Once a database connection is established, you'll need to rely on Python DB API methods like `cursor()`, `fetchone()` and `fetchall()` - as well as perform manual extraction of the results - to be able to successfully run raw SQL queries.

Listing 8-60 illustrates SQL queries using the Python DB API in the context of Django.

Listing 8-60. Django raw SQL queries with connection() and low-level DB API methods

```
from django.db import connection

# Delete record
target_id = 1
with connection.cursor() as cursor:
    cursor.execute("DELETE from items_item where id = %s", [target_id])

# Select one record
salad_item = None
with connection.cursor() as cursor:
    cursor.execute("SELECT * from items_item where name='Red Fruit Salad'")
    salad_item = cursor.fetchone()

# DB API fetchone produces a tuple, where elements are accessible by index
salad_item[0] # id
salad_item[1] # name
salad_item[2] # description

# Select multiple records
all_drinks = None
with connection.cursor() as cursor:
```

```
    cursor.execute("SELECT * from items_drink")
    all_drinks = cursor.fetchall()

# DB API fetchall produces a list of tuples
all_drinks[0][0] # first drink id
```

The first statement in Listing 8-60 imports `django.db.connection`, which represents the `default` database connection defined in the `DATABASES` variable in `settings.py`. Once you have a `connection` reference to the Django database, you can start to make use of the Python DB API, which generally starts with the use of the `cursor()` method.[8]

The first raw SQL query in Listing 8-60 opens a `cursor` on the `connection` and executes the `cursor.execute()` method to perform a delete operation. Because delete queries don't return results, the operation is considered concluded after the calling the `cursor.execute()` method

---

■ **Tip** If you declare multiple database reference in DATABASES, you can cause the django.db.connections reference to create a cursor on a specific database, instead of the default:

from django.db import connections

cursor = connections['analytics'].cursor() # Cursor connects to 'analytics' DB

The second raw SQL query in Listing 8-60 first declares the `salad_item` placeholder variable to store the results of the raw SQL query. Once this is done, another `cursor` is opened on the `connection` to execute a select operation using the same `cursor.execute()` method. Because select queries return a result, an additional call is made on the `cursor.fetchone()` method to extract the results of the query and assign them to the placeholder variable. Note the `fetchone()` method is used because it's expected the raw SQL query will return a single record result.

Next, observe how the results of raw SQL query in `salad_item` are accessed by an index. Since the Python DB API `cursor.fetchone()` method makes no use of field names or other references, you have to know the order in which record fields are returned, a process that can be particularly cumbersome for raw SQL with many fields.

The third raw SQL query in Listing 8-60 first declares the `all_drinks` placeholder variable to store the results of the raw SQL query. Once this is done, another `cursor` is opened on the `connection` to execute anther select operation using the same `cursor.execute()` method. Because select queries return a result, an additional call is made on the `cursor.fetchall()` method to extract the results of the query and assign them to the placeholder variable. Note the `fetchall()` method is used because it's expected the raw SQL query will return multiple record results.

Next, observe how the results of raw SQL query in `all_drinks` are accessed by multiple indexes. Since the Python DB API `cursor.fetchall()` method makes no use of field names or other references, the first index represents a record in the result and the second index represents a field value from a given record.

Model Managers

As you've learned throughout the examples presented in this and the previous chapter, a Django model's `objects` reference or default model manager offers an extensive array of functionalities to execute database operations.

---

[8] `https://en.wikipedia.org/wiki/Cursor_(databases)`

Under most circumstances, Django models don't require any modifications to their default model manager or `objects` reference. However, there can be circumstances where the need arises to customize a Django model's default model manager or inclusively create multiple model managers.

Custom and Multiple Model Managers

One of the main reasons to create custom Django model managers is to add custom manager methods, to make the execution of recurring queries on a model easier.

For example, running queries such as `Item.objects.filter(menu__name='Sandwiches')` or `Item.objects.filter(menu__name='Salads')` is simple, but if you start writing these same queries over and over, the process can become tiresome and error prone. This is particularly true for raw SQL queries, which take more time to write and have a higher degree of complexity.

A custom manager method allows you to write a query once as part of a model, and later invoke the custom manager method - just like other model manager methods (e.g., `all()`, `filter()`, `exclude()`) - to trigger the query. Listing 8-61 illustrates a custom model manager class with a custom method, including a model that uses it, in addition to various model manager calls.

Listing 8-61. Django custom model manager with custom manager methods

```
from django.db import models

# Create custom model manager
class ItemMenuManager(models.Manager):
    def salad_items(self):
        return self.filter(menu__name='Salads')

    def sandwich_items(self):
        return self.filter(menu__name='Sandwiches')

# Option 1) Override default model manager
class Item(models.Model):
    menu = models.ForeignKey(Menu, on_delete=models.CASCADE)
    name = models.CharField(max_length=30)
    ...
    objects = ItemMenuManager()

# Queries on default custom model manager
Item.objects.all()
Item.objects.salad_items()
Item.objects.sandwich_items()

# Option 2) Create new model manager field and leave default model manager as is
    menu = models.ForeignKey(Menu, on_delete=models.CASCADE)
    name = models.CharField(max_length=30)
    ...
    objects = models.Manager()
    menumgr = ItemMenuManager()
```

```
# Queries on default and custom model managers
Item.objects.all()
Item.menumgr.salad_items()
Item.menumgr.sandwich_items()
# ERROR Item.objects.salad_items() # 'Manager' object has no attribute 'salad_items'
# ERROR Item.objects.sandwich_items() # 'Manager' object has no attribute 'sandwich_items'
Item.menumgr.all()
```

The first class in Listing 8-61 is the `ItemMenuManager` that functions as a custom model manager. Notice how this class inherits its behavior from the `models.Manager` class, which is what gives it model manager behavior. Next, the `ItemMenuManager` class declares two methods that return `QuerySet` results. Notice how the class methods reference `self` - representing the model class instance - and call standard model methods to trigger database queries.

It's worth mentioning custom model managers don't necessarily need to use native model queries or return `QuerySet` data structures, and custom model managers can equally contain any logic (e.g., Python DB API calls) or return any data structure (e.g., Python tuples).

Once you have a custom model manager there are two options to assign it to a model class. The first option, illustrated in Listing 8-61, consists of overriding a model's default model manager `objects` and explicitly assigning it a custom model manager. Once this is done, you can use the same `objects` reference to call the custom model manager methods. In addition, notice in Listing 8-61 that even when overriding the default model manager `objects`, a model continues to have access to the built-in model manager methods (e.g., `all()`) because the custom model inherits its behavior from the parent `models.Manager` class.

Next, Listing 8-61 illustrates the second option to integrate a custom model manager. This option consists of adding a new model field to reference a custom manager and leave the default manager `objects` as is. In this case, the custom model manager methods become accessible through the new field reference (e.g., `Item.menumgr.salad_items()`) and the `objects` reference continues to work with its default behavior.

■ **Tip** When you declare multiple model managers in a model, you can set the default model manager using the default_manager_name meta option. See the previous chapter for additional details on model meta options.

■ **Warning** If you don't define a default model manager in a multi-manager model, Django choose the first manager declared in the model. This can have unexpected behaviors in model operations that can't explicitly choose model managers (e.g., dumpdata) unlike queries that can use dot notation to choose a model manager.

Custom Model Managers and QuerySet Classes with Methods

Model managers are closely tied to methods that return `QuerySet` data structures. As you've seen, nearly all methods chained to the default model manager `objects` (e.g., `all()`, `filter()`) generate `QuerySet` data structures. When you create custom model managers, it's possible to override the default behavior for these `QuerySet` methods, as well as create your own custom `QuerySet` classes and methods.

One of the most important `QuerySet` methods in model managers is the `get_queryset()` method, used to define a model's initial `QuerySet` or what's returned by a model manager's `all()` method. In custom model managers, the `get_queryset()` method is particularly important because it lets you filter the initial `QuerySet` depending on the purpose of a model manager.

Listing 8-62 illustrates multiple custom model managers that define custom logic for the get_queryset() method.

Listing 8-62. Django custom model managers with custom get_queryset() method

```
class SanDiegoStoreManager(models.Manager):
    def get_queryset(self):
        return super(SanDiegoStoreManager, self).get_queryset().filter(city='San Diego')

class LosAngelesStoreManager(models.Manager):
    def get_queryset(self):
        return super(LosAngelesStoreManager, self).get_queryset().filter(city='Los Angeles')

class Store(models.Model):
    name = models.CharField(max_length=30)
    ...
    objects = models.Manager()
    sandiego = SanDiegoStoreManager()
    losangeles = LosAngelesStoreManager()

# Call default manager all() query, backed by get_queryset() method
Store.objects.all()
# Call sandiego manager all(), backed by get_queryset() method
Store.sandiego.all()
# Call losangeles manager all(), backed by get_queryset() method
Store.losangeles.all()
```

The first two classes in Listing 8-62 represent custom model managers; however, notice that unlike the custom model manager in Listing 8-61, both the SanDiegoStoreManager and LosAngelesStoreManager classes define the get_queryset() method. In both cases, the get_queryset() method returns a QuerySet generated by calling the parent model manager get_queryset() method (i.e., all()) - via the super() method - and applying an additional filter() to the parent depending on the purpose of the custom model manager (e.g., get stores by city).

Once the custom managers are defined, Listing 8-62 declares the custom model managers as separate fields in the Store model class. Finally, in Listing 8-62 you can see calls made to each of the model managers using the all() method, which return the appropriate filtered results depending on the logic of the backing get_queryset() method.

An alternative to multiple custom model managers is to create a single custom manager and rely on a custom QuerySet class and methods to execute the same logic, a technique that's illustrated in Listing 8-63.

Listing 8-63. Django custom model manager with custom QuerySet class and methods

```
class StoreQuerySet(models.QuerySet):
    def sandiego(self):
        return self.filter(city='San Diego')

    def losangeles(self):
        return self.filter(city='Los Angeles')

class StoreManager(models.Manager):
    def get_queryset(self):
        return StoreQuerySet(self.model, using=self._db)
```

```
    def sandiego(self):
        return self.get_queryset().sandiego()

    def losangeles(self):
        return self.get_queryset().losangeles()

class Store(models.Model):
    name = models.CharField(max_length=30)
    ...
    objects = models.Manager()
    shops = StoreManager()

Store.shops.all()
Store.shops.sandiego()
Store.shops.losangeles()
```

The StoreQuerySet class in Listing 8-63 is a custom QuerySet class that defines the sandiego() and losangeles() methods, both of which apply additional filters to its base QuerySet. Once you have a QuerySet class, it's necessary to associate it with a custom model manager. In Listing 8-63, you can see the StoreManager class represents a custom model manager, which defines its get_queryset() method to set its initial data through the custom StoreQuerySet class.

Next, notice how the custom model manager StoreManager class defines the additional sandiego() and losangeles() methods, which are hooked up to call the methods by the same name in the custom StoreQuerySet class.

Finally, the custom model manager StoreManager is set up as the shops field in the Store model class, where you can observe how calls are made via the shops reference to trigger the query methods backed by the custom StoreQuerySet class.

As helpful as the technique in Listing 8-63 is to cut down on the amount of model managers, if you look carefully at Listing 8-63, there's still a fair amount of redundancy declaring similar named methods for both a custom model manager and a custom QuerySet class.

To cut down on redundant methods when using custom model managers and custom QuerySet classes, the latter type of class offers the as_manager() method to automatically convert a QuerySet class into a custom model manager, a technique that's illustrated in Listing 8-64.

Listing 8-64. Django custom model manager with custom QuerySet converted to manager

```
class StoreQuerySet(models.QuerySet):
    def sandiego(self):
        return self.filter(city='San Diego')

    def losangeles(self):
        return self.filter(city='Los Angeles')

class Store(models.Model):
    name = models.CharField(max_length=30)
    ...
    objects = models.Manager()
    shops =  StoreQuerySet.as_manager()

Store.shops.all()
Store.shops.sandiego()
Store.shops.losangeles()
```

The example in Listing 8-64 defines the same custom QuerySet class as the one in Listing 8-63; however, notice the lack of a custom model manager class. Instead, the Store model definition in Listing 8-64 directly references the custom StoreQuerySet class and calls the as_manager() on it to convert the QuerySet class into a model manager. Finally, notice how the calls made via the shops reference are identical to the ones in Listing 8-63. In this manner, the technique in Listing 8-64 saves you the additional work of creating explicit custom model managers if you're using custom QuerySet classes.

Custom Reverse Model Managers for Related Models

Earlier in the CRUD relationship records subsection, you learned how models that have relationships between one another use reverse queries or _set syntax to execute operations from the model that doesn't have the relationship definition.

These reverse operations are executed by a model manager dubbed RelatedManager, which is a subclass of a model's default manager. This means all reverse queries or _set syntax calls are based on the objects model manager reference or whatever default model manager is used by a model.

If you configure a default model manager on a model, then all the reverse operations on a model will automatically use this same manager. However, it's possible to define a custom model manager exclusively for reverse operations, while ignoring the default model manager. This technique consists of explicitly declaring a model manager as part of the reverse operation, as shown in Listing 8-65.

Listing 8-65. Django custom model manager for reverse query operations

```
from django.db import models

class Item(models.Model):
    ...
    objects = models.Manager() # Default manager for direct queries
    reverseitems = CustomReverseManagerForItems() # Custom Manager for reverse queries

# Get Menu record named Breakfast
breakfast_menu = Menu.objects.get(name='Breakfast')

# Fetch all Item records in the Menu, using Item custom model manager for reverse queries
breakfast_menu.item_set(manager='reverseitems').all()
# Call on_sale_items() custom manager method in CustomReverseManagerForItems
breakfast_menu.item_set(manager='reverseitems').on_sale_items()
```

Listing 8-65 first declares the Item model with its default objects model manager and a custom model manager assigned to the reverseitems field. Next, a query is made to get a Menu record, followed by various queries to get the Menu record's related Item records via the reverse _set syntax.

However, notice how the reverse query operation in Listing 8-65 with _set syntax uses the manager argument to indicate which model manager to use for reverse operations; in this case, the reverseitems model manager is used to execute the queries, instead of the default objects model manager.

CHAPTER 9

Django Model Forms and Class Views

In the previous two chapters you learned how Django models are used to move data between a relational database and a Django project. Although this is the main purpose of Django models, there's another important set of functionalities fulfilled by Django models that isn't tied directly to a database.

In this chapter you'll learn how to create Django forms parting from Django models, a process that further extends Django's DRY (Don't Repeat Yourself) principle. You'll learn how a Django model can produce a Django form, including its fields, validations, and also save its data to a database, all without writing many of the form scaffolding logic described in Chapter 6.

Next, you'll learn about Django class-based views with models. Although you can continue to use the Django view techniques covered in Chapter 2 – just like the form techniques in Chapter 6 – with a firm grasp of Django models, you can further apply the Django DRY principle to views. You'll learn how to create class-based views to execute model CRUD operations, in turn, reducing the amount of logic required to incorporate model CRUD operations in views.

Django Model Form Structure and Workflow

Django models represent the standard way to move data into and out of a database. But as you've learned throughout the previous two chapters, the phase of moving data into and out of a database requires you to programmatically manipulate model records (e.g., inside view methods in `views.py` files) to execute the needed CRUD operation on a model.

While this is a perfectly valid workflow for any web framework, you can improve this process of moving data into and out of a database by linking Django models to a more natural input/output mechanism: forms.

Once you programmatically create enough Django model records in real-life projects, you'll see a pattern emerge: the logic behind most Django model operations is dictated by user interactions. Either an end user creates an `Order` model record, an end user reads a `Store` model record, an administrator updates a `Menu` model record, or an administrator deletes an `Item` model record. And what do these end users and administrators use to communicate these model operations? Exactly, forms in a user interface (UI).

Now let's take a look at the flip side of linking forms to models. In Chapter 6 you learned about Django forms, but did you realize what's the most likely operation you're going to do with the form data after its processed? You're most likely to save it to a database, which involves Django models.

So in the spirit of Django's DRY principle, model forms offer a way to use a Django model as the foundation to produce a Django form to execute CRUD operations on a Django model. In other words, instead of creating a stand-alone Django form and then creating the necessary 'glue' code to create a Django model instance, or vice versa, creating a stand-alone Django model and then creating the necessary form to do CRUD operations on a model record, Django model forms allow you to not repeat yourself.

D. Rubio, *Beginning Django*, https://doi.org/10.1007/978-1-4842-2787-9_9

Create Django Model Forms

Back in Chapter 6 you created a Django form to capture a name, email, and comment. Next, we'll redesign this form as a model form to be able to quickly save the data to a database.

The first step to create a model form is to create a model as the foundation for the data. Listing 9-1 illustrates a Django model class and immediately after a Django model form created from the model.

■ **Tip** Consult the book's accompanying source code to run the exercises, in order to reduce typing and automatically access test data.

Listing 9-1. Django model class and model form

```
from django import forms

class Contact(models.Model):
      name = models.CharField(max_length=50,blank=True)
      email = models.EmailField()
      comment = models.CharField(max_length=1000)

class ContactForm(forms.ModelForm):
      class Meta:
            model = Contact
            fields = '__all__'
```

The first important aspect of Listing 9-1 is the Django model follows the standard model syntax, with three fields that use model fields to restrict the type of data stored by the model. The model in Listing 9-1 is kept simple to better illustrate model forms, but it's possible to add any other model functionality you learned in the previous two chapters (e.g., validators, clean methods, Meta options).

Next in Listing 9-1 is the `ContactForm` class that represents the form and which inherits its behavior from the `django.forms.ModelForm` class, the last of which is what makes it a model form. Notice the `ContactForm` class lacks any form fields like those you learned in Chapter 6 in Table 6-2; instead it declares a `Meta` class section like the one used in models.

The `Meta` class section for the `ContactForm` specifies two options: `model` and `fields`. The `model` option indicates which model to use to generate the form, in this case, the `Contact` model also in Listing 9-1. The `fields` option indicates which model fields to use to generate the form, in the case, `'__all__'` tells Django to use all the model `fields` in the model.

The powerful aspect of `ContactForm` in Listing 9-1 is it uses two statements to create a form that reflects the same field types as the `Contact` model. Not only does this avoid repeating yourself (e.g., typing in explicit form fields), the form fields also inherit the validation behaviors of the model (e.g., `models.EmailField()` get translated into `forms.EmailField`). But I'll describe more details and options about this model-to-form inheritance behavior shortly, once I finish describing the basics of model forms.

Once you have a model form class, you might be wondering how does its processing differ from a standard Django form? Very little actually; the same concepts you learned in Chapter 6 to process, validate, and lay out forms are just as valid for model forms, as shown in Listing 9-2.

Listing 9-2. Django model form processing

```
# views.py method to process model form
def contact(request):
    if request.method == 'POST':
        # POST, generate bound form with data from the request
        form = ContactForm(request.POST)
        # check if it's valid:
        if form.is_valid():
            # Insert into DB
            form.save()
            # redirect to a new URL:
            return HttpResponseRedirect('/about/contact/thankyou')
    else:
        # GET, generate unbound (blank) form
        form = ContactForm()
    return render(request,'about/contact.html',{'form':form})

# See chapter 6 for form layout template syntax in about/contact.html
```

In Listing 9-2 you can see the view method sequence follows the same pattern as a standard Django form. When a user makes a GET request on the view method, an *unbound* form instance is created that is sent to the user and rendered via the `about/contact.html` template. Next, when a user submits the form via a POST request, a *bound* form is created using the `request.POST` argument, which is then validated using the `is_valid()` method. If the form values are invalid, the *bound* form with errors is returned to the user so he can correct the mistakes, and if the form values are valid, in the specific case of Listing 9-2, the user is redirected to the `/about/contact/thankyou` page.

However, there's one important processing difference in model forms that's bolded out in Listing 9-2. After a form's values are determined to be valid, a call is made to the `save()` on the model form instance. This `save()` method is tied to a form's backing model `save()` method, which means the form data is structured as a model record and saved to the database.

As you can realize, this process to create and process a model form is a real time saver vs. having to a create and process a stand-alone form and a stand-alone model.

Django Model Form Options and Field Mapping

Now that you understand the basic operation of model forms, let's take a look at its various options. Most model form options are declared in the Meta class statement, as you saw in Listing 9-1. However, it's also possible to declare regular form fields, to either override the default model field behavior or include new form fields altogether.

Model Form Required Options: Model and Fields or Exclude

Model forms inherit their behavior from the `forms.ModelForm` class - instead of the standard `forms.Form` class - therefore Django always expect a model on which to base the form, which is the purpose of the meta `model` option. Therefore a `model` option value is always a requirement of model forms.

Django doesn't expect the structure of a model to fit perfectly with a form, to the point Django also expects you to explicitly tell it which fields of the backing model should or shouldn't become part of the model form. This is achieved with either the `fields` option – to indicate which model fields become part of the model form – of the `exclude` option – to indicate which model fields shouldn't become part of the model form. The `fields` or `exclude` option is always required, even when a model form will contain all fields of the backing model. Notice how the model form example in Listing 9-1 declares the option `fields='__all__'` to create a model form that captures the same set of fields as its backing model.

When you declare a model form with something other than `fields='__all__'` (e.g., a shortened list of model fields) or the `exclude` option (e.g., a list of model fields to omit in the form), be aware that you're willfully and potentially breaking a model's rules. For example, by default all model fields are required, so if you create a model form that omits certain fields – either with `fields` or `exclude` – the form itself can appear normal, but the model form will never successfully finish its standard workflow, unless you manually add the omitted fields. Under such circumstances, end users will see an 'invalid form error' because the model part of the form is broken due to a required model field value. The upcoming section on model form validation and initialization describes how to manually add omitted field values to model forms.

As you can see, you can create a model form with more or less fields than its backing model. In addition, it's also possible to add new fields to a model form – which aren't part of a backing model – as well as customize the default form field produced by a model field.

In order to describe a solution to these last two scenarios, the next section describes the different form fields produced by each model field – so you can determine if you need to customize the default behavior - and the subsequent section describes how to customize and add new fields to a model form.

Model Form Default Field Mapping

Models forms follow certain rules to transform model field data types – described in Table 7-1 – into form field data types – described in Table 6-2. In most cases, model field data types get transformed into mirror-like equivalent form field data types. For example, if a model field uses the `models.CharField` data type, a model form converts this field to a `forms.CharField` data type.

Table 9-1 illustrates the model form mapping used between model data types and form data types. Note that data types with mirror-like data type mappings between models and forms are enclosed in the first line in Table 9-1.

Table 9-1. *Model form data type mapping between models and forms*

Model field	Form field
models.BooleanField	forms.BooleanField
models.DateField	forms.DateField
models.DateTimeField	forms.DateTimeField
models.DecimalField	forms.DecimalField
models.EmailField	forms.EmailField
models.FileField	forms.FileField
models.FilePathField	forms.FilePathField
models.FloatField	forms.FloatField
models.ImageField	forms.ImageField
models.IntegerField	forms.IntegerField
models.IPAddressField	forms.IPAddressField
models.GenericIPAddressField	forms.GenericIPAddressField
models.NullBooleanField	forms.NullBooleanField
models.SlugField	forms.SlugField
models.TimeField	forms.TimeField
models.URLField	forms.URLField
models.AutoField models.BigAutoField	Not represented in the form, because Auto-model fields are generated by the database.
models.BigIntegerField	forms.IntegerField, with min_value set to -9223372036854775808 and max_value set to 9223372036854775807)
models.CharField	forms.CharField, with max_length set to the model field's max_length and empty_value set to None if null=True
models.CommaSeparatedIntegerField	forms.CharField
models.ForeignKey	forms.ModelChoiceField
models.ManyToManyField	forms.ModelMultipleChoiceField
models.PositiveIntegerField	forms.IntegerField, with min_value set to 0
models.PositiveSmallIntegerField	forms.IntegerField, with min_value set to 0
models.SmallIntegerField	forms.IntegerField
models.TextField	forms.CharField, with widget=forms.Textarea

As you can see in Table 9-1, over 50% of Django model data types map directly to equivalent form data types. Most of the remaining model data types map to slightly adjusted form data types to better fit the backing model type (e.g., `models.PositiveIntegerField` maps to a `forms.IntegerField` but with a form `min_value` value of 0).

It's only four model data types in Table 9-1 that don't map directly to form data types described in Chapter 6 in Table 6-2. The `models.AutoField` and `models.BigAutoField` model data types are never represented in model forms, for the simple reason their values are auto-assigned by a database, so they have no place to be input in forms. The `models.ForeignKey` and `models.ManyToManyField` model data types represent model relationships, which means their data comes from separate models. In turn, the `models.ForeignKey` and `models.ManyToManyField` model data types don't map to regular form field for strings or numbers, but rather form fields that represent other model data, which is the purpose of the special form data types: `forms.ModelChoiceField` and `forms.ModelMultipleChoiceField`. These two last form fields are described in the later subsection on model forms with relationships.

■ **Tip** To consult the HTML produced by a form field data type (e.g., <input type="text" ...> consult Table 6-2, which contains the mapping between form fields and form widgets, the last of which produces the actual form HTML markup.

Model Form New and Custom Fields: Widgets, Labels, help_texts, error_messages, field_classes, and localize_fields

Now that you know how all model fields are transformed into form fields in a model form, let's address how to add and customize form fields in a model form.

Adding a new form field to a model form is as simple as declaring a form field as if it were a regular form. It's also possible to customize the default form field data type used by a model field data type (i.e., the mappings in Table 9-1), by declaring a new form field with the same name as a model field, to take precedence over the default model-form field mapping.

Listing 9-3 illustrates the Django model class and model form from Listing 9-1, updated to include a new form field and a form field that overrides a default model-form field mapping.

Listing 9-3. Django model form with new and custom field

```
from django import forms

def faq_suggestions(value):
      # Validate value and raise forms.ValidationError for invalid values
      pass

class Contact(models.Model):
      name = models.CharField(max_length=50,blank=True)
      email = models.EmailField()
      comment = models.CharField()

class ContactForm(forms.ModelForm):
      age = forms.IntegerField()
      comment = forms.CharField(widget=forms.Textarea,validators=[faq_suggestions])
      class Meta:
            model = Contact
            fields = '__all__'
```

Listing 9-3 first adds the new age form field to capture an integer value in the form. Although the underlying `Contact` model is never aware of the age field or value, with this modification the model form will require this field to be provided as part of the form workflow.

Next in Listing 9-3 is the `comment` form field, which overrides the underlying model field by the same name. In this case, overriding the `comment` form field has the purpose of adding a custom `widget`, as well as adding a custom `validators` method to verify the `comment` value before the form is deemed valid - note that both the `widget` and `validators` options are standard form options described in Chapter 6.

The form field overriding mechanism in Listing 9-3 has both an advantage and disadvantage. The advantage is you get full control of the form field to define any options. The disadvantage is a model field option's (e.g., `max_length`) - that would be passed to the form field - are lost and need to be redeclared as part of the new form field statement.

To preserve a model field's underlying behavior and still be able to customize certain form field options, model forms support additional meta class options besides the `model`, `fields`, and `exclude` options. Listing 9-4 illustrates a model form's additional meta options to override the default model-form field mapping, while keeping the underlying model field behavior.

Listing 9-4. Django model form with meta options to override default form field behavior

```
from django import forms

class Contact(models.Model):
      name = models.CharField(max_length=50,blank=True)
      email = models.EmailField()
      comment = models.CharField()

class ContactForm(forms.ModelForm):
      class Meta:
            model = Contact
            fields = '__all__'
            widgets = {
               'name': models.CharField(max_length=25),
               'comment': form.Textarea(attrs={'cols': 100, 'rows': 40})
            }
            labels = {
               'name': 'Full name',
               'comment': 'Issue'
            }
            help_texts = {
               'comment': 'Provide a detailed account of the issue to receive a quick answer'
            }
            error_messages = {
               'name': {
               'max_length': "Name can only be 25 characters in length"
                }
            }
            field_classes = {
               'email': EmailCoffeehouseFormField
            },
            localized_fields = '__all__'
```

The most important aspect of the meta model form options in Listing 9-4 is they're pluralized names of the form field options described in Chapter 6. The highlighted model form meta options in Listing 9-4 are pluralized because they can declare options for multiple form fields as a dictionary, where each key represents the form field name and its value the option value.

For example, the `widgets` and `labels` meta options in Listing 9-4 define custom widgets and labels for both the `name` and `comment` model form fields. The `help_texts` meta option defines the `help_text` option for the `comment` model form field, while the `error_messages` meta option declares a custom form error message for the `max_length` key error on the `name` model form field.

Next, the `field_classes` meta option in Listing 9-4 is used to declare a custom form field for the `email` model form field. Finally, the `localized_field` meta option in Listing 9-4 is set to `__all__` to tell Django to localize (i.e., convert into a different language) all model form fields. If the `localized_field` option is omitted, then model form fields are not localized. It's worth mentioning you can selectively localize certain model form fields by passing a list of model form fields to the `localized_field` option, just like it's done with the `fields` and exclude options.

Django Model Forms with Relationships

As you learned in the previous two chapters, Django models can have relationships between one another, which in turn makes models have a data type (e.g., `ForeignKey`, `ManyToManyField`) that references records in another model.

When models containing such data types are used in the context of model forms, Django relies on two special form fields. By default, `ForeignKey` model fields are converted to `ModelChoiceField` form fields, and `ManyToManyField` model fields are converted to `ModelMultipleChoiceField` form fields.

The benefit of the `ModelChoiceField` and `ModelMultipleChoiceField` form fields is that they generate a form field based on a Django model query. So instead of manually populating a form field with model data, the `ModelChoiceField` and `ModelMultipleChoiceField` form fields generate a friendly HTML `<select>/<option>` input field with model records.

ModelChoiceField and ModelMultipleChoiceField Form Field Options: queryset, empty_label, to_field_name, and label_from_instance

---

■ **Tip** `ModelChoiceField` and `ModelMultipleChoiceField` are standard form fields usable on any Django form that requires model data. They are used by default on model forms with relationships, but they're not restricted to model forms (i.e., forms inherited from `forms.ModelForm`).

■ **Note** `ModelChoiceField` and `ModelMultipleChoiceField` being standard form fields (i.e., part of the Django `forms` package), also accept the standard form options: required, widget, label, initial, help_text, and limit_choices_to – described in Chapter 6.

Since `ModelChoiceField` and `ModelMultipleChoiceField` form fields use model records to source their data, they unequivocally require a model query. For model forms that inherit their behavior from `forms.ModelForm` and their underlying models contain a `ForeignKey` or `ManyToManyField` model field, this model query is set automatically. For example, if an `Item` model contains a `ForeignKey` to a `Menu` model, an `Item` model form presents all `Menu` records in a form to allow users to select a single `Menu` record. Similarly, if a `Store` model contains a `ManyToManField` to an `Amenity` model, a `Store` model form presents all `Amenity` records in a form to allow users to select multiple `Amenity` records.

While this behavior is acceptable in most circumstances, it can be necessary to provide an explicit query to `ModelChoiceField` or `ModelMultipleChoiceField` form fields, either when you need to filter the default behavior to use all model records on a model form field or when these form fields are used in a regular form (i.e., that inherits `forms.Form`).

Listing 9-5 illustrates the two techniques to set a model query on either the `ModelChoiceField` and `ModelMultipleChoiceField` form fields using the `queryset` option.

Listing 9-5. Django model form and standard form with custom query for ModelChoiceField and ModelMultipleChoiceField form fields

```
from django import forms
from coffeehouse.stores.models import Amenity
```

```
class Menu(models.Model):
    name = models.CharField(max_length=30)
    def __str__(self):
        return "%s" % (self.name)

class Item(models.Model):
    menu = models.ForeignKey(Menu, on_delete=models.CASCADE)
    name = models.CharField(max_length=30)
    description = models.CharField(max_length=100)

class ItemForm(forms.ModelForm):
    menu = forms.ModelChoiceField(queryset=Menu.objects.filter(id=1))
    class Meta:
        model = Item
        fields = '__all__'

class StoreForm(forms.Form):
    name = forms.CharField()
    address = forms.CharField()
    amenities = forms.ModelMultipleChoiceField(queryset=None)
    def __init__(self, *args, **kwargs):
        super(StoreForm, self).__init__(*args, **kwargs)
        self.fields['amenities'].queryset = Amenity.objects.filter(name__contains='W')
```

The first technique in Listing 9-5 defines an inline queryset value by overriding the menu field with a custom ModelChoiceField() on the ItemForm model form. In this case, instead of the ItemForm model form having a menu field with all Item records, the menu field is restricted to only the Item record with id=1.

The second technique in Listing 9-5 defines an empty queryset value on a standard form that uses a forms.ModelMultipleChoiceField() form field on the amenities field. But inside the form's __init__ method, the amenities field is set to a query that restricts its records to Amenity records that contain the letter W.

It's worth mentioning, both queryset techniques illustrated in Listing 9-5 are equally valid in both model forms and regular forms, as well as ModelChoiceField() and ModelMultipleChoiceField() form fields.

By default, ModelChoiceField() form fields that don't define an initial value are generated with the empty HTML <option>---------</option> choice as the default field value. It's possible to customize the value of this empty option with the empty_label option (e.g., empty_label='Please select a value', to output <option>Please select a value</option>). It's also possible to disable the inclusion of this empty option with empty_label=None.

By default, both ModelChoiceField() and ModelMultipleChoiceField() form fields generate their HTML <select>/<option> input field values from a model record's primary key value (i.e., id) and model __str__ method representation. For example, given the Menu model definition in Listing 9-5, an HTML <select>/<option> input field for this model would look like the following snippet:

```
<select name="menu" required id="id_menu">
     <option value="" selected>---------</option>
     <option value="1">Breakfast</option>
     <option value="2">Salads</option>
     <option value="3">Sandwiches</option>
     <option value="4">Drinks</option>
</select>
```

Note each `<option>` value corresponds to a record's primary key `id` value and the `<option>` text corresponds to a record's `name` field returned by the model's `__str__` method.

It's possible to customize the `<option>` value used in both `ModelChoiceField()` and `ModelMultipleChoiceField()` form fields with the `to_field_name` option. For example, setting `to_field_name='name'` in the context of this last snippet, changes the HTML `<select>`/`<option>` input field to the format `<option value="Breakfast">Breakfast</option>`.

■ **Caution** Using a to_field_name value breaks the underlying model form's ability to be saved to the database, since the model's relationship value is set to a different value than the primary key expected by the model relationship.

In addition to customizing the `<option>` value, it's also possible to customize the `<option>` text in form fields to something other than a model's `__str__` method, by overriding a `label_form_instance` method in either a `ModelChoiceField()` and `ModelMultipleChoiceField()` form field. Listing 9-6 illustrate a custom form field designed for this purpose.

Listing 9-6. Django custom form field to customize <option> text for ModelChoiceField and ModelMultipleChoiceField form fields

```
from django import forms
from django.forms import ModelChoiceField

class MenuModelChoiceField(ModelChoiceField):
    def label_from_instance(self, obj):
        return "Menu #%s) %s" % (obj.id,obj.name)

class ItemForm(forms.ModelForm):
    menu = MenuModelChoiceField(queryset=Menu.objects.all())
    class Meta:
        model = Item
        fields = '__all__'

# HTML menu form field output
<select name="menu" id="id_menu" required>
  <option value="" selected>---------</option>
  <option value="1">Menu #1) Breakfast</option>
  <option value="2">Menu #2) Salads</option>
  <option value="3">Menu #3) Sandwiches</option>
  <option value="4">Menu #4) Drinks</option>
</select>
```

The first step in Listing 9-6 creates the `MenuModelChoiceField` custom form field that inherits its behavior from the `ModelChoiceField` form field and defines an implementation for the `label_from_instance` method. In this case, the `label_from_instance` method tells Django to generate `<option>` text values prefixed with the `Menu #` static string, followed by a model's `id` and `name`. Note this same technique can be used to customize a `ModelMultipleChoiceField`, just make sure to change the custom form field's inheriting class.

Next, the MenuModelChoiceField custom form field in Listing 9-6 is added to the ItemForm model form in the same listing through the menu field. Because MenuModelChoiceField is a custom ModelChoiceField form field, it's necessary to specify an explicit queryset value to populate the form field, which in this case corresponds to all Menu model records.

Finally, Listing 9-6 illustrates the HTML <option> text output for the menu field follows the pattern defined in the custom MenuModelChoiceField custom form field.

Django Model Form Processing

Now that you have a solid understanding of the various model form options, it's time to take a deeper look at model form processing, which was briefly introduced in Listing 9-2.

The most important factor to take into account when processing model forms is you're working with two entities: a form and a model. In the model form processing example presented in Listing 9-2, this fact isn't too obvious, mainly because the form fits the backing model perfectly. However, when you modify any of the model form parts, working with a single reference that represents both a form and a model can require more forethought.

Model Form Initialization: Initial and Instance

Model forms can use two initialization parameters: initial and instance. The initial argument works just like the standard initial form argument - described in Chapter 6 - providing the initial values for an *unbound* form. The instance argument is used to initialize a model form with a model instance, which in turn is also used to initialize the values of an *unbound* form.

In all model forms, as you learned in the previous sections, form definitions take precedence over any underlying model definitions. This means all model form values in the initial argument take precedence over values defined via the instance argument. Listing 9-7 illustrates a model form initialization sequence using both the initial and instance parameters.

Listing 9-7. Django model form initialization with initial and instance

```
from coffeehouse.items.models import Item

preloaded_item = Item.objects.get(id=1)

# Model form from Listing 9-6, initialize with instance
form = ItemForm(instance=preloaded_item)

# Unbound form set up with instance values
form.as_p()
  <p>
   <label for="id_menu">Menu:</label>
        <select name="menu" required id="id_menu">
            <option value="">---------</option>
            <option value="1" selected>Menu #1) Breakfast</option>
            <option value="2">Menu #2) Salads</option>
            <option value="3">Menu #3) Sandwiches</option>
            <option value="4">Menu #4) Drinks</option>
         </select>
  </p>
```

```
  <p>
    <label for="id_name">Name:</label>
          <input type="text" name="name"
               value="Whole-Grain Oatmeal" required maxlength="30" id="id_name" />
    </p>
    # Remaining fields committed for brevity

# Model form from Listing 9-6, initialize with instance and override with initial
form2 = ItemForm(initial={'menu':3},instance=preloaded_item)

# Unbound form set up with instance values
form2.as_p()

# Unbound form set up with instance values, but overridden with initial
form2.as_p()
  <p>
   <label for="id_menu">Menu:</label>
        <select name="menu" required id="id_menu">
            <option value="">---------</option>
            <option value="1">Menu #1) Breakfast</option>
            <option value="2">Menu #2) Salads</option>
            <option value="3" selected>Menu #3) Sandwiches</option>
            <option value="4">Menu #4) Drinks</option>
         </select>
  </p>
   # Remaining fields committed for brevity
```

The first step in Listing 9-7 is to obtain an `Item` model record to populate the `ItemForm` model form; in this case, a query is made to get the `Item` model record with `id=1`. Next, the `Item` model record is used to initialize the model form with the instance values. In Listing 9-7, the form is output with the standard `as_p()` form method, where you can confirm the form fields are preselected to reflect the underlying model record.

Next in Listing 9-7 is an initialization sequence for the same `ItemForm` model form, but which also uses the `initial` argument in combination with the `instance` argument. In this case, because the `initial` argument provides the `'menu':3` value, the unbound form's `menu` field is set to a value of `3`, instead of the model record's instance `menu` value of `1`. Thus confirming the `initial` argument values take precedence over `instance` argument values.

Note that it's equally valid to only use the `initial` argument - without the `instance` argument - to initialize a model form as if it were a regular form. At the initialization phase of a model form, the model part of the form is unaware of any values, it's only until the model form enters its validation phase the underlying model is made of aware of any form values.

Model Form Validation

Similar to model form initialization, model form validation can appear to be intertwined because you're dealing with a single variable that references both a form and a model. But as long as you're aware of the fundamental steps of form validation - described in Chapter 6 - and model validation - described in Chapter 7 - model form validation is straightforward.

Back in Listing 9-2, you learned how a model form is converted to a *bound* form (i.e., a form containing user data) by passing the `request.POST` value in a view method (e.g., `ContactForm(request.POST)`). Once you have a *bound* form, the standard Django form validation workflow continues to apply for model forms: a call is made to the `is_valid()` method on the form reference to validate the user submitted data against *form* validation rules. If any of the *form* rules don't comply, an `errors` dictionary is added to the form reference with the causes, which makes its way back to the user as a re-rendered form with the errors. If the `is_valid()` method succeeds, the processing logic of the model form can move to the next step.

Once a model form passes the `is_valid()` method test, you can actually use the same standard form `cleaned_data()` method to gain access to a dictionary with the contents of the valid form data (e.g., `form.cleaned_data()` contains `{'name': '...','email': '...','comment': '...', }`). But since you're working with a model form, the step you're more likely take is to use the form data to further interact with a model.

To facilitate this process, Django adds the `instance` field to the form reference, containing the form data structured as an instance of the underlying model of the model form. The `instance` field is particularly important when you need or must manipulate the model data prior to attempting a model operation. And this is the most critical aspect of the model form validation process: even after the form `is_valid()` method passes and the data is used to structure a model instance in the `instance` field, this model instance data must still undergo model validation or risk being rejected by the backing model validation rules.

For straightforward model form scenarios, where a model and form map directly to one another - like the one in Listing 9-2 - manipulating the `instance` field is unnecessary (e.g., Right after the form `is_valid()` method passes, you can call the `save()` method on the `form` reference to save the model instance in `instance`). But for model forms where the model and form differ in the amount of fields, you'll need to perform additional logic after the form `is_valid()` method passes and before a called is made to the model form's `save()` method.

Listing 9-8 illustrates two validation procedures for a model form where the form omits fields from the underlying model.

Listing 9-8. Django model form with reduced form that requires model update before saving

```
from django import forms
from django.conf import settings

class Contact(models.Model):
      user = models.ForeignKey(settings.AUTH_USER_MODEL, null=True, default=None)
      name = models.CharField(max_length=50,blank=True)
      email = models.EmailField()
      comment = models.CharField()

class ContactForm(forms.ModelForm):
      class Meta:
            model = Contact
            exclude = ['user']

# Option 1) Form model processing with missing value assigned with instance
         if form.is_valid():
            # Check if user is available
            if request.user.is_authenticated():
                # Add missing user to model form
                form.instance.user = request.user
            # Insert into DB
            form.save()
```

```
# Option 2) Form model processing with missing value assigned after model form sequence
          if form.is_valid():
          # Save instance but don't commit until model instance is complete
          # form.save() returns a materialized model instance that has yet to be saved
          pending_contact = form.save(commit=False)
           # Check if user is available
          if request.user.is_authenticated():
              # Add missing user to model form
              pending_contact.user = request.user
          # Insert into DB
          pending_contact.save()
```

The Contact model in Listing 9-8 is similar to the model class used in previous listings, but has the additional user field to register a Django user as part of the model record. Next, in Listing 9-8 is the ContactForm model form - based on this last Contact model - which uses the exclude option to omit the user model field from the form.

Because you're purposely omitting the user field from the model form, an end user will have no way of providing it - even in the unlikely case he would know his internal user. Therefore, as part of the validation process, it's necessary to update the model to contain the internal user, which is always available in the request reference of a view method.

In the first validation sequence in Listing 9-8, you can see that after the model form passes the is_valid() method, a quick check is made to confirm if the user is authenticated; if so, the model's instance reference is accessed to update the user model field. Once this is done, the model form's backing instance contains a value for the omitted user field and upon calling the save() method, the model record is saved with values for all its model fields.

The second validation sequence in Listing 9-8 uses the commit=False to materialize the model instance of the model form without saving it to the database. Once this is done, the model form's work is done, so you're left with a basic model record instance that needs to be updated and saved to the database. You can see in Listing 9-8 an identical check is made to confirm if the user is authenticated, if so, the unsaved model record user reference is updated and a final called is made to the model's save() method to commit the record to the database.

Django Model Formsets

Just as standard Django forms can be grouped together as a set in what's called a formset, Django model forms can also be grouped into what's called a model formset. Similarly, just as Django model forms resemble standard Django forms, model formsets also have a lot of similarities with standard formsets.

Up next, I'll describe the particularities of model formsets building on the knowledge presented in the last part of Chapter 6 on standard formsets. So if you're unfamiliar with formset terms (e.g., factory and management form), go back and read this last section, as the following assumes you have prior knowledge on these basic formset concepts.

Model Formset Factory

The modelformset_factory() method is the centerpiece to working with model formsets. The modelformset_factory() method can accept up to 19 arguments, 9 of which are identical to standard formsets and the remaining ones specific to model formsets. The following snippet illustrates all the names and default values for each argument in the modelormset_factory() method, with bolded text representing model formset specific options.

```
modelformset_factory(model, queryset=model.objects.all(),
                  form=ModelForm,fields=None, exclude=None,
                 formset=BaseModelFormSet, extra=1, can_order=False, can_delete=False,
                 max_num=None, min_num=None, validate_max=False, validate_min=False,
                 widgets=None, localized_fields=None,labels=None,
                 help_texts=None, error_messages=None,
                 field_classes=None,formfield_callback=None)
```

As you can confirm in this snippet, the only required argument (i.e., that doesn't have a default value) for the `modelformset_factory()` method is `model`. The meaning for each argument is the following:

`model`.- Defines the model class on which to create a formset.

`queryset`.- Defines the queryset to create a formset. By default, all model records are used to create the formset (i.e., the `model.objects.all()` queryset if used).

`fields`.- Defines the model form fields to include as part of the model to create the model formset - just like the `fields` meta model form option.

`exclude`.- Defines the model form fields to omit as part of the model to create the model formset - just like the `exclude` meta model form option.

`widgets`.- Defines overriding widgets for the model form to create the model formset - just like the `widgets` meta model form option.

`localize_fields`.- Defines model form fields to localize (i.e., support multiple languages) to create the formset - just like the `localize_fields` meta model form option.

`labels`.- Defines overriding label for the model form to create the model formset - just like the `labels` meta model form option.

`help_text`.- Defines overriding help text for the model form to create the model formset - just like the `help_texts` meta model form option.

`error_messages`.- Defines overriding error messages for the model form to create the model formset - just like the `help_texts` meta model form option.

`field_classes`.- Defines overriding field classes for the model form to create the model formset - just like the `field_classes` meta model form option.

`formsetfield_callback`.- Defines a method to execute prior to creating a form field from a model field. Generally used to customize a model form field - as described in the earlier model form section - in the context of a formset.

■ **Tip** See Chapter 6 for details on the additional modelformset_factory option, which were already described in the standard formsets section.

Given that model formset logic is a combination of the model form techniques described earlier and formset techniques described in Chapter 6, I won't readdress the same techniques once again. You can look over the book's source code for a working model formset example in the source code for Chapter 9 under the `online` app.

Class-Based Views with Models

Back in Chapter 2, you learned how class-based views allow you to create views that operate with object-oriented programming (OOP) principles (e.g., encapsulation, polymorphism and inheritance) leading to greater reusability and shorter implementation times. Now that you know how Django models work, we can address class-based views that integrate with models described in the last part of Table 2-10.

Unlike standard Django views - explored in the early sections of Chapter 2 - which allow open-ended logic to process a request and generate a response, class-based views with models encapsulate the logic performed against Django models in a more modular way.

For example, the logical patterns to create, read, update, and delete model instances in a standard view method, generally follow a very consistent workflow: get input data from a url or form, execute CRUD operation on the model, and send the response to a template.

In the spirit of Django's DRY principle, class-based views with models offer a way to cut down on the boilerplate code used in standard view methods and use class fields and methods to define the workflow used for Django model CRUD operations.

Create Model Records with the Class-Based View CreateView

As you've learned up to this point, the creation of Django model instances in real-life projects comes accompanied by a series of constructs that can include model forms, GET/POST request processing, and the use of templates, among other things.

The Django `CreateView` class-based view is specifically designed to cut down on the amount of boilerplate code needed to perform the creation of a model record. Listing 9-9 illustrates a class-based view that uses the `CreateView` class.

Listing 9-9. Django class-based view with CreateView to create model records

```
# views.py
from django.views.generic.edit import CreateView
from .models import Item, ItemForm
from django.core.urlresolvers import reverse_lazy

class ItemCreation(CreateView):
    model = Item
    form_class = ItemForm
    success_url = reverse_lazy('items:index')

# models.py
from django import forms
from django.db import models

class Menu(models.Model):
    name = models.CharField(max_length=30)

class Item(models.Model):
    menu = models.ForeignKey(Menu, on_delete=models.CASCADE)
    name = models.CharField(max_length=30)
    description = models.CharField(max_length=100)

class ItemForm(forms.ModelForm):
    class Meta:
        model = Item
        fields = '__all__'
        widgets = {
            'description': forms.Textarea(),
        }

# urls.py
from django.conf.urls import url
from coffeehouse.items import views as items_views
```

```
urlpatterns = [
    url(r'^new/$', items_views.ItemCreation.as_view(), name='new'),
]

# templates/items/item_form.html
    <form method="post">
        {% csrf_token %}
        {{ form.as_p }}
        <button type="submit" class="btn btn-primary">Create</button>
    </form>
```

The first part in Listing 9-9 illustrates the `ItemCreation` class-based view that inherits its behavior from the `CreateView` class. Notice this view lacks a `request` reference, processing logic, or `return` statement, all of which were common in the standard view methods described in Chapter 2. So what is the `ItemCreation` class-based view actually doing?

Because you know beforehand you want to create a model record, the `CreateView` class – used by the `ItemCreation` class-based view – supports all the necessary boilerplate logic and requires a minimum set of code to fulfill its model record creation logic.

The `ItemCreation` class-based view in Listing 9-9 uses the `model` field to tell Django to create `Item` model records. In addition, the `form_class` field specifies the `ItemForm` form – also declared in Listing 9-9 – which is used to create model records. In addition, the `success_url` field is used to return control to the `item:index` url when model record creation is successful.

WHY REVERSE_LAZY IN CLASS-BASED VIEWS, INSTEAD OF REVERSE?

Due to the simultaneous import order of models, views, and urls in class-based views, using the standard reverse() method to resolve url names can result in the error: *django.core.exceptions. ImproperlyConfigured: The included URLconf '-----' does not appear to have any patterns in it. If you see valid patterns in the file then the issue is probably caused by a circular import.*

The reverse_lazy method ensures any reverse url name resolution is attempted only after all models, views, and urls have been properly imported; therefore it's the common choice in the context of class-based views.

You may still be left wondering, where are the `save()` and `is_valid()` methods for the `ItemCreation` class-based view in Listing 9-9 if it's creating model records? By default there aren't any. Because you *just* want to create a model record, the parent `CreateView` class takes care of this supporting logic.

The next part in Listing 9-9 contains the `urly.py` file with the hook to set up the class-based view into the application. In this case, the `ItemCreation` class-based view is set to run on the `/new` url and is declared as part of the `url()` method by using the class-based view `as_view()` method – note this url set up technique is identical for all class-based views and was described toward the end of Chapter 2 for class-based views without models.

So what happens when a user visits the `/new` url? Control is sent to the `ItemCreation` class-based view. And because this view's purpose is to create an `Item` model record, the class-based view looks for a template to render the form, under the `TEMPLATES` directory path of a project following the convention `<app_name>/<model_name>_form.html`.

In the last part of Listing 9-9, you can see the template `templates/items/item_form.html`, where `templates` represents a `TEMPLATES` directory path value, `items` the app name, and `item` the model name defined for the class-based view. In addition, notice the contents of the `item_form.html` template use a standard form layout, which you can adjust like any Django form.

So where is the POST form handler and error handling in Listing 9-9? By default, there isn't any either. Once a user gets an unbound form illustrated at the bottom of Listing 9-9, the form processing and validation is taken care of behind the scenes by the `ItemCreation` class-based view. If the form contains errors, the template is re-rendered - like any other form - using the same template in Listing 9-9. If the form data is valid, form processing is deemed successful and the class-based view creates an `Item` model record - like a model form - redirecting control to the `item:index` url defined in the class-based view `success_url` field.

As you can see in this example, a class-based view that inherits its behavior from the `CreateView` class, cuts down the boilerplate code needed to a create model record.

CreateView Fields and Methods

While at first glance a class-based view that inherits its behavior from the `CreateView` class can appear to be inflexible, it's possible to override its default behaviors like any Django construct.

As it turns out, the `CreateView` class inherits its behavior from many other Django class-based views, which is what gives the `CreateView` class - and its implementing child classes like the class-based view in Listing 9-9 - its behind-the-scene powers. The `CreateView` class inherits its behavior from the following class-based view classes:

```
django.views.generic.detail.SingleObjectTemplateResponseMixin
django.views.generic.base.TemplateResponseMixin
django.views.generic.edit.BaseCreateView
django.views.generic.edit.ModelFormMixin
django.views.generic.edit.FormMixin
django.views.generic.detail.SingleObjectMixin
django.views.generic.edit.ProcessFormView
django.views.generic.base.View
```

So why are these classes even important? Because they provide the default behavior for all `CreateView` class-based views. The scant fields declared in the `ItemCreation` class-based view in Listing 9-9 are only three fields for `CreateView` class-based views. It's possible to declare over a dozen more fields and methods - that belong to this past list of classes - to provide behaviors, such as using another template other than `<app_name>/<model_name>_form.html`; specifying the content type for the response (e.g., `text/csv`); custom methods to run when a model form is valid or invalid; as well as declaring custom methods to manually execute GET and POST workflow logic.

■ **Note** A `CreateView` class-based view inherits many fields and methods from its parent classes. The following options are the most common ones; for an exhaustive list consult each of the `CreateView` parent classes.

Basic CreateView options: Model, form_class, and success_url fields

As you've already seen in Listing 9-9, the essential logic fulfilled by a `CreateView` class-based view is to create a model record using a form, which in turn requires a basic set of parameters. First, the `model` field is basic to the whole operation, because a `CreateView` class-based view must know beforehand which type of model record to create. Second, the `form_class` is also a basic parameter, because a user must be presented with a form to capture the data to create the model record.

Finally, because successfully creating a model record entails notifying a user about the action and moving away from the form page, the `success_url` field is also a basic part of a `CreateView` class-based view to indicate where to redirect a user after a model record is created.

Customize template name, MIME type and context: template_name and content_type fields and get_context_data( ) method

Sometimes relying on the `CreateView` class-based view template naming convention `<app_name>/<model_name>_form.html` is unfeasible, either because you have a preexisting template to reuse or simply because you don't like the default convention. You can declare the `template_name` field as part of a `CreateView` class-based view to override this convention. Similarly, it's also possible to override the default MIME type used by a class-based view response - if the template contains something other than `text/html` (e.g., `text/csv`) - using the `content_type` field as part of a `CreateView` class-based view.

In addition, you can alter the context data passed to a class-based view template by defining an implementation of the `get_context_data()` method. This last process is common when you need to pass additional data to a template - besides the `form` reference - or change the actual `form` reference to another name.

Listing 9-10 illustrates a `CreateView` class-based view that makes use of the `template_name` and `content_type` fields, as well as the `get_context_data()` method.

Listing 9-10. Django class-based view with CreateView with template_name, content_type, and get_context_data()

```
# views.py
from django.views.generic.edit import CreateView
from .models import Item, ItemForm, Menu

class ItemCreation(CreateView):
    template_name = "items/item_form.html"
    context_type = "text/html"
    model = Item
    form_class = ItemForm
    success_url = reverse_lazy('items:index')
    def get_context_data(self,**kwargs):
        kwargs['special_context_variable'] = 'My special context variable!!!'
        context = super(ItemCreation, self).get_context_data(**kwargs)
        return context
```

You can see in Listing 9-10 the `template_name` and `content_type` fields are declared as part of the class-based view. In this particular case, both field values are assigned their default values - making them redundant - for simplicity; but you can adjust accordingly to your needs.

The `get_context_data()` method in Listing 9-10 first adds the custom `special_context_variable` key to make it available to the class-based view template (i.e., `items/item_form.html`). Next, a call is made to the parent class's `get_context_data()` method (i.e., `CreateView`) to run its context set up logic, which consists of setting up the `form` reference which is also used in the template. Finally, the `context` reference with all the template context values is returned by the `get_context_data()` method for use inside the template.

As you can see in Listing 9-10, by simply adding fields and overriding methods in a `CreateView` class-based view, you can easily start changing its default behavior.

Customize form initialization and validation: Initial field, get_initial( ), get_form( ), form_valid( ), and form_invalid( ) methods

The initial field on a CreateView class-based view works just like a standard form's initial argument to specify default values for an unbound form. For example, declaring the field initial = {'size':'L'} on a CreateView class-based view sets its form's size field to L.

Form initialization can sometimes require more complex requirements than a single line statement, in which a CreateView class-based view also offers the get_initial() method. The get_initial() method functions like the __init__ method used in standard forms - in that you can introduce open-ended logic to set up default values - but is intended solely to set up initial values and to return a dictionary of values - unlike the __init__ method where you can introduce other actions besides default form values (e.g., change widgets, add validation).

Listing 9-11 illustrates the use of the initial argument and get_initial() method on a CreateView class-based view.

Listing 9-11. Django class-based view with CreateView with initial and get_initial()

```
# views.py
from django.views.generic.edit import CreateView
from .models import Item, ItemForm, Menu

class ItemCreation(CreateView):
    initial = {'size':'L'}
    model = Item
    form_class = ItemForm
    success_url = reverse_lazy('items:index')
    def get_initial(self):
        initial_base = super(ItemCreation, self).get_initial()
        initial_base['menu'] = Menu.objects.get(id=1)
        return initial_base
```

The first step in Listing 9-11 set the initial field to set the class-based view's form size field to L. Next, the get_initial() method is declared to add another default value to a class-based view form.

Inside the get_initial() method, the first step is to call the parent class's get_initial() method (i.e., CreateView) to run its initial set up logic; this ensures the class's initial field value (i.e., {'size':'L'}) is taken into account to as part of the initial value. Next, the initial_base reference is updated to set the form's menu field to the Menu record with id=1. Finally, the get_initial() method in Listing 9-11 returns a dictionary containing both the initial field value set by the class-based view and the custom form value set in its body.

The get_form() method of a CreateView class-based view is designed to tap into the full initialization process of a form and not just on setting its default values like the initial field and get_initial() method. This makes get_form() method suited to perform broader form initialization tasks like setting form widgets and validation initialization, like its done in the __init__ method in standard forms. Inclusively, it's possible to use the get_form() method to specify default form values and forgo the use of initial and get_initial() altogether. Listing 9-12 illustrates the use of the get_form() method in a CreateView class-based view.

Listing 9-12. Django class-based view with CreateView with get_form()

```
# views.py
from django.views.generic.edit import CreateView
from .models import Item, ItemForm, Menu

class ItemCreation(CreateView):
    initial = {'size':'L'}
    model = Item
    form_class = ItemForm
    success_url = reverse_lazy('items:index')
    def get_form(self):
        form = super(ItemCreation, self).get_form()
        initial_base = self.get_initial()
        initial_base['menu'] = Menu.objects.get(id=1)
        form.initial = initial_base
        form.fields['name'].widget = forms.widgets.Textarea()
        return form
```

The first step in the get_form() method in Listing 9-12 is to call the parent class's get_form() method (i.e., CreateView) to get the base form. Next, a call is made to the class-based view's get_initial() method to get its initial form value, as well as set up a default value for the form's menu field using a model query. In this case, the form initialization form dictionary has the same values as those in Listing 9-11.

Next, the form initialization dictionary is assigned to the base form using the standard initial form reference. Finally, before returning an instance of the form class, a custom widget is set on the form's name field, overriding the default widget of the form name field.

In addition to initialization tasks, the form validation process for a CreateView class-based view can also be customized. The form_valid() and form_invalid() methods are used to access the points at which a class-based view form is deemed successful or erroneous, respectively. Listing 9-13 illustrates an example that uses the form_valid() and form_invalid() methods in a CreateView class-based view.

Listing 9-13. Django class-based view with CreateView with form_valid() and form_invalid()

```
# views.py
from django.views.generic.edit import CreateView
from django.http import HttpResponseRedirect
from django.contrib import messages
from .models import Item, ItemForm, Menu

class ItemCreation(CreateView):
    initial = {'size':'L'}
    model = Item
    form_class = ItemForm
    success_url = reverse_lazy('items:index')
    def form_valid(self,form):
        super(ItemCreation,self).form_valid(form)
        # Add action to valid form phase
        messages.success(self.request, 'Item created successfully!')
        return HttpResponseRedirect(self.get_success_url())
    def form_invalid(self,form):
        # Add action to invalid form phase
        return self.render_to_response(self.get_context_data(form=form))
```

As you can see in Listing 9-13, the `form_valid()` method gains access to the form instance via its `form` input argument, which in turn allows you to perform actions on the form when it passes its validation phase. In this case, no action is taken on the form itself to simplify things, but an additional piece of logic is added to illustrate the customization process.

The first step in the `form_valid()` in Listing 9-13 is a call to the parent class's `form_valid()` method (i.e., `CreateView`) to run its form validation setup logic, this ensures the base class's form validation is run first to verify any form rule violations (e.g., add errors to the form). If a call to the parent's `form_valid()` method detects a rule violation, then the class's `form_valid()` method (i.e., the one Listing 9-13) short-circuits and falls back to the `form_invalid()` method. If the parent's `form_valid()` method passes, the logic in Listing 9-13 continues to add a Django message framework success message to present to a user.

■ **Tip** It's also possible to add Django message framework success messages to a class-based view form validation process through a mixin. Mixins for class-based views are described in the last section of this chapter.

Finally, because you're handling a valid form workflow, the `form_valid()` method in Listing 9-13 must explicitly redirect a user to a location to finish its work. In this case, a standard Django `HttpResponseRedirect` method is used with the class-based view's `get_success_url()` method, the last of which gets the class-based view `success_url` field value.

The `form_invalid()` method in Listing 9-13 does nothing in particular to handle an invalid form. It simply does the minimum amount work - by means of class-based view methods - which is to return control to the same template location and add the context that contains the form with errors to present to a user.

As you can see, the benefit of the `form_valid()` and `form_invalid()` methods in a `CreateView` class-based view is they allow you to customize the form validation workflow, without the need to modify other parts of a `CreateView` workflow (e.g., saving the form data to the database).

Customize view method workflow: get() and post() methods

Besides the previous customization options for a `CreateView` class-based view, it's also possible to get absolute control over the workflow done by a class-based view with either the `get()` or `post()` methods. The `get()` method is used to tap into the HTTP GET workflow associated with a class-based view, whereas the `post()` method is used to tap into the HTTP POST workflow associated with a class-based view.

Although the use of the `get()` or `post()` methods can offer some of the greatest flexibility to a class-based view, they also require to explicitly declare the initialization, validation, and redirect sequences of a class-based view. This means class-based views that use either the `get()` or `post()` methods can resemble more the standard open-ended Django views - described in Chapter 2 - than the succinct class-based view presented earlier in Listing 9-9.

Still, sometimes the appeal of class-based views is so great, the use of the `get()` or `post()` methods is warranted. Listing 9-14 illustrates an example that uses the `get()` and `post()` methods in a `CreateView` class-based view.

Listing 9-14. Django class-based view with CreateView with get() and post()

```
# views.py
from django.views.generic.edit import CreateView
from django.shortcuts import render
from django.contrib import messages
```

```
class ItemCreation(CreateView):
    initial = {'size':'L'}
    model = Item
    form_class = ItemForm
    success_url = reverse_lazy('items:index')
    template_name = "items/item_form.html"
    def get(self,request, *args, **kwargs):
        form = super(ItemCreation, self).get_form()
        # Set initial values and custom widget
        initial_base = self.get_initial()
        initial_base['menu'] = Menu.objects.get(id=1)
        form.initial = initial_base
        form.fields['name'].widget = forms.widgets.Textarea()
        # return response using standard render() method
        return render(request,self.template_name,
                      {'form':form,
                       'special_context_variable':'My special context variable!!!'})

    def post(self,request,*args, **kwargs):
        form = self.get_form()
        # Verify form is valid
        if form.is_valid():
            # Call parent form_valid to create model record object
            super(ItemCreation,self).form_valid(form)
            # Add custom success message
            messages.success(request, 'Item created successfully!')
            # Redirect to success page
            return HttpResponseRedirect(self.get_success_url())
        # Form is invalid
        # Set object to None, since class-based view expects model record object
        self.object = None
        # Return class-based view form_invalid to generate form with errors
        return self.form_invalid(form)
```

You can see in Listing 9-14 that both the `get()` and `post()` methods have access to a `request` input – an `HttpRequest` instance – like standard view methods. This `request` reference allows class-based views access to request data, such as HTTP meta data (e.g., user's IP address), which is a topic described in detail in Chapter 2.

The first step in the `get()` method in Listing 9-14 is to create an unbound form using the parent class's `get_form()` method (i.e., `CreateView`). Because the `get()` method gives you full control over the workflow, it would be equally valid to create an unbound form using standard form syntax (e.g., `form = ItemForm()`), but since it's a class-based view, the example leverages a class-based view construct. Once the unbound form is created, a series of initial values and a custom widget is set on the form, just like it's done in the previous class-based view examples.

Once the unbound form is ready, notice the `return` statement of the `get()` method uses the standard `render()` method used in regular view methods. In this case, the `render()` method redirects control to the class-based view template and sets the template context with the unbound `form` and an additional `special_context_variable` variable to use in the template.

Next, the `post()` method in Listing 9-14 is tasked with processing the form with user data. The first step in the `post()` method is to get a bound form instance using the class-based view `get_form()` class. Similarly to the `get()` method, it would be equally valid to create a bound form using standard form syntax (e.g., `form = ItemForm(request.POST)`).

With a bound form instance, a check is made to verify if the user provided form data is valid, just like it's done with standard forms (e.g., `form.is_valid()`). If the form data is valid, a call is made to the parent class's `is_valid()` method (i.e., `CreateView`), which ensures the core logic of a class-based view is executed when a form is valid (e.g. saving the form data to a database). Here it's possible once again to use any standard model construct, but calling the parent class's `is_valid()` method is easier to execute this routine logic to create a model object record. Once the routine validation logic is complete, a success message is added to present to an end user and a redirect is made to the class-based view's success url. If the form data is invalid, the class-based view's object field is set to `None` - since class-based views expect to handle an object record instance in POST processing - and control is returned using the class-based `form_invalid()` method that takes care of the underlying details vs. using the `render()` method to create a standard view method response.

As you can now understand from this example in Listing 9-14, a `CreateView` class-based view can be just as flexible as a standard view method. It's simply a matter of knowing and understanding the different fields and methods supported by a `CreateView` class-based view. Of course, if you feel the custom logic for a `CreateView` class-based view becomes too unwieldy, you can always fall back to a standard view method presented back in Chapter 2.

Read Model Records with the Class-Based Views ListView and DetailView

Similar to the process of creating model records, the process to read model records also follows a near identical process for all models: create a query to get model record(s) and then use a template to display the model record(s). The Django `ListView` and `DetailView` class-based views are specifically designed to cut down on the amount of boilerplate code needed to display a list of Django model records and a single Django model record, respectively.

The `ListView` class-based view can quickly set up a query for a list of model records and display them in a template. Listing 9-15 illustrates a class-based view that uses the `ListView` class-based view.

Listing 9-15. Django class-based view with ListView to read list of records

```
# views.py
from django.views.generic.list import ListView
from .models import Item

class ItemList(ListView):
    model = Item

# urls.py
from django.conf.urls import url
from coffeehouse.items import views as items_views

urlpatterns = [
    url(r'^$',items_views.ItemList.as_view(),name="index"),
]

# templates/items/item_list.html
  {% regroup object_list by menu as item_menu_list %}
  {% for menu_section in item_menu_list %}
   <li>{{ menu_section.grouper }}
    <ul>
        {% for item in menu_section.list %}
```

```
        <li>{{item.name|title}}</li>
        {% endfor %}
    </ul>
    </li>
{% endfor %}
```

The first definition in Listing 9-15 is the `ItemList` class, which inherits its behavior from the `ListView` class-based view class. The `model` field in the `ItemList` class set to `Item` tells Django to generate a list of all `Item` model records (e.g., `Item.objects.all()`).

Next, the `ListView` class-based view is hooked up to a root url regular expression - `r'^$'` - using the `as_view()` method, the last of which is available on all class-based views and was also used in the past section to set up a `CreateView` class-based view.

Finally, the last part in Listing 9-15 illustrates the template `item_list.html` that generates a loop over the `object_list` reference, the last of which is the default context variable used by a `ListView` class-based view that contains the model record list.

Recapping, the most important default behaviors of a `ListView` class-based view are the following:

The list of records is made from all records of the model defined in the `model` option.

The template to render the list of records uses the convention `<app_name>/<model_name>_list.html` under the `TEMPLATES` directory path of a project.

The context variable passed to a template (i.e., the one containing the records) is named `object_list`.

As you can see in this example, a `ListView` class-based view cuts down the boilerplate code needed to present a list of model records to one field.

The `DetailView` class-based view is another record reading construct, designed to quickly set up a single record query and present the results in a template. Listing 9-16 illustrates a class-based view that uses the `DetailView` class.

Listing 9-16. Django class-based view with DetailView to read model record

```
# views.py
from django.views.generic. import DetailView
from .models import Item

class ItemDetail(DetailView):
    model = Item

# urls.py
from django.conf.urls import url
from coffeehouse.items import views as items_views

urlpatterns = [
    url(r'^(?P<pk>\d+)/$',items_views.ItemDetail.as_view(),name="detail"),
]

# templates/items/item_detail.html
<h4> {{item.name|title}}</h4>
<p>{{item.description}}</p>
<p>${{item.price}}</p>
<p>For {{item.get_size_display}} size: Only {{item.calories}} calories
{% if item.drink %}
and {{item.drink.caffeine}} mg of caffeine.</p>
{% endif %}
</p>
```

The first definition in Listing 9-16 is the `ItemDetail` class, which inherits its behavior from the `DetailView` class-based view class. The `model` field in the `ItemDetail` class is to `Item`, which tells Django to get an `Item` model record. Unlike the `ListView` class-based view class in Listing 9-15 that reads all model records, a `DetailView` class-based view class must always limit its model query to a single record, which is where the class-based view url definition comes into play.

The `DetailView` class-based view in Listing 9-16 is hooked up to a root url regular expression - `r'^$'` - using the `as_view()` method - just like other class-based views - but notice the url definition contains the `(?P<pk>\d+)` url parameter, which gets passed to the class-based view to delimit the model query to a single record.

For example, if a request is made on the url `/items/1/`, the `1` is assigned to the pk parameter, which is passed to the classed-based view, to build the model query `Item.objects.get(pk=1)` that gets the `Item` model record with `pk=1` - note the `pk` field stands for primary key, which is generally equivalent to the `id` field.

In this manner, as the url requests made on the `DetailView` class-based view change (e.g. `/items/2/`, `/items/3/`), so does the backing query made for a model a record, and with it the record returned to be displayed in the template.

Finally, the last part in Listing 9-16 illustrates the template `item_detail.html` that outputs various fields of the `item` reference that represents the model record. In this case, the `item` reference is used because the default context variable used by a `DetailView` class-based view for a model record is the name of the model itself.

Recapping, the most important default behaviors of a `DetailView` class-based view are the following:

The model record is determined based on the `model` option and the url pk parameter that delimits the query to a single record based on the model's primary key.

The template to render the record uses the convention `<app_name>/<model_name>_detail.html` under the `TEMPLATES` directory path of a project.

The context variable passed to a template (i.e., the one containing the record) is named after the `model` of the class-based view (e.g., if `model=Item`, the context variable is named `item`).

As you can see in this example, a class-based view that inherits its behavior from the `DetailView` class cuts down the boilerplate code needed to present a single model record.

ListView Fields and Methods

Similar to the `CreateView` class-based view presented earlier, it's possible to override many of default behaviors of a `ListView` class-based view.

As it turns out, the `ListView` class-based view inherits its behavior from many other Django class-based views, presented in the following list:

```
django.views.generic.list.MultipleObjectTemplateResponseMixin
django.views.generic.base.TemplateResponseMixin
django.views.generic.list.BaseListView
django.views.generic.list.MultipleObjectMixin
django.views.generic.base.View
```

■ **Note** A `ListView` class-based view inherits many fields and methods from its parent classes. The following options are the most common ones; for an exhaustive list consult each of the `ListView` parent classes.

Basic ListView option: Model field

As you saw in Listing 9-15, the essential logic fulfilled by a `ListView` class-based view is to create a list of records from a model. Therefore the `model` field option is essential to indicate on which model to create a record list.

The next sections describe how to customize a `ListView` class-based view, including how to delimit and generate multiple pages for a list of records, as well as how to override other default behaviors.

Customize template context reference name: context_object_name

In Listing 9-15, you can see the template of the `ListView` class-based view uses the rather unfriendly context variable named `object_list`. This is the default behavior, but to help template editors, it's possible to use a different context variable to contain the list of records.

The `context_object_name` field is used to define a custom context variable name to manipulate the list of records inside a template (e.g., `context_object_name = 'item_list'`).

■ **Tip** A `ListView` class-based view also inherits its behavior from many of the same classes as the `CreateView` class described earlier. Therefore, you can also use the `template_name` field to specify a custom template name; the `content_type` field to specify a MIME type; and the `get_context_data()` method to alter the context used by a template.

Customize record list: Queryset and ordering fields and pagination behavior

By default, a `ListView` class-based view generates a list for all records that belong to a model. While this behavior is reasonable, it can also be necessary to create a `ListView` class-based view that returns more limited criteria, in which case it's necessary to delimit the backing model query. The `queryset` field is used to define a custom query to generate a list of records.

Another helpful option to customize a record list is to specify the field order in which to generate the record list. Similar to the standard `order_by()` method used in model queries, a `ListView` class-based view can specify the `ordering` field to define the sort order of a record list.

Listing 9-17 illustrates the use of the `queryset` and `ordering` fields in a `ListView` class-based view.

Listing 9-17. Django class-based view with ListView to reduce record list with queryset

```
# views.py
from django.views.generic.list import ListView
from .models import Item

class ItemList(ListView):
    model = Item
    queryset = Item.objects.filter(menu__id=1)
    ordering = ['name']
```

As you can see in Listing 9-17, the `queryset` field is assigned a standard model query to produce `Item` records with a `menu id=1`. In this manner, the resulting record list passed by `ListView` the class-based view to the template only contains `Item` records that match these criteria. In addition, Listing 9-17 also makes use of the `ordering = ['name']` field, which in this case ensures the query to generate the record list is sorted by the `Item` model's `name` field.

Although the queryset option is helpful to delimit the size of the record list presented by a ListView class-based view, sometimes it's necessary to deal with a large record list and still be able to delimit the amount of results displayed in a template. For such scenarios, you can use pagination to split out a large record list over multiple pages.

Since pagination by definition depends on the use of multiple pages, it forces you to adjust not only a ListView class-based view definition, but also the url structure and template used by the class-based view to support multiple pages. Listing 9-18 illustrates a pagination example for a ListView class-based view, which is based on the example from Listing 9-15.

Listing 9-18. Django class-based view with ListView to read list of records with pagination

```
# views.py
from django.views.generic.list import ListView
from .models import Item

class ItemList(ListView):
    model = Item
    paginate_by = 5

# urls.py
from django.conf.urls import url
from coffeehouse.items import views as items_views

urlpatterns = [
    url(r'^$',items_views.ItemList.as_view(),name="index"),
    url(r'^page/(?P<page>\d+)/$',items_views.ItemList.as_view(),name="page"),
]

# templates/items/item_list.html
  {% regroup object_list by menu as item_menu_list %}
{% for menu_section in item_menu_list %}
   <li>{{ menu_section.grouper }}
    <ul>
        {% for item in menu_section.list %}
        <li>{{item.name|title}}</li>
        {% endfor %}
    </ul>
    </li>
{% endfor %}

 {% if is_paginated %}
    {{page_obj}}
 {% endif %}
```

The relevant pagination logic in Listing 9-18 is in bold. First off, the paginate_by = 5 is added to the class-based view definition, which tells Django to limit the record list to 5 records per page. Since the ListView class-based view will require a page number to display records beyond the first 5 records of query – since pages are limited to 5 – the natural place to obtain a page number is through a url (e.g., /page/1/ to create a list with the first 5 records of a query, /page/2/ to create a list with the records 6 through 10, etc.).

Next in Listing 9-18, you can see a new url definition with the `(?P<page>\d+)` parameter hooked up the `ListView` class-based view. This url definition allows a request that matches the regular expression pattern (e.g., `/page/1/,/page/2/`) to pass the url page parameter value to the class-based view. When a `ListView` class-based view detects a url page parameter value with the presence of the `paginate_by` option, it adjusts the query for the record list to return the appropriate set of records to a template based on the page (e.g:, `/page/1/` generates a list of records from 1 to 5 of the overall query, `/page/2/` generates a list of records from 6 to 10 of the overall query, etc.).

Finally, the last section in Listing 9-18 represents the backing template for a `ListView` class-based view that uses pagination. The `{% is_paginated %}` tag and `{{page_obj}}` context reference are used to let users know on which page of the overall record list they're on.

■ **Tip** A `ListView` class-based view can also use the `get()` class-based view method to get full control over the view workflow. See the previous section on the `CreateView` class-based view, which describes how to use it and its implications.

DetailView Fields and Methods

Like other class-based views, a `DetailView` class-based view can also be created with custom fields and methods to override their default behaviors.

As it turns out, the `DetailView` class inherits its behavior from many other Django class-based views, which are described in the following list:

```
django.views.generic.detail.SingleObjectTemplateResponseMixin
django.views.generic.base.TemplateResponseMixin
django.views.generic.detail.BaseDetailView
django.views.generic.detail.SingleObjectMixin
django.views.generic.base.View
```

■ **Note** A `DetailView` class-based view inherits many fields and methods from its parent classes. The following options are the most common ones; for an exhaustive list consult each of the `DetailView` parent classes.

Basic DetailView options: Model field and url with pk parameter

As you saw in Listing 9-16, the essential logic fulfilled by a `DetailView` class-based view is to get a model record and display it in a template. Therefore the `model` field is one of the essential pieces to this type of class-based view and must always be provided.

In order to get a specific model record, a `DetailView` class-based view must also define a url parameter that helps it select a model record. By default, this url parameter must be named `pk` and its value is used to perform a query on the `model` value using the `pk` field, which is generally equivalent to a model's `id` field.

■ **Tip** A `DetailView` class-based view also inherits its behavior from many of the class-based view classes described earlier. Therefore, you can also use the `template_name` field to specify a custom template name; the `content_type` field to specify a MIME type; the `get_context_data()` method to alter the context used by a template; as well as the `context_object_name` field to declare a different context variable to access a record in a template.

Customize url and query parameters: pk_url_kwarg, slug_field and slug_url_kwarg

By default, a `DetailView` class-based view expects a url argument named pk to determine on which model record to make a query by its primary key. However, if you already have a preexisting url or simply don't like this inexpressive url parameter name, you can assign a custom url parameter with the `pk_url_kwarg` field.

For example, setting `pk_url_kwarg='item_id'` on a `DetailView` class-based view, allows a url to be defined as `url(r'^(?P<item_id>\d+)/$',items_views.ItemDetail.as_view())` vs. the default `url(r'^(?P<pk>\d+)/$',items_views.ItemDetail.as_view())`.

Even though performing the record query of a `DetailView` class-based view with the pk field is a common practice - given the pk field is generally an integer field with a database index to increase lookup performance - sometimes in can be necessary to perform the record query of a `DetailView` class-based with another model field (e.g., to create more user/SEO-friendly urls like `/item/capuccino/`, instead of `/item/1/`).

Listing 9-19 illustrates a `DetailView` class-based view that uses the `slug_field` option to allow a model record query to be made against a model field other than pk.

Listing 9-19. Django class-based view with DetailView and slug_field option

```
# views.py
# views.py
from django.views.generic import DetailView
from .models import Item

class ItemDetail(DetailView):
    model = Item
    slug_field = 'name__iexact'

# urls.py
from django.conf.urls import url
from coffeehouse.items import views as items_views

urlpatterns = [
    url(r'^(?P<slug>\w+)/$',items_views.ItemDetail.as_view(),name="detail"),
]

# Template identical to listing to template in Listing 9-16
```

The first important aspect in Listing 9-19 is that the url definition has a url parameter named `slug` that matches any word pattern due to the `w+` regular expression. This means urls such as `/items/espresso/` and `/items/latte/` match this url, unlike the prior `DetailView` class-based url definition that uses the pk parameter to match numeric values with d+ regular expression.

When a `DetailView` class-based view receives a url parameter named `slug`, it signals the class-based view that the model record query should done on a model field other than pk. Because this `slug` value can be ambiguous (e.g., it can represent one of several model field values, such as name, cost, or description), it's necessary to qualify which model field the `slug` value represents, which is the purpose of `slug_field` field.

In the case of Listing 9-19, the `slug_field` field is set to `name__iexact`, which tells the `DetailView` class-based view to perform a case-insensitive model query with the `slug` value on the `Item` model `name` field. The case-insensitive query is provided by the `__iexact` lookup and is important in case the database record values are mixed case (e.g., the url `/items/capuccino/` would match an `Item` name record `capuccino`, `Capuccino`,,or `CAPUCCINO`. Without case inventivenesses, the `Item` name record would need to be exactly `capuccino` to match the url).

Although not presented in the sample in Listing 9-19, another option available for a `DetailView` class-based view is the `slug_url_kwarg` option, which has a similar to the `pk_url_kwarg` option described earlier.

By default, a `DetailView` class-based view that uses a slug query (i.e., non pk query) expects a url argument named `slug` to determine on which model field to make a query to obtain a record. However, if you already have a preexisting url or simply don't like this inexpressive url parameter name, you can assign a custom url parameter with the `slug_url_kwarg` field.

For example, setting `slug_url_kwarg='item_name'` on a `DetailView` class-based view, allows a url to be defined as `url(r'^(?P<item_name>\w+)/$',items_views.ItemDetail.as_view())` vs. the default `url(r'^(?P<slug>\w+)/$',items_views.ItemDetail.as_view())`.

■ **Tip** A `DetailView` class-based view can also use the `get()` class-based view method to get full control over the view workflow. See the previous section on the `CreateView` class-based view that describes how to use it and its implications.

Update Model Records with the Class-Based View UpateView

When you update a Django model record, the typical process involves fetching the model record you want to update from a database, presenting the model data in a form so a user can make changes, and finally saving the changes back to the database. The Django `UpdateView` class-based view is specifically designed to cut down on the amount of boilerplate code needed to update a Django model record.

Due to its functionality, the `UpdateView` class-based view operates like a combination of the `CreateView` - which creates a model record through a form - and the `DetailView` - which displays a model record. Listing 9-20 illustrates an example of an `UpdateView` class-based view.

Listing 9-20. Django class-based view with UpdateView to edit a record

```
# views.py
from django.views.generic import UpdateView
from .models import Item

class ItemUpdate(UpdateView):
    model = Item
    form_class = ItemForm
    success_url = reverse_lazy('items:index')

# urls.py
from django.conf.urls import url
from coffeehouse.items import views as items_views
```

```
urlpatterns = [
    url(r'^edit/(?P<pk>\d+)/$', items_views.ItemUpdate.as_view(), name='edit'),
]

# templates/items/item_form.html
<form method="post">
        {% csrf_token %}
        {{ form.as_p }}
        <button type="submit" class="btn btn-primary">
          {% if object == None%}Create{% else %}Update{% endif %}
        </button>
</form>
```

The first definition in Listing 9-20 is the ItemUpdate class that inherits its behavior from the UpdateView class-based view class. The model field in the ItemUpate class sets a value to Item, which tells Django to update Item model records. In addition, because you're dealing with an update operation, the Item model record must be presented in a form - which is the purpose of the from_class option - as well as define a success url to redirect a user if an update is successful, which is the purpose of the success_url option.

Next in Listing 9-20 is the url definition that hooks up the UpdateView class-based view class. Because an UpdateView class-based view must present a specific model record to edit, it relies on a url parameter to limit a query to a single record. In this case, notice the url contains the pk url parameter that gets passed to the class-based view - just like it's done with a DetailView class-based view.

For example, if a request is made for the url /items/edit/1/, 1 is passed as the pk argument to the UpdateView class-based view, which in turn performs the query Item.objects.get(pk=1) to retrieve the record and present it in a form for editing.

Finally, the last part in Listing 9-20 illustrates the template item_form.html that displays the record inside a form to edit. One important aspect of the default UpdateView class-based view template is that it's the same default template used by a CreateView class-based view. This is because both class-based views share the same parent class-based view class for this functionality, not to mention the purpose of the form is the same (e.g., the form in a CreateView class-based view is sent empty for a user to fill in new record data, where as the form in a UpdateView class-based view is sent pre-filled with a record to update the record data).

For this reason, the template in Listing 9-20 is almost identical to the template in Listing 9-9 used in a CreateView class-based view. The minor difference is that if the template detects the presence of the object variable in its context, it means the UpdateView class-based view is passing a record for editing and the form button is set to Update; otherwise, if no object variable is present, it means the CreateView class-based view is calling the template and the form button is set to Create.

Recapping, the most important default behaviors of an UpdateView class-based view:

The model record to update is determined based on the model option and a url pk parameter that delimits the query to a single record based on the model's primary key.

The template to render a form to update a record uses the convention <app_name>/<model_name>_form.html under the TEMPLATES directory path of a project, noting it's the same default template used by CreateView class-based views, for which you can rely on the presence of the object context variable to determine if it's the UpdateView calling the template.

The context variable passed to a template (i.e., the one containing the record) is named object, albeit the form is automatically populated with this record value.

As you can see in this example, a class-based view that inherits its behavior from the UpdateView class, cuts down the boilerplate code needed to edit a model record.

UpdateView Fields and Methods

Like other class-based views, UpdateView class-based views can also be created with custom fields and methods to override their default behaviors.

As it turns out, the UpdateView class inherits its behavior from many other Django class-based views, presented in the following list:

```
django.views.generic.detail.SingleObjectTemplateResponseMixin
django.views.generic.base.TemplateResponseMixin
django.views.generic.edit.BaseUpdateView
django.views.generic.edit.ModelFormMixin
django.views.generic.edit.FormMixin
django.views.generic.detail.SingleObjectMixin
django.views.generic.edit.ProcessFormView
django.views.generic.base.View
```

■ **Note** An UpdateView class-based view inherits many fields and methods from its parent classes. The following options are the most common ones; for an exhaustive list consult each of the UpdateView parent classes.

Basic UpdateView options: Model, form_class and success_url fields, and url with pk parameter

As you saw in Listing 9-20, the essential logic fulfilled by an UpdateView class-based view is to get a model record and display it in a form for editing. Therefore the model field is one of the essential pieces for this type of class-based view and must always be provided. In addition, because a record is updated via form, it's also necessary to specify a form through the form_class option, as well as a success url through the success_url option for when an update is successful.

In order to get a specific model record, an UpdateView class-based view must also define a url parameter that helps it select a model record to edit. By default, this url parameter must be named pk and its value is used to perform a query on the model value using the pk field, which is generally equivalent to a model's id field.

■ **Tip** An UpdateView class-based view also inherits its behavior from many of the class-based view classes described earlier. Therefore, you can also use the template_name field to specify a custom template name; the content_type field to specify a MIME type; the get_context_data() method to alter the context used by a template; as well as the context_object_name field to declare a different context variable to access a record in a template.

In addition, because an UpdateView class-based view requires obtaining a model record, it can also use the pk_url_kwarg field to accept a different url parameter named differently than pk; the slug_field field to specify an alternative record query field; and the slug_url_kwarg field to accept a different url parameter named differently than slug.

Finally, an UpdateView class-based view can also use the get() and post() class-based view methods to get full control over the view workflow. The previous class-based view sections describe how to use all these class-based view fields and methods.

Delete Records with the Class-Bases View DeleteView

When you delete a Django model record, besides executing the actual delete operation, it's generally a good practice to present a confirmation page to a user. The Django `DeleteView` class-based view is specifically designed to cut down on the amount of boilerplate code needed to delete a model record, while presenting a confirmation page. Listing 9-21 illustrates a `DeleteView` class-based view example.

Listing 9-21. Django class-based view with DeleteView to delete record

```
# views.py
from django.views.generic.edit import DeleteView
from .models import Item

class ItemDelete(UpdateView):
    model = Item
    success_url = reverse_lazy('items:index')

# urls.py
from django.conf.urls import url
from coffeehouse.items import views as items_views

urlpatterns = [
    url(r'^delete/(?P<pk>\d+)/$', items_views.ItemDelete.as_view(), name='delete'),
]

# templates/items/item_confirm_delete.html
  <form method="post">
        {% csrf_token %}
        Do you really want to delete "{{ object }}"?
        <button class="btn btn-primary" type="submit">Yes, remove it!</button>
  </form>
```

The first definition in Listing 9-21 is the `ItemDelete` class, which inherits its behavior from the `DeleteView` class-based view class. The `model` field in the `ItemDelete` class sets a value to `Item`, which tells Django to delete `Item` model records. In addition, because you'll want users to confirm the delete operation, the `success_url` option must also be declared to specify where to take users after the delete operation is successful.

Next in Listing 9-21 is the url definition that hooks up the `DeleteView` class-based view class. Because a `DeleteView` class-based view must be told which model record to delete, it relies on a url parameter to provide this query delimiter. In this case, notice the url contains the pk url parameter that gets passed to the class-based view – just like it's done with a `DetailView` class-based view.

For example, if a request is made for the url `/items/delete/1/`, `1` is passed as the pk argument to the `DeleteView` class-based view, which in turn performs the query `Item.objects.get(pk=1)` to prepare the record for deletion.

Finally, the last part in Listing 9-21 illustrates the `item_confirm_delete.html` template that is used for the user-facing deletion sequence. Notice this template contains a pseudo-form (i.e., no form fields) with a question and submit button. The reason for this pseudo-form is the `item_confirm_delete.html` template has a dual function.

If an HTTP GET request is made on a DeleteView class-based view, a page with this pseudo-form is returned to the user presenting him with the question Do you really want to delete "{{ object }}"?, where object is the model record to be deleted. If the user clicks on this pseudo-form submit button, it issues an HTTP POST request - notice the <form method="post"> tag - to the same DeleteView class-based view, which invokes the actual delete procedure. In this manner, this template with a pseudo-form allows a user to confirm if he really wants to delete the record after hitting a url delete link (e.g., /items/delete/1/), instead of immediately deleting a record when hitting a url delete link.

Recapping, the most important default behaviors of a DeleteView class-based view are the following:

The model record to delete is determined based on the model option and a url pk parameter that delimits the query to a single record based on the model's primary key.

The template to render a form to update a record uses the convention <app_name>/<model_name>_confirm_delete.html under the TEMPLATES directory path of a project.

The context variable passed to a template (i.e., the one containing the record to delete) is named object.

An HTTP GET request on a DeleteView class-based view presents the confirmation page from the <app_name>/<model_name>_confirm_delete.html template. An HTTP POST request on a DeleteView class-based view performs the actual delete procedure.

As you can see in this example, a class-based view that inherits its behavior from the DeleteView class, cuts down the boilerplate code needed to delete a model record.

DeleteView Fields and Methods

Like other class-based views, a DeleteView class-based view can also be created with custom fields and methods to override their default behaviors.

As it turns out, the DeleteView class inherits its behavior from many other Django class-based views, presented in the following list:

```
django.views.generic.detail.SingleObjectTemplateResponseMixin
django.views.generic.base.TemplateResponseMixin
django.views.generic.edit.BaseDeleteView
django.views.generic.edit.DeletionMixin
django.views.generic.detail.BaseDetailView
django.views.generic.detail.SingleObjectMixin
django.views.generic.base.View
```

■ **Note** A DeleteView class-based view inherits many fields and methods from its parent classes. The following options are the most common ones; for an exhaustive list consult each of the DeleteView parent classes.

Basic DeleteView options: Model and success_url fields and url with pk parameter

As you saw in Listing 9-21, the essential logic fulfilled by a DeleteView class-based view is to get a model record and delete it while presenting a confirmation page. Therefore the model field is one of the essential pieces to this type of class-based view and must always be provided. In addition, because a record is set to be deleted, it's also necessary to specify a success url through the success_url option to redirect a user after the record is deleted.

In order to get a specific model record, a `DeleteView` class-based view must also define a url parameter that helps it select a model record to delete. By default, this url parameter must be named pk and its value is used to perform a query on the `model` value using the pk field, which is generally equivalent to a model's `id` field.

■ **Tip** A `DeleteView` class-based view also inherits its behavior from many of the class-based view classes described earlier. Therefore, you can also use the `template_name` field to specify a custom template name; the `content_type` field to specify a MIME type; the `get_context_data()` method to alter the context used by a template; as well as the `context_object_name` field to declare a different context variable to access a record in a template.

In addition, because a `DeleteView` class-based view requires obtaining a model record, it can also use the `pk_url_kwarg` field to accept a different url parameter named differently than `pk`; the `slug_field` field to specify an alternative record query field; and the `slug_url_kwarg` field to accept a different url parameter named differently than `slug`.

Finally, a `DeleteView` class-based view can also use the `get()` and post() class-based view methods to get full control over the view workflow. The previous class-based view sections describe how to use all these class-based view fields and methods.

Class-Based Views with Mixins

Although all class-based views that operate on models typically follow the same workflow to create, read, update, and delete model records, it's fair to say that after seeing the previous class-based view sections, you'll often find yourself adjusting the default behavior of class-based views.

While it can be perfectly reasonable to adjust the methods and fields of a class-based view a couple of times, it can get tiresome if you need to do it over and over to obtain the same functionality across dozens or hundreds of class-based views.

Nowhere is this more evident than when you're forced to define a `get()` or `post()` method in a class-based view, to include some functionality that's not supported in a class-based view (e.g., `CreateView`, `ListView`, `DetailView`, `UpdateView`, `DeleteView`), which requires typing in a long-winded workflow that can turn out to be repetitive if done multiple times. To cut down on repetitive customizations in the context of class-based views, you can use *mixins*.

For starters, you've already used mixins in the context of class-based views, even if you didn't realize it. If you looked closely at the class-based view classes that provide the behaviors to the model class-based views described in previous sections, you may have noticed many include the term *mixin* in their name (e.g., `ModelFormMixin`, `FormMixin`, `SingleObjectMixin`).

A software mixin is a construct that allows *inheritance-like* behavior between classes, noting the emphasis on *inheritance-like*. When you use class inheritance, a parent-child class relationship is often described with the 'is a' term (e.g., if a Drink class inherits its behavior from an Item class, a Drink *is an* Item). A mixin class, on the other hand, allows a class to adopt the behaviors of a mixin class without the 'is a' behavior.

In other words, a mixin class is a way to add functionality to classes, with the mixin class serving as a reusable component. For example, you can have a mixin Checkout class used by a Store class and OnlineStore class, which allows the functionality of the mixin class to be reused in any other class. Notice that for mixin classes, the inheritance 'is a' behavior doesn't apply, you can't say a Store *is a* Checkout or an OnlineStore *is a* Checkout, it's more of 'uses a' behavior. Therefore although mixin classes - semantically speaking - are used to inherit behaviors, technically speaking they don't use inheritance as it's commonly known in software engineering, hence the use of the term *inheritance-like*.

So why are mixins important to class-based views? It turns out, all of the base class-based view classes you learned about in the previous section are built on class-based views mixins. This not only means you can mix and match mixins to create custom class-based views, but you can also create or reuse other mixins to enhance the functionality of class-based views.

Earlier when you learned about the `CreateView()` class-based view, you may recall the examples in Listing 9-13 and 9-14 added a Django framework success message to inform a user when a record was created. In the case of Listing 9-13, this required tapping into the `form_valid()` class-based view method to add this message, while in the case of Listing 9-14, this required tapping into the `post()` class-based view method. Although both approaches are perfectly valid, declaring either of these methods in a class-based view for the sole purpose of adding a Django framework success message is a lot of work.

By using a mixin on a class-based view, you can simplify the addition of Django framework success messages in a class-based view to a single field, without the need to customize more elaborate methods and/or add logic to a class-based view.

Listing 9-22 illustrates a `CreateView` class-based view that uses a mixin to support this functionality to add a Django framework success message to a class-based view response.

Listing 9-22. Django class-based view with CreateView and mixin class

```
# views.py
from django.views.generic.edit import CreateView
from django.contrib.messages.views import SuccessMessageMixin
from .models import Item, ItemForm

class ItemCreation(SuccessMessageMixin,CreateView):
    model = Item
    form_class = ItemForm
    success_url = reverse_lazy('items:index')
    success_message = "Item %(name)s created successfully"
```

■ **Caution** Mixin classes should always be declared first to take precedence over coarser grained class-based views classes in the context of multiple inheritance class-based views (e.g. `class ItemCreation(SuccessMessageMixin,CreateView)`).

The first important aspect of Listing 9-22 is the `import` statement for the `SuccessMessageMixin` mixin class, which is what gives any class-based view the ability to easily add success messages. Next, the `SuccessMessageMixin` mixin class is added to the `ItemCreation` class, along with the `CreateView` class-based view to give the class-based view its core functionality. Notice the mixin class is added to the class-based view using standard Python inheritance syntax.

Once the `ItemCreation` class-based view gains access to the `SuccessMessageMixin` mixin class behavior, all that's needed to generate a success message is to define the actual message in the `success_message` field. In this manner, when a success operation occurs in the context of the class-based view (e.g., the `success_url` is triggered), the class-based view automatically adds the `success_message` value to the request to display to an end user.

As you can see in Listing 9-22, the process to add a Django framework success message to a class-based view is greatly simplified and made reusable by means of a mixin class. This is particularly true, when you compare it to the approaches taken in Listings 9-13 and 9-14, consisting of overriding class-based view methods that require a lot of typing - many repetitive - to fulfill a simple task.

CHAPTER 10

■ ■ ■

Django User Management

In this chapter you'll learn about Django administers users, groups, and permissions. You'll learn how to conditionally display content depending on a user, how to restrict urls and class-based views, as well as how to manage CRUD (Create-Read-Update-Delete) permissions for Django model records based on user permissions.

In addition, you'll also learn how to customize Django's built-in user model to support additional data fields, as well as how to automate user management tasks like signup, password reminders, and password reset emails. Finally, you'll learn how to create custom authentication back ends to validate user credentials with different technologies, including allowing users to access a Django application with a Facebook, Google, or Twitter account.

Introduction to the Django User System

The Django user system is based on the django.contrib.auth package built in to the Django framework. In this section you'll learn about the core concepts offered by this package, which is the default user system used by a variety of Django apps including the Django admin.

User Types, Subtypes, Groups, and Permissions

There are two main types of Django user classes: User and AnonymousUser. If a user authenticates himself (i.e., provides a valid username/password) Django recognizes him as a User. On the other hand, if a user just surfs an application without any authentication, Django recognizes him as an AnonymousUser.

Any User can be further classified into one of various subtypes:

- superuser.- The most powerful user with permissions to create, read, update, and delete data in the Django admin, which includes model records and other users.

- staff.- A user marked as staff can access the Django admin. But permissions to create, read, update, and delete data in the Django admin must be given explicitly to a user. By default, a superuser is marked as staff.

- active.- All users are marked as active if they're in good standing. Users marked as inactive aren't able to authenticate themselves, a common state if there's a pending post-registration step (e.g., confirm email) or a user is banned and you don't want to delete his data.

© Daniel Rubio 2017

D. Rubio, *Beginning Django*, https://doi.org/10.1007/978-1-4842-2787-9_10

Django also offers the concept of a Group class to grant a set of users the same set of permissions without having to assign them individually. For example, you can grant permissions to a group and then assign users to the group to make permission management easier. In this manner, you can revoke or add permissions in a single step to a set of users, as well as quickly give new users the same permissions.

In addition, you can assign Django permissions granularly to a User or Group in order for them to do CRUD (Create-Update-Delete) records on Django models, a process that is done through Permission model records. Or you can also assign coarser-grained Django permissions on URL/view methods or template content to grant access to a User, Group, or even Permission assignee.

Now that you know the basic concepts behind Django's user system, let's explore the more common operations associated with Django users in greater detail.

Create Users

The first user you'll want to create is a superuser. If you already set up the Django admin in Chapter 1, then you'll already have a project superuser. Either way, I'll recap the process here since you can have any number of superusers. Listing 10-1 illustrates the various ways in which you can create a superuser.

■ **Tip** Consult the book's accompanying source code to run the exercises, in order to reduce typing and automatically access test data.

Listing 10-1. Create Django superuser

```
[user@coffeehouse ~]$ python manage.py createsuperuser
Username (leave blank to use 'admin'):
Email address: admin@coffeehouse.com
Password:
Password (again):
Superuser created successfully.

[user@coffeehouse ~]$ python manage.py createsuperuser --username=bigboss
                     --email=bigboss@coffeehouse.com
Password:
Password (again):
Superuser created successfully.

[user@coffeehouse ~]$ python manage.py shell
Python 2.7.3 (default, Apr 10 2013, 06:20:15)
[GCC 4.6.3] on linux2
Type "help", "copyright", "credits" or "license" for more information.
(InteractiveConsole)
>>> from django.contrib.auth.models import User
>>> user = User.objects.create_superuser(username='angelinvestor',
                                 email='angelinvestor@coffeehouse.com',
                                 password='seedfunding')
>>>
```

■ **Note** A Django username must be unique; preexisting usernames are rejected.

As you can see in Listing 10-1, you can create a superuser with the `createsuperuser` command in the `manage.py` utility, where you're asked for a username, email. and password. And you can also create a superuser with the same `createsuperuser` command using inline arguments `--username` and `--email`, in which case you're only prompted for a password.

In addition, it's also possible to create a superuser through the Django shell using the `User` model class with the `create_superuser()` method. Notice how the `create_superuser()` method requires the same username, email, and password arguments.

When you create a superuser in any of these ways, the user is also automatically set as a staff member and marked as a active, so you don't need to take any additional steps to access the Django admin - which requires staff member permissions - or proceed with authentication, which requires a user to be marked as active.

Sometimes you just want to create a regular user, in which case you can use Django's shell utility and create a user directly through the `User` model. This process is illustrated in Listing 10-2.

Listing 10-2. Create regular Django user through shell

```
[user@coffeehouse ~]$ python manage.py shell
Python 2.7.3 (default, Apr 10 2013, 06:20:15)
[GCC 4.6.3] on linux2
Type "help", "copyright", "credits" or "license" for more information.
(InteractiveConsole)
>>> from django.contrib.auth.models import User
>>> user = User.objects.create_user(username='downtownbarista',
                                    email='downtownbarista@coffeehouse.com',
                                    password='cappuccino')
>>> user.is_staff
False
>>> user.is_active
True
>>> user.is_superuser
False
```

As you can see in Listing 10-2, after you gain access to the Django shell you import the `User` model class and invoke the `create_user()` method with the username, email, and password arguments. The result of the `create_user()` method contains the newly created user.

To confirm the `create_user()` method generates a regular user, you can see in Listing 10-2 a call to the various `User` model attributes, confirming the user is neither staff or superuser and is just marked as active.

Finally, it's also possible to create users through the Django admin. To do this you'll first need to make sure you have superuser access to the Django admin. Once you access the Django admin, you'll see a screen like the one in Figure 10-1, click on the 'Users' link. The 'Users' link takes you to a screen like the one in Figure 10-2, click on the button 'Add User+' in the top right. The 'Add User+' button takes you to a screen like the one in Figure 10-3 where you can introduce the credentials for a new user.

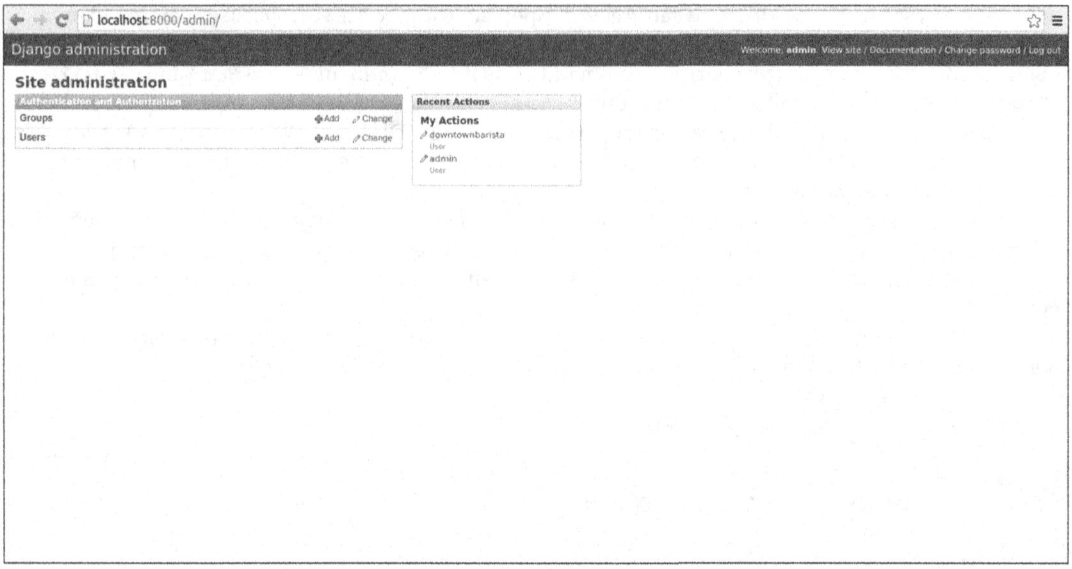

Figure 10-1. *Django admin site home page*

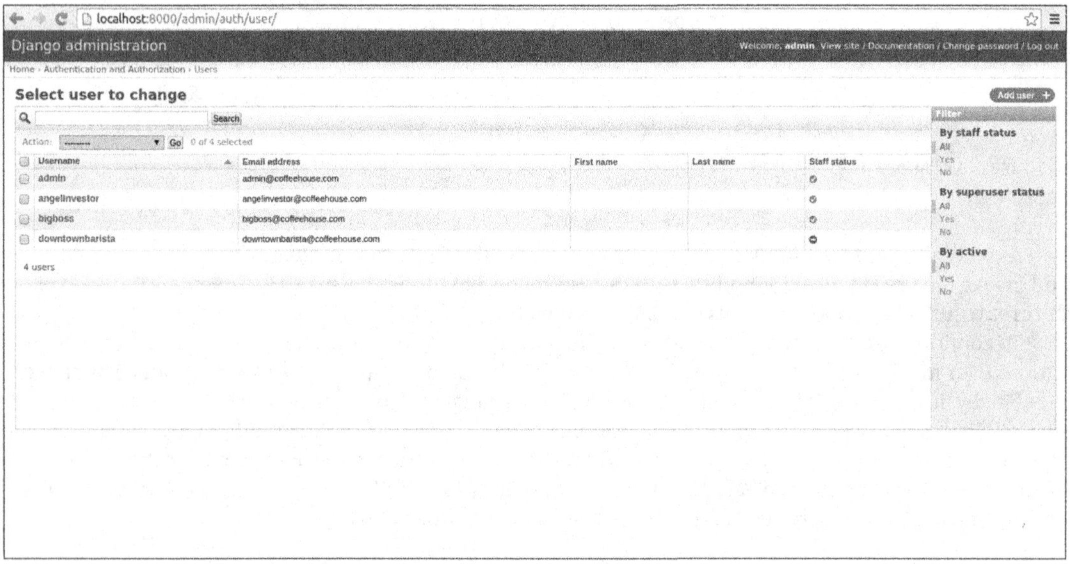

Figure 10-2. *Django admin Users list*

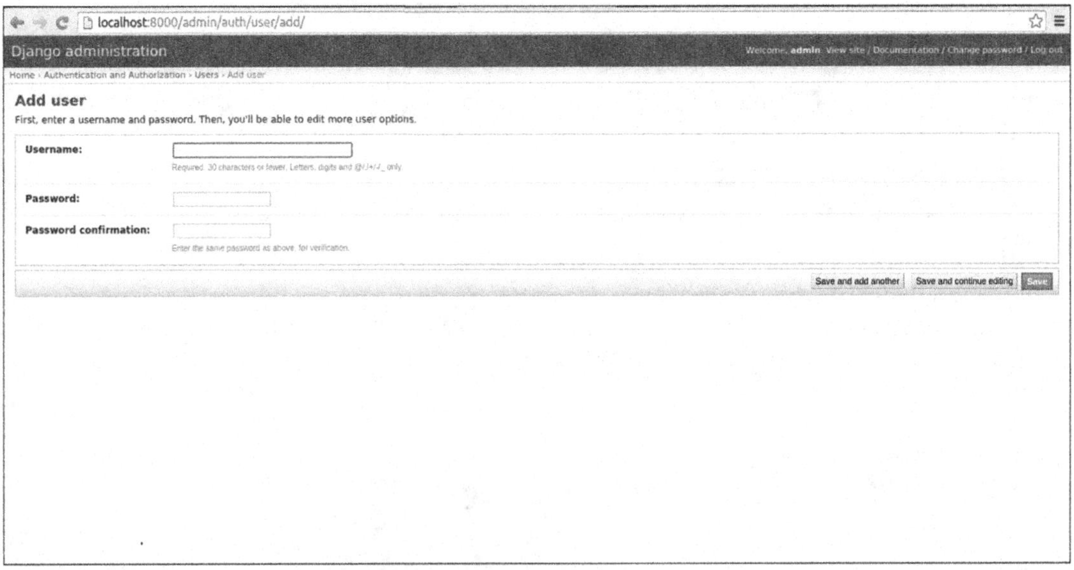

Figure 10-3. *Django admin to create new user*

If you wish to change the subtype (i.e. superuser, staff) of a user created in this manner, you can also do it in the Django admin, a process that's described in the next section.

Manage Users

Once a user is in a Django application, you'll end up managing him. This management can be either revoking his privileges, adding to his privileges, or even editing his profile information. You can manage Django users in two ways, in the Django admin or by manipulating a `User` model in the Django shell or directly in your application.

The easiest way to manage users is directly in the Django admin. Once you access the Django admin you'll see a screen like the one in Figure 10-1, if you click on the 'Users' link you'll be taken to a screen like the one in Figure 10-2 that contains a list of Django users. Each Django user presented in Figure 10-2 has his username as a link, and if you click on this link you'll be taken to the user's page, which is illustrated in Figures 10-4, 10-5, and 10-6 where you can edit a user's profile.

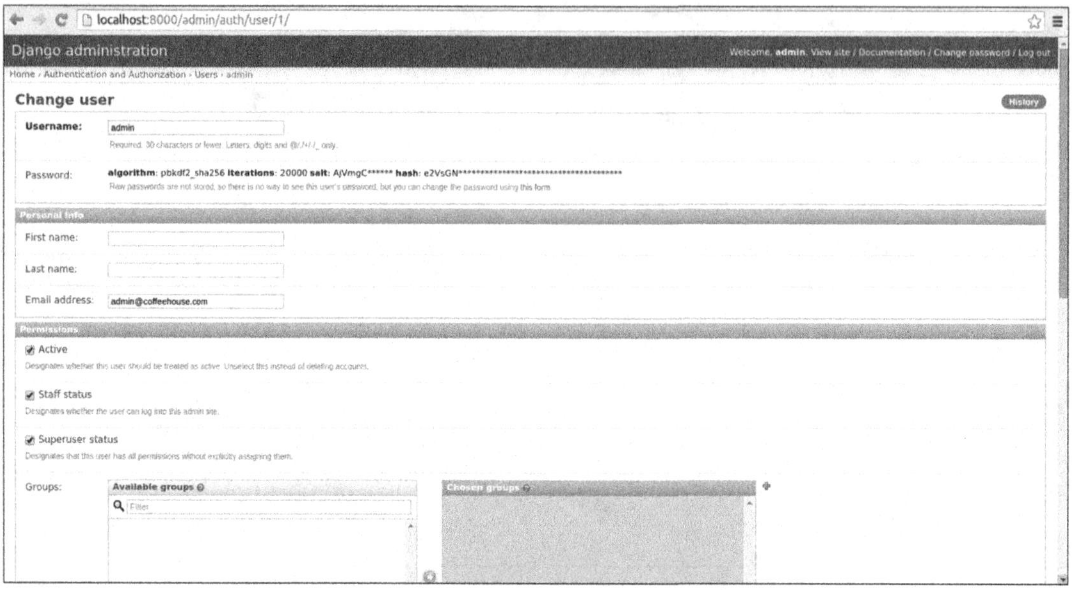

Figure 10-4. Django admin change user page - Part 1

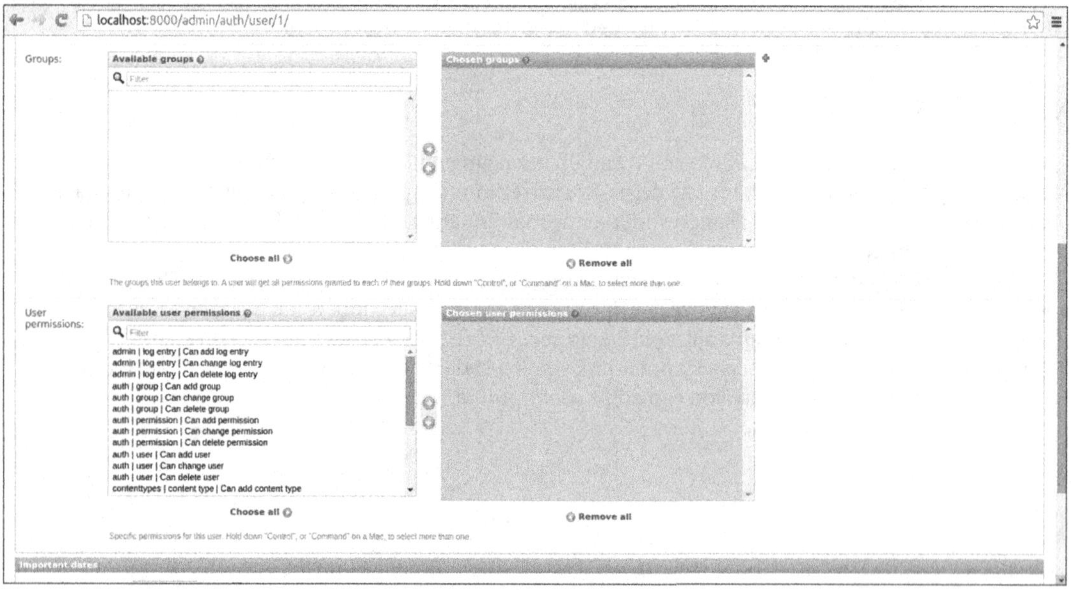

Figure 10-5. Django admin change user page - Part 2

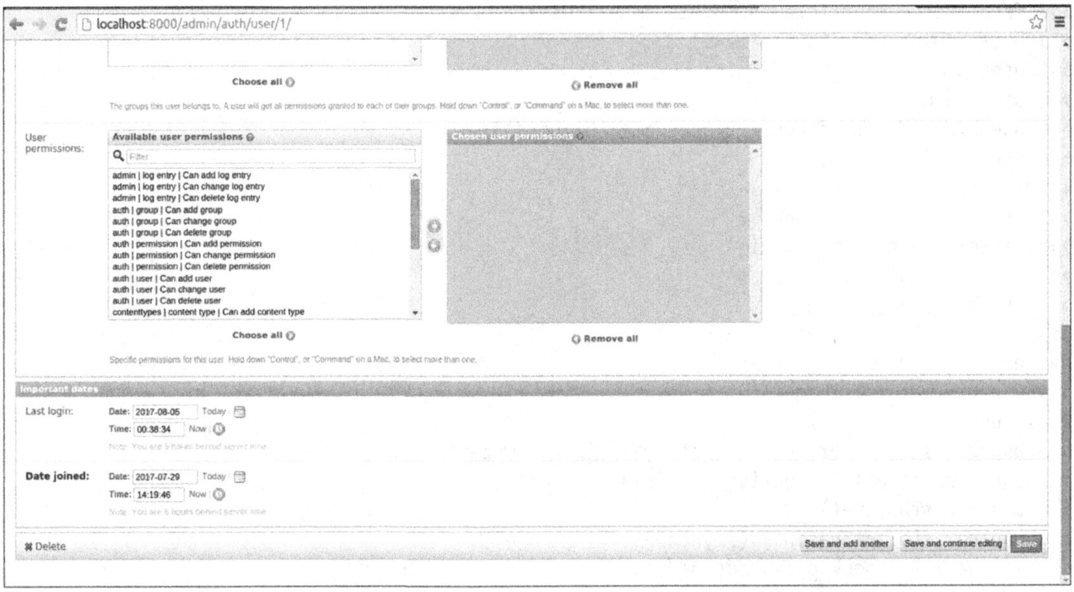

Figure 10-6. Django admin change user page - Part 3

The first part of a user's profile that you can edit is illustrated in Figure 10-4. Here you can edit his username, his password - by clicking on the 'this form' link at the end of the small text - his first name, his last name, as well as his email. In addition, you can see there are three check boxes where it's possible to change a user's active, staff, and superuser status.

If you scroll down, you'll see the second part of a user's profile that you can edit, which is illustrated in Figure 10-5. Here you can assign a user to different groups, as well as assign a user individual CRUD permissions over Django models. Here I would advise you to carefully evaluate the need to assign individual CRUD permissions to a user; a more flexible approach is to create groups and assign them CRUD permissions and then assign users to groups, this way the permissions become easier to track and reusable for other users.

If you scroll further down to the end, you'll see the third part of a user's profile that you can edit, which is illustrated in Figure 10-6. Here you can view and update a user's last login, as well as the date a user was created. At the bottom right of the page, you can see the various save buttons to store any changes made to the page. And in addition, at the bottom left there's a 'Delete' button to remove a user completely; however, I would advise you to consider just unchecking a user's active status to restrict access. This last step is sufficient to block a user from accessing an application again and it keeps his other data untouched in case you want to undo the action.

Another option to modify a user's profile is to directly manipulate his `User` model record. As illustrated in Listing 10-3, you first make a query for the desired user and then modify the model attributes or execute one of the `User` model helper methods.

Listing 10-3. Manage Django user through shell

```
[user@coffeehouse ~]$ python manage.py shell
Python 2.7.3 (default, Apr 10 2013, 06:20:15)
[GCC 4.6.3] on linux2
Type "help", "copyright", "credits" or "license" for more information.
(InteractiveConsole)
```

```
>>> from django.contrib.auth.models import User
>>> user = User.objects.get(id=1)
>>> user.username = 'superadmin'
>>> user.save()
>>> userbig = User.objects.get(username='bigboss')
>>> userbig.is_superuser
True
>>> userbig.superuser = False
>>> userbig.first_name = 'Big'
>>> userbig.last_name = 'Boss'
>>> userbig.save()
>>> userbig.is_superuser
False
>>> userbig.get_full_name()
u'Big Boss'
>>> userbarista = User.objects.get(email='downtownbarista@coffeehouse.com')
>>> userbarista.email ='barista@coffeehouse.com'
>>> userbarista.save()
>>> userbarista.set_password('mynewpass')
>>> userbarista.check_password('oldpass')
False
>>> userbarista.check_password('mynewpass')
True
```

As you can see in Listing 10-3, you can modify the same `User` profile values as those presented in the Django admin in Figures 10-4, 10-5, and 10-6. Just be aware that because you're making a query, any changes made to fields must be followed by a call to the `save()` method on the reference for fields to be persisted. Tables 10-1 and Table 10-2 contain a full list of fields and methods available on the `User` model.

Table 10-1. *Django django.contrib.auth.models.User fields*

Field	Description
username	(Required) 30 characters or fewer and can contain alphanumeric, _, @, +, . and - characters.
first_name	(Optional) 30 characters or fewer.
last_name	(Optional) 30 characters or fewer.
email	(Optional) Email address.
password	(Required) A hash of, and metadata about, the password. Note that Django doesn't store the raw password.
groups	A many to many relationship to django.contrib.auth.models.Group
user_permissions	A many to many relationship to django.contrib.auth.Permission.
is_staff (Boolean)	Designates whether a user can access the admin site.
is_active (Boolean)	Designates whether a user is considered active.
is_superuser	(Boolean) Designates whether a user has all permissions without explicitly assigning them.
last_login	A datetime of the user's last login, set to NULL if the user has never logged in.
date_joined	A datetime designating when the account was created. Is set to the current date/time by default when the account is created.

Table 10-2. *Django django.contrib.auth.models.User methods*

Method	Description
get_username()	Returns the username for the user. Since the User model can be changed for another, this method is the recommended approach instead of referencing the username attribute directly.
is_anonymous()	For a User this method always returns False; it's only used as a way to differentiate between User and AnonymousUser.
is_authenticated()	For a User this method always returns True, as it's only used to find out whether the user has gone through the AuthenticationMiddleware (representing the currently logged-in user).
get_full_name()	Returns the first_name and the last_name fields, with a space in between.
get_short_name()	Returns the first_name.
set_password (raw_password)	Sets the user's password to the given raw string, taking care of the password hashing. Note that when the raw_password is None, the password is set to an unusable password, as if set_unusable_password() were used.
check_password (raw_password)	Returns True if the given raw string is the correct password for the user, talking care of the password hashing for making the comparison.
set_unusable_password()	Marks the user as having no password set. Note this isn't the same as having a blank string for a password. check_password() for this user will never return True. This is helpful if authentication takes place against an existing external source (e.g., LDAP directory).
has_usable_password()	Returns False if set_unusable_password() has been called for the user.
get_group_permissions (obj=None)	Returns a set of group permission strings for the user. If the obj is passed, only returns the group permissions for the specific object.
get_all_permissions (obj=None)	Returns a set of group and user permission strings for the user. If the obj is passed, only returns the group permissions for the specific object.
has_perm (perm, obj=None)	Returns True if the user has the specified permission, where perm is in the format <app label>.<permission codename>". Note if the user is inactive, this method always returns False. If the obj is passed, the check occurs on the specific object and not on the model.
has_perms (perm_list, obj=None)	Returns True if the user has each of the specified permissions, where each perm is in the format <app label>.<permission codename>". Note if the user is inactive, this method always returns False. If the obj is passed, the check occurs on the specific object and not on the model.
has_module_perms (package_name)	Returns True if the user has permissions in the given package (i.e., the Django app label). If the user is inactive, this method always returns False.
email_user (subject, message, from_email=None, **kwargs)	Sends an email to the user. If from_email is None, Django uses the DEFAULT_FROM_EMAIL in settings.py. Also note this method relies on Django's send_mail() method to which it passes the **kwargs argument. See the Django email shortcut methods for more details on the send_mail() method and **kwargs values,

■ **Tip** User model data is stored in the database table auth_user.

PASSWORD STRENGTH OPTIONS

By default, Django enforces password follow certain rules, such as not being similar to a username, containing a minimum amount of characters, avoiding common words, and forcing passwords to consist of more than numbers. These password rules are defined in a project's settings.py file in the AUTH_PASSWORD_VALIDATORS variable, as follows:

```
AUTH_PASSWORD_VALIDATORS = [
    {
        'NAME': 'django.contrib.auth.password_validation.UserAttributeSimilarity
                Validator',
    },
    {
        'NAME': 'django.contrib.auth.password_validation.MinimumLengthValidator',
    },
    {
        'NAME': 'django.contrib.auth.password_validation.CommonPasswordValidator',
    },
    {
        'NAME': 'django.contrib.auth.password_validation.NumericPasswordValidator',
    },
]
```

This list of validators can be edited to suit the needs of a project, by either removing certain rules or inclusively making them more strict with options.[1]

Create and Manage Groups

Django groups can be created in the Django admin. With a superuser account, access the Django admin and you'll see a screen like the one in Figure 10-1, and click on the 'Groups' link. The 'Groups' link takes you to a screen like the one in Figure 10-7, and then click on the button 'Add Group+' in the top right. The 'Add Group+' button takes you to a screen like the one in Figure 10-8 where you can create a new group introducing its name.

[1]https://docs.djangoproject.com/en/1.11/topics/auth/passwords/#included-validators

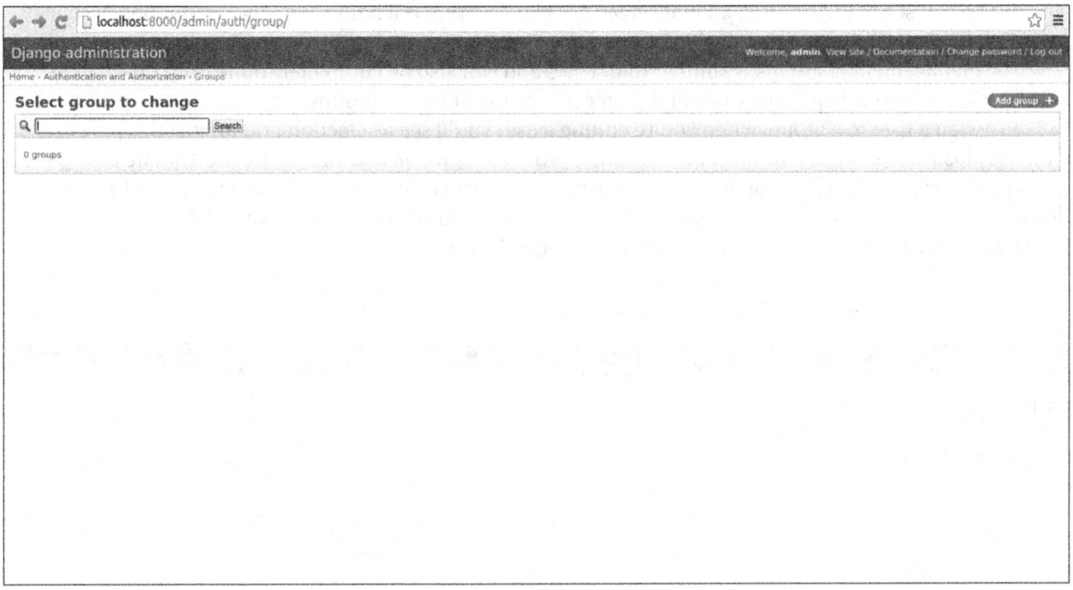

Figure 10-7. *Django admin Groups list*

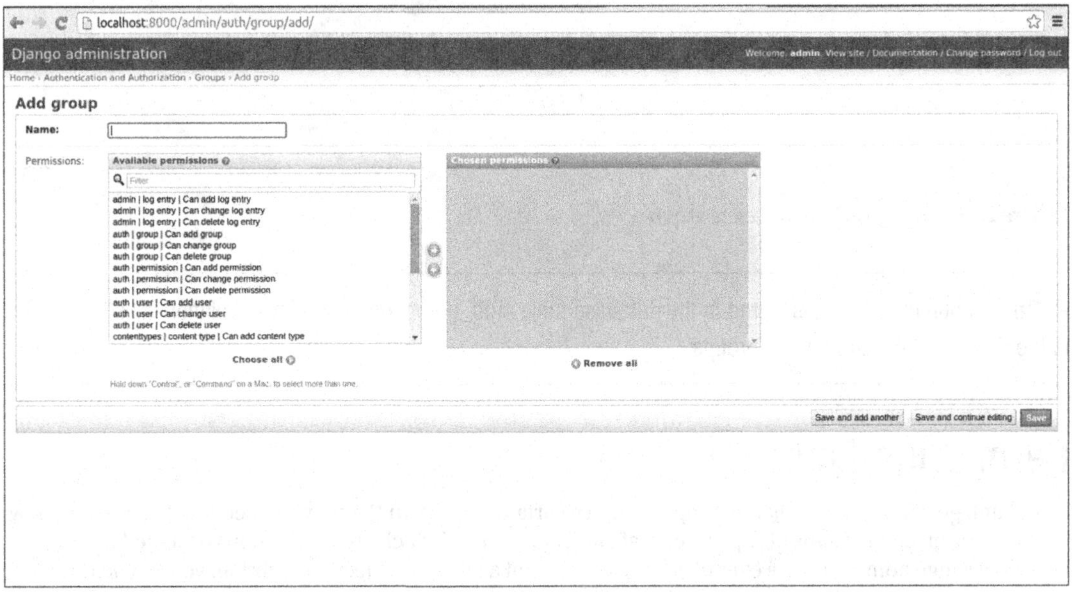

Figure 10-8. *Django admin to create new group*

As you can see in Figure 10-8, all that's need to create a group is a name and you can optionally specify permissions given to the group to do CRUD operations on Django models in the application.

The management of groups is simpler than users and can also be completely done from the Django admin. What you'll end up doing most of the time is assigning users to groups.

To assign a user to a group, when you're editing a user you'll see a selection grid for just this purpose, which is illustrated in Figure 10-5. To edit a group's properties - name and Create-Delete-Update Django model permission - you can do so from the same page where you created it illustrated in Figure 10-8. To delete a group from the Groups list illustrated in Figure 10-7, you select the group you wish to delete and select the action from the drop-down list, as illustrated in Figure 10-9.

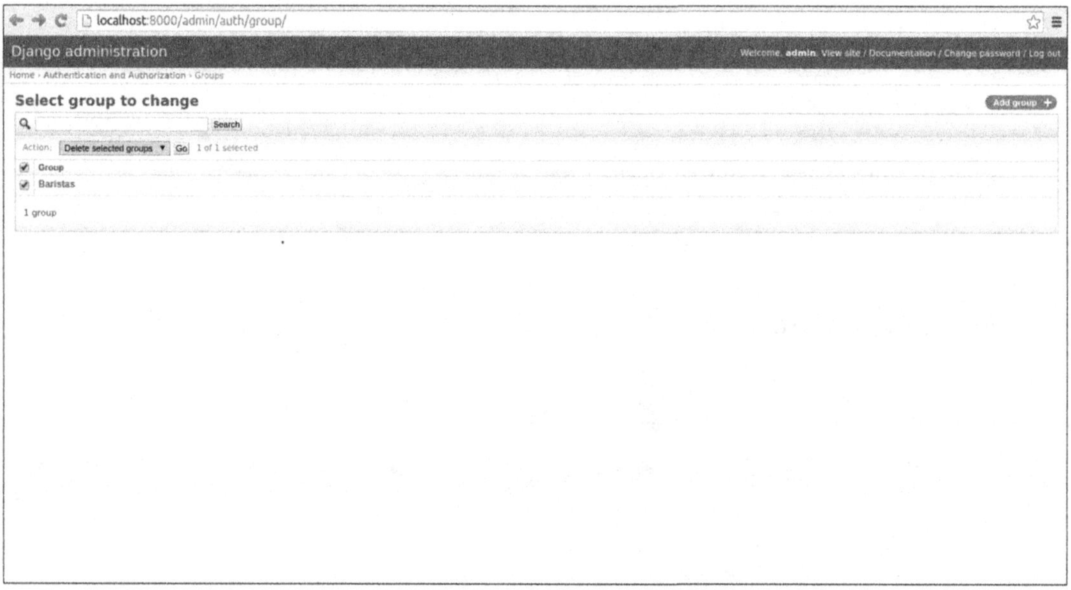

Figure 10-9. *Django admin to delete group*

■ **Tip** Group model data is stored in the database table auth_group. And User-Group relationships is stored in the database table auth_user_groups.

Permission Types

By default, permissions in a Django project enforce certain actions. In the previous section, you learned how users can be given the status of superuser, staff, and active, all of which are permissions designed to work with the Django admin and the overall access workflow of a Django project. In addition, you also learned how users or groups can be given the ability to create, delete, or update Django model records, all of which are permissions assigned to individual Django models.

In this section, I'll expand on the topic of permissions and describe the default behaviors of permissions, as well as how to create your own permissions for other purposes.

User Permissions: Superuser, Staff, and Active

In the previous section, you learned how to assign Django users different subtypes: superuser, staff, and active. The following is a list of permissions associated with each of these user subtypes:

- superuser.- Permission to create, read, update, and delete users in the Django admin, as well as create, read, update, and delete all Django model records in a project through the Django admin.
- staff.- Permission to access the Django admin. Even if a user is marked as a superuser, a user must also be marked as staff to access the Django admin. Users marked as staff must be given additional permissions on each Django model to execute tasks.
- active.- Permission to log in into the application (Django admin or elsewhere). An inactive user is effectively barred from using his credentials to authenticate into a Django project. For example, in order to access the Django admin a user must be marked as active - in addition to staff. Also, any section of a Django project (e.g., view or template) can be marked to require active status, forcing users to log in.

All three user subtypes are stored in the database as part of the `User` model, subtypes that can be confirmed by using the methods in Table 10-2 that belong to the `User` model. Although `User` permissions are heavily used in the Django admin, this doesn't mean they're restricted to it. For example, it's possible to rely on a `User` permissions like superuser, staff, or active to allow or deny access to other parts of a Django project (e.g., a link in a template, a url/view method, or others actions).

The next section on permission enforcement describes these processes in detail. Next, I'll describe another type of permissions that is associated with Django models.

Model Permissions: Add, Change, Delete, and Custom

Model permissions are linked to the ability to create, delete, or update Django model records. In the first section of this chapter, you can see in Figure 10-5 a selection grid to assign `add`, `change`, and `delete` permissions on individual models to each user in a Django project. And in Figure 10-8, you can see an equivalent selection grid to assign these same type of `add`, `change`, and `delete` permissions on individual models for each group in a Django project.

These `add`, `change`, and `delete` permissions are managed at the database level through permission model records, records that are automatically created when you run a Django model's first migration. Managing these types of permissions once they're created is very straightforward, as the assignment is made directly on a user - illustrated in Figure 10-5 - or group illustrated in Figure 10-8.

■ **Tip** Model permission data is stored in the database table auth_permission, which also references the django_content_type table that maintains a list of installed Django models. In addition, model permission-user relationships are stored in the database table auth_user_user_permissions and model permission-group relationships are stored in the database table auth_group_permissions.

Similar to the behavior of user permissions, model permissions aren't necessarily restricted to model operations. For example, it's perfectly possible to allow or deny access to a view or a template section if a user or group has a certain model permission (e.g., if a `User` has the ability to create a `Store` model or change an `Item` model, and allow access to a page or link).

But again, the next section on permission enforcement describes these processes in detail. Next, I'll describe how to customize model permissions for Django models.

Model Meta permission options: default_permissions and permissions

Sometimes the need can arise to change the default permissions given to a model. By default, all Django models are given the add, change, and delete permissions. Although it's up to an administrator to grant these permissions to users and groups, sometimes it can be necessary to eliminate some or all of these permissions from a Django model (e.g., eliminate the presence of the change and delete permissions from a data-sensitive model).

In addition, sometimes it can also be necessary to add custom permissions to a model that doesn't fit the default add, change, and delete permissions (e.g., permissions such as give_refund or can_hire, to assign users/groups permissions to access certain parts of an application).

To alter the default permissions given to a model (i.e., add, change, and delete), you can use a model's meta class default_permissions field. In addition, you can add custom permissions to a model's permissions through a model's meta class permissions field.

Listing 10-4 illustrates a model class that makes use of the model meta permissions and default_permissions fields.

Listing 10-4. Customize a Django model's permissions with default_permissions and permissions

```
class Store(models.Model):
    name = models.CharField(max_length=30)
    address = models.CharField(max_length=30,unique=True)
    city = models.CharField(max_length=30)
    state = models.CharField(max_length=2)
    class Meta:
        default_permissions = ('add',)
        permissions = (('give_refund','Can refund customers'),('can_hire',
        'Can hire employees'))
```

Notice in Listing 10-4 the Store model's default_permissions field is set to ('add',), which effectively removes the change and delete permissions. If you add this model meta statement, you'll notice the Store model's default permissions change, as illustrated in the UI Figure 10-10.

In addition, in Listing 10-4 notice the model meta permissions field sets two custom permissions: give_refund and can_hire, where each custom permission is composed of a tuple with the first element representing the code – used in the database – and the second element a friendly UI name. If you add this model meta statement, you'll notice the Store model adds these two custom permissions, as illustrated in the UI Figure 10-10.

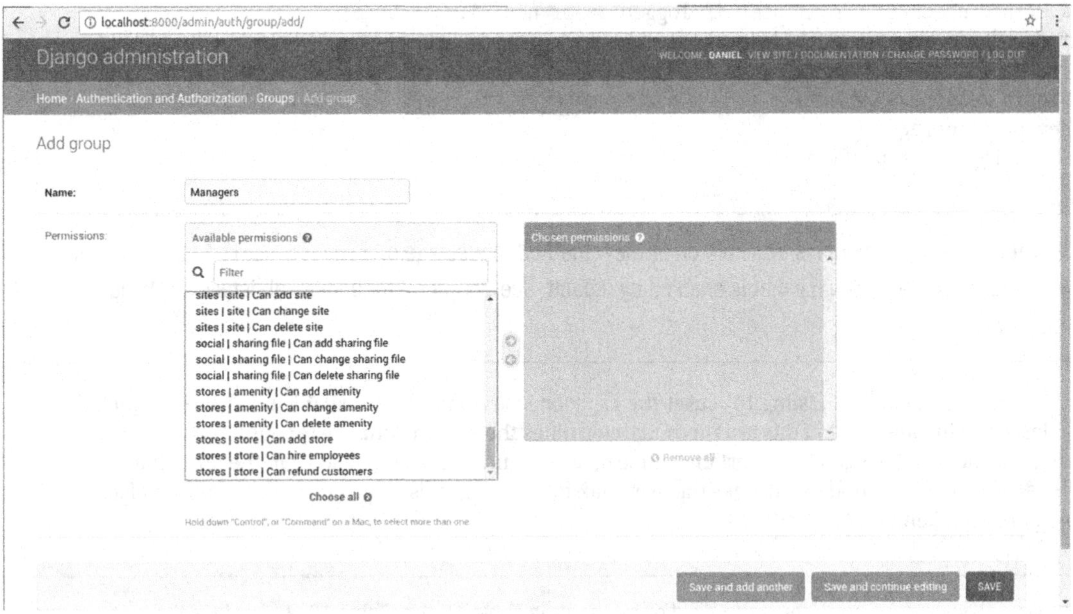

Figure 10-10. *Custom default model permissions and custom model permissions*

Permission Checks and Enforcement

Now that you know about the different types of Django permissions, we can explore how to leverage these permissions outside out of their primary context (i.e., user permissions outside the Django admin and model permissions outside of Django CRUD operations).

Up next, you'll learn how to change and enforce Django permissions in views, urls, templates, models, and class-based views.

View Method Permission Checks

Because view methods process incoming requests and dispatch responses to end users, they represent an ideal location to enforce permission checks. For example, you can use a permission check on a view method to return different content, depending if a user is logged in (i.e., is a `User` vs. an `AnonymousUser`) or is a superuser, staff, or active subtype.

Listing 10-5 illustrates a permission check inside the logic of a view method to return different results based on a user's login status, as well as another variation that uses a decorator to restrict view method access based on a user's login status.

Listing 10-5. Permission check in view methods with internal checks and @login_required

```
# Internal check to see if user is anonymous or not
def homepage(request):
    if request.user.is_anonymous():
        # Logic for AnonymousUser
    else:
        # Logic for User
```

```
# Method check to see if user is logged in or not (i.e. a User)
from django.contrib.auth.decorators import login_required

@login_required
def profile(request):
    # Logic for profile
```

■ **Note** The User model is available on all view method requests (e.g., request.user), thanks to Django's AuthenticationMiddleware that is enabled by default. See Chapter 2 for additional details on Django middleware.

The first example in Listing 10-5 uses the is_anonymous() method available on all User models - described in Table 10-2. If this last method determines the user making the request is anonymous - meaning he hasn't logged in - a certain course of action and response is taken. On the other hand, if the is_anonymous() method determines the user making the request is logged in, another course of action and response is taken.

■ **Tip** You can use any User model field or method - in Table 10-1 or Table 10-2 - besides the is_anonymous method to perform a check (e.g., is_staff, is_superuser).

The second example in Listing 10-5 uses the @login_required() decorator to restrict the entire view method to logged-in users (i.e., requests that have User and blocks requests with AnonymousUser). This last technique is helpful when known beforehand the view method doesn't require a conditional permission workflow like the first example in Listing 10-5.

Permissions checks on view methods can also be performed to verify if a user complies with a certain permission test. For example, a view method can be blocked to users that belong to a certain group or to users that have certain model permissions. Listing 10-6 illustrates three additional view method permission checks using the @user_passes_test and @permission_required decorators.

Listing 10-6. Permission check in view methods with @user_passes_test and @permission_required

```
# Method check to see if User belongs to group called 'Barista'
from django.contrib.auth.decorators import user_passes_test
from django.contrib.auth.models import Group

@user_passes_test(lambda u: Group.objects.get(name='Baristas') in u.groups.all())
def dashboard(request):
    # Logic for dashboard

# Explicit method check, if User is authenticated and has permissions to change Store model

# Explicit method with test
def user_of_stores(user):
    if user.is_authenticated() and user.has_perm("stores.change_store"):
        return True
    else:
        return False
```

```
# Method check using method
@user_passes_test(user_of_stores)
def store_manager(request):
    # Logic for store_manager

# Method check to see if User has permissions to add Store model

from django.contrib.auth.decorators import permission_required

@permission_required('stores.add_store')
def store_creator(request):
    # Logic for store_creator
```

The first example in Listing 10-6 uses the `@user_passes_test` decorator and defines an inline test. The snippet `lambda u: Group.objects.get(name='Baristas') in u.groups.all()` fetches the `Group` model record with the name `Baristas` and checks if the requesting user belongs to this group. If the requesting user does not belong to the `Baristas` group then the test fails and access is denied; otherwise the user is allowed to run through the view method.

The second example also uses the `@user_passes_test` decorator, but instead of defining an inline test it relies on the `user_of_stores()` method to perform the test logic. This is particularly helpful if the test is complex, which can make it hard to follow inline logic, compared to having a regular method. As you can also see in Listing 10-6, the `user_of_stores()` verifies if the user is authenticated and also if he has update permissions on the `Store` model - note the string `stores.change_store` is the syntax used by Django's Permission model records.

The last example in Listing 10-6 uses the `@permission_required` decorator that is designed to validate if a user has a given `Permission` record. In this case, notice the decorator has the input string `stores.add_store` that indicates that only users that have permission to add a `Store` model can run through the view method.

WHAT HAPPENS WHEN A USER FAILS A PERMISSION CHECK?

For internal validation checks (e.g., those made in the body of a method, such as `if request.user.is_anonymous():`) you have absolute control, so you can redirect a user to any page or add flash messages to display on a template.

For the decorator validation checks `@login_required`, `@user_passes_test`, and `@permission_required` the default failure behavior is to redirect a user to Django's login page. Django's default login page URL is `/account/login/`, a value that can be overridden with the `LOGIN_URL` variable in `settings.py`, details of which I'll provide in an upcoming section.

For the `@permission_required` decorator, it's also possible to redirect a failed test to Django's HTTP 403 (Forbidden) page by adding the `raise_exception=True` attribute (e.g., `@permission_required('stores.add_store',raise_exception=True)`).

URL Permission Checks

In certain circumstances you can have a Django workflow that doesn't involve a view method and simply sends control from a URL directly to a static template. In such cases, it's also possible to enforce permission checks directly on URL definitions. Listing 10-7 illustrates similar validation checks like the ones in Listings 10-5 and 10-6 applied to URL definitions in `urls.py`.

Listing 10-7. Permission checks in urls.py for static templates

```
from django.conf.urls import  include, url
from django.views.generic import TemplateView

from django.contrib.auth.decorators import login_required,permission_required,user_passes_
test
from django.contrib.auth.models import Group

urlpatterns = [
      url(r'^online/baristas/',
         user_passes_test(lambda u: Group.objects.get(name='Baristas') in u.groups.all())
         (TemplateView.as_view(template_name='online/baristas.html')),name="onlinebaristas"),
      url(r'^online/dashboard/',
         permission_required('stores.add_store')
         (TemplateView.as_view(template_name='online/dashboard.html')),name="onlinedashboard"),
      url(r'^online/',
         login_required(TemplateView.as_view(template_name='online/index.html')),name='online'),
]
```

As you can see in Listing 10-7, after you import the required decorators you just need to integrate the validation tests in the URL definition. The `@user_passes_test` and `@permission_required` decorators are declared as stand-alone methods followed by the URL definition (e.g., `user_pass_test()(TemplateView.as_view...))`. The `@login_required` decorator though takes the `TemplateView` statement as its input. It should be pointed out the behavior for failed tests in Listing 10-7 is the same as those in Listings 10-5 and 10-6, described in the sidebar "What Happens When a User Fails a Permission Check?'"

Another possibility that can arise for validation checks is to perform them on a group of view methods/ URLs, so that instead of adding a decorator to each individual view method - as illustrated in Listing 10-6-- you only do it once for a whole group. This view method/URL grouping process is particularly common when defining URLs in `urls.py` through the `include()` method. Listing 10-8 illustrates how to enforce validation checks on sets of urls that use the `include()` method.

Listing 10-8. Permission checks in urls.py for include() definitions

```
from django.conf.urls import include, url
from django.core.urlresolvers import RegexURLResolver, RegexURLPattern

class DecoratedURLPattern(RegexURLPattern):
    def resolve(self, *args, **kwargs):
        result = super(DecoratedURLPattern, self).resolve(*args, **kwargs)
        if result:
            result.func = self._decorate_with(result.func)
        return result
```

```
class DecoratedRegexURLResolver(RegexURLResolver):
    def resolve(self, *args, **kwargs):
        result = super(DecoratedRegexURLResolver, self).resolve(*args, **kwargs)
        if result:
            result.func = self._decorate_with(result.func)
        return result

def decorated_includes(func, includes, *args, **kwargs):
    urlconf_module, app_name, namespace = includes
    patterns = getattr(urlconf_module, 'urlpatterns', urlconf_module)
    for item in patterns:
        if isinstance(item, RegexURLPattern):
            item.__class__ = DecoratedURLPattern
            item._decorate_with = func

        elif isinstance(item, RegexURLResolver):
            item.__class__ = DecoratedRegexURLResolver
            item._decorate_with = func

    return urlconf_module, app_name, namespace

from django.contrib.auth.decorators import login_required,permission_required,user_passes_test
from django.contrib.auth.models import Group

from coffeehouse.items.urls import urlpatterns as drinks_url_patterns

urlpatterns = [
    url(r'^items/',
       decorated_includes(login_required,include(items_url_patterns,namespace="items"))),
    url(r'^stores/',
      decorated_includes(permission_required('stores.add_store'),
      include('coffeehouse.stores.urls',namespace="stores"))),
    url(r'^social/',
      decorated_includes(user_passes_test(lambda u: Group.objects.get(name='Baristas') in
      u.groups.all()),
      include('coffeehouse.social.urls',namespace="social"))),
]
```

Because Django doesn't have built-in support for permissions checks in `include()` definitions, you can see in Listing 10-8 we first define two custom classes followed by the custom method `decorated_includes`. If you follow the sequence in Listing 10-8, you can see the `decorated_includes()` method accepts two input arguments, first the permission test (e.g., `login_required`, `permission_required`) and then the standard `include()` method with the URL definitions. It should also be pointed out the behavior for failed tests in Listing 10-8 is the same as those in previous listings, described in the sidebar "What Happens When a User Fails a Permission Check?"

Template Permission Checks

Another permission check available in Django projects is in templates, a process that's helpful if you want to show/hide content (e.g., links) based on a user's permissions. Listing 10-9 illustrates a series of Django template syntax examples.

Listing 10-9. Permission checks in templates

```
{% if user.is_authenticated %}
   {#  Content for authenticated users  #}
{% endif %}

{% if perms.stores.add_store %}
   {#  Content for users that can add stores #}
{% endif %}

{% for group in user.groups.all %}
   {% if group.name == 'Baristas'  %}
        {# Content for users with 'Baristas' group #}
   {% endif %}
{% endfor %}
```

■ **Note** The user and perms variables used to perform permissions checks in templates are available thanks to Django's auth context processor, which is enabled by default - see Chapter 3 details on the use of Django context processors.

You can see in Listing 10-9 all of the template syntax examples use the user and perms variables to perform a conditional permission check. The first example checks to see if the user is authenticated through is_authenticated. The second example verifies if perms - which holds a user's permissions - has access to create Store model records, using Django's Permission syntax stores.add_store. And the third example in Listing 10-9 loops over a user's groups, to check if the user is in the Baristas group; if it's, it outputs content for this type of user.

■ **Tip** Loops in Django templates to check a property are very inefficient. Although the last example in Listing 10-9 works, it's a very inefficient mechanism. A better solution is to create a custom filter and perform a direct query in the filter (e.g., {% if user|has_group:"Baristas" %}, with the has_group filter containing the bulk of the logic check). In this case I opted for the syntax in Listing 10-9 to keep everything in one place, but be aware the more efficient solution for this type of logic is to use a custom filter described in Chapter 3.

Class-Based View Permission Checks

As you learned toward the end of Chapter 2 and in Chapter 9, class-based views provide better reusability and encapsulation for the logic contained in view methods. However, due to the way class-based views are composed, they require a different approach to check permissions than regular view methods presented in Listings 10-5 and 10-6.

Although you can technically check permissions in class-based views – just like it's done in standard view methods – by defining a class-based view's get() and/or post() methods, this technique also forces you to declare the bulk of a view's logic, which is inefficient in a class-based view if all you're trying to do is incorporate permission checks.

Listing 10-10 illustrates a series of options to perform permission checks in class-based views.

Listing 10-10. Permission checks in class-based views

```
from django.views.generic import ListView
from django.views.generic.detail import DetailView
from django.views.generic.edit import CreateView, UpdateView, DeleteView
from django.utils.decorators import method_decorator
from django.core.urlresolvers import reverse_lazy
from django.contrib.messages.views import SuccessMessageMixin

from django.contrib.auth.decorators import login_required,user_passes_test
from django.contrib.auth.models import Group

from django.contrib.auth.mixins import LoginRequiredMixin, UserPassesTestMixin,
PermissionRequiredMixin

class ItemList(LoginRequiredMixin,ListView):
    model = Item
    context_object_name = 'items'
    template_name = 'items/index.html'

class ItemDetail(UserPassesTestMixin,DetailView):
    model = Item
    pk_url_kwarg = 'item_id'
    template_name = 'items/detail.html'
    def test_func(self):
        return self.request.user.is_authenticated

class ItemCreation(PermissionRequiredMixin,SuccessMessageMixin,CreateView):
    model = Item
    form_class = ItemForm
    success_url = reverse_lazy('items:index')
    success_message = "Item %(name)s created successfully"
    permission_required = ('items.add_item',)

@method_decorator(login_required, name='dispatch')
class ItemUpdate(SuccessMessageMixin,UpdateView):
    model = Item
    pk_url_kwarg = 'item_id'
    form_class = ItemForm
    success_url = reverse_lazy('items:index')
    success_message = "Item %(name)s updated successfully"

@method_decorator(user_passes_test(lambda u: Group.objects.get(name='Baristas') in u.groups.
all()), name='dispatch')
class ItemDelete(DeleteView):
    model = Item
    pk_url_kwarg = 'item_id'
    success_url = reverse_lazy('items:index')
```

The first class-based view in Listing 10-10 ItemList uses the LoginRequiredMixin mixin to enforce that only logged-in users are able to access the class-based view. The second class-based view ItemDetail uses another mixin named UserPassesTestMixin to ensure that only users that pass a permission test are allowed to access the class-based view. To define a permission test for a class-based view that uses the UserPassesTestMixin mixin, notice the test_func() method is used. This last method gains access to a user - via self.request - and returns a True or False value based on the test, which in Listing 10-10 consists of simply calling is_authenticated.

The third class-based view in Listing 10-10 ItemCreation uses the PermissionRequiredMixin mixin to enforce only users that have certain model permissions are allowed access to the class-based view. To declare model permissions on a class-based view that uses the PermissionRequiredMixin mixin, the permission_required option is used with a tuple value of permissions. In the case of Listing 10-10, the ('items.add_item',) value follows the model permission syntax <app_name>.<app_permission>, ensuring only users that have permission to add Item records to the items app are allowed access the class-based view.

The last two class-based views in Listing 10-10 ItemUpdate and ItemDelete make use of the @method_decorator decorator to enforce class-based permissions. The @method_decorator decorator is specifically designed to apply standard view method decorators - like the ones used in Listings 10-5 and 10-6 - to class-based view methods, accepting two arguments: a decorator and the class-based view method on which to apply the decorator. In the case of Listing 10-10, you can see the ItemUpdate class-based view applies the login_required decorator to the dispatch() method to only allow logged-in users to access the class-based view. And the ItemDelete class-based view applies the user_passes_test decorator to the dispatch() method to only allow users that belong to the Baristas group access to the class-based view.

User Authentication and Auto-Management

In the first section of this chapter you learned how to create users. But recall that for this process to work, you either had to use a Django command-line tool or the Django admin. These techniques, while valid, are not intended and won't scale for end users that visit an application.

Similarly, up to this point in the chapter, the only location for users to log in and log out has been through the Django admin authentication form. This last form is not an ideal location for end users either, not only because it lacks a layout made for an application, but also because it's not intended for users who never plan to interact with a project's database.

If you plan on end users authenticating themselves into an application, you need to provide a way for users to sign up, a way for users to log in, and log out as well as a way for users to remember and change their passwords. The same django.contrib.auth package that supports the User model also includes a series of prebuilt constructs designed to create user authentication workflows.

The first prebuilt mechanism available to authenticate users is a set of urls that allow users to log in and log out of an application, allow users to change their password, as well as allow users to reset their password supported by an email notification.

Listing 10-11 illustrates how to add the full set of django.contrib.auth urls to the main urls.py file - using an include statement - as well as the equivalent individual url statements in case you want to selectively pick and choose which urls to use in a project.

Listing 10-11. Configure urls from django.contrib.auth package

```
from django.conf.urls import url
from django.contrib.auth import views

# Option 1 to include all urls (See option 2 for included urls)
urlpatterns = [
    url(r'^accounts/', include('django.contrib.auth.urls')),
]
```

```
# Option 2) (Explicit urls, all included in django.contrib.auth)
urlpatterns = [
    url(r'^accounts/login/$', views.LoginView.as_view(), name='login'),
    url(r'^accounts/logout/$', views.LogoutView.as_view(), name='logout'),

    url(r'^accounts/password_change/$', views.PasswordChangeView.as_view(), name='password_change'),
    url(r'^accounts/password_change/done/$', views.PasswordChangeDoneView.as_view(),
     name='password_change_done'),

    url(r'^accounts/password_reset/$', views.PasswordResetView.as_view(), name='password_reset'),
    url(r'^accounts/password_reset/done/$', views.PasswordResetDoneView.as_view(),
    name='password_reset_done'),
    url(r'^accounts/reset/(?P<uidb64>[0-9A-Za-z_\-]+)/(?P<token>[0-9A-Za-z]
    {1,13}-[0-9A-Za-z]{1,20})/$',
        views.PasswordResetConfirmView.as_view(), name='password_reset_confirm'),
    url(r'^accounts/reset/done/$', views.PasswordResetCompleteView.as_view(),
    name='password_reset_complete'),
]
```

The first option in Listing 10-11 configures all the `django.contrib.auth` urls on the `accounts` url. This begets the question, why the `accounts` url? Because, by default all `django.contrib.auth` actions use this url as their root (e.g., in previous sections, recall that attempting to access resources that require login performs a redirect to `/accounts/login`). So by using this url `include()` statement with `django.contrib.auth.urls`, all `django.contrib.auth` actions get a functioning url, which are also backed by the necessary view method logic! But more on view method logic shortly.

Because the url `include()` statement has a 'use all urls or none' behavior, the second option in Listing 10-11 represents the use of granular url statements to configure the same `django.contrib.auth` urls. This last option is helpful if you want to disable certain `django.contrib.auth` urls but still keep other `django.contrib.auth` urls active (e.g., disable password changing urls, but keep login and logout urls).

As you can see, using either option in Listing 10-11 provides you with a quick solution to hook up `django.contrib.auth` actions to urls, the latter of which are also hooked up to default class-based views that are also part of the `django.contrib.auth` package.

Login and Logout Workflow

The entry points into the login and logout workflows - as you can see in Listing 10-11 - are the `/accounts/login/` and `/accounts/logout/` urls, respectively. If a call is made on the `/accounts/login/` url the `django.contrib.auth.views.LoginView` class-based view is triggered, and if a call is made on the `/accounts/logout/` url the `django.contrib.auth.views.LogoutView` class-based view is triggered.

Like all Django built-in class-based views, both the `LoginView` and `LogoutView` class-based views require little to nothing in terms of code and configuration. The only thing they both require is a template to present a login form and a template with a logout success message, respectively.

The `LoginView` class-based view looks for the template `registration/login.html` under a directory defined as part of the `TEMPLATES/DIRS` variable in `settings.py`. And the `LogoutView` class-based view looks for the template `registration/logout.html`, also under a directory defined as part of the `TEMPLATES/DIRS` variable in `settings.py`.

■ **Tip** See the book's accompanying source code for the layout and fields required by the `registration/login.html` and `registration/logout.html` templates.

The login workflow offers two configuration options in `settings.py` that allow you to modify its behavior without the need to customize the `LoginView` class-based view. The `LOGIN_URL` variable defaults to `/accounts/login/` and is used as the url where users are redirected when they attempt to access resources that require authentication and aren't logged in. The `LOGIC_REDIRECT` variable defaults to `/accounts/profile/` and is the url where users are redirected to after a successful log in. The `django.contrib.auth` package provides no entry point for the `/accounts/profile/` url, so you must either configure this url or simply change it to a different location (e.g., `LOGIN_REDIRECT='/'` to redirect users to the home page after a successful login).

The logout workflow supports the `LOGOUT_REDIRECT` variable in `settings.py` to define where users are taken when they log out. The `LOGOUT_REDIRECT` variable defaults to `/accounts/logout/`, but can be updated to redirect users to a different location (e.g., `LOGOUT_REDIRECT='/'` to redirect users to the home page after they log out).

Other than creating the templates, setting up the urls - described in Listing 10-11 - and optionally changing the login url location and login/out redirect behaviors, there is nothing else you need to do to enable the login and logout workflows provided by the `django.contrib.auth` package. If you want a user to log in, simply point them to the `/accounts/login/` url and if you want them to log out point them to the `/accounts/logout/` url. All the other workflow details (e.g., authentication, password verification, error form handling, session expiration) are taken care of by the `LoginView` and `LogoutView` class-based views.

Password Change Workflow

The password change workflow requires two url entry points: the `/accounts/password_change/` url that triggers the `PasswordChangeView` class-based view and the `/accounts/password_change/done/` url that triggers the `PasswordChangeDoneView` class-based view.

The `PasswordChangeView` class-based view looks for a template containing a form to change passwords in `registration/password_change_form.html` under a directory defined as part of the `TEMPLATES/DIRS` variable in `settings.py`. And the `PasswordChangeDoneView` class-based view looks for a template containing a success message in `registration/password_change_done.html`, also under a directory defined as part of the `TEMPLATES/DIRS` variable in `settings.py`.

■ **Tip** See the book's accompanying source code for the layout and fields required by the `registration/password_change_form.html` and `registration/password_change_done .html` templates.

Other than creating the templates and setting up the urls - described in Listing 10-11 - there is nothing else you need to do to enable the password change workflow provided by the `django.contrib.auth` package. If you want a user to change his password, simply point them to the `/accounts/password_change/` url. All the other workflow details (e.g., password verification, database update, form error handling) are taken care of by the `PasswordChangeView` and `PasswordChangeDoneView` class-based views.

Password Reset Workflow

The password reset workflow consists of two sub-workflows. The first sub-workflow captures a user's email and sends him an email with a link to reset his password. The second sub-workflow processes the reset link and validates a new password for the user.

The first sub-workflow uses the `/accounts/password_reset/` url, which triggers the `PasswordResetView` class-based view and the `/accounts/password_reset/done/` url, which triggers the `PasswordResetDoneView` class-based view. The second sub-workflow uses the `/accounts/reset/` url, which triggers the `PasswordResetConfirmView` class-based view and the `/accounts/reset/done/` url, which triggers the `PasswordResetCompleteView` class-based view.

The PasswordResetView class-based view looks for a template containing a form to reset a user's password in registration/password_reset_form.html and the PasswordResetDoneView class-based view looks for a success message template in registration/password_reset_done.html, both under a directory defined as part of the TEMPLATES/DIRS variable in settings.py. For the second sub-workflow, the PasswordResetConfirmView class-based view looks for a template with a form to introduce a new user password in registration/password_reset_confirm.html and the PasswordResetCompleteView class-based view looks for a success message template in registration/password_reset_complete.html, both under a directory defined as part of the TEMPLATES/DIRS variable in settings.py.

By default, the password reset workflow generates an email with instructions to take a user to the second sub-workflow to reset his password. Also by default, the reset email contains a link to the domain localhost:8000, which can be customized by installing the Django site django.contrib.sites app (e.g., add django.contrib.sites to INSTALLED_APPS and SITE_ID=1 in settings.py, and update the site with id 1 in the Django admin to reflect a new domain). Additionally, you can define a custom email layout in the registration/password_reset_email.html template and place it under a directory defined as part of the TEMPLATES variable in settings.py.

■ **Tip** See the book's accompanying source code for the layout and fields required by the registration/password_reset_form.html, registration/password_reset_done.html, registration/password_reset_confirm.html, registration/password_reset_complete.html, and registration/password_reset_email.html templates.

Other than creating the templates and setting up the urls - described in Listing 10-11 - and optionally changing the default email layout, there is nothing else you need to do to enable or allow users to remember their passwords using workflow provided by the django.contrib.auth package. If you want a user to remember his password, simply point them to the /accounts/password_reset/ url. All the other workflow details (e.g., email token validation, password verification, database update, form error handling) are taken care of by the PasswordResetView, PasswordResetDoneView, PasswordResetConfirmView, and PasswordResetCompleteView class-based views.

User Signup Workflow

Users can sign up automatically to a Django application with the help of a few constructs from the django.contrib.auth package. Although the user signup workflow is not as baked in to the django.contrib.auth package as the previous user-related workflows, it's still easy to create.

The first step to create a user signup workflow is to configure a url entry point to allow users to create an account, as illustrated in Listing 10-12.

Listing 10-12. Configure url for user sing up workflow

```
# urls.py main
from django.conf.urls import url
from django.contrib.auth import views

from coffeehouse.registration import views as registration_views

urlpatterns = [
    url(r'^accounts/', include('django.contrib.auth.urls')),
    url(r'^accounts/signup/$',registration_views.UserSignUp.as_view(),name="signup"),
]
```

Listing 10-12 illustrates a url accessible at /accounts/signup/, in addition to all the urls provided by the django.contrib.auth package that include the previous user-related workflows. Notice the /accounts/signup/ url is set to be processed by the UserSignUp class-based view from the coffeehouse.registration app, which means it's a class-based view you need to create for the project.

Listing 10-13 illustrates the UserSignUp class-based view tasked with the user signup workflow, which automates the creation of User model records, which was previously done using the Django command-line tool or the Django admin.

Listing 10-13. Signup workflow fulfilled by custom CreateView class-based view

```
from django.core.urlresolvers import reverse_lazy
from django.http import HttpResponseRedirect
from django.contrib.messages.views import SuccessMessageMixin

from django.contrib.auth.forms import UserCreationForm
from django.contrib.auth.models import User
from django.contrib.auth import authenticate, login

class UserSignupForm(UserCreationForm):
    email = forms.EmailField(required=True)
    class Meta:
        model = User
        fields = ("username", "email", "password1", "password2")

class UserSignUp(SuccessMessageMixin,CreateView):
    model = User
    form_class = UserSignupForm
    success_url = reverse_lazy('items:index')
    success_message = "User created successfully"
    template_name = "registration/signup.html"
    def form_valid(self, form):
        super(UserSignUp,self).form_valid(form)
        # The form is valid, automatically sign-in the user
        user = authenticate(self.request, username=form.cleaned_data['username'],
                                          password=form.cleaned_data['password1'])
        if user == None:
            # User not validated for some reason, return standard form_valid() response
            return self.render_to_response(self.get_context_data(form=form))
        else:
            # Log the user in
            login(self.request, user)
            # Redirect to success url
            return HttpResponseRedirect(self.get_success_url())
```

The UserSignUp class-based view in Listing 10-13 is a standard CreateView class-based view that uses the mixin SuccessMessageMixin - if you're unfamiliar with this type of class-based view to create model records or the concept of mixins, see the previous chapter, which explains both these topics.

The UserSignUp class-based view sets the model option to User to tell Django to create django.contrib.auth.models.User records. Next, the form_class option is set to UserSignupForm that is also defined in Listing 10-13. Followed are the success_url and success_message options to indicate a url and success message when a User record is created, as well as the template_name to specify a template with the form presented to capture the User fields.

The custom UserSignupForm model form in Listing 10-13 is based on the UserCreationForm from the django.contrib.auth package. From a practical standpoint, the UserSignUp class-based view could have used UserCreationForm as its form_class, however, this last built-in form only contains username and password fields. In this case, to solicit an email as part of the user signup process, the custom UserSignupForm model form adds the email field to the base UserCreationForm form class. Note that because the backing User model already includes an email field, no modification is required to the model.

In order to automatically sign in users once a User model record is created, the UserSignUp class-based view includes custom logic in its form_valid() method. In the case of Listing 10-13, the authenticate method from the django.contrib.auth package is invoked with the form values, verifying the credentials are valid. If the credentials are valid – which given the workflow should be 100% of the time, unless an unforeseen hacking event takes place – the authenticate method returns a User instance and immediately executes the login method – also from the django.contrib.auth package – which creates a session (i.e., signs in) the user, after which control is redirected to the success page of the class-based view. In the unforeseen event the authenticate method doesn't return a User instance, the form_valid() method returns its standard payload, which is the validated form.

As you can see from Listings 10-12 and 10-13, you can create a user signup workflow to let users create their own accounts and lift the administrative burden of creating user accounts from the Django admin or Django command-line tool.

■ **Tip** The signup workflow in Listing 10-13 is permissive in the sense it doesn't verify emails and automatically signs users in. This was done for simplicity and may work for most projects as is. But you can add extra safeguards to the signup workflow (e.g., send a verification link, set users to inactive until verification link is clicked) by adding this logic to the different class-based view methods, before or after the User record is created.

■ **Tip 2** The Django allauth package, described later in this chapter, has built-in support for email verification.

Custom User Model Fields

The default Django User model (i.e., django.contrib.auth.models.User class), uses a minimum set of data fields, which include username, email, first_name, last_name, date_joined, and last_login; in addition to the permission related fields password, is_superuser, is_staff, and is_active.

While these last fields are enough for Django's built-in user functionality, they can fall short if you're expecting to store additional user data (e.g., age, telephone, address). There are two approaches to support additional user data: create a separate model to store additional data and create a user relationship to it (i.e., a User with a ForeignKey) or override the default django.contrib.auth.models.User class to create a custom user class.

Listing 10-14 illustrates the first technique by creating an additional model to store extra user data and creating a relationship to the django.contrib.auth.models.User class.

Listing 10-14. Model with extra user fields related to default Django user model

```
from django.contrib.auth.models import User
from django.db import models
```

```
class UserExtra(models.Model):
    user = models.ForeignKey(User)
    age = models.IntegerField(blank=True,null=True)
    telephone = models.CharField(max_length=15,blank=True,null=True)
```

The `UserExtra` model in Listing 10-14 functions like any other model with a `ForeignKey` data type, and as such, has some performance and maintenance implications when used in these circumstances. On the negative side, the user data is distributed in two database tables. One table for `User` records and another for `UserExtra` records, which inevitably requires two queries or a join query to obtain all data for a given user – see Chapter 7 for queries across model relationships. On the positive side, this technique keeps a project's default Django `User` model class intact, requiring no additional configuration or development effort.

Next, let's take a look at the second technique that consists of creating a custom user class, a process that's illustrated in Listing 10-15.

Listing 10-15. Custom User model to override default Django User model

```
# models.py (app registration)
from django.contrib.auth.models import AbstractUser
from django.db import models

class CoffeehouseUser(AbstractUser):
    age = models.IntegerField(blank=True,null=True)
    telephone = models.CharField(max_length=15,blank=True,null=True)

# admin.py (app registration)
from django.contrib import admin
from .models import CoffeehouseUser

class CoffeehouseUserAdmin(admin.ModelAdmin):
    pass

admin.site.register(CoffeehouseUser, CoffeehouseUserAdmin)

# settings.py
AUTH_USER_MODEL = 'registration.CoffeehouseUser'
```

The first section in Listing 10-15 shows the `CoffeehouseUser` class to be used as the custom user class. Notice the class inherits its behavior from the `AbstractUser` class that gives it the same fields and behaviors as the default `User` class (e.g., `username`, `email`, etc.). Next, the `CoffeehouseUser` class declares the age and `telephone` fields using standard model fields, giving the custom user class two more fields than the default `User` class.

Because the custom `CoffeehouseUser` class will override a project's default `User` class, this means the default `django.contrib.auth.models.User` class is no longer used. Therefore, you must configure Django to use the custom `CoffeehouseUser` class anywhere user logic is required.

The second section in Listing 10-15 shows the Django admin configuration necessary to access the new custom user class from the Django admin and be able to create, read, update, and delete users, just like it's done with the standard `django.contrib.auth.models.User` model class. Note the next chapter covers Django admin configuration in greater detail.

Finally, the third section in Listing 10-15 shows the Django `settings.py` file with the `AUTH_USER_MODEL` set to `registration.CoffeehouseUser`, where `registration` represents the app name and `CoffeehouseUser` the custom user model. This last configuration ensures user logic made throughout a project is made on the `CoffeehouseUser` model and not the default `User` model.

Once you run the migration operation with this custom user model class and configurations from Listing 10-15, you'll see Django project users gain two additional fields.

■ **Caution** Custom user model implementations like the one in Listing 10-15 should only be done at the outset of a project (i.e., one of the first project migrations).

Because a user model plays such a central role in managing access to a Django project, you should not attempt to implement custom user models like the one in Listing 10-15 midway through a project. Doing so runs the risk of breaking dependencies - foreign keys - used by other models to refer to default `django.contrib.auth.models.User` model records; in addition, this also changes the underlying database table where user data is stored. By implementing a custom user model at the outset of a project, you guarantee any possible model dependencies made on a user are done against custom user records and user data is stored in a single database table from the outset.

In fact, if you plan to use a custom user model, but don't know which new fields to add at the outset, you can create a placeholder user model like the following:

```
class CoffeehouseUser(AbstractUser):
    pass
```

This snippet creates a model identical to the default `django.contrib.auth.models.User` class, but lays the groundwork to create user dependencies on the custom model, while allowing the ability to add fields to the custom model as they're needed with standard migrations like any other model.

Finally, another factor to take into account when using a custom user model - which isn't obvious in Listing 10-15 - is how to reference a custom user model in other places of a project. When you use the default `User` class, the statement `from django.contrib.auth.models import User` is commonplace in `models.py` and `views.py` files to reference a user, but with a custom model this reference is no longer applicable.

To support custom user models, Django offers the helper method `get_user_model` that returns a reference to whatever user model is defined in the `AUTH_USER_MODEL` variable in `settings.py`. In this manner, you can use the statement `from django.contrib.auth import get_user_model` to obtain a reference to a project's user model from anywhere in a project. The next section contains an example that uses the `get_user_model` method.

Custom Authentication Back Ends

An authentication process is important because it determines which users are allowed access to an application. The default authentication process used by Django consists of comparing a username and password - provided on a web form - against `User` records in a database. If the username and password match against a `User` record, the authentication process is deemed successful, but if the values don't match, then the authentication process is deemed a failure.

Django itself includes a series of built-in authentication back-end classes[2] to support variations of this authentication process. In addition, in the final section of this chapter I'll introduce you to the allauth Django package that supports a series' authentication back ends (e.g., authentication against social media accounts).

---

[2]https://docs.djangoproject.com/en/1.11/ref/contrib/auth/#module-django.contrib.auth.backends

But to illustrate the concept of a custom authentication back end from the ground up, I'll create a simple authentication back end that relies on emails for authentication and can use any user type (i.e., custom user models or the default User model).

By default, Django projects use the django.contrib.auth.backends.ModelBackend authentication back-end class, designed to compare username and password sets - provided by an end user - against a project's users in a database. Now ask yourself, what do you think is easier to remember as a login credential, a username or an email? If you're like most people in this day in age, you're more likely to have answered email.

Listing 10-16 illustrates a custom authentication back end that is able to authenticate users by means of an email credential and not the default username.

Listing 10-16. Custom authentication back end to support authentication with email

```
# models.py (registration app)
from django.contrib.auth import get_user_model

class EmailBackend(object):
    def authenticate(self, request, username=None, password=None, **kwargs):
        User = get_user_model()
        try:
            user = User.objects.get(email=username)
        except User.DoesNotExist:
            return None
        else:
            if getattr(user, 'is_active', False) and  user.check_password(password):
                return user
        return None
    def get_user(self, user_id):
        User = get_user_model()
        try:
            return User.objects.get(pk=user_id)
        except User.DoesNotExist:
            return None

# setting.py
AUTHENTICATION_BACKENDS = ['django.contrib.auth.backends.ModelBackend',
                           'coffeehouse.registration.models.EmailBackend']
```

Listing 10-16 declares the EmailBackend class for the custom authentication back end. Like all custom authentication back-end classes, you must declare at minimum the authenticate() and get_user() methods, where the first method is used to define the authentication logic and the second to return the user of the request.

The authenticate() method gains access to both the username and password fields provided by an end user, as part of the base authentication workflow. Next, you can see the authenticate() method gains access to a project's user model relying on the get_user_model() method helper, which ensures that even if a project uses a custom user model, the authentication workflow is done on the correct user class, as described in the previous section.

Once a reference is obtained to a project's user class, notice the authenticate() method performs a query for a user on the email field with the provided username, which effectively allows the username value provided by a user to be treated as an email field for authentication purposes. If a user matches the email provided as the username value, then the try-except-else block in Listing 10-16 performs a call to check_password()

to validate the password against the matching user. If the password matches, `authenticate()` returns the authenticated user, and if the password doesn't match `authenticate()` returns `None`.

The final section in Listing 10-16 is the `AUTHENTICATION_BACKENDS` variable in `settings.py`, which is assigned a list of authentication back-end classes. In this case, the default `django.contrib.auth.backends.ModelBackend` class is kept to ensure the default authentication workflow of username/password is attempted first. Next, the custom `EmailBackend` authentication back-end class from Listing 10-16 is added, to ensure the authentication workflow is done treating the input data as an email/password set.

As you can see from this example in Listing 10-16, by adding this simple custom authentication back-end class, you can allow users to introduce either their username or email to authenticate themselves in a Django application.

■ **Tip** If you use the custom authentication back-end class in Listing 10-16, change the username label in the login form to 'Username/Email' to notify users they can use both.

User Management with Django allauth

As you've see throughout this chapter, the `django.contrib.auth` package provides a great deal of functionality to manage users and groups, permissions, as well as authentication workflows. But as you've probably also realized, the `django.contrib.auth` package can also suffer from a lot of legacy behaviors that don't work well for web applications in today's day and age. For example, `django.contrib.auth` doesn't support things like social authentication - which is almost a requirement in today's Internet - in addition, `django.contrib.auth` is also designed to work with usernames out of th -box - and not emails - which is also a very outdated practice.

Still because the `django.contrib.auth` package is built into Django, there are often many Django packages (e.g., the Django admin and other third-party packages) that assume a Django project uses the `django.contrib.auth` package and its functionalities.

So on the one hand, it's essential you keep using the `django.contrib.auth` package to maintain user management compatibility across other Django packages that expect the presence of `django.contrib.auth`, but on the other, you don't want to be stuck with 2005 practices asking users to provide usernames and not allowing them to authenticate with social media accounts.

Among the many third-party packages and potential solutions available to solve this Django user management integration, the Django allauth package offers one of the best features set (e.g., social authentication and email based users), as well as the best integration with the `django.contrib.auth` package. So up next, I'll describe the setup process for the Django allauth package.

Install and Set Up django-allauth

To install the Django allauth package, use the following `pip` statement:

```
pip install django-allauth
```

Once you make the installation, let's create a base Django allauth configuration with the intent to fulfill the following user management features:

- Use email as the primary user identifier, but maintain username credentials for compatibility with other packages (e.g., Django admin).
- Require email verification to avoid junk users.
- Set the foundations to add Django social authentication (Facebook, Google, Twitter.)

Listing 10-17 illustrates the necessary additions to make to a project's `settings.py` file, to enable a base Django allauth configuration with these features.

Listing 10-17. Base Django allauth settings.py configuration

```
# Ensure the 'django.contrib.sites' is declared in INSTALLED_APPS
# And also add the allauth, allauth.account and allauth.socialaccount to INSTALLED_APPS

INSTALLED_APPS = [
    # Django sites app  required
    'django.contrib.sites',
    'allauth',
    'allauth.account',
    'allauth.socialaccount',
]

# Ensure SITE_ID is set sites app
SITE_ID = 1

# Add the 'allauth' backend to AUTHENTICATION_BACKEND and keep default ModelBackend
AUTHENTICATION_BACKENDS = [ 'django.contrib.auth.backends.ModelBackend',
                           'allauth.account.auth_backends.AuthenticationBackend']

# EMAIL_BACKEND so allauth can proceed to send confirmation emails
# ONLY for development/testing use console
EMAIL_BACKEND='django.core.mail.backends.console.EmailBackend'

# Custom allauth settings
# Use email as the primary identifier
ACCOUNT_AUTHENTICATION_METHOD = 'email'
ACCOUNT_EMAIL_REQUIRED = True
# Make email verification mandatory to avoid junk email accounts
ACCOUNT_EMAIL_VERIFICATION = 'mandatory'
# Eliminate need to provide username, as it's a very old practice
ACCOUNT_USERNAME_REQUIRED = False
```

In addition to the changes in Listing 10-17 to the `settings.py` file, you'll also need to register the Django allauth url entry points in the main `urls.py` file. Listing 10-18 illustrates the changes you need to make to the main `urls.py` file.

Listing 10-18. Django allauth url configuration urls.py

```
urlpatterns = [
    ...
    url(r'^accounts/', include('allauth.urls')),
    ...
]
```

As you can see in Listing 10-18, the url regular expression tells Django to mount the Django allauth `allauth.urls` urls under the `/accounts/` path, just like it's done for the standard Django `django.contrib.auth` package urls back in Listing 10-11.

Django allauth uses the same url patterns and behaviors almost exactly as the standard `django.contrib.auth` package. This means Django allauth configures its login page at the `/accounts/login/` url and the logout page at the `/accounts/logout/` url. Django allauth does include a series of new urls in its `include()` statement from Listing 10-18 (e.g., email verification), but I'll describe these new urls as we move forward.

Similarly, the same `settings.py` variables used for authentication purposes by the standard `django.contrib.auth` package are also applicable to Django allauth. For example, you can set `LOGIN_URL` to override the default `/accounts/login/` url location and you can also set the `LOGIN_REDIRECT_URL` that defaults to the `/accounts/profile/` url. In fact, just like the `django.contrib.auth` package, Django allauth doesn't include the `/accounts/profile/` url entry point, so you may as well override the `LOGIN_REDIRECT_URL` variable in `settings.py` to point to another url (e.g., `LOGIN_REDIRECT_URL='/'` to redirect the user to the home page after a successful login).

Finally, once you've followed these configuration steps, you need to do the following miscellaneous steps to ensure Django allauth runs correctly:

- Run `python manage.py migrate` from the command line, to ensure all the database tables required by Django allauth are created.
- Ensure the `django.contrib.sites` package reflects the application's domain. By default, the `django.contrib.sites` defaults to the domain `example.com`, you can change this value in the Django admin to ensure certain features (e.g., email) use the correct application domain.

First Log In and Log Out with Superuser in Django allauth

First, create a Django superuser using any of the techniques outlined at the start of this chapter in Listing 10-1 and take note of the email. Next, go straight to the `/accounts/login/` url and you'll see a page like the one illustrated in Figure 10-11.

Figure 10-11. *Django allauth defult login screen*

Now let's pause for a second and contemplate what Django allauth just provided. Figure 10-11 illustrates a login page for which you didn't even have to create its template – unlike the `django.contrib.auth` log in workflow. In addition, notice the login form in Figure 10-11 asks for an email credential and you didn't even need to create a custom authentication back end to support this functionality either.

Next, introduce the superuser email/password into the sign-in form in Figure 10-11 and click on the 'Sign in' button, if the credentials are correct, you'll be redirected to a 'Verify your E-mail address' page. This is by design, remember in Listing 10-17 the base Django allauth configuration enforce email verification (`ACCOUNT_EMAIL_VERIFICATION = 'mandatory'`); therefore until the user's email address is verified, access is denied.

If you're using the same email settings described in Listing 10-17 – to send emails to the console – you will see an email like the one in Listing 10-18 where you're running the Django development server.

Listing 10-18. Confirm email for new user in django-allauth

```
MIME-Version: 1.0
Content-Type: text/plain; charset="utf-8"
Content-Transfer-Encoding: 7bit
Subject: [coffeehouse.com] Please Confirm Your E-mail Address
From: webmaster@localhost
To: cashier@coffeehouse.com
Date: Wed, 12 Aug 2018 00:57:50 -0000
Message-ID: <20180812005750.15177.32621@laptop>

Hello from coffeehouse.com!

You're receiving this e-mail because user daniel at example.com has given yours as an e-mail
address to connect their account.

To confirm this is correct, go to http://localhost:8000/accounts/confirm-email/1aflixsbb6sn1
4hptkntiyrgvk1r0pppqsurx6fxrs6wmlb96u8y3gotxzep0qie/

Thank you from coffeehouse.com!
coffeehouse.com
```

Copy and paste the verification link in the email to your browser. Once you click on the verification link, you'll be asked to confirm the user's email. When you click on the 'Confirm' button to make the final verification, you'll be sent to the `/accounts/login/` url once again showing a small flash message indicating the account was confirmed.

Now reintroduce the superuser email/password into the sign-in form in Figure 10-11 once again and click on the 'Sign in' button. This time you'll be redirected to `/accounts/profile/` url or the url defined in the `LOGIN_REDIRECT_URL` variable in `settings.py`.

At this point, you're logged into the application as a superuser using the login workflow form provided by Django allauth. Next, go directly to the Django admin `/admin/` url and you can confirm you're able to access it directly! In this case, there's no need to reauthenticate yourself using the Django admin form, because you already logged in using the Django allauth workflow.

Finally, in order to log out of the application you can visit the `/accounts/logout/` url, where you'll be presented with a confirmation question asking if you're sure you want to log out, and clicking on the 'Sign out' button materializes the log out action.

As you can see from this exercise, Django allauth provides very tight integration with the standard login workflow used by the Django admin and the `django.contrib.auth` package, on top of the features already outlined: email verification, built-in templates, built-in authentication workflow with email, and backward compatibility with usernames.

User Signup with Django allauth

If you review the `/accounts/login/` url illustrated in Figure 10-11, you can see there's a 'Sign up' link that takes you to the URL `/accounts/signup/`. Click on this link, and you'll be presented with a form that asks for an email and a password to create a user account.

Once you fill out the form, click on the 'Sign up' button. If the submission is successful, you'll be redirected to the 'Verify your E-mail address' page. This is the same behavior described in the previous section, due to Django allauth requiring email verification before allowing access to an application.

Similarly, proceed to inspect the email generated by Django allauth and copy-paste the verification link to complete the user sign up process. Next, you can proceed to log in with this user's credentials, which default to a regular user.

An interesting point about this signup process that may not be obvious, is Django allauth creates a user using only his email, which raises some questions: What happens if this user later becomes a superuser or staff member to access the Django admin? Will the Django admin login form that relies on usernames not work? Nothing of the sort; it will work as expected.

Behind the scenes, Django allauth creates a regular Django user and integrates it with Django allauth features (e.g., email login, social authentication). This built-in integration is an excellent feature because you get all the benefits of Django allauth, plus users get to keep Django's default user management where the same user can get Django admin access, superuser and staff permissions, ability to belong to groups, and permission assignment.

The convention Django allauth uses to create usernames is to take an email's local part (i.e., anything before @) as the username handle. For cases where multiple emails with the same name create an account, Django allauth assign a digit to the username (e.g.`nancy@coffeehouse.com=nancy`, `nancy@hotmail.com=nancy2`, `nancy@gmail.com=nancy3`).

Password Reset and Change with Django allauth

One of the most common management tasks required by users is often related to passwords, whether it's resetting their password because they forgot it or changing it for security reasons. Django allauth provides built-in support for both these password scenarios. If you go to the `/accounts/password/reset/` url, you'll see a form where a user can introduce his email to reset his password.

Once you introduce an email on this last form, click on the 'Reset My Password' button and Django allauth sends a confirmation email like the one in Listing 10-19 with a password reset link.

Listing 10-19. Reset email for new password django-allauth

```
MIME-Version: 1.0
Content-Type: text/plain; charset="utf-8"
Content-Transfer-Encoding: 7bit
Subject: [coffeehouse.com] Password Reset E-mail
From: webmaster@localhost
To: nancy@coffeehouse.com
Date: Wed, 19 Aug 2018 03:05:09 -0000
Message-ID: <20180819030509.15780.98825@laptop>

Hello from coffeehouse.com!

You're receiving this e-mail because you or someone else has requested a password for your
user account at coffeehouse.com.
It can be safely ignored if you did not request a password reset. Click the link below to
reset your password.
```

```
http://localhost:8000/accounts/password/reset/key/5-44f-0f6fbf1251fd33ee4b40/

Thank you for using coffeehouse.com!
coffeehouse.com
-----------------------------------------------------------------------------
```

Next, if you click on the reset link in the email, you'll be taken to another page where you can introduce a new password. After you click on the 'Change password' button, and if the process is successful, you'll see a password confirmation flash message indicating the user password was updated.

The other option available in django-allauth related to passwords is to allow a user to change their password while they're logged in. If you go to the `/accounts/password/change/` url, you'll see a screen with a form to introduce a new password. After you click on the 'Change Password' button, you'll see a confirmation message on the same screen indicating the user password was updated.

Add and Change User Email with Django allauth

To aid users in the possibility of changing their initial email signup address, Django allauth has a dedicated page to manage email addresses. If you go to the `/accounts/email/` url, you'll see the page illustrated in Figure 10-12.

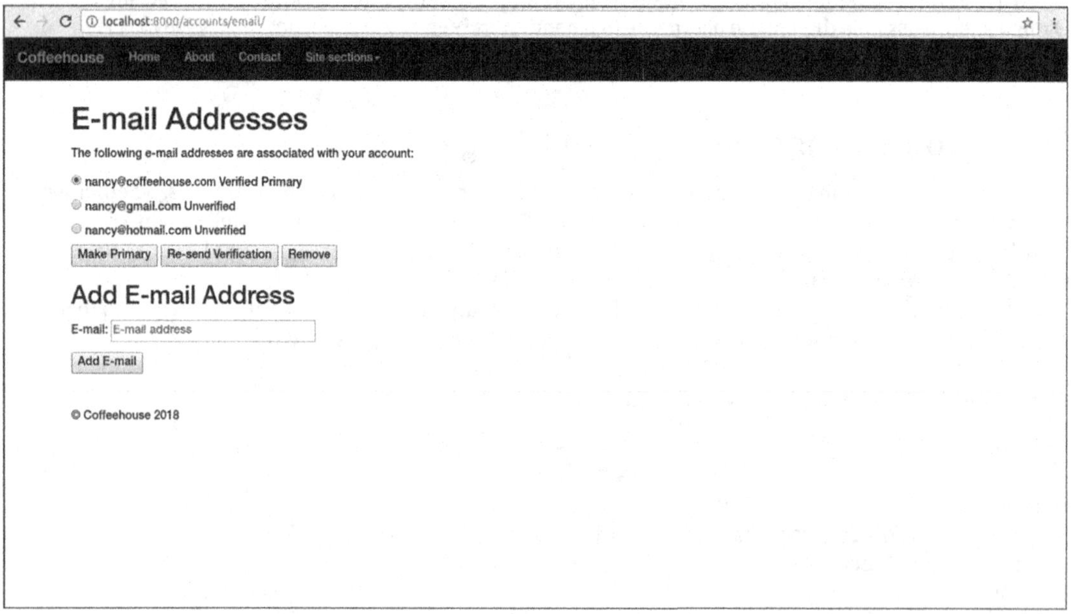

Figure 10-12. *Django allauth email management*

As you can see in Figure 10-12, in addition to the possibility of adding other emails to the account, a user can also change his primary email, resend a verification for an email, or even remove an email associated with an account.

Change Templates for Django allauth

The Django allauth built-in templates provide basic functionality as you've seen in the previous sections. All the built-in templates inherit their behavior from a template named `base.html` and their content is enclosed in `{% block content %}{% block %}`. This means you can create a template called `base.html` in your Django project with all the elements you wish (e.g., custom colors, header menu) and declare the `{% block content %}{% block %}` in it and the Django allauth built-in templates are rendered in this context.

If you want to fully customize the templates used by Django allauth (e.g., to include mobile-friendly forms or some other deep change), you can provide overriding templates in your Django project.

Django allauth relies on over 15 HTML templates and 6 email templates; for this reason, it's easier if you copy the Django allauth default templates to your Django project and then modify them as needed. You should ensure the Django allauth templates are copied with their original `account` subfolder that should be accessible under a `DIRS` value of the `TEMPLATES` variable in `settings.py`. Depending on your Python installation, the default Django allauth templates can be found on the path `/lib/python3.5/site-packages/allauth/templates/`.

■ **Tip** See the book's accompanying source code, which includes the layout of all Django allauth templates.

Models and Database Tables Behind Django allauth

Although Django allauth leverages Django's default user model `django.contrib.auth.models.User` or a custom user model if it's provided as part of the `AUTH_USER_MODEL` configuration, Django allauth relies on a series of new models to support its advanced user management features. Figure 10-13 illustrates the Django admin showcasing the series of Django allauth models.

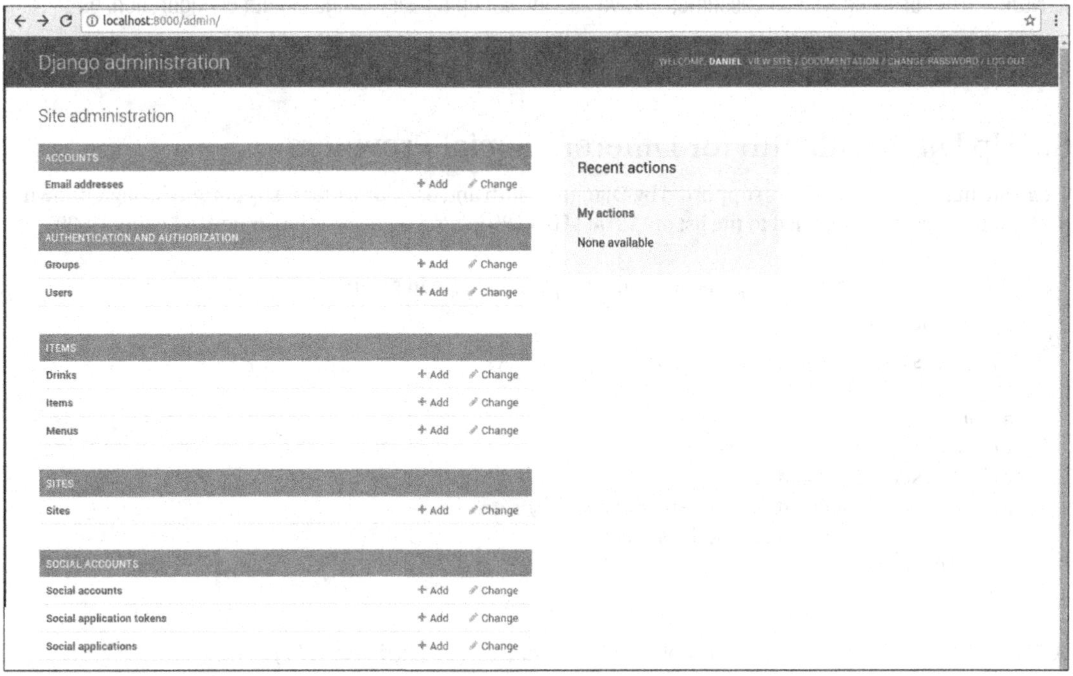

Figure 10-13. *Django admin with models for django-allauth*

The first Django allauth inclusion illustrated in Figure 10-13 corresponds to the 'Accounts' app, which includes the 'Email addresses' model. The 'Email addresses' model keeps track of emails, their association to user model records (e.g., `django.contrib.auth.models.User`), the primary email status, as well as an email's verification status. It should be noted 'Email addresses' model records are stored in the `account_emailaddress` database table.

It's also worth mentioning that in Figure 10-13 you can see the standard 'User' and 'Group' models from the `django.contrib.auth.models.User` package. Django allauth continues to make use of a project's user model to store core user data (e.g., passwords)

The second set of Django allauth models included in Figure 10-13 correspond to social accounts, which are used to allow Django authentication on social media sites (e.g., Facebook, Google, Twitter), which is the topic of the next and last section in this chapter.

Social Authentication with Django allauth

Social authentication involves creating workflows - also known as applications - on third-party sites (e.g., Facebook, Google, Twitter) to allow users of such sites the ability to reuse their identity to access external resources - which in our case will be Django applications. This ability is a very valuable feature in Django applications, because it allows users to register in a few clicks, instead of going through a more involved registration process.

At the most basic level, social authentication processes involve tokens that are authorized by users, which are then exchanged between third-party sites and the requesting party (i.e., your Django application) to indicate a user's consent. In addition, depending on the application and its configuration, the requesting party (i.e., the Django application) can solicit basic user information (e.g., email), as well as more elaborate information (e.g., a user's friends in a Facebook application) from the third-party site.

■ **Note** The following sections assumes you've already set up a base Django allauth configuration, as described in the previous section.

Set Up Django allauth for Different Social Providers

There are many social providers supported by Django allauth and each provider is supported through its own package that needs to be added to the list of `INSTALLED_APPS` in `settings.py` as illustrated in Listing 10-20.

Listing 10-20. Social provider app installation for Django allauth in settings.py

```
INSTALLED_APPS = [
    # Django sites framework is required
    'django.contrib.sites',
    'allauth',
    'allauth.account',
    'allauth.socialaccount',
    'allauth.socialaccount.providers.facebook',
    'allauth.socialaccount.providers.google',
    'allauth.socialaccount.providers.twitter',
]

SOCIALACCOUNT_PROVIDERS = {'facebook': {}, 'google':{}, 'twitter':{}}
```

As you can see in Listing 10-20, the last three apps in the INSTALLED_APPS list correspond to three social providers: Facebook, Google, and Twitter. Adding these providers to INSTALLED_APPS is the first step to enable them in social authentication with Django allauth.

In addition to the google, facebook, and twitter apps, Django allauth also supports over 50 other social authentication workflows from various providers[3] under the same allauth.socialaccount.providers package.

In Listing 10-20 you can also see the SOCIALACCOUNT_PROVIDERS variable with a dictionary of keys that correspond to each social provider. Each key has an empty dictionary value that will eventually contain provider-specific configuration options. In the next sections, I'll describe how to set up each social provider and fill in these configuration values.

■ **Caution** Don't add social provider configurations to settings.py until you have real connection parameters to social providers. You'll get errors due to the missing configuration in the login page and other workflow authentication pages.

In addition to the configuration parameters in SOCIALACCOUNT_PROVIDERS, you'll also need to add a social provider's application credentials as 'Social applications' model records through the Django admin. Go to the Django admin and click on the 'Social applications' model - shown in Figure 10-13.

Next, you'll be presented with a screen like the one in Figure 10-14 where you can edit and add social applications, and click on the 'Add social application' button in the top right button. On this page, you'll see a screen like the one in Figure 10-15 where you can select a social provider and introduce various values associated with a social application (e.g., name, client id, secret key). For the moment we don't have any of these values, but keep this Django admin page open, because next I'll describe where to get the values for each of the three social providers you added to the INSTALLED_APPS variable in Listing 10-20.

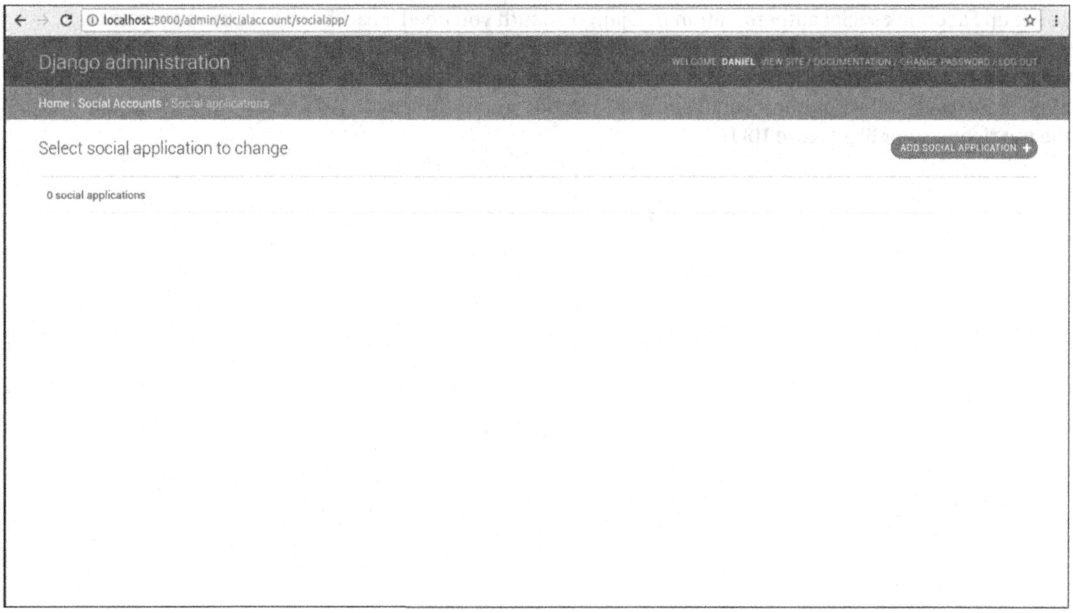

***Figure 10-14.** Django social application list page*

---

[3]http://django-allauth.readthedocs.io/en/latest/providers.html

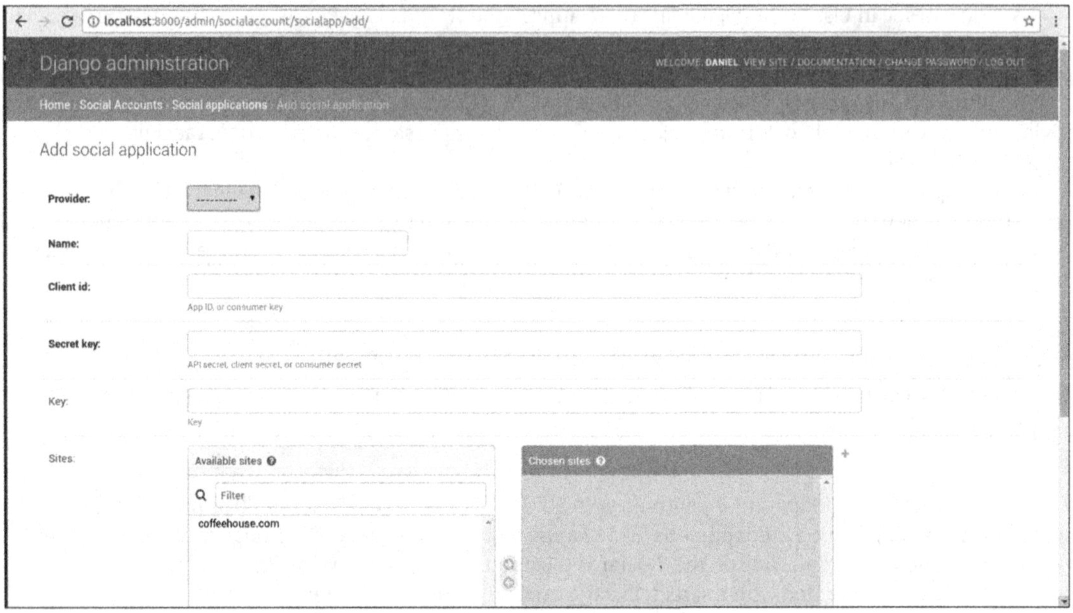

Figure 10-15. *Django social application create/edit page*

Set Up Facebook with Django allauth

To set up Facebook social authentication in Django allauth you need a Facebook account to create an application on their site. Head over to `https://developers.facebook.com/apps`. If you've previously created a Facebook application you'll see a screen like the one in Figure 10-16, but if you've never created an application then you won't see a list of applications, but you'll still see the 'Add a New App' green button in the top right corner like Figure 10-16.

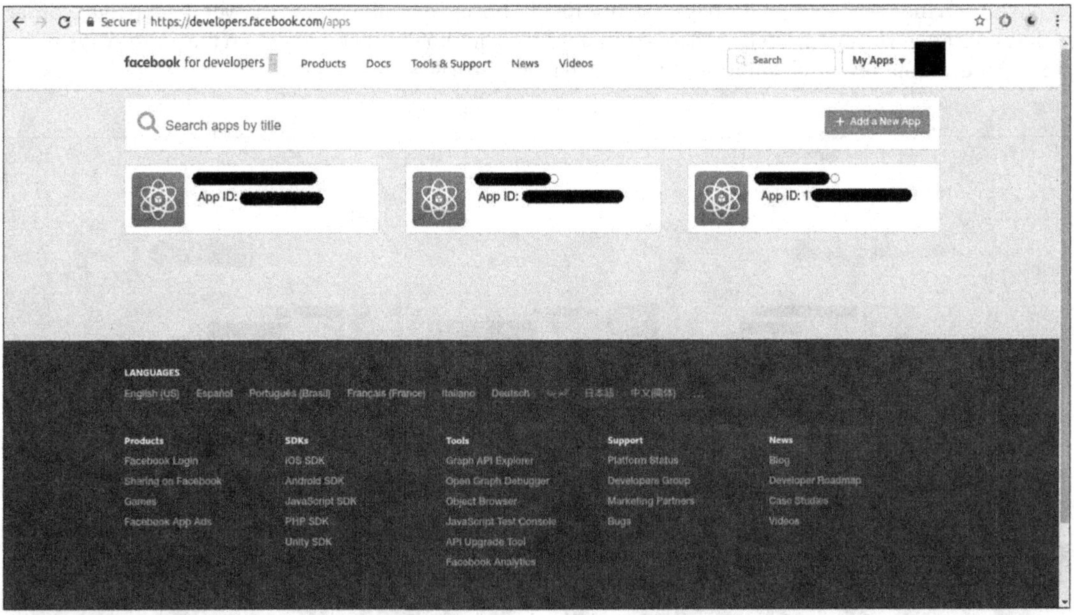

Figure 10-16. Facebook application list page

Click on the 'Add a New App' button in the top right corner of Figure 10-16 and you'll see a pop-up like the one in Figure 10-17. Fill out the two options for the app name (e.g., Coffeehouse) and contact email and click on the 'Create App ID' button.

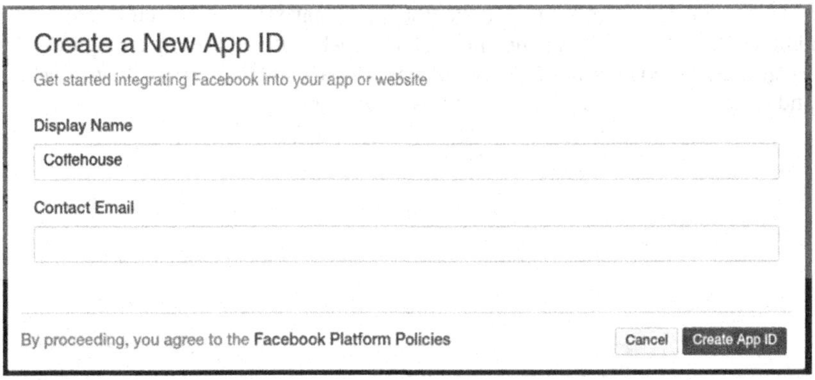

Figure 10-17. Facebook create application pop-up

When you click on the 'Create App ID' button, the app is created and you're taken to the app's main page. Next, let's go back to the page with the list of apps – illustrated in Figure 10-16 – by clicking on the 'See all apps' button on the left-column drop-down or by just visiting the `https://developers.facebook.com/apps` url again – you can come back later to app's main page by clicking on the app on the page with the list of apps.

While on the Facebook app list page - Figure 10-16 - hover your mouse pointer over the top right corner of the application you just created until an arrow appears, click on the arrow, and from the pop-up menu click on the 'Create Test App' option as illustrated in Figure 10-18.

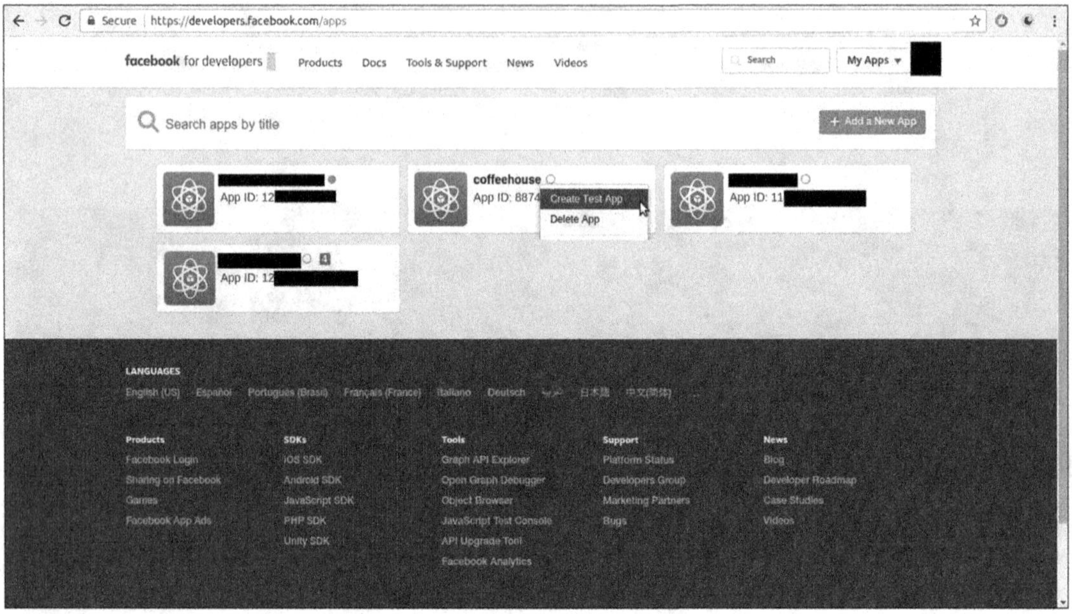

***Figure 10-18.** Facebook created test application pop-up menu*

Next, a pop-up appears where you can assign a name to the test app or leave the default name; choose accordingly. Upon termination, you'll see a screen like the one in Figure 10-19 with all the app configuration parameters. If you don't see Figure 10-19, go back to the Facebook app list page in Figure 10-16, hover over the top right corner again, and select the test application from the pop-up menu.

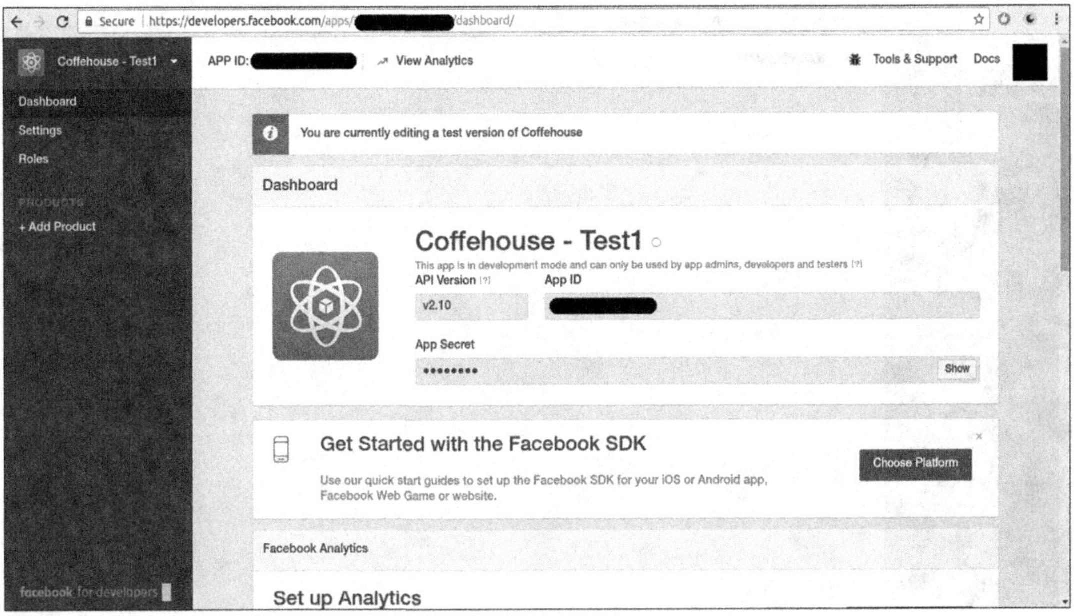

Figure 10-19. *Facebook test app main page*

In Figure 10-19, you can see there's an 'App ID' value, as well as a hidden 'App Secret' value you can see by clicking on the 'Show' button. In addition, on the left-hand side you can see a series of tabs to further customize an application's parameters. Click on the 'Settings'/'Basic' menu in the left-hand column.

While on the 'Settings'/'Basic' menu, in the center bottom of the page you'll see a large button '+ Add platform,' as shown in Figure 10-20. Click on the '+ Add platform' button and in the pop-up menu select the 'Website' option. This adds a 'Website' box above the '+ Add platform' button, in this box's input field add the url of your Django application (e.g., `http://localhost`) to tell Facebook to accept login request from this domain – as illustrated in Figure 10-20 – and in addition, on the 'App Domains' input field near the top of the page also add the url of you Django application – as it's also illustrated in Figure 10-20.

Figure 10-20. *Facebook test app configuration for authorized domain requests*

Next, go to the Django admin and in the 'Social applications' model create/edit page - illustrated in Figure 10-15 - create a Facebook application by selecting 'Facebook' from the provider list, introduce a friendly name in the 'Name' box, introduce the Facebook 'App ID' value in the 'Client Id' box, and introduce the Facebook 'App Secret' value in the 'Secret key' box.

Next, open your Django project's `settings.py` file and update the `SOCIALACCOUNT_PROVIDERS` variable with the Facebook configuration parameters illustrated in Listing 10-21.

Listing 10-21. Facebook social provider configuration for Django allauth in settings.py

```
SOCIALACCOUNT_PROVIDERS =  { 'facebook':
                               {'METHOD': 'oauth2',
                                'SCOPE': ['email'],
                                'AUTH_PARAMS': {'auth_type': 'reauthenticate'},
                                'LOCALE_FUNC': lambda request: 'en_US',
                                'VERSION': 'v2.4'
                               }
                           }
```

The settings in Listing 10-21 are the most basic set of values to run Facebook authentication, but there are many other options you can consult in the Django allauth documentation. Next, start your Django application and visit the `/accounts/login/` page to attempt to log in, you will see a page like the one illustrated in Figure 10-21.

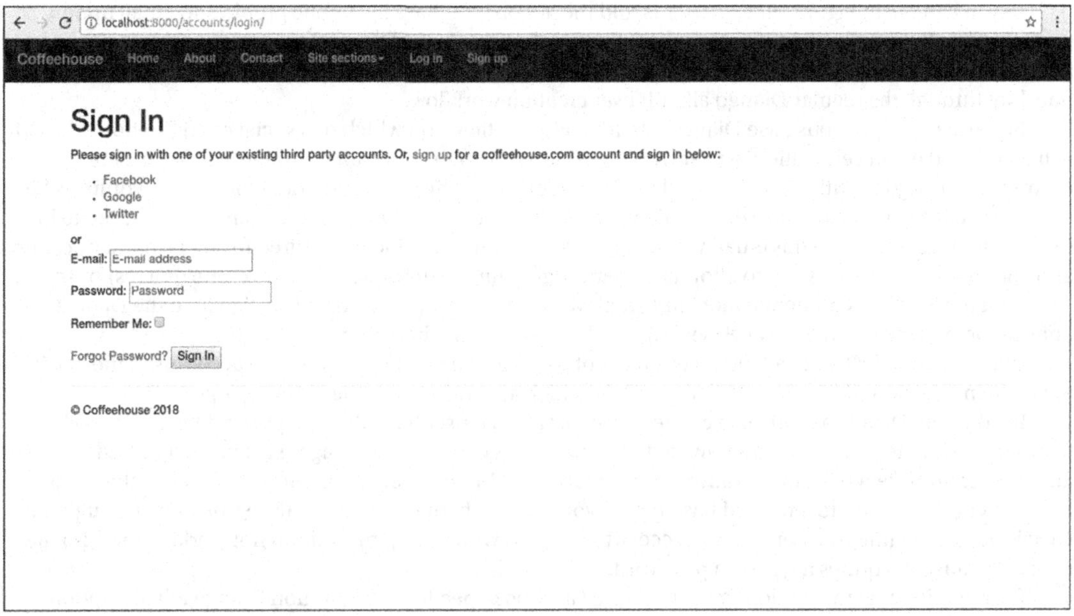

Figure 10-21. *Django login with social authentication options*

As you can see in Figure 10-21, unlike the login page from the Django allauth-based configuration, there are now options to sign up with Facebook, Google, and Twitter. Click on the Facebook link and you'll be redirected to a Facebook page to grant authorization, as illustrated in Figure 10-22.

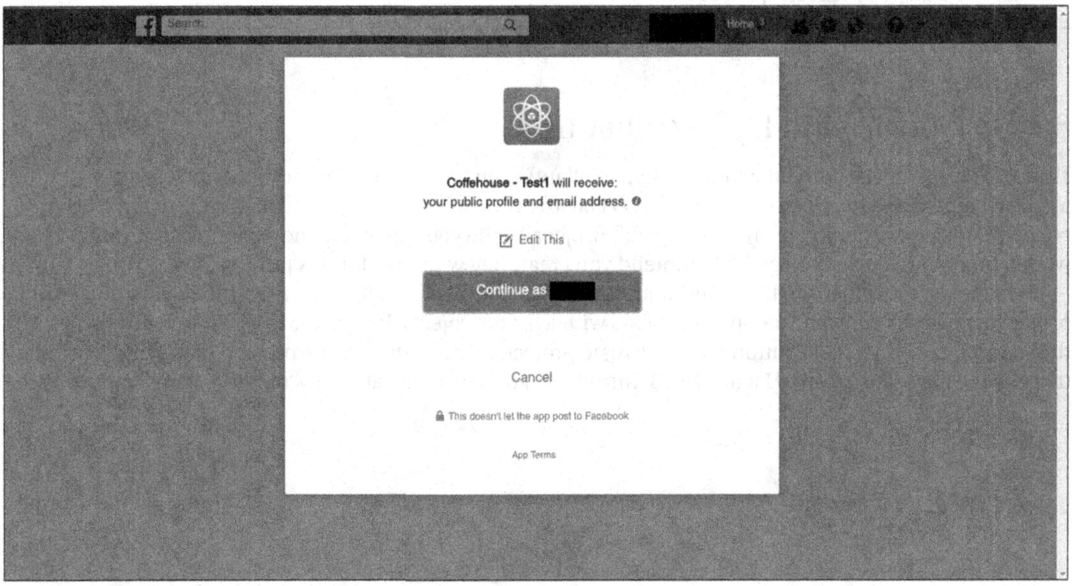

Figure 10-22. *Facebook social authorization pop-up*

As you can see in Figure 10-22, a user is told the action will share his public profile and email upon confirmation. If the user clicks 'Continue as...' Facebook contacts the Django application with a token and the user's information (i.e., public profile info and email). At this juncture, Django allauth creates a user and puts him through the regular Django allauth user creation workflow.

Because of the previous base Django allauth configuration - on which this social configuration is based - that enforced email verification, a user won't be able to log in to application until he verifies his email account via Django allauth, irrespective of the Facebook authentication workflow. Once a user confirms his email through a verification link sent by Django allauth, a user is marked as verified and can proceed to log in to the application - note this email verification process is not specific or required for social authentication and you can disable it you want to allow automatic login immediately after Facebook returns a response.

With the Facebook authentication and email verification complete, a user can sign in to the Django application by clicking on the 'Facebook' sign-in link at any time thereafter.

Under the hood, Django allauth keeps track of social authentication tokens and accounts in the 'Social application tokens' and 'Social accounts' models, which are both accessible in the Django admin.

In addition, Django allauth also creates a regular Django user (e.g., the `django.contrib.auth.models.User` kind) with the Facebook workflow, so the same user is capable of leveraging Django's standard authentication system (e.g., to become superuser or staff). Note however that this type of user relies on a Facebook authorization token - and has no password - so authentication must always be done through the social Facebook authentication link in `/accounts/login/`, with the Django admin not working for this type of user because it requires a typed-in password.

Bear in mind that in addition to the multiple Facebook-specific configuration Django allauth options that are beyond the scope of this discussion, there are other social authentication concepts (e.g., token revocation, callback URLs) that you'll need to explore and configure on your own - given they are not Django specific - to offer a streamlined social authentication process to end users.

■ **Note** The previous procedure is done as a Facebook 'Test application' – see Figure 10-18. For the live version of a Django application, you must perform this identical procedure on the primary (i.e., non-test) channel of the same Facebook application.

Set Up Google with Django allauth

To set up Google social authentication in Django allauth, you'll need a Google account to create an application on their site. Head over to `https://console.developers.google.com/`. If you've previously created Google projects you'll land on a default project. While you can create the social authentication workflow on any Google project, I recommend you create a new project for this purpose.

On the top menu bar - to the right-hand side of the 'Google APIs' logo - there's a menu with the default project name: click on it, and a pop-up appears with a list of projects. Inside this last pop-up and besides the search box is a '+' (plus) button named 'Create project'. Click on the 'Create project' button and you'll be taken to the page illustrated in Figure 10-23. Introduce a project name and click on the 'Create' button.

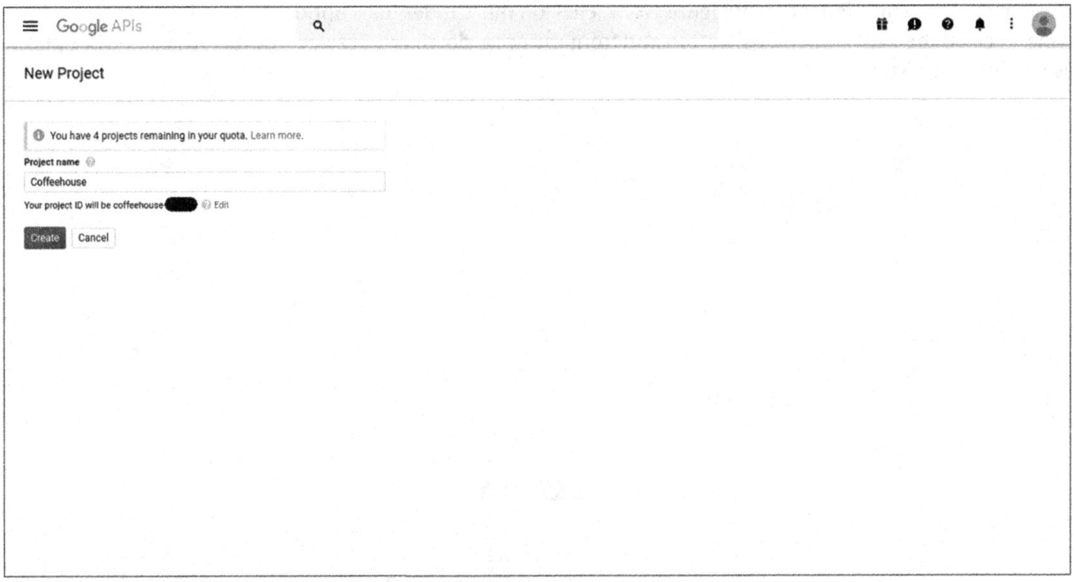

Figure 10-23. *Google create project page*

After you click on the 'Create button,' you'll be taken to the project's home page shown in Figure 10-24. Ensure you're placed in the project you just created verifying the name of the selected project in top menu bar – to the right-hand side of the 'Google APIs' logo. If it's not the correct project, click on project and from the pop-up select the appropriate project from the list of projects.

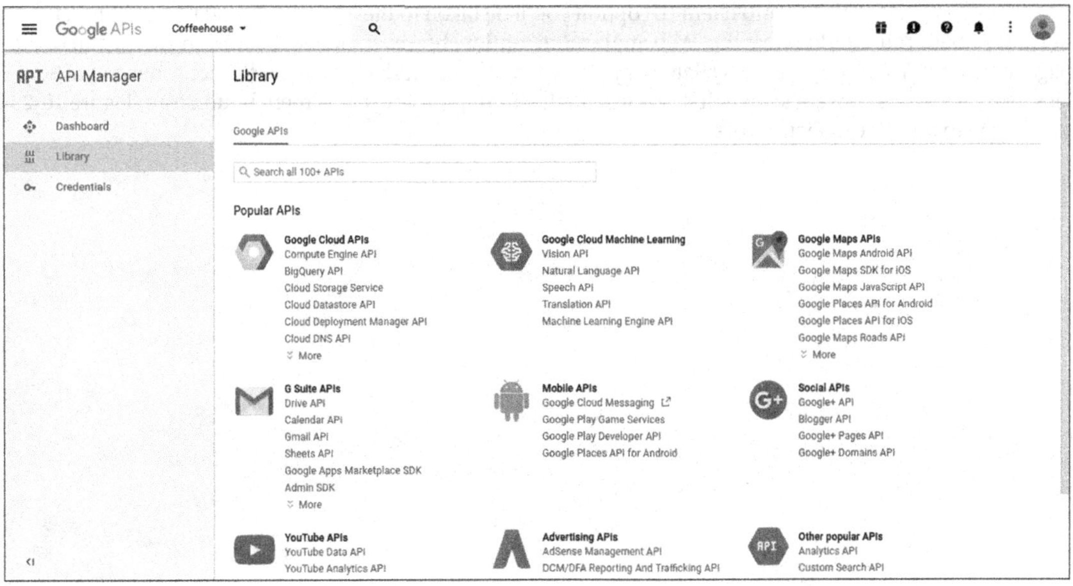

Figure 10-24. *Google project main page*

On the left-hand side menu of Figure 10-24, click on the 'Credentials' option. Next, on the center of the page, click on the 'Add credentials' button and from the drop-down menu select the 'OAuth client ID' option as illustrated in Figure 10-25.

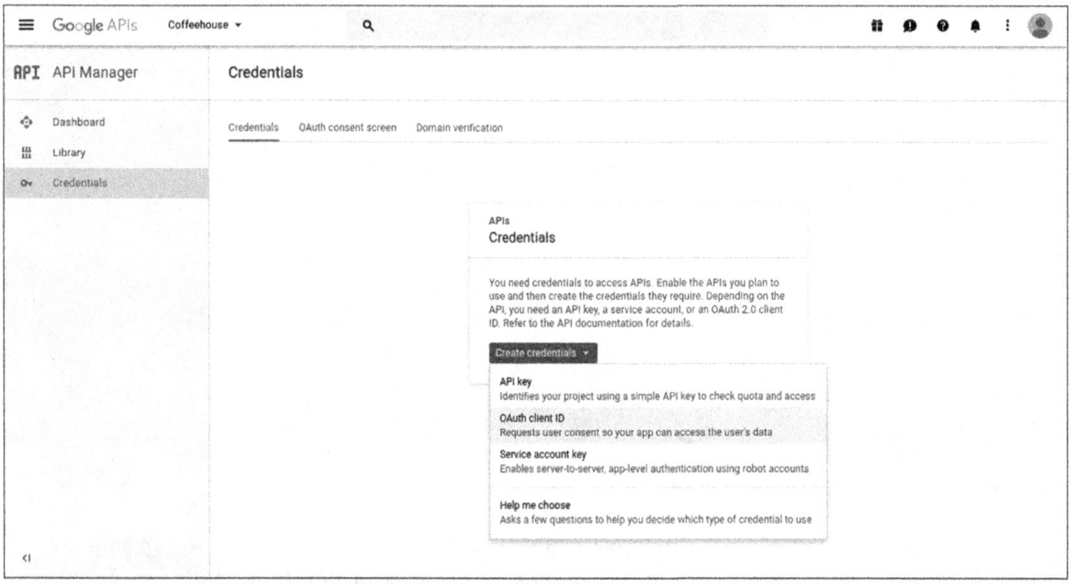

Figure 10-25. *Google project Oauth client ID option*

Once you click on the 'OAuth client ID' option you'll be taken to the 'Create Client ID' page illustrated in Figure 10-26. You should select the 'Web application' option; however, notice the warning at the top of the page indicating 'To create an OAuth client ID, you must first set a product name on the consent screen.' So let's take care of this consent screen first, so click on the 'Configure consent screen' button from Figure 10-26 to take you to the page in Figure 10-27.

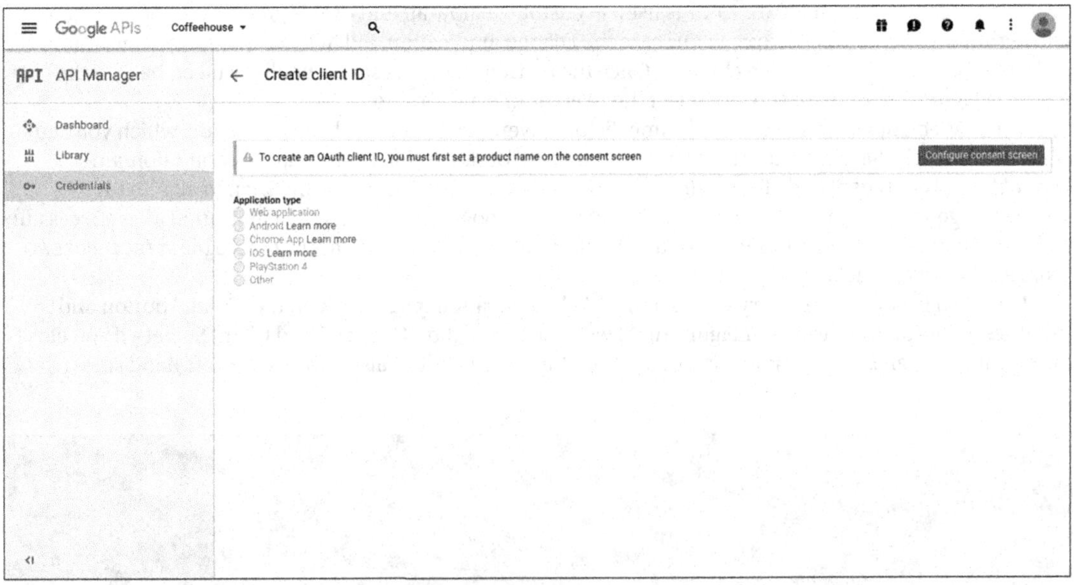

Figure 10-26. Google project create client ID page

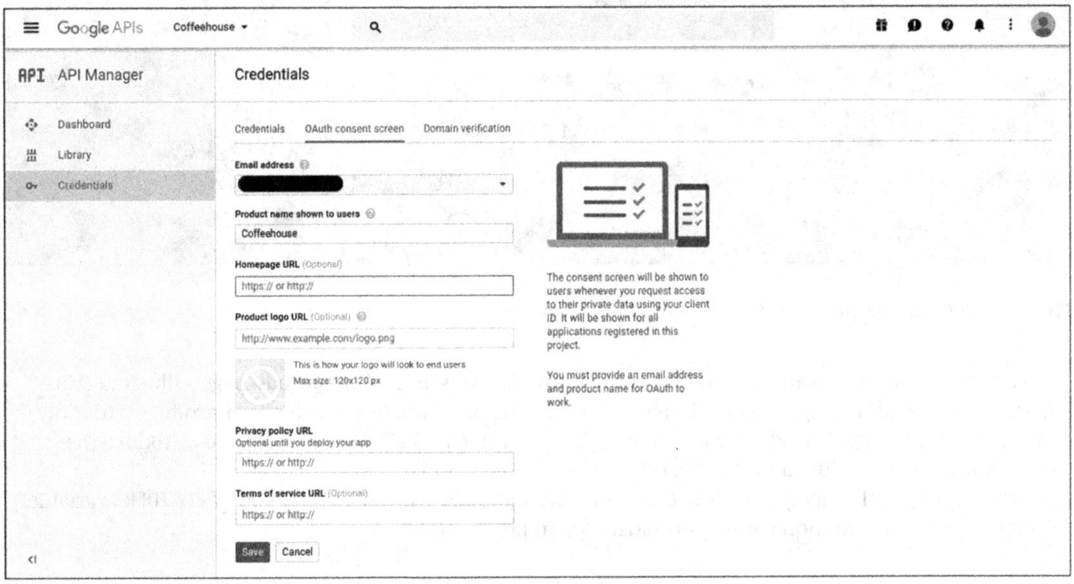

Figure 10-27. Google project OAuth consent screen

The consent screen in Figure 10-27 is used to customize how an end user is greeted by Google when seeking authorization from an app, in our case the Django application. Fill in the required 'Product name shown to users' field and save the changes. Once the consent screen is saved, you'll be taken back to the screen in Figure 10-26 where you can select the 'Web Application' option.

In the 'Web application' page, the 'Name' field is given the default 'Web client 1' value, which you can adjust accordingly. Set the 'Authorized JavaScript origins' option to the Django application's domain (e.g., `http://localhost`) and also set the 'Authorized redirect URIs' option to the Django allauth url `/accounts/google/login/callback/`, which is here that Google will contact the application after successful authentication – note this last value must use a full-qualified domain (e.g., `http://localhost/accounts/google/login/callback/`).

Once you input the necessary values in the 'Web application' page, click on the 'Create' button and you'll see a pop-up like the one in Figure 10-28 with the application Client ID and Client Secret - if you close the pop-up you can later access the same values in the main 'Credentials' menu on the left-hand side.

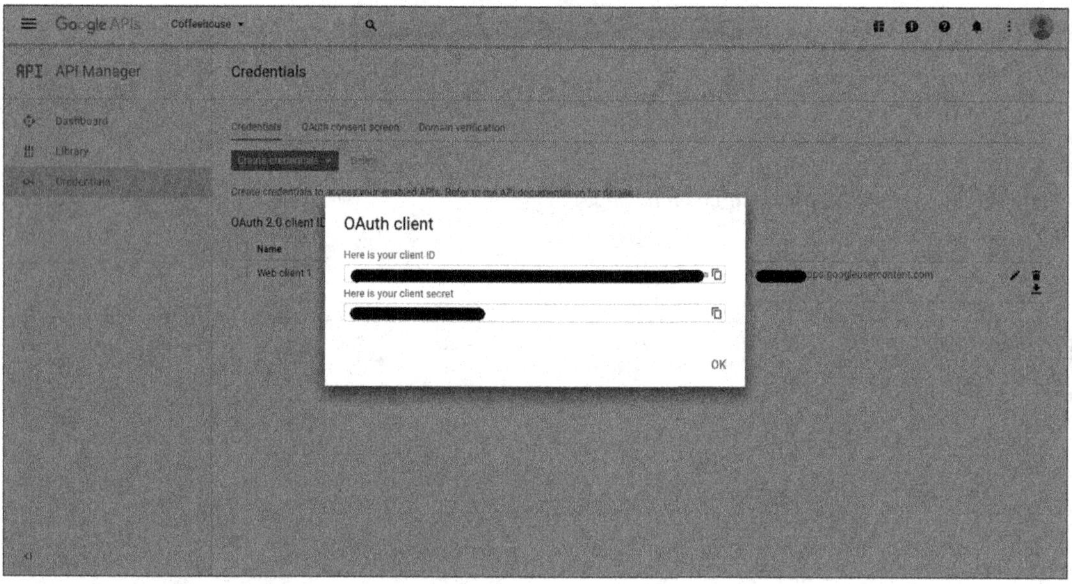

Figure 10-28. *Google project Client ID and Client Secret*

Next, go to the Django admin and in the 'Social applications' model create/edit page – illustrated in Figure 10-15 – create a Google application by selecting 'Google' from the provider list, introduce a friendly name in the 'Name' box, introduce the Google 'Client ID' value in the 'Client Id' box, and introduce the Google 'Client Secret' value in the 'Secret key' box

Next, open your Django project's `settings.py` file and update the `SOCIALACCOUNT_PROVIDERS` variable with the Google configuration parameters illustrated in Listing 10-22.

Listing 10-22. Google social provider configuration for django-allauth in settings.py

```
SOCIALACCOUNT_PROVIDERS = { 'google':
                             { 'SCOPE': ['email'],
                               'AUTH_PARAMS': { 'access_type': 'online' }
                             }
                          }
```

The settings in Listing 10-22 are the most basic set of values to run Google authentication, but there are many other options you can consult in the Django allauth documentation. Next, start the Django application and visit the `/accounts/login/` page – in Figure 10-21 – to attempt a Google login. Click on the 'Google' signup link and you'll be redirected to a Google grant authorization page, illustrated in Figure 10-29.

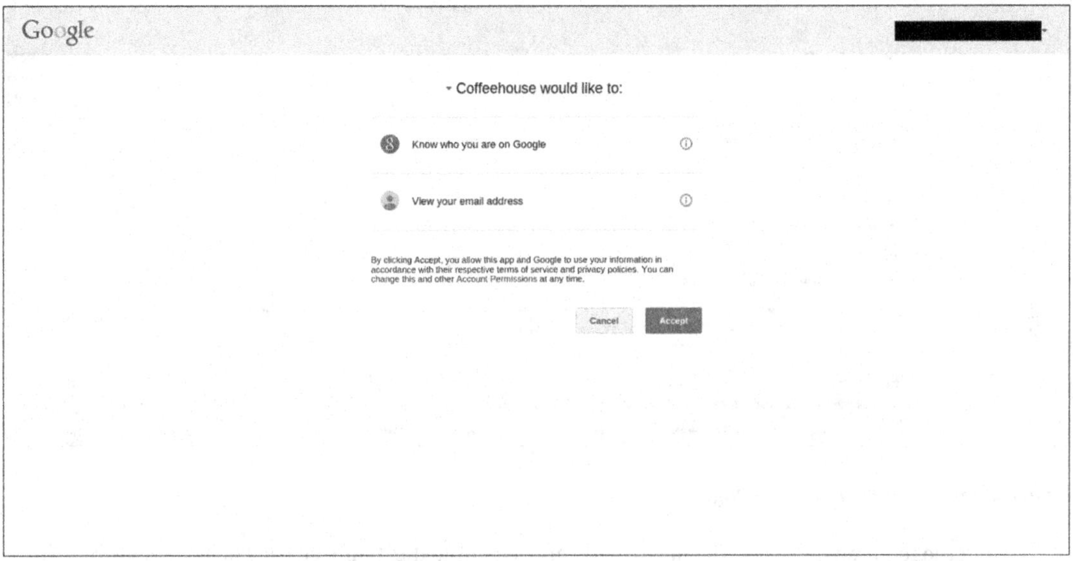

Figure 10-29. *Google social authorization page*

As you can see in Figure 10-29, a user is informed he will share who he is and his email upon confirmation. If the user clicks 'Accept,' Google contacts the Django application with a token and the user's information (i.e., public profile info and email). At this juncture, Django allauth creates a user so he's able to sign into the Django application by simply clicking on the 'Google' sign-in link every time.

Because Google itself requires on valid emails to work, it's implied a user authenticating via Google uses an active and valid email, therefore Django allauth skips the email verification process and automatically marks a user as verified - unlike Facebook authentication, where users can keep using Facebook with a stale and potentially invalid email.

Under the hood, Django allauth keeps track of social authentication tokens and accounts in the 'Social application tokens' and 'Social accounts' models, which are both accessible in the Django admin.

In addition, Django allauth also creates a regular Django user (e.g., the `django.contrib.auth.models.User` kind) with the Google workflow, so the same user is capable of leveraging Django's standard authentication system (e.g., to become superuser or staff). Note, however, this type of user relies on a Google authorization token – and has no password – so authentication must always be done through the social Google authentication link in `/accounts/login/`, with the Django admin not working for this type of user because it requires a typed-in password.

Set Up Twitter with Django allauth

To set up Twitter social authentication in Django allauth you'll need a Twitter account to create an application on their site. Head over to `https://apps.twitter.com/app/new` and you'll see a screen like the one in Figure 10-30 to create a Twitter app.

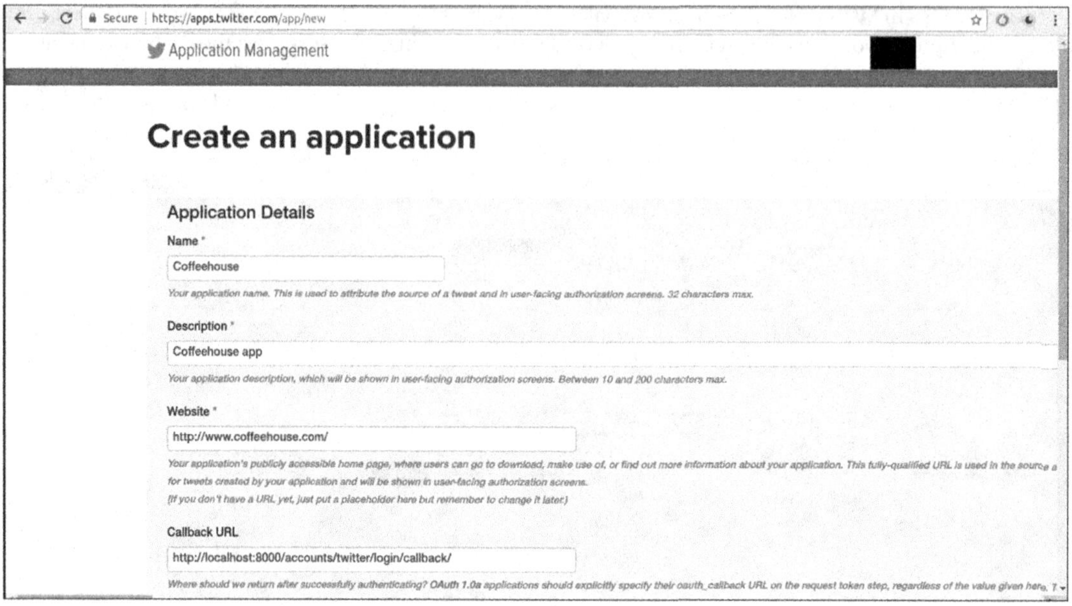

Figure 10-30. *Twitter create app page*

Fill out the required details for the new Twitter app, ensuring the 'Callback URL' field is set to `http://localhost:8000/accounts/twitter/login/callback/`, which is where Twitter will contact the Django application upon successful authentication. Create the application and you'll be redirected to the Twitter application's main page. Next, click on the 'Keys and Access Tokens' tab, where you'll see a screen like the one in Figure 10-31.

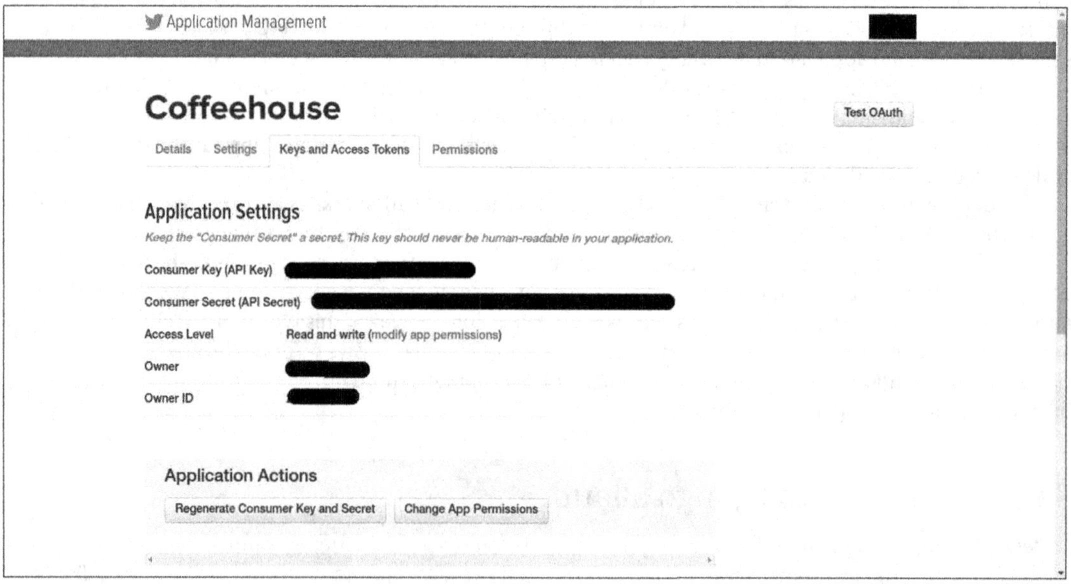

Figure 10-31. *Twitter app Key and Access Tokens page*

Next, go to the Django admin and in the 'Social applications' model create/edit page - illustrated in Figure 10-15 - create a Twitter application by selecting 'Twitter' from the provider list, introduce a friendly name in the 'Name' box, introduce the Twitter 'Consumer Key (API Key)' value in the 'Client Id' box, and introduce the Twitter 'Consumer Secret' value in the 'Secret key' box.

Django allauth doesn't support any Twitter configuration options as part of the `SOCIALACCOUNT_PROVIDERS` variable in settings.py, so you can skip this configuration step.

Next, start your Django application and visit the `/accounts/login/` page - in Figure 10-21 - to attempt to Twitter login. Click on the 'Twitter' sign in link and you'll be redirected to a Twitter grant authorization page, illustrated in Figure 10-32.

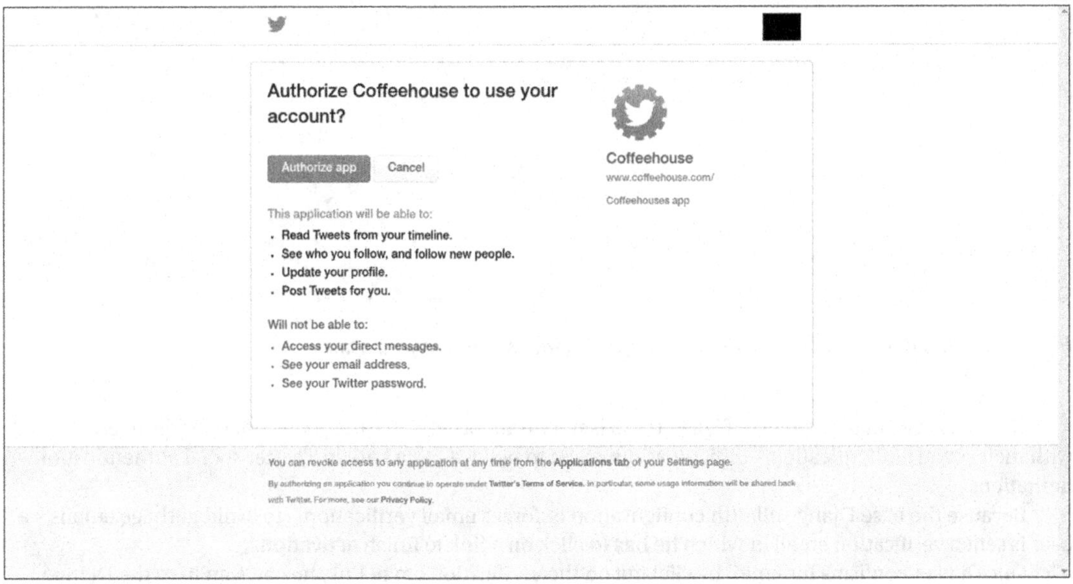

Figure 10-32. *Twitter social authorization page*

As you can see in Figure 10-32, a user is told he will share tweets and other information upon confirmation. If the user clicks 'Authorize app', Twitter contacts the Django application with a token and the user's information (i.e., public profile info). At this juncture, the user is redirected back to the site and Django allauth asks a user for his email to finish the account creation process, as illustrated in Figure 10-33.

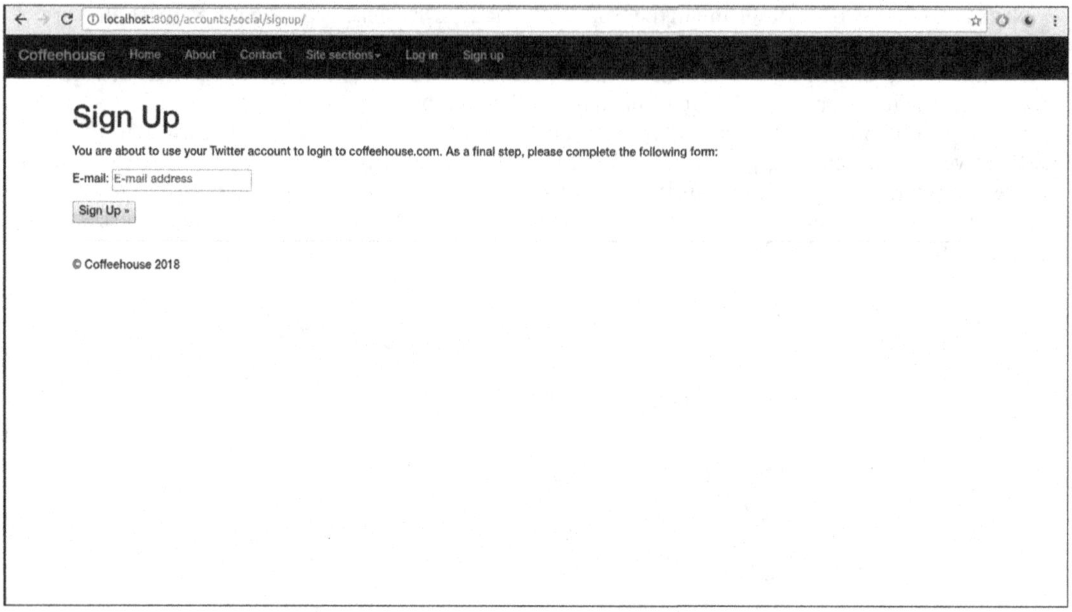

Figure 10-33. *Django allauth email request after Twitter social authorization*

Note this last email request in Figure 10-33 is necessary because Twitter does not provide an email with their social authentication - difficult as it may be to believe, it's a known Twitter social authentication limitation.

Because the base Django allauth configuration enforces email verification - to avoid garbage emails - a user is sent a verification email in which he has to click on a link to finish activation.

Once a user confirms his email by clicking on the verification email link, he can sign in to the Django application by clicking on the 'Twitter' sign-in link at any time. Under the hood, Django allauth keeps track of social authentication tokens and accounts in the 'Social application tokens' and 'Social accounts' models, which are both accessible in the Django admin.

In addition, Django allauth also creates a regular user (e.g., the `django.contrib.auth.models.User` kind) with the Twitter workflow, so the same user is capable of leveraging Django's standard authentication system (e.g., to become superuser or staff). Note however that this type of user relies on a Twitter authorization token - and has no password - so authentication must always be done through the social Twitter authentication link in `/accounts/login/`, with the Django admin not working for this type of user because it requires a typed-in password.

CHAPTER 11

■ ■ ■

Django admin Management

The Django admin is a user-friendly application to administer the contents of a relational database linked to a Django project. Although the Django admin is almost effortless in terms of setting it up – as described in Chapter 1 – there are multiple configuration options you'll learn in this chapter to create more powerful Django admin displays and functionalities.

In this chapter you'll first learn how to register Django models in the Django admin. Next, you'll learn how to display records in the Django admin and use techniques like ordering, inline editing, pagination, search and actions buttons, among other things. In addition, you'll learn how to customize Django admin forms and relationships to easily create, update, and delete model records with the Django admin.

Next, you'll learn how to customize Django admin pages through configuration fields and custom templates, as well as how to add custom data and override Django admin class methods and fields to create the most flexible Django admin pages possible. Finally, you'll learn how to configure and enforce Django admin permissions, as well as how to create multiple Django admin site instances.

Set Up Django Models in the Django admin

Although the Django admin provides an excellent management tool for a Django project's database, simply creating and installing Django models isn't enough to access their data in the Django admin.

In order to access Django model records in the Django admin you must register and configure Django models in `admin.py` files. An `admin.py` file is automatically placed inside a Django app – alongside the `models.py` and `views.py` files – when you create an app.

Although you can technically use a single `admin.py` to register and configure all Django models - just like you can have a single `models.py` to define all Django models - it's a recommended practice that each Django app uses its own `admin.py` file to manage its corresponding model defined in `models.py`.

There are three ways to register a Django model for the Django admin in admin.py files, all of which are illustrated in Listing 11-1.

Listing 11-1. Register Django models in admin.py file

```
from django.contrib import admin
from coffeehouse.stores.models import Store

# Option 1 - Basic
admin.site.register(Store)

# Option 2 - Allows customizing Django admin behavior
class StoreAdmin(admin.ModelAdmin):
    pass
```

© Daniel Rubio 2017
D. Rubio, *Beginning Django*, https://doi.org/10.1007/978-1-4842-2787-9_11

```
admin.site.register(Store, StoreAdmin)

# Option 3 - Decorator
@admin.register(Store)
class StoreAdmin(admin.ModelAdmin):
      pass
```

The first option in Listing 11-1 provides basic Django model registration and consists of declaring a Django model class as the input of the `admin.site.register` method. If you don't require customizing the default Django admin behavior for a model, this option is sufficient.

The second option in Listing 11-1 makes use of a Django admin class that inherits its behavior from the `admin.ModelAdmin` class. In this case, you can see the class is empty, but it's possible to customize the Django admin behavior, as I'll describe throughout this chapter. Once the Django admin class is declared, it must be registered and associated with a Django model using the same `admin.site.register` method in option one, where the first argument is the Django model and the second argument is the Django admin class.

The third option in Listing 11-1 makes use of a Django admin `@admin.register` decorator. The syntax difference between option three and option two is that the registration and association takes place decorating the Django admin class with `@admin.register` where the decorator takes the Django model as its argument.

It's worth mentioning that although options two and three are functionally equal, using the `@admin.register` decorator - option three - has the limitation that you can't reference the Django admin class in its `__init__()` method (e.g., `super(StoreAdmin, self).__init__(*args, **kwargs)`), which is an issue in Python 2 and for certain designs; if you're in this situation then you must use option two to register a model with the `admin.site.register` method.

Now that you know how to register Django models in the Django admin, I'll describe the various options available to customize the Django admin behavior through a Django admin class. To make it easier to look for custom options, I'll classify the options into two main sections: 'Read record options' and 'Create,update,delete record options' to cover the entire scope of CRUD operation options available in the Django admin, in addition to including subsections to group functionality under each main section.

Django admin Read Record Options

When you're on the main page of the Django admin and click on a Django model, you're taken to a page that shows the record list of that specific model. Figures 11-1 and 11-2 illustrate this record list page for a `Store` model.

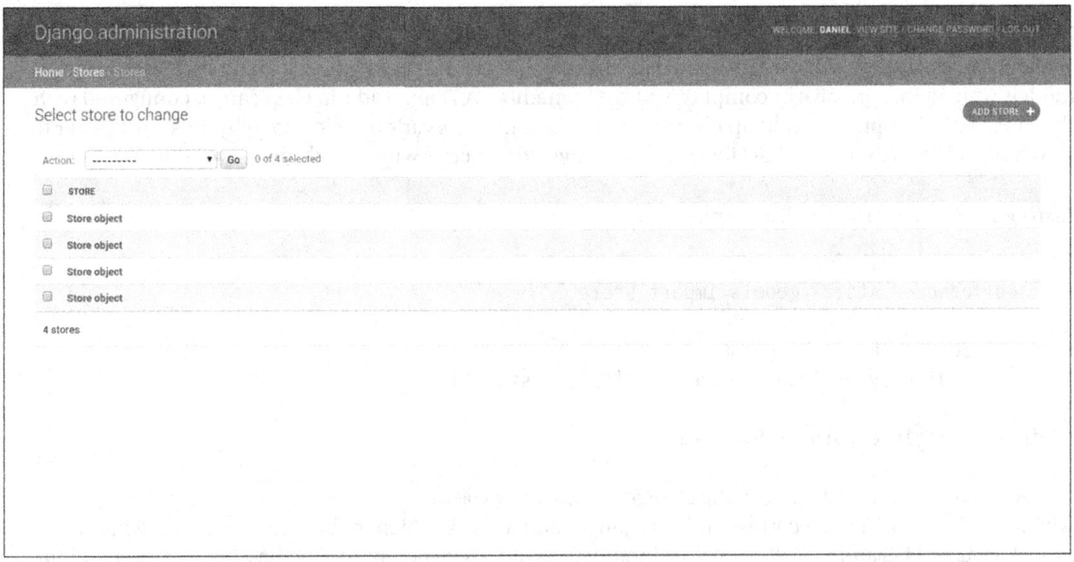

Figure 11-1. *Django admin record list page with no model __str__ definition*

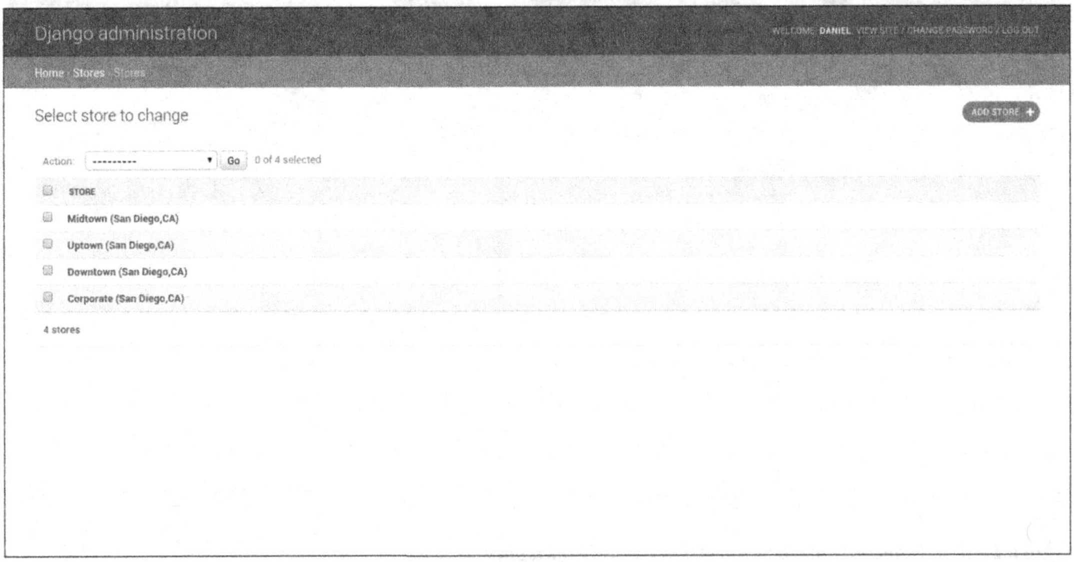

Figure 11-2. *Django admin record list page with model __str__ definition*

As you can see in Figures 11-1 and 11-2, each Django model record is displayed with a string. By default, this string is generated from the `__str__()` method definition of the Django model, as described in Chapter 7. If the `__str__` method is missing from a Django model, then the Django admin displays the records like Figure 11-1 as 'Store object'; otherwise it returns the result generated by the `__str__` method for each record - which in this case of Figure 11-2 is the name, city, and state attributes of each `Store` record.

Record Display: list_display, format_html, empty_value_display

While the basic display behavior presented in Figures 11-1 and 11-2 is helpful, it can be very limited for models with an inexpressive or complex `__str__()` method. A Django admin class can be configured with the `list_display` option to split up the record list with a model's various fields, thereby making it easier to view and sort records. Listing 11-2 illustrates a Django admin class with the list_display option.

Listing 11-2. Django admin list_display option

```
from django.contrib import admin
from coffeehouse.stores.models import Store

class StoreAdmin(admin.ModelAdmin):
      list_display = ['name','address','city','state']

admin.site.register(Store, StoreAdmin)
```

As you can see in Listing 11-2, the Django admin `StoreAdmin` class defines the `list_display` option with a list of values. This list corresponds to Django model fields, which in this case are from the `Store` model. Figures 11-3 and 11-4 illustrate the modified record list layout by adding the `list_display` option.

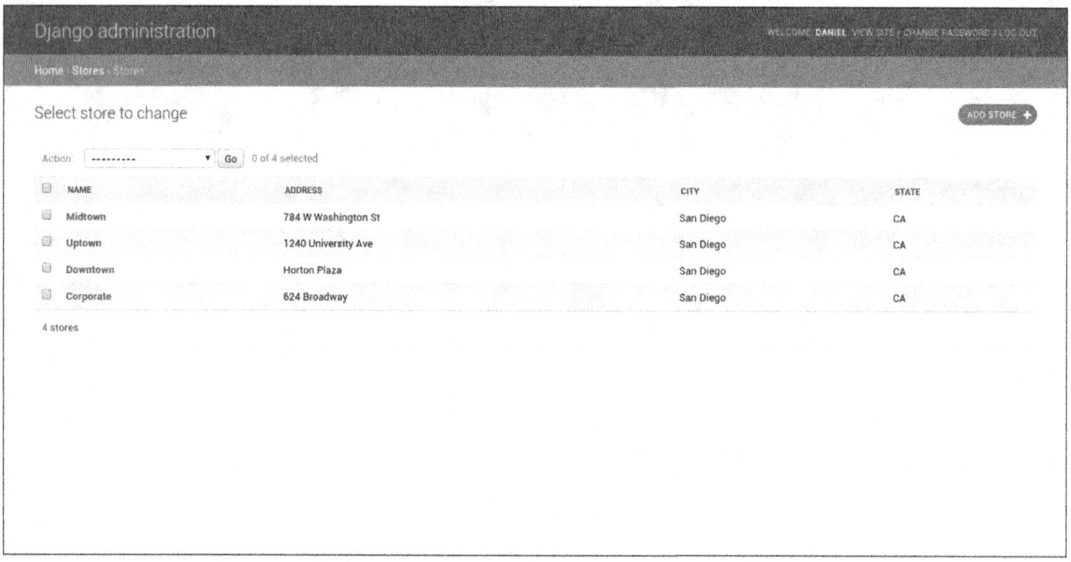

Figure 11-3. *Django admin record list page with list_display*

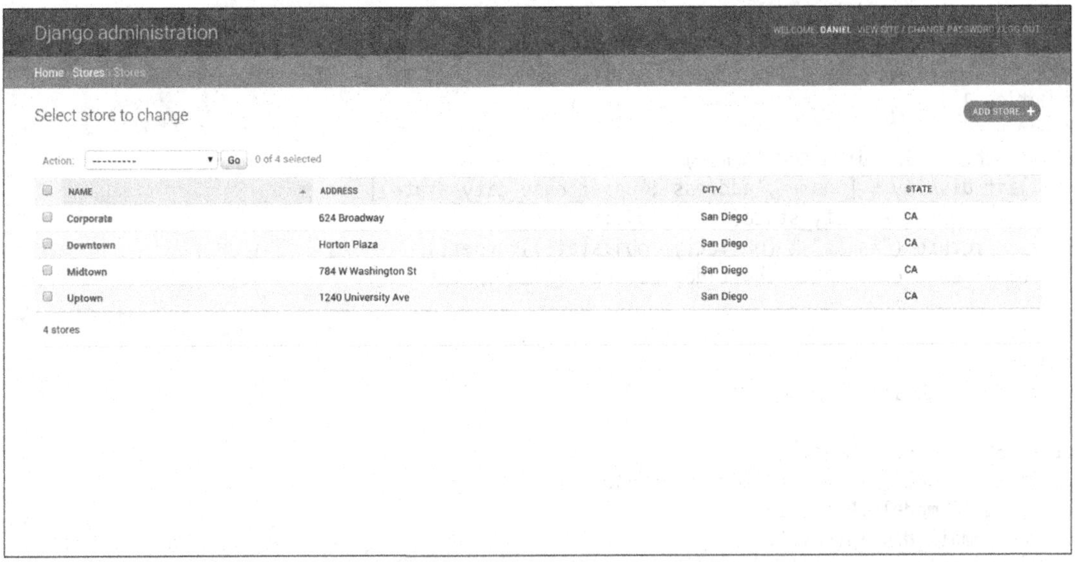

Figure 11-4. *Django admin record list page with model list_display sorted*

■ **Tip** If you want to keep displaying the value generated by a Django model through its `__str__` method in the Django admin, it's valid to add it to the `list_display` option (e.g., `list_display = ['name','__str__']`).

In Figure 11-3 you can see a much cleaner record list layout where each of the fields declared in list_display has its own column. In addition, if you click on any of the column headers - which represent model fields - the records are automatically sorted by that attribute, a process that's illustrated in Figure 11-4 and which greatly enhances the discoverability of records.

Besides supporting the inclusion of Django model fields, the `list_display` option also supports other variations to generate more sophisticated list layouts. For example, if the database records are not homogeneous (e.g., mixed upper and lowercase text) you can generate a callable method to manipulate the records and display them in the Django admin in a uniform manner (e.g., all uppercase). Additionally, you can also create a callable that generates a composite value from record fields that aren't explicitly in the database (e.g., domain names belonging to email records) that makes the visualization of the record list more powerful in the Django admin. Listing 11-3 illustrates several of these callable examples using several method variations.

Listing 11-3. Django admin list_display option with callables

```
from django.contrib import admin
from coffeehouse.stores.models import Store

# Option 1
# admin.py
def upper_case_city_state(obj):
    return ("%s %s" % (obj.city, obj.state)).upper()
upper_case_city_state.short_description = 'City/State'
```

```
class StoreAdmin(admin.ModelAdmin):
      list_display = ['name','address',upper_case_city_state]

# Option 2
# admin.py
class StoreAdmin(admin.ModelAdmin):
    list_display = ['name','address','upper_case_city_state']
    def upper_case_city_state(self, obj):
        return ("%s %s" % (obj.city, obj.state)).upper()
    upper_case_city_state.short_description = 'City/State'

# Option 3
# models.py
from django.db import models

class Store(models.Model):
    name = models.CharField(max_length=30)
    email = models.EmailField()
    def email_domain(self):
        return self.email.split("@")[-1]
    email_domain.short_description = 'Email domain'

# admin.py
class StoreAdmin(admin.ModelAdmin):
      list_display = ['name','email_domain']
```

In Listing 11-3 you can see three callable variations that are all acceptable as `list_display` options. Option one in Listing 11-3 is a callable that's declared outside a class and is then used as part of the `list_display` option. Option two declares the callable as part of the Django admin class and then uses it as part of the `list_display` option. Finally, option three declares a callable as part of the Django model class that is then used as part of the `list_display` option in the Django admin class. Neither approach in Listing 11-3 is 'better' or 'inferior' than the other; the options simply vary in the syntax and arguments used to achieve the same result, you can use whatever approach you like.

On certain occasions you may want to render HTML as part of a record list in the Django admin (e.g., add bold <b> tags or colored <span> tags). To include HTML in these circumstances, you must use the `format_html` method because the Django admin escapes all HTML output by default - since it works with Django templates. Listing 11-4 illustrates the use of the `format_html` method.

Listing 11-4. Django admin list_display option with callable and format_html

```
# models.py
from django.db import models
from django.utils.html import format_html

class Store(models.Model):
    name = models.CharField(max_length=30)
    address = models.CharField(max_length=30,unique=True)
    city = models.CharField(max_length=30)
    state = models.CharField(max_length=2)
    def full_address(self):
        return format_html('%s - <b>%s,%s</b>' % (self.address,self.city,self.state))
```

```
# admin.py
from django.contrib import admin
from coffeehouse.stores.models import Store

class StoreAdmin(admin.ModelAdmin):
      list_display = ['name','full_address']
```

When a model field uses a `BooleanField` or `NullBooleanField` data type, the Django admin displays an "on" or "off" icon instead of `True` or `False` values. In addition, when a value for a field in `list_display` is `None`, an empty string, and for cases when a field in `list_display` is any empty iterable (e.g., list), Django displays a dash -, as illustrated in Figure 11-5.

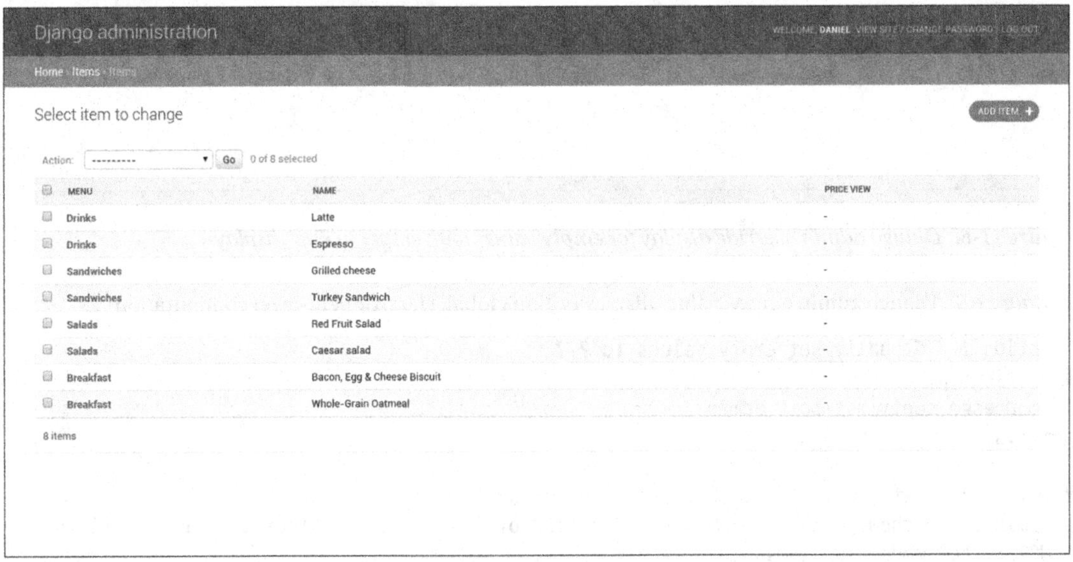

***Figure 11-5.** Django admin default display for empty values*

It's possible to override this last behavior with the `empty_value_display` option as illustrated in Figure 11-6. You can configure the `empty_value_display` option to take effect on all Django admin models, on a specific Django admin class, or individual Django admin fields as illustrated in Listing 11-5.

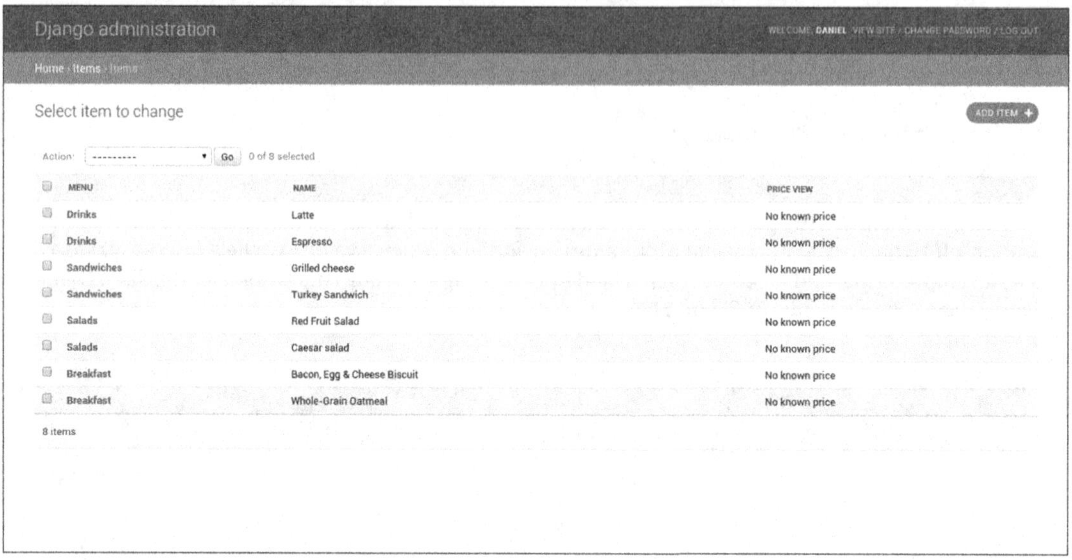

Figure 11-6. *Django admin override display for empty values with empty_value_display*

Listing 11-5. Django admin empty_value_display option global, class, or field-level configuration

```
# Option 1 - Globally set empty values to ???
# settings.py
from django.contrib import admin
admin.site.empty_value_display = '???'

# Option 2 - Set all fields in a class to 'Unknown Item field'
# admin.py to show "Unknown Item field" instead of '-' for NULL values in all Item fields
# NOTE: Item model in items app

class ItemAdmin(admin.ModelAdmin):
    list_display = ['menu','name','price']
    empty_value_display = 'Unknown Item field'

admin.site.register(Item, ItemAdmin)

# Option 3 - Set individual field in a class to 'No known price'
class ItemAdmin(admin.ModelAdmin):
    list_display = ['menu','name','price_view']
    def price_view(self, obj):
         return obj.price
    price_view.empty_value_display = 'No known price'
```

Record Order: admin_order_field and ordering

When you use custom fields in `list_display` (i.e., fields that aren't actually in the database, but are rather composite or helper fields calculated in Django), such fields can't be used for sorting operations because sorting takes places at the database level. However, if an element in `list_display` is associated with a database field, it's possible to create an association for sorting purposes with the `admin_order_field` option. This process is illustrated in Listing 11-6.

Listing 11-6. Django admin with admin_order_field option

```
# models.py
from django.db import models
from django.utils.html import format_html

class Store(models.Model):
    name = models.CharField(max_length=30)
    address = models.CharField(max_length=30,unique=True)
    city = models.CharField(max_length=30)
    state = models.CharField(max_length=2)
    def full_address(self):
        return format_html('%s - <b>%s,%s</b>' % (self.address,self.city,self.state))
    full_address.admin_order_field = 'city'

# admin.py
from django.contrib import admin
from coffeehouse.stores.models import Store

class StoreAdmin(admin.ModelAdmin):
      list_display = ['name','full_address']
```

As you can see in Listing 11-6, the `admin_order_field` declaration tells Django to order the model records by `city` when attempting to perform a sort operation in the Django admin through the composite `full_address` field. Note that it's also possible to add a preceding - to the `admin_order_field` value to specify descending order (e.g., `full_address.admin_order_field = '-city'`), just like it's done in standard model sort operations.

By default, record list values are sorted by their database `pk` (primary key) field – which is generally the id field – as you can appreciate in Figure 11-3 (i.e., record `pk 1` at the bottom and record `pk 4` at the top). And if you click on any of the header columns the sort order changes as you can see in Figure 11-4.

To set a default sorting behavior - without the need to click on the header column - you can use the Django admin class `ordering` option or the Django model meta `ordering` option that you learned about in Chapter 7. If no ordering option is specified in either class then `pk` ordering takes place. If the `ordering` option is specified in the Django model meta option, this sorting behavior is used universally and if both a Django model and Django admin class have `ordering` options, then the Django admin class definition takes precedence.

The `ordering` option accepts a list of field values to specify the default ordering of a record list. By default, the `ordering` behavior is ascending (e.g., Z values first@bottom, A values top@last), but it's possible to alter this behavior to descending (e.g., A values first@bottom, Z values top@last) by prefixing a - (minus sign) to the field value. For example, to produce a record list like the one if Figure 11-4 by default you would use `ordering = ['name']` and to produce an inverted record list of Figure 11-4 (i.e., Uptown at the top and Corporate at the bottom) you would use `ordering = ['-name']`.

Record Links and Inline Edit: list_display_links and list_editable

If you look at some of the past figures you'll notice there's always a generated link for each item in the record list. For example, in Figure 11-2 you can see each 'Store' record is a link that takes you to a page where you can edit the 'Store' values, similarly in Figure 11-4 you can see the 'Store' name field is a link that takes you to a page where you can edit the 'Store' values, and in Figure 11-6 you can see each 'Menu' name field is a link that takes you to a page where you can edit the 'Menu' values.

This is a default behavior that lets you drill-down on each record, but you customize this behavior through the `list_display_links` option to generate no links or inclusively more links. Listing 11-7 illustrates two variations of the `list_display_links` option and Figures 11-7 and 11-8 the respective interfaces.

Listing 11-7. Django admin with list_display_links option

```
# Sample 1)
# admin.py
from django.contrib import admin
from coffeehouse.stores.models import Store

class StoreAdmin(admin.ModelAdmin):
      list_display = ['name','address','city','state']
      list_display_links = None

admin.site.register(Store, StoreAdmin)

# Sample 2)
# admin.py
from django.contrib import admin
from coffeehouse.items.models import Item

class ItemAdmin(admin.ModelAdmin):
    list_display = ['menu','name','price_view']
    list_display_links = ['menu','name']

admin.site.register(Item, ItemAdmin)
```

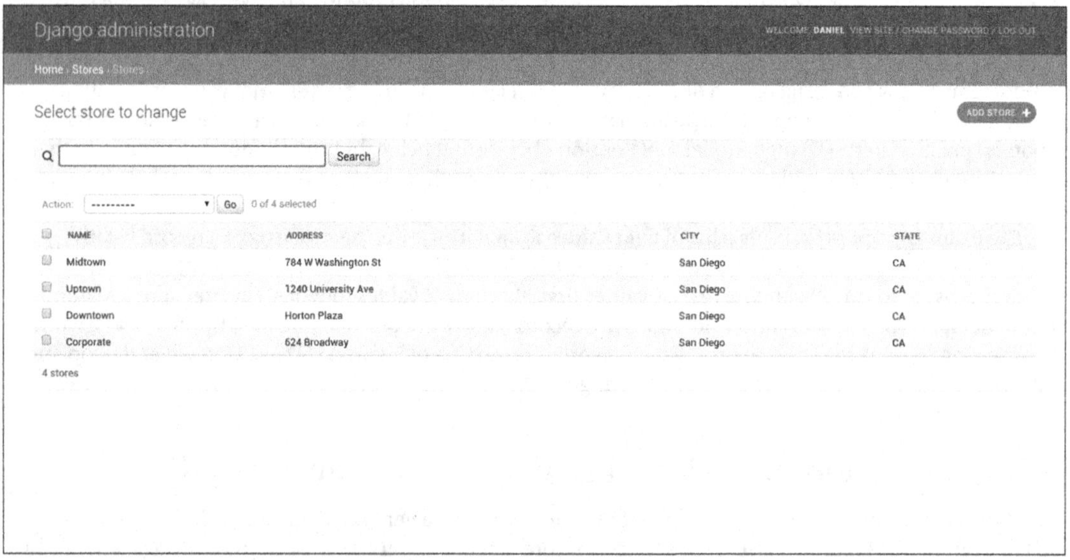

Figure 11-7. *Django admin no links in records list due to list_display_links*

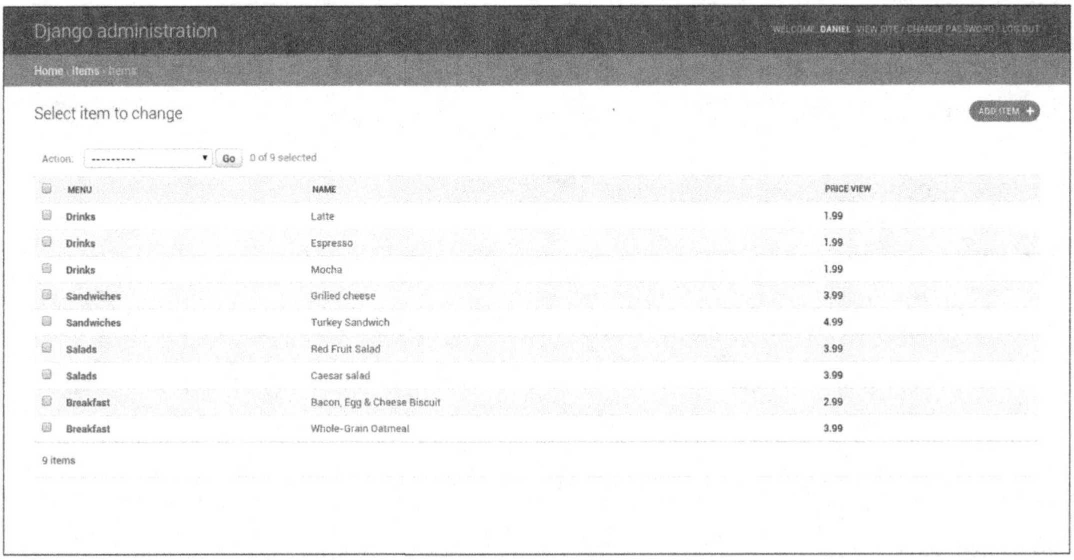

Figure 11-8. *Django admin multiple links in records list due to list_display_links*

The first sample in Listing 11-7 illustrates how the `StoreAdmin` class is set with `list_display_links = None` that results in the page presented in Figure 11-7 that lacks links. The second sample in Listing 11-7 shows the `ItemAdmin` class with the `list_display_links = ['menu','name']` that tells Django to generate links on both `menu` and `name` fields values and which results in the page presented in Figure 11-8 that contains multiple links.

The need to click on individual links on a record list to edit records can become tiresome if you need to edit multiple records. To simplify the editing of records, the `list_editable` option allows Django to generate inline forms on each record value, effectively allowing the editing of records in bulk without the need to leave the record list screen. Listing 11-8 illustrates the use of the list_editable option and Figure 11-9 the respective interface.

■ **Note** Technically list_editable is a Django admin update option, but since the update is done inline and on a page designed to read records, it's included here.

Listing 11-8. Django admin with list_editable option

```
# admin.py
from django.contrib import admin
from coffeehouse.stores.models import Store

class StoreAdmin(admin.ModelAdmin):
      list_display = ['name','address','city','state']
      list_editable = ['address','city','state']

admin.site.register(Store, StoreAdmin)
```

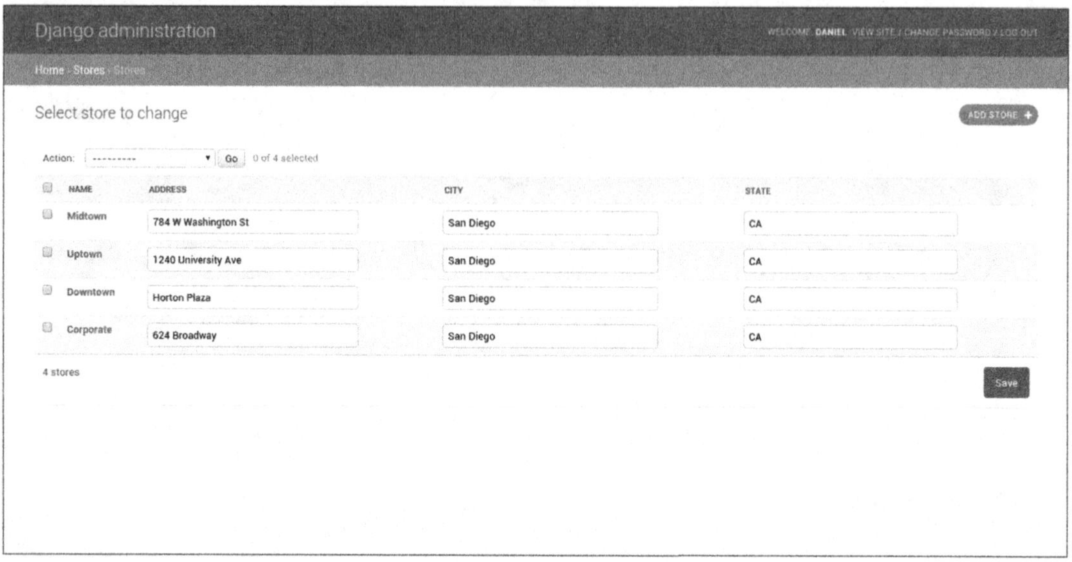

Figure 11-9. *Django admin editable fields due to list_editable*

In Listing 11-8 you can see the `list_editable = ['address','city','state']` option, which tells the Django admin to allow the editing of `address`, `city.` and `state` values in the record list. In Figure 11-9 you can see how each of these field values in the record list is turned into an editable form and toward the bottom of the page the Django admin generates a `'Save'` button to save changes when an edit is made.

It's worth mentioning that any field value declared in the `list_editable` option must also be declared as part of the `list_display` option, since it's not possible to edit fields that aren't displayed. In addition, any field values declared in the `list_editable` option must not be part of the `list_display_option`, since it's not possible for a field to be both a form and a link.

Record Pagination: list_per_page, list_max_show_all, paginator

When record lists grow too large in the Django admin, they are automatically split into different pages. By default, the Django admin generates additional pages for every 100 records. You can control this setting with the Django admin class `list_per_page` option. Listing 11-9 illustrates the use of the list_per_page option and Figure 11-10 shows the corresponding record list generated by the configuration in Listing 11-9.

Listing 11-9. Django admin with list_per_page option

```
# admin.py
from django.contrib import admin
from coffeehouse.items.models import Item

class ItemAdmin(admin.ModelAdmin):
    list_display = ['menu','name','price']
    list_per_page = 5

admin.site.register(Item, ItemAdmin)
```

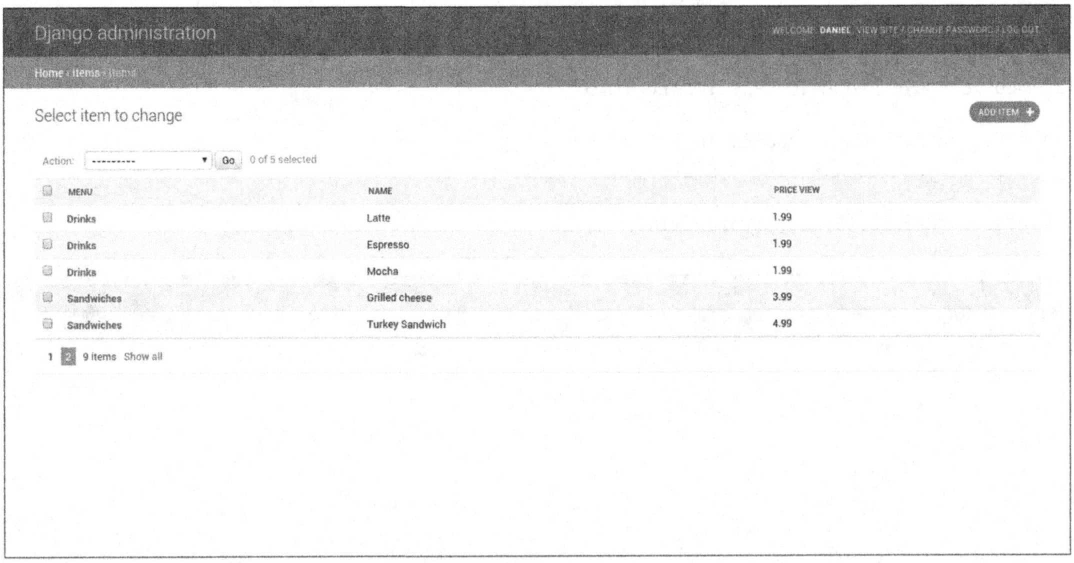

Figure 11-10. *Django admin list_per_page option limit to 5*

As you can see in Figure 11-10, the display of nine records is split into two pages due to the `list_per_page = 5` option illustrated in Listing 11-9. In addition to the page icons at the bottom left of Figure 11-10, notice the right-hand side of these icons is a 'Show all' link. The 'Show all' link is used to generate a record list with all the records in a single page. But note that because this additional database operation can be costly, by default, the 'Show all' link is only shown when a record list is 200 items or less.

You can control the display of the 'Show all' link with the `list_max_show_all` option. If the total record list count is less than or equal the `list_max_show_all` value the 'Show all' link is displayed, if the total record list count is above this number then no 'Show all' link is generated. For example, if you declare `list_max_show_all = 8` option to Listing 11-9 then no 'Show all' link would appear in Figure 11-10 because the total record list count is 9.

The Django admin uses the `django.core.paginator.Paginator` class to generate the pagination sequence, but it's also possible to provide a custom paginator class through the paginator option. Note that if the custom paginator class does not inherit its behavior from `django.core.paginator.Paginator` then you must also provide an implementation for `ModelAdmin.get_paginator()` method.

Record Search: search_fields, list_filter, show_full_result_count, preserve_filters

The Django admin also supports search functionality. The Django admin class `search_fields` option adds search functionality for text model fields through a search box – see Table 7-1 for a list of Django model text data types. Listing 11-10 illustrates a Django admin class with the search_fields option and Figure 11-11 illustrates how a search box is added to the top of the record list.

Listing 11-10. Django admin search_fields option

```
from django.contrib import admin
from coffeehouse.stores.models import Store

class StoreAdmin(admin.ModelAdmin):
      search_fields = ['city','state']

admin.site.register(Store, StoreAdmin)
```

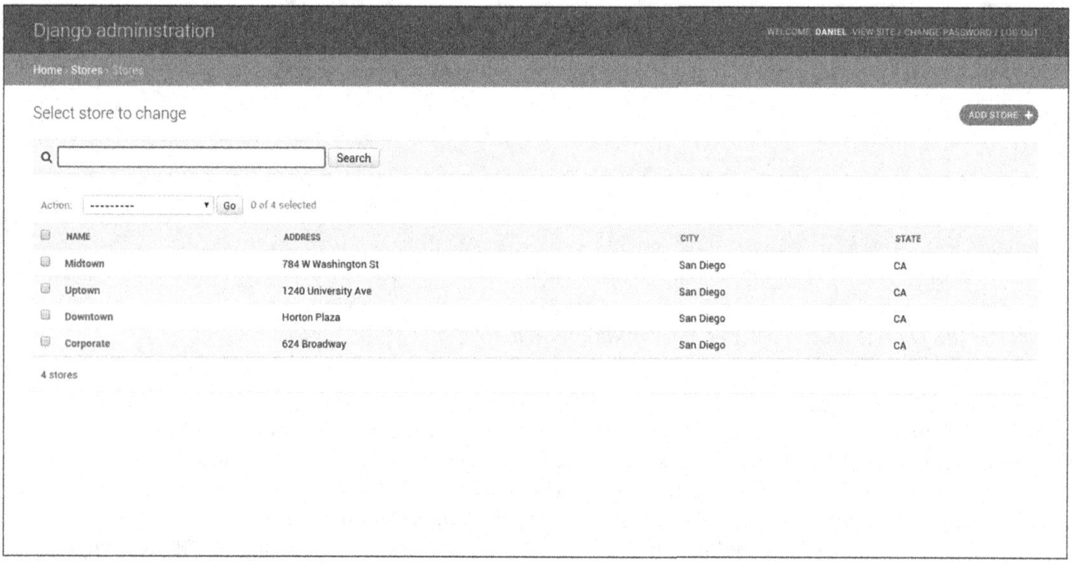

Figure 11-11. *Django admin search box due to search_fields option*

In Listing 11-10 the city and state fields are added to the `search_fields` option, which tell the Django admin to perform searches across these two fields. Be aware that adding too many fields to the `search_fields` option can result in slow search results, due to the way Django executes this type of search query. Table 11-1 presents different `search_fields` options and the generated SQL for a given search term.

Table 11-1. *Django search_fields options and generated SQL for search term*

search_fields option	Search term	Generated SQL condition
search_fields = ['city','state']	San Diego	WHERE (city ILIKE '%San%' OR state ILIKE '%San%') AND (city ILIKE '%Diego%' OR state ILIKE '%Diego%')
search_fields = ['^city','^state']	San Diego	WHERE (city ILIKE 'San%' OR state ILIKE 'San%') AND (city ILIKE 'Diego%' OR state ILIKE 'Diego%')
search_fields = ['=city','=state']	San Diego	WHERE (city ILIKE 'San' OR state ILIKE 'San') AND (city ILIKE 'Diego' OR state ILIKE 'Diego')
*search_fields = ['@city','@state']	San Diego	(Full-text search) WHERE (city ILIKE '%San%' OR state ILIKE '%San%') AND (city ILIKE '%Diego%' OR state ILIKE '%Diego%')

** Full-text search option only supported for MySQL database*

As you can see in Table 11-1, the `search_fields` option constructs a query by splitting the provided search string into words and performs a case insensitive search (i.e., `SQL ILIKE`) where each word must be in at least one of the search_fields. In addition, notice in Table 11-1 it's possible to declare the `search_fields` values with different prefixes to alter the search query.

By default, if you just provide model field names to `search_fields`, Django generates a query with SQL wildcards `%` at the start and end of each word, which can be a very costly operation, since it searches across all text in a field record. If you prefix the `search_field` with a ^ - as illustrated in Table 11-1 - Django generates a query with an SQL wildcard `%` at the end of each word, making the search operation more efficient because it's restricted to text that starts with the word patterns. If you prefix the search_field with a = - as illustrated in Table 11-1 - Django generates a query for an exact match with no SQL wildcard `%`, making the search operation the most efficient, because it's restricted to exact matches of the word patterns. Finally, if you're using a MySQL database, it's also possible to add the `@` prefix to `search_fields` to enable full-text search.

POWER SEARCHES, NON-TEXT SEARCHES, AND OTHER BACK ENDS FOR DJANGO ADMIN SEARCHES

Search engines offer various kinds of power search syntax to customize search queries, but the Django admin `search_fields` option doesn't support this type of syntax. For example, in a search engine it's possible to quote the search term `"San Diego"` to make an exact search for both words, but if you attempt this with the Django admin search, Django attempts to search for literal quotes: `"San"` and `"Diego"` separately. To tweak the default search_fields behavior you must use the options presented in Table 11-1 or `ModelAdmin.get_search_results()`.

The default search behavior for a Django admin class can be customized to any requirements with the `ModelAdmin.get_search_results()` method that accepts the request, a queryset that applies the current filters, and the user-provided search term. In this manner, you can generate non-text searches (e.g., on Integers) or rely on other third-party tools (e.g., Solr, Haystack) to generate search results.

The `list_filter` option offers quicker access to model field values and works like pre-built search links. Unlike the `search_fields` option, the `list_filter` option is more flexible in terms of the data types it can work with and accepts more than just text model fields (i.e., it also supports Boolean fields, date fields, etc.). Listing 11-11 illustrates a Django admin class with the `list_filter` option and Figure 11-12 illustrates the list of filters generated on the right-hand side of the record list.

Listing 11-11. Django admin list_filter option

```
from django.contrib import admin
from coffeehouse.items.models import Item

class ItemAdmin(admin.ModelAdmin):
    list_display = ['menu','name','price']
    list_filter = ['menu','price']

admin.site.register(Item, ItemAdmin)
```

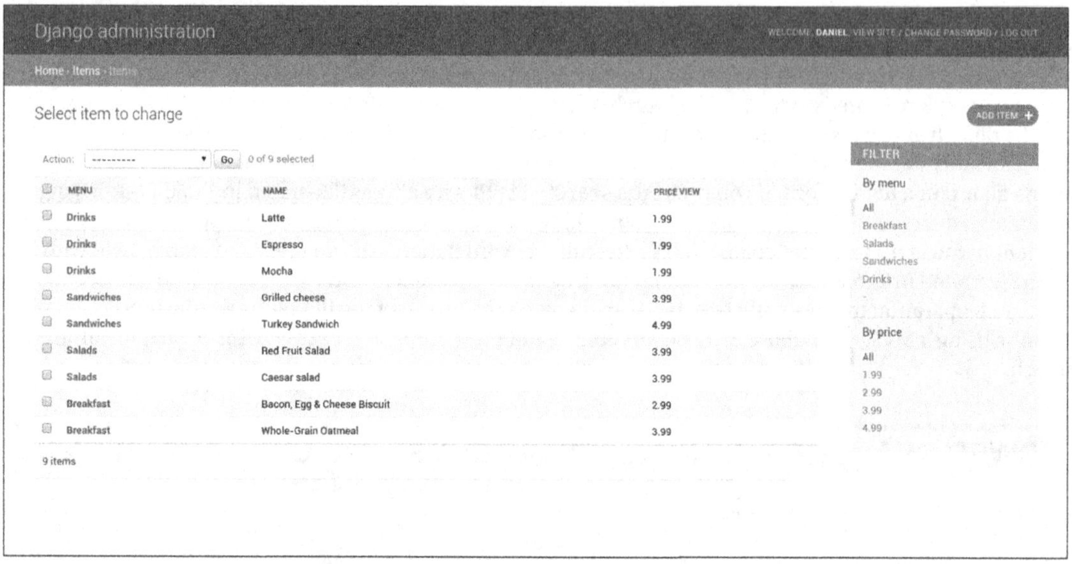

***Figure 11-12.** Django admin list filters due to search_fields option*

In Listing 11-11 the list_filter option is declared with the menu and price fields, which tell Django to create filters with these two fields. As you can appreciate in Figure 11-12, on the right-hand side of the record list is a column with various filters that includes all the values for the `menu` and `price` field values. If you click on any of the filter links, the Django admin displays the records that match the filter in the record list, a process that's illustrated in Figures 11-13, 11-14, and 11-15.

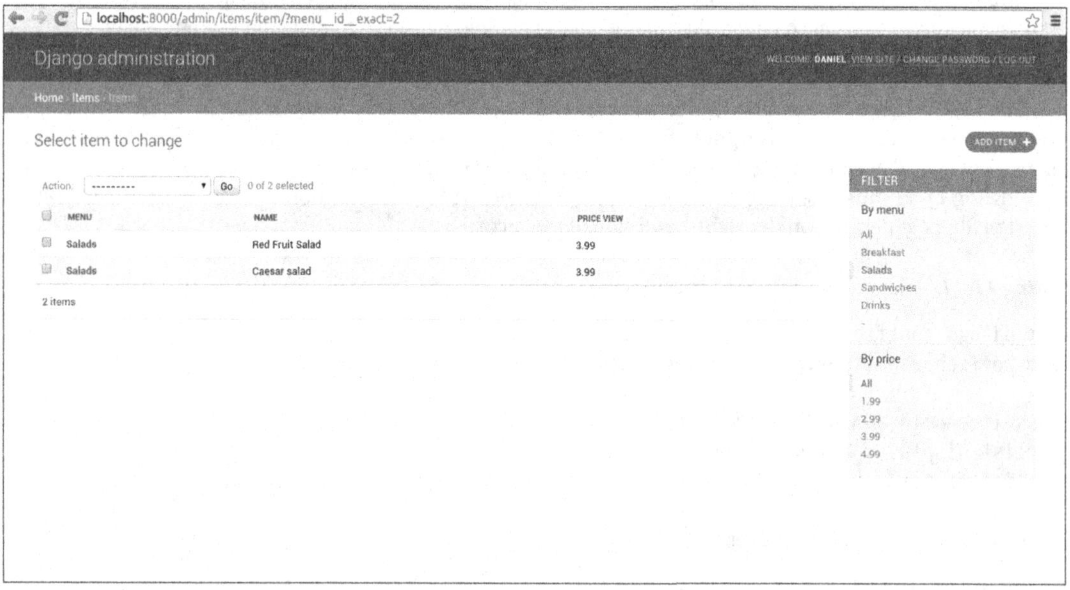

***Figure 11-13.** Django admin list with single filter*

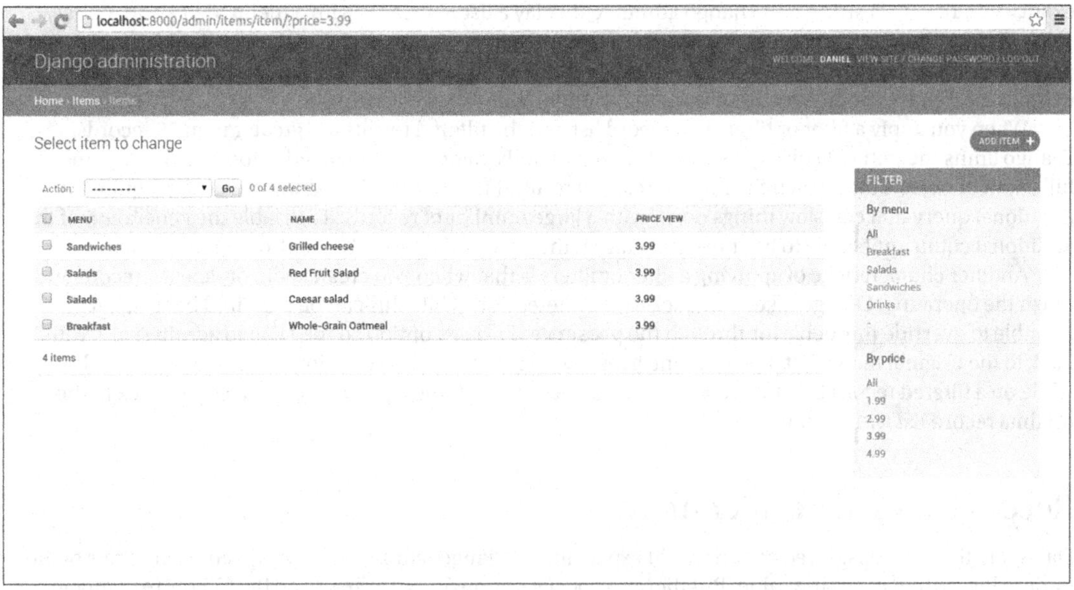

Figure 11-14. *Django admin list with single filter*

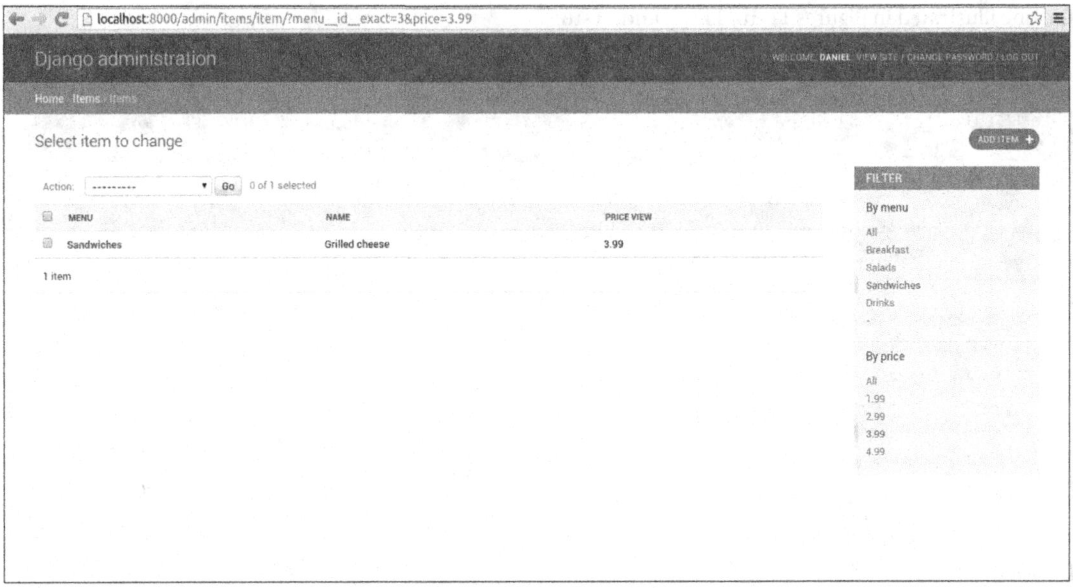

Figure 11-15. *Django admin list with dual filter*

An interesting aspect of Django admin filters that can be seen in Figure 11-15 is that you can apply multiple filters, making it easier to drill-down into records that match very specific criteria.

In addition, if you look at fFgures 11-13, 11-14, and 11-15 you can see how filters are reflected as URL query strings. For example, in Figure 11-13 the `?menu__id__exact=2` string is appended to the URL, which tells Django admin to display a list of records with a menu `id` of `2`; in Figure 11-15 the `?menu__id__` exact=3&price=3.99 string tells Django admin to display a list of records with a menu id of 3 and a price value of 3.99. This URL argument syntax is based on the same syntax used to make standard Django model queries -- described in Chapter 8 - and which is helpful to generate more sophisticated filters 'on the fly' without the need to modify or add options to the underlying Django admin class.

When you apply a filter or filters to a record list and the filtered results are greater than 99 records, Django limits the initial display to 99 records and also adds pagination, but in addition also displays the full count of objects that match the filter(s) (e.g., 99 results (153 total)). This additional count requires an additional query that can slow things down with a large number of records. To disable the generation of this additional count applicable to filter use you can set the show_full_result_count option to False.

Another characteristic of applying a filter or filters is that when you create, edit, or delete a record and finish the operation, Django takes you back to the filtered list. While this can be a desired behavior, it's possible to override this behavior through the preserve_filters option so the Django admin sends you back to the original record list. If you set the preserve_filters = False option in a Django admin class while on a filtered record list and create, edit, or delete a record, the Django admin takes you back to the original record list with no filters.

Record Dates: date_hierarchy

Dates and times are displayed as you would expect in the Django admin UI, as string representations of the underlying Python datetime value. But there's a special option for DateField and DateTimeField model data types that works like a specialized filter. If you use the date_hierarchy option on a Django admin class and assign it a field that's a DateField or DateTimeField (e.g., date_hierarchy = 'created', where timestamp is the name of the field), Django generates an intelligent date filter at the top of the record list like the one illustrated in Figures 11-16, 11-17, and 11-18.

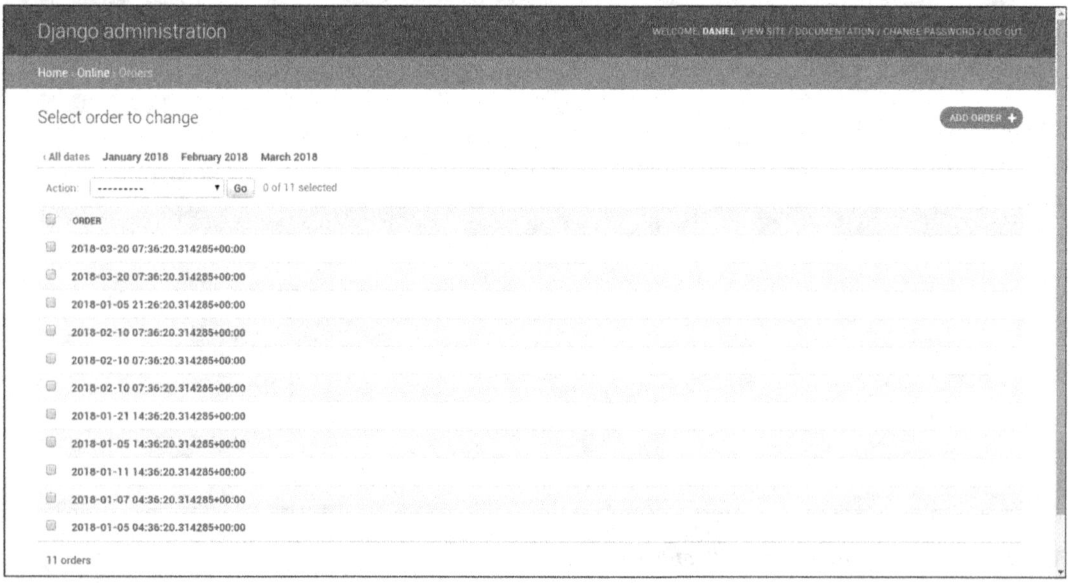

Figure 11-16. *Django date filter by month with date_hierarchy*

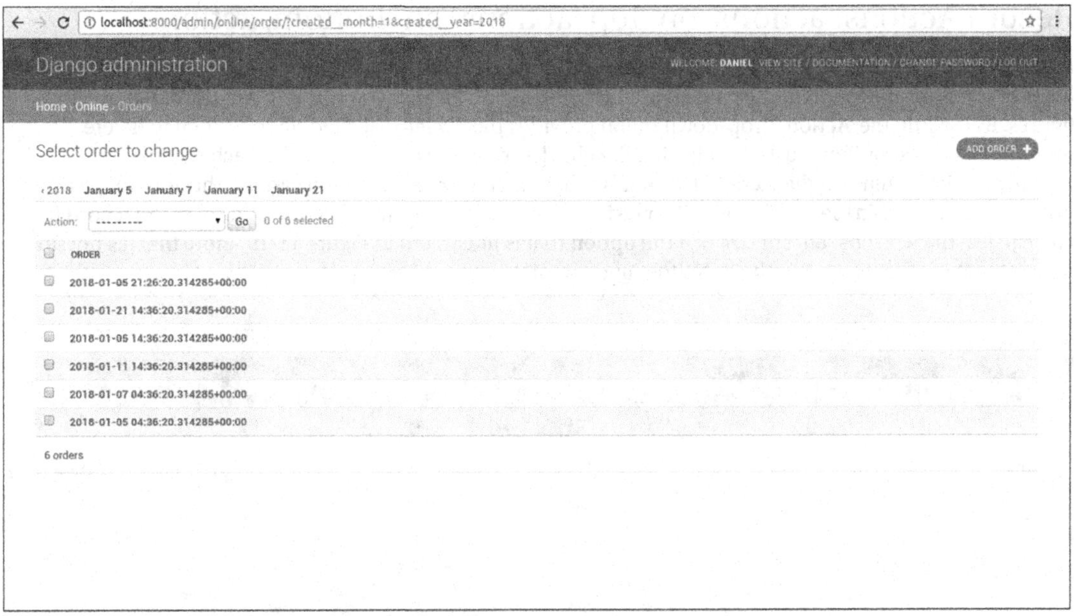

***Figure 11-17.** Django date filter by day with date_hierarchy*

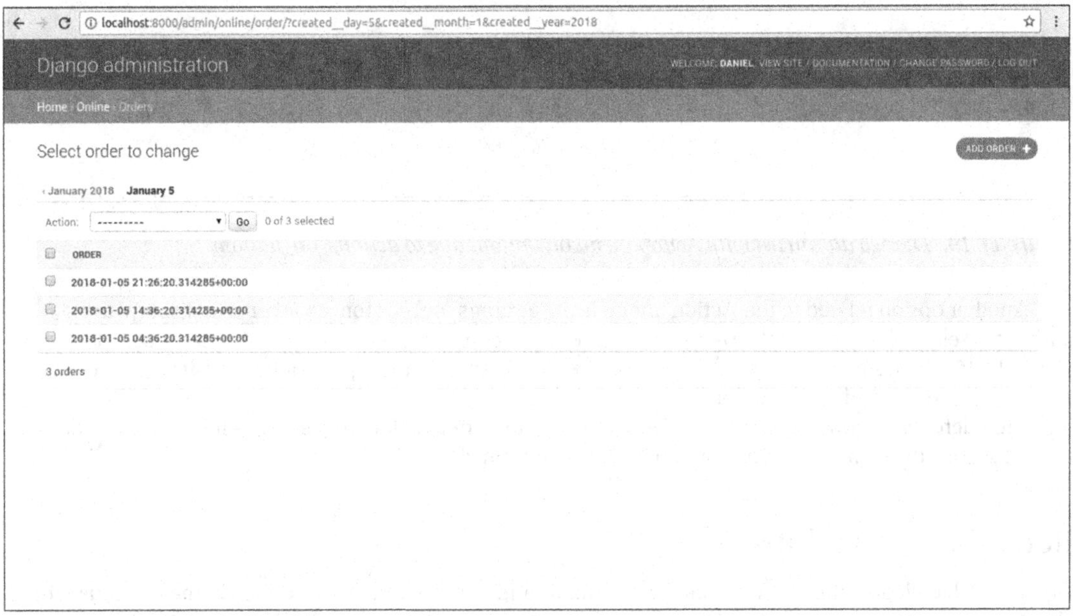

***Figure 11-18.** Django date filter single day with date_hierarchy*

As you can see in Figures 11-16, 11-17, and 11-18, the intelligent behavior comes from the fact that upon loading the record list, Django generates a unique list of the available months or days corresponding to the values of the `date_hierarchy` field. If you click on any of the options of this filter list, Django then generates a unique list of records that matches the values of the month or day in the filter list.

Record Actions: actions_on_top, actions_on_bottom, actions

Besides the ability to click on an item in a Django admin record list to edit or delete it, at the top of the record list there's a drop-down menu preceded with the word 'Action', which you can see in many of the previous figures. By default, the 'Action' drop-down menu provides the 'Delete selected options' item to delete multiple records simultaneously by selecting the check box on the left-hand side of each record.

If you wish to remove the 'Action' menu from the top of the record list you can use the `actions_on_top` options and set it to `False`. In addition, if you wish to add the 'Action' menu to the bottom of the record list you can use the `actions_on_bottom = True` option that is illustrated in Figure 11-19 - note that it's possible to have an 'Action' menu on both the bottom and top of the record list page.

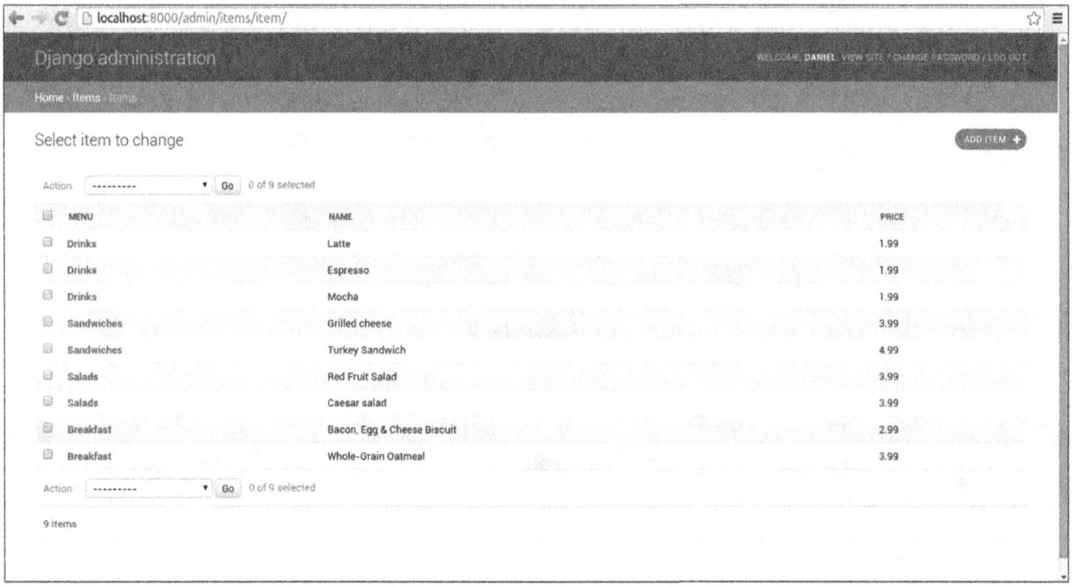

***Figure 11-19.** Django admin list with Action menu on bottom due to actions_on_bottom*

Another option related to the 'Action' menu is the `actions_selection_counter` that displays the amount of selected records on the right-hand side of the 'Action' menu and which can also be seen in Figure 11-19. If you set `actions_selection_counter = False` then the Django admin omits the amount of selected records related to the 'Action' menu.

Although the 'Action' menu is limited to a single action - that of deleting records - it's possible to define a list of actions through the `actions` option in Django admin classes.[1]

Record Relationships

Django model relationships – one to one, one to many, and many to many – described in the previous model chapters, have certain behaviors in the context of Django admin classes and the Django admin that are worth describing separately in the following subsections.

[1]`https://docs.djangoproject.com/en/1.11/ref/contrib/admin/actions/`

Display: list_display (continued)

When you have a one to many relationship and declare the related `ForeignKey` field as part of the `list_display` option, the Django admin uses the `__str__` representation of the related model. This last behavior is presented in Figure 11-5 with a list of `Item` records, where the `Item` model defines the `menu` field with `models.ForeignKey(Menu)` and thus the output of the field is the `Menu` model `__str__` method.

The `list_display` option can't accept a `ManyToManyField` field *directly* because it would require executing a separate SQL statement for each row in the table; nevertheless it's possible to integrate a `ManyToManyField` into `list_display` through a custom method in a Django admin class, a process that's illustrated in Listing 11-12 and Figure 11-20.

Listing 11-12. Django admin list_display option with ManyToManyField field

```
# models.py
from django.db import models

class Amenity(models.Model):
    name = models.CharField(max_length=30)
    description = models.CharField(max_length=100)

class Store(models.Model):
    name = models.CharField(max_length=30)
    address = models.CharField(max_length=30)
    city = models.CharField(max_length=30)
    state = models.CharField(max_length=2)
    email = models.EmailField()
    amenities = models.ManyToManyField(Amenity,blank=True)

# admin.py
from django.contrib import admin
from coffeehouse.stores.models import Store

class StoreAdmin(admin.ModelAdmin):
    list_display = ['name','address','city','state','list_of_amenities']
    def list_of_amenities(self, obj):
        return ("%s" % ','.join([amenity.name for amenity in obj.amenities.all()]))
    list_of_amenities.short_description = 'Store amenities'

admin.site.register(Store, StoreAdmin)
```

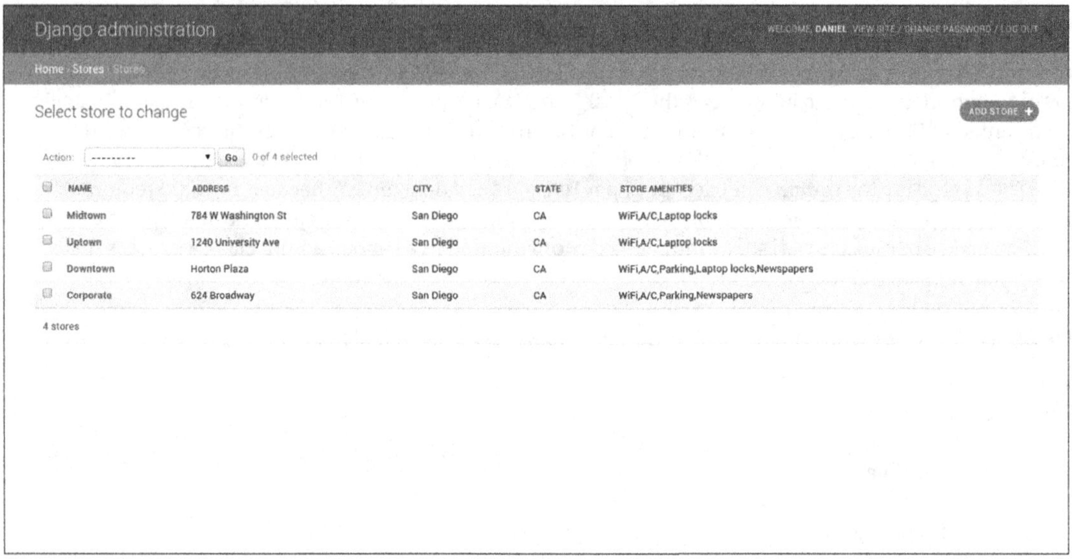

Figure 11-20. *Django admin list_display option with ManyToManyField field*

In Listing 11-12 you can see the `Store` model has a `ManyToManyField` field with the `Amenity` model. In order to present the values of the `ManyToManyField` field in the Django admin through `list_display` you can see it's necessary to create a custom method that makes an additional query for these records. Figure 11-20 presents the rendered Django admin record list for this `ManyToManyField` field. Be aware this design can place a heavy burden on the database because it requires an additional query for each individual record.

Order: admin_order_field (continued)

The `admin_order_field` option also supports sorting on fields that are part of related models. For example, in Listing 11-13, you can see the `admin_order_field` option is applied to a field that's part of the model with a `ForeignKey` field relationship.

Listing 11-13. Django admin admin_order_field option with ForeignKey field

```
# models.py
class Menu(models.Model):
    name = models.CharField(max_length=30)
    creator = models.CharField(max_length=100,default='Coffeehouse Chef')
    def __str__(self):
        return u"%s" % (self.name)

class Item(models.Model):
    menu = models.ForeignKey(Menu)
    name = models.CharField(max_length=30)

# admin.py
from django.contrib import admin
from coffeehouse.stores.models import Store
```

```
class ItemAdmin(admin.ModelAdmin):
    list_display = ['menu','name','menu_creator']
    def menu_creator(self, obj):
        return obj.menu.creator
    menu_creator.admin_order_field = 'menu__creator'

admin.site.register(Item, ItemAdmin)
```

The most important thing worth noting about Listing 11-13 is the double underscore to specify the field menu__creator, which tells the Django admin to access a field in the related model - note this double underscore is the same syntax used to perform queries in Django model relationships queries described in Chapter 8.

Search: search_fields and list_filter (continued), admin.RelatedOnly FieldListFilter, list_select_related

Two other Django admin class options that support the same double underscore syntax (a.k.a. "follow notation") to work across relationships are search_fields and list_filter. This means you can enable search and generate filters for related models (e.g., search_fields = ['menu__creator']).

A variation of the list_filter option that only applies to model relationships is admin.RelatedOnlyFieldListFilter. When model records that belong to a relationship can span beyond a single relationship, it can lead to the creation of unneeded filters.

For example, let's take a relationship between Store and Amenity models; you can generate Django admin filters for Amenity values on the Store record list, but if the Amenity model records are generic and used beyond the Store model (e.g., Amenity values for Employees) you'll see inapplicable filter values in the Store record list. The use of the admin.RelatedOnlyFieldListFilter prevents this, a process that's illustrated in Listing 11-14 and Figures 11-21 and 11-22.

Listing 11-14. Django admin list_filter option with admin.RelatedOnlyFieldListFilter

```
# admin.py
class StoreAdmin(admin.ModelAdmin):
    list_display = ['name','address','city','state','list_of_amenities']
    list_filter = [['amenities',admin.RelatedOnlyFieldListFilter]]
    def list_of_amenities(self, obj):
        return ("%s" % ','.join([amenity.name for amenity in obj.amenities.all()]))
    list_of_amenities.short_description = 'Store amenities'
```

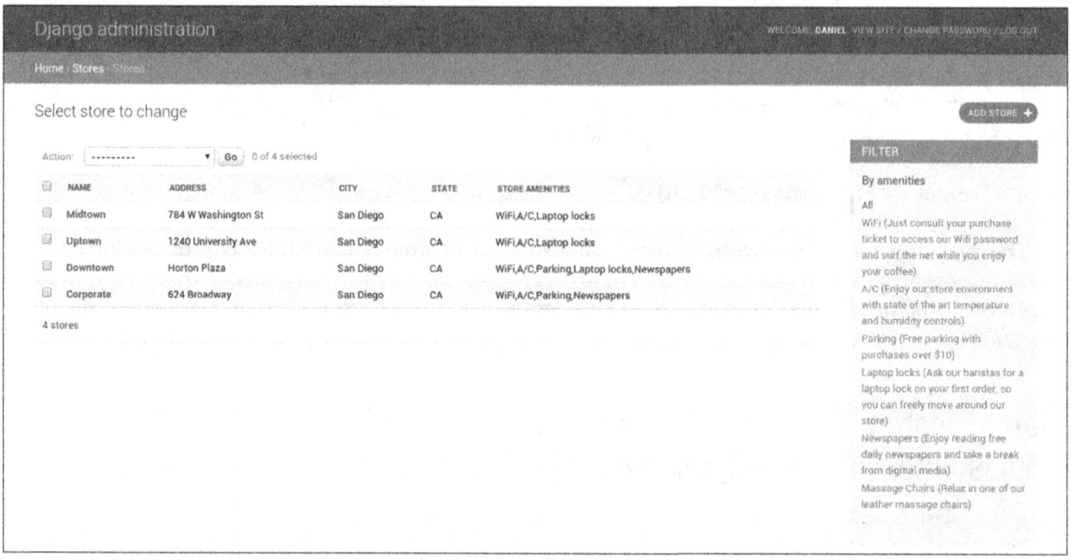

Figure 11-21. *Django admin list_filter option with no RelatedOnlyFieldListFilterDjango*

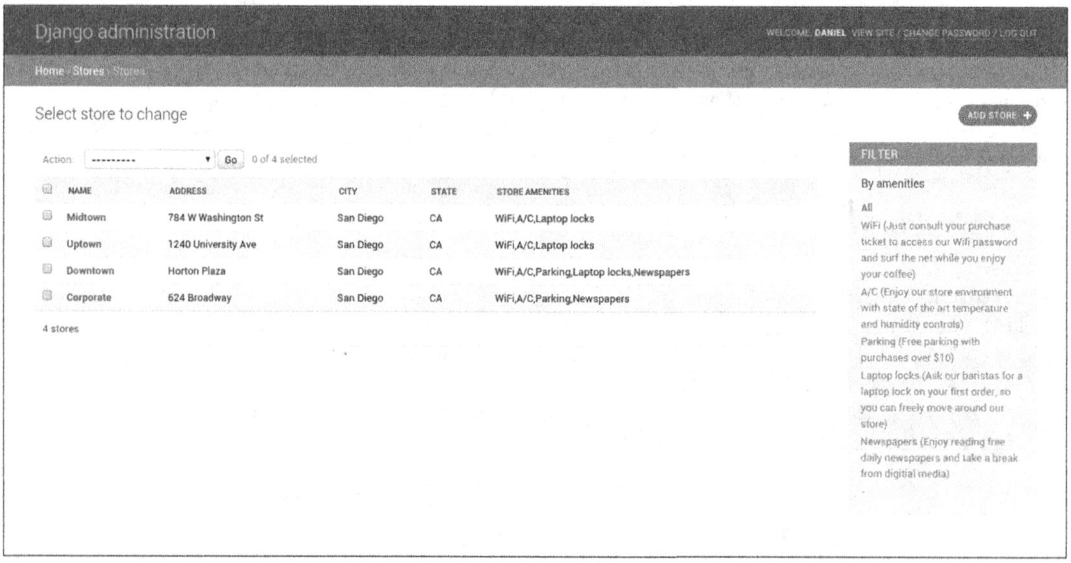

Figure 11-22. *Django admin list_filter option with RelatedOnlyFieldListFilter*

In Listing 11-14 notice how the field to generate filters on - in this case `amenities` - is wrapped in its own list along with `admin.RelatedOnlyFieldListFilter`. To understand the difference between the use and absence of `admin.RelatedOnlyFieldListFilter` look at Figures 11-21 and 11-22. In Figure 11-21 notice the last filter on the list is 'Massage Chairs' - an `Amenity` record - and yet no `Store` record on the main list has this Amenity. To eliminate this inapplicable filter from the `Store` record list you can use `admin.RelatedOnlyFieldListFilter` and get the results from Figure 11-22, which only show `Amenity` filters related to `Store` records.

Finally, another option that's applicable to Django admin classes with model relationships is the `list_select_related`. The `list_select_related` option functions just like the `list_select_related` option used in queries involving relationships, to reduce the amount of database queries that involve relationships (e.g., it creates a single complex query, instead of later needing to issue multiple queries for each relationships).The `list_select_related` option can accept a Boolean or list value. By default, the `list_select_related` option receives a `False` value (i.e., it's not used). Under the hood, the `list_select_related` option uses the same `select_related()` model method to retrieve related records, described in Chapter 8.

If `list_select_related = True` then `select_related()` is always used. For finer-grained control of `list_select_related` you can specify a list, noting that an empty list prevents Django from calling `select_related()` at all and any other list values are passed directly to `select_related()` as parameters.

Django admin Create, Update, Delete Record Options

Besides Django admin read record options, primarily used to modify the main page of every model in the Django admin (i.e., where the list of records for each model is presented), there are other Django admin pages used to create, update and delete Django model records that also support a series of options.

When you click on the 'Add <model name>' button on the top right of every Django admin page that presents model records, you're taken to a form-like page where you can provide values for a new record – illustrated in Figure 11-23 – and when you click on a record in a Django admin record list, you're also taken to a form-like page where you can edit or delete field values for the record – illustrated in Figure 11-24.

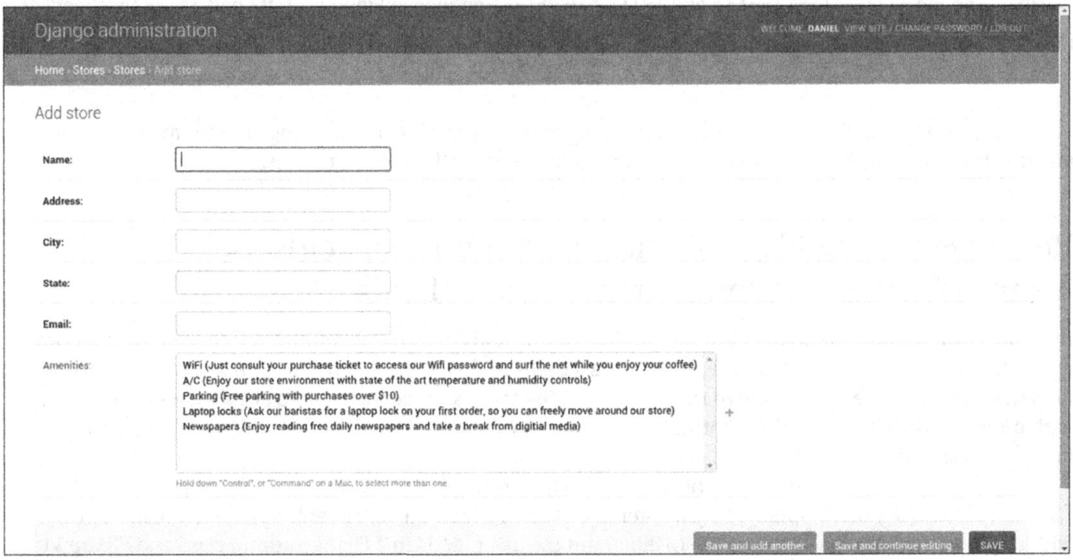

Figure 11-23. *Django admin page to create model record*

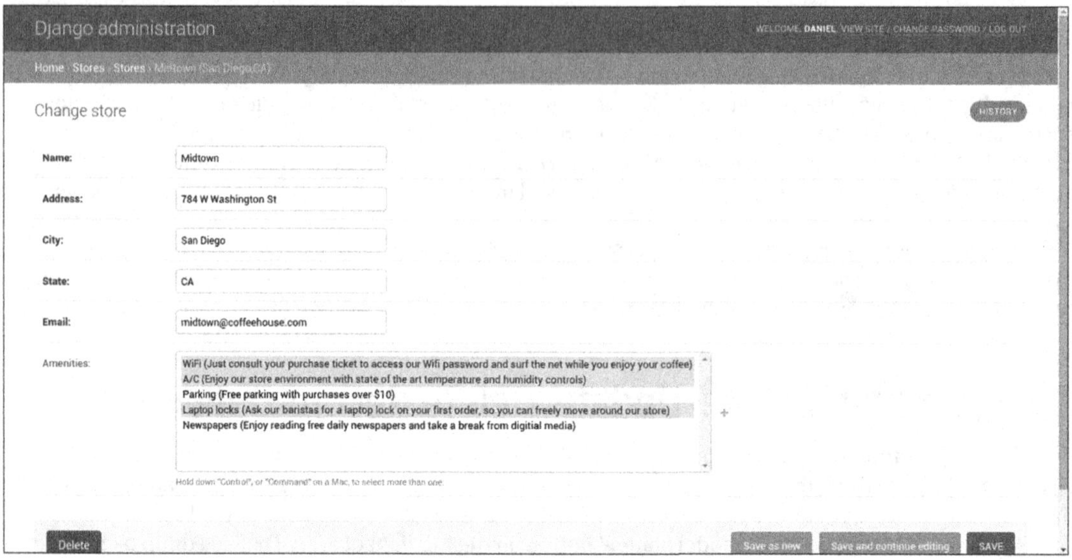

Figure 11-24. *Django admin page to edit or delete model record*

■ **Tip** See the `filter_horizontal` and `filter_vertical` options in Figures 11-37 and 11-38 for friendlier UIs for the amenities field shown in Figures 11-23 and 11-24.

In the next subsections I'll describe the various options available in the Django admin to create, update, and delete records, which is worth noting, is the same page for all three operations.

Record Forms: fields, readonly_fields, exclude, fieldsets, formfield_overrides, form, prepopulated_fields

By default, the Django admin generates a form for all the fields in a Django model you're working on. For example, in Figures 11-23 and 11-24 you can see six fields in the Django admin form that correspond to six field definitions for the `Store` Django model. Behind the scenes, since the Django admin uses forms filled with model records, Django admin forms operate and have options that are almost identical to the model forms described in Chapter 9.

The first option available to alter the amount of Django admin form fields vs. its backing model is the `fields` option. The `fields` option lets you alter the order in which the form fields appear or create a form with a subset of model fields. Listing 11-15 illustrates the use `fields` in a Django admin class and Figure 11-25 illustrates the UI generated by Listing 11-15.

Listing 11-15. Django admin fields option for Django admin forms

```
class StoreAdmin(admin.ModelAdmin):
      fields = ['address','city','state','email']

admin.site.register(Store, StoreAdmin)
```

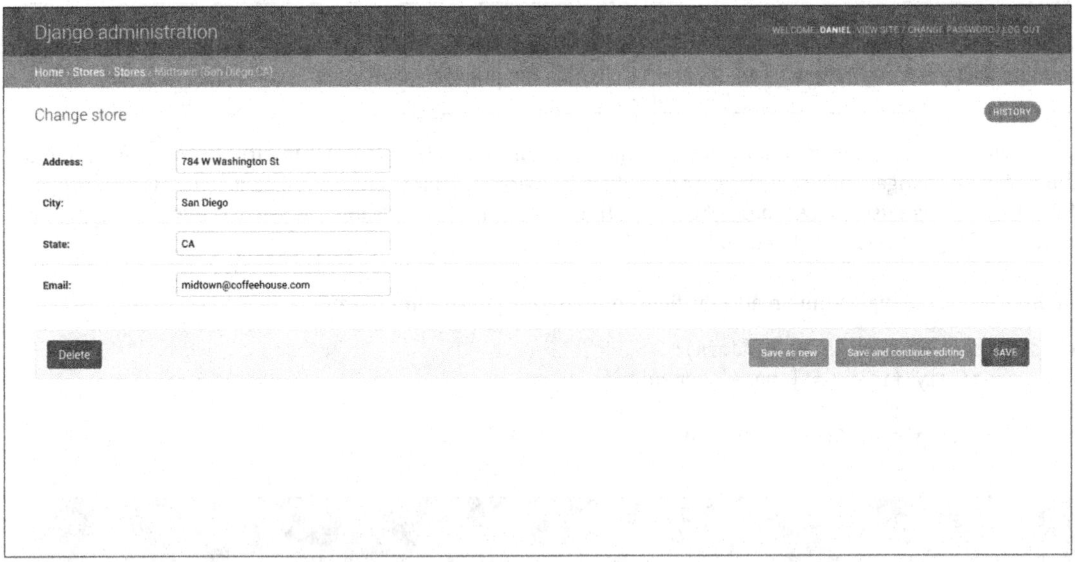

***Figure 11-25.** Django admin fields option for Django admin forms*

In Listing 11-15 you can see the `fields` option contains four fields vs. six fields in the original backing `Store` Django model; and in Figure 11-25 you can confirm that the Django admin form is generated with just four fields.

Another variation of the same `fields` option for Django admin forms is combining multiple form fields into the same UI line. This is easily achieved by nesting fields in their own tuple. For example, if you define `fields = ['address',('city','state'),'email']`, the `city` and `state` forms fields are generated on the same line in the form, as illustrated in Figure 11-26.

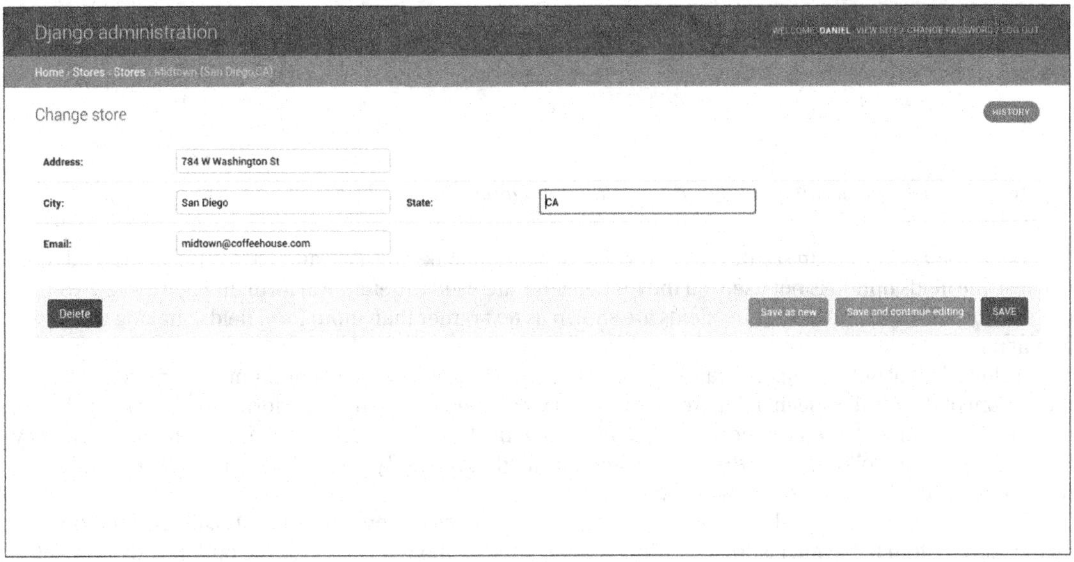

***Figure 11-26.** Django admin fields option with wrapped fields for Django admin forms*

■ **Tip** The list_editable option creates an inline form to edit records without the need to enter a dedicated form page like the one in Figures 11-25 and 11-26. See the previous section on 'Record links and inline edit'.

As helpful as the `fields` options is, on other occasions it can be necessary to display a form field but not allow it to be changed, because omitting a field altogether may lead to confusion. To disallow the editing of a form field you can use the `readonly_fields` option. Listing 11-16 illustrates the use of the `readonly_fields` option and Figure 11-27 its UI layout.

Listing 11-16. Django admin readonly_fields option for Django admin forms

```
class StoreAdmin(admin.ModelAdmin):
    readonly_fields = ['name','amenities']

admin.site.register(Store, StoreAdmin)
```

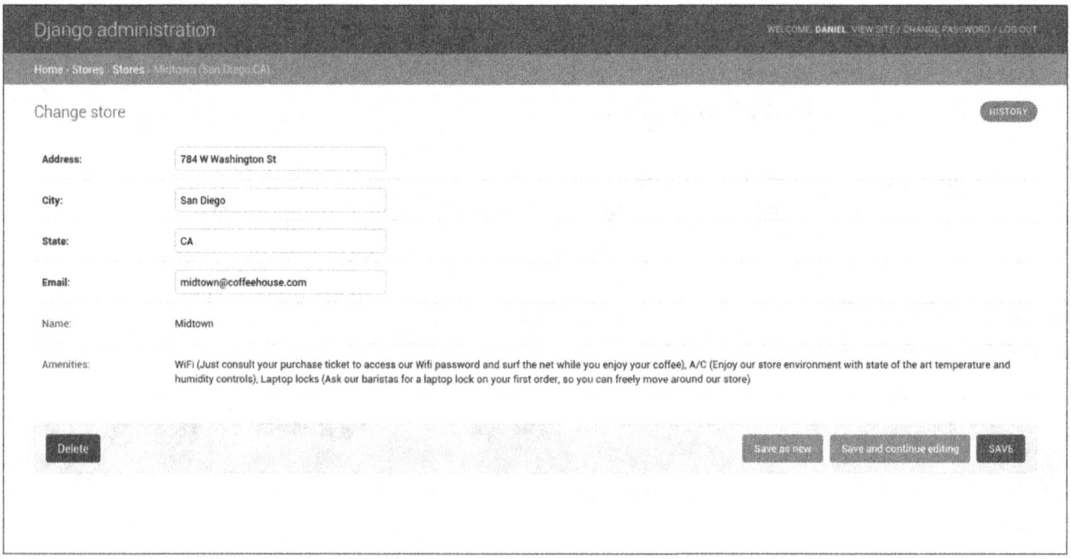

Figure 11-27. *Django admin readonly_fields option for Django admin forms*

In Listing 11-16 you can see the `readonly_fields` option make the `name` and `amenities` fields read only. Because the fields option is not used, all the model fields are used to generate a form. In Figure 11-27 you can see how the `name` and `amenities` fields are shown as text rather than input form fields, making them uneditable.

A side effect of only using the `readonly_fields` option is that these field definitions are placed at the bottom of the form, as seen in Figure 11-27. If you want to maintain the same form field order as the original Django model, then you need to explicitly define the form fields using the `fields` option, in this way the form field order follows the `fields` option and any field in `readonly_field` is displayed as read only, respecting the field position set in the `fields` option.

Besides supporting model field names, the `readonly_fields` option also supports callable methods to further add custom behavior. Listing 11-17 illustrates the use of the `readonly_fields` option with a callable and Figure 11-28 the UI layout.

Listing 11-17. Django admin readonly_fields option with callable for Django admin forms

```
from django.utils.safestring import mark_safe

class StoreAdmin(admin.ModelAdmin):
    fields = ['name','address',('city','state'),'email','custom_amenities_display']
    readonly_fields = ['name','custom_amenities_display']
    def custom_amenities_display(self, obj):
        return mark_safe("Amenities can only be modified by special request, please contact
        the store manager at %s to create a request" % (obj.email,obj.email))
    custom_amenities_display.short_description = "Amenities"

admin.site.register(Store, StoreAdmin)
```

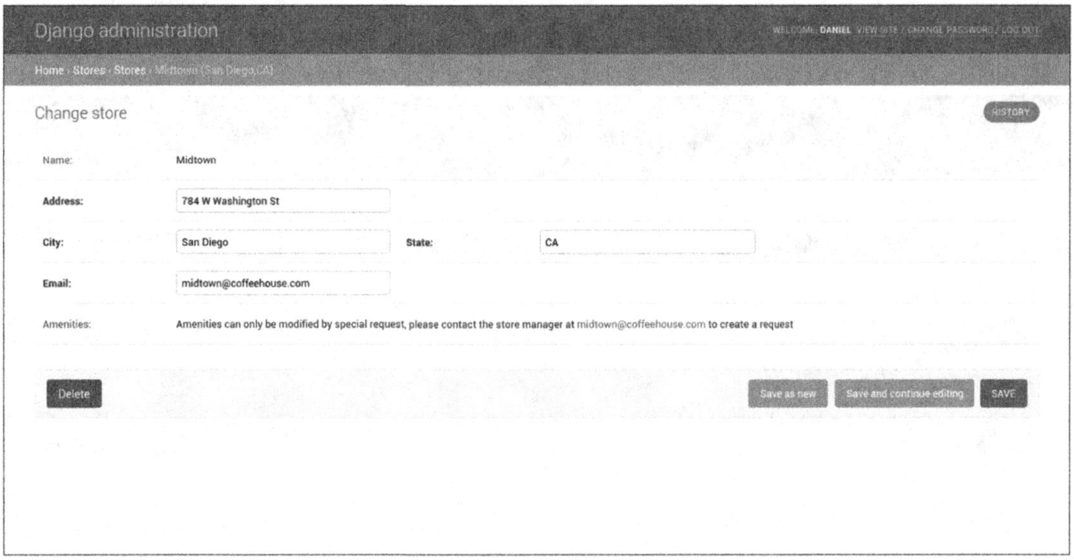

Figure 11-28. *Django admin readonly_fields option for Django admin forms*

In Listing 11-17 you can see the `readonly_fields` option uses the `custom_amenities_display` callable to create a custom field. In Figure 11-28 toward the bottom, you can see this new custom field - in place of the original `amenities` field - which shows a friendlier message than Figure 11-27 and is also uneditable.

The `exclude` option for forms in Django admin classes is complementary to the `fields` option. Whereas the `fields` option requires it to explicitly create of list of fields to include in a Django admin form, and the `exclude` offers the inverse behavior, requiring it to explicitly list fields that shouldn't be part of a Django admin form. For example, for a Django model with the fields a,b,c the Django admin class fields = ('a','b') option is equivalent to the exclude = ('c') option (i.e., both options generate the same Django admin form).

The `fieldsets` option for Django admin classes provides greater control over the layout of pages used to create and edit records in the Django admin. Unlike the `fields` option that can alter the order of form fields or even nest form fields on the same line - as illustrated in Figure 11-26 - the `fieldsets` option works with the fields option to divide a page into sets. Listing 11-18 illustrates the use of the `fieldsets` option and Figures 11-29 and 11-30 the corresponding layout.

Listing 11-18. Django admin fieldsets option for Django admin forms

```
from django.utils.safestring import mark_safe

class StoreAdmin(admin.ModelAdmin):
    fieldsets = [
        ['Store general information', {
            'fields': ['name', 'email']
        }],
        ['Store location options', {
            'classes': ['collapse'],
            'fields': ['address',('city', 'state')],
        }],
    ]

admin.site.register(Store, StoreAdmin)
```

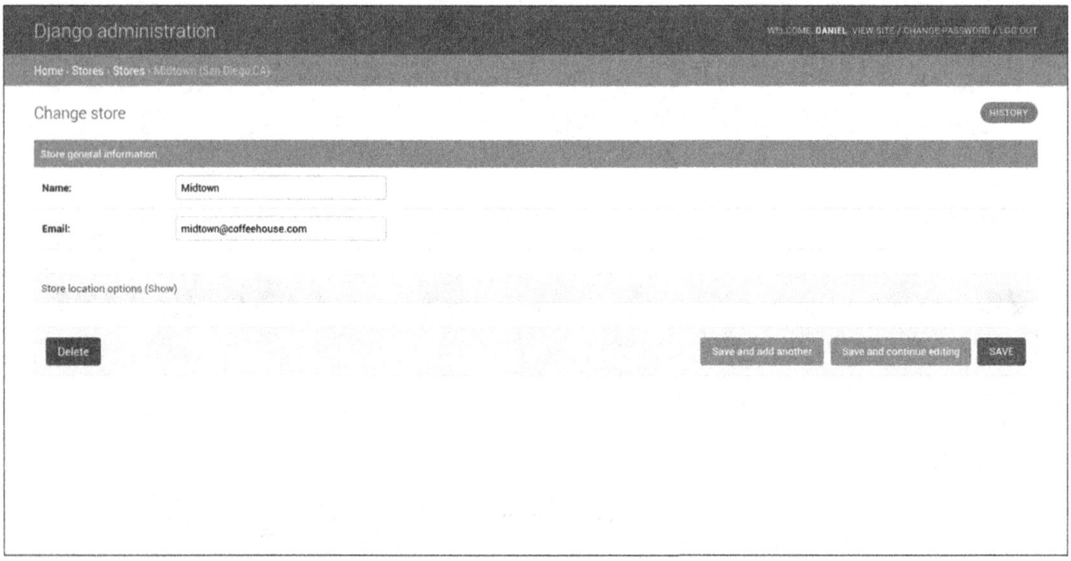

Figure 11-29. *Django admin fieldsets option for Django admin forms*

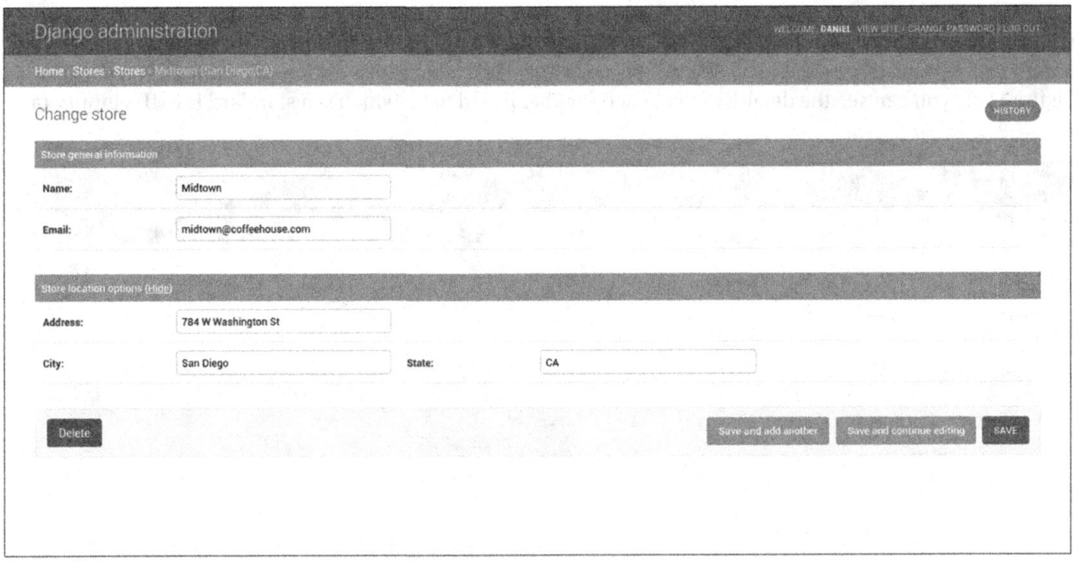

Figure 11-30. *Django admin fieldsets option for Django admin forms (collapsed)*

In Listing 11-18 you can see the `fieldsets` options accepts a list value composed of two lists, where each list represents a section of the Django admin page as illustrated in Figures 11-29 and 11-30. Each of the internal lists is made up by a first argument that represents the title or header of the section and a second argument that's a dictionary. This last dictionary itself contains values assigned to a field's key - which functions just like the `fields` option described previously - and a `classes` key that gives the section certain behaviors through CSS classes. In this case, you can see the second section in Listing 11-18 indicates `'classes': ['collapse']`, which tells Django to make the section collapsible, in Figures 11-29 and 11-30 you can appreciate this collapsed and un-collapsed behavior.

In addition to the `collapse` option used in the `classes` key in `fieldsets`, another helpful CSS class option is `wide`, which adds more horizontal space between fields. Note that it's valid to add any number of CSS classes to the `classes` key, either CSS classes included with the Django admin (i.e., `collapse` and `wide`) or even custom CSS classes.

The `formfield_overrides` option provides a way to override the default form widgets associated with a Django model field in a Django admin form. By default, all Django model fields have a given widget assigned to them for the purpose of generating a form – a topic discussed in Chapter 9, specifically Table 9-1. However, if you feel the default widget for a given model field is inadequate for the Django admin, you can use the `formfield_overrides` option as illustrated in Listing 11-19.

Listing 11-19. Django admin formfield_overrides option for Django admin forms

```
from django.contrib import admin
from coffeehouse.items.models import Menu

class MenuAdmin(admin.ModelAdmin):
    formfield_overrides = {
        models.CharField: {'widget': forms.Textarea}
    }

admin.site.register(Menu, MenuAdmin)
```

The formfield_overrides option in Listing 11-19 tells the Django admin to use the forms.Textarea widget - which generates a standard HTML <textarea> tag - for all model fields that use the CharField. In Figure 11-32 you can see the effects of applying the formfield_overrides option of Listing 11-19, whereas in Figure 11-31 you can see the default widget used for CharField field, which is a standard HTML <input> tag.

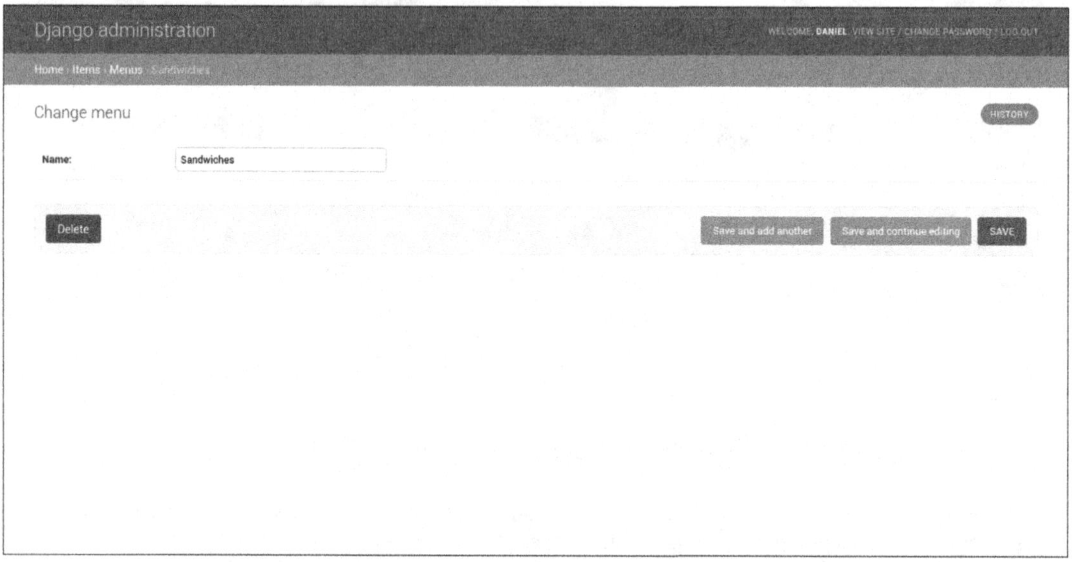

***Figure 11-31.** Django admin default CharField field display in Django admin form*

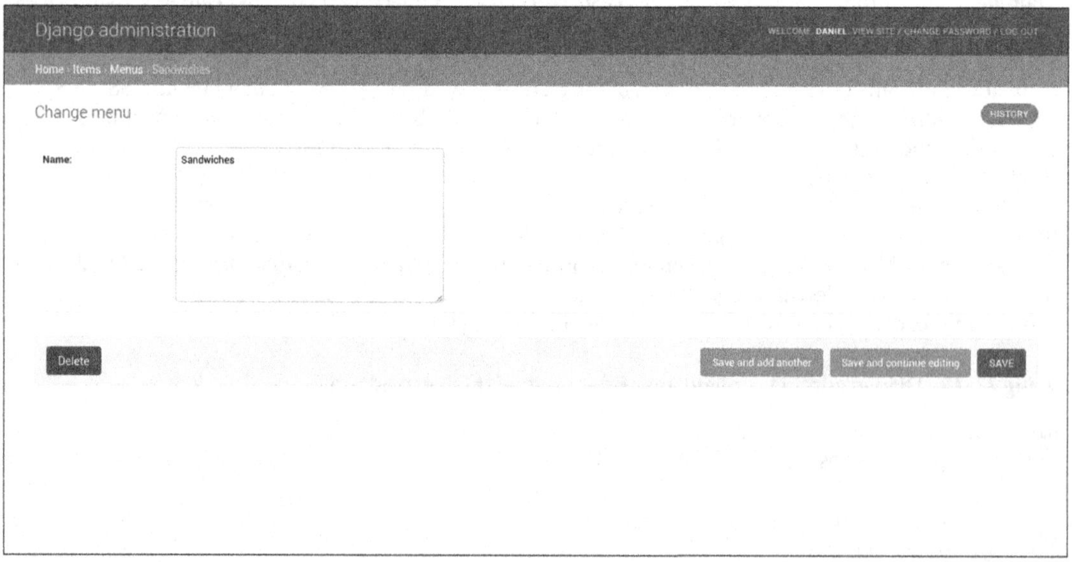

***Figure 11-32.** Django admin custom CharField field display in Django admin form using formfield_overrides*

While all the previous options allow you to tweak parts of a form used in the Django admin, sometimes it's necessary to create a form from scratch for the Django admin instead of tweaking the underlying form generated by the Django model (e.g., if you require custom validation for the Django admin form). To specify a custom form for a Django admin class you can use the `form` option.

Finally, one more option associated with Django admin forms that's specific to models that require slug field values is `prepopulated_fields`. If you're unfamiliar with the term 'slug', in the simplest terms a slug field value is a machine-friendly representation of a string, for example, uppercase letters are converted to lowercase and special characters like spaces are converted to dashes. Through the `prepopulated_fields` option, you can tell Django that while a user types in a value for a given field in a Django admin form, it automatically fills another field in the form with the slug representation of the first.

For example, for the `prepopulated_fields = {'address': ['city','state']}` option, if a user types in a value of San Diego into the city form field and CA in state, Django fills the `address` form field with the value of `san-diego-ca`. It's worth mentioning this functionality is achieved through JavaScript integrated into the Django admin and also that the `prepopulated_fields` option doesn't accept `DateTimeField`, `ForeignKey`, or `ManyToManyField` fields as backing model data types.

Actions, Links, and Positions: save_on_top, save_as(Clone records), save_as_continue and view_on_site

At the bottom of each form page to create, update, and delete Django model records are all the buttons to perform actions on the page: 'Delete', 'Save and add another', 'Save and continue editing', and 'Save', all of which are illustrated in Figure 11-33. If a form is too large it can be difficult to reach these action buttons without scrolling down, so to solve this scenario Django admin classes support the `save_on_top` option, which creates the same action buttons at the top of the page as illustrated in Figure 11-34. Note that to generate the layout in Figure 11-34 you use `save_on_top = True`.

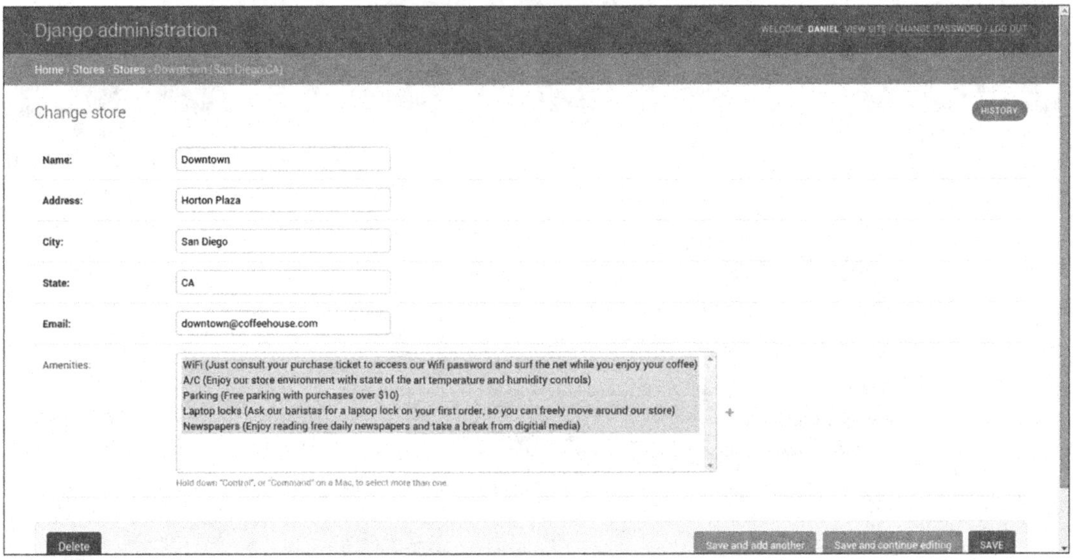

***Figure 11-33.** Django admin standard action button on form page*

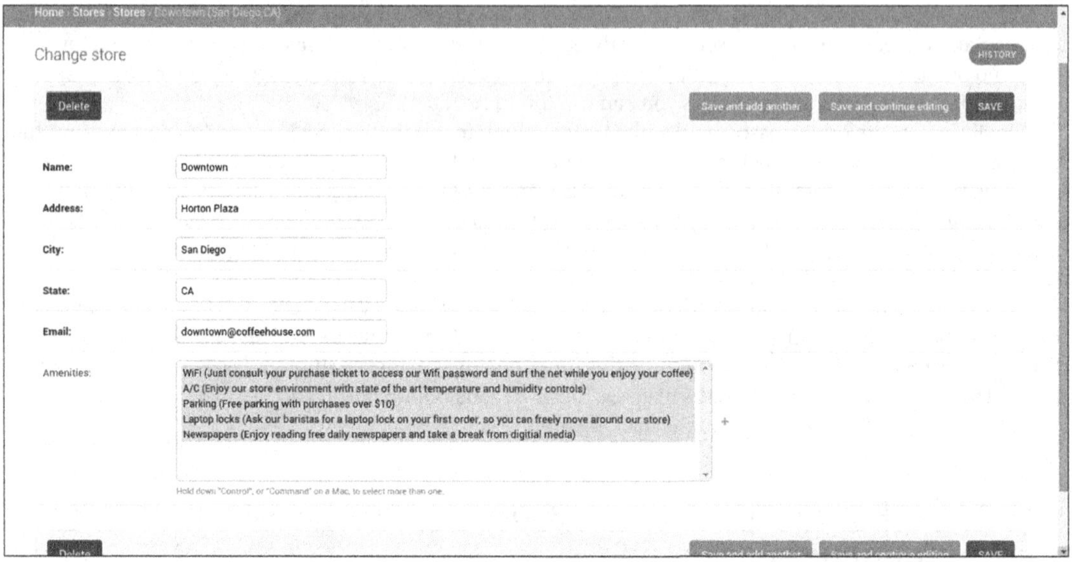

Figure 11-34. *Django admin save_on_top option on form page*

Sometimes the need can arise to generate an identical or almost identical record from a preexisting record in the Django admin. Because copy-pasting values from one form to another in the Django admin can be a time-consuming and error-prone process, Django admin classes also support the `save_as` option to clone preexisting model records. If you set the `save_as = True` option on a Django admin class, Django replaces the 'Save and add another' button with the 'Save as new' button, as illustrated in Figure 11-35.

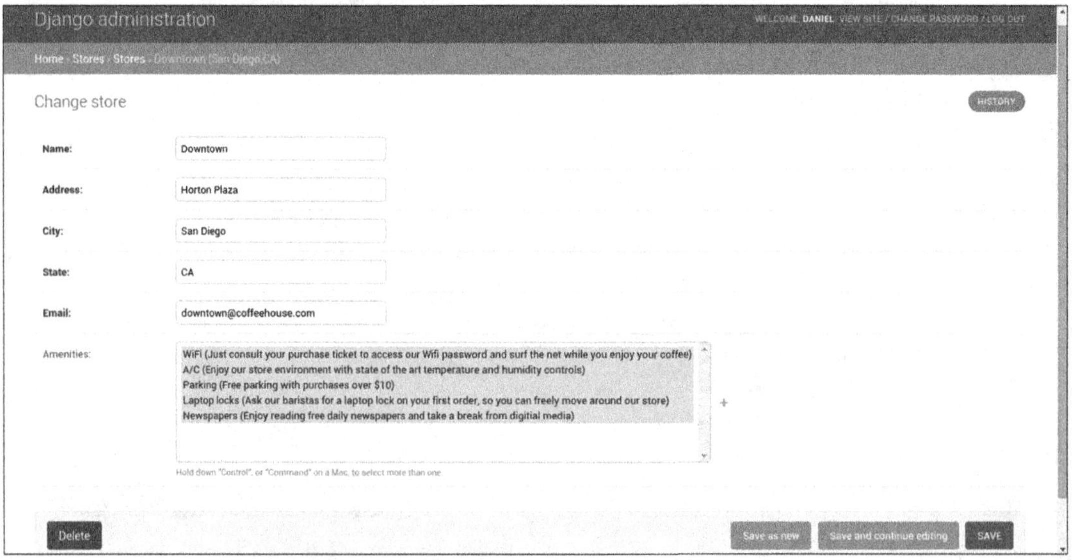

Figure 11-35. *Django admin save_as (Clone) option on form page*

If you click on the 'Save as new' button illustrated in Figure 11-35, Django saves an identical record - effectively cloning the record you see on screen - using a different `id` value to differentiate between the two. Note that if the underlying Django model prohibits this action (e.g., fields must be unique), the operation does not take place and an error is thrown indicating the cause.

When you use the `save_as = True` option and perform the action of cloning a record (i.e., clicking on the 'Save as new' button), the Django admin keeps you on the form of the newly cloned record in case you want to change it further. You can use the `save_as_continue = False` option, to tell the Django admin to redirect you to the main model list page after cloning a record.

Django model classes support an instance method called `get_absolute_url()` that makes it possible to resolve the public URL of a record via a Django model's fields (e.g., the URLs `/store/1/`, `/store/2/`, `/store/3/` fit a pattern, where each number represents a Store `id` value, in which case the `get_absolute_url()` method for the `Store` model would return `/store/<store_record_id>`. In the Django admin, the `get_absolute_url()` method is tied directly to a link that aids in viewing the record at its public URL destination, and Figure 11-36 illustrates this link in the top right corner.

***Figure 11-36.** Django admin 'View on site' button due to get_absolute_url() Django model method*

In Figure 11-36, the 'View on site' button in the top right generates a link based on the Django model's `get_absolute_url()` method, as well as the current record's value defined in this last method. In this manner, in a single click you're able to visualize the record you're editing in the Django admin at its public URL destination. If you wish to disable this button you can add the `view_on_site = False` option to the Django admin class. Note that if the underlying Django model class does not define the `get_absolute_url()` method, no button is displayed, irrespective of the `view_on_site` value.

Relationships: filter_horizontal, filter_vertical, radio_fields, raw_id_fields, inlines

Django model relationships tasks related to create, update, and delete operations, also have certain behaviors in the context of Django admin classes that are worth describing separately.

When you use a `ManyToManyField` field on a Django model and access it in the Django admin, Django generates HTML <select>/<option> form tags to choose the values for the `ManyToManyField` field - as illustrated at the bottom of Figures 11-23 and 11-24. However, because this type of selection method can be cumbersome for large lists, the Django admin offers the `filter_horizontal` and `filter_vertical` options to generate separate panels to make value selection easier. Figure 11-37 illustrates the layout of the `filter_horizontal` option and Figure 11-38 illustrates the layout of `filter_vertical` option.

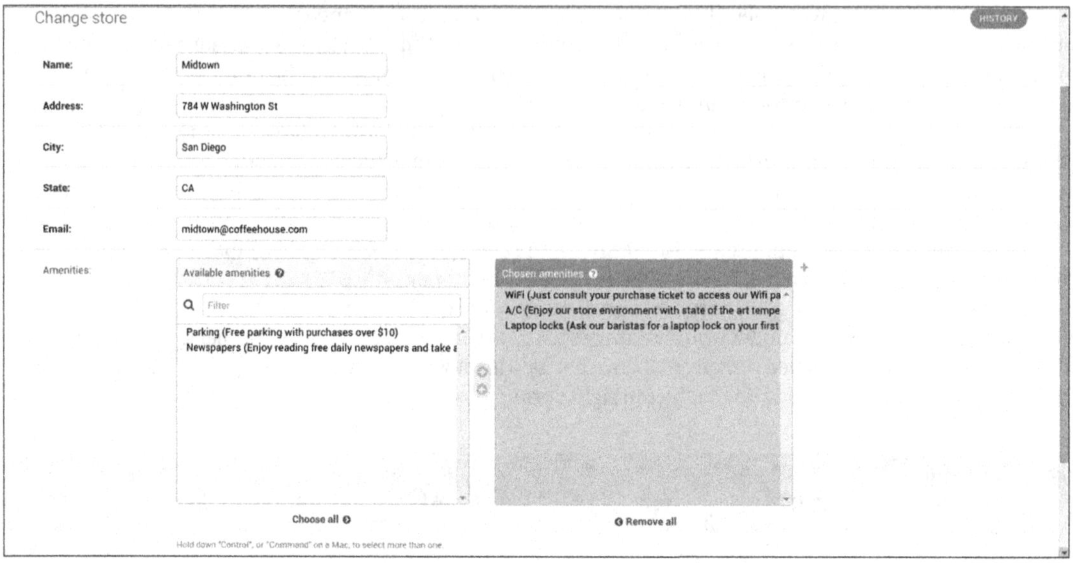

***Figure 11-37.** Django admin filter_horizontal option for ManyToManyField*

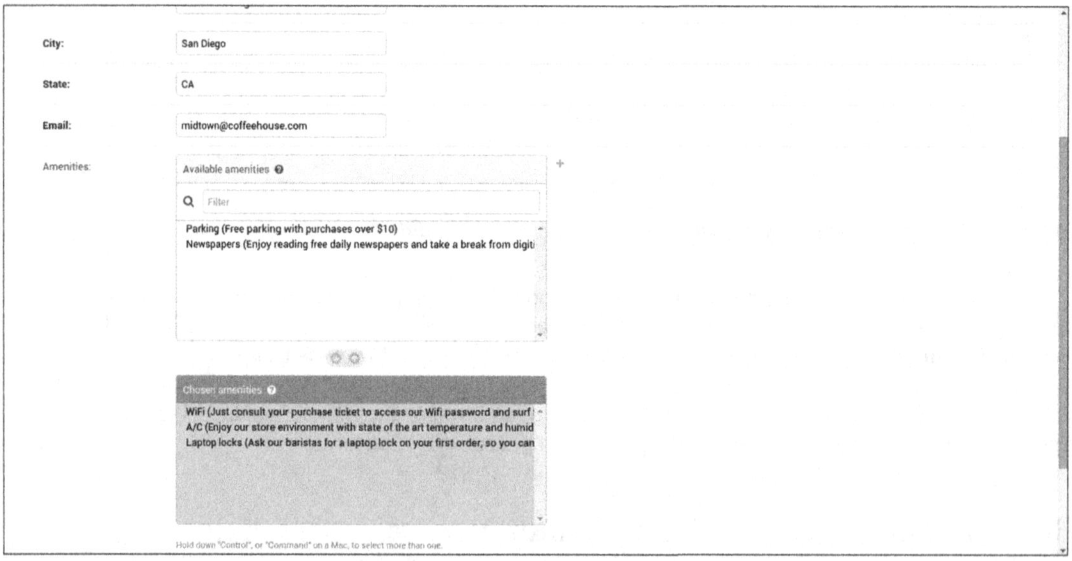

***Figure 11-38.** Django admin filter_vertical option for ManyToManyField*

In Figures 11-37 and 11-38 you can see there are two panels to select and unselect values for a given `ManyToManyField`, with the only difference being `filter_horizontal` stacks the panels horizontally - in Figure 11-37 - and `filter_vertical` stacks the panels vertically - in Figure 11-38.

Assuming the `ManyToManyField` field is named `amenities`, to achieve the layout in Figure 11-37 you would declare `filter_horizontal = ['amenities']` and to achieve the layout in Figure 11-38 you would declare `filter_vertical = ['amenities']`.

When you use a `ForeignKey` model data type or the `choices` option in a Django model field and access it in the Django admin, Django also generates HTML <select>/<option> form tags to choose the value for the `ForeignKey` field - as illustrated at the top of Figure 11-39.

Figure 11-39. *Django admin default select list for ForeignKey or choices option*

A Django admin class can change this default layout with the `radio_fields` option to generate a layout with HTML radio buttons. Listing 11-20 illustrates the two alternatives for the `radio_fields` option in a Django admin class and Figures 11-40 and 11-41 the UI layouts.

Listing 11-20. Django admin radio_fields option for ForeignKey field

```
from django.contrib import admin
from coffeehouse.items.models import Item

# Option 1 (Horizontal)

class ItemAdmin(admin.ModelAdmin):
    radio_fields = {"menu": admin.HORIZONTAL}

admin.site.register(Item, ItemAdmin)

# Option 2 (Vertical)

class ItemAdmin(admin.ModelAdmin):
    radio_fields = {"menu": admin.VERTICAL}

admin.site.register(Item, ItemAdmin)
```

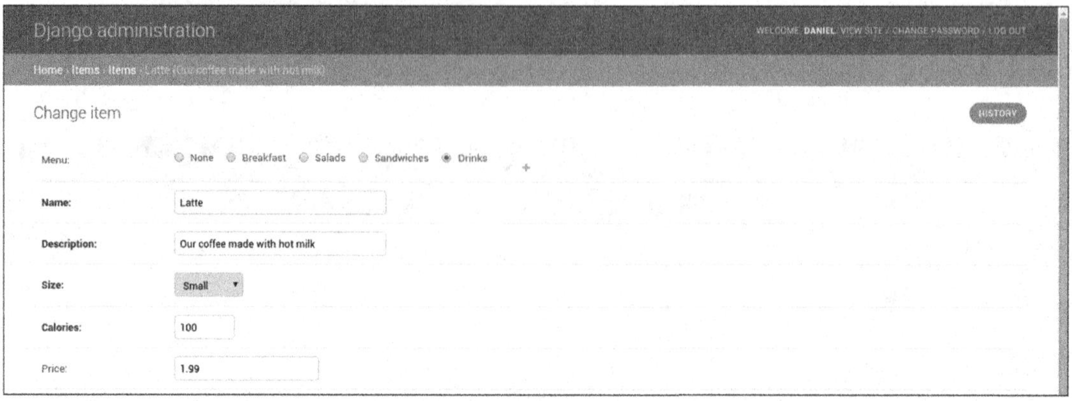

***Figure 11-40.** Django admin horizontal radio_fields option for ForeignKey or choices option*

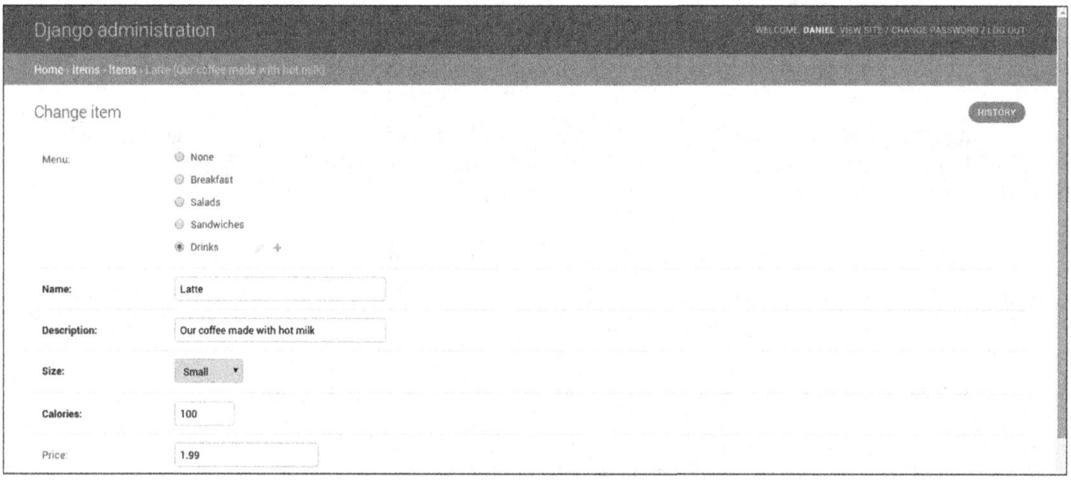

***Figure 11-41.** Django admin vertical radio_fields option for ForeignKey or choices option*

In Listing 11-20 you can see option one defines the `radio_fields` value with the `{"menu": admin.HORIZONTAL}` dictionary, where `menu` represents the `ForeignKey` field or a field with the `choices` option and `admin.HORIZONTAL` is the orientation of the radio fields - this option generates a layout like the one in Figure 11-40. Option two in Listing 11-20 defines the `radio_fields` in a similar way except it uses the `admin.VERTICAL` value to tell the Django admin to generate a vertical layout for the radio fields as illustrated in Figure 11-41.

Another Django admin alternative for `ForeignKey` or `ManyToManyField` fields is the `raw_id_fields` option, which as its name implies relies on the raw `id` field value(s) to assign a `ForeignKey` value or `ManyToManyField` values. Figure 11-42 illustrates how a `raw_id_fields` option looks like in the Django admin.

Figure 11-42. *Django admin raw_id_fields option for ForeignKey or ManyToManyField option*

As you can see in Figure 11-42, the Django admin generates a basic text box where you can assign id values, aided by the adjacent magnifying glass button that allows you to search for and select values. Assuming the ForeignKey or ManyToManyField field is named menu, to achieve the layout in Figure 11-42 you would declare raw_id_fields = ["menu"]. Note that for a ForeignKey field the acceptable value is a single id and for a ManyToManyField field you can also introduce a list of ids separated by commas (i.e., a CSV).

Finally, we come to the Django admin class inlines option, designed for reverse models relationships. When you create or edit a model with a relationship in the Django admin, if this is done on the model with the relationship field definition (i.e., ForeignKey or ManyToManyField), the Django admin displays the related model values inline or adds a '+' button to add new model values, as shown in Figure 11-37 - for ForeignKey menu values - and Figure 11-39 - for ManyToMany amenities values. However, when you attempt to edit or create values on the reverse model relationship (i.e., the model that doesn't have the relationship field) the Django admin only shows the model by itself as shown Figure 11-31. It's possible to edit or create related model values on a reverse model relationship with the inlines option.

The inlines option first requires you to create a Django admin TabularInline or StackedInline class, both of which are subclasses of the InlineModelAdmin class, which is a more specialized version of the standard admin.ModelAdmin class used to create standard Django admin classes. Once you have TabularInline or StackedInline class, you can declare it as part as the value of the inlines option.

Listing 11-21 illustrates two Django admin examples that use a TabularInline and StackedInline class on models that have a one to many and many to many relationship.

Listing 11-21. Django admin inlines option for ForeignKey and ManyToManyField field

```
# admin.py (ForeignKey)
from django.contrib import admin
from coffeehouse.items.models import Item, Menu

class ItemInline(admin.TabularInline):
    model = Item

class MenuAdmin(admin.ModelAdmin):
    list_display = ['name']
    inlines = [
        ItemInline,
    ]
```

```
admin.site.register(Menu, MenuAdmin)

# admin.py (ManyToManyField)
from django.contrib import admin
from coffeehouse.stores.models import Store, Amenity

class StoreInline(admin.StackedInline):
    model = Store.amenities.through

class AmenityAdmin(admin.ModelAdmin):
    inlines = [
        StoreInline,
    ]

admin.site.register(Amenity, AmenityAdmin)
```

The first example in Listing 11-21 illustrates the `ItemInline` class, which inherits its behavior from built-in `TabularInline` class. Because this last class is designed to represent a model in the Django admin, it also declares the `model` field with the `Item` model class. Next, the `MenuAdmin` class is a standard Django admin class designed for the `Menu` model class, but notice it uses the `inlines` option with the `ItemInline` class. Because of this last configuration, when you go to edit or create `Menu` model record in the Django admin, all `Item` model records associated with a given `Menu` model record are displayed inline as illustrated in Figure 11-43.

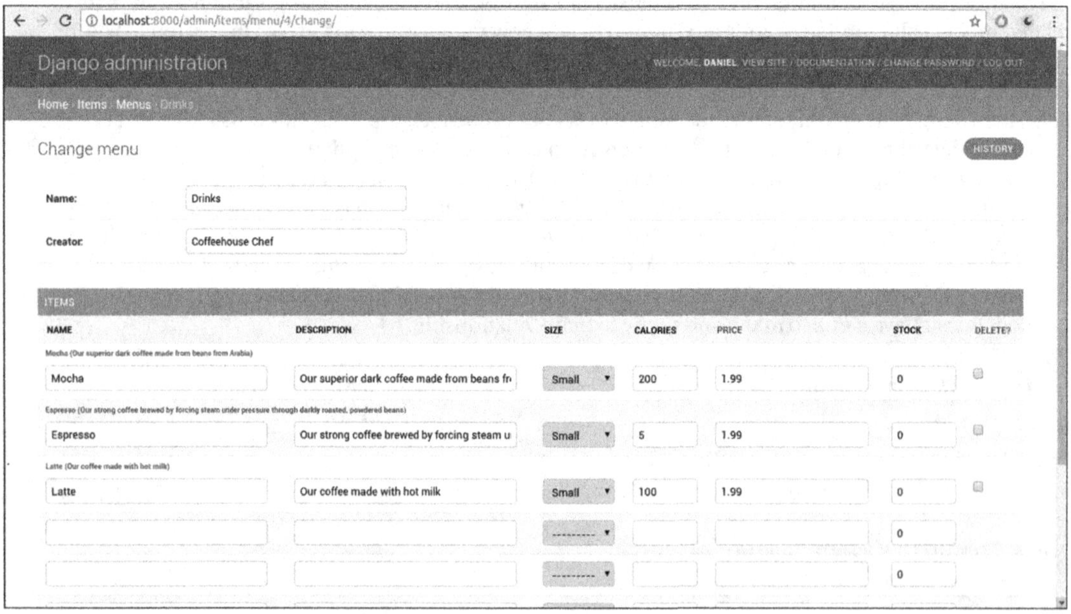

***Figure 11-43.** Django admin inlines option with TabularInline for ForeignKey*

As you can see in Figure 11-43, in addition to the standard Django admin form to edit or create `Menu` records, there's also a formset displaying all `Item` model records for the given `Menu` record; in this case, the formset contains `Item` records that belong to the `Drinks Menu` record. Also notice the form fields for each form in the formset in Figure 11-43 are inlined as tabs, which is a behavior provided by the `TabularInline` class.

The second part of Listing 11-21 illustrates the `StoreInline` class that inherits its behavior from built-in `StackedInline` class. Because this last class is designed to represent a model in the Django admin, it also declares the `model` field with the `Store.amenities.through` model class, this additional model syntax – `amenities.through` – is necessary because the `Store` to `Amenity` model is a many to many relationship. Note the `through` keyword is standard for many to many relationship queries and is described in the earlier Django model chapters.

Next, the `AmenityAdmin` class is a standard Django admin class designed for the `Item` model class, but notice it uses the `inlines` option with the `StoreInline` class. Because of this last configuration, when you go to edit or create an `Amenity` model record in the Django admin, all `Store` model records associated with a given `Amenity` model record are displayed inline as illustrated in Figure 11-44.

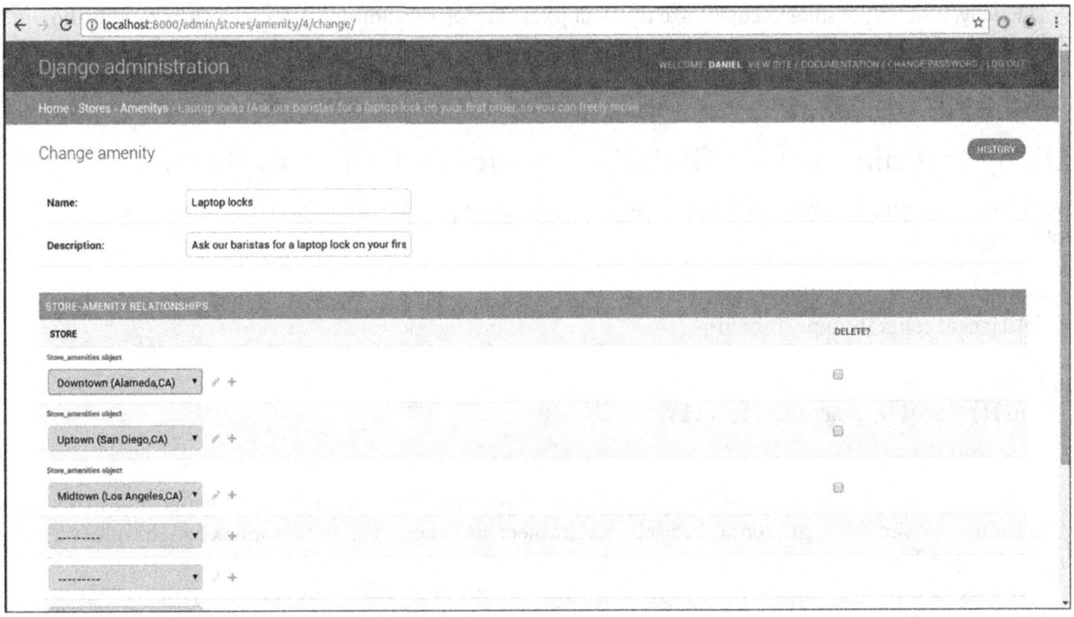

Figure 11-44. *Django admin inlines option with StackedInline for ManyToManyField*

As you can see in Figure 11-44, in addition the standard Django admin form to edit or create `Amenity` records, there's also a formset displaying all `Store` model records for the given `Amenity` record; in this case, the formset contains `Store` records that have the `Amenity Laptop locks` record. Also notice the form fields for each form in the formset in Figure 11-43 are inline stacks, which is a behavior provided by the `StackedInline` class.

■ **Tip** `InlineModelAdmin` classes (i.e., `TabularInline` or `StackedInline`) in addition to the `model` option, also support standard Django admin class – `admin.ModelAdmin` – options described earlier (e.g., `form`, `fields`, `exclude`), as well as standard formset options described in Chapter 6 and model formset options described in Chapter 9 (e.g., `formset`, `extra`, `max_num`, `min_num`).[2]

Django admin Custom Page Layout, Data, and Behaviors

In addition to the Django admin class options described in previous sections, there are multiple ways to customize the layout, data, and behaviors of Django admin pages. You can customize certain global values used across all Django admin pages without the need to modify any Django template. But in addition, it's also possible to customize any template used by a Django admin page - like the log in, log out, password update, display record, and create/update/delete record page - to alter its layout (e.g., modify the default blue CSS skin or component positions in the page).

Finally, it's also possible to customize the data passed to Django admin pages, as well as modify the default behavior run by Django admin pages (e.g., CRUD actions) by means of methods and fields declared as part of a Django admin class.

Django admin Custom Global Values for Default Templates

By default, the Django admin is configured as part of a Django project's `urls.py` file, as shown in the following snippet:

```
from django.conf.urls import url
from django.contrib import admin

urlpatterns = [
    url(r'^admin/', admin.site.urls),
]
```

While `admin.site.urls` - from the `django.contrib` package - lets you set up the Django admin on the `/admin/` url, the same `django.contrib.admin.site` object also allows you to customize certain values used by all Django admin pages.

Listing 11-22 illustrates how to customize several Django admin fields through the `django.contrib.admin.site` object.

Listing 11-22. Django admin django.contrib.admin.site object to customize fields

```
from django.conf.urls import url
from django.contrib import admin

admin.site.site_header = 'Coffeehouse admin'
admin.site.site_title = 'Coffeehouse admin'
admin.site.site_url = 'http://coffeehouse.com/'
admin.site.index_title = 'Coffeehouse administration'
admin.empty_value_display = '**Empty**'
```

[2]`https://docs.djangoproject.com/en/1.11/ref/contrib/admin/#inlinemodeladmin-options`

```
urlpatterns = [
    url(r'^admin/', admin.site.urls),
]
```

■ **Tip** It's also possible to define the custom admin field values in Listing 11-22 inside the `settings.py` file. Simply import `django.contrib.admin` and declare the admin fields to centralize them with other custom configurations in `settings.py`.

As you can see in Listing 11-22, before declaring `admin.site.urls` as a `url` statement, there are a series of declarations on the `admin.site` object that are also part of the `django.contrib` package:

- `admin.site.site_header`.- Defines the title used across all Django admin pages (e.g., in the navy blue header and login page). See Figures 11-45 and 11-46.
- `admin.site.site_title`.- Defines the title used across all Django admin pages, as part of the HTML title. See Figures 11-45 and 11-46.
- `admin.site.site_url`.- Defines the domain (e.g., `coffeehouse.com`) to use as part of the Django admin 'View site' link, to easily access the live site from the Django admin. See Figure 11-45.
- `admin.site.index_title`.- Defines the title of the main Django admin page. See Figure 11-45.
- `admin.empty_value_display`.- Defines the default value to display when a Django admin model value is empty.

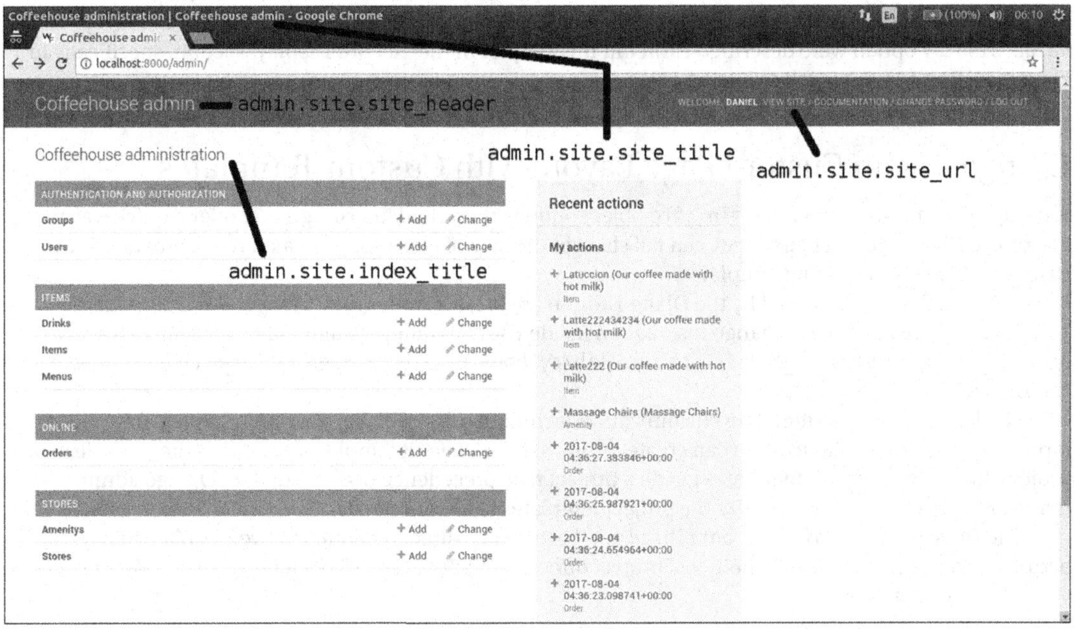

Figure 11-45. *Django admin main index with custom global values*

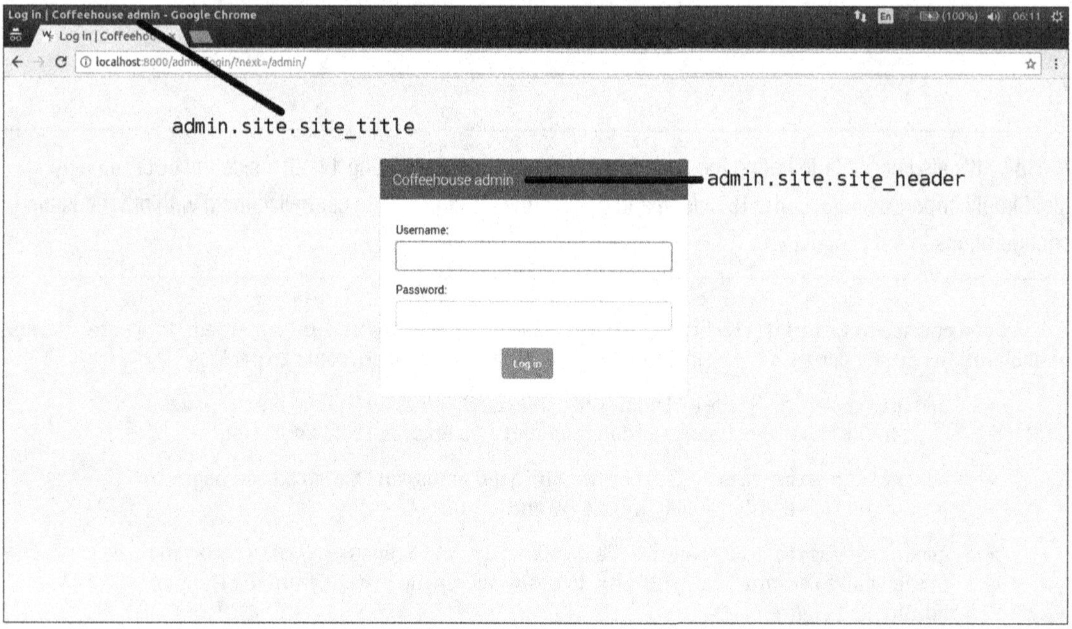

Figure 11-46. *Django admin login page with custom global values*

As you can see in Figures 11-45 and 11-46, with a few simple statements like the ones in Listing 11-22, you can customize the Django admin template content, without the need to interact with templates or HTML.

It's worth noting the `admin.empty_value_display` option described in Listing 11-22 is applied to all Django admin models when a record field contains an empty value. Examples of the `admin.empty_value_display` option were described earlier in this chapter in the 'Record Display' section, specifically in Figures 11-5 and 11-6, as well as Listing 11-5.

Django admin Custom Page Layout with Custom Templates

Although the `django.contrib.admin.site` object options presented in Listing 11-22 offer a quick way to customize Django admin pages, they can fall short in the face of more sophisticated requirements, in which case you must rely on custom templates.

The default templates used by the Django admin are located under the `/django/contrib/admin/templates/` directory of your Django installation inside your operating system's or virtual env Python environment (e.g., `<virtual_env_directory>/lib/python3.5/site-packages/django/contrib/admin/templates/`).

Similar to the Django template customization techniques described in previous chapters (e.g., Django form widgets, Django allauth), you can create a copy of these default templates and place them inside your project. In this manner, the templates inside a project take precedence over the default Django admin templates, where you can customize the project templates to fit your needs.

The Django admin `/django/contrib/admin/templates/` directory contains two template folders: `admin` and `registration`. Copy them to a project directory that's part of a `DIRS` folder of the `TEMPLATES/DIRS` variable in `settings.py`.

■ **Tip** See the book's accompanying source code that includes the layout of all Django admin templates.

All the Django admin templates inherit their behavior from the `admin/base_site.html` template, which itself inherits its behavior from the `admin/base.html` template. If you're unfamiliar with how Django template inheritance works, look over Chapter 3, which describes this topic.

If you open the `admin/base.html` template, you can see the core structure behind every Django admin page, such as the HTML <head> section (e.g., CSS files, meta tags), navigation header, and message notification block, among other things. Therefore, you can modify the `admin/base.html` template to include custom CSS or JavaScript files to alter the 'look & feel' of every Django admin page.

In addition to the `admin/base.html` template, there are many other templates inside the `admin` and `registration` directories whose functions are described in the following list:

- `admin/404.html` and `admin/500.html`.- Defines the layout for Django admin not found and error pages (i.e., HTTP 404 and HTTP 500), respectively.
- `admin/index.html`.- Defines the layout for Django admin index pages, on the main page - shown in Figure 11-45 - as well as those for app indexes showing all models.
- `admin/change_list.html`.- Defines the layout for Django admin list pages, those used to read records, shown from Figures 11-1 to 11-22.
- `admin/change_form.html`.- Defines the layout for Django admin form pages, those used to create, update, and delete records, shown from Figures 11-23 to 11-44.
- `admin/login.html`.- Defines the Django admin login page, shown in Figure 11-46.
- `registration` folder.- Contains templates for the various Django admin page password change actions, as well as the Django admin logout page layout.

■ **Note** Other pages in the `admin` folder not described in this list (e.g., `filter.html`, `object_history.html`) are more granular templates – included as part of the larger templates in this list – which you can customize as necessary.

As you can see, by creating a copy of the Django admin templates and placing them in your project, you can fine-tune the layout of every Django admin page by modifying its backing template. An important modular behavior worth mentioning about the Django admin `index.html`, `change_list.html` and `change_form.html` templates, is how they can be applied to individual Django admin apps or models.

By default, if you provide a custom layout for the `admin/index.html`, `admin/change_list.html` or `admin/change_form.html` templates, these templates are used for all apps and models in the Django admin (i.e., globally). However, sometimes it can be necessary to customize Django admin index pages, list pages, or form pages for only certain apps (e.g., `stores` app) or inclusively an individual model (e.g., `Item` model).

To define a custom Django admin template for all models in an app, you can create a Django admin template and place it under the template path `admin/<app_name>/` (e.g., `admin/stores/change_list.html` to define a `change_list.html` template for all `stores` app models).

To define a custom Django admin template for a single model, you can create a Django admin template and place it under the template path `admin/<app_name>/<model>/` (e.g., `admin/items/item/change_list.html` to define a `change_list.html` template to use on the `Item` model of the `items` app).

■ **Note** Only the templates admin/index.html-admin/app_index.html, change_form.html, change_list.html, delete_confirmation.html, object_history.html, and popup_response.html can be customized on a per app and per model basis.

Django admin Custom Static Resources

If you customize the Django admin admin/base.html template in your project with custom CSS or JavaScript files, these static resources take effect on every Django admin page. While this can be a desired effect in certain circumstances, in other cases, it can be necessary to only apply custom static resources to certain Django admin pages.

Django admin classes support the Media class to define both CSS and JavaScript files and include them on all pages associated with a given Django admin class. The advantage of using the Media class on a Django admin class is that you don't need to deal with templates or HTML markup, with the Django admin automatically loading the static resources as part of every admin page linked to an admin class. Listing 11-23 illustrates a Django admin class that makes use of the Media class.

Listing 11-23. Django admin class with Media class to define custom static resources

```
from django.contrib import admin
from coffeehouse.items.models Item

class ItemAdmin(admin.ModelAdmin):
      list_per_page = 5
      class Media:
            css = {
                "screen": ("css/items/items.css",)
            }
            js = ("js/items/items.js",)

admin.site.register(Item, ItemAdmin)
```

As you can see in Listing 11-23, the Media class supports the css and js fields to declare both CSS and JavaScript static files, respectively. In the case of css, Listing 11-23 declares a dictionary, where the key corresponds to the CSS media type and the value is a tuple with a CSS file. For the case of js, Listing 11-23 declares a tuple pointing to a JavaScript file. All files declared as part of a Media class are automatically searched for in Django's static file directory paths - as described in Chapter 5.

The final outcome of Listing 11-23 is that all Django admin pages associated with the ItemAdmin admin class (e.g., index.html, change_list.html, change_form.html) will include an additional CSS import statement (e.g., <link href="/static/css/items/items.css" type="text/css" media="screen" rel="stylesheet" />), as well as an additional JavaScript import statement (e.g., <script type="text/javascript" src="/static/js/items/items.js"></script>).

It's worth pointing out that while you can include any third-party CSS or JavaScript library in a Django admin page (e.g., Bootstrap, D3), Django admin pages already include the popular jQuery 2.2 library under the django.jQuery namespace to fulfill certain functionalities. The Django admin uses a jQuery namespace, to let you import any other jQuery library version in Django admin pages without fear of conflict. If you want to leverage the included Django admin jQuery library for your own custom JavaScript, you must wrap your JavaScript logic in this namespace, as illustrated in the following snippet:

```
(function($) {
    // Custom JavaScript logic leveraging the Django admin built-in jQuery libray
    $(document).ready(function() {
       $('.deletelink').on('click',function() {
            if( !confirm('Are you sure you want to delete this record ?')) {
              return false;
           }
       });
    });
})(django.jQuery); // <-- Note wrapping namespace
```

As you can see in this last snippet, by wrapping your custom JavaScript logic in the `django.jQuery` namespace, it gains access to the Django admin built-in jQuery library (i.e., the custom JavaScript logic gains access to the jQuery $ scope).

GRAPPELLI PROJECT – AN OUT-OF-BOX DJANGO ADMIN SUPPLEMENT

If you want try a different 'look & feel' for the Django admin, without having to write custom templates or supporting CSS & JavaScript files, there are various Django apps designed for this purpose.

One of the most popular apps is the 'Grappelli Project'.[3] Grappelli uses the 'Compass' CSS authoring Framework to include additional Django admin features like: auto-complete, inline sortable 'drag & drop' and support for jQuery plug-ins, among other things.

Django admin Custom Data and Behaviors with admin Class Fields and Methods

Although the modification of Django admin templates allows you to generate any type of Django admin page layout, it can still fall short for cases where you need to include custom data in Django admin pages (e.g., add data from another model for reference) or override the default CRUD behaviors of Django admin pages (e.g., perform a custom audit trail for delete actions).

Django admin classes like the ones you've written in this chapter since Listing 11-1, rely on over two dozen fields - all of which you explored in the previous sections in this chapter as Django admin read options and create/update/delete options - and over three dozen methods[4] to define a Django admin page's default data and behaviors.

In a very similar way to how you can customize the default behaviors and data used by Django class-based views - described in Chapter 9 - Django admin classes can also define their own custom fields and methods to override their default data and behaviors.

The bulk of this chapter already covered all the Django admin class fields to customize Django admin page behaviors, so I won't readdress them once again. However, I will provide examples of the most common Django admin class methods to illustrate how to add custom data and override other default behaviors in Django admin pages.

[3]http://grappelliproject.com/
[4]https://docs.djangoproject.com/en/1.11/ref/contrib/admin/#adminsite-methods

Listing 11-24 illustrates a Django admin class that uses a custom implementation of the changelist_view() method - which adds custom data to access in the underlying Django admin change_list.html template - as well as a custom implementation of the delete_view() method - to execute custom logic when a delete action is taken on a Django admin class.

Listing 11-24. Django admin class with custom changelist_view() and delete_view() methods

```
from coffeehouse.stores.models import Store

class StoreAdmin(admin.ModelAdmin):
    search_fields = ['city','state']
    def changelist_view(self, request, extra_context=None):
        # Add extra context data to pass to change list template
        extra_context = extra_context or {}
        extra_context['my_store_data'] = {'onsale':['Item 1','Item 2']}
        # Execute default logic from parent class changelist_view()
        return super(StoreAdmin, self).changelist_view(
            request, extra_context=extra_context
        )
    def delete_view(self, request, object_id, extra_context=None):
        # Add custom audit logic here
        #
        # Execute default logic from parent class delete_view()
        return super(StoreAdmin, self).delete_view(
            request, object_id, extra_context=extra_context
        )

admin.site.register(Store, StoreAdmin)
```

As you can in Listing 11-24, both the changelist_view() and delete_view() methods are declared inline with the Django admin search_fields option you learned earlier. In this case, the changelist_view() method in Listing 11-24 is triggered whenever you visit the list view page of the Store model in the Django admin (e.g., illustrated in Figure 11-10). Notice the changelist_view() method adds a custom value to the extra_context variable, which is then returned as part of the response, in this case it's a hard-coded value, but you can equally add any type of data like a model query or third-party API call to pass to the Django admin page. Because of this last workflow, the list view page of the Store model (i.e., the change_list.html template) can gain access to custom data to display as part page.

The delete_view() method in Listing 11-24 is triggered whenever you delete a Store model in the Django admin. In this case, the delete_view() method in Listing 11-24 simply triggers the default action of deleting a record by calling the parent class's delete_view() method, but you can see how it's possible to execute custom logic (e.g., create an audit trail) whenever a delete action is performed on a Store model in the Django admin.

As I've already mentioned, Django admin classes rely on over three dozen methods to implement their default behavior, all of which you can customize to suit your requirements. Given the amount of custom variations that this amount of methods can generate, you can use the example in Listing 11-24 as a guide and consult the footnote in the previous page for other methods you can customize in Django admin classes.

Django admin CRUD Permissions

By default, the Django admin allows access to users with superuser and staff permissions - in case you've never heard of the terms Django superuser, Django staff, or Django permissions, see the previous chapter that describes Django user management.

A Django superuser, as its name implies, means it's a user with 'super' permissions. By extension, this means a superuser has access to any page in the Django admin, as well as permissions to Create, Read, Update, and Delete any type of model record available in the Django admin. Because Django superusers represent an 'all or nothing' proposition, the Django admin is also designed to allow access to Django staff users.

Any Django user marked as staff is given access to the Django admin, but nothing else, unless explicitly given permissions, as illustrated in Figure 11-47.

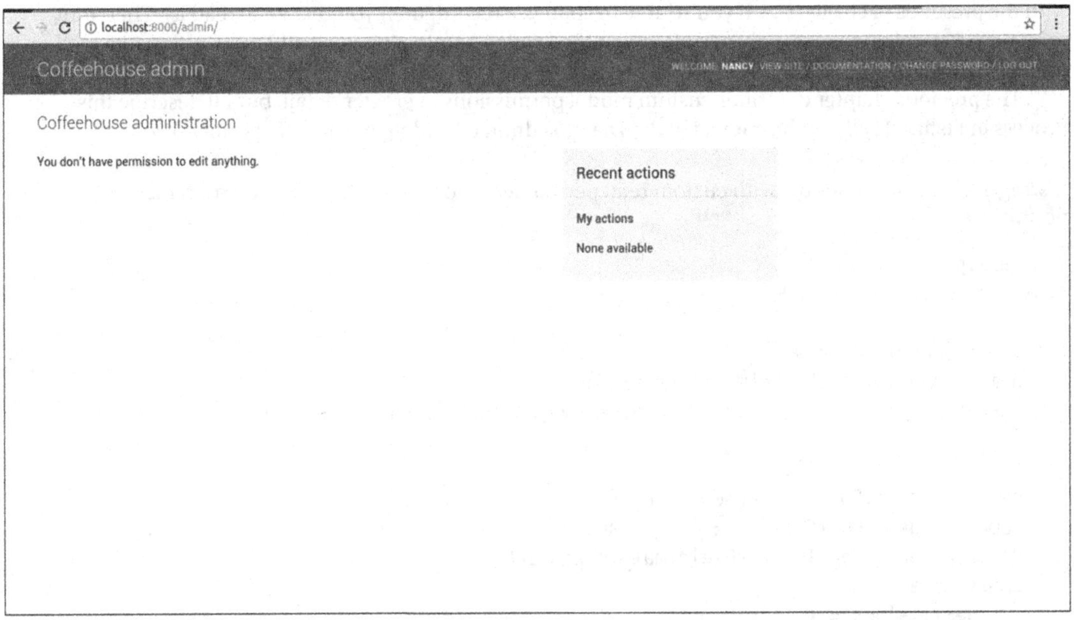

Figure 11-47. *Django admin main page for staff user with no permissions*

As you can see in Figure 11-47, the main Django admin page is empty. Although this scenario of an empty Django admin main page can also present itself when you have no registered models in a project's `admin.py` files, this case represents a scenario for a staff user with no explicit model permissions.

In order for staff users to gain access to Django admin pages, they must be given explicit permissions by means of model permissions, given Django admin pages operate on the basis of CRUD model actions (e.g., a Django admin page to create model records, a Django admin page to delete model records).

By default, all Django models are given `add`, `change`, and `delete` permissions, which you can assign to staff users. As a consequence, each of these model permissions represents an access permission for a Django admin page.

For example, if a staff user is given the `delete` permission on a model, it means he's also given access to delete records of said model in the Django admin. Similarly, if a staff user is given the add permission on a model, it means he's given access to the create record page of said model in the Django admin. Finally, if a staff user is given the change permission on a model, it means he's given access to the edit record page of said model in the Django admin.

■ **Note** Granting a `delete` permission to a user on a given model also requires granting the `change` permission to fulfill the delete action in the Django admin. This is because the Django admin delete action is available on the Django admin record change page.

As you can deduce from this behavior, by using staff users and model permissions, you can allow very fine-grained access to different sections of the Django admin, instead of the 'all or nothing' Django admin superuser behavior.

Still, Django admin staff users have one important missing behavior: the ability to allow read only access for model records in the Django admin. Because Django models default to having `add`, `change` and `delete` permissions (i.e. CUD [Create, Update, Delete] behaviors), a `read` permission is deemed implicit with the presence of change (i.e. if you're able to change a record, then you're able to read it). Therefore, to achieve a standalone read-only permission in the Django admin, you must add a custom model read permission (i.e. the missing R in CRUD).

The previous chapter describes custom model permissions in greater detail, but I'll describe this process in Listing 11-25 for the context of the Django admin by adding a read only permission.

Listing 11-25. Django model with custom read permission and Django admin class enforcing read permission

```
# models.py
from django.db import models

class Menu(models.Model):
    name = models.CharField(max_length=30)
    creator = models.CharField(max_length=100,default='Coffeehouse Chef')

class Item(models.Model):
    menu = models.ForeignKey(Menu, on_delete=models.CASCADE)
    name = models.CharField(max_length=30)
    description = models.CharField(max_length=100)
    class Meta:
        permissions = (
            ('read_item','Can read item'),
        )

# admin.py
from django.contrib import admin

from coffeehouse.items.models import Item

class ItemAdmin(admin.ModelAdmin):
      list_per_page = 5
      list_display = ['menu','name','menu_creator']
      def get_readonly_fields(self, request, obj=None):
        if not request.user.is_superuser and request.user.has_perm('items.read_item'):
            return [f.name for f in self.model._meta.fields]
```

```
        return super(ItemAdmin, self).get_readonly_fields(
            request, obj=obj
        )

admin.site.register(Item, ItemAdmin)
```

The first step highlighted in Listing 11-25 is the `Item` model with a custom permission named `read_item` with the friendly name `'Can read item'`. After you run the `Item` model in Listing 11-25 through its corresponding migration, the `Item` model will get a custom `read_item` permission. Next, create a staff user and assign it both the `read_item` and built-in change permission of `Item` model. Once a staff user is given these permissions, you must enforce the Django admin class for the `Item` model only allow read access to users with these permissions.

When a user is given the `change` permission on a model, the Django admin grants a user access to the Django admin form page, which is used to update records of a given model and is shown from Figures 11-23 to 11-44. But since you want to restrict the update functionality to read only, you must set this page's form fields to read only, which is the purpose of the `get_readonly_fields()` method in the second part of the Listing 11-25.

By defining an admin class with a custom `get_readonly_fields()` method, you can tell the Django admin under which circumstances you want to set a Django admin page's form fields to read only. In this case, you can see the logic of the `get_readonly_fields()` method in Listing 11-25 uses the `is_superuser()` and `has_perm()` methods the determine if the calling party is not a superuser (i.e. staff) and if the user has the `read_item` permission on the `Item` model. If this last rule is true, then the `get_readonly_fields()` method sets all the model form fields to read-only, which is the whole purpose the `get_readonly_fields()` method. If this last rule is false, then the `get_readonly_fields()` method returns its default behavior calling the parent class's default `get_readonly_fields()` method.

As you can see with this brief exercise, by using custom Django admin class methods in conjunction with standard and custom Django model permissions, there are no limitations to restricting or allowing CRUD operations in the Django admin.

Multiple Django admin Sites

Throughout this chapter, you've learned the Django admin site is activated under the `/admin/` url using `django.contrib.admin.site.urls`. In addition, the Django admin site also requires the definition of Django admin classes to be placed inside a Django project's app `admin.py` files and registered using one of the techniques described in Listing 11-1 (e.g. `django.contrib.admin.site.register(Store,StoreAdmin)`)

While this is the standard practice for almost all Django admin site installations, this process can differ for cases when you want or need to set up multiple Django admin sites. This of course begets the question 'Why would you want or need multiple Django admin sites ?'

Mulitple Django admin sites are helpful because they let you separate the access locations for different types of users or groups. For example, you can have a Django admin site designed to let employees perform CRUD operations across different models, while having a completely different Django admin site designed to let providers perform more limited CRUD operations across another set of models.

If you maintain a single Django admin site, creating a solution for multiple types of users and models can be very difficult as you only have user permissions to enforce CRUD operation access, as described in the previous section. With multiple Django admin sites, you can register models in one or both admin sites depending on your requirements.

The first step to create multiple Django admin sites is to create multiple instances of the `django.contrib.admin.AdminSite` class, as illustrated in Listing 11-26

Listing 11-26. Django admin multiple sites accessible on different urls

```
# urls.py (Main directory)
from django.conf.urls import include, url
from django.views.generic import TemplateView

from django.contrib import admin
admin.site.site_header = 'Coffeehouse general admin'

from coffeehouse.admin import employeeadmin, provideradmin

urlpatterns = [
url(r'^$',TemplateView.as_view(template_name='homepage.html'),name="homepage"),
url(r'^admin/', admin.site.urls),
url(r'^employeeadmin/', employeeadmin.urls),
url(r'^provideradmin/', provideradmin.urls),
]

# admin.py (Main directory)
from django.contrib.admin import AdminSite

class EmployeeAdminSite(AdminSite):
    site_header = 'Coffeehouse Employee admin'
employeeadmin = EmployeeAdminSite(name='employeeadmin')

class ProviderAdminSite(AdminSite):
    site_header = 'Coffeehouse Provider admin'
provideradmin = ProviderAdminSite(name='provideradmin')
```

First, notice Listing 11-26 declares the standard Django admin with the `django.contrib.admin` class in `urls.py`, including a custom `site_header` value to mount the Django admin on the standard `/admin/` url. Next, two custom Django admin instances are configured on their own urls - `/employeeadmin/` and `/provideradmin/` - using a `urls` reference that corresponds to a custom `django.contrib.admin.AdminSite` class.

Both the `EmployeeAdminSite` and `ProviderAdminSite` custom Django admin site classes are defined in their own `admin.py` file in the top level directory of the project (i.e. alongside the main `urls.py` file). Notice how each of the custom Django admin site classes inherits its behavior from the `django.contrib.admin.AdminSite` class. Next, observe how each instance of the `AdminSite` classes in Listing 11-26, also defines the `site_header` field to define a custom header for each Django admin site instance, just like it's done with the standard Django admin site.

At this juncture, if you visit either the `/employeeadmin/` and `/provideradmin/` urls for the custom Django admins, you'll access a main Django admin page like the one in Figure 11-47. The reason you'll see an empty Django admin page in both cases, is because each custom Django admin site still doesn't have any models registered to it.

To register Django admin classes with a custom Django admin site, you can use any of the techniques already described in Listing 11-1. The difference though is you must register a Django admin class with an instance of a specific Django admin site (e.g. `employeeadmin`, `provideradmin`) instead of the default `django.contrib.admin` class, as illustrated in Listing 11-27.

Listing 11-27. Django admin class registration on multiple Django admin sites

```
# admin.py (stores app)
from django.contrib import admin
from coffeehouse.stores.models import Store,Amenity

class StoreAdmin(admin.ModelAdmin):
    search_fields = ['city','state']

# Default model registration on main Django admin
admin.site.register(Store, StoreAdmin)

# Model registration on custom Django admin named provideradmin
from coffeehouse.admin import provideradmin
provideradmin.register(Store, StoreAdmin)

# admin.py (items app)
from django.contrib import admin
from coffeehouse.items.models import Menu

class MenuAdmin(admin.ModelAdmin):
    list_display = ['name','creator']

# Default model registration on main Django admin
admin.site.register(Menu, MenuAdmin)

# Model registration on custom Django admin named provideradmin
from coffeehouse.admin import employeeadmin
employeeadmin.register(Menu, MenuAdmin)
```

Notice in Listing 11-27, that in addition to the default Django admin class registration done through `admin.site.register`, the `Store` class is registered with the custom `provideradmin` Django admin class and the `Menu` class is registered with the custom `employeeeadmin` Django admin class, both of which are the custom Django admin classes declared in Listing 11-26.

As you can see in Listing 11-27, it's perfectly valid to register the same Django admin class on multiple Django admin sites, a process that allows you to selectively access certain models under different Django admin sites.

■ **Caution** Multiple Django admin sites don't preclude user permissions, authentication or url visibility. By default, all Django users can use the same credentials and are assigned the same permissions across multiple Django admin sites. This means it's up to you to enforce effective model permissions across all Django admin sites, limit model registration for each Django admin site, as well as avoid easy to guess Django admin urls to avoid unintended access.

CHAPTER 12

■ ■ ■

REST Services with Django

Representational state transfer (REST) services or simply RESTful services have become one of the most popular techniques in web development since they first appeared in the year 2000. While there's a long background story on REST services,[1] which I won't get into here, the appeal and explosive growth of REST services in web development is simply due to how they solve a common problem in an easy and reusable manner.

In this chapter, you'll learn about the options available to create REST services with Django, including plain Python/Django REST services and framework specific REST services. In addition, you'll learn how to create REST services with plain Python/Django packages and when they're preferable over using framework specific REST services packages. In addition, you'll also learn how to create and use some of the most important features of REST services created with the Django REST framework, as well as incorporate essential security into Django REST framework services.

REST Services in Django

A REST service provides access to data through an end point or Internet URL making no assumption about who uses it (e.g., an IoT device, a mobile phone or, a desktop browser); this means there's no device or environment requirements to access REST services – all you need is Internet access.

On top of this, because REST services operate on Internet URLs, they provide a very intuitive access scheme. For example, the REST service URL /products/ can mean 'get all product data', while the URL /products/10/20/ can mean get all data for products with a price between 10 and 20 and the URL /products/drinks/ get all product data in the drinks category.

The power of this last approach is there's no steep learning curve (e.g., language syntax, complex business logic) to access REST service variations that solve elaborate data queries. Because of these features and versatility, REST services work as a reusable data backbone across a wide array of areas and applications. For example, practically the entire web API (Application Programming Interface) world operates around REST web services, because by definition an API must provide a device/environment neutral way for customers to access their functionality. In fact, there's a high chance most web sites you visit make use of REST services in one way or another, a practice that allows web site operators to reuse the same data and then format it for users on desktop browsers, IoT devices, mobile applications, RSS feeds, or any other target like Accelerated Mobile Pages(AMP).[2]

With this brief overview of REST services, let's start with the simplest option available to create REST services in Django.

[1]https://en.wikipedia.org/wiki/Representational_state_transfer
[2]https://www.ampproject.org/

© Daniel Rubio 2017
D. Rubio, *Beginning Django*, https://doi.org/10.1007/978-1-4842-2787-9_12

Standard View Method Designed as REST Service

You can actually create a REST service in Django with just the Django package and Python's core packages, with no need to install any third-party package. Listing 12-1 illustrates a standard Django url and view method designed to function as a REST service.

Listing 12-1. Standard view method designed as REST service

```
# urls.py (In stores app)
from coffeehouse.stores import views as stores_views

urlpatterns = [
    url(r'^rest/$',stores_views.rest_store,name="rest_index"),
]

# views.py (In stores app)
from django.http import HttpResponse
from coffeehouse.stores.models import Store
import json

def rest_store(request):
    store_list = Store.objects.all()
    store_names = [{"name":store.name} for store in store_list]
    return HttpResponse(json.dumps(store_names), content_type='application/json')

# Sample output
# [{"name": "Corporate"}, {"name": "Downtown"}, {"name": "Uptown"}, {"name": "Midtown"}]
```

The url statement in Listing 12-1 defines an access pattern on the `stores` app under the `rest` directory (i.e., final url `/stores/rest/`). This last url statement is hooked up to the `rest_store` view method – also in Listing 12-1 – which makes a query to get all `Store` records from the database, then creates a list comprehension to generate a list of store names from the resulting query and finally uses Django's `HttpResponse` to return a JSON response with the store names using Python's `json` package. The design in Listing 12-1 is one of the simplest REST services you can create in Django and has some important points:

- Serialization.- Notice the `Store` query is not used directly in the response, but rather a list comprehension is created first. This is done to serialize the data into an appropriate format. Due to the way Django queries are built, results may not be naturally serializable, so a list comprehension is used to ensure the data is a standard Python dictionary that can be converted to JSON with the json package. I'll provide more details on why serialization is an important piece of working with REST services in the following sidebar.
- Response handling.- Notice the use of Django's low-level `HttpResponse` method vs. Django's more common `render()` method to generate a response. While it's possible to use Django's `render()` method and further pass the data to a template to format the response, for most REST services this is unnecessary as responses tend to be raw data (e.g., JSON, XML) and can be generated without a backing template. In addition, notice in Listing 12-1 the `HttpResponse` uses the `content_type` argument that adds the HTTP Content-Type `application/json` header telling the requesting party the response is JSON. The HTTP Content-Type response value is important because it avoids consumers having to guess how to process a REST service response

(e.g., another Content-Type option can be `application/xml` for REST services with XML responses). HTTP response handling for Django view methods is discussed in greater detail in Chapter 2.

- (No) Query parameters.- For simplicity, the view method in Listing 12-1 has no parameters, so it provides a very rigid output (i.e., all stores in a JSON format).

ERROR: IS NOT JSON/XML SERIALIZABLE

One of the most common errors you're likely to encounter when you create REST services in Django is the 'Is not JSON/XML serializable' error. This means Django isn't capable of serializing (i.e., representing/converting) the source data into the selected format – JSON or XML. This error happens when the source data is made up of objects or data types that can produce undetermined or ambiguous serializing results.

For example, if you have a `Store` model class with relationships, how should Django serialize these relationships? Similarly, if you have a Python `datetime` instance how should Django serialize the value, as DD/MM/YYYY, DD-MM-YYYY, or something else? In every case, Django never attempts to guess the serialization representation, so unless the source data is naturally serializable – as in Listing 12-1 - you must explicitly specify a serialization scheme – as I'll explain next – or you'll get the 'Is not JSON/XML serializable' error.

Now that you have a brief understanding of a simple REST service in Django, let's rework the REST service in Listing 12-1 to make use of parameters so it can return different data results and data formats.

Listing 12-2. Standard view method as REST service with parameters and different output formats

```
# urls.py (In stores app)
from coffeehouse.stores import views as stores_views

urlpatterns = [
    url(r'^rest/$',stores_views.rest_store,name="rest_index"),
    url(r'^(?P<store_id>\d+)/rest/$',stores_views.rest_store,name="rest_detail"),
]

# views.py (In stores app)
from django.http import HttpResponse
from coffeehouse.stores.models import Store
from django.core import serializers

def rest_store(request,store_id=None):
    store_list = Store.objects.all()
    if store_id:
        store_list = store_list.filter(id=store_id)
    if 'type' in request.GET and request.GET['type'] == 'xml':
        serialized_stores = serializers.serialize('xml',store_list)
        return HttpResponse(serialized_stores, content_type='application/xml')
    else:
        serialized_stores = serializers.serialize('json',store_list)
        return HttpResponse(serialized_stores, content_type='application/json')
```

The first thing that's different in Listing 12-2 is an additional url statement that accepts requests with a `store_id` parameter (e.g., `/stores/1/rest/`, `/stores/2/rest/`). In this case, the new url is processed by the same `rest_store()` view method to process the stores index from Listing 12-1 (i.e., `/stores/rest/`)

Next, the view method in Listing 12-2 is a modified version of the view method in Listing 12-1 that accepts a `store_id` parameter. This modification allows the REST service to process a url request for all stores (e.g., `/stores/rest/`) or individual stores (e.g., `/stores/1/rest/` for store number `1`). If you're unfamiliar on how to set up Django urls with parameters, see Chapter 2, which describes url parameters.

Once inside the view method, a query is made to get all `Store` records from a database. In case the method receives a `store_id` value, an additional filter is applied on the query to limit the results to the given `store_id`. This last query logic is perfectly efficient due to the way Django queries work - if you're unfamiliar with the behavior in Django queries, see Chapter 8 "Understanding a QuerySet" section.

Next, an inspection is made on the `request` to see if it has the `type` parameter with an `xml` value. If a request matches this last rule (e.g., `/stores/rest/?type=xml`), then an XML response is generated for the REST service; if it doesn't match this last rule, then a JSON response - the default - is generated for the REST service.

While the example in Listing 12-2 also uses `HttpResponse` and the `content_type` argument just like Listing 12-1, notice the data is prepared with Django's `django.core.serializers` package that is designed to make data serialization easier - unlike the REST service in Listing 12-1 that required pre-processing the query data with a listing comprehension and then using Python's `json` package to complete the process.

The use of `django.core.serializers` is very simple in Listing 12-2. The `serialize()` method is used, which expects the serialization type as its first argument (e.g., `'xml'` or `'json'`) and the data to serialize as the second argument (e.g., the `store_list` reference that represents the query). There's much more functionality behind the `django.core.serializers` package (e.g., filters) that I won't explore here to keep things simple, but Figures 12-1 and 12-2 show two sample results from the REST service in Listing 12-2.

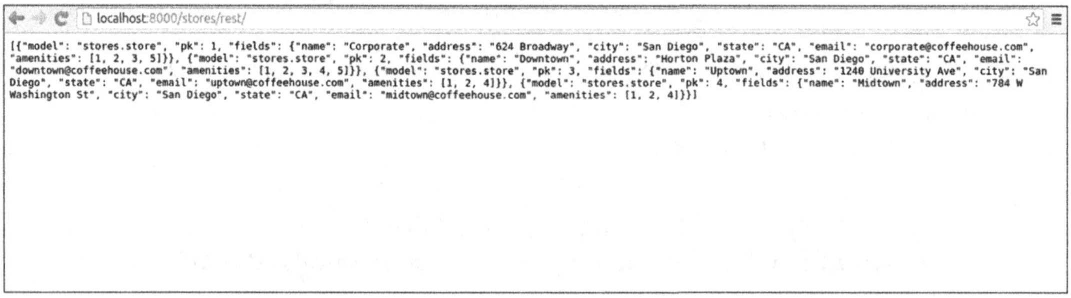

Figure 12-1. *JSON output from Django REST serviceXML output from Django REST service*

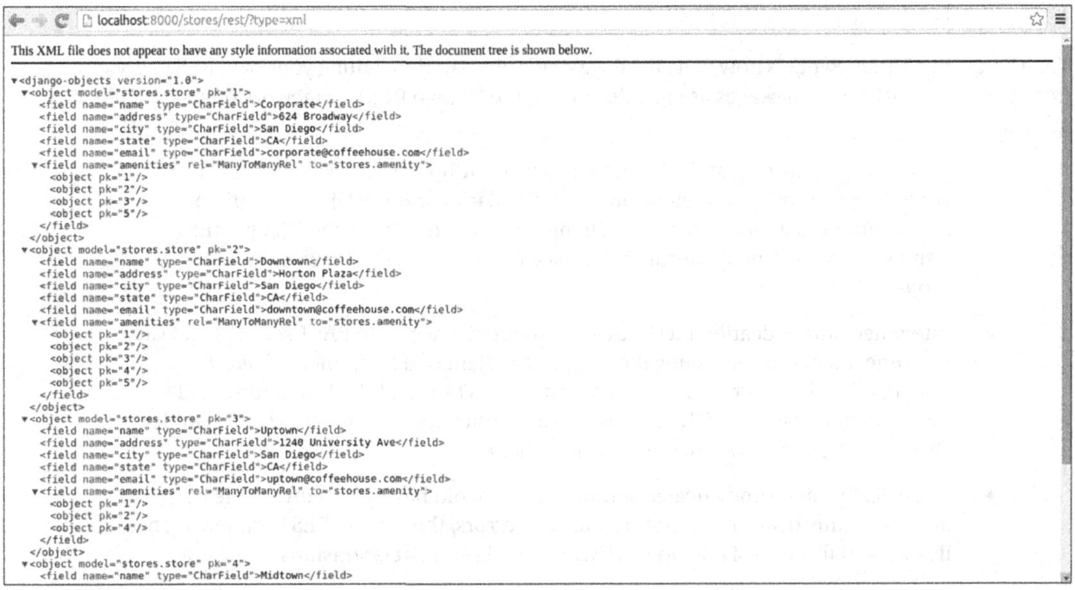

***Figure 12-2.** XML output from Django REST service*

As you can see in Figures 12-1 and 12-2, Django is capable of serializing a query and outputting its result as a REST service response in either JSON or XML, with just the few lines in Listing 12-2. It's likely these few lines from Listing 12-2 can take you a long way toward building your own REST services in Django, but if you've never done REST services or plan to use REST services as the centerpiece of an application or web site, you should pause to analyze your requirements.

Because REST services solve a common problem in an easy and reusable manner, they tend to suffer from scope creep, a characteristic where changes appear to be never ending and functionality is always 'not quite finished'. After seeing this initial Django REST service example, ask yourself the following questions:

- Do you need to support REST services for more than a couple of Django model types? (e.g., Store,Drink,Employee).
- Do you need to customize the JSON/XML response to something that doesn't map directly to Django model records? (e.g., use a custom schema, filter certain attributes).
- Do you need to provide a friendly interface for users, describing what a REST service does and what parameters it accepts?
- Do you need to support some kind of authentication mechanism so the REST service isn't publicly available?
- Do you need REST services to support more than just displaying data or read operations? (e.g., update and delete operations)?

If you said yes to most of the previous questions, then your REST services undertaking is beyond basic. While you could continue building on the example in Listing 12-2 - using a standard Django view method and additional Python packages - to support all of the previous scenarios, supporting these more elaborate REST services features in Django is a path many have gone down before, to the point there are dedicated frameworks for just this purpose.

Django REST Framework[3]

The Django REST framework is now in its third version. Compared to writing your own REST services from plain Python/Django packages as I just described, the Django REST framework offers the following advantages:

- A web browsable interface.- Provides a user-friendly descriptive page for all REST services (e.g., input parameters, options). Similar to how the Django admin provides a near effortless interface to view a Django project's database, the Django REST framework offers a near effortless interface for end users to discover a Django project's REST services.
- Integrated authentication mechanisms.- To restrict access to REST services and save you time integrating authentication logic, the Django REST framework is tightly integrated with authentication mechanisms like OAuth2, HTTP Signature, HTTP digest authentication, JSON Web Token Authentication, and HAWK (HTTP Holder-Of-Key Authentication Scheme), among others.
- More flexible and sophisticated serializers.- To avoid having to reinvent the wheel and constantly deal with 'Is not serializable' errors, the Django REST framework has its own serializers designed to work with complex data relationships.

These are just some of the core benefits of using the Django REST framework. As you can realize, if you plan to create more than a couple of REST services, investing the time to learn the Django REST framework is well worth the time vs. dealing with the scaffolding code necessary to deploy REST services using plain Python/Django packages.

Django Tastypie Framework[4]

The Django Tastypie framework emerged as an alternative to the Django REST framework. Although the Django Tastypie framework is in its 0.14 version, don't let the pre-1.0 release number fool you: the Django Tastypie framework has been in development since 2010. Although both the Django Tastypie framework and Django REST framework can potentially produce the same results, the Django Tastypie framework has these differences:

Tastypie provides more default behaviors, making it simpler to configure and set up REST services than with the Django REST framework.

Tastypie is still the second most used Django REST package[5] - albeit it gets half the downloads of the Django REST framework - so it's still an attractive option for many Django projects.

Tastypie was originally developed by the same creators of Django haystack, which is still the most popular Django search package[6] - so Tastypie operates on some very solid Python/Django fundamentals.

Even though the Django Tastypie framework is not as mainstream as the Django REST framework, if you feel overwhelmed creating REST services with the latter, you can always try out the former to arrive at a faster REST solution rather than building your REST services from scratch with plain Python/Django packages.

---

[3]`http://www.django-rest-framework.org/`
[4]`http://tastypieapi.org/`
[5]`https://djangopackages.org/grids/g/rest/`
[6]`https://djangopackages.org/grids/g/search/`

Django REST Framework Concepts and Introduction

The Django REST framework is distributed as a standard Python package. So to get started, you need to install the Django REST framework with the command: `pip install djangorestframework`.

Once you install the Django REST framework package, add it to the `INSTALLED_APPS` list variable in your Django project's `settings.py` file with the name `rest_framework`. Once this is done, you can start working with the Django REST framework. Next, let's walk through the core concepts and creation process of a REST service using the Django REST framework.

Serializers and Views

Serializers are one of the main building blocks of the Django REST framework used to define the representation of data records, which are generally based on Django models. As described in the previous section on Introduction to REST services options for Django, Python records can have ambiguous data representations (e.g., a record with a `datetime` value can be represented as DD/MM/YYYY, DD-MM-YYYY, or MM-YYYY) and a serializer removes any uncertainty about how to represent a record. Listing 12-3 illustrates a Django REST framework serializer using one of its `serializers` package.

Listing 12-3. Serializer class based on Django REST framework

```
# coffeehouse.stores.serializers.py file
from rest_framework import serializers

class StoreSerializer(serializers.Serializer):
    name = serializers.CharField(max_length=200)
    email = serializers.EmailField()
```

As you can see in Listing 12-3, a Django REST framework serializer is a standard Python class, which in this case, inherits its behavior from the Django REST framework's `serializers.Serializer` class. Next, inside the serializer class are a set of fields that use the data types from the `serializers` package of the same Django REST framework. Notice the similar structure between this Django REST framework serializer class and Django model classes or Django form classes (i.e., they inherit their behavior from a parent class and use different fields to represent different data types like character and email fields).

The example in Listing 12-3 is one of the simplest Django REST framework serializer classes possible, because it only has two fields and inherits its behavior from the very basic `serializers.Serializer` class. But just as with Django models and forms, as you progress with the Django REST framework, you'll find yourself using more advanced data types, as well as creating serializers with more sophisticated base classes than `serializers.Serializer`. I'll describe a more advanced serializer shortly. Next let's explore a view in the context of the Django REST framework.

Serializer classes by themselves do nothing and must be integrated with views that do the bulk of the REST service logic (i.e., handle incoming requests, query a database for data), which then use serializers to transform data. In the first section in this chapter, you learned how a regular Django view method can be turned into REST services. While it's perfectly possible to use a Django REST framework serializer class - like the one in Listing 12-3 - in a regular Django view method, the Django REST framework also provides an additional view syntax - illustrated in Listing 12-4 - to make it easier to build REST services.

Listing 12-4. Django view method decorated with Django REST framework

```
from coffeehouse.stores.models import Store
from coffeehouse.stores.serializers import StoreSerializer

from rest_framework.decorators import api_view
from rest_framework.response import Response

@api_view(['GET','POST','DELETE'])
def rest_store(request):
    if request.method == 'GET':
        stores = Store.objects.all()
        serializer = StoreSerializer(stores, many=True)
        return Response(serializer.data)
    elif request.method == 'POST':
        ... #logic for HTTP POST  operation
    elif request.method == 'DELETE':
        ... #logic for HTTP DELETE operation
```

First notice the method in Listing 12-4 is a regular Django view method, but it uses the `@api_view` decorator from the Django REST framework. The arguments to `@api_view` indicate which HTTP REST methods to support - see Chapter 2 or Chapter 6 for details on the topic of HTTP methods in Django or wikipedia's REST entry,[7] as HTTP methods is a generic REST concept rather than a Django/REST topic. Next, inside the view method, a series of conditions are executed to process the different HTTP request methods that form the REST service.

If a GET request is made on the view method, a query is made to get all `Store` model records. However, notice in this case of Listing 12-4, it uses the `StoreSerializer` from Listing 12-3 to transform the Django queryset. In addition, the `return` statement uses the Django REST framework `Response` method instead of Django's standard `HttpResponse` or `render` methods.

More importantly, notice both the request and response logic in Listing 12-4 lacks any kind of REST output format (e.g., JSON, XML). By leveraging the Django REST framework, you no longer need to deal with the low-level details of detecting or handling output formats-- this is taken care of directly by the REST framework and based on how you make requests to the REST service, which I'll describe shortly.

Next, the `rest_store()` view method in Listing 12-4 must be configured to become accessible at a url. A line like `url(r'^rest/$',stores_views.rest_store,name="rest_index")` added to the app's `urls.py` file solves this issue. Once you do this, if you access the URL you'll see a result like the one in Figure 12-3.

---

[7]`https://en.wikipedia.org/wiki/Hypertext_Transfer_Protocol#Request_methods`

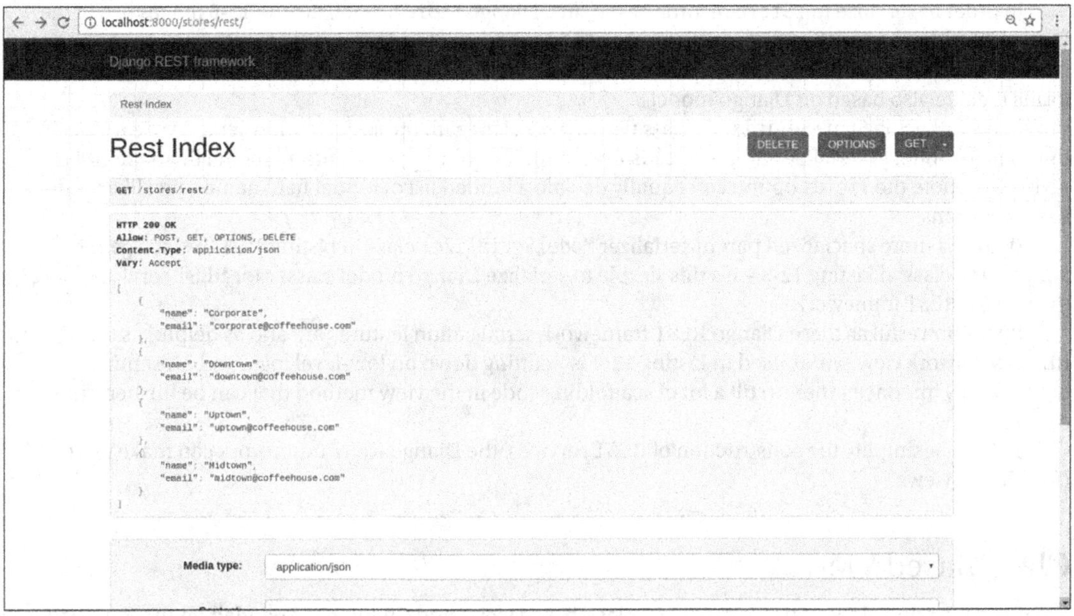

Figure 12-3. *Django REST framework main service response*

■ **Caution** If you get the error `'TemplateDoesNotExist at /stores/rest/ rest_framework/api.html'` instead of the page in Figure 12-3, it means you haven't added the REST framework to your project's `INSTALLED_APPS` as described at the start of this section (e.g., `INSTALLED_APPS = ['rest_framework']`).

As you can see in Figure 12-3, the REST framework service response is very informative and pretty compared to Django's basic `HttpResponse` response generated by the Django REST service created in the initial section of this chapter.

For example, you can see the different options offered by the REST service and invoke its various operations in a few clicks. Also notice the output from the REST service only has `Store` objects with two fields due to the `StoreSerializer` definition in Listing 12-3. Next, let's modify the serializer class to output complete `Store` records. Listing 12-5 shows an updated serializer class based on Listing 12-3.

Listing 12-5. Serializer class using Django model based on Django REST framework

```
from rest_framework import serializers

from coffeehouse.stores.models import Store

class StoreSerializer(serializers.ModelSerializer):
    class Meta:
        model = Store
        fields = '__all__'
```

In order to serialize full Store records based on a Django Store model, Listing 12-5 makes use of the Django REST framework ModelSerializer class to simplify the serializer syntax. More importantly, notice how the REST framework StoreSerializer class in Listing 12-5 uses syntax that's identical to Django model forms that are also based on Django models.

In this case, the StoreSerializer class uses a Meta class with the model option set to Store to specify the Django model to serialize and the fields option set to __all__ to indicate all model fields should be serialized - note the fields option can equally declare a limited list of model field names, just like it's done in model forms.

With this more specialized parent serializer ModelSerializer class in Listing 12-5 - vs. the generic Serializer class in Listing 12-3 - it's this simple to serialize Django model classes for REST services using the Django REST framework.

But as powerful as these Django REST framework serialization features are and as helpful as the Django REST framework view syntax used in Listing 12-4 is - cutting down on low-level logic and presenting a user-friendly interface - there's still a lot of scaffolding code in the view method that can be further trimmed down.

To further simplify the construction of REST services, the Django REST framework can make use of class-based views.

Class-Based Views

Chapter 2 introduced the concept of Django class-based views and Chapter 8 expanded on the topic with class-based views that use Django models to perform CRUD operations. Since the principles of class-based views in Django have already been covered, I'll assume you have a minimum level of familiarity with the topic; if not, then go back to these other chapters to learn the basics.

Listing 12-6 illustrates a class-based view based on a REST framework class, which simplifies the earlier standard view method - in Listing 12-4 - decorated with @api_view from the REST framework.

Listing 12-6. Django REST framework class-based views

```
from coffeehouse.stores.models import Store
from coffeehouse.stores.serializers import StoreSerializer

from rest_framework.views import APIView
from rest_framework.response import Response

class StoreList(APIView):

    def get(self, request, format=None):
        stores = Store.objects.all()
        serializer = StoreSerializer(stores, many=True)
        return Response(serializer.data)

    def post(self, request, format=None):
        ...
        #logic for HTTP POST operation

    def delete(self, request, format=None):
        ...
        #logic for HTTP DELETE operation
```

Notice in Listing 12-6 how the class inherits its behavior from the Django REST framework `APIView` class. This allows the class to contain various methods representing each of the REST service's HTTP methods (i.e., GET,POST, DELETE), - similar to how it's done with standard Django class-based views that handle multiple HTTP methods (e.g., form processing).

As you can see, Listing 12-6 produces much more readable REST services logic, compared to the regular Django view method in Listing 12-4, which requires you to manually inspect a request and perform conditional statements. The logic inside the `get` method in Listing 12-6 uses the same Django REST framework syntax used in Listing 12-4, so there's nothing new.

In the same way you must hook up a regular Django view method to a url, you must also associate a Django REST framework class-based view to make it accessible on a certain url. Listing 12-7 illustrates a `urls.py` file with the syntax to access the REST service class-based view from Listing 12-6.

Listing 12-7. Django URL definition linked to Django REST framework class-based views

```
from django.conf.urls import url
from coffeehouse.store import stores_views

urlpatterns = [
    url(r'^$',stores_views.index,name="index"),
    url(r'^rest/$',stores_views.StoreList.as_view(),name="rest_index"),      ]
```

In Listing 12-7 you can see the `urls.py` file declares the `r'^rest/$'` url pattern is mapped to the Django REST framework `StoreList` class using the `as_view()` method, which is a staple of all Django class-based views to link them to a url. In this manner, if an HTTP GET request is made on the `/stores/rest/` url, it's handled by the `get()` method of the class-based view and if an HTTP POST request is made on the same `/stores/rest/`, it's handled by the `post()` method of the class-based view.

It's worth mentioning that hitting a url backed by a REST framework class-based view like the one in Listing 12-6 also produces the same interface shown in Figure 12-3, which is produced by the standard view method from Listing 12-4.

Now, as helpful as REST framework class-based views are to simplify REST service logic, class-based views still require you to write all of the logic behind each method. For example, in the `get()` method in Listing 12-6 a query is made to get all `Store` records, then serialize the data, and finally return a response. For the `post()` method in Listing 12-6, you would similarly need to insert/update a `Store` record with the provided data and with the `delete()` method you would need to delete a `Store` record with the provided data.

Once you write a couple of class-based views with the Django REST framework, you'll realize there's a constant pattern behind each type of view method (e.g., read a record, serialize it, and return a response). On top of this, you'll also come to realize what a close relationship there is between REST methods (e.g., GET,POST and DELETE) and the operations they execute on Django models (i.e., Create-Read-Update-Delete (CRUD) operations).

To avoid having to constantly write the same CRUD operations and boilerplate logic for different Django objects associated with REST services, the Django REST framework following Django's DRY (Don't Repeat Yourself) principle and Django's class-based model view principle offers another construct: *mixins*.

Mixins and Generic Class-Based Views

A mixin is used to encapsulate and reuse the same logic and be able to use it in a class-based view. For example, instead of writing the same logic from Listing 12-6 - get all records, serialize them, and generate a response - over and over for different REST services (e.g., `Item`, `Drink`, or `Store` services); you can use the `mixins.ListModelMixin` class and quickly achieve the same result.

I won't go into greater detail about mixin classes here, mainly because mixin classes are not as widely used as other Django REST framework options, not to mention Django mixins were already described in Chapter 9 in the context of class-based views that use models.

For most Django framework REST services, you'll either end up using class-based views - to get full control over the logic - or a more succinct approach based on mixins called 'mixed-in generic class views.' Listing 12-8 illustrates an equivalent mixed-in generic class view based on the class-based view from Listing 12-6.

Listing 12-8. Django mixed-in generic class views in Django REST framework

```
from coffeehouse.stores.models import Store
from coffeehouse.stores.serializers import StoreSerializer

from rest_framework import generics

class StoreList(generics.ListCreateAPIView):
    queryset = Store.objects.all()
    serializer_class = StoreSerializer
```

Notice Listing 12-8 is even more succinct than prior iterations of the same REST service. In this case, the generic class name `ListCreateAPIView` is indicative of what the class produces - A REST view to generate a list - based on the `queryset` option that specifies to get all `Store` records and the `serializer` option that points to the `StoreSerializer` class in Listing 12-5.

Just as before and even though you now have a REST service composed of a couple of lines, the Django REST framework can further extend Django's DRY principle with the use *view sets* and *routers*.

View Sets and Routers

The generic class view in Listing 12-8 is pretty powerful for just three lines, but it's just one class to display a list of `Store` records. Let's assume you now need to create a REST service to a display a specific `Store` record, another REST service to update a `Store` record, and yet another REST service to delete `Store` records. In this scenario, you would need to create three more generic class views and three more URL mappings to roll out this basic CRUD functionality. But instead of creating separate view classes for each case, you can instead rely on a Django REST framework view set.

A Django REST framework view set, as its name implies, is a group of views. To create a Django REST framework view set all you need to do is create a class that inherits its behavior from one of the Django REST framework's classes intended for this purpose. Listing 12-9 illustrates a view set created with the `ModelViewSet` class.

Listing 12-9. Django viewset class in Django REST framework

```
from coffeehouse.stores.models import Store
from coffeehouse.stores.serializers import StoreSerializer

from rest_framework import viewsets

class StoreViewSet(viewsets.ModelViewSet):
    queryset = Store.objects.all()
    serializer_class = StoreSerializer
```

Listing 12-9 is as short as the REST service class in Listing 12-8, but besides the class name change, it's the parent ModelViewSet inherited class that gives this REST service a whole new dimension. Using this class alone, a REST service is automatically hooked up to display a Store record list, as well as to create, read, update, or delete individual Store records.

Because a view set generates multiple views, you're still left with the issue of configuring each view to a url, in which case the easiest path is to use a Django REST framework router. A router is to a view set what a url statement is to class-based view: a way to hook up an end point. Listing 12-10 illustrates the urls.py file set up with a Django REST framework router.

Listing 12-10. Django URL definition with Django REST framework router for view set

```
from django.conf.urls import include, url
from coffeehouse.stores import views as stores_views

from rest_framework import routers

router = routers.DefaultRouter()
router.register(r'stores', stores_views.StoreViewSet)

urlpatterns = [
    url(r'^rest/', include(router.urls,namespace="rest")),
    ]
```

■ **Caution** View set and router combinations automatically create sensitive REST end points (e.g., delete and update), which by default are accessible to anyone. See the next section on REST framework security to restrict these service end points.

The first step in Listing 12-10 is to initiate a router with routers.DefaultRouter() and then register the different view sets with it. As you can see in Listing 12-10, the router registration process uses the router.register method that accepts two arguments: the first argument indicates the REST url prefix - in this case stores - and a second argument to specify the view set - in this case the StoreViewSet class from Listing 12-9.

Next, you can see the router is assigned using Django's standard url and include methods. In this case, the router instance is assigned under the r'^rest/' url, which means the final root url of the Store view set becomes /rest/stores/ as shown in Figure 12-4.

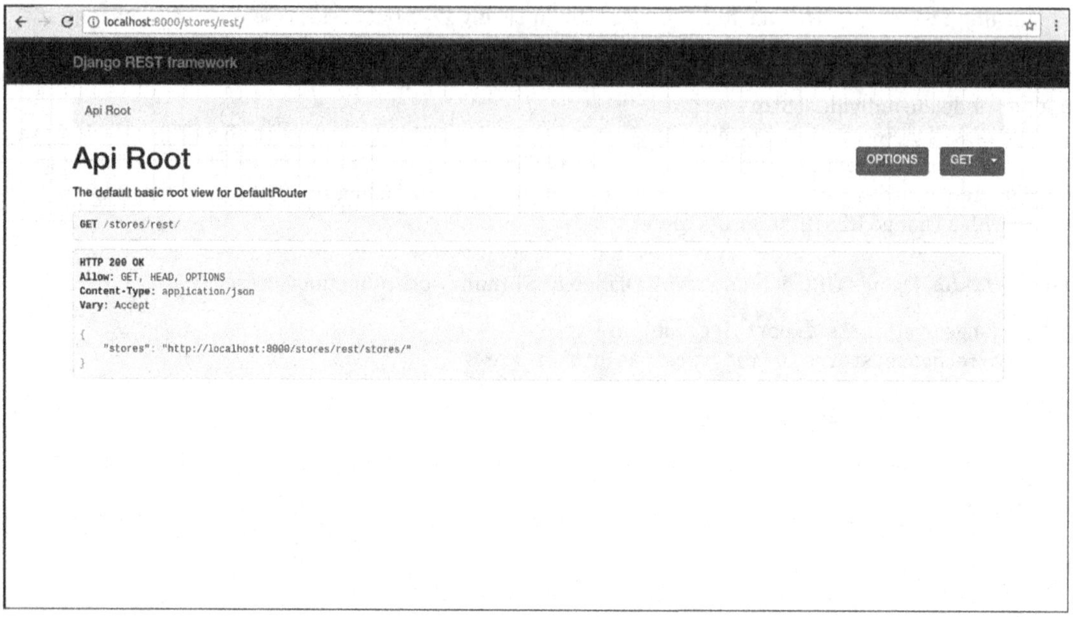

Figure 12-4. *Django REST framework view set main page*

As you can see in Figure 12-4, the REST framework presents a default Api Root page. You can further navigate to other urls under the Api Root page (i.e., `/stores/rest/`) to perform other CRUD actions associated with the view set (e.g., an HTTP GET request on `/stores/rest/stores/` to get a list of all `Store` records, an HTTP GET request on `/stores/rest/stores/1/` to get the `Store` record with `id=1`, or an HTTP DELETE request on `/stores/rest/stores/2/` to delete the `Store` record with `id=3`).

And with this description of view sets and routers, we conclude the coverage of basic concepts needed to set up REST services with the Django REST framework. Now that you're familiar with the basics, in the next section you'll learn how to secure REST services built with the Django REST framework.

Django REST Framework Security

Although the Django REST framework represents a great time saver to create REST services that allow access to an application's data, you need to be careful you don't inadvertently allow access to data or functionalities you didn't mean to. Using the wrong class or configuration parameter with the Django REST framework can leave your application open to a security risk, even though the Django REST framework is fundamentally secure.

Set Up REST Framework Services Permissions

By default, all REST framework services are open to *anyone*, so long as they know or discover a REST service end point (i.e., the url). While this default behavior is convenient, it can also represent a grave security threat, particularly if you create REST framework services with sensitive operations (e.g., Update or Delete actions) or view sets - such as the one in Listing 12-9 - which automatically create end points that support sensitive operations.

The default REST framework permission can be configured through the `REST_FRAMEWORK` variable in `setting.py` file, via the `DEFAULT_PERMISSION_CLASSES` option. Out of the box, the REST framework sets this option to use the `rest_framework.permissions.AllowAny` class, as illustrated in the following snippet:

```
REST_FRAMEWORK = {
    'DEFAULT_PERMISSION_CLASSES': (
        'rest_framework.permissions.AllowAny',
    )
}
```

This means that unless you define a `DEFAULT_PERMISSION_CLASSES` option in your Django project's `settings.py` file, all REST framework services are open to the public. To lock down access to REST services to the public, you can change the REST framework's default permission strategy.

Listing 12-11 illustrates the `DEFAULT_PERMISSION_CLASSES` option set to the `rest_framework.permissions.IsAuthenticated` class, which enforces that only users logged in via Django's built-in user system - described in Chapter 10 - be allowed access to REST framework services.

Listing 12-11. Django REST framework set to restrict all services to authenticated users

```
REST_FRAMEWORK = {
    'DEFAULT_PERMISSION_CLASSES': (
        'rest_framework.permissions.IsAuthenticated',
    )
}
```

In addition to the `rest_framework.permissions.IsAuthenticated` class, the REST framework also supports the classes in Table 12-1 to be part of the `DEFAULT_PERMISSION_CLASSES` option.

Table 12-1. *Django REST framework permission classes*

REST framework permission class	Description
rest_framework.permissions.AllowAny	(Default) Allows access to anyone.
rest_framework.permissions.IsAuthenticated	Allows access to logged-in users via Django's built-in user system.
rest_framework.permissions.IsAdminUser	Allows access to Django admin users, based on Django's built-in user system.
rest_framework.permissions.IsAuthenticatedOrReadOnly	Allows read access to anyone (logged in or not), but requires logging in to perform non-read operations.
rest_framework.permissions.DjangoModelPermissions	Allows access to logged-in users, but also requires that said users have the necessary add/change/delete model permissions on which the REST service operates with.
rest_framework.permissions.DjangoModelPermissionsOrAnonReadOnly	Just like the DjangoModelPermissions class, but allows read access to anyone (logged in or not).
rest_framework.permissions.DjangoObjectPermissions	Similar to the DjangoModelPermissions class, except it works per-object permissions on models on which the REST service operates with.

As you can see in Table 12-1, the REST framework provides various classes to set the default access permission for all REST services in a project. For example, if you're fine allowing public read access to a project's REST services but want to restrict more sensitive REST services operations, the `IsAuthenticatedOrReadOnly` and `DjangoModelPermissionsOrAnonReadOnly` classes from Table 12-1 are good alternatives for the `DEFAULT_PERMISSION_CLASSES` option.

Still, by relying on the `DEFAULT_PERMISSION_CLASSES` option you give every REST service in a project the same access permission. What if you want to provide a more flexible or strict permission strategy for one or two services? The REST framework also supports specifying more granular permissions on individual REST services, using the same classes in Table 12-1.

Listing 12-12 illustrates a modified version of the REST service from Listing 12-4 that uses `@permission_classes` decorator to specify a different permission strategy than the global `DEFAULT_PERMISSION_CLASSES` option.

Listing 12-12. Django view method decorated with Django REST framework and @permission_classes decorator

```
from coffeehouse.stores.models import Store
from coffeehouse.stores.serializers import StoreSerializer

from rest_framework.decorators import api_view, permission_classes
from rest_framework.permissions import IsAuthenticated
from rest_framework.response import Response

@api_view(['GET','POST','DELETE'])
@permission_classes((IsAuthenticated, ))
def rest_store(request):
    if request.method == 'GET':
        stores = Store.objects.all()
        serializer = StoreSerializer(stores, many=True)
        return Response(serializer.data)
```

As you can see in Listing 12-12, the standard view method in addition to being decorated with `@api_view` is also decorated with `@permission_classes`. In this case, the `@permission_classes` decorator is set with the `IsAuthenticated` class values, ensuring this REST service permission strategy take precedence on the service over the default service permission in `DEFAULT_PERMISSION_CLASSES` option.

Listing 12-13 illustrates a modified version of the REST service from Listing 12-9 that uses permission_classes field to specify a different permission strategy than the global `DEFAULT_PERMISSION_CLASSES` option.

Listing 12-13. Django viewset class in Django REST framework and permission_classes field

```
from coffeehouse.stores.models import Store
from coffeehouse.stores.serializers import StoreSerializer
from rest_framework.permissions import IsAuthenticated

from rest_framework import viewsets

class StoreViewSet(viewsets.ModelViewSet):
    permission_classes = (IsAuthenticated,)
    queryset = Store.objects.all()
    serializer_class = StoreSerializer
```

As you can see in Listing 12-13, the REST framework view set method makes use of the `permission_classes` field. In this case, the `permission_classes` field is set with the `IsAuthenticated` class values, ensuring this REST service permission strategy takes precedence on the service over the default service permission in `DEFAULT_PERMISSION_CLASSES` option.

Set Up REST Framework Login Page

By default, if a user attempts to access a REST framework via a browser and doesn't have the necessary permissions, a user is presented with a warning page like the one in Figure 12-5.

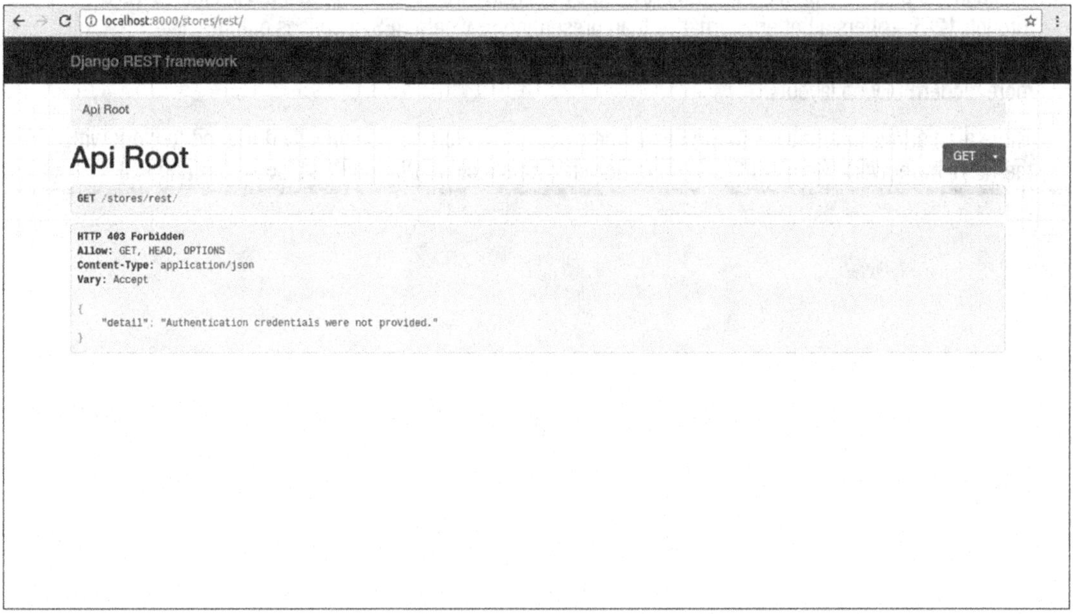

Figure 12-5. *Django REST framework access denied page*

Although Figure 12-5 represents a standard access denied page, it has one glaring omission: it's a dead end with no link to let users log in. If a user reaches the page in Figure 12-5, he needs to manually go to a Django login page in either the application or the Django admin, to provide his credentials and then go back to the REST service to access it.

This last workflow creates an unnecessary burden on users, which is why the REST framework provides an easy way to integrate a login page – including a login/logout link on all its pages – that's tied directly to the same authentication back end of the Django admin.

Listing 12-14 illustrates a Django project's main urls.py that declares the REST framework's urls to automatically activate its built-in login page and links.

Listing 12-14. Django REST framework url declaration to enable log in

```
from django.conf.urls import include, url
urlpatterns = [
    url(r'^rest-auth/', include('rest_framework.urls',namespace='rest_framework')),
]
```

In Listing 12-14 you can see `rest_framework.urls` is configured with Django's standard `include()` statement and `namespace` argument, in addition to being configured on the `rest-auth/` url, the last of which you can change to any url pattern of your choosing.

With this addition to a Django project's main `urls.py` file, all REST framework pages are generated with a login link in the top right corner, which takes users to a login page accessibly under the login path of the url configuration (e.g., if `url(r'^rest-auth/')`, the login page is available at `/rest-auth/login/`).

ENHANCED REST FRAMEWORK USER INTERFACE OPTIONS

Although the built-in user interface (UI) provided by the REST framework – presented in Figures 12-3 through 12-5 – offers a better alternative than presenting raw data REST services output – like Figures 12-1 and 12-2 – the REST framework UI is still rather rudimentary when you compare it to more modern UI web layouts.

There are various alternatives to the REST framework UI, which are specifically designed to work with the REST framework. Some of the more mature projects include Django REST Swagger[8] and DRF Docs.[9]

[8]`http://marcgibbons.github.io/django-rest-swagger/`
[9]`http://drfdocs.com/`

APPENDIX A

Python Basics

Python, like most programming languages, has certain behaviors that can confuse anyone who is new to the language. This appendix contains an overview of the Python features that are most important to understand for anyone who wants to create Django applications and who is already familiar with another programming language (e.g., Ruby, PHP).

In this appendix you'll learn about Python strings, Unicode, and other annoying text behaviors; Python methods and how to use them with default, optional, *args, and **kwargs arguments; Python classes and subclasses; Python loops, iterators, and generators; Python list comprehensions, generator expressions, maps, and filters; as well as how to use the Python lambda keyword for anonymous methods.

Strings, Unicode, and Other Annoying Text Behaviors

Working with text is so common in web applications that you'll eventually be caught by some of the not-so-straightforward ways Python interprets it. First off, beware there are considerable differences in how Python 3 and Python 2 work with strings.

Python 3 provides an improvement over Python 2, in the sense there are just two instead of three ways to interpret strings. But still, it's important to know what's going on behind the scenes in both versions so you don't get caught off-guard working with text. Listing A-1 illustrates a series of string statements run in Python 2 to showcase this Python version's text behavior.

Listing A-1. Python 2 literal unicode and strings

```
Python 2.7.3 (default, Apr 10 2013, 06:20:15)
[GCC 4.6.3] on linux2
Type "help", "copyright", "credits" or "license" for more information.
>>> import sys
>>> sys.getdefaultencoding()
'ascii'
>>> 'café & pâtisserie'
'caf\xc3\xa9 & p\xc3\xa2tisserie'
>>> print('\xc3\xa9')
é
>>> print('\xc3\xa2')
â
```


D. Rubio, *Beginning Django*, https://doi.org/10.1007/978-1-4842-2787-9

The first action in Listing A-1 shows the default Python encoding that corresponds to ASCII and which is the default for all Python 2.x versions. In *theory*, this means Python is limited to representing 128 characters, which are the basic letters and characters used by all computers - see any ASCII table for details.[1] This is just in *theory* though, because you won't get an error when attempting to input a non-ASCII character in Python.

If you create a string statement with non-ASCII characters like `'café & pâtisserie'`, you can see in Listing A-1 the é character is output to `\xc3\xa9` and the â character is output to `\xc3\xa2`. These outputs, which appear to be gibberish, are actually literal Unicode or UTF-8 representations of the é and â characters, respectively. So take note that even though the default Python 2 encoding is ASCII, non-ASCII characters are converted to *literal* Unicode or UTF-8 representations.

Next in Listing A-1 you can see that using the `print()` statement on either of these character sequences outputs the expected é or â characters. Behind the scenes, Python 2 offers the convenience of inputting non-ASCII characters in an ASCII encoding environment, by automatically encoding strings into *literal* Unicode or UTF-8 representations. To confirm this behavior, you can use the `decode()` method, as illustrated in Listing A-2.

Listing A-2. Python 2 decode unicode and u" prefixed strings

```
Python 2.7.3 (default, Apr 10 2013, 06:20:15)
[GCC 4.6.3] on linux2
Type "help", "copyright", "credits" or "license" for more information.
>>> 'café & pâtisserie'.decode('utf-8')
# Outputs: u'caf\xe9 & p\xe2tisserie'
>>> print(u'\xe9')
# Outputs: é
>>> print(u'\xe2')
# Outputs: â
```

In Listing A-2 you can see the statement `'café & pâtisserie'.decode('utf-8')` outputs `u'caf\xe9 & p\xe2tisserie'`. So now the same string decoded from Unicode or UTF-8 converts the é character or `\xc3\xa9` sequence to `\xe9` and the â character or `\xc3\xa2` sequence to `\xe2`. More importantly, notice the output string in Listing A-2 is now preceded by a `u` to indicate a Unicode or UTF-8 string.

Therefore the é character can really be represented by both `\xc3\xa9` and `\xe9`, it's just that `\xc3\xa9` is the *literal* Unicode or UTF-8 representation and `\xe9` is a Unicode or UTF-8 character, representation. The same case applies for the â character or any other non-ASCII character. The way Python 2 distinguishes between the two representations is by appending a `u` to the string. In Listing A-2 you can see calling `print(u'\xe9')` - note the preceding `u` - outputs the expected é and calling `print(u'\xe2')` outputs the expected â.

This Python 2 convenience of allowing non-ASCII characters in an ASCII encoding environments works so long as you don't try to forcibly convert a non-ASCII string that's already loaded into Python into ASCII, a scenario that's presented in Listing A-3.

Listing A-3. Python 2 UnicodeEncodeError: 'ascii' codec can't encode character

```
Python 2.7.3 (default, Apr 10 2013, 06:20:15)
[GCC 4.6.3] on linux2
Type "help", "copyright", "credits" or "license" for more information.
>>> 'café & pâtisserie'.decode('utf-8').encode('ascii')
```

[1] `https://www.cs.cmu.edu/~pattis/15-1XX/common/handouts/ascii.html`

```
Traceback (most recent call last):
  File "<stdin>", line 1, in <module>
UnicodeEncodeError: 'ascii' codec can't encode character u'\xe9' in position 3: ordinal not
in range(128)
```

In Listing A-3 you can see the call `'café & pâtisserie'.decode('utf-8').encode('ascii')` throws the `UnicodeEncodeError` error. Here you're not getting any convenience behavior – like when you input non-ASCII characters – because you're trying to process an already Unicode or UTF-8 character (i.e., `\xe9` or `\xe2`) into ASCII, so Python rightfully tells you it doesn't know how to treat characters that are outside of ASCII's 128-character range.

You can, of course, force ASCII output on non-ASCII characters, but you'll need to pass an additional argument to the `encode()` method as illustrated in Listing A-4.

Listing A-4. Python 2 encode arguments to process Unicode to ASCII

```
Python 2.7.3 (default, Apr 10 2013, 06:20:15)
[GCC 4.6.3] on linux2
Type "help", "copyright", "credits" or "license" for more information.
>>> 'café & pâtisserie'.decode('utf-8').encode('ascii','replace')
# Outputs: 'caf? & p?tisserie'
>>> 'café & pâtisserie'.decode('utf-8').encode('ascii','ignore')
# Outputs: 'caf & ptisserie'
>>> 'café & pâtisserie'.decode('utf-8').encode('ascii','xmlcharrefreplace')
# Outputs: 'caf&#233; & p&#226;tisserie'
>>> 'café & pâtisserie'.decode('utf-8').encode('ascii','backslashreplace')
# Outputs: 'caf\\xe9 & p\\xe2tisserie'
```

As you can see in Listing A-4, you can pass a second argument to the `encode()` method to handle non-ASCII characters: the `replace` argument so the output uses ? for non-ASCII characters; the `ignore` argument to simply bypass any non-ASCII positions; the `xmlcharrefreplace` to output the XML entity representation of the non-ASCII characters; or the `backslashreplace` to add a backlash allowing the output of an escaped non-ASCII reference.

Finally, Listing A-5 illustrates how you can create Unicode strings in Python 2 by prefixing them with the letter `u`.

Listing A-5. Python 2 Unicode strings prefixed with u''

```
Python 2.7.3 (default, Apr 10 2013, 06:20:15)
[GCC 4.6.3] on linux2
Type "help", "copyright", "credits" or "license" for more information.
>>> u'café & pâtisserie'
u'caf\xe9 & p\xe2tisserie'
>>> print(u'caf\xe9 & p\xe2tisserie')
café & pâtisserie
```

In Listing A-5 you can see the `u'café & pâtisserie'` statement. By appending the `u` to the string you're telling Python it's a Unicode or UTF-8 string, so the output for the characters é and â are `\xe9` and `\ xe2`, respectively. And by calling the `print` statement on the output for this type of string preceded by `u`, the output contains the expected é and â letters.

Now let's explore how Python 3 works with unicode and strings in Listing A-6.

Listing A-6. Python 3 unicode and string

```
Python 3.5.2 (default, Nov 17 2016, 17:05:23)
[GCC 5.4.0 20160609] on linux
Type "help", "copyright", "credits" or "license" for more information.
>>> import sys
>>> sys.getdefaultencoding()
'utf-8'
>>> 'café & pâtisserie'
'café & pâtisserie'
```

As you can see in Listing A-6, the encoding is UTF-8 or Unicode, which is the default for all Python 3.x versions. By using UTF-8 or Unicode as the default, it makes working with text much simpler. There's no need to worry or deal with how special characters are handled; everything is handled as UTF-8 or Unicode. In addition, because the default is Unicode or UTF-8, the leading u on strings is irrelevant and not supported in Python 3.

Next, let's move on to explore the use of Python's escape character and strings. In Python, the backslash \ character is Python's escape character and is used to escape the special meaning of a character and declare it as a literal value.

For example, to use an apostrophe quote in a string delimited by quotes, you would need to escape the apostrophe quote so Python doesn't confuse where the string ends (e.g., `'This is Python\'s "syntax"'`). A more particular case of using Python's backslash is on those special characters that use a backslash themselves. Listing A-7 illustrates various strings that use characters composed of a backslash so you can see this behavior.

Listing A-7. Python backslash escape character and raw strings

```
>>> print("In Python this is a tab \t and a line feed is \n")
In Python this is a tab and a line feed is

>>> print("In Python this is a tab \\t and a line feed is \\n")
In Python this is a tab \t and a line feed is \n
>>> print(r"In Python this is a tab \t and a line feed is \n")
In Python this is a tab \t and a line feed is \n
```

In the first example in Listing A-7 you can see the `\t` character is converted to a tab space and the `\n` character to a line feed (i.e., newline). This is the actual character composition of a tab - as a backslash followed by the letter t - and a line feed -- as a backslash followed by the n. As you can see in the second example in Listing A-7, in order for Python to output the literal value `\t` or `\n` you need to add another backslash - which is after all Python's escape character.

The third example in Listing A-7 is the same string as the previous ones, but it's preceded by `r` to make it a Python *raw* string. Notice that even though the special characters `\t` and `\n` are not escaped, the output is like the second example with escaped characters.

This is what's special about Python raw strings. By preceding a string with `r`, you tell Python to interpret backslashes literally, so there's no need to add another backslash like the second example in Listing A-7.

Python raw strings can be particularly helpful when manipulating strings with a lot of backslashes. And one particular case of strings that rely a lot on backslashes is regular expressions. Regular expressions are a facility in almost all programming languages to find, match, or compare strings to patterns, which makes them useful in a wide array of situations.

The crux of using Python and regular expression together is they both give special meaning to backslashes, a problem that even the Python documentation calls The Backslash Plague.[2] Listing A-8 illustrates this concept of the backslash plague and raw strings in the context of Python regular expressions.

Listing A-8. Python backslash plague and raw strings with regular expressions

```
>>> import re
# Attempt to match liternal '\n', (equal statement: re.match("\\n","\\n") )
>>> re.match("\\n",r"\n")
# Attempt to match liternal '\n', (equal statement: re.match("\\\\n","\\n") )
>>> re.match("\\\\n",r"\n")
<_sre.SRE_Match object at 0x7fedfb2c7988>
# Attempt to match liternal '\n', (equal statement: re.match(r"\\n","\\n") )
>>> re.match(r"\\n",r"\n")
<_sre.SRE_Match object at 0x7fedfb27c238>
```

In Listing A-8, we're trying to find a regular expression to match a literal `\n` - in Python syntax this would be `r"\n"` or `"\\n"`. Since regular expressions also use \ as their escape character, the first logical attempt at a matching regular expression is `"\\n"`, but notice this first attempt in Listing A-8 fails.

Because we're attempting to define a regular expression in Python, you'll need to add an additional backslash for Python and yet another one to escape the regular expression, bringing the total to four backslashes! As you can see in Listing A-8, the regular expression that matches a literal `\n` is the second attempt `"\\\\n"`.

As you can see in this example, dealing with backslashes in Python and in the context of regular expression can lead to very confusing syntax. To simplify this, the recommended approach to define regular expressions in Python is to use *raw* strings so backslashes are interpreted literally. In the last example in Listing A-8, you can see the regular expression `r"\\n"` matches a literal `\n` and is equivalent to the more confusing regular expression `"\\\\n"`.

■ **Note** Python's escape character and raw string behavior is the same in both Python 2 and Python 3.

Methods Arguments: Default, optional, *args, and **kwargs

Methods are one of the most common things you'll create in Python. Declared with the syntax def <method_name>(arguments) and called with the syntax result = <method_name>(input), what can be tricky to understand about Python methods is their argument/input syntax.

The obvious way you define and call methods is to have the same number of arguments on both sides, but this is far from most real-world cases where data can be missing or the number of arguments can change based on the circumstances. Listing A-9 illustrates a basic method definition with multiple calls using different syntax.

[2]https://docs.python.org/3/howto/regex.html#the-backslash-plague

Listing A-9. Python method definition and call syntax with * and **

```
def address(city,state,country):
    print(city)
    print(state)
    print(country)

address('San Diego','CA','US')
address('Vancouver','BC','CA')

us_address = ('San Diego','CA','US')
address(*us_address)

canada_address = {'country':'US','city':'San Diego','state':'CA'}
address(**canada_address)
```

The `address` method in Listing A-9 represents the most obvious syntax with three input parameters. Next, you can see two calls are made to the method also with the also obvious syntax: `address('San Diego','CA','US')` and `address('Vancouver','BC','CA')`. Following these calls are another two calls made with the not-so-obvious syntax `address(*us_address)` and `address(**canada_address)`.

A variable preceded with * is called a *positional argument* and tells Python to unpack the tuple assigned to it, which in turn passes each value as an individual argument. A variable preceded with ** is called a *keyword argument* and tells Python to unpack the dictionary assigned to it, which in turn passes each value as an individual argument.

As you can confirm in Listing A-9, the `us_address` variable is in fact a three-item tuple that is then used as the input argument in `address(*us_address)`. And the `canada_address` variable is in fact a three-item dictionary that is then used as the input argument in `address(**canada_address)`.

An interesting behavior of the values in ** is they don't have to follow a strict order (i.e., as expected by the method). Because these values are classified by keyword in a dictionary, Python can map each keyword according to the expected method argument order. This is unlike the values in * that need to be in the same order expected by a method, which is why they're called *positional arguments* because position matters.

Another important Python method syntax is making an argument optional. In Listing A-10 the `address_with_default` method uses a `default` argument value for `country`, which in turn makes it optional.

Listing A-10. Python method optional arguments

```
def address_with_default(city,state,country='US'):
    print(city)
    print(state)
    print(country)

address_with_default('San Diego','CA')
address_with_default('Vancouver','BC','CA')
address_with_default(**{'state':'CA','city':'San Diego'})
```

The first call in Listing A-10 `address_with_default('San Diego','CA')` only provides two input arguments and the call still works, even though the `address_with_default` method definition declares three input arguments. This is because the missing `country` argument takes the default method value `US`.

The second call in Listing A-10 `address_with_default('Vancouver','BC','CA')` provides all three input arguments with the third value effectively overriding the default method value `US` for `CA`. Finally, the third call in Listing A-10 `address_with_default(**{'state':'CA','city':'San Diego'})` uses the ** syntax to unpack an inline dictionary with two values, and the missing argument `country` takes the default method value `US`.

In addition to using the positional * syntax for calling methods, it's also possible to use this same syntax to define method arguments, as illustrated in Listing A-11.

Listing A-11. Python method positional argument

```
def vowels(*args):
    print("*args is %s" % type(args))
    print("Arguments %s " % ', '.join(args))

vowels('a')
vowels('a','e')
vowels('a','e','i')
vowels('a','e','i','o')
vowels('a','e','i','o','u')
```

Notice the method in Listing A-11 `def vowels(*args)` uses the * syntax to define the method argument. The * character has the same meaning described earlier, which is to unpack the values in a tuple. In this case, by using it in a method argument, it gives the method the flexibility to accept any number of arguments. You can confirm this flexibility by seeing the various calls to the `vowels()` method in Listing A-11, which take from one to five arguments.

Because you can't directly reference input arguments with a positional argument - unless you manually split them - Listing A-12 shows another method that first defines a standard input variable and then declares a positional argument.

Listing A-12. Python method with standard and positional argument

```
def address_with_zipcode(zipcode,*args):
    print(zipcode)
    print("*args is %s" % type(args))
    print("Arguments %s " % ', '.join(args))

address_with_zipcode(92101,'100 Park Boulevard','San Diego','CA','US')
address_with_zipcode('V6B 4Y8','777 Pacific Boulevard','Vancouver','BC','CA')
```

As you can confirm with the various calls made to `address_with_zipcode()` in Listing A-12, the first value is assigned to the first input variable and the rest of the values are assigned to the positional argument. Listing A-13 illustrates yet another method syntax that uses a keyword argument in the method definition.

Listing A-13. Python method with keyword argument

```
def address_catcher(**kwargs):
    print("**kwargs is %s" % type(kwargs))
    print("Keyword arguments %s " % ', '.join(['%s = %s' % (k,v) for k,v in kwargs.items()]))

address_catcher(zipcode=92101,street='100 Park Boulevard',city='San Diego',state='CA',
country='US')
address_catcher(postalcode='V6B 4Y8',street='777 Pacific Boulevard',city='Vancouver',
province='BC',country='CA')
```

Notice the method in Listing A-13 uses the ** syntax to define the method argument. The ** character has the same meaning described earlier, which is to unpack the values in a dictionary. In this case, by using it in a method argument, it gives the method the flexibility to accept any number of keyword arguments. You can confirm this flexibility by seeing the various calls to `address_catcher()` in Listing A-13, which use different keys; one call uses `zipcode` and `state`, while the other uses `postalcode` and `province`.

Finally, Listing A-14 illustrates a method that uses a standard input variable, a positional argument, and a keyword argument.

Listing A-14. Python method with standard, positional and keyword argument

```
def address_full(country,*args,**kwargs):
    print(country)
    print("*args is %s" % type(args))
    print("Arguments %s " % ', '.join(args))
    print("**kwargs is %s" % type(kwargs))
    print("Keyword arguments %s " % ', '.join(['%s = %s' % (k,v) for k,v in kwargs.items()]))

address_full('US','100 Park Boulevard','San Diego',state='CA',zipcode=92101)
address_full('CA','777 Pacific Boulevard','Vancouver',province='BC',postalcode='V6B 4Y8')
```

If you look over the sample calls to `address_full()` method in Listing A-14, you'll see this process works by assigning input values as the method slots requires. The first input value is always assigned to the standard input variable `country`, the next input values up to the first `keyword=value` are assigned to the positional argument `*args`, and all the input values with a `keyword=value` syntax are assigned to the keyword argument `**kwargs`. Be aware the input sequence when you use all three types of input types must always follow this order to avoid ambiguity.

■ **Note** The * and ** characters are what really matter in Python methods. Syntax wise you're more likely to encounter the references *args and **kwargs, but what really matters are the * and ** characters. To Python, you can equally declare *foo and **bar; however, the names *args and **kwargs are so prevalent you're more likely to encounter these than custom names.

Classes and Subclasses

Python classes are used to give greater structure and object-orientated facilities to many projects, so it's important to have a firm grasp on class behaviors and syntax. Even if you've used object-orientated design in other language like Java or PHP, Python has some particularities that you need to understand. Listing A-15 shows a simple Python class.

Listing A-15. Python class syntax and behavior

```
class Drink():
      """ Drink class """
      def __init__(self,size):
            self.size = size
      # Used to display object instance
      def __str__(self):
            return 'Drink: size %s' % (self.size)
      # Helper method for size in ounces
      def sizeinoz(self):
            if self.size == "small":
                  return "8 oz"
```

```
        elif self.size == "medium":
            return "12 oz"
        elif self.size == "large":
            return "24 oz"
        else:
            return "Unknown"

thedrink = Drink("small")
print(thedrink)
print("thedrink is %s " % thedrink.sizeinoz())
```

The first thing to notice about Listing A-15 is it uses the Python `class` keyword to declare the start of a Python class. Next, you can see various class methods that are declared with the same `def` keyword as standard Python methods. Notice all the class methods use the `self`-argument to gain access to the class/object instance, a construct that's prevalent in almost all Python classes, since Python doesn't grant access to the instance transparently in class methods like other object-oriented languages (e.g., in Java you can just reference this inside a method without it being a method argument).

Now let's move on the some calls made on the Drink class in Listing A-15. The first call in Listing A-15 `Drink("small")` creates an instance of the `Drink` class. When this call is invoked, Python first triggers the `__init__` method of the class to initialize the instance. Notice the two arguments `__init__(self,size)`. The self variable represents the instance of the object itself, while the `size` variable represents an input variable provided by the instance creator, which in this case is assigned the `small` value. Inside the `__init__` method, the `self.size` instance variable is created and assigned the `size` variable value.

The second call in Listing A-15 `print(thedrink)` outputs the `thedrink` class instance that prints `Drink: size small`. What's interesting about the output is that it's generated by the class method `__str__`, which as you can see in Listing A-15 returns a string with the value of the `size` instance variable. If the class didn't have a `__str__` method definition, the call to `print(thedrink)` would output something like `<__main__.Drink object at 0xcfb410>`, which is the rather worthless/unfriendly in-memory representation of the instance. This is the purpose of the `__str__` method in classes, to output a friendly instance value.

The third call in Listing A-15 `print("thedrink is %s " % thedrink.sizeinoz())` invokes the `sizeinoz()` class method on the instance and outputs a string based on the `size` instance variable created by `__init__`. Notice the `sizeinoz(self)` method declares `self` - just like `__init__` and `__str__` - to be able to access the instance value and perform its logic.

Now that you have a basic understanding of Python classes, let's explore Python subclasses. Listing A-16 illustrates a subclass created from the `Drink` class in Listing A-15.

Listing A-16. Python subclass syntax and behavior

```
class Coffee(Drink):
    """ Coffee class """
    beans = "arabica"
    def __init__(self,*args,**kwargs):
        Drink.__init__(self,*args)
        self.temperature = kwargs['temperature']
    # Used to display object instance
    def __str__(self):
        return 'Coffee: beans %s, size %s, temperature %s' % (self.beans,self.size,self.
        temperature)

thecoffee = Coffee("large",temperature="cold")
print(thecoffee)
print("thecoffee is %s " % thecoffee.sizeinoz())
```

Notice the class Coffee(Drink) syntax in Listing A-16, which is Python's inheritance syntax (i.e., Coffee is a subclass or inherits its behavior from Drink). In addition, notice that besides the subclass having its own __init__ and methods, it also has the beans class field.

Now let's create some calls on the Coffee subclass in Listing A-16. The first call in Listing A-16 Coffee("large",temperature="cold") creates a Coffee instance that is a subclass of the Drink instance. Notice the Coffee instance uses the arguments "large",temperature="cold" and in accordance with this pattern, the __init__ method definition is def __init__(self,*args,**kwargs).

Next is the initialization of the parent class with Drink.__init__(self,*args); the *args value in this case is large and matches the __init__ method of the parent Drink class. Followed is the creation of the self.temperature instance variable, which is assigned the value from kwargs['temperature'] (e.g., the value that corresponds to the key temperature).

The second call in Listing A-16 print(thecoffee) outputs the thecoffee class instance which prints Coffee: beans arabica, size large, temperature cold. Because the Coffee class has its own __str__ method, it's used to output the object instance - overriding the same method from the parent class - if there were no such method definition, then Python would look for a __str__ method in the parent class (i.e., Drink) and use that, and if no __str__ method were found, then Python would output the in-memory representation of the instance.

The third and final call in Listing A-16 print("thecoffee is %s " % thecoffee.sizeinoz()) invokes the sizeinoz() class method on the instance and outputs a string based on the size instance variable. The interesting bit about this call is it demonstrates object-orientated polymorphism, and the Coffee instance calls a method in the parent Drink class and works just like if it were a Drink instance.

Loops, Iterators, and Generators

Loops are one of the most common programming constructs. In Python, though, there are a series of subtle loop behaviors that are essential to grasp in order to understand some of Python's more advanced features. First let's start by exploring the typical for loop syntax applied to a Python string, list, and dictionary, which is illustrated in Listing A-17.

Listing A-17. Python implicit iterator behavior

```
astring = 'coffee'
coffee_types = ['Cappuccino','Latte','Macchiato']
address = {'city':'San Diego','state':'CA','country':'US'}

# Standard for loop, with implicit iterator
for letter in astring:
    print(letter)

# Loop with enumerator (counter)
for counter,letter in enumerate(astring):
    print(counter,letter)

# Standard for loop, with implicit iterator
for coffee in coffee_types:
    print(coffee)

# Loop with enumerator (counter), starting at 1
for counter,coffee in enumerate(coffee_types,start=1):
    print(counter,coffee)
```

```
# Standard for loop, with implicit iterator
for key,value in address.items():
    print(key,value)

# Standard for loop, with implicit iterator
for address_key in address.keys():
    print(address_key)

# Standard for loop, with implicit iterator
for address_value in address.values():
    print(address_value)
```

As you can see in Listing A-17, the standard for loop syntax in Python is `for <item> in <container>`. In each case, the for loop steps through uninterrupted through every `<item>` in the `<container>`, where the `<item>` varies depending on the `<container>` (e.g., for a string `<container>` the `<items>` are letters, for a list `<container>` the `<items>` are list elements).

In addition to the standard for syntax, Listing A-17 also make use of three special methods. The first one is the built-in Python function `enumerate()`, which functions as a counter. In the second and fourth examples you can see the `<container>` is wrapped in the `enumerate()` method, which gives the loop access access to a counter variable that's declared alongside the `<item>` variable. By default, the `enumerate()` counter starts at 0 but can be set to start at any number by using the `start` argument. In addition, Listing A-17 also makes use of the dictionary `keys()` and `items()` methods, which extract a list of dictionary keys and values, respectively.

Although the examples in Listing A-17 are straightforward, there is more going on behind the scenes. When you create for loops like the ones in Listing A-17 the `<container>` on which you're creating, the loop actually uses a construct called an *iterator*. To advance through the `<container>`, Python uses the iterator's `__next__` method to walk through each of the items in the `<container>`. Because there's no syntax related to the iterator or `__next__` method, these for loops are said to use *implicit iterators*.

Iterators are such an important concept in Python, they're first-class citizens with built-in support in the language, just like strings, integers, lists, and dictionaries. In addition, to support iterators, other data types must implement what's called the iterator protocol, which is why you can automatically invoke a for loop on strings, lists, dictionaries, and other data structures without actually seeing an iterator or `__next__` method.

To further illustrate the concept of iterators, let's explore a set of similar examples to the ones in Listing A-18 but this time with *explicit iterators*.

Listing A-18. Python explicit iterator behavior

```
astring = 'coffee'
coffee_types = ['Cappuccino','Latte','Macchiato']

# Create explicit iterators
astring_iter = iter(astring)
coffee_types_iter = iter(coffee_types)

# Print iterator types
print(type(astring_iter))
print(type(coffee_types_iter))

# Call next() to advance over the iterator
# In Python 2 next() works the same (e.g. astring_iter.next() )
# In Python 3 __next__() works the same (e.g. astring_iter.__next__() )
```

```
>>> next(astring_iter)
'c'
>>> next(astring_iter)
'o'
>>> next(astring_iter)
'f'
>>> next(astring_iter)
'f'
>>> next(astring_iter)
'e'
>>> next(astring_iter)
'e'
>>> next(astring_iter)
Traceback (most recent call last):
  File "<stdin>", line 1, in <module>
StopIteration

# Call next() to advance over the iterator
# In Python 2 next() works the same (e.g. coffee_types.next() )
# In Python 3 __next__() works the same (e.g. coffee_types.__next__() )
>>> next(coffee_types_iter)
'Cappuccino'
>>> next(coffee_types_iter)
'Latte'
>>> next(coffee_types_iter)
'Macchiato'
>>> next(coffee_types_iter)
Traceback (most recent call last):
  File "<stdin>", line 1, in <module>
StopIteration

order_numbers = iter([1,2,3,4,5,6,7,8,9,10])
# Get order number
next(order_numbers)
# Do other stuff
next(order_numbers)
# Do other stuff
next(order_numbers)
```

The first two lines in Listing A-18 declare a string and list. Next, you can see both values are wrapped with the built-in Python function `iter()` that's used to create an explicit iterator. To advance or walk through an iterator, you use the Python built-in function `next()` on the iterator reference - or you can also use the iterator's `next()` method in Python 2 or the iterator's `__next__()` method in Python 3. As you can see in Listing A-18, each time `next()` is called on the iterator reference, it advances to the next item just like a for loop, until it reaches the end and throws `StopIteration` when no more items are present.

Now that you've seen both implicit and explicit iterators, you might be left wondering what's the point of explicit iterators and calling `next()` to advance each time? The point is that explicit iterators give you the opportunity to pause and get the next element whenever you want, whereas for loops with implicit iterators just run through the elements uninterrupted.

This opportunity to pause and get the next element when you need a powerful feature is best illustrated with the last example in Listing A-18. You can see at the end of Listing A-18 the `order_numbers` iterator is a list of numbers. Next, a call is made to the `next()` method on the `order_numbers` iterator to fetch the next item only when its needed, giving us the ability to continue doing other work in between fetching items.

As powerful a concept as pausing an iteration is, the last iterator example in Listing A-18 has some flaws. First, it's a long list of values that won't scale for hundreds or thousands of items, which is problematic both in terms of hard-coding the values, as well as keeping them in memory. In addition, using the `iter()` method and declaring everything as a global iterator variable can lead to debugging and scoping issues. A cleaner and more efficient solution to achieve the same result is to use a *generator*.

A generator is an iterator embodied as a function. In a standard function - like those described in the past section - you call the function and it runs uninterrupted until it finds `return` or reaches the end and returns `None` by default. In a generator function - which is simply called generators - you can integrate pauses into a function so that each time it's called, it's a continuation of the previous call. In addition, generators have the ability to generate values on-demand - which is how they get their name - so they're much more efficient when it comes to handling large data ranges.

Listing A-19 illustrates a series of generators and their critical piece, which is Python's `yield` keyword.

Listing A-19. Python generator behavior

```
def funky_order_numbers():
    yield 100
    yield 350
    yield 575
    yield 700
    yield 950

order_numbers = funky_order_numbers()
print(type(order_numbers))
# Call next() to advance over the generator
# In Python 2 next() works the same (e.g. order_numbers.next() )
# In Python 3 __next__() works the same (e.g. order_numbers.__next__() )
>>> next(order_numbers)
100
...
...
>>> next(order_numbers)
950
>>> next(order_numbers)
Traceback (most recent call last):
  File "<stdin>", line 1, in <module>
StopIteration

def generate_order_numbers(n):
    for i in range(1,n):
        yield i

regular_order_numbers = generate_order_numbers(100)
# Call next() to advance over the generator
# In Python 2 next() works the same (e.g. regular_order_numbers.next() )
# In Python 3 __next__() works the same (e.g. regular_order_numbers.__next__() )
```

```
>>> next(regular_order_numbers)
1
...
...
>>> next(regular_order_numbers)
99
>>> next(regular_order_numbers)
Traceback (most recent call last):
  File "<stdin>", line 1, in <module>
StopIteration

def generate_infinite_order_numbers(n):
    while True:
          n += 1
          yield n

infinite_order_numbers = generate_infinite_order_numbers(1000)

# Call next() to advance over the generator
# In Python 2 next() works the same (e.g. infinite_order_numbers.next() )
# In Python 3 __next__() works the same (e.g. infinite_order_numbers.__next__() )
>>> next(infinite_order_numbers)
1001
...
...
# next() never reaches end due to infinite 'while True:' statement
```

The first generator in Listing A-19 `funky_order_numbers()` is unconventional in trying to illustrate the use of `yield`, which is a combination of return and stop behavior. Once you assign a generator to a reference, you can start stepping through the generator with Python's built-in function `next()` - or you can also use the generator's `next()` method in Python 2 or the generator's `__next__()` method in Python 3.

The first time a `next()` call is made, the generator gets to `yield 100`, where it returns `100` and stops until `next()` is called again. On the second `next()` call the generator gets to `yield 350`, it returns `350`, and stops until `next()` is called again. This process goes on until the last `yield` statement is reached and Python return `StopIteration` - just like it does with iterators.

Using multiple `yield` statements and hard-coding values in a generator is rarely done, so the second generator in Listing A-19 gives more justice to the name generator. The generator `generate_order_numbers(n)` accepts an input number and then creates a loop from 1 to `n`, where each iteration returns `yield i`, where `i` is the iteration number.

As you can see in Listing A-19, the first step is to assign the generator to a reference by initializing it with a number. Once the assignment is made, you walk through the generator calling the `next()` method and each time it returns the current counter until you reach the initialization number. An interesting behavior of generators is they generate their return values on-demand, so in this case even if you initialize the generator with a large number, say `10000000`, the generator doesn't create a `10000000` element list that takes up memory, it generates and returns values as they're needed.

The third generator in Listing A-19 `generate_infinite_order_numbers()` is designed to never end. The generator `generate_infinite_order_numbers(n)` accepts an input number and then creates an infinite loop to return `yield n+i` on each iteration. In the same way as the other generators, you call the `next()` method on the reference and each time it returns a subsequent value. Because of the `while True:` statement that represents an infinite loop, this generator never ends and thus never returns `StopIteration`.

List Comprehensions, Generator Expressions, Maps, and Filters

List comprehensions offer a concise way to express Python operations that involve lists. Although you can express the same logic using standard for loops and if/else conditionals, there's a high probability you'll eventually encounter or use a list comprehension because of its compact nature. Listing A-20 illustrates a series of list comprehensions, as well as their equivalent standard syntax representation.

Listing A-20. Python list comprehensions

```
country_codes = ['us','ca','mx','fr','ru']
zipcodes = {90003:'Los Angeles',90802:'Long Beach',91501:'Burbank',92101:'San
Diego',92139:'San Diego',90071:'Los Angeles'}

# Regular syntax
country_codes_upper_std = []
for country_code in country_codes:
    country_codes_upper_std.append(country_code.upper())

# Equivalent ist comprehension
country_codes_upper_comp = [cc.upper() for cc in country_codes]

# Regular syntax
zip_codes = []
for zipcode in zipcodes.keys():
    zip_codes.append(zipcode)

# Equivalent ist comprehension
zip_codes_comp = [zc for zc in zipcodes.keys()]

# Regular syntax
zip_codes_la = []
for zipcode,city in zipcodes.items():
    if city == "Los Angeles":
        zip_codes_la.append(zipcode)

# Equivalent list comprehension
zip_codes_la_comp = [zc for zc,city in zipcodes.items() if city == "Los Angeles"]

# Regular syntax
one_to_onehundred = []
for i in range(1,101):
    one_to_onehundred.append(i)

# Equivalent  list comprehension
one_to_onehundred_comp = [i for i in range(1,101)]
```

As you can see in Listing A-20, the syntax for list comprehensions is `[<item_result> for item in container <optional conditional>]`. At first you'll need some time to get accustomed to the syntax, but eventually you'll find yourself using it regularly because it takes less time to write than equivalent regular code blocks.

The last example in Listing A-20 produces a list with the numbers 1 to 100, and it's an interesting example because it's an inefficient approach for most cases that require a number series. In the past section, you learned how generators can create on-demand sequences requiring little memory vs. ordinary lists that require more memory to store data. While you could use the generator syntax from the previous section, Python also has a shorthanded notation for generators named *generator expressions,* which is illustrated in Listing A-21.

Listing A-21. Python generator expressions

```
one_to_onehundred_genexpression = (i for i in range(1,101))
print(type(one_to_onehundred_genexpression))
one_to_onehundred_genexpression.next()
one_to_onehundred_genexpression.next()

first_fifty_even_numbers = (i for i in range(2, 101, 2))
first_fifty_even_numbers.next()
first_fifty_even_numbers.next()

first_fifty_odd_numbers = (i for i in range(1, 101, 2))
first_fifty_odd_numbers.next()
first_fifty_odd_numbers.next()
```

As you can see in Listing A-21, the syntax is almost identical to list comprehensions; the only difference is generator expressions use parentheses `()` as delimiters, instead of brackets `[]`. Once you create a generator expression, you simply call the `next()` method on its reference to get the next element in the generator.

As helpful as list comprehensions are at reducing the amount of written code, there are two other Python constructs that operate like list comprehensions and are helpful for cutting down even more code or for cases where the logic for list comprehensions is too complex to make them understandable.

The `map()` function can apply a function to all the elements of a container and the `filter()` function produces a new container with elements that fit certain criteria. Listing A-22 presents some of the list comprehension from Listing A-20 with the `map()` and `filter()` functions.

Listing A-22. Python map() and filter() examples

```
country_codes = ['us','ca','mx','fr','ru']
zipcodes = {90003:'Los Angeles',90802:'Long Beach',91501:'Burbank',92101:'San
Diego',92139:'San Diego',90071:'Los Angeles'}

# List comprehension
country_codes_upper_comp = [cc.upper() for cc in country_codes]

# Helper function
def country_to_upper(name):
    return name.upper()

# Map function
country_codes_upper_map = map(country_to_upper,country_codes)

# List comprehension
zip_codes_la_comp = [zc for zc,city in zipcodes.items() if city == "Los Angeles"]
```

```
# Helper function
def only_la(dict_item):
    if dict_item[1] == "Los Angeles":
       return True

# Filter function
zip_codes_la_filter_dict_items = filter(only_la,zipcodes.items())
print(zip_codes_la_filter_dict_items)
zip_codes_la_filter = [tup[0] for tup in zip_codes_la_filter_dict_items]
```

As you can see in Listing A-22, the syntax for the map() function is map(<method_for_each_element>, <container>). This technique helps keep a cleaner design, maintaining the logic in a separate method and the invocation of said method on every element contained in the map() method itself. The map() function produces the same type of input container, but with each of its elements altered by its first argument or logic method.

The syntax for filter() is filter(<method_to_evaluate_each_element>,<container>). In Listing A-22 you can see the container is a dictionary and the only_la() helper function is used to evaluate each container element and return True if the second tuple value (i.e., the dictionary value) is "Los Angeles."

Unlike the map() function that uses the results of its logic method, the filter() function only checks for True or False values. If the logic method on a container element evaluates to True, the element becomes part of the new container as is (i.e., in this case the dictionary item), if the logic method on a container element evaluates to False then the element is discarded. Finally, in Listing A-22 you can see that because the filter() function returns dictionary items, an additional list comprehension is made to get the desired key values (i.e., zip codes) as a list.

Lambda Keyword for Anonymous Methods

Python uses the lambda keyword to define inline or anonymous methods. It's mostly used when you want method behavior (e.g., input variables and scope protection) but want to avoid declaring a full-fledged method with def because the logic is too simple; want to minimize written code; or want to keep the logic in a single location.

Similar to list comprehensions that are not essential but are widely used to simplify iteration logic, the lambda keyword is also not essential but is widely used to incorporate method-like behavior with a simpler syntax. To get accustomed to the lambda keyword, when you see a statement like lambda x: <logic_on_x> just make the mental transformation to def anon_method(x): <logic_on_x>.

Listing A-23 illustrates various lambda examples based on past examples.

Listing A-23. Python lambda examples

```
country_codes = ['us','ca','mx','fr','ru']
zipcodes = {90003:'Los Angeles',90802:'Long Beach',91501:'Burbank',92101:'San
Diego',92139:'San Diego',90071:'Los Angeles'}

# Map function with lambda
country_codes_upper_map = map(lambda x: x.upper(),country_codes)

# Filter function with lambda
zip_codes_la_filter_lambda_dict_items = filter(lambda (zipcode,city): city == "Los
Angeles",zipcodes.items())
print(zip_codes_la_filter_lambda_dict_items)
zip_codes_la_filter = [tup[0] for tup in zip_codes_la_filter_lambda_dict_items]
```

Index

A, B

D. Rubio, *Beginning Django*, https://doi.org/10.1007/978-1-4842-2787-9

C

D

E

F, G

H, I

J, K

N, O

P, Q

U

V

W

X, Y

Z

Printed in the United States
By Bookmasters